Internet Jurisdiction

Internet Jurisdiction

Law and Practice

JULIA HÖRNLE

OXFORD
UNIVERSITY PRESS

OXFORD
UNIVERSITY PRESS

Great Clarendon Street, Oxford, OX2 6DP,
United Kingdom

Oxford University Press is a department of the University of Oxford.
It furthers the University's objective of excellence in research, scholarship,
and education by publishing worldwide. Oxford is a registered trade mark of
Oxford University Press in the UK and in certain other countries

First Edition published in 2021

Impression: 6

Published in the United States of America by Oxford University Press
198 Madison Avenue, New York, NY 10016, United States of America

British Library Cataloguing in Publication Data

Data available

Library of Congress Control Number: 2020934590

ISBN 978–0–19–880692–9

Printed and bound by
CPI Group (UK) Ltd, Croydon, CR0 4YY

To those who are prepared to swim against the prevailing current to seek deeper understanding.

Foreword

Reading *Internet Jurisdiction: Law and Practice* reminded me of the concluding words by Martti Koskenniemi in *Sovereignty in Fragments* (CUP, 2010): 'In the context of war, economic collapse, and environmental destruction, sovereignty points to the possibility, however limited or idealistic, that whatever comes to happen, one is not just a pawn in other people's games but, for better or for worse, the master of one's own fate.' At a time when appeal to sovereignty tends to invoke ideas of populism, nationalism, xenophobia, and insularity, Koskenniemi's words are a powerful reminder of its liberal, democratic, and idealistic aspirations of self-governance. Sovereignty gives us a way to self-govern *and* to agree to disagree, and thus for a multitude of communities to live peacefully together. The topic of jurisdiction in its transnational settings is quintessentially about implementing that self-governance against socio-economic or socio-technical global landscapes that make it messy. The rise of the internet and global network society has amplified that messiness by several orders of magnitude. The task of disentangling those transnational online knots in all their innumerable instantiations – from civil disputes (IP, contract, defamation, data protection) to criminal and regulatory infractions (hate or terrorist speech, gambling), from investigation and adjudication to enforcement jurisdiction – is painstaking, and yet vital for constructing and reconstructing those national spaces of sovereignty. This monograph engages in that task with patience and confidence; by drawing on a huge number of legislative and judicial examples from across the (Western) world, the discussion shows us, the readers, how national spaces are – in law and practice – reasserting themselves against the online forces of globalization. Although different states set their legislative priorities very differently, what they do have in common is the urge to defend their national cultural, political or economic domains.

Internet Jurisdiction: Law and Practice also shows courage – a courage that has become a hallmark of many internet law academics – in daring to challenge entrenched legal disciplinary boundaries. By covering competence questions under private international law *and* under public international law, Julia's monographs continues a tradition that has formidable forefathers, notably Michael Akehurst (1972) and Frederick A Mann (1964, 1984), and has recently been revived by, for example, Alex Mill's *Confluence of Public and Private International Law* (2009), but remains a deeply subversive act amongst traditionalists – despite the common roots of the two disciplines. The advantages of an integrated approach are numerous. Practically, it means there is no need to impose artificial silos on regulatory activities that are pervasive in the transnational (online) sphere and for which the private or public categorizations are fairly unimportant. Classically, whilst questions about intermediary liability are neither on their face nor traditionally connected to the topic of jurisdiction, in the internet context they have become (and rightly so) a staple part of the jurisdictional discussion (Chapter 3). Online intermediaries – whether search engines, social media platforms, e-commerce sites or internet access providers - are the new 'border guards' on whom the burden to effectively 'enforce' national laws, via notice-and-takedown or blocking orders, rests. This burden ultimately flows from the territorially strictly delimited enforcement jurisdiction of states under public international law. The 'enforcement' obligations of local intermediaries over foreign content extend across a wide spectrum of harms as covered by civil, criminal, and regulatory laws, and there is a little to be gained from compartmentalizing them. Equally, ambiguously private or public substantive legal areas, most pertinently data protection law, need not be squeezed out of the inquiry on the ground of being poor fit. As data protection law has become the epitome of IT regulation, it also perfectly illustrates how jurisdictional wrangling embodies a contest between different normative settlements by different states (nicely covered in Chapter 7) upon which online transnationality exerts a 'natural' pressure towards a convergence.

A comparative public and private international law perspective on internet transnationality is also helpful in exposing the political and economic drivers behind the rules of private international law which are all too often treated as mere neutral, technical rules with no wider collective purpose or agenda, and purely concerned with what is just and fair as between the parties. Yet, the (un)willingness of a court to let a transnational dispute on copyright or defamation law (see Chapters 8–12) slip its national net can be vividly understood as capturing not just the private interests of the parties, but important collective interests when juxtaposed against an international law framing of jurisdiction, which is more explicitly embedded in the vigilantly guarded self-interests of states. In reverse, doctrines or principles such as comity or *forum non conveniens* from the private sphere are useful to understand state practice in the deciding whether to prosecute an international online crime or not (Chapter 4). At the same time, their strongly permissive nature reveals their weak claim to being rules or doctrines properly so called, rather than merely descriptive labels for the wide judicial or executive discretion exhibited in transnational wrangling (with intra-EU relations being an important exception).

In as much as *Internet Jurisdiction: Law and Practice* takes a comprehensive perspective on internet jurisdiction, it also shows acute awareness of the limits of that perspective. The fact is that much transnational regulation or quasi-regulation of the internet simply falls outside the jurisdictional inquiry, or a state-based perspective (Chapter 2). In other words, sovereignty is after all waning, or at least being shared with other overlapping regulatory spaces. Here the concept of 'global law' provides a useful terrain for contesting the effective coverage and relevance of state law vis-à-vis alternatives, such as online dispute resolution systems. More interestingly, the growing practice by states to 'instruct' online platforms to not only deal with illegal content, but harmful content that falls short of illegality, presents a peculiar form of delegation of authority to these private corporate actors to fix their own meanings of right and wrong, and then enforce them, often at a global level. As Julia observes, such private regulation creates inroads into our freedoms without the normal safeguards provided by the rule of law or by human rights entitlements whose focus is government not governance. Again, the limits of state jurisdiction vis-à-vis alternative non-state orders are disempowering, given that corporate actors are only and rather imperfectly held accountable by the market. Opting out of their orders is generally not a realistic option.

Internet Jurisdiction: Law and Practice leaves much room for argument – as any good monograph should. Readers might, for example, ponder the accuracy of constructing the internet as 'borderless' and 'decentralised'. It seems both true and not true. It seems not true if one considers that the complementary legal constructs of territory and borders have, for some time, been implemented and indeed 'protected' by 'border guards' other than those literally standing on the border. Every time a bank applies a national rule to an international money transfer, it guards the sovereign national banking space. The internet has its very own border guards. For example, when Google responds to a European right-to-be-forgotten request on its search engine, it creates and recreates borders around an EU online space and delineates it from other national online spaces from which such requests cannot be made. Jumping to the end of the monograph, a reader might also ponder whether the argument that some jurisdictional discordances may be solved or lessened through states' self-restraint or better co-ordination between them, is rather too optimistic. The phenomenon of regulatory arbitrage, where companies use and abuse different levels of state regulation for forum shopping or tax avoidance, is long-standing and hardly in the interests of states collectively (even if it benefits individual ones) and yet, it has seen fairly little progress by way of effective inter-state cooperation. What are the forces, if any, that make the internet, or some areas of online transnationality, exceptional in this respect? In its ambitious comprehensiveness and in its willingness to combine micro and macro analysis, Internet Jurisdiction: Law and Practice provides an excellent platform for engendering debate on internet jurisdiction (and the many areas with which it intersects) for years to come.

Uta Kohl
Professor of Law, Southampton Law School
Author of Jurisdiction and the Internet (CUP, 2007)

Preface

The fundamental clash between the internet enabling borderless data flows and national laws whose authority ends at a territorial border has intrigued me since I started teaching the LLM course Internet Law at Queen Mary University of London in 2001. Before that, while working as a solicitor at Eversheds Brussels Office and meeting with EU Commission officials in various fora discussing the drafts of what was to become the E-commerce Directive 2000/31/EC and the Brussels Jurisdiction Regulation 44/2001, I realized the chasm between the Internal Market objective and legal doctrines in private international law. While the latter had the objective of preserving a fair balance between claimants and defendants in civil cases, the former had the objective of harnessing the economic opportunities, which e-commerce was about to bring in terms of cross-border trade within the EU. In many ways, this conflict encapsulates two different understandings of the function of law. On the one hand, the function of law is to balance different stakeholders' interests and, through this balance, implement fundamental values of a society. This balance is influenced by cultural and political considerations, which in turn differ from nation state to nation state. On the other hand the function of law is to increase transactional efficiency thereby leading to greater economic wealth. Greater overall wealth is achieved through cross-border trade which then leads to conflicts between national legal systems. While legal systems are closed to each other in the sense that they exist in parallel universes, the necessary cross-border interaction inevitably leads to conflicts between legal systems. These conflicts are not new, but they have been exacerbated and multiplied by the characteristics of the internet as a borderless communications medium to the extent that the self-sufficiency of the nation state has been shaken at its roots. This book analyses these conflicts with respect to rules on jurisdiction and the applicable law, from multiple vantage points: civil and commercial law, criminal law and regulatory laws with a focus on the specific challenges caused by the internet, and more recently social media and cloud computing. I found the analysis intellectually stimulating, but at the same time deeply frustrating as the solution to these legal challenges can only partly be addressed by changing the legal rules themselves, as legal systems cannot reach beyond themselves. I hope that readers likewise find this book intellectually satisfying in its legal analysis and in providing a comparison between different approaches to jurisdiction and conflicts of law questions in the internet era.

Finally, no woman is an island – I would like to take this opportunity to express my gratitude to a number of individuals who have helped me in my journey of writing this book. First of all I would like to thank Professor Giovanni Sartor who invited me to stay at the European University Institute in 2017, Professor Thomas Hoeren who kindly hosted me at the Institute for Information, Telecommunications and Media Law, University of Münster in 2017 and Professor Ulrich Sieber who enabled me to spend a research period at the fantastic research facilities of the Max Planck Institute for Foreign and International Criminal Law in Freiburg during 2018, supported by a generous grant of the Max Planck Gesellschaft. My thanks also go to the German Academic Exchange Service for their grant financing my stay at the University of Münster. I would also like to applaud the editorial team at Oxford University Press for their support and editing of this book. Furthermore, I am grateful for the research assistance of Asma Al Abbarova, Lisa Engelbrecht, Zita Heuer, and grateful for the co-operation with my two co-contributors of chapters, Dr Ioannis Revolidis and Dr Elif Kuşkonmaz. Moreover, I pay tribute to the LLM and PhD students who I have been lucky to teach over the last twenty years at Queen Mary University of London and my fantastic colleagues at the Centre for Commercial Law Studies, Professors Chris Reed, Ian Walden, Christopher Millard, Anne Flanagan, Gavin Sutter, and Laura Edgar. Finally, I would like to express my gratitude to my partner, Sean Wilcox, who has supported my book writing and research spells, here and abroad, and tolerated the resultant stress-levels and anti-social absorption.

Table of Contents

Table of Cases

INTERNATIONAL

Court of Justice of the European Union

European Human Rights Reports

General Court/Court of First Instance

Permanent Court of International Justice

NATIONAL COURTS

Australia

United States

Table of Legislation

STATUTORY INSTRUMENTS

OTHER LEGISLATION

Australia

Austria

Belgium

California

Canada

Denmark

France

Germany

Illinois

Netherlands

New Zealand

Russia

Singapore

United States

COUNCIL OF EUROPE INSTRUMENTS

EU PRIMARY LAW

EU SECONDARY LAW

Decisions

Directive

Regulations

INTERNATIONAL/MULTILATERAL AGREEMENTS

BILATERAL AGREEMENT

REGIONAL CONVENTIONS &INSTRUMENTS

NON-REGIONAL MLA AGREEMENT

1
A Brief Introduction

This book is about the Jurisdictional Challenge created by the internet. The internet and its manifold applications have fundamentally changed how we interact, conduct business, conclude contracts, consume media content, and provide news and other information. Much of these interactions and relationships take place across a geographical border and therefore raise questions of jurisdictional competence.

The entertaining eighteenth-century adventure stories of the Baron von Münchausen are part of German folklore.[1] In one of his fantastic, hyperbolic adventure stories, he tells the story of how he escaped a swamp, in which he and his horse had been drowning, by pulling himself up on his own hair. This is a good metaphor for the relationship between national legal systems and the internet. The internet stands here for the swamp, potentially in more than one sense, and the Baron pulling on his own hair stands for the national legal systems trying to solve the Jurisdictional Challenge caused by the borderless internet. The argument underlying this metaphor is that national law systems on their own cannot solve the borderless nature of the internet. The force of pulling on the hair does not defy the gravity of the planet Earth. National law likewise has limited force in respect of a transnational network of networks spanning the globe.

Remoteness is inherently built into the client–server architecture of the internet, in that resources can be provided and consumed from any point in the network of networks. Hand-in-hand with this remoteness comes the distributed nature of harm caused by internet dissemination: since the same resource can be accessed, streamed, or downloaded from many locations simultaneously, harms may be spread across multiple jurisdictions.

The ubiquity of the internet has multiplied with the introduction of cloud computing and mobile computing, whose use in turn has been enabled by ubiquitous broadband access and wireless networking. Another feature of the internet is decentralization of the network architecture, which has been an intentional feature of the internet since its inception, in order to provide for resilience of the internet as a communication tool and to defeat central control of communications and traffic flows, allowing for unimpeded, free flow of information. This decentralization has been augmented by more recent technologies such as peer-to-peer file sharing applications, avoiding a central hosting server, or blockchain technologies, which allow decentralized sharing and recording of information under conditions of pseudonymity.

Another feature of the internet is that it has enabled user-generated content. The networking capabilities introduced by social media platforms mean that users can now share content across the globe and across different platforms in seconds. Since

[1] GA Bürger, *Die Abenteuer des Freiherrn von Münchhausen* (Anaconda 2010).

Internet Jurisdiction. Julia Hörnle, Oxford University Press (2021). © Julia Hörnle.
DOI: 10.1093/oso/9780198806929.001.0001

everyone (and not only commercial entities) can now be publishers of information and sellers of products, this has further decentralized interactions and concomitantly, the potential for liability and disputes between users.

Furthermore, while traditionally business have marketed and distributed their products along national and regional territories, adopting their business strategies according to the markets targeted, some products—especially if they can be downloaded online—are now not necessarily targeted at any particular market. The internet has destroyed many traditional business models, such as subscription models, and replaced them with the exploitation of personal data through tracking and profiling of individual users, so that marketing is based on online behaviour patterns. This development makes it more difficult to assess whether a particular product or behaviour has been targeted at a particular jurisdiction, as some commercial activity may be targeted at everywhere and nowhere in particular.

The remoteness of the internet, its ubiquity, the increasing decentralization of many internet applications, and the geographical spread of harms transmitted online are the features of modern technology that have caused the Jurisdictional Challenge, that is, the situation where multiple courts may be competent or no court may be competent. In addition to the question of jurisdiction of the courts, the competence of other authorities to govern the internet arises. Legislators and regulators may equally find it difficult to judge the ambit of their authority over online interactions. Moreover, cross-border enforcement of the law is subject to major obstacles, as this book demonstrates. Law continues to be made and enforced at the level of nation states and international law provides the interface between different national legal systems. However, this interface is comparatively thin and riddled with political considerations.

Traditionally, private international law providing the rules within the national legal order on the recognition and enforcement of foreign civil judgments, the rules on jurisdiction of the civil courts and the applicable law, and international law, providing the principles for jurisdiction in respect of public law, were regarded as separate disciplines. However, the internet provides a Jurisdictional Challenge for both. Therefore, this book crosses the lines between private and public law and looks at the jurisdictional principles pertaining to both, in order to gain insights from both public and private law situations.

Chapter 2 conceptualizes the notion of jurisdiction in different context, framing jurisdiction in relation to territoriality and sovereignty. Chapter 3 explains how the use of local service providers for enforcement (gatekeeper regulation) is a response to the enforcement problems caused by the Jurisdictional Challenge and how this gatekeeper regulation means that increasingly positive duties of care are imposed on communication service providers. Chapter 4 examines the jurisdictional principles under international law in the light of increasing transborder cybercrime and highlights the need for better international coordination as an enormous challenge of the international law system. Chapter 5 analyses the jurisdiction of the criminal courts by comparing the jurisdictional rules in Germany and England, highlighting the similarity of the challenges and the differences in approach of both countries. Chapter 6 discusses the intractable problem of cross-border digital investigations of crime, where the evidence is located in the cloud. It examines traditional Mutual Legal Assistance, extended application of domestic investigative powers and the new system of bilateral executive agreements introduced by the Cloud Act. One of the areas of law most affected by the Jurisdictional Challenge is data protection and therefore Chapter 7 examines data protection regulation and the jurisdiction of regulatory authorities within the EU. Chapter 8 provides a general overview and examination of the harmonized private international law rules in the EU. Chapter 9 follows with a critical analysis of the US approach to jurisdiction and conflicts of law under the due process clause of the US Constitution and how the conflicts of law principles have been applied to internet cases. Chapter 10 contrasts the rules on consumer jurisdiction in e-commerce cases in the EU and the US. The Jurisdictional Challenge has been particularly prominent in online privacy and defamation cases, given the ease of online publication and therefore Chapter 11 examines private international law in the EU, UK, and Germany in respect of the infringement of online privacy and defamation. Equally prominent and complex questions have arisen in respect of the private international law rules for intellectual property infringement, which are examined in Chapter 12. Finally, Chapter 13 brings together the insights from the examination of the Jurisdictional Challenge in the previous chapters and points to a combination of factors for overcoming it.

2

"Head in the Clouds": The Clash between Territorial Sovereignty, Jurisdiction, and the Territorial Detachment of the Internet

1. Different contexts of the term "jurisdiction"

The essence of jurisdiction is lawful authority to "state the law" (the Latin meaning of the term "jurisdiction"). Authority implies competence, the competence of the executive (government, independent regulatory agencies) to enforce the law (enforcement jurisdiction), the competence of the legislator to pass laws and other legislation (prescriptive jurisdiction), and the competence of the courts to adjudicate disputes (adjudicative jurisdiction).[1] But authority implies also the requirement of subjects over which the authority is exercised (or, as Dorsett and McVeigh put it, the "listeners" to whom the law is stated[2]). Finally, jurisdiction as "authority" also raises the question of who has conferred the authority in the first place. In Western political thinking this was derived from God (eg with the French Sun King Louis XIV as the divine ruler) or in more recent times, in the age of democracy, it is the people who give this authority.[3]

Historically it may be useful to remember that in Medieval and in Renaissance Europe several independent systems of law applied in parallel on the same territory (eg ecclesiastical law, the common law, the law merchant) leading to questions of the delimitation of each authority.[4] These authorities coexisted independently within the same territory.

From a lawyer's point of view, jurisdiction is a known term of art and it is only on closer reflection that it becomes clear that the term is complex and multi-faceted.[5] The underlying reason is that "jurisdiction" has different meanings in different contexts and lawyers using the term are not always precise as to which meaning or context they refer to. So, in one sense, jurisdiction is also a muddled concept, which this first section is attempting to conceptualize.

[1] JH Beale, "The Jurisdiction of a Sovereign State" (1923) 36 Harvard Law Review 241—"the power of a sovereign to affect the rights of persons, whether by legislation, by executive decree, or by the judgment of a court."

[2] S Dorsett and S McVeigh, *Jurisdiction* (Routledge 2012) ch 2.

[3] See discussion in Dorsett and McVeigh (n 2) 10–11; S Sassen, *Losing Control? Sovereignty in the Age of Globalization* (Columbia University Press 1996) 2 and the Universal Declaration of Human Rights 1948, Art 21(3): "The will of the people shall be the basis of government," The Declaration of Independence of the Thirteen United States of America 1776: "deriving their just powers from the consent of the governed."

[4] Dorsett and McVeigh (n 2)18.

[5] C Ryngaert, *Jurisdiction in International Law* (2nd edn, Oxford University Press 2015) 5; J Crawford, *Brownlie's Principles of Public International Law* (8th edn, Oxford University Press 2012) 448.

Internet Jurisdiction. Julia Hörnle, Oxford University Press (2021). © Julia Hörnle.
DOI: 10.1093/oso/9780198806929.001.0001

There are essentially four different contexts in which the term is used: (1) public international law, (2) private international law, (3) the criminal justice system, and (4) regulatory jurisdiction. What makes the opaqueness of the term worse is that it relates to four distinct and specialist areas of law, whose discourse is separate to a degree, and seldom are all four meanings of jurisdiction discussed together in synthesis. This is precisely what this book aims to achieve in the context of the internet, where jurisdictional issues are paramount.

The first context is public international law—the law of nations or international law. Jurisdiction here refers to the competence of a state to govern matters on its territory and provides the link between the sovereign government and its territory, and ultimately its people. Since states are sovereign and independent from each other, the exercise of state power encroaching on another state's sovereignty is likely to lead to conflict.[6] It is one of the functions of jurisdiction under international law to avoid such conflicts, as far as possible. Thus, jurisdiction confers "entitlements" of power to states[7] and at the same time delimits this power. For this purpose, public international law has developed high-level principles that serve as the justification for states assuming jurisdiction over matters on their territory and largely link the matter to the territory by means of "connecting factors."[8] These principles do not lead to a unique or exclusive allocation of jurisdiction to one state, with the consequence that more than one state may claim jurisdiction over a subject matter (overlapping jurisdiction).[9] If a state exceeds its jurisdiction, by not bringing its jurisdictional claim within one of the recognized principles of jurisdiction, the international community may frown on this exercise of jurisdiction as "extraterritorial" or "exorbitant."[10] However, it is disputed amongst scholars whether the "extraterritorial" assumption of jurisdiction is illegal under international law as is sometimes assumed by English and German scholars.[11] In the US this issue was disputed: Section 421 of the Restatement Third stated that it was not clear whether the principles governing jurisdiction to adjudicate were dictated by international law. By contrast, the draft of the Restatement Fourth states that rules of personal jurisdiction appertain exclusively to the domestic law of the US.[12] It also states that international law does not impose restrictions on jurisdiction to adjudicate, the only remedy another state has is not to recognize or enforce a judgment rendered by a US court if it considers the basis of jurisdiction exorbitant.[13]

The state claiming "extraterritorial" jurisdiction can usually provide some sort of territorial connecting factor by pointing to effects or impact within its own territory.[14]

[6] Ryngaert (n 5) 6.

[7] R Higgins, *Problems and Process: International Law and How We Use It* (Clarendon Press 1994) 146.

[8] Discussed in Chapter 4.

[9] Restatement of the Law Fourth—the Foreign Relations Law of the US, Jurisdiction, Tentative Draft No 2 (22 March 2016) s 211, 47: "multiple jurisdictional bases may also combine to establish a genuine connection between the state and the subject of its regulation. Bases of jurisdiction often overlap in practice."

[10] Restatement of the Law Fourth—the Foreign Relations Law of the US Jurisdiction, Tentative Draft No 2 (22 March 2016) s 302 Reporters Notes, 111.

[11] Council of Europe, Report: European Committee on Crime Problems, Extraterritorial Jurisdiction Strasbourg 1990, 25–26; Ryngaert points to a pejorative meaning of the term, often expressing criticisms about the long arm of US law: Ryngaert (n 5) 8.

[12] Restatement of the Law Fourth—the Foreign Relations Law of the US Jurisdiction, Tentative Draft No 2 (22 March 2016) s 302 Reporters Notes, 118.

[13] ibid 111.

[14] Ryngaert (n 5) 6–7.

A clearer distinction should be made between location (of an activity, of persons, of effects) and the nature of the connection to territory.[15] This is discussed in more detail later.[16]

This is the first function of jurisdiction in the context of public international law: it aims at restricting a state's power to its territory and it allows each state to assert power over its territory. However it has two more functions: jurisdiction also allows a state to represent its people (and those under its control) at the international level[17] (second function of jurisdiction) and especially in the modern (post World War II) sphere of international human rights it may also imply state responsibility[18] (third function of jurisdiction). For those states who have signed/ratified the European Convention of Human Rights the scope of human rights obligations is co-extensive with their jurisdiction.[19] The mere fact that a state has authority and exercises control over a person may give rise to such obligations in certain circumstances.[20] Furthermore, jurisdiction may impose positive and negative obligations on states to protect human rights even outside specific treaty obligations (although this is disputed).[21]

The second context is private international law, which refers to the domestic rules (usually part of a state's civil procedure law) governing civil and commercial disputes between private parties with a cross-border dimension. Private international law is not "international" law as such, but the domestic interface with international cases. In particular, first, it covers the competence of a domestic court to hear and decide a particular dispute (court jurisdiction); secondly, the question of which legal system's law that court uses to decide the case (applicable law); and thirdly, the question of whether a particular court decision will or will not be recognized and enforced (enforcement). Thus, private international law consists of the triumvirate of jurisdiction, applicable law, and enforcement. In the area of private law, there is no bar to a domestic court (eg the English High Court) applying foreign law (eg German law) as the applicable law to a dispute,[22] so that jurisdiction and applicable law do not necessarily relate to the same legal system.[23] The rules of private international law are metaphysical and methodological in that they come prior to the application of the material law to the issues in dispute and are used in order to pinpoint the law(s) used to solve the dispute.[24]

15 D Svantesson, *Extraterritoriality in Data Privacy Law* (ExTuto Publishing 2013) 85–86.

16 Chapter 4.

17 Crawford (n 5) 448.

18 G Noll, "Theorizing Jurisdiction" in A Orford and F Hoffmann (eds), *The Oxford Handbook of the Theory of International Law* (Oxford University Press 2016) 600–17.

19 Art 1 ECHR; *Jaloud v Netherlands* (47708/08) (2015) 60 EHRR 29; *Pisari v Moldova and Russia* (42139/12) unreported 19 October 2015 (ECHR); *Al-Skeini v United Kingdom* (55721/07) (2011) 53 EHRR 18.

20 *Al-Skeini v United Kingdom* (55721/07) (2011) 53 EHRR 18, para 137: "It is clear that, whenever the State through its agents exercises control and authority over an individual, and thus jurisdiction, the State is under an obligation under Art 1 to secure to that individual the rights and freedoms under Section 1 of the Convention that are relevant to the situation of that individual." And para 149.

21 This is not further explored in this book, but see C Tomuschat, "Obligations Arising for States Without or against their Will" (1993) 241 Recueil des Cours 195– 369.

22 Although the foreign law is treated as a matter of fact on which evidence is heard.

23 A difference is made between procedural law and substantive law, with the procedural law of the forum applying to the dispute, see Chapter 11.

24 H Muir Watt, "Theorizing Private International Law" in A Orford and F Hoffmann (eds), *The Oxford Handbook of the Theory of International Law* (Oxford University Press 2016) 862–81.

The third and fourth contexts relate to public law, namely the criminal justice system and regulatory or administrative law. This area of jurisdiction is about national law empowering the criminal justice agencies to act in cases with a cross-border dimension. With respect to the criminal justice system, a distinction can be made between investigative jurisdiction, the jurisdiction of the criminal courts and enforcement jurisdiction. Investigative jurisdiction refers to the competence of the police and prosecution authorities to gather intelligence, investigate a crime, and prepare the prosecution of a suspect, in particular where relevant data and evidence is located in a foreign territory. In the pre-internet days this issue arose only rarely as it is clear that public authorities of one state would have no jurisdiction to physically enter foreign territory to carry out investigations (unless specific mutual assistance arrangements are in place). By contrast in the internet era it is technically possible to access and search foreign servers remotely without entering the territory and to ask foreign intermediaries (internet service providers) for direct assistance.[25] Cross-border cooperation in criminal investigations also raises difficult questions as to which country's criminal procedure law applies to the investigation to ensure due process (this was one of the issues in the *Megaupload* case).[26] Enforcement jurisdiction is concerned with jurisdiction in extradition cases (where the requesting state must show that it has jurisdiction to try the case) and the principle of *ne bis idem*[27] as well as jurisdiction in the context of seizure of foreign assets.

Regulatory jurisdiction is about the question of when a regulatory body is competent to apply its powers to a foreign entity—whether *ex ante* through a licensing or authorization regime or *ex post* through the imposition of a fine or administrative penalty (or other sanction) for non-compliance with the rules and standards imposed by the regulator. One of the defining characteristics of public law jurisdiction is that a public body only ever applies its own laws, never foreign law.[28]

2. State sovereignty

The concept of "sovereignty" describes a state's power over its territory and, as a corollary, over the permanent population and activities located in that territory. One of the defining features of sovereignty is that each state is legally equal (ignoring *de facto* economic and political power) and independent from each other.[29] This structure of ordering international relations is traced back to the end of the Thirty Year War in 1648 and the Peace of Westphalia in Europe, which accepted that states have sovereignty, in the sense of exclusive power, within their territorial borders to determine their own affairs.

[25] Further discussed in Chapter 6.
[26] Further discussed in Chapter 6.
[27] Discussed in Chapter 4.
[28] U Kohl, *Jurisdiction and the Internet* (2007) 56
[29] Crawford (n 5) 447; see also Art 4 Declaratory Theory of Statehood as set out in Arts 1 and 3 of the Montevideo Convention on Rights and Duties of States, 26 December 1933, 165 LNTS 19, http://www.oas.org/juridico/english/treaties/a-40.html, accessed on14/7/2020, and Art 2(1) of the UN Charter.

Max Weber defined statehood as a community that asserted its power monopoly over a given territory (ie the legitimate power to use physical force).[30]

Moreover, sovereignty is bound up with the principle of self-determination on the international plane[31] as famously set out in President Woodrow Wilson's Fourteen Points on his vision of the world post World War I: that the world "be made safe for every peace-loving nation which (...) wishes to live its own life, determine its own institutions, be assured of justice and fair dealing with the other peoples of the world."[32]

Thus understood, sovereignty is tied to the international law principle of non-interference in the sense that each state's power is limited to its own territory and any overreaching is a breach of the sovereignty of *another* state and therefore it can be said that it identifies a relation to other states.[33] This principle of non-interference is also the basis on which the US courts have developed the presumption against extraterritoriality in US statutory interpretation as set out in the 1909 US Supreme Court decision of *American Banana v United Fruit Company* limiting the territorial scope of the Sherman Act to US territory. In this case, Mr Justice Holmes held that to apply any law other than the *lex locus delicti* would not only be unfair to the person acting in the foreign territory but would also be contrary to the principle of non-interference, which is part of the principle of comity between nations.[34]

Another of the defining features of sovereignty is that, at least in principle, a state is a legally independent agent of international law and has no superior authority above itself. Therefore, legal obligations under international law arise by the state limiting its sovereignty by joining an international organization or signing a treaty.[35] While it is clear that states have to comply with the treaty obligations they have entered into ("pacta sunt servanda"), for a long time sovereignty under international law was held to be absolute (as long as it does not infringe onto another state's sovereignty).[36]

However, it is disputed to what extent states are bound by international law frameworks (customary international law, humanitarian law, or human rights law) without having submitted themselves to, or having acquiesced into, such frameworks.[37] Furthermore, more recently, investor–state arbitration tribunals have held that transnational investment agreements should be interpreted against the state, to the benefit of the private investor. This is an example of the phenomenon of globalization where private law adjudication corals the sovereignty of nation states through an expansive interpretation of international law (in this case an investment treaty). Furthermore, the UN Charter recognizes that the maintenance of international peace and security is more important than the unlimited sovereignty of states by recognizing that even non-members of the UN have an obligation to act in accordance

[30] M Weber "Politics as a Vocation" (1918) translated in Weber's *Rationalism and Modern Society*. Translated and edited by Tony Waters and Dagmar Waters (Palgrave Macmillan 2015).

[31] UN Charter Art 1(2).

[32] Preamble, 8 January 2018, http://avalon.law.yale.edu/20th_century/wilson14.asp accessed on 14/7/2020.

[33] Crawford (n 5) 447; see also UN Charter of 26 June 1945, Art 1(2).

[34] 213 US 347, 356 (1909).

[35] Crawford (n 5) 448.

[36] *Case of the S.S. Lotus (Fr. v. Turk.)* PCIJ Rep Series A No 10.

[37] Crawford (n 5) 448.

with the Principles laid out in the Charter if this is necessary for international peace and security.[38]

The difference between sovereignty and jurisdiction is that sovereignty describes the power to rule, whereas jurisdiction describes the authority of a state to rule.[39] The root of the word *jurisdiction*[40] implies that it relates to making, adjudicating, interpreting, and enforcing the law.[41] Jurisdiction is therefore connected to law (as opposed to mere might or *imperium* or power without limit[42]) and also to the rightful lawmaker, law adjudicator, or law enforcer and the rule of law. *Jurisdiction* is thus connected to legitimacy, legal institutions, and rule-making.[43]

Hannah Arendt, writing on authority in the modern age (and since jurisdiction is about authority this is directly relevant to jurisdiction), clarifies the meaning of the political concept of authority by distinguishing it from coercion by force and persuasion through arguments. In her view authority is always hierarchical, whereas persuasion is based on egalitarianism. While both coercion and authority are hierarchical in structure, the crucial difference is that submission to authority is based on *external legitimization* (religious dogma and faith, a constitution, democratic elections, and/or tradition), whereas coercion is based on *force or power*. She associates coercion with totalitarianism and unlimited power of a ruler over its people and distinguishes this from governance based on authority, where, if the external legitimization is removed (because of the diminishing influence of religion or loss of tradition or lack of recognition of a government by its people), authority implodes.[44] She therefore makes clear that authority is very different from the power of violence: "where force is used, authority itself has failed"[45] and "the difference between tyranny and authoritarian government has always been that the tyrant rules in accordance with his own will and interest, whereas even the most draconic authoritarian government is bound by laws."[46]

Sovereignty is about the power of a state over its territory and people, whereas jurisdiction is concerned with authority to state the law. The distinction is played out in the international law field by the process of recognition of states as being equal among equals.[47] A state that cannot establish an effective administration over its territory based on law (eg a state torn apart by a civil war) may not be recognized as having jurisdiction by other states or certain (but not all) acts of that state will not be recognized by other states. However, this threshold is low: normally other states will recognize a state that exercises effective power over its territory and people, without inquiring

[38] Art 2(6) and (7).
[39] Crawford (n 5) 448.
[40] "Juris dicere" is saying the law, see Ryngaert (n 5).
[41] Noll (n 18) 600–01.
[42] Dorsett and McVeigh (n 2) 11.
[43] In the context of the jurisdiction of Contracting States to the European Convention on Human Rights and its applicability to checkpoint in areas of war and civil unrest see L Raible, "The Extraterritoriality of the ECHR" (2016) 2 European Human Rights Law Review 161–68, 166–67.
[44] H Arendt, *Between Past and Future: Six Essays in Political Thought* (Penguin Classics Paperback 2006) 91–98.
[45] ibid 92.
[46] ibid 97.
[47] See also Sassen (n 3) Reprint 2014, 61.

whether governance is based on the rule of law and/or legitimate, as this would be seen as an internal matter for the people within the state. Furthermore, recognition is frequently tied up with territorial disputes, ethnic disputes, or ideological differences between states, which are of a purely political nature.[48] In other words, states may only recognize another state if it is in their political interest and recognition can be used to avoid obligations under international law. Thus, it is controversial whether recognition by other states is constitutive or merely declaratory for statehood and jurisdiction.[49] Crawford considers recognition as merely declaratory: "states cannot by their independent judgment remove or abrogate any competence of other states established by international law."[50] Therefore the distinction between sovereignty and jurisdiction discussed above may be more theoretical and less practical, both in political and legal terms.

Jurisdiction (authority) may in fact simply be the legal consequence of sovereignty (power). Thus understood, the legal conception of the relationship between sovereignty, statehood, and jurisdiction is this: statehood arises automatically if certain legal criteria are fulfilled cumulatively[51] and sovereignty (defined as independent power and effective governance and administration in a state) is one of these criteria for statehood[52] applied with others such as state territory, permanent population. Jurisdiction, in turn is one of the automatic *consequences of statehood*, that is, the legal competence of the state to act internally (authority over its population) and externally (interaction with other states).[53]

3. State sovereignty, national identity in the context of globalization

This book contains a legal analysis of how digital technology has impacted on the legal concept of jurisdiction in all its facets. The brief discussion of globalization in this section provides a much-needed theoretical background to the legal stage, painting the larger picture from a political and socio-economic point of view. The difficulty here is that there is a burgeoning literature on globalization in the social sciences, which it is difficult to do justice to in a few pages. Nevertheless, a summary of some of the key themes provides new insights into why exactly the complex phenomenon of globalization leads to various challenges to the Westphalian system, sovereignty over territory, and jurisdiction. Arguably the Westphalian system has failed completely in regulating credit and financial markets to provide stability at the end of the twentieth century. According to Susan Strange, for example, "a dangerous gap is therefore opening up

[48] As examples one may consider the non-recognition by certain States of Taiwan, Kosovo, East Germany 1949–90, or Palestine.
[49] Crawford (n 5) 145–46.
[50] ibid 146.
[51] Declaratory Theory of Statehood as set out in Arts 1 and 3 of the Montevideo Convention on Rights and Duties of States, 26 December 1933, 165 LNTS 19, http://www.oas.org/juridico/english/treaties/a-40.html accessed on 14/7/2020.
[52] Crawford (n 5) 134–35.
[53] ibid 127–36 on statehood.

between the international institutions that are unable or unwilling to discipline the banks, the hedge and pension fund managers and the markets, and the national systems of supervision and control whose reach is not long enough or quick enough to prevent trouble."[54] Zygmunt Bauman argues that modernity has created the illusion of "being in control," which is challenged by what he calls "the new world disorder" after the end of the Cold War, which has created a "field of scattered and disparate forces" with the consequence that no-one seems to be in control any longer.[55] According to him globalization occurs in a kind of no-man's land, which stretches "beyond the reach of the design and action capacity of anybody's in particular."[56] John Ruggie in 1993 even links the new paradigm in international relations to the postmodern condition in society more generally.[57] Bauman furthermore argues that nation states' base was a tripod of military, economic, and cultural sovereignty and that the three legs of this tripod are now broken.[58]

However, it should be added that the legal notion of sovereign equality of states has always been a legal fiction and an oversimplification of economic realities—trading and economic conditions, to an extent, have always limited a state's sovereignty (certainly for the weaker state). Bauman also points out that states have always formed groups and alliances, thus voluntarily surrendering a degree of sovereignty, and that states have never been entirely self-sufficient.[59]

This section summarizes the key features of globalization and examines the jurisdictional challenges arising therefrom. Globalization is a buzzword and was debated as such from the 1990s onwards.[60] Bauman states that globalization is not an intellectually clear concept, but rather refers to a generalized *perception* of world affairs as having an "indeterminate, unruly and self-propelled character," which is contrasted with the decline of the nation state.[61]

As Manfred Steger points out, the term is used to describe both a process and a condition.[62] Although globalization is a complex phenomenon, Steger identifies four elements. The first element is the creation of new and the multiplication of existing networks and connections that transcend traditional borders. Secondly, globalization involves the expansion and augmentation of transnational social, economic, and political connections, activities, and relationships. Thirdly, social relations are intensified in such a way that events happening far away can shape local responses.[63] Finally, the

[54] S Strange, "The Westfailure System" (1999) 25(3) Review of International Studies 345–54, 350.

[55] Z Bauman, *Globalisation The Human Consequences* (Columbia University Press 1998) 57–58.

[56] ibid 60.

[57] JG Ruggie, "Territoriality and Beyond: Problematizing Modernity in International Relations" (1993) 41(1) International Organization 139–74, 140, 144–48.

[58] Bauman (n 55) 61–64.

[59] ibid 64.

[60] M Steger, *Globalization* (Oxford University Press 2013) 1; albeit that there's much earlier research literature, see eg JG Ruggie, "International Responses to Technology: Concepts and Trends" (1975) 29(3) International Organization 557–83.

[61] Bauman (n 55) 59.

[62] Steger (n 60) 9.

[63] An example for this is the British truck driver Dave Duncan who spontaneously set up a fundraising page to help the family of the Polish truck driver Lukasz Urban who was murdered in the Berlin terrorist attack in December 2016 after he tried to stop the truck being driven into the Christmas market by the terrorist, https://www.gofundme.com/lukaszurban accessed on 14/7/2020.

fourth element is that globalization does not only impact material, objective social, political, and economic structures but also affects human identity, leading to people having both local and global identities.[64] Since the political system had been organized almost exclusively on the basis of geographical territories and borders for several centuries, populations have developed a "sense of belonging" to their particular nation state. This sense of belonging to a particular nation state formed peoples' collective identities by establishing the notion of a familiar "us" and a foreign "them."[65] While globalization is likely to have some impact on the shaping of national identity, for large parts of the population it may well mean that a negative reaction to the process of globalization means an augmentation of a sense of national identity and increased attachment to the nation state. One of (no doubt) several explanations for the majority vote to leave the EU in the UK Referendum in June 2016 was precisely that a fear of the consequences of globalization (and in particular anti-migration sentiments) motivated voters to vote for what the Leave Campaign called "taking back" control over social, political, and economic matters by the nation state.[66] Hannah Arendt examines the link between authority, identity, and tradition and finds that human beings need permanence and durability because we are mortal and that national roots provide this much-needed link between identity and authority.[67] To the extent that globalization uproots people's identity and sense of belonging, the reaction is negative and leads to a loss of feelings of security. In fact, it has been discussed in the literature that globalization may actually accentuate people's sense of national identity and lead to a rejection of a global, multicultural identity.[68]

Furthermore, globalization leads to or at least contributes to growing inequality[69] and a race to the bottom as a consequence of increased competition and growing economies of scale (enabled through technology), causing insufficient investment in sectors providing middle-income jobs, which is partly also caused by the hypermobility of capital that is following the lure of short-term profits on a global basis. These developments have the effect of depleting the middle classes in developed nations and discouraging the development of a strong middle class in developing countries.[70]

Commentators point in particular to two economic drivers of globalization: global financial markets and the mobility of capital,[71] "the geographic dispersal of firms'

[64] Steger (n 60) 14–15; Sassen (n 3) Reprint 2014, 38.

[65] Steger (n 60) 60.

[66] It is highly doubtful whether leaving the EU will achieve this, but this is another matter not discussed here.

[67] Arendt (n 44) 93–95.

[68] Sassen (n 3) Reprint 2014 Preface.

[69] The richest eight persons in the world (Bill Gates, Amancio Ortega, Warren Buffett, Carlos Slim Helú, Jeff Bezos, Mark Zuckerberg, Larry Ellison, and Michael Bloomberg) own more wealth than the poorest 50 per cent of humanity (3.6 million people), according to the Oxfam Report 2017; interestingly six out of these eight men have made their wealth in the IT and communications and information sectors, sectors in which network effects lead to dominance and concentration of power. The same Report states that 1 per cent of the richest own more than 99 per cent of the rest of the world's population, see Oxfam, "An Economy for the 99%" Report published on 16 January 2017, http://policy-practice.oxfam.org.uk/publications/an-economy-for-the-99-its-time-to-build-a-human-economy-that-benefits-everyone-620170 accessed on 14/7/2020.

[70] Sassen (n 3) Reprint 2014, 39–40; Strange (n 54) 346.

[71] ibid 349.

factories, offices, service outlets and markets," and the "global assembly line in manufacturing," including the use of special export processing zones[72] and offshoring of clerical work and call centres.[73] The purpose of these forms of offshoring is frequently precisely to avoid taxation, business laws, and regulations and ultimately the jurisdiction of a particular state. Saskia Sassen terms this a form of extraterritoriality:[74] "it creates a space economy that goes beyond the regulatory umbrella of the state."[75] This leads to an economy where the factories, services, and outlets required for production are highly dispersed geographically, but are also integrated in a centralized and streamlined corporate system, with centralized top-level control and corporate services, frequently situated in a developed country.[76] Global financial markets as another driver of globalization have risen exponentially, partly through the use of online forms of communication, which enable transmission of financial information and funds across the globe in seconds, partly through increased connectivity.[77] Since states have less control over the regulation of financial markets, short-term investment in financial markets dominates over long-term investment in production. This in turn means that economies are driven by the dictates of financial markets, so that in the words of *Keynes* "the position is serious when enterprise becomes the bubble on a whirlpool of speculation. When the capital development of a country becomes a by-product of the activities of a casino, the job is likely to be ill-done."[78]

Nevertheless, it is disputed in the literature on globalization to what extent globalization in fact reduces the nation state—in most areas the nation state continues to be the "political container of modern social life."[79] It seems unlikely that globalization spells the death of the nation state or the current international order any time soon, but it has led to significant changes *within* the nation state.[80] Globalization is changing the "form, power and functions" of the state.[81] Sassen argues that globalization has been formed and enabled by institutions *within* nation states who did become the active conduit to allow globalization to occur in the first place.[82] Examples of such institutions from the legal field are the pre-eminence of contract in US common law (eg over consumer protection regulation) and the pre-dominance of international

[72] Special free trading zones in developing economies to promote manufacturing processes and employment with exemption from taxes and business regulations to encourage foreign direct investment and employment, see UNCTAD, Enhancing the Contribution of Export Processing Zones to the Sustainable Development Goals, UN 2015 4; in 2015 there were about 4000 such zones, see *The Economist* "Special Economic Zones-Political Priority, Economic Gamble" (2015), http://www.economist.com/news/finance-and-economics/21647630-free-trade-zones-are-more-popular-everwith-politicians-if-not accessed on 14/7/2020.

[73] Sassen (n 3) Reprint 2014 7–8.

[74] ibid 14.

[75] ibid 9.

[76] ibid 10.

[77] ibid 12, 46.

[78] JM Keynes, *General Theory of Employment, Interest and Money* (Macmillan Cambridge University Press 1936) ch 12 quoted (partly) in Sassen (n 3) Reprint 2014, 45.

[79] Steger (n 60) 61, 65.

[80] J Baylis, S Smith, and P Owens, "Globalization and the Post-cold War Order" in J Baylis and S Smith (eds), *The Globalization of World Politics* (6th edn, Oxford University Press 2013) 513–26, 513, 523.

[81] ibid.

[82] S Sassen, *Territory, Authority, Rights: From Medieval to Global Assemblages* (Princeton University Press 2006) 222–71.

commercial arbitration to solve cross-border commercial disputes outside the state courts. Therefore changes in the legal systems of nation states have acted as enablers of economic globalization. Bauman states that the new global economic players seek political fragmentation and weak states as this serves their interests of avoiding taxes, achieving deregulation, and avoiding law enforcement. These players need states to achieve a degree of security but they want the state to be weak.[83]

For this discussion in particular, two roots of globalization are particularly relevant. First, the neoliberal political choices made by governments in the 1980s to liberalize global financial markets (eg currency, bond, and capital markets) and to deregulate many economic sectors, which in turn enabled economic globalization.[84] Second, the rise of technology (developments in telecommunications and the internet) and in particular digitalization led to a staggering increase in denationalization of transactions and speeding up of transactions in addition to causing a direct jurisdictional and regulatory challenge and deregulation of markets.

It is clear that global trade and mobility of capital (Bauman calls this the extraterritoriality of capital leading to feeble and impotent states[85]) are restricting the capacity of governments to establish and impose local standards.[86] States have less control over economic policy (eg devaluing their currency)[87] and less money for social welfare and redistribution of some wealth for public purposes (eg due to reduced ability to collect tax).[88] It is for this reason that globalization leads to great enrichment and great impoverishment at the same time.[89]

On a conceptual level, globalization has three immediate impacts on the concept of jurisdiction.

First, since globalization makes it difficult for states to make and enforce laws and rules and leads to new forms of social, political, and economic ordering across borders, even if it does not mean the end of the nation state, it does mean that *de facto* states have less power and therefore impacts on their sovereignty. With respect to the internet, states also have less enforcement power, as enforcement becomes more complex, resource intensive, and expensive. This leads to a loss of sovereignty of states. Thus, enforcement of the law is frequently confined to the local level.

Second, and as a consequence, it directly impacts on state governments' authority, since if states have less power to regulate their affairs voters may question the utility to vote or participate in the democratic political processes. "There may be little point in holding national and local politicians accountable through elections if these politicians remain relatively powerless to exercise influence over global corporations, global technology, global environmental changes or the global financial system."[90] Therefore globalization undermines national democratic processes and as a consequence the authority (and jurisdiction) of states.

[83] Bauman (n 55) 68.
[84] Sassen (n 3) Reprint 2014, 18, 29.
[85] Bauman (n 55)) 67.
[86] Steger (n 60) 66.
[87] Bauman (n 55) 65.
[88] Sassen (n 3) Reprint 2014, 6, 48–49; Strange (n 54)352
[89] Bauman (n 55) 72.
[90] Baylis, Smith, and Owens (n 80) 522.

Third, territory as a connecting factor to authority and jurisdiction has become less significant. The extent to which this statement is true, is debated in the literature. Jack Goldsmith and Tim Wu, for example, argue that people, institutions, data centres, and activities continue to be physically grounded within the territory of nation states.[91] But there are a number of factors that explain why territory is less relevant in the world of the twenty-first century. The territorial links may be opaque or obscure in the sense that the physical location of the activities or actors subject to the law may be difficult to pin down. Additionally, some territories are more global than others, in the sense that they connive with global actors by disapplying their national, local law and creating denationalized spaces, which are governed by different, frequently private norms.[92] Moreover, internet technologies allow for activities taking place in one state to be controlled remotely from a location in another state. Examples include a remotely controlled lights-out data centre or the provision of online gambling services remotely provided from another state.[93]

Fourth, in a globalized world activities are more likely to have effects inviting regulation/the application of criminal law in several states, not merely the state in which the activity is carried out.[94]

Fifth, because of the multitude of connections and distributed enterprises in a globalized world, law enforcement (enforcement or executive jurisdiction) is more expensive and/or resource intensive, with the consequence that states may consider applying and enforcing their laws to be impractical or are forced to focus on narrow enforcement priorities.[95]

Finally, this leads to the political dimension of the jurisdictional challenge: states are reluctant to admit their reduced sovereignty and authority and are concerned about being accused of acting extraterritorially and therefore proceed with a degree of caution so as to not expose their lack of authority. This leads to further confusion about the limits of their authority and principles of jurisdiction.

4. Global law?

Global law is another buzzword, simultaneously an oxymoron, since, if law is defined as legal rules made by the nation state, the term "global law" is a contradiction in itself. William Twining criticizes the use of the adjective "global" in phrases such as "global law" as "globababble" for being vague, ambiguous, and misleading and the purpose of which is hype and exaggeration.[96] However, it is clear that global law is not the same as international law: international law is part of global law, but global law goes beyond public international law. As we have seen, international law is concerned with relationships between states and universal obligations associated with statehood, whereas some forms of global law are implemented by private parties for private parties.

[91] J Goldsmith and T Wu, *Who Controls the Internet?* (Oxford University Press 2006).
[92] Sassen (n 3) Reprint 2014 9.
[93] Discussed further in Chapters 3 and 15.
[94] Discussed further in Chapters 3 and 4.
[95] Discussed further in Chapters 3, 5, 7, 8, and 15.
[96] See eg W Twining, "Intimations of Global Law (Publication Review)" (2016) Public Law 540–44.

Global law could be understood in one of three ways. The first one would be to regard it as a solution to a problem; in that sense it is the floss supplementing the toothbrush, in that it can get to transnational spaces where national laws (the toothbrush) cannot reach. Thus, understood global law becomes a form of risk management in transnational transactions and relationships, addressing regulatory challenges arising from differences in legal cultures. This understanding of the term also means that global law becomes an instrument (however rudimentary and imperfect at present) for addressing emerging global problems[97] such as climate change, global economic crises, or technology regulation through Codes of Practice.[98]

Secondly, another sense of the phrase are rules and norms that are part of the core of all legal systems such that they are effectively of universal application. For example, an argument that is made in relation to international human rights and humanitarian law is precisely that fundamental norms form the core of all legal systems. More generally it may be described as an attempt to find the common core or digest of all legal systems through comparison and legal approximation in the hope of extracting the common denominator, which could then be described as a form of global law.[99] Understood in this way comparative law becomes a tool for the quest of finding the global law. Depending on how this quest is undertaken, the risk here is that it either is too focused on one dominant cultural legal tradition including its transplants (eg English common law or Western civil law) or that the commonalities between worldwide legal systems (and religions and cultures) are greater than commonly assumed, so that this quest becomes a self-defeating exercise.[100] Understood in this way, global law could become an answer to finding the applicable law.

Thirdly, the phrase can be used to describe a study of phenomena that share certain characteristics, namely governance in transnational situations. This section examines global law as a range of phenomena, but it approaches the field of study from the opposite end: the question here is not whether global law exists based on these phenomena, but whether national forms of governance within states are being slowly replaced and/or supplemented by, relatively speaking, more global forms of governance (rule-making, standard setting, and rule enforcement). It seems that state actors and national law as such are becoming less and less self-contained and independent and national law is operating in tandem with regulatory forms situated outside the nation state, such as global law governance.[101]

The field of study termed "global law" can therefore be understood as new forms of governance not attached to a national law, but which are nevertheless rule-based. These are specialized, particular phenomena rather than systemic changes.[102] Furthermore, global law is applied and not theoretical—it is a potential way of addressing global problems and regulatory challenges, not a philosophical quest on the essential characteristics and the fundamental nature of law(s).[103] Global law can

[97] W Twining, *Globalisation and Legal Scholarship* (Wolf Legal Publishers 2011) 46–48.

[98] See further Chapter 3.

[99] eg the Common Frame of Reference for European Private Law or the work of the International Institution for the Unification of Private Law (UNIDROIT).

[100] Twining (n 97) 19.

[101] N Walker, *Intimations of Global Law* (Cambridge University Press 2015) 16.

[102] Sassen (n 3) Reprint 2014, 18.

[103] D Priel, "Two Models of General Jurisprudence" (2013) 4(4) Transnational Legal Theory 512–23, 514.

therefore also be described as both an aspirational idea and a transnational practice.[104] Furthermore, the debate about global law is also epistemic—it informs our thinking about law outside the traditionally recognized systems of national and international law.[105]

Scholars in the political science field when discussing global governance and global law point to the rise in the presence and activities of national and international non-government organizations (NGOs), cross-border social movements, and international cooperation efforts between states at the national, regional, and municipal levels.[106]

Globalization optimists point to the emerging sphere of a global civil society and argue that from these beginnings cosmopolitan, democratic, tolerant, and accountable governance structures will develop.[107] This vision is idealistic or, more likely, utopian, as it does not take into account who holds power in a globalized world, how this power is or is not subjected to checks and balances, and how those in power act in their own self-interest. This vision also does not consider the feasibility of global democracy,[108] the impact of opposition and resistance to globalizing forces, sometimes leading to irrational, counterproductive results,[109] and the power structures in a world of globalized states more generally.

From a legal point of view, global law as a field of study comprises the development and enforcement of rules (and norms) outside the traditional national legal systems in order to regulate a multitude of transnational transactions and relationships. Global law in this sense need not be completely outside the existing national or international legal order, but is at least partially independent from it. In fact, one of the defining features of the notion of global law is that it does not derive its authority from its provenance or source, but from "global relevance and resonance" through consensus-building dialogue or through approximation.[110]

More generally the purpose of global law is to enable the expansion of the economy beyond the national borders while minimizing legal transaction risks,[111] by overcoming differences in legal cultures and making enforcement of rules and norms effective by avoiding conflicts of law.

For the purposes of this section I distinguish between five different forms of global law. First, law-making and enforcement by international (inter-governmental) or supranational organizations, which are strategically placed to overcome the limitations of national law but frequently rely on lengthy and slow consensus-based procedures (agreements, treaties, guidelines, and model laws), followed by national implementation procedures. Second, formal (treaty-based) and informal (ad-hoc) cooperation between governments is used to overcome some of the regulatory challenges of

104 Walker (n 101) 1.
105 ibid 26–27.
106 Steger (n 60) 67–70; Baylis, Smith, and Owens (n 80) 522.
107 Steger (n 60) 70–73; D Held, A McGrew, D Goldblatt, and J Perraton, *Global Transformations* (Stanford University Press 1999).
108 Baylis, Smith, and Owens (n 80) 522.
109 Steger (n 60) 73.
110 Walker (n 101) 19–20.
111 Sassen (n 3) Reprint 2014, 17.

globalization processes. The examples are endless, but of relevance to internet regulation are, for instance, mutual assistance in transborder criminal matters,[112] Interpol,[113] the European Cybercrime Centre,[114] the OECD's International Consumer Protection Enforcement Network,[115] the European Advertising Standards Alliance,[116] and data sharing in respect of passenger name records between the US/Canada/Australia and the EU.[117] Many of these cooperation efforts do now occur outside the traditional diplomatic channels between central governments and instead take place at the regional or municipal level or between specialized agencies.

A third instance of global law is rule-making and standard setting by multinational corporate entities, where transnational companies provide for rules and standards within their own corporate network, for example, codes and terms implemented by social media companies to regulate content online.[118]

Fourth, contracts and private law play an ever-increasing role in regulating transborder transactions and relationships. Some of these forms of governance are laws in a traditional, doctrinal sense, for example, contract law, but used in a field where one would expect state-made public law to govern. Some of the rules are not law strictly speaking (sometimes termed "softlaw"[119]), such as Codes of Conduct or Privacy Policies. Different instances of regulation by private law can be distinguished: for example, a trade or industry association divulging Codes of Conduct or other rules for its international members, which are binding the members through contract (ie the promise to comply in exchange for membership and the use of the associated branding, such as trademark protected trustmarks).

A second example is online cloud provider platforms,[120] through their Terms and Conditions, Acceptable Use Policies, End-user Licence Agreements (EULAs), Privacy

[112] eg the European Convention on Mutual Assistance in Criminal Matters of 20 April 1959, Strasbourg ETS No 030 (Council of Europe); ASEAN Treaty on Mutual Legal Assistance in Criminal Matters of 29 November 2004, Kuala Lumpur

[113] The International Police Organisation, eg using the International Child Sexual Exploitation (ICSE) database to identify and rescue child sex abuse victims worldwide and prosecute their abusers locally, https://www.interpol.int/en/Crimes/Crimes-against-children/International-Child-Sexual-Exploitation-database Accessed on 14/7/2020.

[114] Set up by Europol in 2013 providing capacity building and training, digital forensics, and operational support across borders, https://www.europol.europa.eu/about-europol/european-cybercrime-centre-ec3 accessed on 14/7/2020.

[115] https://www.icpen.org accessed on 14/7/2020.

[116] A network of co-regulatory bodies regulating advertising in various EU Member States, providing for a cross-border complaints system (infringing advertising), http://www.easa-alliance.org/about-easa accessed on 14/7/2020.

[117] Agreement between the US and the EU on the use and transfer of passenger name records to the US Department of Homeland Security of 14 December 2011, signed in Brussels, OJ L215/5; Agreement between the European Community and the Government of Canada on the processing of Advance Passenger Information and Passenger Name Record Data, OJ L82/15 published on 21 March 2006 and Agreement between the European Union and Australia on the processing and transfer of Passenger Name Record (PNR) data by air carriers to the Australian Customs and Border Protection Service of 29 September 2011, OJ L186/4.

[118] See further Chapter 3.

[119] B Peters and J Karlsson Schaffer, "The Turn to Authority Beyond States" (2013) 4(3) Transnational Legal Theory 315–35, 317.

[120] eg e-commerce platforms such as eBay, Amazon, Uber, and Airbnb; social media platforms such as Facebook (Instagram, WhatsApp) or Twitter; content sharing (YouTube, Flickr) or gaming platforms (such as Steam).

Policies, and other contractual clauses imposing a private law regulatory regime on end-users, regulating not only the contractual relationship between the end-user and the online provider, but also the conduct of end-users amongst themselves. This effectively creates a regulatory system for the online environment, regulating public law matters such as illegal content, cybercrime, data protection, consumer protection, cybersecurity, and protection of intellectual property, as well as more private law matters such as liability and contractual rights (and their exclusion).[121]

This phenomenon of using private law, contractual mechanisms, and soft-law as a regulatory tool has also been described as "self-regulation," that is, the establishment of standards and rules and their enforcement by providers or by the relevant business sector.

Its purpose is to avoid conflicts of law and conflicts of jurisdiction in transnational transactions and relationships. Another purpose can be to achieve clarity and reduce legal uncertainty. Self-regulation, especially in technology markets moving at lightning speeds, is also used to capture the technical and business expertise within the industry for the purposes of regulation. This helps providers to protect their own legitimate interests, manage risk, improve standards, and establish user trust. Thus understood, self-regulation can be used for players to distinguish their offering on the market as trustworthy.

However, its purpose can also be the opposite: evading the application of stricter (consumer, privacy, product liability, environmental) standards set by (certain) nation states. Thus, self-regulation can also be a tool to avoid stringent regulation through an attempt at pre-empting the states' regulatory initiative and exploiting their inability to enforce the national law effectively across borders. To the extent that this happens, self-regulation may lead to regulation at the lowest acceptable denominator and a race to the bottom (in terms of regulatory standards). Self-regulation can be criticized on the basis that it is essentially self-serving the interests of the person who drafts the rules (the platform provider or the relevant industry), especially if not all stakeholders are effectively represented and involved in drafting the private legal regime. If these contractual, private legal norms are imposed by the more powerful party on the weaker and are drafted and enforced without transparency or accountability, it is misleading to bestow the authority of law on them.[122] Furthermore, there may be doubts about the enforceability and effectiveness of self-regulation and concerns about its compliance with fundamental human rights norms such as privacy or non-discrimination.

Finally, global law may also refer to private dispute resolution systems, avoiding jurisdictional challenges where the competent court is unclear or can be disputed between the parties. An example for this is the success story of international commercial arbitration (and more recently, investment arbitration) as the preferred dispute resolution procedure for transnational disputes. Fabian Gélinas has described it as "global and meta-normative, much like contract."[123] He argues that legitimacy of arbitration

[121] Although it should be noted that this regulatory system is of course interacting with national laws such as consumer protection or intellectual property or data protection and privacy laws and that many if not most of these platforms *do* adapt their contractual clauses to the regions or countries they target their services to and rarely will rely on purely "global" contractual clauses.

[122] Peters and Karlsson Schaffer (n 119) 324.

[123] F Gélinas, "Arbitration as Transnational Governance by Contract" (2016) 7(2) Transnational Legal Theory 181–98.

stems not only from the private law concept of consent of the parties, but from the function of arbitration as adjudication complying with the rule of law and due process (reasons, rationality, and coherence).[124] Arbitration has effectively emerged as a means of transnational governance by contract.[125] The widespread adoption of the New York Convention on Arbitration ensuring the cross-border enforceability of arbitration agreements and awards has been the key to this success.[126] However, as Gélinas points out, arbitration is a private–public law hybrid, not merely an instrument of private law.[127]

The final chapter of this book will discuss to what extent these global law phenomena are apt in overcoming the regulatory and jurisdictional challenges posed by internet technologies and applications.

5. Nexus to territory: territoriality, interests, and connecting factors; extraterritoriality

The current system of jurisdiction is largely based on territoriality, based on the so-called Westphalian international order, which allowed each sovereign to determine affairs within their territory to the exclusion of other sovereigns (principle of non-interference), crystallized in the 1648 Westphalian Peace terminating the period of religious wars in Europe (Thirty Years War). This was a shift of paradigm from the Medieval and Renaissance periods in Europe where there was no exclusive sovereignty based on territory, allowing for a degree of pluralist legal systems coexisting in parallel within the same territory, based on adherence to religious authority (the Catholic Church in pre-reformation Europe), kinship (allegiance to the local rulers), citizenship, or trading or other relationships (eg membership in the Hanseatic League or a religious order).[128] Thus, laws coexisted in a territory with shifting hierarchies (eg canon law, common law, law merchant, municipal laws, etc). Therefore exclusive territorial jurisdiction is not inevitable or immutable: jurisdiction based on a territorial basis may not be exclusive, allowing for pluralist legal systems coexisting within the same territory.[129] Which system of jurisdiction prevails (exclusive territory or pluralism within the territory) depends on the relative power of the sovereign in a territory and the external forces reaching into that territory. To the extent that the process of globalization leads to a weakening of state sovereigns' exclusive power, it may cause a return towards a more pluralist system of jurisdiction in state territories.

However, territorial jurisdiction has been strongly entrenched in legal doctrine, as exemplified by Chief Justice Marshall's dictum in *Schooner Exchange v McFaddon*: "the jurisdiction of the nation within its own territory is necessarily exclusive and absolute."[130]

124 ibid.
125 ibid.
126 ibid.
127 ibid.
128 Ryngaert (n 5) 50–54; Ruggie (n 57) 150.
129 Sassen (n 3) 3; Ruggie (n 57) 149.
130 11 US (7 Cranch) 116, 136–37 (1812).

Under the Westphalian system of territorial sovereignty, jurisdiction is directly or indirectly connected to a state's territory: for a state to claim jurisdiction over a matter it has to demonstrate a clear nexus of the matter with its territory. This nexus can consist of (1) clear connecting factors such as person acting, objects (such as property), actions, or effects located on the territory combined with (2) legitimate interests of the state to assume jurisdiction.[131]

But even if (which is not the case) international law obligations or a state's national law imposed a strict obligation of only assuming jurisdiction if the matter to be regulated occurred on the territory (such as the principle of *locus delicti*) the connecting factors are by no means clear in all cases. For example, in the context of a particular crime it may be difficult to pinpoint a single conduct or an act to a particular territory.[132] By way of illustration, in the context of blackmail, defined under English law as "making any unwarranted demand with menaces,"[133] if the criminal act is the sending of a WhatsApp message by a sender in England to a recipient in Germany, it is difficult to determine the location where the demand with menaces was made. Furthermore, some offences consist of an act and the consequences resulting from the act and the act may take place in a jurisdiction different from the jurisdiction(s) where the result(s) occur(s). With such types of "two-step" offences it may be difficult to determine with certainty the *locus delicti*.[134] The required nexus to territory may not be clear or more than one place may establish such a nexus, but the nexus is required under the doctrine of territoriality.

If such a nexus cannot be shown a state may be accused of interfering with the affairs of another state and applying its law "extraterritorially."[135] However, because of the difficulty of pinpointing the connecting factor(s) states claim that effects or impacts on the territory are sufficient to provide the link.

Some scholars, however, go even further by arguing that in the postmodern globalized world, where many legal conflicts are likely to be multijurisdictional by their nature, that is, have credible connection factors to many jurisdictions, reliance by one state on one connecting factor to assert jurisdiction implicates extraterritoriality.[136] They criticize the concept of territoriality exercised by linking territory to connection factors as a legal method for finding jurisdiction.[137]

This brings the discussion to the concept of extraterritoriality. The term is frequently used in this pejorative sense, criticizing a state for asserting exorbitant jurisdiction beyond the affairs connected to its own territory, in particular in US and common law scholarship. US scholars have defined the claim of extraterritoriality as "resistance" to state authority made by actors with particular interests to promote (eg

131 The detailed principles for asserting jurisdiction are discussed in Chapter 4 and Chapter 6, but see eg in relation to property or persons within territory the US Supreme Court case of *Pennoyer v Neff* 95 US 714, 722–23 (1877).

132 AJ Colangelo, "A Unified Approach to Extraterritoriality" (2011) 97 Virginia Law Review 1019–109, 1040.

133 Section 21 Theft Act 1968 (example based on *Treacy v DPP* [1971] AC 537(HoL)).

134 Further discussed in Chapter 6.

135 *Treacy v DPP* [1971] AC 537(HoL) 561 (Lord Diplock).

136 Colangelo (n 132)1044; Svantesson (n 15).

137 Colangelo (n 132)1044.

a defendant in a criminal trial)[138] or, it has been defined, more pragmatically, where an act occurs outside the territory of the US, the US claims to regulate that foreign act.[139] Extraterritoriality has also been defined as the (claimed) "competence of a state to make, apply and enforce rules of conduct in respect of persons, property or events beyond its territory."[140]

Part of the confusion about the use of the term extraterritoriality stems from the fact that the concept of territoriality as a legitimate ground for jurisdiction is also a proxy for authority over the people on a territory. To the extent that territoriality thus becomes synonymous with power over territory, extraterritorial jurisdiction becomes an oxymoron.[141]

However, since not all legitimate bases of jurisdiction are based on territoriality (such as the active personality principle or the universality principle),[142] it is by no means clear that extraterritorial assumption of jurisdiction is contrary to international law.[143] German authors state that the passing of extraterritorial laws is principally permissible under international law with the consequence that in the regulation of a particular subject matter more than one state can be competent. It is acknowledged that this may lead to conflicts, which in turn makes it necessary for states to exercise restraint, for example, through the doctrine of comity.[144]

In fact, certain forms of extraterritoriality have been well-recognized under international law. A historical example (among European states) is the creation of extraterritorial enclaves on the territory of another state, such as those created by European States (and the US) in their trading relationships with the Ottoman Empire, and later, China.[145] A second example is the right of embassy: when states started to claim territorial exclusivity and other sovereign players of international law (states and international organizations) were allowed to set up embassies, effectively tiny territories of another state within the territory of the granting state and usually on a reciprocal basis.[146] When Edward VI insisted that the new English prayer book should be used in all churches on English soil, Charles V refused to accept such an edict—hence the fiction arose that the church service was not taking place on the territory, but that (chapels in) embassies constituted "little islands of alien sovereignty."[147]

[138] HL Buxbaum, "Territory, Territoriality and the Resolution of Jurisdictional Conflict" (2009) 57 American Journal of Comparative Law 631, 635.

[139] Colangelo (n 132) 1020.

[140] M Kamminga, "Extraterritoriality" in R Wolfrum (ed), *The Max Planck Encyclopedia of Public International Law* (online edn, Oxford University Press 2010).

[141] In the context of the jurisdictional scope of the ECHR, see Raible (n 43) 167.

[142] See discussion in Chapter 4 and M Martyniszyn, "On Extraterritoriality and the Gazprom Case" (2015) 36(7) European Competition Law Review 291–94, 291; U Kohl *Jurisdiction and the Internet* (Cambridge University Press 2007) 39.

[143] C Kuner, "Data Protection and International Jurisdiction on the Internet" Part II (2010) 18(3) International Journal of Law and Information Technology 227–47, 241; Svantesson (n 15) 84–85 makes a clear distinction between "exorbitant" and "extraterritorial" claims to jurisdiction. See also Council of Europe, European Committee on Crime Problems "Extraterritorial Criminal Jurisdiction," Report Strasbourg 1990, 25–26.

[144] P Uecker, *Extraterritoriale Regelungshoheit im Datenschutzrecht* (Nomos 2017) 26; H-J Ziegenhain, *Extraterritoriale Rechtsanwendung und die Bedeutung des Genuine-Link-Erfordernisses* (München 1992) 3.

[145] Ryngaert (n 5) 61.

[146] Sassen (n 3) 4.

[147] Ruggie (n 57) 165 quoting G Mattingly, *Renaissance Diplomacy* (Penguin Books 1964).

Furthermore, the European Court of Human Rights (ECHR) has recognized that there are "exceptional circumstances capable of giving rise to the exercise of jurisdiction by a Contracting State outside its own territorial boundaries."[148]

In Europe territoriality became the main principle of jurisdiction and was espoused by seventeenth-century and eighteenth-century philosophers and the Enlightenment project as the most rational and fair basis for jurisdiction (in particular in criminal law, where the principle of the place of the commission of the crime became the dominant basis for jurisdiction and applicable law[149]).[150] Unlike the English common law, however, continental legal systems have never relied exclusively on the territoriality principle. In practice, the active and passive personality principle (nationality of the offender/the victim), the presence/residence of the offender in the jurisdiction, the protective principle, and the vicarious principle all played a role.[151] In particular, the emphasis on the territoriality principle did not hinder European states from exercising jurisdiction based on the active personality principle.[152]

By contrast, historically, in England the courts limited themselves strictly to the territoriality principle.[153] Cedric Ryngaert calls it the "bedrock principle of jurisdiction in England."[154] As discussed further in Chapter 5, the English courts for a long time limited criminal jurisdiction to cases where the last act to complete the offence took place in England.[155] Territoriality is also a matter of statutory interpretation: the English courts apply a strong presumption that English law does not apply to acts done outside the territory.[156] This presumption is rebuttable and can therefore be overridden by specific statutory provisions.[157] In fact, in modern times the presumption has been replaced by specific statutory provisions, for example, in respect of murder in section 9 of the Offences against the Person Act 1861 and section 4 of the Suppression of Terrorism Act 1978. Section 9 of the 1861 Act expressly applies to murder committed abroad by English nationals. The 1978 Act gives effect to the European Convention on the Suppression of Terrorism[158] and expands the jurisdictional reach of offences listed to any of the contracting states, regardless of the nationality (or residence) of the offender.[159] Section 4 was used in a conviction for murder of a Lithuanian national, unrelated to an act of terrorism. He had driven in a van to England, kidnapped his ex-wife there, and murdered her somewhere on the way

148 *Al-Skeini v United Kingdom* (55721/07) (2011) 53 EHRR 18, paras 131–32.

149 *Forum Delicti Commissi* and *Lex Loci Delicti*.

150 Ryngaert (n 5) 54–65—he refers to P Ayrault, *L'Ordre, formalité et instruction judiciare* (1642); Montesquieu, *De L'Esprit des Lois* (1758); JJ Rousseau Le Contrat Social ou Principes du Droit Politique (1762); S Pufendorf, *De Jure Naturae et Gentium Libri* (1688); C Wolff, *Jus Gentium Methodo Scientifica Pertractatum* (1746); H Grotius, *De Jure Belli ac Pacis* (1625); T Hobbes, *The Leviathan* (1688).

151 Ryngaert (n 5) 55, 56, 58.

152 ibid 61.

153 *R v Keyn* LR 2 Ex D 63, 13 cox CC 403 (1876); *Mac Leod v Attorney General for New South Wales* [1891] AC 455, 458 (Lord Halsbury): "All crime is local. The jurisdiction over the crime belongs to the country where the crime is committed"; *Treacy v DPP* [1971] AC 537 (HoL) 552 (Lord Morris): "the general principle of the common law in England is that the exercise of criminal jurisdiction does not extend to acts committed on land abroad."

154 Ryngaert (n 5) 63.

155 Chapter 6.

156 *Treacy v DPP* [1971] AC 537 (HoL) 551 (Lord Reid), 552 (Lord Morris).

157 Ryngaert (n 5) 64.

158 Council of Europe, 27 January 1977, ETS 090.

159 This applies to a whole range of criminal offences (not necessarily terrorism related): murder, manslaughter, rape, kidnapping, abduction, firearms and explosives, terrorist financing, etc.

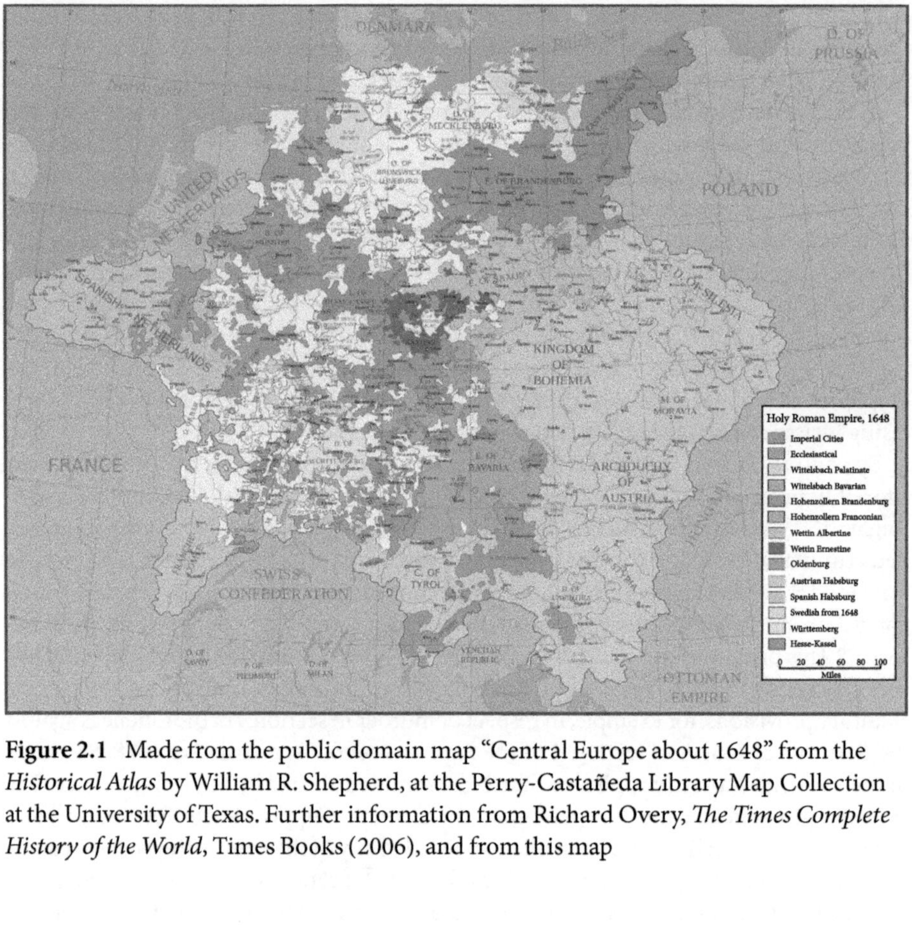

Figure 2.1 Made from the public domain map "Central Europe about 1648" from the *Historical Atlas* by William R. Shepherd, at the Perry-Castañeda Library Map Collection at the University of Texas. Further information from Richard Overy, *The Times Complete History of the World*, Times Books (2006), and from this map

from England to Poland (where he disposed of the body). The Court of Appeal confirmed that the English courts had jurisdiction and could apply English criminal law in this case regardless of where the murder had in fact taken place (as all the countries through which the van had travelled were contracting states).[160]

The difference between the common law in England and continental Europe can be explained by two interconnected factors: (1) geography and (2) differences in criminal procedure. Foremost in the minds of continental jurists was the risk of impunity when an offender slipped across borders, thus removing himself from the jurisdiction of the state where the offence had been committed.[161] The map in Figure 2.1 illustrates this geographical aspect in respect of central Europe where some small states prevailed.

By contrast, the common law in England was less concerned about offenders fleeing the island location, but put more emphasis on the due process right of offenders to be tried by a local jury of peers (as witnesses to the local crime)[162]—hence the importance

[160] *R v Venclovas* [2014] Crim L R 684.

[161] C Ryngaert (n 5) 60–61, referring to A Matthaeus, *De Criminibus* (1644) arguing that jurisdiction could also be based on residence and place of arrest, but that the *lex loci delicti* should apply.

[162] *Treacy v DPP* [1971] AC 537 (HoL) 558 (Lord Diplock): "the historical origins of these rules date back to the embryonic stage of development of English trial by jury. Jurors originally combined the functions of

of the exclusive jurisdiction of the forum in the territory where the crime had been committed.[163]The English courts have also upheld the presumption against extraterritoriality relying on the principle of non-interference with the sovereignty of other states.[164] However, this only applies if the criminal conduct has taken place outside the jurisdiction and has had no harmful consequences within the jurisdiction.[165]

In the US, early cases after the 1776 Declaration of Independence emphasized the principle of territoriality as the basis for jurisdiction and applicable law, as a defence mechanism for asserting the newly independent status of the former British colonies. In these cases the courts condemn the extraterritorial assertion of jurisdiction as contrary to international law.[166] The 1787 US Constitution reflects the strong emphasis on the common law principle of territoriality by requiring that crimes should be tried in the state where the crime has been committed.[167]

As the US emerged as the dominant world power after 1945, the doctrine against extraterritoriality took on a different colour: the courts move away from a strict interpretation of the territoriality principle, expanding the reach of US law and US courts. For example, in the 1945 Second Circuit *Alcoa* decision[168] US courts found jurisdiction in antitrust cases where the foreign conduct takes *effect* in the US.[169] Similarly, in *Hartford Fire Insurance Co* the Supreme Court held that the US District Court should not have declined jurisdiction and applied the Sherman Act to a British reinsurer notwithstanding that the reinsurer was acting legally under its own domestic law.[170]

In the US the concept of jurisdiction distinguishes between prescriptive jurisdiction (whether a US statute can be applied) and the jurisdiction of the courts over a person, which is then further divided into personal jurisdiction (relating to a specific dispute) and general jurisdiction (which subjects the person to the jurisdiction of the US courts generally).[171] The discussion on extraterritoriality takes place mainly in the context of prescriptive jurisdiction,[172] that is, whether a particular US statute applies. Three areas in particular seem prominent here: (1) antitrust law (the Sherman Act), (2) the Alien Tort Statute (ATS), and (3) securities regulation (Securities and Exchange Act 1934).

The approach of the US courts to the question of extraterritoriality has been shaped by six legal doctrines.

knowers of facts as well as triers of facts and the prisoner was entitled to have his guilt determined by jurors drawn [from the local area]."

[163] C Ryngaert (n 5) 62–65.

[164] Sassen (n 3) Reprint 2014 7–8.

[165] *Treacy v DPP* [1971] AC 537(HoL) 561 (Lord Diplock) 564.

[166] *Rose v Himley* 8 US (4 Cranch) 241 (1808); *Schooner Exchange v McFadden* 11 US (7 Cranch) 116 (1812); *The Appolon* 22 US (9 Wheat) 362 (1824); *The Antelope* 10 Wheat 66 (1825).

[167] US Constitution, 1 Stat 10 Art III s 2.

[168] *US v Alcoa* 148 F2d 416 (2nd Circuit 1945).

[169] Contrast this with the earlier case of *American Banana Co v United Fruit Co* 213 US 347, 29 S Ct 511 (1909).

[170] *Hartford Fire Ins. Co. v California* 509 US764, 796 (1993): "it is well established by now that the Sherman Act applies to foreign conduct that was meant to produce and did in fact produce some substantial effects in the US" (Justice Souter delivering the Opinion of the Court—Justice Scalia filed a dissenting Opinion finding the assertion of jurisdiction unreasonable).

[171] See further the discussion in Chapter 9.

[172] *Hartford Fire Ins. Co. v California* 509 US 764, 812 (1993).

The first doctrine derives from the *Charming Betsy* canon of cases, which have established the principle that US legislation must be interpreted in such a way that it does not conflict with US obligations under international law (eg the principle of non-interference).[173]

Second, from this statutory rule of construction developed[174] the more recent doctrine of the presumption against extraterritoriality: "it is a long-standing principle of American law that legislation of Congress, unless a contrary intent appears, is meant to apply only within the territorial jurisdiction of the US."[175]

This doctrine means that the courts, when interpreting the jurisdictional reach of a statute, use the presumption that the statute does not apply extraterritorially unless this was clearly indicated by the legislator.[176] It is used to decide whether US legislation regulates conduct taking place abroad. The presumption against extraterritoriality protects against unintended clashes with the laws of other nations, which could lead to international discord.[177]

However, since few statutes expressly state that they apply extraterritorially, at the level of the US Court of Appeals and below, the courts were prepared to infer that Congress had intended extraterritorial application, and deduced such intention from the context of the statute and whether the extraterritorial application is reasonable.[178]

For example, in respect of litigation under §10 (b) Securities and Exchange Act 1934, the courts have pointed to policy considerations justifying a statute's extraterritorial reach, such as the need to protect American investors in the case of foreign shares traded on US stock exchanges.[179] This was later rationalized into two tests: (1) the "effects" test, whether the wrongful conduct had substantial effect in the US or upon US citizens, and (2) the "conduct" test, whether the wrongful conduct occurred in the US.[180] But the application of the tests became very uncertain and inconsistent, without clear statutory basis.[181]

[173] *Murray v Schooner Charming Betsy* 2 Cranch 64, 118 2 L Ed 208 (1804).

[174] Colangelo (n 132) 1060.

[175] *EEOC v Arabian American Oil Co.* 499 US 244, 248; 111 S Ct 1227 (1991); *Foley Bros, Inc v Filardo* 336 US 281, 285; 69 S Ct 575 (1949).

[176] Ryngaert (n 5) 68–69; *Morrison v National Australia Bank Ltd* 561 US 247, 130 S Ct 2869 (2010); *RJR Nabisco Inc v European Community* 136 S Ct 2090, 2100 (US Supreme Court Decision of 20 June 2016); Restatement of the Law Fourth—the Foreign Relations Law of the US Jurisdiction, Tentative Draft No 2 (22 March 2016) s 203 "US courts interpret federal statutory provisions to apply only within the territorial jurisdiction of the United States unless there is a clear indication of congressional intent to the contrary."

[177] *EEOC v Arabian American Oil Co* 499 US 244, 248, 111 S Ct 1227 (1991); *RJR Nabisco Inc v European Community* 136 S Ct 2090, 2100 (US Supreme Court Decision of 20 June 2016).

[178] *Schoenbaum v Firstbrook* 405 F 2d, at 206 (2nd Cir 1968); *Leasco Data Processing Equip. Corp. v Maxwell* 468 F 2d 1326, 1334 (2nd Cir 1972); *Bersch v Drexel Firestone, Inc* 519 F 2d 974, 985 (2nd Cir 1975); *SEC v Kasser* 548 F 2d 109, 116 (3rd Cir 1977); *Grunenthal GmbH v Hotz* 712 F 2d 421, 424–25 (9th Cir 1983); *Kauthar SDN BHD v Sternberg* 149 F 3d 659, 667 (7th Cir 1998); Restatement (Third) of the Foreign Relations Law of the United States ss 402, 403, 416 (1986).

[179] *Schoenbaum* 405 F 2d 208–09.

[180] As described by Justice Scalia in *Morrison v National Australia Bank* 561 US . 247, 257, 130 S Ct 2869 (2010), referring to *SEC v Berger* 322 F 3d 187, 192–93 (2003), see also S Choi and L Silberman, "Transnational Litigation and Global Securities Class-Action Lawsuits" (2009) Wisconsin Law Review 465–505, 469.

[181] Justice Scalia in *Morrison v National Australia Bank* 561 US 247, 258–59, 130 S Ct 2869 (2010); Choi and Silberman (n 180) 467–68.

Therefore in the judgment of *Morrison v National Australia Bank* the US Supreme Court has returned to a stricter interpretation of the legislative presumption against extraterritoriality and held that, if there is no affirmative indication in the relevant legislation (§10(b) Securities and Exchange Act 1934) that it applies extraterritorially, it did not.[182] This return to a stricter approach against extraterritoriality may be prompted by a wish to discourage foreign litigants using precious US enforcement resources.[183]

Furthermore, in *Kiobel v Royal Dutch Petroleum Co*[184] the US Supreme Court also upheld the presumption against extraterritoriality. In this case Nigerian citizens resident in the US sued Nigerian, Dutch, and British corporations under the ATS for aiding and abetting[185] the Nigerian government in violations of international law on the territory of Nigeria. The ATS provides that "[t]he district courts shall have original jurisdiction of any civil action by an alien for a tort only, committed in violation of the law of nations or a treaty of the United States."[186] For a plaintiff to sue under the ATS there has to be a clear cause of action in that there has to be a violation of an international norm, which is "specific, universal and obligatory."[187] The ATS does not create a new cause of action, but simply confers jurisdiction on the US federal courts, but its jurisdictional nature does not defeat the presumption of extraterritoriality, which still applies.[188]

In *Kiobel* the US Supreme Court found that historically the ATS was intended to apply to international law obligations such as providing safe passage to foreigners or the diplomatic immunity of ambassadors *within the US* or to offences such as piracy on the High Seas, which by their nature do not conflict with the rights of other sovereigns.[189] It held that the presumption applied, since there was nothing in the text of the ATS that evinced a clear indication of extraterritoriality. Furthermore, mere corporate presence of the defendant corporations in the US was not sufficient to overcome the presumption, which therefore was not rebutted.[190]

One exception to the extraterritorial presumption are crimes, of which the government is a victim, where the US Supreme Court has held that it is in the nature of these offences that extraterritorial jurisdiction can be assumed even if this is not stated explicitly in the statute.[191] However, some US scholars have argued that *Morrison* and

[182] 561 US 247, 255, 130 S Ct 2869 (2010).
[183] Ryngaert (n 5) 86.
[184] 133 S Ct 1659 (2013) 1663–69 (Roberts CJ).
[185] This case (and many similar cases brought in the US dealing with corporations assisting governments in foreign human rights abuses by supplying vehicles, computers, or military equipment etc) of course also raises the question of corporate liability, *Kiobel* 621 F 3d 111, 148 (2d Cir 2010) (Cabranes, J and Jacobs, CJ)—no corporate liability. For cases where corporate liability was found, see *Flomo* 643 F 3d 1021; *Sarei v Rio Tinto* 671 F 3d 736, 764–65 (9th Cir 2011) (en banc), vacated on other grounds: 133 S Ct 1995, 185 L Ed 2d 863 (2013); *Exxon* 654 F 3d 57; *Romero v Drummond Co* 552 F 3d 1303, 1315 (11th Cir 2008); *In re South African Apartheid Litigation* 15 F Supp 3d 454 at 461 (US District Court SDNY 2014).
[186] 28 USC s 1350.
[187] *Sosa v Alvarez-Machain* 542 US 692, 732, 124 S Ct 2739 (2004).
[188] *Kiobel* 133 S Ct 1659 (2013) 1663–64 (Roberts CJ).
[189] *Kiobel* 133 S Ct 1659 (2013) 1666–67 (Roberts CJ).
[190] 133 S Ct 1659 (2013) 1666–69 (Roberts CJ).
[191] *United States v Bowman* 260 US 94, 97–98 (1922), see also *United States v Siddiqui*, 699 F 3d 690, 700 (2d Cir 2012) ("The ordinary presumption that laws do not apply extraterritorially has no application to

Kiobel may also affect extraterritorial jurisdiction in criminal cases.[192] In *RJR Nabisco Inc v European Community* the US Supreme Court has applied the presumption against extraterritoriality in a criminal case.[193]

The stricter application of the presumption against extraterritoriality closes the court doors in the face of foreign litigants deprived of a claim under US law, making it less likely, for example, for claims about human rights abuses being brought under US law.[194]

The third one is a recent re-enforcement of the doctrine of territoriality by strengthening the focus on the most relevant connecting factors. The background to this is that the distinction between territorial and extraterritorial assumption of jurisdiction is not always clear. A discussion of extraterritoriality can be avoided by using broad grounds of jurisdiction and finding connection factors that tie the matter to be regulated to US territory (so the case is framed within the concept of territoriality). Thus, in some cases the courts have avoided approving extraterritorial application of the law by using wide jurisdictional principles to justify the territorial application of US law by classifying the case as domestic.[195] This approach has been restricted by a recent lane of cases.

In *RJR Nabisco Inc v European Community*[196] the US Supreme Court has established a new two-step test to square territoriality and extraterritoriality in multijurisdictional cases. First, the court must examine whether the legislation itself gives a clear, affirmative indication that it applies extraterritorially. *If* this is the case, the court must then determine the limits of the foreign, extraterritorial application as stated in the legislation *itself*. However, if the legislation does not show the required indication that it applies extraterritorially, the court must then consider territoriality—in other words, it must consider whether the case can properly be said to be a domestic application of the legislation. For this, the court must determine the *focus* of the conduct complained of.[197] If the conduct relevant to the statute's focus occurred in the US, then the case involves a permissible domestic, territorial application of the statute. But if the main conduct occurred on foreign territory, then it is not permissible to apply the domestic statute, even if other, related conduct occurred in the US, as the application otherwise would be extraterritorial.[198] In this case the US Supreme Court has therefore restricted territorial application of US law to cases where the conduct (not the results or the effects) occurred in the US and therefore limited the use of wide jurisdictional principles. Similarly, in *Morrison* the Supreme Court found that the focus of the statute was the regulation of a securities exchange—thus this was the relevant connecting factor

criminal statutes") and *United States v Al Kassar*, 660 F 3d 108, 118 (2d Cir 2011) ("The presumption that ordinary acts of Congress do not apply extraterritorially, does not apply to criminal statutes").

[192] D Keenan and S Shroff, "Taking the Presumption against Extraterritoriality Seriously in Criminal Cases After Morrison and Kiobel" (2013) 45 Loyola University Chicago Law Journal 71–122, 74.

[193] 136 S Ct 2090, 2099–101 (US Supreme Court Decision of 20 June 2016).

[194] *RJR Nabisco Inc v European Community* Case Review [November 2016] 130 Harvard Law Review 487.

[195] eg *Goldberg v UBS AG* 690 F Supp 2d 92 105–06 (EDNY 2010) (defendant owning property in the US and passive personality principle).

[196] 136 S Ct 2090 (US Supreme Court Decision of 20 June 2016).

[197] Restatement of the Law Fourth—the Foreign Relations Law of the US Jurisdiction, Tentative Draft No 2 (22 March 2016) s 203 Comment (b).

[198] At 2099–101.

(in Australia), and not the deceptive conduct (which had taken place in the US).[199] Thus, in recent cases the courts have focused on the central connecting factors and not just any connection with the territory of the US.

The fourth doctrine that is relevant is the US Constitutional doctrine of the separation of powers, which leaves the competence over relations with foreign states to the political branches, not the judiciary.[200] This means that it is not for the courts to reach a decision on whether a statute should be applied extraterritorially[201] and is the rationale behind the presumption against extraterritoriality: "The presumption against extraterritorial application helps ensure that the Judiciary does not erroneously adopt an interpretation of U.S. law that carries foreign policy consequences not clearly intended by the political branches."[202]

Fifth, the US Constitution confers powers on US state organs (and in particular Congress exercising its legislative power) to act extraterritorially in certain instances via the Foreign Commerce Clause,[203] the Offence Clause,[204] and the Necessary and Proper Clause concerning the implementation of international law into national law.[205] The matters covered by these powers are likely to include matters that are not confined to US territory and allows Congress to expand its legislative reach beyond US territory. For example, the Foreign Commerce Clause supports the extraterritorial reach of the Computer Fraud and Abuse Act[206] or that of the Sherman Act[207] or of the Racketeer Influenced and Corrupt Organizations Act (RICO).[208] However, the foreign commerce connection must be anchored in the US, that is, the conduct must concern foreign commerce between a foreign country *and the US*, not just commerce between two foreign countries.[209] Furthermore, in *Morrison* the US Supreme Court held that a general reference in the statute to "foreign commerce" appearing in the definition of interstate commerce was not sufficient to defeat the presumption against extraterritoriality.[210]

Finally, if US law is applied extraterritorially, the question of due process arises and in particular whether the assertion of extraterritorial jurisdiction by the US courts is in breach of the Fifth Amendment of the US Constitution. As a matter of principle, the US Constitution does not impose a bar on the extraterritorial application of US law

[199] *Morrison v National Australia Bank* 561 US 247, 266–67; 130 S Ct 2869 (2010).

[200] Colangelo (n 132) 1037; Keenan and Shroff (n 192) 91–92.

[201] *Sosa v Alvarez-Machain* 542 US 692, 727, 124 S Ct 2739 (2004): "The possible collateral consequences of making international rules privately actionable argue for judicial caution."

[202] *Kiobel* 133 S Ct 1659 (2013) 1664 (Roberts CJ).

[203] US Constitution Art I, s 8, cl 3, giving Congress the power to regulate commerce with foreign nations.

[204] US Constitution Art I, s 8, cl 10, giving Congress the power to define and punish offences against the Law of Nations.

[205] US Constitution Art I, s 8, cl 18, giving Congress the power to effectuate treaties entered into by the executive arm of government.

[206] 18 USC s 1030. Fraud and related activity in connection with computers—this protects computers which are used in or affecting foreign commerce or communication of the US, regardless of whether that computer is located outside the US, s 1030 (e)(2)(B).

[207] 15 USC s 1 and *Hartford Fire Ins. Co. v California* 509 US 764, 813–14 (1993).

[208] RICO creates an offence of using income from a pattern of racketeering activity in an enterprise "which is engaged in, or the activities of which affect, interstate or foreign commerce," 18 USC s 1962(a).

[209] *RJR Nabisco Inc v European Community* 136 S Ct 2090, 2103–05 (US Supreme Court Decision of 20 June 2016).

[210] *Morrison v National Australia Bank Ltd* 561 US 247; 130 S Ct 2869, 2881–83 (2010).

as such.[211] However, if an individual has no legitimate expectations that US law may apply to their conduct and the imposition of US law and jurisdiction would be arbitrary and fundamentally unfair, since there is no sufficient nexus to US territory the due process guarantee in the Fifth Amendment may mean that a law cannot be applied against an individual extraterritorially.[212] This is further discussed in Chapter 10 in the context of personal and general jurisdiction.

The doctrine of extraterritoriality like the doctrine of comity[213] can be used to limit the protection of US interests impaired by conduct by non-US persons as well as to limit the protection of foreign, non-US interests impaired by the conduct of US entities (*Kiobel*, *Nabisco*, *Morrison*). The trend by US courts is to apply the doctrine of extraterritoriality unless the conduct is focused on US connecting factors, which means that foreign, non-US persons might find it harder to obtain redress before the US courts under US legislation. As the doctrine of comity is used to limit the application and enforcement of US law in cases with a strong foreign connection. For example, the US District Court in *Doe I et al v Cisco*,[214] US and Chinese citizens, domiciled in China and the US, and practitioners of Falun Gong brought claims under the ATS and the Electronic Privacy Communications Act (ECPA)[215] based on *Ciscos* design of networking hardware enabling surveillance, tracking, and prosecution of Chinese dissidents. The plaintiffs had been subjected to torture and other human rights abuses because of their following of Falun Gong and they alleged that Cisco "knowingly, purposefully and intentionally designed, implemented and helped to maintain the Golden Shield system in collaboration with" the Chinese Communist Party and Public Security officers across China, under the direction and control of Cisco in San Jose.[216] The Court allowed the defendants' motion to dismiss on the basis of the US Supreme Court decision in *Kiobel* that the conduct occurred in China and was therefore extraterritorial. Although the Court found that "it is not clear what circumstances will 'touch and concern the territory of the United States' in such a way that is sufficient to overcome the presumption against extraterritoriality,"[217] the Court focused on the human rights abuses as the relevant conduct (not the design of the networking technologies enabling surveillance and tracking) and found that these human rights abuses did not "touch and concern" the territory of the US.[218] In respect of the ECPA claim, the court upheld the argument of

[211] *United States v Felix-Gutierrez* 940 F 2d 1200, 1204 (9th Cir 1991); *United States v King* 552 F 2d 833,850 (9th Cir 1976).

[212] *United States v Clark* 435 F 3d 1100, 1108–09 (9th Cir 2006); *United States v Yousef* 327 F 3d 56, 111–12 (2d Cir 2003); *United States v Perez-Oviedo* 281 F 3d 366, 369–77 (5th Cir 2002); Colangelo (n 132) 1104.

[213] See discussion in Chapter 9.

[214] 66 F Supp 3d 1239 (US District Court ND California 2014).

[215] § 2512(1) of the ECPA, which prohibits the sending through the mail or interstate commerce of, or the manufacture, assembly, possession, or sale of device that renders it primarily useful for the purpose of the surreptitious interception of wire, oral, or electronic communications.

[216] ibid 1242.

[217] ibid 1245.

[218] ibid 1246–47; this can be contrasted with *Sexual Minorities Uganda v Lively* 960 F Supp 2d 304 (US District Court Massachusetts 2013) where the defendant was also US domiciled and the conduct partly occurred in the US.

the defence[219] that the surveillance technologies had been designed in the course of Cisco's normal business conduct (and could be used generally for crime prevention purposes).[220] In respect of the aiding and abetting claims the US District Court held that the plaintiffs had not shown that the defendants' product had a sufficiently substantial effect on the perpetration of the human rights abuses or that Cisco knew that their product was used beyond "normal" security purposes.[221] The Court was clearly concerned not to provide a precedent for US technology exporters to be liable for privacy and even more serious human rights abuses perpetrated by foreign governments or other nefarious uses of their technology by foreign entities. This first instance decision shows how the doctrine of extraterritoriality is used to bar claims under US law by (foreign and US) plaintiffs against a US defendant. Here the conduct occurred both in the US (design and collaboration) and abroad (Chinese implementation of the technology for surveillance and tracking and human rights abuses). It is used to shield a US company from liability for the effects of their commercial conduct (designing and selling surveillance and tracking technologies abroad) and allows them to turn a blind eye to how this technology will be used by the purchaser. However, the case has been appealed to the US Court of Appeals where it is currently pending.[222]

A prominent area where extraterritoriality has been discussed is information privacy and data protection, as online data storage and processing is frequently conducted remotely (cloud computing) and may in fact be difficult to pinpoint to any particular location. Many laws regulating this area therefore apply to foreign entities. For example, US state law requiring data breach notifications applies to foreign-based entities if they conduct business in the relevant state.[223] In the EU, the General Data Protection Regulation applies if a foreign entity offers goods or services to EU residents or tracks their online behaviour.[224]

Another area where extraterritoriality has been discussed and developed as part of legal doctrine is competition law. Initially states regularly protested against the US adopting an effects doctrine to justify its assertion of jurisdiction in cases where anti-competitive conduct by foreign companies agreed and co-ordinated from foreign jurisdictions has harmful anti-competitive effects on the US market, which are direct, substantial, and foreseeable.[225] However, in the 1985 *Wood Pulp* decision the European Court adopted a similar approach to extraterritorial jurisdiction and found jurisdiction on the basis that the anti-competitive agreement was implemented in the EEC market through direct sales. This was extended to cases where there were no direct sales in the EU in *Intel*. In *Gencor* (merger control) and in *Intel* (anti-competition)

[219] 18 USC s 2512 (2)(a).
[220] ibid 1249.
[221] ibid 1248.
[222] https://www.eff.org/deeplinks/2016/04/ciscos-latest-attempt-dodge-responsibility-facilitating-human-rights-abuses-export accessed on 14/7/2020.
[223] eg s 1798 82 (a)(California).
[224] See discussion in Chapters 7 and 11.
[225] Martyniszyn (n 142) 292; see eg the *amicus curae* brief in *Hartford Fire Ins. Co. v California* 509 US 764.

the Court has held that immediate, substantial, and foreseeable effects are sufficient for the EU to have jurisdiction.[226] A number of jurisdictions have included similar versions of this effects doctrine in their national competition legislation.[227]

[226] Case C-89/85 *A Ahlstrom Osakeyhtio v Commission of the European Communities* [1988] ECR 5193 (Wood Pulp); case T-102/96 *Gencor Ltd v Commission of the European Communities* [1999] ECR II-753; case T-286/09 *Intel Corp v European Commission* EU:T:2014:547; [2014] 5 CMLR 9.

[227] Martyniszyn (n 142) 292.

3

The Jurisdictional Challenge Answered—Enforcement through Gatekeepers on the Internet

1. The "out-of-reach" problem

This chapter examines the consequences of the jurisdictional challenge of the internet for the enforcement of public law, such as content regulation and criminal law relating to illegal content.[1] Internet applications such as websites, mobile apps, peer-to-peer file sharing, cyberlockers, and social media have enabled the remote sharing of illegal content and criminal interaction between people around the globe and across national borders. This global spread of illegal activities means that the laws of many different countries are potentially engaged and that no state alone can act against all infringers without international cooperation. In respect of illegal content, the internet effectively has led to the decentralization of criminal activity, which is scattered across many different jurisdictions.

Moreover, the remote provision of services and content from outside a particular state means that national law can be easily evaded and circumvented, as it may be impossible to enforce the law against the creator and uploader of the content or other person directly responsible for the online activity (such as the operator of unauthorized online gambling or the distributor of child sexual exploitation and abuse (CSEA) materials), as this person is outside the jurisdiction, and therefore outside the reach of enforcement. Furthermore, the software application and the content may be stored and processed in the cloud in a foreign state, moved between states, or shards of the information may be stored in different jurisdictions.[2] As a consequence, the immediate objects of enforcement (the illegal content itself or the person responsible) are out of reach of the law enforcement authorities and law enforcement therefore cannot take place at source, even where content is targeted at the enforcement jurisdiction. This lack of jurisdiction leads to lack of enforcement. For example, in our research on the regulation of online gambling, some regulators stated that they cannot approach foreign communications service providers and social media providers not established within their jurisdiction.[3]

[1] This chapter does not discuss gatekeeper enforcement in the context of intellectual property enforcement.

[2] *In re Search Warrant No. 16-960-M-1*, No 16-960, 2017 US Dist LEXIS 131239, at 3–4 (ED Pa 17 August 2017).

[3] J Hörnle et al, EU Study "Evaluating Regulatory Tools for Enforcing Online Gambling Rules and Channelling Demand towards Controlled Offers" (29 January 2019) DOI 10.2873/253036 https://publications.europa.eu/en/publication-detail/-/publication/6bac835f-2442-11e9-8d04-01aa75ed71a1/language-en/format-PDF/source-98923888 accessed on 16/7/2020.

Internet Jurisdiction. Julia Hörnle, Oxford University Press (2021). © Julia Hörnle.
DOI: 10.1093/oso/9780198806929.001.0001

Because of the decentralization and the remote targeting, enforcement takes place against entities facilitating or enabling dissemination of illegal content or the illegal activities instead of the primary perpetrators. These entities in the internet law enforcement context are local intermediaries such as internet service providers, search engines, or payment services providers established within the same jurisdiction as the law enforcement authority. This strategy is used to overcome the "out of reach" problem caused by decentralization and remote targeting. Or as Jack Balkin has phrased it, "that infrastructure, largely held in private hands, is the central battleground over free speech in the digital era."[4]

In this way, *local* intermediaries become the "gatekeepers" of the internet for the purposes of public law enforcement.[5] Gatekeepers quite literally are "entities that decide what [or who] shall or shall not pass through a gate" and the term has been coined by the social psychologist Kurt Lewin in 1943 in a different context.[6] Information and communication science has used the notion of the gatekeeper in order to explain how news and information is filtered before it is distributed by mass media.[7]

However, the law has also used the concept of gatekeepers to explain regulatory enforcement models and legal responsibility for content provided by others. Gatekeepers have no control over illegal information or activities but are in a position to prevent or minimize its distribution.[8] In the law enforcement context the position of the gatekeeper derives from the concept of secondary liability. While the gatekeeper is not liable for a law infringement, the gatekeeper may prevent or disrupt the illegal activity if they take appropriate measures, and therefore the law in certain circumstances may impose on them a duty of care to take such measures. As a consequence, this model of regulation has been described as decentred.[9]

In the context of regulation, gatekeepers have been described as "non-state actors with the capacity to alter the behaviour of others in circumstances where the state has limited capacity to do the same."[10] This model of regulation attaches to those who facilitate or enable infringements carried out by others. Legal responsibility is based on the principle that gatekeepers know about and facilitate the infringement and/or on the principle that gatekeepers could prevent the illegal activity and financially profit from it, or simply that they are in a position where they can take reasonable measures against an infringement.[11] Legal responsibility in this context does not necessarily

[4] JM Balkin, "Old-School/New-School Speech Regulation" (2014) 127 Harvard Law Review 2296–342, 2296.

[5] J Zittrain, "Internet Points of Control" (2003) 44 Boston College Law Review 653–88, 655; E Laidlaw, "A Framework for Identifying Internet Information Gatekeepers" (2010) 24(3) International Review of Law, Computers & Technology 263–76.

[6] K Lewin, "Forces Behind Food Habits and Methods of Change" (1943) 108 Bulletin of National Research Council 35–65.

[7] K Barzilai-Nahon, "Gatekeeping: A Critical Review" (2009) 43 Annual Review of Information Science and Technology 433–78, 434.

[8] Laidlaw (n 5) 264.

[9] B Morgan and K Yeung, *An Introduction to Law and Regulation: Text and Materials* (Cambridge University Press 2007) 280.

[10] Laidlaw (n 5) 264.

[11] For example, under US copyright law, *contributory* liability in tort arises from intentionally inducing or encouraging direct copyright infringement and *vicarious* liability in tort arises from profiting from direct infringement while declining to exercise a right to stop or limit it, *Metro-Goldwyn-Mayer Studios Inc v Grokster Ltd* 545 US 913, 930; 125 S Ct 2764 (27 June 2005); however, subjective or objective knowledge

mean that gatekeepers are liable in the sense that they are liable for compensatory damages in tort, or punitive measures under administrative or criminal law, but that they can be ordered to take proactive steps to prevent or minimize the illegal activity.[12] However, as will be argued, increasingly lawmakers and judges move towards imposing a positive duty of care on intermediaries to proactively take measures and/or impose liability.[13]

In addition to the jurisdictional "out-of-reach" problem concerning enforcement, regulators are additionally confronted with a conflicts-of-law problem with content disseminated across many different legal systems, if not globally. This raises the question of which law applies to content that can be assessed anywhere via the internet. There are two fundamental approaches to addressing conflicts of law. The first is to find a local connecting factor and apply the regulator's national law.[14] The second approach is to rely on terms and conditions imposed by social media platforms on their users as a form of self-regulatory "community regulation."[15] As discussed later, many legal instruments for gatekeeper regulation in the EU or at national level adopt a mixture of both approaches.[16]

Gatekeeper liability overcomes the jurisdictional challenges of internet law enforcement, if the service provider is established within the same jurisdiction as the regulator. Hence, this chapter examines how different laws have imposed legal obligations and specific liability on service providers and how this mechanism is used to overcome the jurisdictional out-of-reach problem.

2. Internet gatekeepers as facilitators of illegal activity?

The internet and its waves of applications—from blogging, to search engines, to social media sites—have enabled unprecedented dissemination and access to an incredible wealth of information, which has enriched everyone's life and transformed the publishing and entertainment sectors, as well as connecting people across the world. But for every bright side there is inevitably a dark side. The internet has likewise enabled the sharing of illegal content and a host of old and new criminal activities. This includes the sharing of CSEA materials;[17] terrorist and extremist

of copyright infringement has to be shown, *Viacom International Inc v YouTube* 676 F 3d 19, 37 (2nd Cir) 5 April 2012.

12 See eg the German concept of *Störerhaftung* developed in the context of determining an online auction platform's responsibility for trademark infringement in the *Rolex Ricardo* judgment BGHZ 158, 236–53 of 11 March 2004, which ordered the platform to filter (in the future) for the same or similar infringements (by eg using keyword filters for the brand).

13 See also G Frosio, "Why Keep a Dog and Bark Yourself?" (2018) 26(1) International Journal of Law and Information Technology 1–33, 3, 7–8.

14 This is the approach taken by the Netzwerkdurchsetzungsgesetz (NetzDG), discussed in section 3.4.1.4.1.

15 Art 4a(1) and (2) AVMS Directive (EU) 2018/1808 of 14 November 2018, OJ L 303, 28.11.2018, 69–92.

16 Proposal for a Regulation on Preventing the Dissemination of Terrorist Content Online of 12 September 2018, COM(2018) 640 final.

17 B Gallagher, "International and Internet Child Sex Abuse: the Typology, Extent and Nature of Known Causes and their Implications for Policy and Practice" (2007) 240 Childright 14–17.

speech;[18] online hate;[19] cyberbullying, online abuse, and harassment;[20] violent and extreme pornography;[21] the sale of illegal weapons; propagation of gang culture and knife crime; and the propagation of self-harm and suicide, to name but a few. The internet is not merely a new tool to share these old forms of illegal content; it has fundamentally revolutionized how we communicate, connect, and interact. It has therefore led to new forms of behaviour engendered by a number of psychological factors: its perceived anonymity or pseudonymity, the immersive or even addictive nature of some applications, the 24/7 convenient access, its "virtual" nature, and the "filter-bubble" silo or echo chamber of many social media applications[22]—the latter due to the targeted nature of communication based on online profiling of individuals. The filter-bubble limits content to what the user seems to be interested in. These psychological factors all lead to, or amplify, certain types of criminal behaviour.[23]

This raises the difficult question of to what extent different types of service providers are, or should be, responsible for illegal content and activities and be shoe-horned into the role of gatekeepers of the internet.

3. Online service provider liability as gatekeepers?

The sheer quantity of data transmitted, processed, and stored means that data cannot be manually checked or controlled through editorial control and therefore internet service providers are rightly given a degree of immunity[24] for the services they provide despite their facilitating role, as there is a well-founded fear that automated filtering mechanisms are apt to infringe freedom of expression/freedom of speech.[25] Under EU law a distinction is made between *internet access providers*, providing mere conduit, and *internet hosting providers*, who process and *store data* on behalf of users.

Article 12(1) of the E-Commerce Directive 2000/31/EC[26] provides that if the service is limited to transmission in a communication network, or access to a communications network, provided the service provider does not initiate the transmission, does not select the receiver, and does not select or change the information to be transmitted,

[18] M-H Maras, "Social Media Platforms: Targeting the Found Space of Terrorists" (August 2017) Journal of Internet Law 3–9; JM Berger and J Morgan, "The ISIS Twitter Census" Center for Middle East Policy Brookings, Analysis Paper No 20 (March 2015).

[19] C Bakalis, "Rethinking Cyberhate Laws" (2018) 27(1) Information and Communications Technology Law 86–110.

[20] J Agate and J Ledward, "Social Media: How the Net is Closing in on Cyberbullies" (2013) 24 (8) Entertainment Law Review 263–68.

[21] J Hörnle, "Countering the Dangers of Online Pornography: Shrewd Regulation of Lewd Content?" (2011) 2(1) European Journal of Law and Technology 1–26.

[22] E Pariser, *The Filter Bubble: How the New Personalized Web Is Changing What We Read and How We Think* (Penguin 2011).

[23] C Reed, "Why Must You be Mean to Me Crime and the Online Persona" (Summer 2010) 13(3) New Criminal Law Review 485–514.

[24] At least under EU and under US law.

[25] A Kuczerawy, "Intermediary Liability & Freedom of Expression: Recent Developments in the EU Notice & Action Initiative" (2015) 31(1) Computer Law & Security Review 46–56, 48–49.; UN General Assembly, Report of the UN Special Rapporteur David Kaye on the Promotion and Protection of the Right to Freedom of Opinion and Expression 6 April 2018, A/HRC/38/35, para 32.

[26] 8 June 2000, OJ L178/1.

it is immune from liability for illegal content. Thus, *internet access providers* have complete immunity concerning the information they provide access to or transmit given their limited control. Imposing an obligation on internet access providers to automatically filter for certain types of general content (such as eg copyright infringing file sharing) would breach Article 12(1).[27] Member States must not impose a general obligation on internet access providers to monitor content,[28] since overbroad monitoring infringes the mere conduit's right to operate a business, users' freedom of expression[29] and their right to privacy.[30] However, Article 12(3) enables the use of specific orders by an administrative authority or court in a Member State to require internet blocking of content (such as a list of URLs) and this can be congruent with freedom of expression, provided safeguards are implemented.[31]

By contrast, *internet hosting providers* have a greater degree of control over content as they may be in a position to take content down and therefore have greater due diligence obligations than mere conduit providers.[32] This means that if they have actual knowledge of illegal activity, or illegal activity is apparent from all the circumstances, they have an obligation to remove the content by way of take down on notice (also referred to as *notice and take down*).[33] Under English law, they may be treated as *common law* publishers.[34]

Like for mere conduit, EU Member States must not impose a *general* obligation to monitor content hosted on their services,[35] as to do so would mean that they lose their role as neutral internet service providers, whose function is automatic, passive, and technical.[36]

This technical role notwithstanding, the administrative authorities or courts may impose *specific* orders[37] to content and take preventative measures against future infringements in order to ensure that content stays down (*notice and stay down*). Notice and stay down involves filtering techniques identifying the same or similar *known* content (by searching for image hashes or phrases) or by closing the accounts of infringing users.[38] However, the delineation between what amounts to general

[27] Case C-70/10 *Scarlet Extended SA v SABAM*, Judgment of 24 November 2011, [2012] ECDR 4; *Bunt v Tilley* [2007] 1 WLR 1243 (QB): internet access providers are not common law publishers, mere conduit defence applies.

[28] Art 15(1) E-Commerce Directive 2000/31/EC.

[29] *Ahmet Yildirim v Turkey* Application 3111/10, Judgment of 18 December 2012, paras 57–70.

[30] Case C-70/10 *Scarlet Extended SA v SABAM*, Judgment of 24 November 2011, [2012] ECDR 4.

[31] *Twentieth Century Fox v BT (Newzbin II)* [2012] 1 All ER 869 (CA); *Ahmet Yildirim v Turkey* Application 3111/10, Judgment of 18 December 2012, para 64.

[32] Case C-18/18 *Eva Glawischnig-Piesczek v Facebook*, Opinion of Advocate General Szpunar of 4 June 2018, ECLI:EU:C:2019:458, para 48.

[33] Art 14(1) E-Commerce Directive 2000/31/EC and Case C-324/09 *L'Oréal v eBay International* [2011] ECR I-6011.

[34] *Tamiz v Google Inc* [2013] 1 WLR 2151, 2163, 2165 (Richards LJ): arguable case that Google hosting a blog becomes a common law publisher under English defamation law after it has received notification; *Davison v Habeeb* [2012] 3 CMLR 104.

[35] Art 15 and Recital 47 E-Commerce Directive 2000/31/EC; Case C-70/10 *Scarlet Extended SA v SABAM* (n 30); Case C-18/18 *Eva Glawischnig-Piesczek v Facebook*, Opinion (n 32) para 35.

[36] *Eva Glawischnig-Piesczek v Facebook*, Opinion (n 32) para 36.

[37] See also Recital 47 E-Commerce Directive 2000/31/EC.

[38] Case C-324/09 *L'Oréal v eBay International* [2011] ECR I-6011, EU:C:2011:474, para 144; *Eva Glawischnig-Piesczek v Facebook*, Opinion (n 32) paras 41–42.

monitoring and specific orders to take down or filter content has been contentious. In *Eva Glawischnig-Piesczek v Facebook*,[39] comments accompanying images of the claimant had been uploaded by a Facebook user insulting the former spokesperson of the Parliamentary Green party of Austria. Facebook refused to take the comments down, despite notification. These disparaging comments formed the basis of a claim in tort (harm to reputation and rights to one's own image) under Austrian law.[40] The claimant successfully applied for an injunction ordering the permanent removal of the comments from Facebook worded as an obligation to cease the publication/dissemination of photographs of the claimant together with the "*same* allegations and/or *equivalent* content."[41] On eventual appeal to the Austrian Supreme Court[42] the Court referred questions as to the delineation between a general obligation to monitor and a mandatory preventative order to remove content in the form of an injunction.

Advocate General Szpunar opined that the delineation should be as follows: first the social media company hosting the comments can be obliged to monitor the same user for equivalent content.[43]

He acknowledged that the notion of "equivalent content" gives rise to interpretational difficulties, especially in the context of insulting or defamatory statements.[44] As a general principle, courts and administrative authorities have to ensure that a removal order is clear, precise, and foreseeable and balances the fundamental rights of the parties involved in a proportionate manner.[45] The Court held that the removal order must contain "specific elements which are properly identified in the injunction, such as the name of the person concerned by the infringement," and "must not, in any event, be such as to require the host provider concerned to carry out an independent assessment of that content," considering that the service provider will use automated tools.[46]

The Court of Justice of the European Union (CJEU) followed the Advocate General by holding that the obligation includes the removal of equivalent information and found that this is information that essentially conveys the same message.[47]

Secondly, the social media company can also be obliged to monitor *all* users for the same content,[48] using keyword filtering.[49] However, an injunction must not contain an obligation to monitor all users and preventing the upload of equivalent content, as this would amount to a general monitoring obligation and would deprive the social media company of its neutral status.[50] Finally, the Advocate General found that an

[39] Case C-18/18 *Eva Glawischnig-Piesczek v Facebook*, Opinion (n 32); Judgment of 3 October 2019, ECLI:EU:C:2019:821.

[40] "lousy traitor of the people," "corrupt oaf," member of a "fascist party."

[41] Opinion para 14.

[42] Oberster Gerichtshof.

[43] Opinion para 72.

[44] ibid paras 67, 70.

[45] ibid para 75 in particular the right to conduct a business in Art 16, freedom of expression in Arts 11 and 7 respect for private and family life; Judgment para 45.

[46] Judgment paras 45–46.

[47] ibid para 41.

[48] This refers to identical content, word for word the same or reposts, Opinion para 56. The Attorney General did not comment on the sameness of the photographs/images.

[49] Opinion paras 57, 59, 61, 63.

[50] ibid para 73; pointing to the disproportionate impact on the freedom to conduct business and freedom of expression, para 74.

obligation to remove equivalent insults posted by *any* user could arise where the social media company has actual or constructive knowledge of these insults depending on the applicable national law, as the immunity under Article 14 does not apply.[51]

Notice and take down and judicial or administrative removal orders have been established in the EU Member States with variations in the precise nature of the action to be taken.[52] One of the main issues with notice and take down has been that content taken down has reappeared quickly, uploaded by the same account, or by a different account. It is for this reason that court or administrative orders may encompass an obligation on internet hosting providers to prevent the uploading of the same or similar or equivalent infringing content through proactive and automated filtering.[53]

By contrast, in the US, internet service providers, both hosting providers and internet access providers, have complete immunity from liability[54] for the illegal content their users upload or the illegal activities their users engage in under the Communications Decency Act,[55] regardless of their state of knowledge (active or constructive).[56]

However, this complete immunity does not apply to copyright infringement, as the Digital Millennium Copyright Act imposes an obligation on *hosting* providers to take content down if they receive notice of copyright infringing activity (notice and take down): but, additionally, they have to reinstate materials if they receive a counter-notice from the user declaring that the content is not infringing.[57] Thus, in the US, where content has been uploaded by a user outside the jurisdiction, gatekeeper liability is limited to copyright infringement, and the jurisdictional out-of-reach problem can only be solved through the gatekeeper if an allegation of copyright infringement can be made. Claimants have used this mechanism in privacy infringement cases and in revenge porn cases. Thus, use of internet hosting providers as gatekeepers has been more limited in the US because of the much stronger protection of free speech[58] under the First Amendment of the US Constitution.[59] This can be contrasted with the European notion of freedom of expression under Article 10 ECHR,[60] which allows Council of Europe States to impose greater[61] restrictions on content infringing the

[51] ibid paras 31, 107.

[52] C Angelopoulos and S Smet, "Notice-and-Fair Balance How to Reach a Compromise between Fundamental Rights in European Intermediary Liability" (2016) 8(2) Journal of Media Law 266–301, 267–69, 286–90.

[53] Case C-324/09 *L'Oréal v eBay International* [2011] ECR I-6011.

[54] This immunity, however, does not apply to federal criminal law, 47 USCA s 230(e)(1). In 2018 the Fight Online Sex Trafficking Act (FOSA) carved out state criminal law and civil law actions in respect of sex trafficking, after a lawsuit by trafficked victims against Backpage had failed, 47 USCA s 230(5).

[55] 47 USCA s 230(c)(1): "No provider or user of an interactive computer service shall be treated as the publisher or speaker of any information provided by another information content provider."

[56] *Zeran v AOL* 129 F 3d 327 (4th Cir 1997); *Blumenthal v Drudge* 992 F Supp 44, 49–53 (DDC 1998); *Batzel v Smith* 333 F 3d 1018 (9th Cir 2003).

[57] 17 USCA s 512(c).

[58] C Bakalis and J Hörnle, "The Role of Social Media Companies in the Regulation of Online Hate Speech" (2020) Studies in Law, Politics and Society (forthcoming).

[59] *Reno v ACLU* 521 US 844 (US Supreme Court 1997) parts of the CDA imposing filtering and age-verification requirements on internet service providers to prevent dissemination of pornography was held to be unconstitutional.

[60] Art 11 Charter of Fundamental Rights of the EU.

[61] Compared to the First Amendment.

rights and legitimate interests of others. For example, in the *Delfi* case,[62] the European Court of Human Rights (ECtHR) held that a fine imposed by a Member State on a media platform that hosted defamatory and racially abusive comments, amounting to hate speech, was not a breach of Article 10, even though the media platform had no knowledge or awareness of these comments and took them down once notified. By contrast, in MTE[63] the ECtHR expressly acknowledged that platform providers have limited control over content hosted on their platform and therefore held that providers' duty to monitor content was a breach of Article 10.[64]

Since many European states restrict freedom of expression in order to protect the rights and legitimate interests of others, they use hosting providers as gatekeepers to enforce (criminal, civil, and administrative) laws protecting such rights and legitimate interests. Since the EU E-Commerce Directive was passed in 2000, technology has significantly developed and a number of cloud providers may be involved in providing hosting services. Hosting in a cloud computing environment[65] usually means that a complex chain of entities, linked through contracts, is involved in providing services,[66] with software-as-a-service (SAAS),[67] platform-as-a-service (PAAS),[68] and infrastructure-as-a-service (IAAS)[69] providers, which are in difference locations. Hence, different aspects of the relevant service may be spread over different servers in many jurisdictions. This makes it more difficult to identify which entity or entities has/have to take down content. This should be the provider with control over the *content* closest to the content provider, who has the function of disseminating the content (eg content delivery networks or social media companies).[70] It is likely to be the entity who has control over determining the service that it provides. Therefore the actual location of the physical servers in a data centre and control over the physical infrastructure is less likely to be relevant for the gatekeeper function than control over content, even if the controller is remote to the physical, real-world place(s) of storage. The complexity of the cloud infrastructure frequently is not adequately reflected in legislative instruments, with the consequence that it is unclear to whom an obligation to take measures attaches. For example, the draft EU Regulation on Preventing the Dissemination of Terrorist Content Online[71] defines a hosting service provider

[62] *Delfi AS v Estonia (64569/09)* [2015] EMLR 26.

[63] *MTE v Hungary (22947/2013)*, Judgment of 2 February 2016, https://hudoc.echr.coe.int/eng#{%22itemid%22:[%22001-160314%22]}, accessed on 16/7/2020, where the Court found that the incriminated comments did not constitute clearly unlawful speech, para 64 and that the applicants never sought the removal of the comments, but went straight to court, para 83.

[64] ibid para 86.

[65] See also P Mell, T Grance *The NIST Definition of Cloud Computing* NIST Special Publication 800-145, National Institute of Standards and Technology, US Department of Commerce, September 2011, https://nvlpubs.nist.gov/nistpubs/Legacy/SP/nistspecialpublication800-145.pdf accessed on 16/7/2020.

[66] C Millard (ed), *Cloud Computing Law* (Oxford University Press 2013) 3–17, 13–15.

[67] End-user applications; ibid 4.

[68] Platforms for developing and deploying software applications; hosting platforms with application management tools; Millard (n 66) 4.

[69] Raw computing resources, such as processing power and storage; computing hardware infrastructure (servers) and tools to help manage those resources; it is essentially computing and storage infrastructure for rental; Millard (n 66) 4.

[70] cf the Australian Criminal Code Amendment applies removal obligations not only to social media services, but also to cloud hosting providers, see (n 207).

[71] Discussed in section 4.1.2.

as "provider of information society services consisting in the storage of information provided by and at the request of the content provider and in making the information stored available to third parties."[72] This definition overlooks that several cloud service providers may be involved. The entity providing mere storage may not have any control whatsoever over the content, to the point even where it may not be able to even identify content, as the content is encrypted.[73]

While in a complex cloud environment it may not be clear which entity is in effect the gatekeeper for regulation, it is equally clear that content regulation increasingly relies on gatekeepers for content control.

4. The use of gatekeeper legislation for specific types of content

4.1 Hosting: from notice and take down to duty of care

A number of take down mechanisms exist in respect of different types of illegal content. In other words, obligations and procedures exist for *specific* types of illegal content (terrorist content, child sex abuse materials, "abhorrent materials"). It is noticeable that initial attempts at creating notice and take down mechanisms defined the relevant materials narrowly. In the last few years the spate of terrorist attacks, and increasing levels of hate crime, have led to an expansion of the type of contents, which are regulated through gatekeeper enforcement. Furthermore, we also see a shift from laws merely providing for a mechanism for notice and take down to laws imposing wider duties on hosting providers to take proactive measures to limit the dissemination of illegal materials, or materials, which are suspected to be illegal.

4.1.1 CSEA materials

Article 25(1) of Directive 2011/92/EU[74] provides that Member States must have systems in place to take measures to ensure the prompt take down of websites disseminating CSEA materials hosted in their jurisdiction and, for those hosted in a foreign state to endeavour to have such materials taken down. In the UK, the Internet Watch Foundation (IWF) has taken down CSEA materials since 1996 and in the year 2018 had removed 105,047 webpages, and as a consequence of its actions it is now believed that well under 1 per cent of child sex abuse images are hosted in the UK.[75]

In addition to the take down of images, the IWF has created a database of hashes of images, after they have been assessed by the IWF as child sex abuse. This database of hashes allows known images of child sex abuse to be identified by their hashes, even if they have been altered, and prevents the reuploading and further dissemination of

[72] Art 2(1), COM(2018) 640 final.

[73] Millard (n 66) 18–35.

[74] Directive 2011/92/EU on Combating the Sexual Abuse and Sexual Exploitation of Children and Child Pornography, OJ L335 of 17 December 2011, 1.

[75] https://www.iwf.org.uk/what-we-do/why-we-exist/our-campaigns; https://www.iwf.org.uk/what-we-do/why-we-exist/our-history accessed on 16/7/2020.

such known images automatically by companies who participate in the scheme. This is based on cloud technology provided by Microsoft in 2016.[76]

Removal of content can *only* occur in the country where it is hosted and therefore it has been recognized that notice and take down of such materials requires international cooperation. For this purpose the INHOPE international network of hotlines has been founded to fight against the dissemination of child sex abuse content, as well as rescue victims and prosecute offenders.[77]

4.1.2 Terrorism-related materials

Another area of high concern is terrorist content and so-called extremist content. The UK Home Affairs Committee concluded in its Nineteenth Report "Roots of Violent Radicalisation"[78] that the internet may well be the main source for radicalization, although not all research points in this direction.[79] It has been pointed out that more research needs to be carried out to better understand the mechanisms of online radicalization and that there is no proven causal link between networking in respect of and consumption of violent extremist content and terrorist radicalization[80] albeit that the internet clearly has created opportunities for radicalization.[81]

In the UK the Terrorism Act 2006[82] provides for a take-down mechanism for content that is "unlawfully terrorism related" and has thereby created an endorsement offence for those who fail to comply with a Notice to remove such "unlawfully terrorism-related" content.[83] This phrase captures content that is a "direct or indirect encouragement[84] or other inducement to the commission, preparation or instigation of acts of terrorism"[85] or is information useful in the commission of terrorist acts[86] and is understood to be disseminated for this purpose.[87] Essentially, a police constable is empowered by the Act to give a Notice when content is "published" in the course of, or in connection with, the provision or use of a service provided electronically,[88] or if such content is transmitted electronically,[89] or where such content is made available online to others that enables them to obtain, read, listen to, or look at the content.[90] However, the Act omits to clearly stipulate *who* the Notice can be given to and *which internet service providers*[91] can be made recipient of such a police Notice. Confusingly,

[76] https://www.iwf.org.uk/our-services/hash-list accessed on 16/7/2020.

[77] http://www.inhope.org/ accessed on 16/7/2020.

[78] Home Affairs Committee "Roots of Violent Radicalisation" 31 January 2012, https://publications.parliament.uk/pa/cm201012/cmselect/cmhaff/1446/144602.htm accessed on 16/7/2020.

[79] ibid para 33.

[80] M Conway, "Determining the Role of the Internet in Violent Extremism and Terrorism: Six Suggestions for Progressing Research" (2017) 40(1) Studies in Conflict and Terrorism 77–98.

[81] Berger and Morgan (n 18).

[82] Ss 3 and 4 Terrorism Act 2006.

[83] S 3(3)(a).

[84] Relating to the ss 1 and 2 offences.

[85] S 3(7)(a).

[86] See eg *R v Brown (Terence Roy)* [2012] 2 Cr App R (S) 10 for selling the "Anarchist Cookbook" through a website.

[87] S 3(7)(b) Terrorism Act 2006.

[88] S 3(1).

[89] Ss 2(2)(e) and 3(1).

[90] Ss 2(2)(d) and 3(1).

[91] Hosting providers or additionally internet access providers?

the actus reus refers to "publication" or causing publication that does not clearly refer to internet service providers who do not have editorial control.[92] Bad parliamentary drafting here leaves the legal obligation of internet service providers unclear.

The Notice must state that the content is "unlawfully terrorism related," demand that the recipient takes the content down or modifies it, and warn that failure leads to criminal liability for endorsing terrorist content.[93] The recipient essentially has to take down the offending content within two working days.[94] Furthermore, the recipient of such a Notice has an additional obligation to ensure that the same or similar content is not reuploaded again and must take active measures to prevent this "repeat statement" (stay down).[95] Awareness (eg through Notice) is part of the *mens rea* of this endorsement offence and the Act contains a defence if the recipient of the Notice has taken every step he/she reasonably could to prevent the repeat statement from becoming available again.[96] Finally, the Notice must be served by hardcopy, either personally or through the post by recorded delivery,[97] which makes it unworkable, because of the issue of speed and the velocity of reposting, retweeting, and so on of content online.

The notice and take down provisions in the UK Terrorism Act have not been used and reliance is instead placed on the "voluntary" cooperation mechanism set up through the Counter-Terrorism Internet Referral Unit (CTIRU).[98]

The EU Counter-Terrorism Directive (EU) 2017/541[99] likewise contains an obligation for all Member States to ensure the prompt take down of "online content constituting a public provocation to commit a terrorist offence."[100] As with CSEA content, this obligation relates to content hosted within the jurisdiction, but Member States must "endeavour" to obtain the removal of such terrorist content hosted in a foreign jurisdiction,[101] through the cooperation mechanism in the form of the EU CTIRUs and Europol.[102] The Directive envisages safeguards for the protection of freedom of expression, such as making the removal transparent and providing judicial redress,[103] thus acknowledging the impact of take down mechanisms on freedom of expression, but without clear guidance as to how content can be reinstated if it has been assessed wrongly or stipulating how and by whom content is taken down. Considering that these schemes are likely to be operated internally by the police without recourse to the

[92] But cf in the defamation context *Tamiz v Google* (n 34) where the CA held that after notification a hosting provider may be a common law publisher—but is this the same in the criminal law context of the Terrorism Act?

[93] S 3(3) Terrorism Act 2006.

[94] S 3(2).

[95] S 3(4).

[96] Ss 3(5) and (6).

[97] S 4.

[98] Home Office "Memorandum to the Home Affairs Committee: Post-Legislative Scrutiny of the Terrorism Act 2006" (2011) 6–7, http://www.official-documents.gov.uk/document/cm81/8186/8186.pdf. accessed on 16/7/2020.

[99] 15 March 2017, OJ L88/6.

[100] Art 21(1): this refers to the harmonized offence under Art 5 of the Directive.

[101] Art 21(1).

[102] The relationship between the UK and Europol after exit from the EU was unclear at the time of writing, but it is likely that the UK's involvement in Europol will substantially change.

[103] Art 21(3).

courts or judicial supervision and without clear transparency[104] as to what content *actually is taken down*, it is questionable whether such safeguards have actually been implemented.

In the UK the CTIRU was set up by the Association of Chief Police Officers and the Metropolitan Police in 2010. The CTIRU's work consists of notifying social media platforms of terrorist-related content for "voluntary" notice and take down under their own terms and conditions with users.[105] The CTIRU largely works in a secretive manner and is not accountable or transparent. Thus, it is unclear whether it only notifies content illegal under UK law (such as the Terrorism Acts 2000 and 2006) or whether its assessment includes more loosely defined terrorist-related content.[106] Since platforms are potentially criminally liable for the endorsement offence discussed above there is a likelihood that, if in doubt, platforms remove content. Thus, notification by the CTIRU is not voluntary, as notification has legal effects.[107] Furthermore, platforms are likely to make the decision whether or not to remove content based on their own community guidelines.[108] Both these facts make it likely that legal content is among the content taken down. Platforms have stated that they refuse to take down 20–30 per cent of content notified by the CTIRU.[109] Arguably the process should be made more transparent, by declaring which content is actually being taken down by reference to the relevant legal provisions, the publication of statistics and annual reports, an explanation of the process of how referrals for removal are made, an independent oversight mechanisms such as a commissioner, and independent review mechanism by sampling of content that has been referred and an appeals process to reinstate content that has been wrongly removed.

A clearer contrast could not exist between the IWF and its clear and narrow remit, and accountability as an independent organization, on the one hand, and the secretive, non-transparent, non-accountable CTIRU whose remit is ultimately unclear, on the other. It also contrasts with the German Network Law Enforcement Act,[110] which contains quality standards and reporting obligations for the actual removal processes for material *illegal under German criminal law*.

An EU Internet Referral Unit was set up at the European Counter-Terrorism Centre at Europol in 2015. This flags terrorist and violent extremist content to "relevant partners," including social media companies, and requests removal of information about migrant smuggling networks. It claims to have assessed 42,066 pieces of content resulting in 40,714 decisions for referral across eighty platforms in ten languages.[111]

[104] As to the importance of transparency in this context, see recommendations in the Report of the UN Special Rapporteur David Kaye on the Promotion and Protection of the Right to Freedom of Opinion and Expression (n 25) paras 52, 64.

[105] Open Rights Group, *UK Internet Regulation: Internet Censorship in the UK Today* 18 December 2018, 11–13; TJ McIntyre, "Internet Censorship in the United Kingdom: National Schemes and European Norms" in L Edwards *Law, Policy and the Internet* (Hart Publishing 2018) 291–330.

[106] ibid.

[107] B Chang, "From Internet Referral Units to International Agreements: Censorship of the Internet by the UK and the EU" (2018) 49(2) Columbia Human Rights Law Review 116–212, 122.

[108] ibid.

[109] ibid.

[110] Discussed in section 4.1.4.1.

[111] As of December 2017, https://www.europol.europa.eu/about-europol/eu-internet-referal-unit-eu-iru accessed on 16/7/2020.

It has now been recognized that referral and removal processes require additional safeguards and international coordination. With this in mind, the EU has published a Proposal for a Regulation on Preventing the Dissemination of Terrorist Content Online on 12 September 2018.[112] Its purpose is to harmonize the procedures for removing and preventing the upload of terrorist content to restrict its dissemination.[113] It is the first legal instrument that has moved from a "notice and take down" approach to a more comprehensive duty of care approach. While the UK will not be a Member State of the EU if this Proposal matures into a directive, the duty of care approach shows clear parallels to the UK approach proposed in the UK White Paper on "Online Harms."

The Proposal is a prime example of gatekeeper regulation by imposing duties of care on *hosting service providers*[114] to deal with terrorist content in one of three ways. First it makes a clear and helpful distinction between removal orders and referrals. Removal orders are issued by the relevant competent national authority and create *binding legal obligations* on *hosting service providers* as gatekeepers to remove terrorist content. The nature of these legal obligations depends on national law and may create administrative,[115] civil,[116] or criminal[117] liabilities. Such removal orders can be issued by administrative authorities or the courts in the Member States, depending on national law, but must be effected *within one hour*.[118] Secondly, the Proposal provides the legal basis for the competent authorities in the EU Member States and Europol to notify hosting service providers of terrorist-related material by way of a *referral*.[119] These referrals leave the decision whether to remove or disable access to the hosting service providers who have to assess the content according to their policies. If hosting services take action as a consequence of such referrals they do so on a *voluntary basis without a legal obligation* or deadline for making the decision.[120] Arguably, this provision of the Draft contradicts the rule of law—if the content is illegal, then a removal order can and should be used, if it is not clear whether or not the content is illegal, public authorities should not notify gatekeepers to take it down. In practice, even in unclear cases, hosting providers are likely to take content down in order to protect themselves from (potential) liability and therefore the apparent voluntariness of the take down mechanism does little to protect freedom of expression, on the contrary. Thirdly, the Proposal requires hosting service providers to take *proactive* measures to protect their services being used for the distribution of terrorist materials.[121] In particular, hosting

[112] Proposal for a Regulation on Preventing the Dissemination of Terrorist Content Online on 12 September 2018 COM(2018) 640 final, 3.

[113] ibid 4.

[114] Art 1(1) "rules on duties of care to be applied by hosting service providers in order to prevent the dissemination of terrorist content"—this raises the question of who is a "hosting service provider" in a cloud computing environment, see discussion in section 3.

[115] S 4 NetzDG.

[116] UK Government White Paper "Online Harms" (8 April 2019) https://www.gov.uk/government/consultations/online-harms-white-paper, accessed on 16/7/2020, discussing the concept of a statutory duty of care, breach of which would be a tort.

[117] eg the UK Terrorism Act 2006, ss 3–4.

[118] Art 4(2).

[119] Art 5(1).

[120] Art 5.

[121] Art 6(1).

service providers would have to use automated tools to prevent the reupload of known terrorist content previously removed, *and* for identifying and removing *new* terrorist content.[122] It is this active content monitoring that goes beyond notice and take down and creates a new duty of care.

Clearly the overwhelming quantity of terrorist content online and the velocity of its dissemination and reupload, reposting, or retweeting makes human review of content extremely challenging; therefore artificial intelligence has to be used. However, artificial intelligence is likely to be inaccurate and cannot make nuanced assessments of context and meaning (understanding irony, criticism, satire).

As a consequence, it is likely that freedom of expression is infringed through the process of automated tools unless these tools are only used to either prevent previously identified content from being reuploaded or to identify new content, which is then double-checked by human review ("human-in-the-loop principle").[123] The EU Commission's Communication[124] on tackling illegal content online outlined the Commission's thinking back in 2017 concerning the achievement of enhanced responsibility of online platforms for illegal content, including incitement to terrorism, but additionally including xenophobic and racist speech, and CSEA materials. It is a response to EU governments' political calls for industry to develop "technology and tools to improve the automatic detection and removal of content."[125] The Communication states that social media companies should take proactive steps to detect and remove illegal content through automated means, but that this *currently requires final vetting through the human-in-the-loop principle.*[126] By contrast, this human-in-the-loop principle has been omitted from the draft Regulation. As currently drafted, the 2018 Proposal does not require that terrorist content that is automatically detected by artificial intelligence is necessarily subject to human review before it is removed or blocked.[127]

The only two safeguards *in respect of automated tools* are that hosting service providers have to ensure that the measures taken must be effective and proportionate[128] (which inaccurate tools are not[129]) and that hosting service providers have to report annually on the use of these tools.[130] The proportionality test here refers to a risk assessment of the nature of the content and exposure level, the fundamental rights of users, and the importance of freedom of expression in open and democratic societies.[131] It is, however, highly doubtful whether *private* entities such as hosting service

[122] Art 6(2).

[123] UN General Assembly, Report of the UN Special Rapporteur David Kaye on the Promotion and Protection of the Right to Freedom of Opinion and Expression (n 25) para 32.

[124] EU Commission COM(2017) 555 final of 28 September 2017, 16.

[125] ibid 2 (European Council of 22–23 June 2017).

[126] ibid 13: "This human-in-the-loop principle is, in general an important element of automatic procedures that seek to determine the illegality of a given content, especially in areas where error rates are high or where contextualisation is necessary."

[127] See the guarded and limiting language in Art 9(2): "where appropriate"; "where a detailed assessment of the relevant context is required."

[128] Art 6(1); Art 3(1) applies the proportionality principle more generally.

[129] Therefore the proportionality principle itself limits automation.

[130] Art 6(2); more transparency is also recommended by the Report of the UN Special Rapporteur David Kaye on the Promotion and Protection of the Right to Freedom of Opinion and Expression (n 25) para 37.

[131] Art 6(1).

providers are best placed to make this assessment.[132] This point raises an important structural problem with gatekeeper regulation. The jurisdictional challenges of content regulation (originators of content are abroad) lead to hosting providers having to act as gatekeepers. This, in turn, shifts content regulation and censorship from the public sector (administrative and judicial authorities) to the private sector, who have to act as guardians of fundamental rights, which is a function they may not be suited to carry out. Thus, what is required is that the automated tools themselves should be vetted by the relevant public authorities, in order to ensure that these tools are both ethical, compliant with fundamental rights, and accurate. While the Proposal contains an oversight mechanism through benchmarks and key objectives,[133] arguably this is not sufficient in itself and should include much greater emphasis on testing and restricting the tools that can be used. In particular, independent researchers should be able to test the automated tools and publish the test results.

Unlike the content-referral activities carried out by the UK CTIRU, at least the nature of the terrorist material is more clearly defined in the Proposal by reference to the public provocation, recruitment, and training offences in the EU Counter-Terrorism Directive (EU) 2017/541.[134] Moreover, it contains three general safeguard mechanisms, the first of which is a transparency provision.[135] This obliges hosting service providers to inform their users that they are using automated tools and to publish annual reports. The competent authority in each Member State must supervise the removal orders and implementation of automated tools.[136] Second, the Proposal includes an obligation for *hosting service providers* to include a complaints mechanism in respect of referrals and automated means of removal, and to reinstate content taken down wrongly.[137] The third and final safeguard is that content providers (users), whose content has been removed or disabled through referrals or through automated tools, need to be informed that this was the case and obtain reasons on request.[138] Member States' authorities can impose a time-limited embargo if the disclosure of information would be prejudicial to public safety, such as the detection, prevention, investigation, and prosecution of a terrorist offence.[139] The Proposal envisages content retention obligations on service providers to ensure that evidence of crime is not lost. It also proposes that content is retained so that it can be reinstated, where removed by error.[140] Moreover, hosting providers have an obligation to notify national police forces or Europol of any terrorist content on their platforms.[141]

Furthermore, the Proposal provides for international coordination of removals orders, bilaterally, multilaterally, and through Europol, in order to avoid duplication and wasted efforts.[142] This is particularly important in the jurisdictional context, as

[132] UN General Assembly, Report of the UN Special Rapporteur David Kaye on the Promotion and Protection of the Right to Freedom of Opinion and Expression (n 25)para 1.

[133] Arts 6(3) and 17(1)(c).

[134] Art 6(3).

[135] Art 8.

[136] Art 4(9).

[137] Art 10.

[138] Art 11(1) and (2).

[139] Art 11(3).

[140] Art 7.

[141] Art 13(4).

[142] Arts 1(1)(b) and 13.

overlapping jurisdictional claims may lead to conflicts. The proposed Regulation would apply to all hosting companies providing services in the EU irrespective of their physical establishment, and thus adopts a "country" of destination approach with regards to the EU as a whole.[143] However, the Proposal further clarifies the meaning of "providing services in the EU" by requiring one of the following additional criteria to show a link to the EU: (1) establishment of the hosting service provider in the EU, (2) significant number of users in one or more EU Member States, or (3) targeting of activities towards one or more Member States.[144] If a hosting service provider is not established within the EU they have to appoint a legal representative and this determines jurisdiction for the competent authority.[145] Otherwise, the competent authority in the EU Member State where the hosting service provider's main or only establishment is located is competent.[146]

Member States' competent authorities must have the powers to impose penalties for non-compliance and in case of persistent failure of a hosting service provider to comply with its legal obligations the maximum penalty is 4 per cent of global business turnover.[147] The European Commission will monitor the application of the Regulation and will establish an expert group to support the implementation, monitoring, and assessment of the Regulation.[148]

Thus, the EU has proposed a detailed and comprehensive regime for regulating hosting service providers' obligations and has established them as gatekeepers for enforcing counter-terrorism laws online. Gatekeepers are forced to have a local presence, that is, an establishment or legal representative, in the EU, if they provide services in the EU; for example, by having substantial numbers of users or targeting their activities to the EU. The Proposal addresses the decentralization of communications in the age of user-generated content by using the hosting service providers as chokepoints for regulation and forcing them to have a local presence. It also addresses the problem of applicable law in respect of globally dispersed user communities by making a clear distinction between the two possibilities of applying national law in respect of local user communities (*removal orders* under Article 4) or relying on self-regulatory terms and conditions promulgated by the hosting provider itself (*referral* under Article 5). The Proposal uses both normative systems for better protection as a double-walled defence mechanism against terrorist content. However, as already discussed, double-protection infringes against the rule of law and is therefore not compatible with freedom of expression.[149] Both removal and referral orders are a form of notice and take down and should therefore be compatible with Article 14 of the E-Commerce Directive.[150] However, to the extent that Article 6 poses an obligation on hosting service providers to actively seek out and identify *new* terrorist content, it is difficult to see how this is compatible with Articles 14(1) and 15(1) despite the protestations of the

[143] Art 1(2).
[144] Art 2(3).
[145] Art 16.
[146] Art 15.
[147] Art 18.
[148] Explanatory Memorandum to the Draft Regulation p 9.
[149] Frosio (n 13)13–14.
[150] See section 3.

draft Regulation to the contrary in Recitals 12, 16, and 19. Thus, the drafters have recognized the conflict between the Proposal and E-Commerce Directive, but have not solved it, other than through semantics, by effectively saying green is green and does not contain any blue. The Proposal can therefore be criticized on two main counts. First, it does not respect the rule of law by providing for an extra-legal "voluntary" referral mechanism[151] (like those carried out by the CTIRU and Europol). Second, by imposing proactive, automated monitoring obligations, it additionally conflicts with the E-Commerce Directive, and ultimately with freedom of expression, unless clearer safeguards will be employed to govern automated content moderation processes.[152] Gatekeeper regulation may lead to infringing the rule of law and unaccountable removal of content.[153] It has also moved from mere notice and take down obligations towards a comprehensive duty of care and proactive technology regulation.

4.1.3 Online gambling and notice and take down

In respect of policing unauthorized online gambling in a country, notice and take down is not an effective enforcement mechanism for a number of different reasons. Operators provide online gambling as a service, that is, the activity of gambling—thus online gambling is not about the dissemination of content by many dispersed users. Our previous examples of gatekeeper regulation concerned regulation of content provided by the users themselves, so-called *user-generated content*. By contrast, gambling regulations is about policing an activity provided by online gambling operators, that is, online casinos, betting exchanges, bookmakers, bingo providers, and so on. These operators target operations remotely into certain jurisdictions and markets. Operators can therefore ensure that their websites are not hosted by entities established in the same jurisdiction as the regulator, or are hosted by content delivery networks, who do little to enforce national gambling regulation. Since the law on gambling and attitudes towards different forms of online gambling vary significantly between countries, including between the Member States of the EU, there is little agreement on how unlicensed gambling websites should be dealt with. With CSEA materials or terrorism-related content there is a consensus that these materials are heinous and therefore there may be more of a morally motivated incentive by some hosting providers to take steps against such materials. Such a consensus does not exist in respect of online gambling and, since the law is fragmented, it is even more difficult to achieve notice and take down internationally. Thus, a regulator in Member State A notifying the competent authorities in Member State B, or even the hosting provider established in Member State C, that they are hosting gambling illegal in State A may not have any effect in achieving a take down.

The 2019 EU Study on gambling enforcement[154] mapped the location of the servers and/or the content delivery networks in respect of the published blacklists of

[151] Unaccountable, private norms, not "prescribed by law," see Report of the UN Special Rapporteur David Kaye on the Promotion and Protection of the Right to Freedom of Opinion and Expression (n 25) para 46.

[152] Report of the UN Special Rapporteur David Kaye on the Promotion and Protection of the Right to Freedom of Opinion and Expression (n 25) para 32; Frosio (n 13) 23–27.

[153] ibid 13–14.

[154] Hörnle et al (n 3).

unlicensed gambling of eleven EU Member States.[155] Unsurprisingly the US is home to the largest number of servers hosting illegal gambling websites from these lists: 40 per cent of websites and 51 per cent of all servers observed were mapped to the US.[156] However, the UK also hosted a large percentage of gambling websites illegal in other EU Member States: 23 per cent of websites on the Greek blacklist and 27 per cent of websites on the Lithuanian blacklist were hosted in the UK.[157] A significant number of gambling websites were also hosted on servers in Malta: 27 per cent of blacklisted websites in Lithuania were hosted in Malta and, overall, 40 per cent of blacklisted websites were hosted in EU Member States.

Interestingly, a small number of content delivery networks hosts a large number of gambling websites. The main US-established content delivery networks were CloudFlare and GoDaddy. In fact, 30 per cent of all servers observed were part of the CloudFlare content delivery network.[158] This may mean that regulatory dialogue and action needs to focus on these content delivery networks, but this would require joined-up coordination efforts with other government departments (such as media or content regulation) within a Member State, as well as strategic international cooperation with like-minded other Member States with uncertain outcomes.

4.1.4 Wider range of contents

The most recent trend is for regulatory instruments to address a number of different illegal or harmful contents applying. This section examines a number of legislative instruments adopting this horizontal approach to gatekeeper regulation.

4.1.4.1 The German Netzwerkdurchsetzungsgesetz (NetzDG)

The legal assumption behind the NetzDG of 2017[159] is that German criminal law[160] applies to social media companies and other hosting providers within its scope of application and German jurisdiction.[161] Thus, the NetzDG does not create new obligations for social media companies and hosting providers as such but instead provides standards for improving complaints mechanisms and notice and take down *procedures*. A study conducted in early 2017 showed that while YouTube managed to remove 90 per cent of criminal content notified, Facebook only removed 39 per cent of such content, and Twitter only 1 per cent.[162] The reluctance of social media companies to take down content, such as hate speech,[163] notified by the police and other authorities quickly and efficiently was the political driver behind the adoption of this

[155] Meaning that the gambling on the listed website domains was illegal in one or more of the following EU Member States: Cyprus, Belgium, Bulgaria, Estonia, Greece, Italy, Latvia, Lithuania, Poland, Romania, and Slovakia.

[156] Hörnle et al (n 3) 52.

[157] ibid.

[158] ibid.

[159] Gesetz zur Verbesserung der Rechtsdurchsetzung in Sozialen Netzwerken vom 1 September 2017, BGBl I 61/2017 p 3352.

[160] The NetzDG refers to specific content-related provisions in the German Criminal Code in s 1(3).

[161] Ss 3–9 St GB, see further Chapter 5, the complexity of the jurisdictional rules makes it difficult to predict with certainty whether German criminal law applies to a given content crime online.

[162] Explanations of the German Government for the NetzDG of 5 April 2017.

[163] N Guggenberger, "Das Netzwerkdurchsetzungsgesetz in der Anwendung" (2017) 70(36) *Neue Juristische Wochenschrift* 2577–82, 2577.

Act. Furthermore, news reports indicated that content moderators at social media companies, who had to make the decisions whether to remove content, had terrible working conditions with little support or training affecting both their welfare and the quality of decisions made.[164] The NetzDG has caused much controversy between those that praise the NetzDG as an assertion of state power over irresponsible internet giants and those that consider it a serious infringement of freedom of speech.[165] Its opponents point to two criticisms: first, the speed of removal required, which makes it likely that the take down process will be automated and therefore inaccurate and, second, the lack of procedure for reinstating content,[166] which has been taken down erroneously.[167]

The Act applies to for-profit internet service providers who operate internet platforms for the purpose of sharing contents or making such contents publicly available, which are defined as "social networks."[168] The Act does not apply to contents over which the social networks have editorial control, one-to-one communication or specialized platforms.[169] Essentially the NetzDG imposes reporting obligations[170] and procedures for content take down[171] for social networks with at least two million registered users in Germany.[172] Social networks have to produce and publish bi-annual reports if they receive more than 100 complaints per calendar year[173] and these reports must contain the following information:[174]

(1) a general description of the measures taken by the social network to suppress illegal activities on the platform;
(2) explanations of the complaints mechanism to achieve notice and take down and the criteria used for deciding whether content is taken down;
(3) number of complaints about illegal contents received providing the numbers for complaints made by individual and institutional complainants, and numbers for each ground for complaint;

[164] https://www.sueddeutsche.de/digital/exklusive-sz-magazin-recherche-inside-facebook-1.3297138 (15 December 2016) accessed on 16/07/2020.

[165] For press coverage along these lines, see eg *Der Spiegel*, "Das Facebook-Gesetz ist erst der Anfang," 30 June 2017, http://www.spiegel.de/netzwelt/netzpolitik/heiko-maas-und-facebook-das-netzdg-ist-erst-der-anfang-die-analyse-a-1155222.html accessed on 16/7/2020. The critique continued after the entry into force of the NetzDG on 1 January 2018, see eg *Die Zeit*, 8 January 2018, https://www.zeit.de/digital/internet/2018-01/netzwerkdurchsuchungsgesetz-bundesregierung-soziale-netzwerke-berichte accessed on 16/7/2020. Two members of the Liberal party have decided in June 2018 to bring an action for constitutional review of the NetzDG, see *Die Zeit*, 10 June 2018, https://www.zeit.de/digital/internet/2018-06/netzdg-netzwerkdurchsetzungsgesetz-klage-fdp accessed on 16/7/2020.

[166] As pointed out by Guggenberger (n 163) 2580, the NetzDG does not prohibit social media companies from taking content that is legal under German law, but infringes the Community Guidelines of the social media company.

[167] https://www.heise.de/newsticker/meldung/NetzDG-im-Bundestag-zwischen-Kapitulation-des-Rechtsstaats-und-Meilenstein-4423284.html (15 May 2019) accessed on 16/7/2020.

[168] S 1(1) NetzDG.

[169] ibid.

[170] S 2.

[171] S 3.

[172] S 1(2).

[173] S 2(1).

[174] ibid.

(4) how the complaints mechanism is organized, staffed, languages used, and qualifications of complaints personnel as well as the training and support provided for such personnel;
(5) the social network's membership in trade associations and whether the trade association maintains a complaints mechanism;
(6) number of complaints for which external legal advice was sought for the decision;
(7) number of complaints that led to the removal or blocking of content further distinguishing between individual and institutional complaints; numbers according to particular grounds for the complaints; number of cases where the social network gave the content provider an opportunity to reply to factual allegations; and how many cases where referred to the recognized self-regulatory complaints bodies in Germany;
(8) the time taken to remove or block content after a complaint (twenty-four hours; forty-eight hours; seven days; longer than seven days), distinguishing between individual and institutional complaints, and the ground for the complaint; and
(9) measures taken to inform the complainant and the content provider about the decision reached.

Furthermore, the NetzDG imposes an obligation for social networks to provide an effective and transparent complaints procedure[175] to deal with illegal contents under German criminal law.[176] Contents that are "obviously illegal" must be removed or blocked within twenty-four hours[177] of receipt of a complaint, unless the social network and the competent prosecution authorities have agreed that the content should remain online for a longer period.[178] Other illegal content must be removed within seven days, unless there are exceptional circumstances.[179] Exceptional circumstances exist if the decision depends on factual circumstances and the social network decides to take a statement from the content provider.[180] Furthermore, exceptional circumstances exist where the social network refers the complaint(s) to a recognized[181] self-regulatory body.[182] If content is taken down it has to be retained for ten weeks after take down for evidence purposes[183] and the social network further has to inform the complainant and the content provider about the decision and give reasons.[184] Moreover, each complaint and any measures taken in response to the complaint must be recorded and the management of the social network provider must supervise the process and offer regular support and training, at least twice a year for staff dealing with complaints.[185] The Act also obliges social networks to appoint a legal representative in

[175] S 3(1).
[176] The NetzDG refers to the relevant criminal provisions in the German Criminal Code, s1(3).
[177] See Guggenberger (n 163) 2579, arguing that this infringes Art 14 E-Commerce Directive 2000/31/EC and freedom of expression.
[178] S 3(2) No 2.
[179] S 3(2) No 3.
[180] S 3(2) No 3(a).
[181] These are certified by the relevant competent administrative authority in Germany, see s 3(6)–(9).
[182] S 3(2) No 3(b).
[183] S 3(2) No 4.
[184] S 3(2) No 5.
[185] S 3(3) and (4).

Germany if they are not established in Germany and creates a supervisory administrative authority.[186]

Finally, the Act provides for sanctions in the shape of administrative fines[187] of up to five million Euro[188] for failure to:

(1) comply with the reporting obligations;
(2) provide a complaints and notice and take down process according to the procedure detailed;
(3) supervise the complaints process;
(4) remedy any defects in the notice and take down process;
(5) provide regular and timely training and support to content moderators;
(6) appoint a legal representative established in Germany who responds to information requests by the administrative authority.[189]

The NetzDG makes clear that these administrative fines can be applied extraterritorially, even if the social network has no establishment in Germany.[190] However, if the social network provider disputes the illegality of the content the administrative authority has to obtain a judicial decision before imposing the administrative fine.[191]

The German NetzDG is an example of gatekeeper regulation *par excellence* by prescribing a procedure for notice and take down and reporting obligations that allow the relevant administrative authority to monitor the enforcement of criminal law, resorting to social networks as gatekeepers to remove illegal content, thus dealing with decentralization and the jurisdictional challenge. Unlike the legislative instruments discussed in sections 4.1.1–4.1.3, the NetzDG applies to a whole range of criminal offences. The negative effects of private entities balancing fundamental rights with criminal enforcement are palpable as there is an incentive to take content down, which is not counter-balanced by a procedure for reinstating content.

4.1.4.2 Audiovisual Media Services Directive (EU) 2018/1808

The Audiovisual Media Services Directive (AVMSD),[192,193] originally called the Television without Frontiers Directive of 1989, has the purpose (amongst others) to harmonize the *minimum* standards applicable to broadcast content and ensuring the free movement of media services across the EU. This was extended to certain "non-linear" (ie non-scheduled) audiovisual content services delivered over the internet

[186] S 5.
[187] S 4.
[188] Other than the appointment of a legal representative for which the maximum fine is Euro 500,000, s 4(2).
[189] S 5.
[190] S 4(3).
[191] S 4(5).
[192] The revised AVMS Directive must be transposed by the EU Member States by 19 September 2020. DCMS consulted on whether UK law should be aligned with the revised AVMS Directive even after UK withdrawal from the EU, see https://assets.publishing.service.gov.uk/government/uploads/system/uploads/attachment_data/file/807651/Audiovisual_Media_Services_Consultation_Document.pdf accessed on 16/7/2020.
[193] AVMS Directive (EU) 2018/1808 of 14 November 2018, OJ L303 pp 69–92.

in 2010, but only to TV-like internet services, leaving internet content largely unregulated (as regards media regulation). However, concerns over terrorist and hate speech videos on YouTube and similar audiovisual services has meant that the latest revision of the Directive now has included video-sharing platforms (containing user-generated content without a person with editorial responsibility) for the first time within the scope of regulation. Social media companies are included in the category of video-sharing platforms, if the sharing of videos is not merely an ancillary or minor part of the functionality they offer.[194] By requiring Member States to regulate content on video-sharing platforms hosting user-generated content, video-sharing platforms become internet gatekeepers for content regulation. The AVMS Directive does this in two ways: by supervised self-regulation and direct regulatory invention in respect of certain types of content.

As to self-regulation, the AVMS Directive envisages and encourages the drawing up of self-regulatory Codes of Conduct[195] by the video-sharing platforms,[196] but it additionally advocates a co-regulatory approach, beyond the self-regulatory approach. Member States must establish regulator(s) to assess the measures taken by the video-sharing platforms themselves.[197]

Article 28b stipulates that EU Member States must take positive measures to ensure protection from four types of content. Firstly, the public must be protected from user-generated videos and advertising containing incitement to violence or hatred against a protected[198] group.[199] Furthermore, the public must additionally be protected from three types of content contained in user-generated videos and advertisements: (1) public provocation to commit a terrorist offence,[200] (2) child pornography,[201] and (3) offences related to racism and xenophobia.[202] Member States *may* impose stricter measures, additionally regulating other types of content, as Germany has done in the NetzDG.[203] Thus, following the implementation deadline for the AVMS Directive on 19 September 2020, Member States have to take *regulatory* measures to curb online hate crime, terrorist content, child sex abuse, and racist material on video-sharing services, as a minimum.

[194] Recital 5, Art 1(1)(aa).

[195] See the existing EU Voluntary Code of Conduct on Countering Hate Speech Online (2016) https://ec.europa.eu/info/policies/justice-and-fundamental-rights/combatting-discrimination/racism-and-xenophobia/countering-illegal-hate-speech-online_en (May 2016) accessed on 16/7/2020—this is essentially a number of commitments including notice and take down.

[196] Art 4a(1) and (2).

[197] Art 28b(5).

[198] Referring to the protected characteristics in Art 21 of the EU Charter of Fundamental Rights: sex, race, colour, ethnic or social origin, genetic features, language, religion or belief, political or any other opinion, membership of a national minority, property, birth, disability, age, or sexual orientation.

[199] Art 28(b).

[200] Art 5 of the Counter-Terrorism Directive (EU) 2017/541 harmonizes the criminal laws in the EU by providing that Member States must make it a criminal offence to incite the terrorist acts listed in Art 3(1) of the Directive, whereby both direct and indirect incitement is sufficient, including the glorification of such terrorist acts, creating a danger that such acts may be committed.

[201] Art 5(4) of the Directive on Combatting the Sexual Abuse and Sexual Exploitation of Children 2011/93/EU.

[202] Art 1 Council Framework Decision on Racism and Xenophobia 2008/913/JHA of 28 November 2008.

[203] Art 28b(6).

However, the AVMS Directive does not stipulate the precise nature of the measures to be taken by the Member States, and only sets out the general principles for taking such measures.[204] While the AVMS Directive is an example of gatekeeper regulation for video-sharing platforms, the implementation in the Member States will vary. But interestingly, the general principles[205] for gatekeeper regulation are similar to the principles set out in the UK White Paper discussed in section 4.1.4.3.

First of all, Member States should adopt a risk-based approach, being informed by the nature of the content and its harmfulness, the intended audience to be protected, as well as the interests of the video-sharing platform, the users who have uploaded the content, and the public interest.[206] Furthermore, the AVMS Directive adopts a practical and proportionate approach, which takes into account the size of the video-sharing platform and the nature of its service. The AVMS Directive states that the measures should *not* comprise "ex-ante control measures" or "upload-filtering of content" in breach of the prohibition on the imposition of general monitoring obligations on hosting services.[207] In other words, automated tools based on artificial intelligence must not be implemented in such a way that they lead to the automated, overbroad filtering of content and general monitoring of all content.[208] This means that such tools must be supplemented by human review and the measures themselves must be specific and targeted, in accordance with Article 14(3) of the E-Commerce Directive.[209] This contrasts with the Proposal for a Regulation on Preventing the Dissemination of Terrorist Content Online discussed earlier, which (in its draft form) does not include a specific requirement for human review.

The AVMS Directive lists the measures that video-sharing platforms must implement by way of co-regulation,[210] such as prohibiting the four types of content[211] in their terms and conditions,[212] to provide for users the opportunity to report and flag such illegal content for notice and take down,[213] providing transparent information as to what the video-sharing platform has done with content reported or flagged,[214] providing age-verification mechanisms for content harmful to children,[215] implementing content rating systems,[216] parental control systems for content harmful to children,[217]

[204] Art 28b(3).
[205] Art 28b(2) and (3).
[206] Art 18b(3).
[207] Art 28b(3); cf Art 15(1) E-Commerce Directive 2000/31/EC: "Member States shall not impose a general obligation on providers (. . .) to monitor the information which they transmit or store, nor a general obligation actively to seek facts or circumstances indicating illegal activity." See also Recital 47.
[208] See also the CJEU case of C-70/10 *Scarlet Extended v SABAM* (n 30) of 24 November 2011, which held that a filtering system searching all content for copyright infringements breaches EU law as being disproportionate to the freedom of expression and privacy.
[209] As already discussed, this permits specific orders by administrative authorities or courts to terminate or prevent an infringement and which also permits procedures "governing the removal or disabling of access to information."
[210] Art 28b(4) and (5).
[211] Listed in Art 28b(1) discussed earlier.
[212] Art 28b(3)(a).
[213] Art 28b(3)(d).
[214] Art 28b(3)(e).
[215] Art 28b(3)(f).
[216] Art 28b(3)(g).
[217] Art 28b(3)(h).

complaints handling measures,[218] and measures to improve digital literacy.[219] Furthermore, the AVMS Directive envisages the use of complaint mechanisms and alternative dispute resolution mechanisms.[220] Finally, the AVMS Directive envisages further Codes of Conduct in respect of hate speech.[221]

While the UK may no longer be part of the EU, the UK White Paper strongly aligns with the approach in the AVMS Directive.

4.1.4.3 The UK White Paper "Online Harms" 2019

The UK White Paper[222] prepares the UK's regulatory framework for online content regulation for the next decades. Like the AVMS Directive and the draft EU Regulation on Preventing the Dissemination of Terrorist Content Online, it has moved on from the implementation of notice and take down (for which the NetzDG is an example) to the establishment of a *duty of care*. The duty of care approach involves imposing *a range of obligations* on hosting providers *as gatekeepers* to minimize the dissemination of harmful content. The regulatory regime envisaged will impose positive obligations to take proactive measures, notwithstanding the fact that service providers have limited control over user-generated content. Hosting providers *themselves* must police their platforms and the legal framework is there to supervise and enforce standards set by the regulator by way of co-regulation. This is similar to the proactive, co-regulatory approach adopted by the EU AVMS Directive, discussed earlier.[223]

The UK instrument to achieve this is the planned statutory duty of care for hosting service providers and a (future) co-regulatory Codes of Conduct will set out the obligations.[224] These Codes of Conduct will be binding as to their result (which is encapsulated in the tool of the statutory duty of care), but companies will be able to deviate as long as their alternative approach will lead to the same standard of protection from "online harms."[225]

The implementation of the Codes of Conduct will be supervised by a new "internet safety"[226] regulator who will have a range of enforcement powers, including the power to demand information, the power to give non-compliant providers substantial fines and impose liability on individual members of senior management.[227] Hosting providers' legal obligations will include: enhancing existing notice and take down mechanisms and proactive content moderation, including the use of artificial intelligence to identify "harmful" content and prevent known child sex abuse and terrorist content

[218] Art 28b(3)(i).
[219] Art 28b(3)(j).
[220] Art 28b(7).
[221] See Art 28b(10).
[222] "Online Harms" (n 116) jointly published by the Home Office and the Department of Culture, Media and Sport on 8 April 2019, https://assets.publishing.service.gov.uk/government/uploads/system/uploads/attachment_data/file/793360/Online_Harms_White_Paper.pdf accessed on 16/7/2020.
[223] See the measures that video-sharing platforms must implement discussed earlier.
[224] "Online Harms" (n 116) 7.
[225] ibid.
[226] To my mind this raises the question whether "internet safety" is an oxymoron and therefore creates false expectations as to what can be achieved, rather than preparing citizens for a less safe world (say, compared to broadcast content).
[227] See "Online Harms" (n 116) 41ff and 59–60.

being made available to users.[228] As a matter of priority, the government will promulgate Codes on CSEA materials and terrorist content, which will have to be agreed by government.[229] Codes in respect of other types of illegal materials must include cooperation and coordination between the regulator and UK law enforcement authorities.[230]

Like the German NetzDG the proposals envisage annual transparency reports.[231] Moreover, the White Paper envisages the use of artificial intelligence in content moderation, but advocates its proportionate and transparent use by hosting providers, including giving independent researchers access to data to examine its fairness in operation.[232] Like the AVMS Directive, the UK White Paper proposes effective and easy-to-use complaints mechanisms, which hosting providers must implement and an independent review mechanism in respect of such complaints by the independent regulator if a large number of users are affected.[233]

The White Paper has an *extremely wide scope* both in respect of the regulated entities and in respect of the content covered. It applies to all companies that "allow users to share or discover user-generated content or interact with each other online."[234] It acknowledges that this means that a very wide range of companies, small and large, and including not only social media platforms, but also file-hosting sites, blogging sites, discussion forums, messaging services and search engines, which are all caught in the net of regulation.[235]

As to the types of content covered, the White Paper addresses not only concerns about illegal content online, but also concerns about a range of "unacceptable" content.[236] It lists a large number of twenty-three "online harms."[237] The ambitious reform goal of the government is to create a regulatory framework that tackles the full range of online harms, rather than just enforcing the criminal law and this distinguishes it from the NetzDG.[238]

The White Paper recognizes that, first, hosting providers as gatekeepers of regulation are key to that aim, and, second, that artificial intelligence has a role to play in content regulation, but that the threats to freedom of expression by technology regulation must be contained through transparency and regulatory oversight. However, surprisingly it does not discuss the jurisdictional conflicts which arise in co-regulation

[228] ibid 64ff.

[229] ibid 41.

[230] ibid 7.

[231] ibid 41.

[232] ibid 8.

[233] ibid 8. This is not expressly stated but presumably this includes reinstatement of material wrongfully taken down as well as complaints about the (continued) presence of harmful content.

[234] ibid 8.

[235] ibid 8, 49ff; purely private communications will not be included—this raises the question of what are private communications: Is a WhatsApp group with fifty users still private?

[236] ibid 5.

[237] Such as CSEA, terrorist content and activity, organized immigration crime, modern slavery, extreme pornography, revenge pornography, harassment and cyberstalking, hate crime, encouraging suicide, incitement to violence, sale of illegal goods such as weapons or drugs, content illegally uploaded from prisons, sexting, cyberbullying, "extremist" content, disinformation, self-harm, and children accessing pornography and other inappropriate material: ibid 31, Table .

[238] ibid 6.

and how to limit the standards developed in the Codes of Practice to the territory of the UK. By ignoring the jurisdictional challenges and extending the scope of the co-regulatory framework to "unacceptable" (as opposed to illegal content) it additionally moves away from the rule of law, and into the realms of private systems of regulation without clearly applicable legal standards, which can be checked in a court of law.

4.1.4.4 Australia

4.1.4.4.1 Schedules 5 and 7 Broadcasting Services Act 1992 Australia has adapted its broadcasting regulations to apply to internet materials in 1999 and 2007. The Australian Communications and Media Authority (ACMA) can serve notices on internet service providers in Australia to take down content that (1) would be refused classification or is rated as X18+, or which is rated as 18+ or as 15+, where no age-verification takes place, or (3) cyberbullying content.

4.1.4.4.2 Criminal Code Amendment (Sharing of Abhorrent Violent Material) Act 2019 In the wake of the terrorist attacks on two mosques in Christchurch, New Zealand, in March 2019, which left fifty-one people dead and was live-streamed by the terrorists on Facebook Live, Australia quickly passed new Federal legislation[239] amending the Criminal Code Act 1995. The political connection is the "Christchurch Call," which the Prime Minister of New Zealand, Jacinda Ardern, and the French President, Emmanuel Macron, led at the G7 meeting in France, seeking international commitments by governments and technology companies to tackle extremist content online.[240]

The Australian Criminal Code Amendment has created two new offences regarding (1) failure by a *content or hosting provider* to expeditiously remove abhorrent violent material and (2) failure by a content, hosting, or internet service provider to refer abhorrent violent material to the Australian Federal Police, if the underlying offence occurred in Australia.

Abhorrent violent conduct is defined as a terrorist act, murder, attempted murder, torture, rape, or kidnapping.[241] Abhorrent violent material is defined as offensive, audio, visual, or audiovisual content, recording or streaming, and which is produced (eg filmed or recorded) by one of the perpetrators or their associates.[242] The offences therefore do not apply if the abhorrent violent conduct is filmed by the victim, a journalist, or a bystander, for example. In practice, it may be difficult to tell from the footage or recording who produced this, which leads to uncertainty for content and hosting providers whether they are obliged to remove or refer such material.

Content services are defined as social media services or designated internet services in accordance with the Enhancing Online Safety Act 2015[243]—these are

[239] Criminal Code Amendment (Sharing of Abhorrent Violent Material) Act No 38/2019, https://www.legislation.gov.au/Details/C2019A00038 came into effect 6 April 2019 accessed on 16/7/2020.

[240] https://www.bbc.co.uk/news/technology-48288353?intlink_from_url=https://www.bbc.co.uk/news/topics/c96 6094wvmqt/christchurch-mosque-shootings&link_location=live-reporting-story (15 May 2019) accessed on 17/7/2020.

[241] S 474.32 Federal Criminal Code.

[242] S 474.31 Federal Criminal Code.

[243] S 474.30.

services enabling online social interaction, allowing users to interact and post content (social media services)[244] or services that deliver to end users, or allows end users to access, material over the internet (designated internet services).[245] Hosting services are storing content for social media and their users, such as cloud providers. Thus, it is important to note that the Australian obligation to remove content does not only apply to social media companies, video-sharing platforms, and search engines, but additionally to cloud storage providers.[246]

First, if an internet service provider, a content service provider, or a hosting service provider is aware that their service can be used to access *particular* abhorrent violent material that depicts conduct that has occurred or is occurring in Australia and does not *refer* the material to the Australian Federal Police within a reasonable time, it commits a criminal offence.[247]

Secondly, a content or hosting service provider commits a criminal offence if it knows or is reckless about abhorrent violent material which can be accessed through its service, or if such material is hosted on its service, and does not ensure the expeditious disabling of access to or removal of the material.[248]

The maximum penalty for individuals is three years' imprisonment and/or a fine and for a company it is 10 per cent of annual global turnover.[249]

Both offences apply extraterritorially, even to content or hosting service providers, which are not established in Australia, the only territorial link to Australia being the accessibility of the abhorrent violent material.[250] However for the non-referral offence, the consent of the Australian Attorney General must be sought if the offending company is not established in Australia or an individual is not an Australian citizen[251] and for the non-removal offence, the consent of the Attorney General must always be sought before a prosecution.[252]

Thus, the Act has created two new criminal offences, which are committed by omission. Or in other words, the Act has created a legal obligation, subject to criminal liability. For the failure to remove offence, the Act requires knowledge, but recklessness *is* sufficient.[253] The *mens rea* requirement will be crucial to understanding the exact scope of the obligations of content and hosting service providers to remove content or disable access to it, as recklessness is essentially about taking an unjustifiable risk.[254] Recklessness as a *mens rea* standard is particularly problematic in relation to offences committed by omission, as it raises the question of what exactly service providers have to do to avoid liability. In the context of gatekeeper regulation, this raises the question

244 S 9 Enhancing Online Safety Act 2015.
245 S 6.
246 S 474.34(5)–(8).
247 S 474.33.
248 S 474.34.
249 S 474.34(9) and (10).
250 Ss 474.33(2), 474.34(2), (3) and (6), (7).
251 S 474.42(1).
252 S 474.42(3).
253 S 474.34(4) and (8).
254 "a person is reckless if he or she is aware of a substantial risk that a circumstance exists, or a result will occur, and, having regard to all the circumstances, it is unjustifiable to take that risk," s 5.4(1) and (2) Criminal Code Act.

of what proactive measures they must take in order to avoid being accused of taking an unjustifiable risk and, *in particular* what type of *artificial intelligence* they have to use to avoid criminal liability. For example, should they block or filter known terrorist content in image- hash databases? Should they block or filter images, which depict CSEA content in image-hash databases?

Ultimately the scope of the recklessness standard will be decided by the courts, but creates legal uncertainty, which is highly problematic given the risk of criminal liability. The Act also provides for the eSafety Commissioner to notify a content or hosting service provider about specified abhorrent violent material on their service.[255] Once a notice has been issued there is a presumption that the content or hosting provider has been reckless and the burden of proof is on the service provider to prove that they have not been reckless, that is, that they have taken all measures to avoid the taking of unjustifiable risks.[256]

Finally, the Act contains a number of defences, such as that the accessibility of the material is necessary for law enforcement, monitoring criminals or court proceedings,[257] necessary for scientific, medical, academic or historical research,[258] professional news or current affairs reporting in the public interest,[259] performance of public duties by a public official,[260] lawful procurement of a change to any matter established by law, policy or practice,[261] or, finally, accessibility of the material is for the development, performance, exhibition or distribution, in good faith, of an artistic work.[262] The Act also makes clear that the provisions must not be applied to the extent that it would infringe on the constitutional freedom of political communication.[263] While these defences seek to balance censorship of abhorrent violent materials with freedom of expression, the assessment of whether a defence applies has to be made by private companies, that is, the service providers under threat of criminal liability. Given the overwhelming quantity of materials online and the difficulty of understanding the wider context of the material, arguably these defences will not function to protect freedom of expression, as service providers have no choice but to err on the side of caution and employ technology to make the decision.

The Australian provisions take gatekeeper regulation one step further in that they do not rely on co-regulation with industry, but instead impose heavy criminal sanctions in respect of the failure to censor abhorrent materials. While the criminal sanctions are limited to some of the *most violent* materials, and are therefore apt to deal with public outrage, it must be questioned whether they are necessarily effective to deal with the increasing problem of radicalizing young people to become terrorists or the commission of any of these violent criminal acts. The harmfulness of ideology (of whatever nature) is not necessarily correlated to the degree of abhorrence or violence

[255] S 474.35.
[256] Ss 474.35(5), (6) and 474.36(5), (6).
[257] S 474.37(1), (2)(a), (b) and (c).
[258] S 474.37(1), (2)(d).
[259] S 474.37(1), (2)(e).
[260] S 474.37(1), (2)(f).
[261] S 474.37(1), (2)(h).
[262] S 474.37(1), (2)(i).
[263] S 474.38(1).

it depicts.[264] Gatekeeper regulation should be limited to the fundamental interests protected by criminal law prohibitions rather than ensuring broadcasting-like content standards, preventing offence and outrage, such as those for example encapsulated in the Ofcom Broadcasting Code (UK).[265] Hence, what should count is the danger emanating from such materials, not necessarily the outrage they may engender. What becomes clear of this discussion is that intermediary gatekeeper regulation requires clear strategic priorities as to content regulation and the formulation of clear standards to ensure legal certainty.

4.1.5 Content regulation point two: hosting as gatekeeping

Having compared different initiatives of gatekeeper content regulation it is evident that laws examined have moved from narrowly tailored and specific content regulation to much broader content regulation: covering a broader range of contents and moving from specific notice and take down obligations[266] to a *duty of care* approach.[267] Notice and take down obligations, albeit that they, too, have an impact on freedom of expression, acknowledge the limited control that social media and hosting providers have over user-generated content and could be described as "Gatekeeper Content Regulation.1." However, notice and take down as an instrument of regulation has had limited effectiveness in fighting illegal and harmful contents online, as materials are reposted and replicated quickly and, depending on the nature of the medium, the impact of the posting may be instantaneous and ephemeral (as tweets, for example, frequently are). The duty of care approach imposes a range of proactive measures, including notice and take down, on service providers hosting or making available content. Thus, gatekeeper regulation imposes responsibility on gatekeepers going beyond the removal or blocking of content.

This duty of care is informed by the concept used in relation to the regulation of physical spaces and bases responsibility on the fact that service providers have created a virtual space as a public space, drawing parallels to health and safety regulatory regimes. Furthermore, they encourage certain types of behaviours and interactions, that is, they are not purely passive hosts of user-generated content. This approach bases responsibility on the precautionary principle, that is, a duty to prevent harm when engaging in or encouraging "risky" endeavours.[268] Another parallel can be drawn between the regulation of broadcast content and internet gatekeeper regulation. Since national broadcasters have to rely on national infrastructure and obtain a licence, which in turn allows regulation of content,[269] broadcasting regulation is a

[264] J Ammar and S Xu, *When Jihadi Ideology Meets Social Media* (Palgrave Macmillan 2018), 25–58.

[265] https://www.ofcom.org.uk/__data/assets/pdf_file/0016/132073/Broadcast-Code-Full.pdf accessed on 17/7/2020, see also s 319 Communications Act 2003 (UK), which requires protection of the public from offensive and harmful material, for example s 319(2)(f).

[266] See eg the Directive 2011/92/EU on Combating the Sexual Abuse and Sexual Exploitation of Children; EU Counter-Terrorism Directive (EU) 2017/541; German NetzDG, discussed in section 4.1.4.1.

[267] See the AVMS Directive, the UK White Paper and the Australian Criminal Code Amendment discussed in section 4.1.4.4.2.

[268] L Woods and W Perrin, "Online Harm Reduction-a Statutory Duty of Care and Regulator" Carnegie Trust UK Report April 2019 5–6, https://d1ssu070pg2v9i.cloudfront.net/pex/carnegie_uk_trust/2019/04/08091652/Online-harm-reduction-a-statutory-duty-of-care-and-regulator.pdf. accessed on 17/7/2020.

[269] S 319 Communications Act 2003 (UK).

classic example of well-established gatekeeper regulation and governments have been seeking to extend some aspects of this type of regulation to the internet.[270] As has already been discussed,[271] since the providers of content are decentralized, difficult to locate, and are likely to be in a foreign jurisdiction, the criminal law cannot easily be enforced. Gatekeepers as the more central nodes in the system are easier to reach as they are more likely to have some link to the domestic jurisdiction- hence the need to step up gatekeeper regulation.

So, while the unenforceability of the law against decentralized content providers may bring about augmented gatekeeper regulation, at the same time this development is a danger for freedom of expression *and* the rule of law.[272]

The rule of law requires that there is a degree of legal certainty, and restrictions of freedom of expression must be prescribed by law. This requires legally defined offences (or torts) and is counter to the vague notion of "harmfulness."[273] Furthermore, the removal of content from public spaces by private caretakers without a clear legal procedure, transparency, accountability, and judicial review[274] is equally contrary to the rule of law.[275] As the UN Special Rapporteur David Kays expresses it in his 2019 Report on content moderation: "This moment calls for radical transparency, meaningful accountability and a commitment to remedy in order to protect the ability of individuals to use online platforms as forums for free expression, access to information and engagement in public life."[276]

The overwhelming quantity of illegal and/or harmful materials also means that the use of technology and automation (including the use of artificial intelligence) are necessary. However, such technologies are inaccurate, as they do not recognize context and technologies such as machine learning techniques are largely opaque. It is for this reason that proactive monitoring leads to pre-publication censorship.[277]

Since many social media companies and hosting providers are globally operating companies, content regulation additionally raises the question of which national laws should be applicable and, if several national laws are applicable, what are the connecting factors to the national territory to delineate between them. This can be separate from the question of the competent court (jurisdiction of the court).

The relationship between jurisdiction and the territorial scope of the law applicable is particularly acute in respect of injunctions, such as judicial removal orders. It is unclear whether injunctions with *extraterritorial* effect are compatible with the notion of comity under international law. A distinction has to be made here between the rules of private international law, on the one hand, and international law, on the other. If a court has jurisdiction under private international law, it may indeed seek to impose a

[270] For which the AVMSD is a classic example.

[271] Section 1.

[272] Frosio (n 13) 13–14.

[273] *Sunday Times v United Kingdom* Series A No 30 (1979-80) 2 EHRR 245, paras 47, 49; *Ahmet Yildirim v Turkey* ECtHR Application 3111/10, Judgment of 18 December 2012, para 57.

[274] *Ekin v France* ECtHR Application 39288/98, Judgment of 17 July 2001, para 58.

[275] Report of the UN Special Rapporteur David Kaye on the Promotion and Protection of the Right to Freedom of Opinion and Expression (n 25) paras 46, 52, 64.

[276] Para 64.

[277] Para 67.

worldwide injunction, effectively applying its national law extraterritorially. In Case C-18/18 *Eva Glawischnig-Piesczek v Facebook*[278] the CJEU examined a reference on the scope of the obligation to remove content illegal in Austria, imposed by an injunction. The Austrian courts had in fact applied a worldwide removal order on Facebook. The Advocate General found that the EU has not harmonized the private international law rules in respect of injunctions, or in fact the private international law rules on applicable law in cases of defamation.[279] He stated that a court competent to adjudicate a dispute under the rules of jurisdiction, such as the harmonized rules in EU Regulation 1215/2012,[280] may impose a universal removal order with extraterritorial effect if its national procedural rules allow it to do so.[281] However, he then limited this finding by saying that courts should exercise self-restraint under the international law doctrine of comity and that "the implementation of the removal obligation should not go beyond what is necessary to achieve the protection of the injured person."[282] The Court followed the Advocate General and held that EU law does not prevent worldwide injunctions available under national law, but that such injunctions have to comply with international law.[283]

The imposition of worldwide cease and desist injunctions can also be seen in the context of intellectual property infringements.[284] In *Google v Equustek* the Canadian Supreme Court in 2017 upheld an interlocutory worldwide injunction to delist search results linking to a competitor's offering allegedly infringing Equustek's Internet Protocol (IP) rights.[285] The Court held that the impact of the injunction on parties outside the territory is a material consideration in deciding whether to grant the injunction, but it does not affect the competent court's *authority* to grant the order.[286] The problem with worldwide removal orders is that the applicable law of the court making the order applies globally and therefore potentially reduces the availability of content to the lowest common denominator. As argued by Advocate General Szpunar, this effect has to be carefully balanced against the need of protecting a claimant from serious harm from illegal conduct (such as defamation, privacy infringement, or IP infringement) and therefore when examining whether an injunction should be granted this should be part of the interests of justice test.

The lack of clarity of which state's laws apply is compounded further by conflict with the providers' own self-regulatory, private rules such as community guidelines, policies, and contractual terms and conditions, all of which provide for further overlaps and potential conflicts of rules. While self-regulation may provide *one set of rules* for the whole of the relevant provider's offer, thus apparently solving the jurisdictional conflicts between nation states' laws, it would impose one set of rules on

[278] See *Eva Glawischnig-Piesczek v Facebook* (n 32).
[279] Paras 78, 93, 96.
[280] See Chapters 8 and 11.
[281] Paras 86, 88.
[282] Para 100.
[283] Paras 49–51.
[284] See further Chapter 12.
[285] *Google Inc v Equustek Solutions Inc*, 2017 SCC 34.
[286] Abella J, quoting Fenlon J at para 30.

many different nations and thereby undermine local values, representation of local stakeholders, and democratic lawmaking. Compared to regulation by criminal law, self-regulation based on standards created by the industry is more apt to reflect the underlying technological limitations and is therefore fairer to the gatekeeper. But it again pushes regulation to the private sector and may make it opaque and less accountable. Private regulation by internet gatekeepers does not necessarily secure greater free speech rights.

All these factors lead to a threat to freedom of expression and the rule of law.[287] The UN Rapporteur recommends that the starting point for tackling the threat to freedom of expression and the rule of law would be the formation of a global Social Media Council,[288] which provides for transparency and accountability by an independent body. Such a body should be independent both of government and of the social media companies, but should have all stakeholders on its board. He further recommends that social media companies should publish detailed rules and their "case-law" in respect of their content moderation and, as far as this rule-making is concerned, engage on a far greater level with the public.[289]

Hosting providers and social networks are not the only gatekeepers in the system, however, additionally internet access providers are another chokepoint for gatekeeper regulation (Figure 3.1).

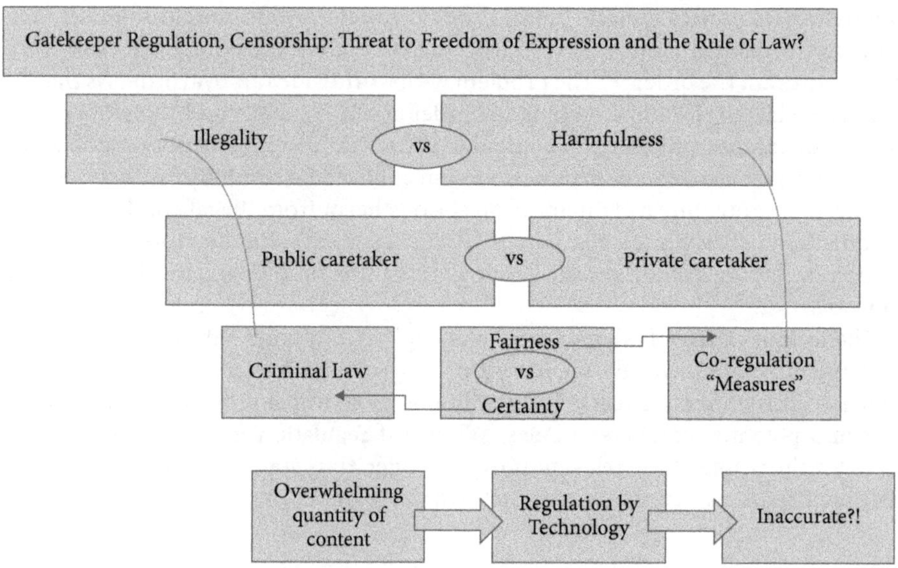

Figure 3.1 Threat to freedom of expression and the rule of law

[287] Report of the UN Special Rapporteur David Kaye on the Promotion and Protection of the Right to Freedom of Opinion and Expression (n 25) para 68.

[288] Paras 63, 72,

[289] Paras 63, 71.

4.2 Internet access providers as local gatekeepers—blocking

The second category of intermediaries who can act as gatekeepers are internet access providers, as they are close to the destination of the information—and hence the point of regulation—and are therefore mostly (but not always) in the same jurisdiction as the regulator.

Internet access providers are communication companies who provide different types of users with access to the internet. They can block certain types of content or websites with the consequence that users cannot access the content or websites. Since internet access providers are licensed by the state, the state may in turn mandate that they block certain types of content or websites.[290] Different mechanisms can be used for blocking: (1) Doman Name System (DNS) blocking, (2) blocking of IP addresses, or (3) specific deep-packet inspection.[291]

DNS blocking is the cheapest method for blocking and the easiest to implement, but on the flipside it can be easily circumvented. It involves disrupting the look up of the IP address corresponding to a particular domain name, which is a function commonly carried out by the internet access provider.[292]

IP addresses identify particular internet connection points were resources can be found—IP blocking involves configuring internet routers in such a way that requests for certain IP addresses will be dropped. IP address filtering is purely based on destination, not on content and, since all web traffic to that destination is blocked, it may lead to considerable overblocking (content that should not have been blocked is included in the block).[293]

A more exact method therefore involves inspecting the content of an internet communication (deep-packet inspection) and searching for certain keywords before a communication is blocked, for example, through the use of a proxy filter. This type of blocking is more precise but also complex and therefore more expensive to implement.[294] However, this type of blocking can be combined with IP address blocking—only traffic relating to "suspect" IP address is routed through the proxy filter, which inspects the content, thus keeping the precision of deep-packet inspection and the lower expense of IP blocking.[295]

Political opposition against the introduction of internet access blocking is aligned to the controversy surrounding internet censorship generally. The introduction of blocking measures can generate considerable political opposition and media controversy.[296] Yana Breindl, in her study of the discourses surrounding legislation

[290] J Zittrain and J Palfrey, "Internet Filtering: The Politics and Mechanisms of Control" in R Deibert and J Palfrey et al (eds), *Access Denied- the Practice and Policy of Global Internet Filtering* (MIT Press 2008) 29–56, 34.

[291] ibid.

[292] S Murdoch and R Anderson, "Tools and Technology of Internet Filtering" in R Deibert, J Palfrey et al (eds), *Access Denied- the Practice and Policy of Global Internet Filtering* (MIT Press 2008) 57–72, 61.

[293] ibid 59.

[294] ibid 60, 62.

[295] ibid 63–64.

[296] K Gracz, "On the Role of Copyright Protection in the Information Society. Anti-ACTA Protests in Poland as a Lesson in Participatory Democracy" (2013) 4 *Journal of Intellectual Property, Information*

introducing internet access blocking of child sex abuse content both in Germany and France, found that opposition against internet access blocking centred round civil society and the media (with the opponents being more vocal in both countries than the proponents) and the opponents managed to frame their arguments and form a well-connected opposition with growing political influence (especially in Germany).[297] She concludes that "Governmental proposals for state regulation of internet blocking create particularly favourable windows of opportunity to manifest opposition towards internet blocking."[298]

There is a general debate as to what extent blocking is appropriate in Western liberal democracies; and this debate is embedded in the discourse on internet governance and freedom of expression. The Open Network Initiative at the Berkman Center for Internet & Society measures and exposes all forms of internet censorship and monitors and measures blocking.[299] Measuring internet censorship is complex and goes beyond measuring blocking and the type of blocking used (DNS, IP, or URL blocking).[300] However, as a matter of good practice internet users should at least know when their internet access has been obstructed through warning messages.[301]

Internet access blocking raises questions of its compatibility with freedom of expression[302] and it has to be implemented in a manner that respects human rights and in particular the proportionality principle and therefore also raises questions of constitutionality. In this context, the non-effectiveness of blocking measures and the ease of circumvention of such measures are often used as arguments that they are not proportionate and that they are not suitable to implement a policy objective. Likewise, the imprecise nature of blocking, in particular overblocking (capturing content which should not be blocked) and underblocking (content which should be blocked not being captured), leads to arguments in the same direction.[303]

In the UK, internet access providers have a duty to act as a gatekeeper under a number of regulatory systems, thus avoiding the jurisdictional enforcement challenge for certain types of internet content. Interestingly, to date there has been less public

Technology and Electronic Commerce Law 22–36; Y Breindl, "Discourse Networks on State-Mandated Access Blocking in Germany and France" (2013) 15(6) Info 42–62.

[297] ibid 49—the Act was overturned in Germany in at the end of 2011; whereas in France internet access blocking in respect of child abuse images was successfully introduced in 2011. Directive 2011/92/EU on Combating the Sexual Abuse and Sexual Exploitation of Children makes internet access blocking optional and subject to safeguards, see discussion in section 4.2.1.

[298] ibid at 59.

[299] See further RJ Deibert and JG Palfrey et al (eds), *Access Denied: the Practice and Policy of Global Internet Filtering* (MIT Press 2009).

[300] S Burnett and N Feamster "Making Sense of Internet Censorship: a New Frontier for Internet Measurement" (2013) 43(3) ACM SIGCOMM Computer & Communications Review 84–89.

[301] ibid 84; see also Art 25(2) of Directive 2011/92/EU.

[302] Chang (n 107); McIntyre (n 105) 315ff; UN General Assembly, Report of the UN Special Rapporteur David Kaye on the Promotion and Protection of the Right to Freedom of Opinion and Expression (n 25) for an in-depth discussion.

[303] WPh Stol, HKW Kaspersen et al, "Governmental Filtering of Websites: the Dutch Case" (2009) 25 Computer Law and Security Review 251–62; Y Akdeniz, "To Block or Not to Block: European Approaches to Content Regulation and Implications for Freedom of Expression" (2010) 26 Computer Law & Security Review 260–72; Breindl (n 296) .

resistance against internet access blocking in the UK compared to some continental European countries such as Sweden, Poland, or Germany.

4.2.1 Blocking of CSEA

Article 25(1) of Directive 2011/92/EU gives EU Member States the option of imposing duties on companies providing internet access in their territories to block access to "to webpages containing or disseminating child pornography." This provision is worded as an option, not a harmonized standard, as internet access blocking is more controversial in some EU Member States than in others.[304] The Article expressly provides for a number of safeguards: the internet access blocking procedures must be transparent, the restrictions must be necessary and proportionate, users must be informed of the blocking, for example, through a landing page and, finally, there must be judicial redress for wrongful blocking. Recital 47 explains the reason for the necessity of blocking measures in legal frameworks with the fact that removal of CSEA content at source is frequently impossible, as the hosting provider may be in a state which is unable or unwilling to instigate notice and take down, or such procedures are too lengthy.

In the UK, the blocking of CSEA is self-regulatory, and laid down in the rules of the IWF, which was set up in 1996 as a self-regulatory body to fight criminal CSEA for internet access providers in the UK and started mandatory blocking in 2004. The IWF cooperates with the police, government agencies, and industry stakeholders but is independent of the government and the police and its remit is narrowly restricted to this type of content. Under the self-regulatory regime of the IWF, internet access providers have committed to blocking CSEA on websites as a last resort where the content is hosted in a foreign jurisdiction and cannot be taken down at source. It uses a combination of IP blocking and deep-packet inspection in a technology developed by British Telecommunications ("BT Cleanfeed"). The URLs are assessed for CSEA by specially trained IWF assessors who are police trained but independent of the police force and who specialize in assessing this type of content. For example, the IWF has reported that in 2018 more than 105,000 websites contained CSEA and almost half (47 per cent) of that content was hosted in the Netherlands.[305] The IWF engages in international collaboration with regulators in other jurisdictions, but where this does not result in the content being taken down internet access providers use their gatekeeper function to block UK users from accessing such material.

4.2.2 Blocking of terrorist content

The EU Counter-Terrorism Directive (EU) 2017/541 encourages Member States to make arrangements for the blocking of access to material that constitutes a public provocation[306] to commit a terrorist offence, when removal of such content at source is not possible.[307] As for the Directive on CSEA, because of the controversy surrounding internet access blocking in many Member States, the Directive makes such legal measures optional, and the Counter-Terrorism Directive provides for the same

[304] See also Akdeniz (n 303) 262.

[305] https://www.bbc.co.uk/news/technology-48022950 accessed on 17/7/2020.

[306] Cross-reference is to Art 5 of the Directive, but not to recruitment or training materials in general.

[307] Art 21(2) and Recital 22.

safeguards for internet access blocking as the Directive on CSEA.[308] It is believed that in the UK the CTIRU compiles a list of webpages (URLs) that cannot be removed at source, which is then included in the family friendly filters given to users as a choice by the major UK internet access providers.[309] Like the list of webpages referred for removal there is no public guidance as to what content is included on the filter list, but the family filters are implemented at user level and are therefore optional.[310]

4.2.3 Pornography and the Digital Economy Act 2017

The Digital Economy Act 2017 imposes an obligation on commercial providers of "hardcore" pornography[311] to ensure that such material is not normally accessible to persons under eighteen years old.[312] The age-verification requirement is enforced by the British Board of Film Classification (BBFC) as the designated regulator with the powers to request information and issue enforcement notices.[313] However, additionally, the Digital Economy Act 2017 uses internet access providers as gatekeepers. The BBFC may give a legally binding notice to internet access providers, ordering them to block hardcore pornography websites not complying with the age-verification requirement as well as websites making available illegal, extreme pornography.[314] The notice by the BBFC may include a requirement to provide a landing page to which the user is redirected.[315] The BBFC has powers to enforce its blocking notices through civil proceedings and internet access providers may challenge such notices through an appeal to the Independent Appeals Panel set up under the Act[316] or by way of judicial review. Part 3 of the Digital Economy Act 2017 was due to come into force on 15 July 2019 but, since the UK government has failed to notify the provisions to the European Commission under Directive 2015/1535, its coming into force has been postponed.[317] At the time of writing the government decided to fold the regulation of "hardcore" pornography into the wider online harms approach.[318]

4.2.4 Website blocking and gambling

The 2019 EU Study on gambling enforcement[319] mentioned earlier also examined website blocking as a gatekeeper enforcement tool in the EU and EEA Member States.[320] From the data and analysis of website blocking used as an enforcement tool to keep out unauthorized internet gambling offers from national markets in the

[308] Art 21(3).
[309] Chang (n 107) 130; McIntyre (n 105) 308.
[310] ibid.
[311] Defined by reference to the BBFC's rating system under the Video Recordings Act 1984, meaning content that was produced principally for the purposes of sexual arousal and is rated with R18, 18 or is not suitable for classification, s 15.
[312] S 14(1) Digital Economy Act 2017.
[313] Ss 18–19.
[314] S 23(1)(a) and (b).
[315] S 23(4).
[316] S 16(6)(d).
[317] https://www.wired.co.uk/article/uk-porn-block-delayed (20 June 2019) accessed on 17/7/2020.
[318] https://www.gov.uk/government/consultations/online-harms-white-paper/online-harms-white-paper accessed on 17/7/2020.
[319] Hörnle et al (n 3).
[320] ibid 28–52.

EU/EEA, it is clear that two-thirds of EU/EEA Member States (67 per cent) use website blocking, and several jurisdictions are currently considering introducing it in their national gambling legislation.[321]

Eighteen EU/EEA Member States (Belgium, Bulgaria, Czech Republic, Cyprus, Denmark, Estonia, France, Greece, Hungary, Italy, Latvia, Lithuania, Poland, Portugal, Romania, Slovakia, Slovenia, Spain) block gambling website at internet access provider level, whereas twelve EU/EEA Member States (Austria, Croatia, Finland, Germany, Ireland, Liechtenstein, Luxembourg, Malta, Netherlands, Norway, Sweden, Great Britain) do not. In the majority of Member States, blocking was based on a blacklist of URLs and DNS or IP blocking.

Those regulators that do not use website blocking state as a reason that they do not have the required legal power for website blocking, that it is deemed ineffective, or that it is politically controversial and considered to be disproportionate.[322] While website blocking can be politically controversial, with the exception of the Czech Republic and Hungary, all regulators that have implemented website blocking measures reported that the introduction of these measures did not stir significant political or legal opposition or controversy.[323]

Despite the potential ineffectiveness of website blocking (circumvention by users and operators), the majority of regulators nevertheless considered it to be an effective enforcement measure. The effectiveness of website blocking lies in three characteristics, the most important of which is the use of a landing page to which users trying to access blocked gambling websites are directed. Such a landing page may be a valuable consumer information tool and could warn consumers about the fact that a particular provider is not operating legally within the jurisdiction, link to alternative legal offers, and warn about financial risks of gambling. Secondly, landing pages allow for traffic analysis, such as where did the user come from and go to next or search terms used, which may give regulators important insights about consumer behaviour. Finally, the website block may prevent *some* illegal gambling. However, website blocking is not completely effective in preventing users from accessing gambling, as circumvention is possible. Moreover, DNS blocking does not block the mobile apps used by many gamblers.

4.2.5 UK White Paper "Online Harms" and website blocking

Taking inspiration from Part 3 of the Digital Economy Act, the White Paper "Online Harms"[324] envisages the introduction of website and app blocking for those internet destinations that do not comply with the standards established in the future Codes of Practice. The White Paper proposed that the regulator would make the decision of which URLs would be included on the block list, but that this enforcement option should only be used for "serious, repeated and egregious" violations. The White Paper puts forward two different options of implementing website blocking in respect of online harms. One would be to make it mandatory for internet access providers to block

[321] Austria, Finland, Norway, and Sweden.
[322] Hörnle et al (n 3).
[323] ibid 33.
[324] Discussed earlier with respect to the "duty of care."

websites or apps following an administrative notice by the regulator. Alternatively, the regulator could publish a black list of non-compliant websites, which internet access providers "could choose to block on a voluntary basis."[325] Thus, the UK government is proposing a very broad blocking mechanism, which potentially includes not only content illegal to possess, but also content which may be harmful, but not illegal to possess (such as obscenity).[326] This form of censorship may take gatekeeper regulation too far and contradicts the rule of law and "prescribed by law" principle of regulation.

4.2.6 Australia and internet access blocking

In Australia, the regulatory regime set up by Schedules 5 and 7 of the Broadcasting Act 1992 allows the ACMA to include relevant content hosted outside the jurisdiction to be included in a block list. Once included in the block list, internet access providers are obliged to include these websites in their filters.

As the examples in the preceding discussion have shown, internet access providers have been made subject to obligations to block illegal or harmful content and are therefore forced to assume the role of gatekeepers for internet censorship, in particular where the content is hosted outside the regulating jurisdiction and cannot therefore be ordered to be taken down.

4.3 Payment services providers, advertisers, and search engines as gatekeepers

Where content is hosted outside the jurisdiction and cannot be successfully taken down, other ancillary service providers may become the gatekeepers for regulation.[327] This strategy is a type of "follow the money" enforcement.[328] Arguably, payment blocking has the potential to be a highly effective enforcement method, since it is much more difficult for content providers to find new ways of streaming their finance than to find another hosting provider.[329] One way of fighting illegal content online is attacking the sources of finance for illegal content providers, such as payment services providers blocking payment, or preventing online advertising on illegal websites providing a source of finance. Furthermore, internet users have to find illegal content online and therefore search engines may be used as gatekeepers to prevent the distribution of illegal content.[330]

Payment services rely on a merchant acquirer giving content providers access to payment and, before content providers are allowed to join the network, the merchant acquirer has to carry out certain due diligence checks to comply with counterterrorism and anti-money laundering rules. This raises the question of how extensive these due diligence checks are and whether they can be used to police the network against providers of illegal content more generally. Payment services providers are

325 "Online Harms" (n 116) 60.
326 S 2 Obscene Publications Act 1959.
327 Balkin (n 4) 2298.
328 A Bridy, "Internet Payment Blockades" (2015) 67(5) Florida Law Review 1523–68, 1528.
329 ibid 1525.
330 Envisaged in the Digital Economy Act 2017 and the UK White Paper "Online Harms" (n 116).

reluctant to become gatekeepers of the internet and resist obligations to police their merchants for the content they provide thus playing a role in censorship.

4.3.1 Digital Economy Act 2017 and the White Paper "Online Harms"

The Digital Economy Act provides for a power of the BBFC to give notice to payment services providers and other "ancillary service providers," such as search engines, in respect of hardcore and extreme pornography material.[331] Ancillary services are defined as services "which enable or facilitate the making available of pornographic material or extreme pornographic material" or advertisers, where the content is financed through advertising.[332] However, the Act does not set out a concrete obligation of the payment services or ancillary service provider to take any specific action. The expectation is that payment services providers and ancillary services take voluntary steps to block a payment, or to remove a search result,[333] or stop advertising, but these measures are voluntary. In a similar fashion, the White Paper "Online Harms" proposes "disruption of business activities" to put pressure on payment and ancillary service providers to withdraw their services which indirectly facilitate the harmful material. The services mentioned in the White Paper are: search results, app stores and advertising links on social media.[334]

The International Centre for Missing and Exploited Children has founded the Financial Coalition against Child Sexual Exploitation in 2006 with the aim of preventing payment to internet services offering CSEA materials. The Financial Coalition includes major banks, credit card providers, electronic payment networks, payment services providers, and internet services providers to eliminate merchants profiting from selling such materials.[335]

4.3.2 Payment blocking of illegal gambling payments

Likewise, gambling regulators have made use of the blocking of financial transactions between players and out of state unauthorized gambling operators, thus extending their jurisdictional reach.[336] This was first introduced in the US by the Unlawful Internet Gambling Enforcement Act of 2006.[337]

As of 2018, in the EU/EEA a total of sixteen Member States have legal frameworks in place requiring payment providers not to process payment transactions for online gambling operators not authorized in their jurisdiction[338]. By contrast, thirteen[339] Member States have no legal framework for payment blocking.[340] However, only half of the Member States that have included payment blocking in their legal frameworks

[331] S 21(1).
[332] S 21(5).
[333] Or move it down in the order of search rankings so that the result moves into oblivion.
[334] "Online Harms" (n 116) 60.
[335] https://www.icmec.org/fcacse/ accessed on 17/7/2020.
[336] Bridy (n 328) 1526.
[337] 31 USC ss 5361–67.
[338] Czech Republic, Denmark, Estonia, France, Germany Greece, Italy, Hungary, Latvia, Lithuania, the Netherlands, Norway, Poland, Romania, Slovakia, and Spain.
[339] Austria, Belgium, Bulgaria, Croatia, Finland, Ireland, Liechtenstein, Luxembourg, Malta, Portugal, Slovenia, Sweden, and the UK.
[340] Hörnle et al (n 3) 58.

actually actively use it in practice,[341] due to the complexity of implementing gatekeeper regulation through payment blocking.[342] This section will examine this complexity.

Payment blocking can be used in order to prevent the gamblers making gambling deposits to operators, or, in order to prevent gambling operators paying winnings to gamblers. In either case, the block is aimed at stopping the transaction from being processed.

Payment blocking obligations can impose two types of gatekeeper regulation: they can either be specific, in the sense that specific transactions have to be prevented, or general, in the sense that payment services providers must comply with a general obligation not to facilitate or promote online gambling services. The problem with the second type of gatekeeper regulation is that it means that payment service providers have to identify all gambling transactions out of the large number of transactions. A general obligation causes uncertainty as to what the due diligence obligations of payment services providers are and such a general obligation puts payment service providers in a difficult position as intermediaries. They would be liable to a customer if they wrongly blocked a transaction and liable under the relevant regulations if they do not block a transaction related to unauthorized online gambling. For this reason is it important that the due diligence obligations are clearly described in the relevant implementing laws.[343] The Dutch Council of State[344] held in December 2017 that section 1(1)(a) of the Dutch Betting and Gambling Act, which prohibits the promotion of unauthorized gambling, is insufficient to impose a payment blocking obligation, so that payment blocking can only be based on voluntary cooperation, that is, payment disruption, which is an alternative to payment blocking.

Payment disruption does not focus on stopping individual funds transfers related to unauthorized gambling, but instead targets the business activities of payment services providers more generally. A prominent example outside the gambling context was the payment blockade of Wikileaks during 2010.[345] The US government threatened action against Wikileaks in connection with the leaks of military and diplomatic cables and Skrill (Moneybookers), PayPal, Visa, and Mastercard refused to process donations for Wikileaks without any formal legal process in either the UK or the US.[346] Julian Assange announced that donations are now made by cryptocurrencies, including Bitcoin, which he claimed was a lucrative investment.[347] This illustrates the continuous mouse and cat game between new technology entrants and regulators, and cryptocurrencies are used as a payment method for both licensed and unauthorized

[341] Czech Republic, Greece, Latvia, the Netherlands, Norway, Poland, Slovakia, and Romania.

[342] Hörnle et al (n 3) 58.

[343] Hörnle et al (n 3) p 69.

[344] Supreme Administrative Court, ECLI:NL:RVS:2017:3571.

[345] Bridy (n 328) 1524–25.

[346] https://www.theguardian.com/media/2010/oct/14/wikileaks-says-funding-is-blocked (14 October 2010), accessed on 17/7/2020; https://www.theguardian.com/commentisfree/cifamerica/2011/oct/27/wikileaks-payments-blockade-dangerous-precedent (27 October 2011); https://www.theguardian.com/commentisfree/2012/nov/23/anonymous-trial-wikileaks-internet-freedom (23 November 2012) accessed on 17/7/2020.

[347] G Synek Techspot https://www.techspot.com/news/71764-wikileaks-thanks-us-government-blocking-credit-card-donations.html (7 November 2017) accessed on 17/7/2020.

online gambling, too.[348] For payment disruption, regulators identify the payment services, which are available in respect of unauthorized online gambling in their jurisdiction, and seek to put pressure on such payment services providers by threatening potential criminal liability as an accessory or in relation to money laundering charges, or by informing the financial regulator at the place where the payment services provider is established.

Whether payment disruption has a degree of success depends on the size and political power of the countries concerned and whether they share similar regulatory goals in respect of online gambling regulation. One concern with payment disruption is that it is based on negotiation between regulators and payment service providers (or other regulators), and therefore is extra-legal and conflicts with the rule of law. Many regulators do not have administrative powers (or resources) to engage in such negotiations in order to put pressure on payment providers. These "informal" mechanisms operate without accountable administrative enforcement decisions, which are subject to judicial review. This is an example of how overcoming the jurisdictional challenge threatens the rule of law.

The complexity of implementing payment blocking is partly due to the fact that a large variety of payment services[349] exists, and this means that frequently a chain of domestic and foreign payment services providers is involved in facilitating the transaction. Furthermore, different EU/EEA Member States have different "payment cultures," that is, internet users in different jurisdictions use different means of payment online, including for gambling transactions. In some states, for example in Italy, cash transactions continue to be popular, which take the form of e-vouchers bought in a gambling retail outlet used for online gambling. Such e-vouchers may not be subject to money laundering regulations because of the closed loop exception or because they are low value.[350]

Gamblers may use a credit or debit card to directly pay a gambling deposit or make a bank transfer. For such *direct* transactions, payment blocking is comparatively easy. The card systems, such as Visa and Mastercard, as part of their due diligence when on-boarding a new online merchant, use merchant category codes (MCCs) to identify the business of the merchant and for gambling this is the MCC 7995. The MCC 7995 allows the issuer (in the country of residence of the gambler) to decline a transaction during the payment authorization process, if gambling is illegal in the country of the issuer. However, payment blocking based on MCC 7995 does not distinguish between cardholder present and cardholder not present transactions, so that it may decline transactions for a user resident in a jurisdiction that prohibits gambling transactions, but who plays, for example, at a land-based casino while on holiday abroad. Moreover, MCC 7995 does not distinguish between different forms of online gambling (such as sports betting, casino games, lotteries, bingo, etc). It is for these reasons that a number of EU/EEA Member States have considered payment blocking based on MCC 7995

[348] Hörnle et al (n 3) 79; C Altaner, "Unregulated Lotteries Are Blockchain's Most Popular Products" (29 August 2018) Gambling Compliance; B Lischke and B Fabian, "Analyzing the Bitcoin Network: the First Four Years" (2016) Future Internet doi:10.3390/fi8010007.

[349] See Payment Services Directive II (EU) 2015/2366 of 25 November 2015, OJ L337, Annex I.

[350] Hörnle et al (n 3) 56.

as overbroad and have decided not to implement such blocking.[351] For direct bank transfers, regulators find the bank details of the recipient online gambling operator and order the banks in their *own* jurisdiction, where the gambler is likely to have his or her bank account, to desist from processing funds transfer to such identified bank accounts. Both payment blocking based on MCC 7995 and blocking based on identified bank account numbers can be circumvented through merchant miscoding or merchants regularly moving their banks accounts. However, arguably, banks and card systems have checking mechanisms in place to minimize such circumvention.

In any case, additional complexity is introduced by the use of further intermediaries and e-payment methods within an international chain of intermediaries, which obfuscates the identity of the merchant, the nature of the transaction, and/or the ultimate recipient of a payment.

For example, digital wallets are used in online gambling transactions. In most scenarios only the gambler and the gambler's bank are located in the same country as the regulator and therefore subject to the regulator's jurisdiction. The digital wallet provider is likely to be in a foreign jurisdiction, outside the reach of the regulator. For this reason, the gatekeeper is likely to be the gambler's domestic bank, as the first intermediary, when foreign digital wallets are used for online gambling transactions.

For example, the gambler may use funds from a bank account and transfer them to his digital wallet and subsequently use the funds in the digital wallet to pay a gambling deposit to an operator. For the purposes of the local bank of the gambler, the recipient of the funds transfer is the digital wallet. Thus, if the gambler uses a payment card to pay the funds into the digital wallet this transaction will not be coded as a gambling transaction. This makes is impossible for the local bank to recognize the transaction as one related to unauthorized online gambling.[352] While the digital wallet provider may recognize the recipient merchant as a gambling operator, the digital wallet provider is likely to be outside the enforcement jurisdiction, and hence out of the reach of the regulator (Figure 3.2).

Both for direct funds transfers and for funds transfers through one or more payment intermediaries, fundamentally, there are three methods[353] to block a payment transaction: (1) for card transactions, using the MCC 7995, (2) for bank transfers the identification of the unauthorized gambling provider's bank accounts, and (3) the targeting of specific transactions. The third option could be used to identify gambling transactions at the gambler's (payer's) end or at the gambling operator's (payee's) end, using several factors using data mining.

Identifying gambling transactions at the gambler's end, the gambler's bank may detect gambling transactions from payment patterns through data mining. At the gambling operator's end, gambling transactions could be identified through the name of the payee as the ultimate recipient of the payment.

[351] ibid 73.
[352] ibid 73.
[353] In 2018, only four EU/EEA Member States have used more than one of these three options: Germany, Greece, Lithuania, and Norway.

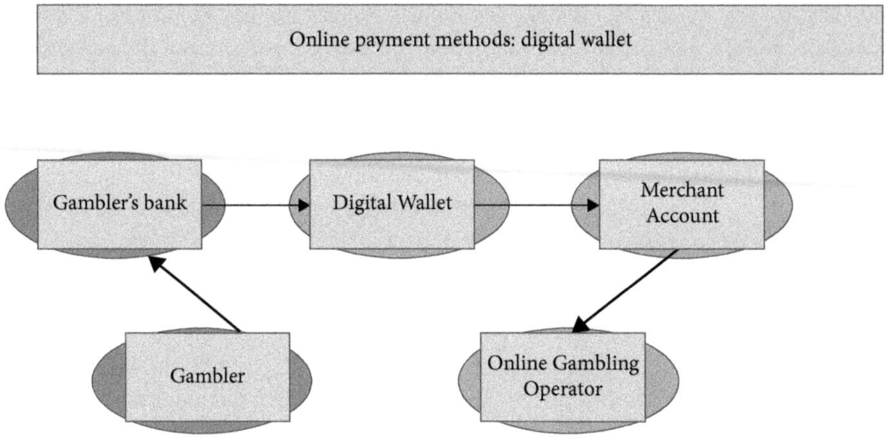

Figure 3.2 Gatekeeper regulation and censorship

The revised 2015 EU Funds Transfer Regulation (FTR),[354] which came into effect on 26 of June 2017, has the ambitious aim of full traceability of non-cash, electronic payments and combines efforts in anti-money laundering and counter-terrorism finance.[355] The European Supervisory Authorities have introduced guidelines on the implementation and interpretation of the FTR.[356] FTR applies to payment services providers established in the EU/EEA Member States who send or receive transfer of funds in any currency.[357] However, there is an exception for prepaid payment cards, e-money instruments, or mobile phone payments.[358] Member States have a discretion not to apply the Regulation to single transactions below Euro 1000, where the payer's provider (eg a bank or credit card issuer) has identified their customer (the payer) through the know your customer (KYC) requirements and can trace the payee through a unique identifier through the contract for goods or services.[359]

Otherwise, the FTR basically introduced a requirement that certain information about the payer and the payee (intended recipient of the payment[360]) must be attached to the transaction as it moves through the chain of payment services intermediaries. As a minimum, *all providers* should know the payee's bank account number (for Single Euro Payments Area (SEPA) payments) and for other payments, the payee's name and bank account number.

The information about the payer comprises the following: (1) the name of the payer, (2) the payer's payment account number (or unique identifier if there is no account),

[354] Regulation (EU) 2015/847 of the European Parliament and of the Council of 20 May 2015 on information accompanying transfers of funds and repealing Regulation (EC) No 1781/2006.

[355] Recital 9 Regulation (EU) 2015/847.

[356] As stipulated by Art 25, https://www.eba.europa.eu/documents/10180/1969371/Joint+Guidelines+to+prevent+terrorist+financing+and+money+laundering+in+electronic+fund+transfers+%28JC-GL-2017-16%29.pdf/, 27 September 2017 accessed on 17/7/2020.

[357] Art 2(1) Regulation (EU) 2015/847.

[358] Art 2(2) Regulation (EU) 2015/847.

[359] Art 2(3) Regulation (EU) 2015/847—presumably this is just another means of ensuring traceability.

[360] Art 3(4) Regulation (EU) 2015/847.

and (3) the payer's address, official personal document number, customer id, or, date and place of birth. The full information about the payee must contain the name of the payee and the payee's payment account number (or unique identifier if there is no account).[361] This information must be obtained by the payer's provider (as the first link in the chain) and firmly attached to the transaction, and if the payer's provider cannot obtain that information it must decline to execute the transaction.[362] The payer's provider also has an obligation to verify the information "from a reliable and independent source."[363] However, the payer's provider need not verify the data if the transaction is below Euro 1000 (but must identify any "linked" transactions), unless the transaction involves cash or anonymous electronic money or there are other grounds for suspicion of money laundering or terrorist financing.[364]

Furthermore, for funds transferred solely within the EU/EEA[365] the minimum information required is limited to the payer's and the payee's payment account numbers.[366] Presumably, the reason for this is to avoid the loss of the advantages of the SEPA.

It is noteworthy that the FTR make clear that the payment service providers only have reporting obligations and duties to disclose information to the authorities competent for the enforcement of Anti-Money Laundering and Counter-Terrorism Financing laws (purpose limitation under data protection law).[367] Likewise, the FTR also make clear that data processed under the Regulation may only be processed for the purposes of countering money laundering and terrorist financing.[368] Therefore the FTR cannot form the *legal* basis for data processing for gambling enforcement purposes.[369] The FTR could form the practical basis and mechanism for the implementation of payment blocking, but it would not be a sufficient legal basis.

However, these provisions in FTR as such would not prevent *national law* in certain EU/EEA Member States to implement due diligence obligations, data exchange, and reporting obligations in respect of the identification of unauthorized gambling transactions, provided a clear, specific, and narrowly circumscribed legal framework is passed to enable the relevant data collection, exchange, and data retention.[370] If this legal framework aligns with the requirements under the FTR, it may be workable in practice.

Any national law would need to be made in such a way that it provides a certain legal basis for the processing of personal data and creating a system that is compliant with the provisions of the General Data Protection Regulation (GDPR) (including limited

[361] Art 4 Regulation (EU) 2015/847.
[362] Art 4(6) Regulation (EU) 2015/847.
[363] Art 4(4) Regulation (EU) 2015/847.
[364] Arts 5(3), 6(2), and 7(4) Regulation (EU) 2015/847.
[365] Where all payment services providers (payer's payment services provider, intermediary payment services provider and the payee's payment services provider) are situated within the EU/EEA.
[366] Art 5(1) Regulation (EU) 2015/847.
[367] Art 14 Regulation (EU) 2015/847.
[368] Art 15(2) Regulation (EU) 2015/847.
[369] M Rossi "Europa—und datenschutzrechtliche Rahmenbedingungen für Maßnahmen des Financial Blocking auf der Grundlage von s 9 Absatz 1 Satz 3 Nummer 4 GlüStV" Research Report (December 2017), who concludes that the provisions in the German Glückspielstaatsvertrag would not be sufficiently specific to serve as the basis for payment blocking.
[370] Art 6(3) GDPR.

retention periods, purpose limitation, impact assessments, etc.).[371] However, there is an express justification in the GDPR that may apply to banks and other payment service providers in Art 6(1)(c), which defines as lawful processing, "processing which is necessary for compliance with a legal obligation to which the controller is subject."

Thus, one could argue that the payer's payment provider, the first payment intermediary in the chain and in the local jurisdiction of the gambling regulator, has information about the payee (the intended recipient) and could use this information in order to identify to which entity the payment is going to (subject to data protection compliance). The first hurdle is the question as to what information is actually contained in the name of the payee: the name itself ("Blues Resort") may not disclose the nature of the business of the payee and may not reflect the actual brand under which the payee is trading.

Finding out the precise nature of the underlying transactions is likely to be challenging, complex, resource-intensive, and costly, but provided resources are invested, not impossible. Further investigation is required and most likely this can only be achieved through information exchanges between the local banks, payment intermediaries, gambling regulators, and financial services regulators. It could also mean that banks and payment intermediaries have to carry out data mining, looking at patterns (such as, but not limited to, amounts paid, frequency, timing of payments, etc.) in order to obtain a clearer picture and to identify a payee who is likely to operate unlicensed online gambling. This is clearly somewhat invasive of privacy and should be proportionate to the legitimate objectives (such as the regulatory risks stemming from online gambling).

However, for payment purposes banks already have extensive duties to carry out checks both in respect of the sender and the recipient of a payment. Banks and payment intermediaries already use data mining in connection with other risk assessments such as AML, CTF, fraud, KYC, and credit reporting on their customers. While there are such screening processes already in place for various purposes, such processes are automated and banks are not naturally equipped to identify a gambling transaction that is deliberately channelled through a sophisticated front. So, for example, if an online gambling operator as part of the KYC checks pretends to be a shoe shop or uses several apparent "shoe shops" to layer transactions, such that the identity checks, business name, address checks, business checks, and so on, and the transaction patterns do not indicate otherwise, because there is a well-structured deception attempt, it may be impossible to block these transactions despite the checks and authorization procedures.

The second hurdle is that a transaction may be carried out in several stages, which may naturally obfuscate the intended recipient. For example, many users of digital wallets pay a deposit in their account (for unspecified purposes) and maintain that credit balance until they decide to spend money at a later stage. For example, if a bank or credit card is used for depositing money in the digital wallet, the payee is the payment intermediary as the intended recipient. In the second stage, when the user pays their stake to the gambling operator, the payee would be the gambling operator, but

[371] Regulation (EU) 2016/679 of 27 April 2016; OJ L119 of 4 May 2016, 1–88.

the payment intermediary may be foreign and unwilling to cooperate with the foreign gambling authority in the player's state. In these two-stage processes (separated by a time-lag) it may simply be impossible for the gambling regulator to order the local blocking of the deposit paid by the player.[372]

Having examined the role of payment services providers as gatekeepers it can be said that implementation of payment blocking and payment disruption is complex, invasive of privacy, and raises concerns from a rule of law point of view. If states are using payment providers as gatekeepers it is necessary to stretch legal obligations to a number of service providers and using several methods (MCCs, bank account numbers, and payer and payee information). Given the complexity of international payment systems, it is unlikely that all unauthorized gambling transactions are blocked.

5. Conclusion

This chapter has examined the use of online intermediaries and ancillary service providers as gatekeepers for content moderation. It has outlined several examples for such gatekeeper regulation in the UK, the EU, and Australia in respect of hosting services, internet access providers (blocking), and payment services. The chapter pointed to the immunities developed for online intermediaries, particularly in the EU. Since hosting service providers are only liable if they have actual or constructive knowledge of illegal content or activity, gatekeeper regulation has been implemented by notice and take down mechanisms. However, given the large quantity of illegal materials, their reposting by the same or a different person, and the velocity of the impact of content online, notice and take down mechanisms have limited effectiveness. It is for this reason that internet access providers have been placed in a gatekeeper role by having obligations to block certain websites. In particular the use of notice and take down mechanisms have been observed in respect of CSEA and terrorist materials. However, legislators and regulators are moving towards much broader notions of gatekeeper regulation. Regulators impose a duty of care on a range of internet service providers, including social media companies hosting user-generated content online, and extend these duties to other forms of "harmful" or "abhorrent content," and expand the range of service providers affected (payment services, advertising, and search engines). As far as hosting services are concerned, the duty of care includes proactive content monitoring and management obligations. Finally, as we have seen, payment providers have also been used as gatekeepers to cut off money streams from illegal content services and this has been discussed by using online gambling as a case study. This has shown the complexity of blocking unauthorized online gambling transactions and the difficulty of tracing transactions through a chain of payment intermediaries.

The decentralization of content provision through user-generated content, internationally acting, powerful social media companies, and remote targeting of internet services have created an enormous jurisdictional challenge for the enforcement of national law. The ensuing conflicts of laws affect both rule-making (multitude of national

[372] Hörnle et al (n 3) 70–73.

laws vs community guidelines) and rule enforcement (criminal or administrative penalties vs content removal). These conflicts of law and the enforcement challenge necessitate closer international cooperation between states and enforcement authorities.

The choice between two types of regulation emerges from the jurisdictional challenge: regulation by the state and self-regulation.[373] Regulation by the state through administrative and criminal law is challenged by conflicts of law and jurisdictional limitations. Self-regulation by the gatekeeper (such as a social media company) avoids the jurisdictional challenge and conflicts of law to some extent, as the rules governing the service provided, such as terms, policies, and community guidelines, are laid down centrally by the gatekeeper and could therefore be called "platform law." This platform law applies to all users in all countries and the gatekeeper implements these rules centrally by removing or blocking content or by closing accounts. Self-regulation additionally has the advantage of being more sensitive to technological developments, as the service provider is controlling both the technology and the "platform law" in tandem.

However, as this chapter has shown, self-regulation raises serious concerns about the rule of law, and therefore our collective and individual freedom. Any restrictions on freedom of expression have to be "prescribed by law," necessary, and legitimate.[374] Self-regulation of content moderation undermines democracy, as it is made by unelected businesses. It does not ensure that all stakeholders are engaged and that rules reflect the public interest, as opposed to powerful social media companies' own business interests. Furthermore, it has taken the decision making away from public institutions such as courts. Self-regulation should be made transparent, accountable, and subject to stakeholder engagement and judicial review processes.

Internet content is regulated by both state and self-regulation in a complex web of overlapping regimes and to the extent that state regulation is coordinated with self-regulation it can also be termed coregulation. This becomes problematic where coregulation turns informal, based on "behind the scenes" negotiation between regulators and private companies. The rule of law demands that state action is transparent, accountable, and subject to judicial review.

Self-regulation or coregulation can take many different forms,[375] for example, the government mandates that industry takes certain measures or adopts certain practices, as a form of mandatory self-regulation. An example for this is the UK White Paper "Online Harms," which mandates the adoption of Codes of Practices. Furthermore, *coerced* self-regulation occurs where the government threatens regulation and industry wards this off by formulating and policing rules. An example of this is the work of the IWF discussed earlier, as without the IWF initiative in 1996 it is likely that the government would have imposed regulatory measures on internet service providers. Another example is the cooperation between social media and CTIRU as a "voluntary" mechanism, backed up by the Terrorism Act.[376]

[373] These are archetypical—many models of regulation are in fact coregulation, combining the two forms.

[374] Art 10(2) European Convention of Human Rights, Art 19(3) International Covenant Civil Political Rights, Art 13(2) American Convention on Human Rights.

[375] J Black, "Constitutionalising Self-Regulation" (1996) 59(1) Modern Law Review 24–55, 27.

[376] McIntyre (n 105) 295–96, 303.

Nevertheless, state regulation continues to be necessary, despite the jurisdictional challenge and the option of coregulation. For state regulation clearer jurisdictional rules connecting an online activity with the regulator are required. The complexity of jurisdictional rules in criminal law has been discussed in Chapter 5. In the context of internet content regulation simpler rules have to be found. One connecting factor could be the IP address of a user when accessing an internet service and the use of geo-blocking.[377] Geo-blocking could help to limit the overreach of removal orders.[378]

It should be pointed out that gatekeeper regulation is more invisible and focuses on preventing the dissemination of illegal content *ex ante*, and not merely its criminalization and deterrence *ex post*,[379] and it is for this reason that it amounts to secretive pre-publication censorship, which makes it so invasive for freedom of expression. Effectively, the infrastructure for freedom of expression is the same infrastructure as the infrastructure for suppression and control of speech.[380] For example, social media companies are the vehicle for user-generated content, but they concomitantly provide the means to control content. This is precisely the challenge of the new paradigm of the jurisdictional challenge.

377 Further discussed in Chapter 13.

378 Case C-18/18 *Eva Glawischnig-Piesczek v Facebook*, Opinion (n 32) para 100.

379 Balkin (n 4) 2340ff.

380 ibid 2341.

4

Criminal Jurisdiction—Concurrent Jurisdiction, Sovereignty, and the Urgent Requirement for Coordination

Julia Hörnle and Elif Mendos Kuskonmaz

1. Introduction

Criminal jurisdiction is concerned with the competence of state authorities to investigate and prosecute criminal offences with cross-border elements, and the competence of the courts to adjudicate such criminal offences. Jurisdiction can be understood as both a power and a duty to prosecute. Rules on jurisdiction must take into account the efficiency of criminal prosecution, the integrity of the criminal justice system and the rights of the defendant, a triangle that is difficult to square.

First of all, it is necessary to distinguish between jurisdiction in respect of investigative powers of the police and prosecution authorities, on the one hand, and the powers of the courts to hear and decide a criminal case, on the other. Jurisdictional questions already arise during the start of criminal investigations as the evidence may be spread over several jurisdictions. However, investigative powers end at a state's border, which does not sit easily with digital evidence hosted in the cloud and access to data stored on foreign computers. Chapter 6 analyses jurisdiction in respect of investigative powers.

Since criminal courts always apply the substantive law of their country, questions of competence of the courts (adjudicative jurisdiction) and applicable law (prescriptive jurisdiction) are congruent. The law of the forum is always applied in criminal cases, in the sense that a court in Country X will always apply the law of Country X, unlike in private law cases, where the courts in Country X apply the law of another Country, Y as the applicable law if the rules of private international law so determine.[1] Chapter 5compares the national rules regarding criminal jurisdiction of the courts and applicable law in Germany and England.

Arguably, criminal jurisdiction in all its forms is one of the core domains of the sovereign powers of a state, and hence states are reluctant to relinquish criminal jurisdiction.[2] However, states' sovereignty is also circumscribed by public international law, which defines the outer limits of state sovereignty, and within which the *national* rules on criminal jurisdiction therefore must remain.[3] National rules can be coextensive

[1] U Kohl, *Jurisdiction and the Internet* (Cambridge University Press 2007) 17.

[2] I Patrone, "Conflicts of Jurisdiction and Judicial Cooperation Instruments: Eurojust's Role" (2013) 14 ERA Forum 215–25, 217.

[3] Kohl (n 1) 16.

Internet Jurisdiction. Julia Hörnle, Oxford University Press (2021). © Julia Hörnle.
DOI: 10.1093/oso/9780198806929.001.0001

with public international law, but they must not contradict the principles under public international law, as this is likely to infringe the sovereignty of another state. However, as discussed in the following sections, the principles for jurisdiction under public international law are both wide and malleable, and are unlikely to substantially restrict or restrain the assertion of competence by state authorities or courts, or the application of national law. This discussion is the focus of this chapter.

For this reason, the public international law principles do not prevent the assertion of jurisdiction by more than one state, so jurisdiction of the criminal courts is not exclusive with the consequence that that concurrent jurisdiction is frequent.[4] In criminal cases, this can be prejudicial to the rights of defendants, as they might be prosecuted and convicted more than once for the same criminal offence. As will be discussed, the rule that a defendant should not be convicted more than once for the same crime is largely inapplicable to cross-border offending.

As this chapter shows there are two main conflicts of jurisdiction. One is the multiple, overlapping claims of jurisdiction between several states and the risk of multiple prosecutions for the same crime. The second conflict is jurisdictional overreach where conduct is a criminal offence in one country, but not in another, and the second country wishes to prosecute. This conflict of jurisdictional overreach and spill-over effects, where a state applies its criminal law to a cross-border criminal offence in such a way that this affects conduct in another state (where that conduct is not criminally illegal), cannot be easily solved through rules of international co-operation and coordination, as it involves a direct conflict between different national laws (and potentially, culture clashes). However, the first conflict of multiple, overlapping claims can be addressed by effective international cooperation.

Therefore associated to questions of jurisdiction is the framework of international criminal coordination of prosecutions and international cooperation in criminal investigations. This chapter examines the coordination of multi-state prosecutions and Chapter 6 examines mutual legal assistance in respect of investigative powers.[5]

2. Jurisdiction under (public) international law

The emphasis on the coexistence of states in international law suggests that principally every state is equal within its own territory. The corollary of this observation is that states respect each other's power in the international legal system. This power is referred to as state sovereignty, which is "the power states do have at any given moment of development of the international legal system."[6] The extent of that power lies within

[4] Expressly recognized eg in the 1972 Council of Europe European Convention on the Transfer of Proceedings in Criminal Matters, Art 2.

[5] Because of lack of space, Chapter 6 does not discuss in any detail international cooperation in the enforcement of criminal punishments, such as surrender, extradition, the EU Arrest Warrant, and the freezing and recovery of criminal assets and proceeds of crime, and international rules against money laundering.

[6] A J Colangelo, "Spatial Legality" (2012) 107(1) Northwestern University Law Review 69–124, 106, see the discussion in Chapter 2.

the term "jurisdiction," which refers to the states' competence "to regulate the conduct of natural and legal persons."[7]

For a state to exercise its jurisdiction there needs to be a link or a connection between that state and the object for which it asserts that jurisdiction.[8] Principles have been developed in order to delineate the bases upon which states are entitled to claim jurisdiction. Those principles are:

(1) the personality principle (concerns the nationality of either perpetrator (active personality) or the victim (passive personality);
(2) the protective principle (focusing on the vital interests of the state for which that state can assert jurisdiction if harmed);
(3) the universality principle (concerns certain criminal offences that deemed to be of such a grave nature, such as genocide, that all states can assert jurisdiction);
(4) the territoriality principle. The importance of these principles is that they articulate which state has jurisdiction over which conduct, or which aspects of that conduct.[9]

The following sections look at these principles in detail and continue by discussing how they are articulated in relation to jurisdiction in cybercrime cases. Since the territoriality principle is "the basis of jurisdiction most often invoked by states,"[10] this section starts with examining that principle before looking at other principles and how these other principles are asserted as grounds of jurisdiction over conduct that occurred beyond the territory of a state (ie extraterritorial jurisdiction).

2.1 The territoriality principle and effects doctrine

The idea of jurisdiction closely relates to state sovereignty, and so is the territoriality principle because it demarcates the boundaries of states' rights to regulate their public order.[11] States hold the authority to regulate persons and matters within their territory. However, in reality, different stages of the same course of conduct may attract claims by different territorial jurisdictions. For example, a cyberattack can be launched in one

[7] J Crawford, *Brownlie's Principles of Public International Law* (Oxford University Press 2012) 456 ("Jurisdiction is not coextensive with state sovereignty, although the relationship between them is close").

[8] BH Oxman, "Jurisdiction of States" in R Wolfrum (ed), *The Max Planck Encyclopedia of Public International Law* (online edn, Oxford University Press 2007) note 10 ("It is unclear whether a State may exercise jurisdiction only where there is a recognized basis for its exercise or, as asserted in The Case of the SS 'Lotus' (France v Turkey), in the absence of any prohibition on its exercise. Whatever the underlying conceptual approach, a State must be able to identify *a sufficient nexus* between itself and the object of its assertion of jurisdiction") (emphasis added).

[9] Oxman (n 8) note 9.

[10] ibid note 13. See also M Byers, *Custom, Power and the Power of Rules* (Cambridge University Press 1999) 64 ("The interests of a State in exercising jurisdiction are usually rooted in its territorial self. This enables States, when seeking to justify specific assertions of jurisdiction through constructive extensions of that principle, to act within an accepted conceptual framework of legality."); M Akehurst, "Jurisdiction in International Law" (1972–73) 46 British Yearbook of International Law 145, 152 ("One of the main functions of a State is to maintain order within its own territory, so it is not surprising that the territorial principle is the most frequently invoked ground for criminal jurisdiction"); A Kaczorowska, *Public International Law* (Routledge 2010) 309.

[11] M Hirst, *Jurisdiction and the Ambit of the Criminal Law* (Oxford University Press 2003) 45.

country, before it infects computers in many different countries. In order to cope with overlapping jurisdictional claims, the territoriality principle can be seen through different lenses. The first lens is the subjective territoriality principle, according to which a state is entitled to enforce its laws for crimes that are initiated in its territory but are completed or consummated outside its territory.[12] The second and more prominent variant of the territorial jurisdiction is the objective territoriality principle, which establishes jurisdiction when any essential element of an offence is consummated within a state's territory.[13] Therefore, if a state wishes to take either approach, the jurisdictional question will boil down to how that particular crime is defined under its national laws, as this definition will decide the essential elements of the criminal offence for the purposes of applying the objective territoriality principle. Since states and their lawmakers ultimately define the ambit of criminal offences, they also decide when the commission of a crime is territorial.

There can also be cases in which the act that is initiated and consummated outside the territory of a state causes some harm to that state (without that harm being one of the essential elements contained in the offence's definition). In order to address this harm-based scenario, the territoriality principle is expanded to recognize the *effects of acts carried out outside the state's territory*, but felt within that state as the connecting factor. The crux of this interpretation, or "the effects doctrine," as it is generally known, is that the effect of acts, although not their initiation or completion itself, occurred in the state claiming jurisdiction.[14]

This effects doctrine was endorsed by the Permanent Court of International Justice (PCIJ) in the *Lotus* case in August 1926 as a basis of state jurisdiction.[15] This case concerned the collision of a French steamer, the Lotus, and a Turkish vessel, the Boz-Kourt, in the high seas, resulting in the deaths of eight Turkish nationals. The survivors were taken to the Lotus who then continued its course to the Turkish port. Upon its arrival, the Turkish officials arrested the French captain of the Lotus who was prosecuted for the charge of manslaughter. His prosecution was based on the 1926 Turkish Criminal Code, which allowed for the jurisdictional exercise over conduct involving a Turkish citizen as the victim (passive personality principle).[16] France disputed this prosecution on the ground that the exercise of jurisdiction by Turkey over an act that had occurred on the high seas violated the principles of public international law.[17] Although the Court applied the objective territoriality principle instead of the effects doctrine when finding the jurisdiction of Turkey here,[18] the fact that it emphasized the allocation of jurisdiction to a state "if one of the constituent elements of the offence, and more especially its *effects*, have taken place"[19] in that state shows that it acknowledged the effects doctrine as part of the objective territoriality principle.

[12] See also Kaczorowska (n 10) 309; G Boas, *Public International Law* (Edward Elgar 2012) 251–53.

[13] Crawford (n 7) 458; Kaczorowska (n 10) 309; Boas (n 12) 251–53.

[14] Oxman (n 8) note 22.

[15] *S.S. Lotus* (*Fr. v. Turk.*) PCIJ Rep Series A No 10 (September 7) .

[16] ibid paras 31–32.

[17] ibid para 7. See also Akehurst (n 10) 155.

[18] When determining the jurisdiction in light of the objective territoriality principle, the Court equated the ships to the territories of the states in question. See *S.S. Lotus* (*Fr. v. Turk.*) (n 15) para 65.

[19] ibid, para 60 (emphasis added).

The *Lotus* case involved the reach of the physical effects of a conduct (ie elements of a criminal offence) to another jurisdiction, but over the years states expanded the effects doctrine to cover non-physical elements. It has been applied specifically in competition law, a field of law where actions of parties may have anti-competitive effects within a state jurisdiction without the parties being physically present.[20] In the following, this chapter examines the effects doctrine under competition law (with no particular focus on criminal law) in order to illustrate how the effects doctrine has developed as a jurisdictional principle.

The US has been the prominent example where the effects doctrine has found support in competition law. In the *Alcoa* decision of 1945, the US Second Circuit Court of Appeals was asked to determine whether non-US companies had liabilities under the Sherman Antitrust Act 1890 for their conduct that occurred beyond the US territory and, if so, whether the agreements signed by them on the aluminium trade would be a breach of that Act.[21] The Act proscribed the following acts as breaches of US competition laws:

> 1. Every contract, combination in the form of trust or otherwise, or conspiracy, in restraint of trade or commerce among the several states, or with foreign nations, is hereby declared to be illegal. 2. Every person who shall monopolise, or combine or conspire with any other person or persons to monopolise any part of the trade or commerce among the several states, or with foreign nations, shall be guilty of a misdemeanour.[22]

The important aspect of the *Alcoa* decision for the jurisdictional queries is that the Court upheld the US jurisdiction for agreements made by foreign companies abroad on the ground that "any state may impose liabilities, even upon persons not within its allegiance, for conduct outside its borders that has *consequences* within its borders which the state reprehends; and these liabilities other states will ordinarily recognize."[23] The agreements in question intended to affect, and indeed affected, imports to and exports from the US.[24] Thus, the economic repercussions of those agreements established the consequential link for the application of US antitrust laws provided that those repercussions were intentional, which included instances where the anti-competition effects were foreseeable.[25] Other jurisdictions than the US were reluctant to endorse the effects doctrine in the field of competition law. The European Court of Justice (ECJ)'s *Wood Pulp* decision is a common example provided in relation to the acknowledgement of the effects doctrine in jurisdictions other than the US, albeit there are different interpretations of the ECJ's observations on the jurisdictional link, arguing that it is not an actual support of the effects doctrine in EU competition

[20] M Jeffrey, "The Implications of the Wood Pulp Case for the European Communities" (1991) 4(1) Leiden Journal of International Law 75–107,76; J Coppel, "A Hard Look at the Effects Doctrine of Jurisdiction in Public International Law" (1993) 6(1) Leiden Journal of International Law 73–90, 73.

[21] *US v Aluminium Co. of America* 148 F 2d 416 (2nd Cir 1945).

[22] Sherman Antitrust Act, 15 USC s 1.

[23] *US v Aluminium Co. of America* (n 21) 443 (emphasis added).

[24] ibid.

[25] Jeffrey (n 20) 88.

law.[26] This decision concerned an appeal against the European Commission's decision to impose a fine on the wood pulp producers and their associations that operated outside the European Community because of their concerted practice to fix prices. Article 85[27] EC Treaty prohibited "all agreements between undertakings, decisions by associations of undertakings and concerted practices which may *affect* trade between Member States and which have as their object or *effect* the prevention, restriction or distortion of competition within the common market." The applicants argued that the European Commission was in breach of public international law when asserting jurisdiction over their activities because it applied Article 85 EC Treaty merely due to the economic repercussions of their activities within the (then) European Community (EC).[28] On this point, the ECJ observed that an Article 85 EC Treaty infringement would have two elements, namely formation of a concerted practice and its implementation.[29] If jurisdictional application of Article 85 EC Treaty relied purely on the place where the concerted practice was formed, this would allow circumvention of the prohibition on anti-competitive conduct. Therefore the decisive factor in determining the jurisdiction of EU competition rules was the *place of implementation*, which provided the most relevant territorial link.[30] Thus, the wood pulp producers and their associations were bound by those rules, even though they operated outside the EC and they had no agent or subsidiaries within the EC, for the reason that their price fixing cartel was effectively implemented within the EC.[31] On the one hand, the Court's interpretation of the implementation of price fixing is reminiscent of the economic repercussion argument in the *Alcoa* decision. On the other hand, it is not an endorsement of effects doctrine as in *Alcoa* because the literal wording of Article 85 EC Treaty suggested that the anti-competitive effects of the practice was the constituent element of the application of EU competition law.[32] In other words, the direct anti-competitive effect of actions within the EU was proscribed as the element of illegality, which fall within the principle of objective territoriality.[33]

Nonetheless, after the *Wood Pulp* decision, the effects doctrine was embraced in the *Gencor* decision.[34] Two South African mining firms, Gencor and Lonrho, decided to merge, but the European Commission informed the firms that the merger

[26] Case 89/85 *Ahlströhm Osakyhtio v Commission* [1988] ECR 519. For arguments that *Wood Pulp* decision was not an explicit endorsement of the effects doctrine see DG Lange and J Byron Sandage, "The Wood Pulp Decision and its Implications for the Scope of EC Competition Law" (1989) 26(2) Common Market Law Review 137–65, 157. ("The Court in Wood Pulp never expressly adopted the effects test. Instead it adhered, perhaps for political reasons, to the fiction that there was some quasi-territorial basis for jurisdiction.")

[27] Now Art 101.

[28] *Ahlströhm Osakyhtio v Commission* (n 26) para 15.

[29] ibid para 16.

[30] ibid para 16.

[31] ibid para 17.

[32] Under EU competition law, the doctrine established by the ECJ in *Wood Pulp* is the "implementation test." For other tests under the same field of law see P Behrens, "The Extraterritorial Reach of EU Competition Law Revisited: The 'Effects Doctrine' before the ECJ" (2016) Discussion Paper No 3/16 Europa-Kolleg Hamburg, Institute for European Integration, Hamburg.

[33] *Ahlströhm Osakyhtio v Commission* (n 26) para 18 ("Accordingly the Community's jurisdiction to apply its competition rules to such conduct is covered by the territoriality principle as universally recognized in public international law.")

[34] Case T 102/96 *Gencor Ltd v European Commission* [1999] ECR-II 753.

was in breach the EC Merger Regulation which applied to "all concentration with a Community dimension."[35] Gencor sought the annulment of this decision before the ECJ, disputing that, among other things, the Regulation was not applicable to them because the concentrations concerned were carried out outside the EU.[36] Rejecting this argument, the ECJ found that the application of EU law "is justified under public international law when it is foreseeable that a proposed concentration will have an *immediate and substantial effect*" in the EU.[37]

In conclusion, the objective territoriality principle has received general support over the years and the effects doctrine that was developed through that principle has also been applied in some jurisdictions, although with some protest from other states.

2.2 Principles of extraterritorial jurisdiction

The territoriality principle is the principal basis upon which states exercise jurisdiction under public international law; but as mentioned at the beginning of this section, there are other principles under public international law according to which states can exercise jurisdiction. These principles are the personality principle (concerns the nationality of either perpetrator or victim), the universality principle (concerns crimes against humanity such as genocide and piracy), and the protective principle (concerns acts jeopardizing the sovereignty or national interest of the state). Because these principles do not refer to the territory of the relevant state to create a nexus between the act in question and the state claiming jurisdiction over it, they are collectively referred to as principles of extraterritorial jurisdiction.[38]

2.2.1 Personality principle

The personality principle has two different branches: the active personality principle (or nationality principle) and the passive personality principle. The active personality principle refers to sustaining a state's jurisdiction over its nationals even when they act abroad, when the person is the national of that state at the time of either the commission of the crime or its prosecution and punishment.[39] Application of this principle is sometimes extended to states' residents.[40] There may be varying reasons for which a state asserts jurisdiction over its nationals, but the core reason is that they owe allegiance to the state whose nationality they hold and thus they remain under the obligation to respect these rules even when abroad.[41] One particular justification for the application of this principle may be where the accused's conduct is not punishable in

[35] EC Merger Regulation 139/2004 of 20 January 2004 OJ L 24/1 Art 1.

[36] *Gencor Ltd v European Commission* (n 34) paras 48–49.

[37] ibid para 90.

[38] C Ryngaert, *Jurisdiction in International Law* (Oxford University Press 2008) 85–133.

[39] Harvard Research on International Law, "Draft Convention on Jurisdiction with Respect to Crime" (1935) 29 American Journal of International Law Supplement 439–651.

[40] eg Terrorism Act 2000 (UK) ss 63B and 63C; Misuse of Drugs Act (Singapore) s 8A; Criminal Code of the Kingdom of Netherlands Art 5.

[41] *Joyce v DPP* [1946] AC 347; Harvard Research on International Law (n 39) 519; Crawford (n 7) 459; Ryngaert (n 38) 90; Kaczorowska (n 10) 317.

the jurisdiction in which it is committed.[42] Also, where a national is present in the state of his or her citizenship, the state may try its own national before the domestic courts, on the basis of the active personality principle, if it refuses to surrender its national to the other state where the crime has been committed, by reason of the *aut dedere aut indicare* principle (the obligation to extradite or prosecute).[43]

The passive personality principle provides the ground for states to assert jurisdiction where the accused is an alien and has committed harmful conduct against the state's nationals from abroad.[44] One of the early examples in which the passive personality principle was disputed in the international arena is the *Cutting* case, in which a US national was charged with defamation by a Mexican court for his defamatory publication in the US about a Mexican national by reason of the application of the passive personality principle under the then valid Mexican law.[45] The case was inconclusive because the Mexican court dropped charges against the US national upon the political pressure from the US Government. Unlike the active personality principle, the endorsement of the passive personality principle has been contentious under international law.[46] The accused cannot anticipate which laws would apply to their acts because in the majority of cases he will not know the nationality of his victim. This would not give a fair notice to the accused exposed to a foreign jurisdiction of whose rules he may not even be aware.[47] Another criticism is that the principle poses a greater intrusion on the sovereignty of the state in which the prohibited conduct occurred or of whose nationality the accused possesses because there are less compelling reasons to assert jurisdiction over a foreigner's activities abroad than over a state's own nationals.[48]

Despite various criticisms against the principle, states have referred to the passive personality principle in sustaining jurisdiction for certain crimes such as terrorism.[49] For example, according to the US Federal Criminal Code, the US has jurisdiction over terrorist acts *targeting* US nationals while they are abroad.[50] In *US v Fawaz Yunis*, the US Supreme Court relied on the passive personality principle in upholding the

[42] Ryngaert (n 38) 89.

[43] Council of Europe Convention on Cybercrime (CETS No 185, Budapest, 2001), Art 22(3); C Ryngaert (n 38) 107.

[44] eg French Penal Code, Arts 113–17. See also Crawford (n 7) 461; Kaczorowska (n 10)322; Akehurst (n 10) 157–59.

[45] Department of State, "Report on Extraterritorial Crime and the *Cutting* Case" (1887) Foreign Relations of the United States 751.

[46] *Case of the S.S. Lotus (Fr. v. Turk.)* (n 15)(dissenting opinions Lord Loder para 108; Lord Finlay paras 201–10; Lord Nyholm paras 218–25; Lord Moore paras 270–79); Harvard Research on International Law (n 39) 579 ("Jurisdiction asserted upon the principle of passive personality without qualifications has been more strongly contested than any other type of competence"); GR Watson, "The Passive Personality Principle" (1993) 28 Texas International Law Journal 1–46, 2–3; J Meyer, "Vicarious Administration of Justice: An Overlooked Basis of Jurisdiction" (1990) 31 Harvard International Law Journal 108–16, 114. ("Ultimately, the passive personality principle should be abandoned.")

[47] Meyer (n 46) 114; Watson (n 46) 22.

[48] Watson (n 46) 16–17; on limiting the application of the principle on the condition that the state in which the prohibited conduct is carried out decides not to prosecute the offender see Watson (n 46) 20–22.

[49] *Arrest Warrant*, ICJ Report 2002 Join Separate Opinion of Judges Higgins, Kooijmans, and Buergenthal para 47 ("Passive personality jurisdiction, for so long regarded as controversial, is now reflected not only in the legislation of various countries ... and today meets with relatively little opposition, at least so far as a particular category of offences is concerned").

[50] 18 USC s 2332 (US).

indictment against a Lebanese citizen for high-jacking a Jordanian airliner in Beirut that had US citizens on board.[51] However, in this case the passive personality principle is limited to cases where US citizens are targeted, which makes the application of US law foreseeable. Moreover, the *aut dedere aut indicare* principle provided under international conventions on certain transnational crimes (eg torture, hijacking, and hostage taking) authorizes the states signatories to apply the passive personality principle.[52]

2.2.2 Protective principle

Another type of extraterritorial jurisdiction is the protective principle, which allows states to claim jurisdiction for acts done abroad based on the vital interests that they seek to protect such as their sovereignty or security. Application of the protective principle does not require a territorial link to the state, nor does it require for the harms to occur there.[53] Neither the nationality of the accused nor that of the victim is relevant.[54] Rather, the state's vital interest constitutes the nexus between the matter concerned and the state exercising jurisdiction over it. The justification of this principle under international law is not in doubt, although states have rarely resorted to it.[55] The exemplary crimes for which states claim jurisdiction on the basis of this principle are treason,[56] illegal immigration,[57] drug-trafficking,[58] and crimes against a state's external security.[59]

2.2.3 Universality principle

The last principle allowing a state to claim extraterritorial jurisdiction is the universality principle. It refers to states' assertion of jurisdiction irrespective of any link between the adjudicating state and the prescribed activity unlike the other principles mentioned earlier.[60] This principle was originally recognized for piracy on the high seas in order to protect international public order and the accused is considered *hostus*

[51] *US v Fawaz Yunis* 681 F Supp 896. Another jurisdictional principle that the US Supreme Court referred to was the universality principle as the perpetrator was apprehended by the US authorities in international seas.

[52] eg Convention of Offences Committed on Board Aircraft (adopted 14 September 1963, entered into force 4 December 1969) 220 UNTS 10106 Art 4(b); Convention for the Suppression of Unlawful Acts Against the Safety of Maritime Navigation (adopted 10 March 1988, entered into force 1 March 1992) 222 UNTS 29004, Art 6(2)(b); UN Torture Convention, (adopted 10 December 1984, entered into force 26 June 1987) 1465 UNTS 85 Art 5(1)(c); International Convention Against the Taking of Hostages (adopted 17 December 1979, entered into force 3 June 1983) 1316 UNTS 205 Art 5(1)(d).

[53] *US v Evans* 667 F Supp 974, 980 (SDNY 1987) ("international law permits jurisdiction under these theories even if the act or conspiracy at issue is thwarted before ill effects are actually felt in the target state").

[54] Akehurst (n 10) 207; Meyer (n 46) 112.

[55] Ryngaert (n 38) 98–99.

[56] eg *Joyce v DPP* [1946] AC 347, 372 ("No principle of comity demands that a state should ignore the crime of treason committed against it outside its territory. On the contrary, a proper regard for its security requires that all those who commit that crime, whether they commit it within or without the realm, should be amenable to its laws.")

[57] eg *Naim v Molvan v AG for Palestine* [1948] AC 531; *Giles v Tumminello* (1969) 38 ILR 120.

[58] eg *US v Alomia-Riascos* 825 F 2d 769 (4th Cir 1987); *US v Gonzalez* 776 F 2d 931 (1995).

[59] eg *Nusselein v Belgium* [1950] 17 ILR 136. See also MR Garcia-Mora, "Criminal Jurisdiction Over Foreigners for Treason and Offenses Against the Safety of the State Committed Upon Foreign Territory" (1957–58) 19 University of Pittsburgh Law Review 567–90, 587.

[60] Ryngaert (n 38) 101; Crawford (n 7) 467.

humani generis (ie evil of mankind).[61] The universality principle was later expanded to cover core crimes against international law such as war crimes, crimes against humanity, genocide, torture, and slavery, which have been subjects of international conventions. The justification for this principle has been based upon the "heinous" nature of these core international crimes,[62] the alleged violations of *jus cogen*,[63] and the need to protect the common interest of the international community as a result of which the prescribing state acts on behalf of all the nations.[64] Despite the sporadic application of the universality principle and the scholarly debate surrounding its rationale,[65] a distinction has been made in the scholarly debate between the universality principle proper and the quasi-universality principle based upon the international agreements that impose the obligation of *aut dedere aut indicare* upon their signatory parties in relation to certain criminal offences.[66] As mentioned earlier, the quasi-universality principle requires states to prosecute the accused if present in their jurisdiction or to extradite him to state willing and able to prosecute. It was argued that when this principle is used to assert jurisdiction in light of the *aut dedere aut indicare* requirement, this is not an exercise of the universality principle proper.

These above-mentioned principles for extraterritorial jurisdiction assertions, save the passive personality principle, have found their ways into criminal laws outlawing cybercrimes and they are discussed in section 3 on developing principles for such crimes.

3. Developing principles for cybercrime: territorial and extraterritorial laws

Cybercrimes as a legal concept refers to different types of criminal offences committed using information technology, computers, and the internet.[67] In general, the concept of cybercrime can be subdivided into three categories.[68] The first subcategory is content- and communication-related crimes, where illegal content is disseminated and obtained by way of computer networks, including criminal intellectual property infringement, child pornography, and hate speech. The second category consists of

[61] *Re Piracy Jure Gentium* [1934] AC 586, 589; Harvard Research on International Law (n 39) 563–64.

[62] eg *Demjanjuk v Petrovsky*, 776 F 2d 571, 582 (6th Cir 1985); *US v Fawaz Yunis* (n 51) 900.

[63] eg *R v Bow Street Metropolitan Stipendiary Magistrate and others, Ex Parte Pinochet Ugarte (No. 3)* [2000] 1 AC 147; see Ryngaert (n 38) 110–15.

[64] M Robinson, *The Princeton Principles on Universal Jurisdiction* (Princeton University Press 2001) 23 ("When national courts exercise universal jurisdiction appropriately, in accordance with internationally recognized standards of due process, they act to vindicate not merely their own interests and values but the basic interests and values common to the international community.")

[65] On arguments for and against the universality principle see JH Marks, "Mending the Web: Universal Jurisdiction, Humanitarian Intervention and the Abrogation of Immunity by the Security Council" (2003–04) 42 Columbia Journal of Transnational Law 445–90, 463–75; Ryngaert (n 38) 106–08.

[66] Ryngaert (n 38) 104–06.

[67] I Walden, *Computer Crimes and Digital Investigations* (Oxford University Press 2016) 11–92; P Kastner and F Megret, "International legal dimensions of cybercrime" in N Tsagourias and R Buchan (eds), *Research Handbook on International Law and Cyberspace* (Edward Elgar Publishing 2015) 190–210, 191; BH Schell and C Martin, *Cybercrime: A Reference Handbook* (ABC Clio 2001) 2.

[68] Walden (n 67) 93–206.

computer integrity crimes, where the computer is the target of the crime, such as hacking, the spreading of malware, and denial-of-service attacks. Finally, the third category is computer-related crimes, where computers and networks are the means enabling the commission of crimes, this includes fraud, forgery, or identity theft.

Because cybercrimes rely on computers and connectivity afforded by the internet, cybercrime can, and typically does, involve a multitude of jurisdictions including in terms of the place where the prohibited conduct is committed as well as where the victims or their property are located.[69] Cybercrime therefore typically can be described as cross-border crime and frequently is multi-jurisdictional.

Three different aspects of the cross-border nature of cybercrime are distinguishable. First, the perpetrator and the victim may be located in two different countries, with the perpetrator remotely targeting their crime to the victim. Perpetrators may use the internet specifically to carry out offences remotely from a different jurisdiction and for hiding their tracks. Second, the criminal conduct may result in harm which is spread across multiple jurisdictions, potentially at a vast scale (such as eg the distribution of a computer virus or child sex abuse or copyright infringing materials, which may be uploaded from one place and then downloaded in many other places). Third, because technology has enhanced communication and cooperation at a distance, the perpetrators themselves may be located in different countries and act as accomplices across national borders.

Consequently, there can be numerous perpetrators or victims of cybercrimes in a multitude of different jurisdictions. Indeed, in November 2016 Europol carried out an investigation against the Avalanche network, that had been used for a variety of criminal activities from phishing to sending malware, with the help of prosecutors and investigators from thirty countries and they identified victims from 189 countries.[70] Therefore the jurisdictional challenge is particularly acute for the investigation and prosecution of cybercrimes and raises the question of how the jurisdictional principles under international law are applied.

3.1 Territoriality principle in exercising jurisdiction over cybercrimes

As the discussion of the jurisdictional principles here has shown, jurisdiction is not exclusive—several states may claim jurisdiction over the same crime concurrently. The geographically irreverent nature of cybercrimes can have two consequences: either *no* state is claiming jurisdiction over criminal conduct (ie a *negative conflict*) or more than one state claims jurisdiction over that conduct (ie *positive conflict* between overlapping or concurrent claims of jurisdiction). The inherent "border defiant" nature

[69] J Goldsmith, "The Internet and the Abiding Significance of Territorial Sovereignty" (1997–98) 5(2) Indiana Journal of Global Legal Studies 475–92, 475. ("More than any other technology, the internet facilitates cheap, fast, and difficult-to-define multi-jurisdictional transactions.")

[70] Europol Review, General Report on Europol Activities (2016–17), https://www.europol.europa.eu/activities-services/main-reports/europol-review-2016-2017, 38–39. Accessed on 16 July 2020.

of cybercrime as discussed earlier challenges the territoriality-based state system and jurisdictional claims, head-on.

The territorially principle essentially connects jurisdictional competence to the territory in which the substantive elements of the offence are committed.[71] The territoriality principle continues to be the main jurisdictional principle that states resort to when assuming jurisdiction over criminal conduct.[72] Indeed, the Council of Europe's Cybercrime Convention, which is the first international treaty addressing the harmonization of substantive and procedural rules on cybercrime, provides that "each Party shall adopt such legislative and other measures as may be necessary to establish jurisdiction over any offence established in accordance with Articles 2 through 11 of this Convention, when the offence is *committed* in its territory."[73] This principle is equally contained in some of the recent EU measures on combatting content crimes such as child abuse images[74] and racism online[75] or on combatting computer integrity offences.[76] It means that, in the first instance, the onus to prosecute is on the state on whose territory the offence is committed. The primacy of territoriality as a jurisdictional principle addresses *negative jurisdictional conflicts* in ensuring that there is *a* state that is competent to prosecute.

However, it does not really assist with positive conflicts of jurisdiction. In many cybercrime cases, more than one state is able to claim jurisdiction based on the territoriality principle. Since any of the elements of the offence may serve as the connection to the territory, and since frequently it is difficult to locate a particular element of the offence, the question of the proper nexus can be complicated to answer.

An illustration of the difficulty of finding the territorial nexus came in the *Yahoo!* decision rendered by a French court in 2000.[77] Yahoo! Inc argued that the French law did not apply to their auction activities because the auction website was operated from and hosted on servers in the US, and argued that therefore the contested conduct was committed solely on the territory of the US. The French Court, on the other hand, held that Yahoo! Inc was bound by the French Criminal Code because it allowed for the

[71] R O'Keefe, *International Criminal Law* (Oxford University Press 2015) 10.

[72] R August, "International Cyber-Jurisdiction: A Comparative Analysis" (2002) 39 American Business Law Journal 531–74, 572; Ryngaert (n 38) 79; J-B Maillart, "The Limits of Subjective Territorial Jurisdiction in the context of Cybercrime" (2018) 19 ERA Forum 375–90, 376 ("the exercise of jurisdiction in the context of cybercrimes remains largely based on the principle of territoriality"). See Art 19(1)(a), Terrorism Directive (EU) 2017/541 of 15 March 2017, OJ L88/6.

[73] Cybercrime Convention Art 22(1)(a) (emphasis added).

[74] Directive 2011/92/EU of the European Parliament and of the Council of 13 December 2011 on combating the sexual abuse and sexual exploitation of children and child pornography, and replacing Council Framework Decision 2004/68/JHA, OJ L335 (17 December 2011) Art 17(1)(a).

[75] Council Framework Decision 2008/913/JHA of 28 November 2008 on combating certain forms and expressions of racism and xenophobia by means of criminal law, OJ L328 (6 December 2008) Art 9(1)(a).

[76] Directive 2013/40/EU of the European Parliament and of the Council of 12 August 2013 on attacks against information systems and replacing Council Framework Decision 2005/222/JHA, OJ L218 (14 August 2013) Art 12(1)(a).

[77] *LICRA and UEJA v Yahoo! Inc. and Yahoo France* (Tribunal de Grande Instance de Paris, 22 May 2000) affirmed in *LICRA and UEFJ v Yahoo! Inc. and Yahoo France* (Tribunal de Grande Instance de Paris, 20 November 2000).

access by internet users in France to auction websites selling Nazi objects. As a result, it ordered Yahoo! Inc to take technical measures to render it impossible for the internet users in France to access to the contested websites.[78]

Regarding content crimes, the prohibiting state might outlaw certain conduct relating to the information concerned such as its publication,[79] advertisement,[80] distribution,[81] or making available[82]—locating such conducts on the internet is frequently difficult. In the French Yahoo! Case, the criminal offence in question was the exposure for sale of the Nazi memorabilia. The Court held that permitting the visualization of the objects in France amounted to that offence.

Furthermore, even if none of the elements of the offence can be located within the territory, a state can nonetheless claim jurisdiction over criminal conduct, if its effects have occurred within the territory.[83] This is because the territoriality principle allows states to assert jurisdiction over criminal conduct abroad that took *effect* within their territory.

The reading of the territoriality principle and the effects doctrine in this context has raised several concerns over the regulation of online content. Firstly, because numerous states can assert territorial jurisdiction, content providers are exposed to multiple jurisdictions. Thus, it might be hard for them to anticipate with which law they have to comply with, as they might not know where the content might produce effects.[84] Related to this, the second concern is spill-over effect of national laws in other jurisdictions for the reason that intermediaries choose to comply with the strictest law, depriving residents of other states of content legal in those states.

Furthermore, jurisdictional claims can additionally arise based on the extraterritorial principles discussed. The primacy of the territoriality principle does *not* mean that extraterritorial principles cannot be used to justify the assumption of jurisdiction to prosecute cybercrimes, in addition to the territoriality principle. This is expressly recognized in Article 22(1)(d) of the Cybercrime Convention, which

[78] The French Court decided for the injunctive relief on the ground that Yahoo! Inc could, although not entirely, identify the geographical location of the users of the auction websites based on the IP addresses, using geolocation technology. This was based on the opinion of a panel of experts in determining the technical feasibility. The Court noted that Yahoo! Inc was aware that it had been targeting those users because, when the auction websites were accessed from the computers located in France, they displayed advertisements *in French*. The expert panel submitted its opinion that it was highly feasible to locate the users, the Court ordered Yahoo! Inc to block the access to the contested website if a user is located in France. For discussions on the background of the case see MH Greenberg, "A Return to Lilliput: The LICRA v. Yahoo—Case and the Regulation of Online Content in the World Market" (2003) 18 Berkeley Technology Law Journal 1191–258.

[79] eg Obscene Publications Act 1959 s 1(1) (UK).

[80] eg Protection of Children Act 1971 s 1(d) (UK).

[81] eg Protection of Children Act 1971 s 19 (UK).

[82] eg Directive 2001/29/EC of the European Parliament and of the Council of 22 May 2001 on the harmonization of certain aspects of copyright and related rights in the information society, OJ L167/10, 22 June 2001, Art 7(1)(b).

[83] An example for this is the Töben case discussed in Chapter 5.

[84] DR Johnson and DG Post, "The Law and Borders: The Rise of Law in Cyberspace" (1996) 48 Stanford Law Review 1367–402, 1375. ("And in Cyberspace, physical borders no longer function as signposts informing individuals of the obligations assumed by entering into a new, legally significant, place. Individuals are unaware of the existence of those borders as they move through virtual borders.")

additionally provides for the active personality principle: "when the offence is committed (...) by one of its nationals, if the offence is punishable under criminal law where it was committed or if the offence is committed outside the territorial jurisdiction of any State."

Article 7 of the UN International Convention on the Suppression of the Financing of Terrorism[85] likewise contains the territoriality principle[86] and the active personality principle (limited to nationality)[87] as mandatory grounds for jurisdiction. Wider grounds are optional for states and include variants of the passive personality principle,[88] the active personality principle in respect of stateless persons extended to habitual residence,[89] or where aircraft is operated by the government of a state (even though registered in another state).[90] These grounds must be notified to the Secretary General of the UN.[91] Furthermore, it establishes that a state where the accused is located should prosecute unless it extradites the accused to a competent state.[92] Finally, Article 7(5) imposes an obligation on states who wish to exercise concurrent jurisdiction to coordinate their actions in respect of prosecution and mutual legal assistance.

Therefore, the primacy of the territoriality principle does not solve the problem of *positive jurisdictional conflicts* for two reasons. First, the territoriality principle is not the *only* principle recognized for establishing jurisdiction. Secondly, the territoriality principle itself may allow more than one state to assume jurisdiction for a particular cybercrime, and more importantly allow them to apply its criminal laws to conduct. This raises problems where laws differ (one law allowing a certain conduct, another law prohibiting it subject to criminal penalties) and such positive conflicts of law cause legal uncertainty as to which laws need to be complied with (contrary to the rule of law and the principle of *nullum crimen sine lege*).[93] In respect of offences prohibiting the publication or distribution of illegal content this overlap of jurisdiction may lead to censorship at the level of the strictest, most restrictive regime. As mentioned earlier in this chapter, there is no prohibition under public international law against concurrent jurisdiction. Thus, as undesirable as it may be, there can be overlapping concurrent jurisdiction over the same conduct.

[85] Ratified at New York 9/12/1999, UNTS Vol 2178, p 197.

[86] Art 7(1)(a) "the offence is committed in the territory of that State" and Art 7(1)(b) "the offence is committed on board a vessel flying the flag of that State or an aircraft registered under the law of that State (...)."

[87] Art 7(1)(c) "the offence is committed by a national of that State."

[88] Art 7(2)(a), (b) and (c).

[89] Art 7(2)(d).

[90] Art 7(2)(e).

[91] Art 7(3).

[92] Art 7(4).

[93] See V Mayer-Schönberger and TE Foster, "A Regulatory Web: Free Speech and the Global Information Infrastructure" (1997) 3 Michigan Telecommunications and Technology Law Review 45–61, 50. ("Yet, the internationality of the Net, as well as the conglomeration of national regulations and their effects on the flow of information on the Net, invariably shapes all communicative activity on it as a whole. Thus, the international aspect of the Net does not remove discussions on the Net from national regulations, but instead subjects them to panoply of varying and contradictory regulations that breed un-certainty.")

3.2 Extraterritorial laws in prescribing cybercrimes

As mentioned at the beginning of this section, public international law provides a jurisdictional latitude for states to regulate matters originating outside its jurisdiction.[94] This has been made possible through the application of the following principles of extraterritorial jurisdiction: the personality (active or passive personality) principle; the protective principle; and the universality principle. This subsection traces how states have used those principles to assert prescriptive jurisdiction over cybercrimes.

As a starting point, the active personality principle is provided under the Cybercrime Convention as an optional extraterritorial jurisdiction.[95] Accordingly, parties to the Convention shall adopt measures in exercising jurisdiction for offences committed "by one of its nationals, if the offence is punishable under criminal law where it was committed or if the offence is committed outside the territorial jurisdiction of any State." It also requires states to exercise jurisdiction over their nationals if those states refuse to extradite their nationals to the requesting state.[96] The Computer Misuse Act 1990 provides for the exercise of jurisdiction over UK nationals (active personality principle) for the computer misuse offences they commit abroad if their contested conduct constituted an offence in the country in which it was committed.[97]

The drafters of the Cybercrime Convention acknowledged extraterritorial jurisdiction. Signatory Parties can assert jurisdiction based on the jurisdictional principles accepted in their domestic law.[98] The protective principle is limited to important national interests and the protection of national sovereignty, but may apply where cybercrimes involve terrorism or threaten national security. One point of concern regarding the use of the protective principle is that because it solely focuses on states' national interests, it may undermine international solidarity.[99]

Certain states such as Germany rely on the universality principles when asserting jurisdiction over the criminal offence of the distribution of child pornography images.[100] Academic circles also use the analogy of piracy as an international crime that transgresses borders (high seas v cyberspace) when supporting for the application of the universality principle for cybercrimes that affect states' infrastructure and national security (eg "cyberterrorism" or attacks on national infrastructure, including "cyberwarfare").[101] However, the transgression of a border alone would not be sufficient to apply the universality principle and therefore it would only apply to those

94 ES Podgor, "International Computer Fraud: A Paradigm for Limiting National Jurisdiction" (2002) 35(2) University of California Davis Law Review 267–318, 302.

95 Art 22(1)(d).

96 Cybercrime Convention Art 24.

97 Computer Misuse Act 1990 s 5(1A) (UK) see further Chapter 5.

98 Cybercrime Convention Art 22(4).

99 HWK Kaspersen, "Cybercrime and Internet Jurisdiction" Discussion Paper (5 March 2009), https://rm.coe.int/16803042b7. Accessed on 16 July 2020.

100 See Chapter 5.

101 KA Gable, "Cyber-Apocalypse Now: Securing the Internet Against Cyberterrorism and Using Universal Jurisdiction as a Deterrent" (2010) 43 Vanderbilt Journal of Transnational Law 57–118, 106; WM Stahl, "The Uncharted Waters of Cyberspace: Applying the Principles of International Maritime Law to the Problem of Cybersecurity" (2011–12) 40 Georgia Journal of International and Comparative Law 247–74, 267–70.

cybercrimes where the perpetrators are deemed as *hostus humani generis*. Moreover, giving states universal jurisdiction over certain cybercrimes does not mean that the states where the offenders are situated are willing and able to prosecute.

4. Resolving jurisdiction conflicts for cybercrimes: limiting the assertion of jurisdiction and coordinating criminal enforcement

Public international law allows states to assert jurisdiction in respect of activities that take place beyond their territories, whether on territorial or extraterritorial grounds. Thus, *several* states may claim jurisdiction for the *same* conduct, which means that there can be concurrent jurisdiction and, therefore jurisdictional conflicts.[102] The corollary impact of these jurisdictional conflicts is that individuals may not know which law applies to them, and in which jurisdiction they have to defend themselves, contrary to the rule of law. As a consequence of conflicts of law, legal uncertainty arises.

Nonetheless, there is yet no rule under public international law prohibiting states from establishing concurrent jurisdiction or prioritizing one principle over another.[103] There is also no international convention or practice allocating criminal jurisdiction to any one state in a given case. This section examines international law principles and frameworks attempting to coordinate which state asserts jurisdiction and prosecutes criminal cases with an international element.

4.1 International comity and the reasonableness principles

Cedric Ryngaert has suggested the principle of international comity, according to which each state respects each other's law, as a method to resolve concurrent jurisdiction in criminal law.[104] In the context of jurisdictional inquiries, comity would mean that a state does not assert jurisdiction over activities that have *stronger link* to other states.[105] The state with the stronger link should assert jurisdiction if it is reasonable to do so considering the interest of other states. Permitting jurisdiction in light of the reasonableness principle has not yet become part of customary international law because of the lack of sufficient state practice supported by *opinio juris* on the matter.[106] According to Ryngaert, "when States exercise jurisdiction reasonably, they appear to do so as a matter of discretion, not out of legal obligation. Reasonableness, if any could be discerned, appears to be 'soft law' that need not guide future State behaviour as a matter of law."[107]

The reasonableness as a criterion to limit states' jurisdiction found doctrinal support in section 403 of the Restatement (Third) of US Foreign Relations Law of 1987.[108]

[102] Ryngaert (n 38) 134.
[103] ibid 128–9.
[104] ibid 147–52.
[105] ibid 148.
[106] ibid 178.
[107] ibid.
[108] Restatement (Third) of Foreign Relations Law of the United States s 403(2).

At its core, the Restatement provides "principles derived from international law, for determining when the US may properly exercise regulatory (or prescriptive) jurisdiction over activities or persons connected with another state."[109] According to section 403, the exercise of jurisdiction would be reasonable depending on:

(1) the nexus between the state and regulated activity on the basis of the place that the activity took place or its substantial, direct, and foreseeable effect upon that state territory;
(2) the links, such as nationality, residence, economic activity between the state and regulated activity;
(3) the character of the activity to be regulated, its importance to the regulating state, the extent to which other states regulate that activity, and the degree to which the desirability of the regulation is generally accepted;
(4) the existence of justified expectations that might be protected or hurt by the regulation;
(5) the importance of the regulation to the international political, legal, or economic system;
(6) the extent to which the regulation is consistent with the traditions of the international system;
(7) the extent to which another state may have an interest in regulating the activity;
(8) the likelihood of conflict with regulation by another state.[110]

Based on these criteria, the state would balance interests, and, if as a result its exercise of jurisdiction is found unreasonable, it would defer jurisdiction to another state with whom it is in jurisdictional conflict. Nevertheless, there are arguments that despite what the drafters of the section 403 assumed at the time, the reasonableness criterion does not constitute a customary international law due to the insufficient state practice and the lack of *opinio juris*.[111]

Drawing on the (Third) Restatement, scholars have put forward different interpretations of the reasonableness standard in determining concurrent jurisdiction. Ryngaert moves beyond the reasonableness criteria enshrined in the (Third) Statement and considers that in untangling the concurrent jurisdiction issues, states may weigh in the protective purpose of the legislation and the principle of subsidiarity according to which "states with the strongest nexus to the case forfeit their right of protest against other States' jurisdictional assertions over that case, if the former States fail to adequately deal with it."[112] Applying to the jurisdictional assertions, "a State, which also entertains a strong nexus with the situation, is *entitled* to exercise jurisdiction if the other State is unable or unwilling to tackle a situation that is, on aggregate, harmful to the regulatory interests of the international community."[113] Thus, when exercising its

[109] *United States v Nippon Paper Indus Co*, 109 F 3d 1, 11 (1st Cir 1997) (Lynch J, dissenting) *cert denied*, 522 US 1044 (1998).
[110] Restatement (Third) of Foreign Relations Law of the United States s 403(2).
[111] DB Massey, "How the American Law Institute Influences Customary Law: The Reasonableness Requirement of the Restatement of Foreign Relations Law" (1997) 22(2) Yale Journal of International Law 416–38, 428–37; Ryngaert (n 38) 180–82.
[112] Ryngaert (n 38) 221.
[113] ibid 186.

jurisdiction (based on either of the principles mentioned in the section), a state may take into account whether in doing so it would address the protective purpose of the legislation. Then, it should consider whether a state with the strongest nexus has failed to assert jurisdiction. If this is the case, it can exercise its jurisdiction on a "subsidiary basis."[114]

The Cybercrime Convention does not further elaborate on how to refine competing jurisdictional claims. It states that in cases of concurrent jurisdiction, "the Parties involved shall … consult with a view to determining the most appropriate jurisdiction for prosecution,"[115] but does not advance the factors that need to be considered when settling those concurrent jurisdictional claims or explain considerations or procedures for coordinating jurisdictional conflicts.[116] Criteria for balancing jurisdiction additionally exist in other international treaties. For example, the Arab Convention on Combating Information Technology Offences[117] states in terms of jurisdictional competence the following order of priority: "State whose security or interests were disrupted by the offence, followed by the State in whose territory the offence was committed, and then by the State of which the wanted person is a national."

Susan Brenner has suggested balancing the following factors for deciding the proper forum to assert jurisdiction:

(1) the place of the commission of the crime;
(2) the place of custody of the accused;
(3) the location of the harm;
(4) nationality of the perpetrator;
(5) strength of the case against the accused;
(6) punishment;
(7) fairness of proceedings and inconvenience.[118]

This list of factors combines the jurisdictional principles under public international law, namely factors connecting the crime to territory (along the lines of the territoriality principle) with factors relating to the nationality of the perpetrator and their location (akin to variations of the active personality principle), the harms to protected interests (objective territoriality principle in the case of result crimes and protective principle), with factors relating to the interests of justice (such as the last two criteria).

For the aim of preventing impunity, the strength of the case against the accused such as availability of evidence and defences that the accused can plead.[119] The strength of the case might be a desirable factor to warrant priority to one state, but this does not mean that this would be the best option to protect the accused's human rights.[120] The punishment factor aims at capturing the seriousness of the crime while delineating the

[114] ibid 216.
[115] Cybercrime Convention Art 22(5).
[116] Cf the EU instruments discussed later.
[117] League of Arab States Art 30(3).
[118] SW Brenner and B-J Koops, "Approaches to Cybercrime Jurisdiction" (2004) 4 Journal of High Technology Law 1.
[119] ibid.
[120] In the European context, this would potentially raise concern over protecting accused's right to a fair trial as protected under Art 6 of the ECHR.

maximum charge that can be brought for the crime concerned.[121] Lastly, the fairness of proceedings and inconvenience can capture concerns over the accused's interests as well as the feasibility of carrying out the proceedings in determining the proper forum to exercise jurisdiction. However, the cost of proceedings in terms of their convenience can only be taken into account once the other factors are equally balanced.

Thus, the Restatement (Third) of Foreign Relations Law of the United States and the proposal by Brenner and Koops envisage a set of criteria that each state incorporates in their national law and uses to decide whether it is best placed to assert jurisdiction. While these reasonableness criteria may guard against *some* unreasonable assertion of jurisdiction, they do not as such *coordinate* states' approaches and therefore do not prevent concurrent jurisdiction. It is also questionable, given the preponderance of considerations of sovereignty and assertion of power by states how useful they are. However, roughly equivalent criteria have also been discussed in the EU.

4.2 EU criminal law coordination

In the EU, Eurojust has issued Guidelines on the factors to be considered when deciding jurisdiction to prosecute and the Council of the EU has passed a Framework Decision.[122] Rules on criminal jurisdiction must be prescribed by law before an offence is committed. If jurisdiction was determined solely by negotiated agreement of the prosecutors on a case-by-case basis this would infringe the due process rule against the arbitrary judge.[123] The dilemma is here that, on the one hand, the rule against an arbitrary forum must be respected, but, on the other hand, a situation has to be avoided where states agree a single place of prosecution and agree to concentrate jurisdiction in one forum, that after a lengthy investigation when the case reaches the court of the agreed forum, the judge rules that he or she has no jurisdiction.[124] This dilemma has not yet been solved.[125]

Eurojust is composed of representatives of EU Member States (and other states) and is the intergovernmental[126] EU coordination body for cross-border criminal prosecution founded in 2002.[127] Given its role in fostering cooperation and coordination of cross-border criminal prosecutions, Eurojust has issued Guidelines for deciding which jurisdiction should prosecute, first issued in 2003 and revised in 2016.[128] The

121 Brenner and Koops (n 118).

122 At time of writing it was too early to tell what impact the UK's withdrawal from the EU would have on its participation in Eurojust mechanisms. It should be noted, however, that non-EU states participate in Eurojust.

123 Patrone (n 2) 215–25, 218.

124 ibid.

125 And arguably could only be solved if states agreed a single set of harmonized jurisdictional rules, which will not happen for political reasons and states' insistence on their sovereignty.

126 See further A Weyembergh et al, "Competition or Co-operation? State of Play and Future Perspectives on the Relations Between Europol, Eurojust and the European Judicial Network" (2015) 6(2) New Journal of European Criminal Law 258–87, 264.

127 See further on Eurojust, Chapter 6.

128 Eurojust, "Guidelines for Deciding Which Jurisdiction Should Prosecute" (Revised 2016), http://www.eurojust.europa.eu/doclibrary/Eurojust-framework/Casework/Guidelines%20for%20deciding%20which%20jurisdiction%20should%20prosecute%20(2016)/2016_Jurisdiction-Guidelines_EN.pdf. Accessed on 16 July 2020.

background to the Guidelines explains that the increase in cross-border crime has inevitably led to more cases where multiple Member States might launch a prosecution or may already have launched separate prosecutions, which can lead to multiple prosecutions of the same defendant.[129] The Guidelines address the issue of multiple prosecutions resulting from concurrent jurisdiction. They do not address conflicts of law, where conduct is a criminal offence in one Member State that wants to prosecute but *not* a criminal offence in another Member State and the crime is linked to the territory of both Member States. This scenario is concerned with the reach of criminal law, and for publication crimes, with restrictions to free speech,[130] but *not* with (potential or actual) multiple prosecutions.

These Guidelines must be seen in the context of Eurojust's coordination role. They are not hard and fast rules about which state is competent, instead they provide guidance[131] in respect of the considerations, which should be taken into account when a Eurojust member assesses its competence to prosecute or when Eurojust is tasked with coordination of prosecution, for example, in the framework of a joint investigation team. Given that states are reluctant to cede sovereign powers to investigate and prosecute crime, a coordination and cooperation approach is likely to be more successful. Thus, currently, Eurojust does not provide a legally binding settlement of jurisdictional conflicts, but its role is instead to prevent such conflicts from arising in the first place.[132] It is for this reason that it is described as a "service provider" (rather than a decision maker).[133]

The Guidelines establish a Smörgås Board of thirteen considerations for coordinating jurisdiction. The very first consideration addresses the fundamental problem that where the commission of a crime and its result are spread over several Member States, several states might claim jurisdiction under the territoriality principle. If this is the case the Guidelines recommend that prosecution should *only* take place where the majority or the most important part of the criminality occurred, or in which the majority or the most important part of the harm was sustained.[134] Thus, this limitation on the territoriality principle contains both a quantitative ("majority") and a qualitative element ("most important"). However, it would be wrong to argue that this first consideration of the Guidelines restricts the use of the territoriality principle in a holistic way, as the Guidelines only apply to prevent multiple prosecutions of the same offence. They are not designed to limit the reach of national criminal law as such.

The second consideration is an important practical consideration, which facilitates prosecution and avoids *in absentia trials*,[135] namely the *location of the suspect or accused person*. Member States are asked to consider whether they can get hold of the accused as a defendant in a criminal trial, and thus the following factors are relevant: the place where the accused was found, nationality or usual place of residence,

[129] ibid 1.
[130] See the discussion in section 2.1.
[131] Eurojust (n 128) 1.
[132] Patrone (n 2) 218, 222–23.
[133] Weyembergh (n 126) 264.
[134] Eurojust (n 128) 3. This is similar to the substantial measure test developed under the rules on jurisdiction under English common law, see Chapter 5.
[135] Which are a violation of due process.

other strong personal connections with a Member State, the possibility of obtaining surrender or extradition, and, finally, the possibility of transferring proceedings to the Member State where the accused is located.[136] The updated 2016 version of the Guidelines, however, recognizes that this consideration has been rendered less important in view of the system of European Arrest Warrants[137] and the mutual recognition of judgments imposing custodial sentences in the EU.[138]

The third consideration is equally an important and practical factor, namely the availability, reliability, and admissibility of the evidence on which the prosecution rests.[139] Related to this is the fourth consideration, namely the availability of evidence through testimony during trial from witnesses, experts, and victims.[140] Thus, when considering which state is best suited for a criminal trial, it should be considered whether witnesses are able to travel to the location of the trial, or whether evidence can be taken remotely through video-conferencing technology. Fifth, it should be considered whether the state concerned is able to offer a witness protection programme, in order to ensure a fair trial and maintain the integrity of the criminal justice process.[141]

The sixth consideration is that the interests of the victim must be taken into account in order to guarantee that the victim is not prejudiced by trial in one state as opposed to another. This includes the possibility for the victim to claim criminal injuries compensation.[142]

Moreover, states should consider, if criminal investigations or proceedings have reached an advanced stage in one state, it may be inappropriate to terminate and transfer proceedings. In fact, delay is one of the due process considerations that must be taken into account under the Guidelines, which stipulate the length of time of criminal proceedings as the eighth relevant factor and the existing legal framework in each jurisdiction as the eighth and ninth relevant factors.[143]

Interestingly the Guidelines equally stipulate factors that should not be considered as part of the decision as to which jurisdiction should prosecute. States should not make the decision on the basis that it is easier to prosecute or that sentences are longer in one state compared to another.[144] Nor should the place of prosecution be determined by the place where it is easier to recover the proceeds of crime.[145] The twelfth, negative, consideration is that the costs of prosecuting and the impact on resources should not be a relevant consideration, unless all other factors are equally balanced. Finally, a state should not refuse to prosecute on the basis that the prosecution is not a priority for the relevant prosecution service or judicial authority.

The Guidelines contain factors more akin to the *forum non conveniens* analysis in civil cases under the common law, based on weighing up the interests of different

136 Eurojust (n 128) 3.

137 Framework Decision 2002/584/JHA.

138 ibid.

139 Eurojust (n 128) 3, the European Investigation Order Directive 2014/41/EU has made this consideration less pressing than before.

140 ibid.

141 ibid 3.

142 ibid 3.

143 ibid 3–4.

144 ibid 4.

145 ibid 4.

stakeholders, the interests of justice and due process considerations. The Guidelines encourage Member States to identify possible multiple prosecutions early on in the process to avoid duplication and wasted resources[146] and to prevent that a prosecution in one country is prejudiced by a prosecution in another country.[147]

The Framework Decision on the Prevention and Settlement of Conflicts of Exercise of Jurisdiction in Criminal Proceedings[148] likewise is a coordination instrument and imposes a duty on the EU Member States to cooperate in settling jurisdictional conflicts.[149] The Framework Decision, like the Guidelines, seeks to prevent unnecessary multiple prosecutions for the same offence.[150] The Framework Decision makes clear in Recital 11 that Member States are not obliged to exercise or relinquish jurisdiction, or to discontinue a prosecution. Obligations under the Framework Decision are limited to information exchange and consultation for coordinating conflicts of jurisdiction, and do not introduce new jurisdictional rules.[151]

If an EU Member State is obliged to prosecute whenever information about a crime has been laid before the relevant authority, the Framework Decision stipulates that this mandatory prosecution requirement has been fulfilled by any (other) Member State starting a prosecution.[152] This reflects that in many EU Member States prosecutors do not have a discretion whether to prosecute a criminal case, once the relevant intelligence is available.

Finally, EU law provides for harmonized jurisdictional rules for a number of *specific types of offences* relevant to cybercrime, such as terrorism, organized crime,[153] child sex offences,[154] and computer misuse.[155] The Terrorism Directive[156] provides in Article 19 two layers: first it lays down a number of rules for jurisdiction of the Member States,[157] even though they are expressed as being without prejudice to the exercise of jurisdiction by a Member State under its own national law, that is, this provision does not amount to a harmonization of the rules on criminal jurisdiction for terrorism offences.[158] Member States should be able to exercise jurisdiction under their national criminal law implementing the Directive, under the territoriality principle,[159] which is mentioned first in order of priority (*sic*), the active personality principle extending

146 See also the Council Framework Decision 2009/948/JHA of 30 November 2009, OJ L328/42.
147 Eurojust (n 128) 2.
148 Council Framework Decision (n 146).
149 Arts 2(1), 5(1), 6(1), and 10(1).
150 Recitals 3 and 12, Art 1(2)(a).
151 Recital 17.
152 Recital 12.
153 Council Framework Decision 2008/841/JHA of 24 October 2008 on the fight against organized crime, Art 7.
154 Directive on combating the sexual abuse and sexual exploitation of children and child pornography 2011/93/EU of 13 December 2011, OJ L335/1, Art 17.
155 Directive on attacks against information systems 2013/40/EU of 12 August 2013, OJ L218/8, Art 12.
156 Art 19., Terrorism Directive (EU) 2017/541 of 15 March 2017, OJ L88/6; previously in the Council Framework Decision 2002/475/JHA of 13 June 2002 Art 9.
157 Art 19(1).
158 Art 19(6): "this Article shall not exclude the exercise of jurisdiction in criminal matters as laid down by a Member State in accordance with its national law."
159 Art 19(1)(a): "where the offence is committed in whole or in part in its territory" and Art 19(1)(b) "where the offence is committed on board a vessel flying its flag or an aircraft registered there."

to nationality, residence, and establishment of legal persons,[160] the protective or representative principle,[161] and the universality principle (within the EU).[162]

Secondly, the Directive explicitly recognizes concurrent jurisdiction and jurisdictional conflicts between the Member States, but mandates the Member States concerned to cooperate "when any of the Member States concerned can validly prosecute on the basis of the same facts." The cooperation must be with the goal of centralizing criminal proceedings in one single Member State, using the assistance of Eurojust to achieve that aim.[163] It then lists the factors taken into account for deciding which Member State should prosecute and the first factor is that some priority should be given to the Member State in whose territory the crime has been committed,[164] or else the Member State whose national or resident the offender is,[165] or else the Member State that is the country of origin of the victims, or finally the Member State in whose territory the accused is found.[166]

Thus, the Directive contains rules on jurisdiction and an obligation to coordinate in cases of concurrent jurisdiction.

As a practical point, for crimes where there are no international rules on jurisdiction and coordination of prosecution, the state where the accused has been apprehended is best able to prosecute in practice, as all other states would require surrender or extradition. However, this state is not necessarily best placed to prosecute in terms of the evidence or closest nexus to the offence. Equally if this state is not prepared to prosecute (eg for the reasons of lack of evidence or political will), and if this state does not extradite, and in the absence of a binding extradition treaty, then no state can effectively prosecute.

However, within the EU framework this practical point has been overcome by the European Arrest Warrant,[167] Eurojust coordination,[168] and special rules such as those in the Terrorism Directive. The Terrorism Directive expressly includes the principle of *aut dedere aut indicare* (to extradite or to prosecute) in Article 19(4), so that Member States have to prosecute if they refuse to extradite the accused, for example, if a Member State refuses to extradite its own citizens.[169] These rules in the Terrorism Directive overcome some of the jurisdictional challenges by ensuring there is at least

[160] Art 19(1)(c): "where the offender is one of its nationals or residents" and Art 19(1)(d): "where the offence is committed for the benefit of a legal person established in its territory."

[161] Art 19(1)(e): "where the offence is committed against the institutions or people of the Member State in question or against an institution, body, office or agency of the Union based in that Member State."

[162] Art 19, Second Sentence: "Each Member State may extend its jurisdiction if the offence is committed in the territory of another Member State."

[163] Art 19(3).

[164] Art 19(3) Second Sentence.

[165] ibid.

[166] ibid.

[167] Framework Decision 2002/584/JHA; since the Framework Decision is a third pillar EC instrument the UK is no longer part of the European Arrest Warrant scheme; however its role in the EAW scheme will only be clear once negotiations have been concluded.

[168] Discussed in section 4.2.

[169] While the UK has no provision that it does not extradite its own citizens, a revision of the Extradition Act in 2013 in s 83A gives the court power in exceptional cases to decide that an extradition should not take place if it decides that a substantial measure of the alleged criminal activity took place in the UK, and it would be in the interests of justice for the extradition not to take place, this was applied in *Love v USA* [2018] EWHC 172 (Admin) and *US v McDaid* [2020] EWHC 1527 (Admin) —this is the so-called forum bar.

one Member State that prosecutes, and if multiple Member States are competent obliges them to coordinate the prosecution and trial of the accused in one single jurisdiction. Thus, at least a framework for cooperation is in place, aided on an institutional level by Eurojust, even though such cooperation is difficult in view of the obstacles of cross-border cooperation.

As regards another set of cybercrime offences, namely child sex offences committed over the internet (such as eg grooming of child victims for sexual abuse, or the dissemination or consumption of child sex abuse materials online[170]), Directive 2011/93/EU equally contains provisions on jurisdictional rules on the basis of which Member States can exercise jurisdiction in Article 17. Curiously though, the Article is headed "Jurisdiction and Coordination of Jurisdiction," the Article does not contain any provisions on *coordination*.[171]

The jurisdictional rules again rank the territoriality principle[172] first and the active personality principle second (limited to nationality of the offender as the connecting factor).[173] Where the offences are committed remotely using internet technologies, Member States should assert jurisdiction on the basis that the accused has *accessed the internet from the territory of the Member State concerned*.[174] Thus, if the accused uploads child sex abuse materials on a server or seeds such material in a peer-to-peer file sharing system, the Member State from which they accesses the internet has jurisdiction under the Directive. Furthermore, if grooming is carried out remotely by using instant messaging or social media, the state in which the accused is physically located could claim jurisdiction under the territoriality principle. Likewise, if a person consumes child sex materials by streaming a video on a mobile device, the Member State where the accused is watching can assume jurisdiction. These three examples are relatively uncontroversial as jurisdiction is established in the location where the accused acted when committing the crime, which is exactly the subjective territoriality principle.

More controversial and difficult is the application of the *objective* territoriality principle[175] based on the connecting factor of internet access.[176] So, the pertinent question is this: If the accused in State Z has uploaded or seeded child sex abuse materials onto a server and they are subsequently downloaded or streamed by consumers of such materials in Member State A, B, C, D, E, and F, can these six Member States assume jurisdiction and prosecute the *foreign uploader* for distributing child sex abuse materials? The wording of Article 17(3) is ambiguous in this respect,[177] but arguably

[170] Arts 5 and 6.

[171] This wording was contained in the original EU Commission Proposal COM(2010)94 final of 29/03/2010.

[172] Art 17(1)(a) "the offence is committed in whole or in part within their territory"

[173] Art 17(1)(b) "the offender is one of their nationals" and for some of the offences this is regardless to whether the offence prosecuted is a criminal offence under the law of the country where it has been committed, Art 17(4) or whether a complaint or denunciation has been filed in that country, Art 17(5).

[174] Art 17(3).

[175] For a discussion of the objective and subjective territoriality principle see section 2.1.

[176] See the debate in Germany in Chapter 5.

[177] Deliberate or not, this is bad, opaque drafting: "Member States shall ensure that their jurisdiction includes situations where an offence (. . .) is committed by means of information and communication technology accessed from their territory, whether or not it is based on their territory." In particular it is not clear what "access" refers to (internet access of the uploader or the downloader) and what the "it" refers to. Is the "it" the server from which the material is distributed?

includes jurisdiction in the state of consumption against the foreign uploader for distribution. If this interpretation is correct, in our example, all six Member States A, B, C, D, E, and F could concurrently prosecute the uploader in State Z, regardless of whether State Z is a Member State of the EU, and regardless of whether the materials is illegal in State Z. The good news of this situation is that, if State Z harbours child sex abuse without effective law enforcement, Member States of the EU could assume jurisdiction to fight this criminality. The bad news of this situation is that there may be six concurrent prosecutions for one crime. While the Directive does not contain any specific obligations to coordinate, Member States could fall back on the cooperation mechanisms provided by Eurojust and Recital 4 expressly refers to the Framework Decision on the Prevention and Settlement of Conflicts of Exercise of Jurisdiction in Criminal Proceedings 2009/948/JHA.

Less well recognized extraterritorial jurisdictional grounds, namely the passive personality principle,[178] or the active personality principle extended to where a legal person is established,[179] or the active personality principle extended to habitual residence,[180] are optional. Member States have to inform the European Commission if they establish jurisdiction on such grounds under their *national* rules.[181]

Regarding computer misuse and attacks against information systems, Directive 2013/40/EU[182] provides for harmonized rules on jurisdiction in Article 12 that mirror those in the Directive 2011/93/EU on child sex offences. It first lists the territoriality principle[183] and the active personality principle (limited to nationality of the offender as the connecting factor).[184] In cross-border attacks against information systems, the offender acts in one state against a/several computer system(s) physically located in another state (or several other states). The Directive then clarifies that the application of the subjective territoriality principle means that both the state in which the offender acts and the state where the computer is located have jurisdiction.[185] Like Directive 2011/93/EU it then requires Member States to notify the European Commission if they establish jurisdiction under national law on two grounds, the active personality principle extended to where a legal person is established,[186] or the active personality principle extended to habitual residence.[187]

Finally, the Council Framework Decision[188] on hate speech contains provisions on jurisdiction along the same formula as the other instruments discussed. It stipulates

[178] Art 17(2)(a) "the offence is committed against one of its nationals or a person who is an habitual resident in its territory."

[179] Art 17(2)(b) "the offence is committed for the benefit of a legal person established in its territory."

[180] Art 17(2)(c) "the offender is an habitual resident in its territory."

[181] As discussed in Chapter 5 Germany applies the universality principle to the dissemination of child pornography.

[182] Directive 2013/40/EU (n 76).

[183] Art 12(1)(a) "where the offence has been committed in whole or in part within their territory."

[184] Art 12(1)(b) "where the offence has been committed by one of their nationals, at least in cases where the act is an offence where it was committed."

[185] Art 12(2), see also the equivalent provisions in the UK Computer Misuse Act discussed in Chapter 5.

[186] Art 12(3)(b) "the offence is committed for the benefit of a legal person established in its territory."

[187] Art 12(3)(a) "the offender has his or her habitual residence in its territory."

[188] 2008/913/JHA of 28 November 2008 on combating certain forms and expressions of racism and xenophobia by means of criminal law, OJ L328 (6 December 2008), Art 9.

first that the territoriality principle is mandatory,[189] followed by the active personality principle (extended to corporations),[190] which is optional.[191] It then contains a similar provision to that found in respect of attacks on information systems, which essentially applies the territoriality principle to crimes committed remotely via computer networks by stipulating that the offence was committed both at the place where the offender was physically acting as well as the place where the computer was located.[192] This makes little sense in the context of dissemination and publication offences. While the computer can be a target in attacks on information systems, publication and dissemination offences are different. The provision in the Framework Decision focuses on the place where the server hosting the material is located, which in the age of cloud computing is fortuitous and arbitrary. As we discuss in Chapter 5 EU Member States have grappled with the difficult question of when a publication or dissemination online can be linked to their territory based on residents in that country accessing that content and have developed various tests (such as targeting or the endangering of public peace in that country). The Framework Decision does not even address this difficult and controversial question of access.

In addition to the EU instruments just discussed, there is a 1972 Council of Europe European Convention on the Transfer of Proceedings in Criminal Matters,[193] which has been ratified or acceded to by twenty-five Member States at the time of writing, including Russia and Turkey, but not by some of the large EU Member States such as France, Germany, Hungary, Italy, Poland, nor, for that matter, by the UK. Because of this lack of ratification, it has been described as "close to useless."[194] The other reason for its limited usefulness is of course that it is not backed up by an institutional framework for cross-border cooperation.

The 1972 Convention does not provide jurisdictional rules as such, but essentially provides a procedure allowing for the transfer of proceedings on request, if the requested state for some reasons is in a better position to prosecute. These reasons are set out in Article 8 and comprise:

(1) that the suspect is ordinarily resident in the requested state;
(2) if the suspect is a national or originates from the requested state;
(3) if the suspect is imprisoned in the requested state;
(4) if proceedings against the suspect are underway in the requested state;
(5) if the most important evidence is in the requested state (or it is otherwise more conducive to finding the truth);
(6) if the sentence in the requested state is more likely to lead to the social rehabilitation of the accused;

[189] Art 9(1)(a) "where the conduct has been committed in whole or in part within its territory" and Art 9(3).

[190] Art 9(1)(b) "where the conduct has been committed by one of its nationals" and Art 9(1)(c) " where the conduct has been committed for the benefit of a legal person that has its head office in the territory of that Member State."

[191] Art (3).

[192] Art 9(2)(b) "(b) the conduct involves material hosted on an information system in its territory, whether or not the offender commits the conduct when physically present in its territory."

[193] ETS 073 of 15 May 1972, which entered into force on 30 March 1978.

[194] Patrone (n 2) 218.

(7) if the presence of the suspect can be ensured at proceedings in the requested state;
(8) if the requesting state considers that it could not enforce a sentence against the suspect if convicted.

In the US, conflicts of jurisdiction arise between the Federal and state jurisdictions, as well as between different state jurisdictions, and multiple prosecutions are possible. In practice, prosecutors cooperate and coordinate prosecutions across the Federal–state jurisdictional line and between states. However, in some instances, a prosecutor at a different jurisdictional level may wish to pursue the peculiar interests of that Federal or other state jurisdiction,[195] notwithstanding an earlier acquittal or conviction by a different Federal or state court. The dual sovereignty doctrine allows this.[196]

In summary then, concurrent criminal jurisdiction in internet cases is not unusual and can lead to multiple prosecutions against the same offender in respect of the same criminal offence. This raises the question of whether the principle of *ne bis in idem*, or double jeopardy can prevent this. As is seen in section 5, this principle has very little application in transnational internet cases.

5. *Ne bis in idem*, the rule against double jeopardy

The principle of *ne bis in idem*, or the rule against double jeopardy is the right not to be tried or punished more than once in the same matter. Justice Black in *Green v US* has explained its rationale as follows:

> the State with all its resources and power should not be allowed to make repeated attempts to convict an individual for an alleged offense, thereby subjecting him to embarrassment, expense and ordeal, and compelling him to live in a continuing sense of anxiety and insecurity, as well as enhancing the possibility that even though innocent he may be found guilty.[197]

The principle closely aligns to the idea of *res judicata*, giving a complex and imperfect decision-making process finality. In cross-border internet cases, *ne bis in idem* is of particular significance in cases where there is concurrent jurisdiction between several states leading to the risk that a defendant is tried, convicted, and punished several times.

One of the key issues is what amounts to the *Idem*. This can relate to the offence (no-one is to be punished for the same *offence* twice) or it can relate to the facts (no-one is to be punished for the same *incident* twice). If *Idem* relates to the offence,[198] a person could be tried consecutively for the same conduct, if the offence is defined

[195] Such interests could be that penalties are more severe or that the offence protects different public interests of that sovereign (such as public peace vs private interests of the victim) or that plea-bargaining means that the defendant is convicted of a lesser charge.

[196] Confirmed in the US Supreme Court *Gamble v US* No 17-646, 587 US_(2019).

[197] *Green v United States* 355 US 184, 187–88; 78 S Ct 221 (1957).

[198] As traditionally interpreted under the common law.

differently in different jurisdictions. For example, in a *cyber-phishing*[199] case, different sovereigns may bring successive prosecutions for computer misuse offences, identity theft offences, and fraud in respect of the same incident, and arguably these different offences protect against different types of threats. Thus understood, the principle is inapplicable, if the successive prosecutions relate to different offences. By contrast, if the *Idem* relates to the facts, successive prosecutions could not be brought for the same incident, even if they relate to differently defined offences. If *Idem* is assessed by the facts of the crime, this then raises a further distinction between conduct and results of a crime. For example, if a person infects multiple computers in multiple jurisdictions through one act launching an attack, the question arises whether this is one single crime (focusing on the conduct) or a separate crime for each and every computer or for each and every jurisdiction affected.[200] The scope of the principle is therefore unclear, especially in respect of the *Idem*.[201]

The principle is widely recognized in national constitutional orders,[202] although its scope and implementation varies widely.[203] For example, in Germany the principle does *not* apply to a foreign conviction and punishment, so that German courts can prosecute and convict a person who has already been punished for the same criminal act and the same criminal offence in a foreign court.[204] Given that Germany can assert jurisdiction based on the active personality principle,[205] this can lead to double punishment where a German national has already been punished in the territorial state. However, the German Court must take into account any punishment imposed in the foreign country in sentencing.[206] The English Courts recognize a foreign criminal judgment of competent jurisdiction barring a successive prosecution for the same crime in the English Courts.[207] On the European regional level, the principle is contained in Article 4 of Protocol 7[208] to the European Convention of Human Rights (ECHR),[209] Article 54 of the Schengen

199 The practice of sending out online communications (via email or social media) enticing an individual to reveal personal identifying information and security credentials such as login details and passwords, with a view to stealing a person's identity, operate a false account, make disclosure of confidential information or commit financial fraud.

200 M O'Floinn, "The Concept of Idem in the European Courts: Extracting the Inextricable Link in European Double Jeopardy Law" (2017) 24 Columbia Journal of European Law 75–109, 95.

201 ibid 77ff.

202 In common law countries through the doctrine of autrefois acquit, which applies to successive prosecutions for the same offence: *Connelly v DPP* [1964] AC 1254 HL; the German Constitution provides in Art 103(3): no-one must be punished more than once for the same act on the basis of the general criminal law.

203 DA Principato, "Defining the "Sovereign" in Dual Sovereignty: Does the Protection against Double Jeopardy Bar Successive Prosecutions in National and International Courts?" (2014) 47 Cornell International Law Journal 767–85,770.

204 BVerfGE 3,248, 252; BVerfGE 12,62, 66; BVerfGE 56, 22, 27; BVerfG 75, 1, 15 and ECLI:DE:BVerfG:2007:rk20071204.2bvr003806.

205 See Chapter 5.

206 S 51(3) St GB, ECLI:DE:BVerfG:2007:rk20071204.2bvr003806.

207 *Rex v Roche* (1775) 1 Leach 134; *Rex v Aughet* (1918) 13 Cr App R 101; *Treacy v DPP* [1971] AC 537 HL 562 (Lord Diplock).

208 Not ratified by Germany, the Netherlands, and the UK (as of 11 February 2020) https://www.coe.int/en/web/conventions/full-list/-/conventions/treaty/117/signatures?p_auth=Hp6a9YeB. Accessed on 16 July 2020.

209 Protocol No 7 to the Convention for the Protection of Human Rights and Fundamental Freedoms, ETS 117, Strasbourg 22 November 1984.

Convention,[210] and Article 50 of the Charter[211] of Fundamental Rights of the EU.[212] *Ne sis in idem* is a due process right and protects both the authority of the first sovereign (as a state interest) and the defendant (as a human right).[213]

Like other international human rights treaties,[214] Article 4 *only* applies to prosecutions under the jurisdiction of the *same* state.[215] Thus, the ECHR does not prevent prosecution by multiple sovereigns with competent concurrent jurisdiction for crimes committed online. The principle under international law only provides protection against successive prosecutions by a *single* sovereign, and, as will be seen below so does US Constitutional law.[216] Thus, as an international law principle, it provides little to no protection from multiple prosecutions in multi-jurisdictional cybercrime cases: "one 'act' could lead an individual to face consecutive punishment for consecutive prosecutions and spend a lifetime defending himself from behind bars."[217]

By contrast, the EU Charter, while referring to the ECHR,[218] is autonomous and firmly placed within the EU legal order.[219] Mutual recognition of criminal laws[220] is the basis for Schengen and the Charter[221] and *ne bis in idem* therefore applies across the whole of the Schengen Members or the EU. Schengen[222] and the Charter[223] therefore have created a transnational *ne bis in idem* in their respective area of application. Both instruments prevent a criminal trial in Member State B, if the defendant has already been acquitted or convicted[224] for the same offence in Member State A. Thus, both Schengen and the Charter are examples of a transnational *ne bis in idem*,[225] going beyond the principle as incorporated in traditional international human rights law.

The Schengen Convention contains certain derogations such as that the criminal act took place in Member State B,[226] or where the offence relates to a specific offence

[210] Convention Implementing the Schengen Agreement of 14 June 1985, OJ L239/19 of 22 September 2000.

[211] Applicable to EU law and the implementation of EU law.

[212] OJ C364/1 of 18 December 2000.

[213] M Luchtman, "The ECJ's Recent Case Law on Ne Bis in Idem: Implications for Law Enforcement in a Shared Legal Order" (2018) 55 Common Market Law Review 1717–50, 1721–22.

[214] Art 14(7) of the ICCPR, Principato (n 203) 772; AJ Colangelo, "Double Jeopardy and Multiple Sovereigns: A Jurisdictional Theory" (2009) 86 Washington University Law Review 769–817, 772.

[215] Art 4(1): "No one shall be liable to be tried or punished again in criminal proceedings *under the jurisdiction of the same State* for an offence for which he has already been finally acquitted or convicted in accordance with the law and penal procedure of that State."

[216] Principato (n 203) 773.

[217] O'Floinn (n 200) 78.

[218] Art 52(3).

[219] G Lo Schiavo, "The Principle of Ne Bis in Idem and the Application of Criminal Sanctions: of Scope and Restrictions" (2018) 14 European Constitutional Law Review 644–63, 656–57.

[220] See the discussion in Chapter 6.

[221] Luchtman (n 213) 1742.

[222] Art 54: "A person whose trial has been finally disposed of in one Contracting Party may not be prosecuted in another Contracting Party for the same acts provided that, if a penalty has been imposed, it has been enforced, is actually in the process of being enforced or can no longer be enforced under the laws of the sentencing Contracting Party."

[223] Art 50: "No one shall be liable to be tried or punished again in criminal proceedings for an offence for which he or she has already been finally acquitted or convicted within the Union in accordance with the law."

[224] And is being punished.

[225] Another example is Art 20 of the Rome Statute of the International Criminal Court, with exceptions where the first trial was in a state not providing for an impartial trial, see further Principato (n 203) 779.

[226] Art 55 (1)(a).

protecting national security or other essential interests in Member State B,[227] or where officials of Member State B carried out the criminal acts.[228] Furthermore, Schengen provides that if Member State B prosecutes it should deduct any sentence, which the defendant has received in Member State A.[229] Thus, the principle applies to concurrent jurisdiction with respect to EU law and within the Schengen area.

Differences between the ECHR 7 Protocol, the Charter, and the Schengen Convention additionally exist in respect of the "idem." Whereas the ECHR 7 Protocol and the Charter refer to "offence," Schengen refers to "the same acts." The Court of Justice of the EU (CJEU) has defined the "idem" in its jurisprudence concerning Schengen as a set of concrete factual circumstances involving the same defendant and inextricably linked together in time and space, the existence of which must be demonstrated in order to secure a conviction or institute criminal proceedings. In brief, in order to fall under the principle the two proceedings must relate to identical facts.[230] The CJEU has held that Article 50 of the Charter prohibits duplication of proceedings and punishments for the "same acts and against the same person."[231] Thus, it has interpreted the word "offence" in the Charter widely, in line with the Schengen Convention.[232]

However, Charter rights, including Article 50, are subject to limitations, which according to the proportionality test in Article 52(1) must be provided for by law and respect the essence of the right. Such limitations must be necessary and genuinely meet general interest objectives of the EU or the need to protect the freedoms and rights of others.[233] This leads to further uncertainties regarding the principle in multi-state cybercrime prosecutions within the Schengen area.

In the US, the principle of *ne bis in idem* exists in the form of the common law rule against *double jeopardy*, which was incorporated in the Fifth Amendment to the US Constitution: "nor shall any person be subject for the same offense to be twice put in jeopardy of life or limb." Double jeopardy only applies if the first court had jurisdiction to try the matter.[234] In a long line of cases the double jeopardy prohibition has been restricted to apply only to prosecutions and convictions by courts of the *same* jurisdiction, under the so-called dual sovereignty doctrine.[235] The syllogism applied

[227] Art 55(1)(b) and (2).

[228] Art 55(1)(c).

[229] Art 56.

[230] Case C-436/04 *Van Esbroeck*, EU:C:2006:165, paras 36, 38 (Schengen); Case C-367/05 *Kraaijenbrink*, EU:C:2007:444, para 36 (Schengen); Case C-524/15 *Menci* ECLI:EU:C:2018:197, para 35 (Charter); Case C-537/16 *Garlsson Real Estate and Others* ECLI:EU:C:2018:193, para 37.

[231] Case C-596/16 *Di Puma* ECLI:EU:C:2018:192, para 38; Case C-537/16 *Garlsson Real Estate and Others* ECLI:EU:C:2018:193, para 27; Case C-524/15 *Menci* ECLI:EU:C:2018:197, para 25; Case C-489/10 *Bonda* EU:C:2012:319, para 37; C-617/10 *Åkerberg Fransson* EU:C:2013:105, para 35.

[232] But even within the EU legal order many questions still exist about the scope of the principle, see O'Floinn (n 200) 83ff.

[233] Art 52(1); Case C-524/15 *Menci* ECLI:EU:C:2018:197, paras 41–46; Case C-537/16 *Garlsson Real Estate and Others* ECLI:EU:C:2018:193, paras 43–48; see also Lo Schiavo (n 219) 659 further on the proportionality test.

[234] *Grafton v US* 206 US 333, 345 (1907).

[235] *Fox v Ohio* 5 How 410 (1847); *Moore v Illinois* 14 How 13, 17 (1852); *US v Lanza* 260 US 377, 382; 43 S Ct 141 (1922); *Abbate v US* 359 US 187, 195; 79 S Ct 666 (1959); *Bartkus v People of State of Illinois* 359 US 121; 79 S Ct 676 (1959); *US v Wheeler* 435 US 313 (1978); *Heath v Alabama* 474 US 82, 92; 106 S Ct 433 (1985); *Gamble v US* No 17-646, 587 US_(2019) (US Supreme Court).

by the US courts is that different jurisdictions (as sovereigns) have their own criminal offences, such that convicting the offender under separate criminal laws does not render the person criminally liable under the same *offence*.[236] The courts in the US have relied on the wording of the Fifth Amendment, which is predicated on the *offence* being the same,[237] not the *conduct* being the same. Thus, *double jeopardy* under US Constitutional Law does not exclude successive prosecutions in courts belonging to different sovereigns, even if the first court has acquitted the defendant.[238] Two sovereigns are different if they derive their authority from distinct sources of power.[239]

Therefore double jeopardy does not apply to multiple, successive convictions by courts of different states,[240] or dual convictions by a state court and a Federal court,[241] even if these convictions are based on the same conduct, the same facts, and all the elements required for a conviction are the same under the offences under the two legal systems.[242] A good illustration is the 2019 US Supreme Court case of *Gamble v US* where Mr Gamble pleaded guilty to an offence under Alabama state law of being in possession of a firearm as a person previously convicted of a crime of violence. Federal prosecutors regarded the sentence as too lenient and commenced a parallel prosecution for the Federal law offence of possession of a firearm by a convicted felon, to which Gamble pleaded guilty and another three years were added to his prison sentence, even though both successive convictions related to the same incident. The majority of the US Supreme Court in *Gamble v US* refused to overturn the longstanding dual sovereignty doctrine, with two judges dissenting.[243] The US Supreme Court affirmed 170 years of precedent.[244] The dual sovereignty doctrine refers back to the notion that a crime can constitute an offence against two sovereigns, which gives each sovereign an independent right to vindicate.[245] In her dissent, Justice Ginsburg argues that the dual sovereignty doctrine should be abandoned, as the powers of both the states and the Federal state have their origin in the people.[246] She argued that the incorporation of the US Constitution in State law, and the expansion of Federal criminal law in recent years causing greater overlap between Federal and state law warrants this.[247] Justice Gorsuch argued that the premise underlying the dual sovereignty doctrine was wrong, that where there were two laws it did not necessarily mean that there were two offences.[248] In his Opinion, "So if two laws demand proof of the same facts to secure a conviction, they constitute a single offense under our Constitution and a second trial is forbidden."[249] Despite these two powerful dissenting opinions, the dual

[236] *Heath* (n 235).
[237] *Gamble* (n 235) 3–5 (Alito J).
[238] *Bartkus* (n 235).
[239] *Heath* (n 235) 82, 88; 106 S Ct 433 (1985); Principato (n 203) 774.
[240] *Heath* (n 235) 82, 87–93; 106 S Ct 433 (1985).
[241] *Gamble v US* No 17-646, 587 US (2019) (Alito J).
[242] State/State or Federal/State.
[243] Justices Ginsburg and Gorsuch.
[244] *Gamble* 2 (Alito J); 14, 17 (Thomas J).
[245] *Gamble* 5, 8 (Alito J).
[246] *Gamble* 3–4 (Ginsburg J dissenting); 22 (Gorsuch J dissenting).
[247] Paras 9–10; para 23.
[248] Gamble 4 (Gorsuch J dissenting).
[249] Para 5.

sovereignty doctrine remains part of US law on double jeopardy, such that the same criminal conduct can give rise to a state and a Federal conviction.

It equally applies to conflicts of jurisdiction between the US and a foreign country.[250] In *Studabaker* the 6th Circuit Court of Appeals held that the conviction of the defendant was not infringing the principle of double jeopardy, even though the defendant had previously been convicted in England and had served time in prison there.[251] The Court applied the dual sovereignty doctrine internationally and since England and the US were different sovereigns, the English conviction in respect of the same serious criminal conduct (internet access of child abuse content, internet grooming and enticing a minor to travel with the intent to engage in criminal sexual activity) did not bar a subsequent second conviction in the US.[252] The 6th Circuit Court held that it was sufficient that the District Court had acknowledged the fact that the defendant had served time in prison in a foreign country when applying the sentencing guidelines.[253] Thus, he could be prosecuted and sentenced again for the same offences after he was deported from England. The Court imposed a further eleven years on Studabaker who had served four and a half years in an English prison. Another example of consecutive prosecutions for hacking in Romania and subsequently in the US is the extradition of "Guccifer" who had revealed sensitive data about politicians in Romania and the US after hacking their personal email and social media accounts.[254]

In the context of multi-jurisdictional cybercrime, the scope of *ne bis in idem* or double jeopardy is not clear and the principle has limited application. Arguments for applying the principle transnationally are due process and fairness considerations from the perspective of the defendant, and accepting the authority of the first court ensuring the finality of court decisions (*res judicata*).[255] However, there may be good reasons to restrict the scope of the principle in the transnational context. First, different legal cultures have very different penalties and sanctions for the same criminal offence. Secondly, courts in different jurisdictions have different evidence adduced to them, including later new evidence or information concerning the offender's previous offending and likelihood to offend again, his or her prospects of rehabilitation or danger to society. Furthermore, different societies and cultures have different perceptions about the seriousness of a particular type of offending. Finally, perceptions as to the reliability and quality of legal proceedings in terms of independence and impartiality of the judiciary and due process may vary between different countries. For these reasons, there is inevitably a local factor pertaining to criminal punishments with the consequence that prosecution, conviction, and punishment, or acquittal of an offender in State A may not completely satisfy the demand for retribution for the same criminal conduct in State B. These open questions surrounding the exact scope

[250] *US v Guzman* 85 F 3d 823, 826 (1st Cir 1996); *US v Riviere* 924 F 2d 1289, 1301–02 (3d Cir 1991); *US v Jeong* 624 F 3d 706, 712 (5th Cir 2010); *US v Richardson* 580 F 2d 946, 947 (9th Cir 1978); *US v Duarte-Acero*, 208 F 3d 1282, 1286–87 (11th Cir 2000); Principato (n 203) 771.

[251] *US v Studabaker* 578 F 3d 423.

[252] Para 430.

[253] Paras 431–32.

[254] https://www.reuters.com/article/us-usa-cyber-guccifer-idUSKCN0W61TX and https://www.justice.gov/usao-edva/pr/romanian-hacker-guccifer-pleads-guilty-computer-hacking-crimes. Accessed on 16 July 2020.

[255] Principato (n 203) 769.

of the *ne bis in idem* principle in transnational cases mean that there is even greater need for transborder cooperation.[256] In the context of EU criminal and administrative regulation Luchtman argues that the guarantee of *ne bis in idem* and its limitations are a "powerful instrument for enforcement integration," and reflective of a transnational legal order.[257] In the EU there is a recognition that the principle of *ne bis in idem* can be restricted, provided this is necessary and subject to a proportionality analysis and a minimization of negative effects.[258] As Lo Schiavo suggests, national authorities must "weigh carefully the scope of duplication of proceedings and penalties in the law."[259]

As O'Floinn has pointed out, the "sameness" criterion (*idem*), whether that relates to the same offence or the same facts, is insufficient to solve the problem of adequate punishment in cross-border offences. The binary choice of whether or not a second prosecution can go ahead does not lead to satisfactory outcomes.[260] The way forward should be the development of principles, which reflect the underlying interests more clearly with less emphasis on sovereignty and more emphasis on coordination between different legal orders.

National rules should provide for a more holistic approach whereby the second court needs to carefully weigh fairness to the defendant against the interests of justice taking into account local factors. Furthermore, greater transnational cooperation should minimize any duplication of fact-finding, and ensure that any punishment resulting from the first set of criminal proceedings are deducted from the punishment imposed by the second set of criminal proceedings.[261] If the first trial leads to an acquittal, the second set of proceedings should be halted, unless there are good reasons to doubt the fact-finding process of the first trial, or the offences prosecuted are substantially different, and the second, subsequent prosecution is in the interests of justice.

6. Conclusion

The international law rules on jurisdiction provide only a loose framework for reigning in jurisdictional competence. In transnational cybercrime cases, even the strict application of the territoriality principle can lead to no state prosecuting a crime (negative conflict of jurisdiction) or multiple prosecutions (positive conflict of jurisdiction). In addition, extraterritorial principles for the assumption of jurisdiction are recognized under international law. As a consequence, jurisdictional concurrency is entrenched

[256] Luchtman (n 213)1741.
[257] ibid.
[258] Lo Schiavo (n 219) 659–60.
[259] ibid 660.
[260] O'Floinn (n 200) 101, who states in the context of the EU legal order that the "problems arise primarily because all double jeopardy answers are being sought from one idem rabbit hole and the concept of idem in Article 50 of the Charter, Article 54 CISA, and A4P7 is being asked to bear a textual load for which none of these provisions were designed."
[261] ECtHR *A and B v Norway*, Applications 24130/11 and 29758/11, Judgment of 15 November 2016, https://hudoc.echr.coe.int/eng#{%22itemid%22:[%22001-168972%22]}, accessed on 16/7/2020; Case C-524/15 *Menci* ECLI:EU:C:2018:197, paras 53, 55; Case C-537/16 *Garlsson Real Estate and Others* ECLI:EU:C:2018:193, paras 55–56.

as a phenomenon in public international law, and in order to address the issue certain factors have been put forward at the national and international levels to determine which state should prosecute and which courts should be competent. Because of the connection between criminal law and sovereignty, it is unlikely that a uniform coherent international system of jurisdiction is developed in the short term. The jurisdictional challenge has two distinct aspects, namely, first, rules about states' competence (jurisdiction in the narrower sense) and, second, rules on international coordination and cooperation in order to deal with jurisdictional overlap and multi-state prosecutions. Multi-state prosecutions of the same defendant in respect of the same criminal offence raise serious questions about due process and fairness to defendants, but also questions about the integrity of the legal order and the authority of the courts. The principle of *ne bis in idem* and *double jeopardy* has no application in transnational cybercrime cases, with the exception of its application within the Schengen area or its application by the English common law courts. Positive and negative conflicts of jurisdiction, and the potential of multiple prosecutions of defendants for the same offence, urgently call for greater international cooperation between states and coordination rules between different legal orders. However, the development of coordination rules in respect of national criminal jurisdiction is very much at its infancy stage. None of the proposals has reached the status of customary international law and much more work needs to be done to coordinate jurisdictional claims. The development of rules about states' competence (jurisdiction in the narrower sense) is even more difficult and hence, even less developed and clashes with states' sovereignty claims. In criminal cases there exists no framework of agreed rules to determine which state's courts have jurisdiction over a crime in case of a positive or negative conflict. The area of prosecution in cross-border cybercrime cases is a space where the factual constellation (who is willing to prosecute and who can apprehend the offender) and the power position and negotiation between states largely determine the outcome. However, efforts such as the institutional coordination through Eurojust improve the situation in the interests of justice. Hopefully therefore the UK will continue its participation in Eurojust after its withdrawal from the EU.

5

Jurisdiction of the Criminal Courts in Cybercrime Cases in Germany and England

This chapter[1] compares and contrasts the domestic rules on jurisdiction of the criminal courts in Germany and England[2] and the applicability of the respective criminal law in each country. As has been seen in Chapter 4, many cybercrimes are transnational in the sense that the criminal conduct and/or its results may be effected in several countries simultaneously. Given the transnational character of much cybercrime, and the fact that the law on the jurisdiction of the criminal courts does not pinpoint a single court as having competence to the exclusion of other national courts, cybercrime harbours a great potential for jurisdictional conflicts. This makes an examination and comparison of the rules on jurisdiction more pertinent.

In public law, the questions of applicable law and competence of the courts merge under the heading of jurisdiction for the simple reason that national courts only apply the relevant national law, with the exception of a conflicts of law situation in which the principle of dual criminality arises. As discussed in this chapter, in some instances where the active or passive personality principle are the basis for jurisdiction, the court has to assess whether conduct is a criminal offence in the foreign place where it was committed and this leads a court to examine that foreign law. The question of jurisdiction arises not only in the context of a criminal prosecution but also in the context of extradition of a fugitive offender, where the requesting state has to show that it has jurisdiction.[3] Depending on the extradition rules in question, a showing of dual criminality is also required in this situation.[4]

Since jurisdiction in criminal prosecutions is concerned with the link between the criminality and the territory (or, in the UK, "keeping the Queen's Peace"[5]), it by necessity focuses on the *actus reus* and, to a lesser extent on the *mens rea* of the criminal offence and thus the constituent elements of the criminal offence. It has been argued that criminal jurisdiction should therefore be considered to be part of the criminal law rather than criminal procedure.[6] In the words of Michael Hirst, "misconduct committed outside the realm cannot ordinarily amount to the *actus reus* of an offence

[1] Chapter 4 has discussed the principles of international law in respect of criminal jurisdiction.
[2] England and Wales.
[3] M Hirst, *Jurisdiction and the Ambit of Criminal Law* (Oxford University Press 2003) 111.
[4] Extradition is not further discussed in this book.
[5] *R v C* [2007] Crim LR 235 (CA) 236.
[6] Hirst (n 3) 2–3.

Internet Jurisdiction. Julia Hörnle, Oxford University Press (2021). © Julia Hörnle.
DOI: 10.1093/oso/9780198806929.001.0001

under English law."[7] German law, likewise, places the rules on the applicability of German criminal law within the substantive law of the Criminal Code, not the criminal procedure rules.[8] Since the territoriality principle links criminal acts and results with the territory, jurisdiction depends on the definition of the criminal offence. This in turn means that lawmakers (parliament, or in common law countries, the courts) control the reach of a country's criminal law, be that territorial or extraterritorial. Under the English common law there is a presumption that Parliament did not intend to confer extraterritorial reach of criminal law, unless it does so *explicitly*, but the doctrine of Parliamentary sovereignty means that Parliament may confer extraterritorial reach on a statute.[9] By contrast, in Germany, the legislature includes relevant extraterritorial provisions in the consolidated Criminal Codes.[10]

As has been seen in Chapter 2 claims of jurisdiction rely on connection factors to a state's territory (and the people living on this territory)—the looser this connection is, the more states are potentially competent, which in turn leads to more jurisdictional conflicts, including the negative consequences associated with such conflicts, such as interference with the affairs of another state, legal uncertainty and the risk of double jeopardy[11] for the accused. These negative consequences can flow from a wide interpretation of the territoriality principle or from the wide application of extraterritorial jurisdiction. Because of the transnational nature of cybercrime these negative consequences are a problem in the context of cybercrime jurisdiction. Conversely, however, a narrow interpretation of the territoriality principle in the cybercrime context may mean that offenders escape justice as they target their crimes remotely from a place where they are unlikely to be prosecuted or by moving between countries.[12]

1. Jurisdiction under German criminal law

1.1 Introduction

German criminal law applies the territoriality principle as the main basis for jurisdiction, but this is only the starting point for the assessment of the jurisdictional competence of the criminal courts. German criminal law also applies the active and passive personality principle, the representative principle, and the universality principle for particular crimes and in particular circumstances. Because of these broad grounds for applying German law extraterritorially to crimes committed on foreign territory, it has been argued that German law should be reformed to limit jurisdictional competences further.[13]

[7] ibid 3.

[8] Other than the rules on international criminal law, they are contained in the Criminal Code (Strafgesetzbuch, StGB); see also T Rotsch, "Der Handlungsort iSd s 9 Abs 1 StGB" (2010) 5 (3) Zeitschrift für Internationale Strafrechtsdogmatik 168–74, 168.

[9] *Treacy v DPP* [1971] AC 537 (CA) 551.

[10] The Criminal Code (StGB) and the Code of International Criminal Law (Völkerstrafgesetzbuch, VStGB).

[11] See also Chapter 4.

[12] See the discussion in Chapters 2 and 4.

[13] *Lackner/Kühl Strafgesetzbuch Kommentar* (29th edn, CH Beck 2018) Vor ss 3–7 para 1.

1.2 Territoriality principle as the main basis for jurisdiction

Jurisdiction in criminal matters is regulated in ss 3–9 of the German Criminal Code (Strafgesetzbuch, StGB). The territoriality principle in s 3 ("German criminal law applies to criminal acts committed on national territory"[14]) is both the main and the starting principle for German conflicts of law in criminal law,[15] but it is supplemented by numerous other principles.[16] Indeed there are so many exceptions to the territoriality principle in German criminal law that Kai Ambos questions whether it can be called the "main" principle.[17] However, some offences provide specifically that the crime has to be committed in Germany itself. An example for this is s 86(1) No 1 StGB, which makes it a criminal offence to disseminate insignia of prohibited[18] associations or parties (such as the swastika) or to use them publicly in publications distributed by the offender or in a public assembly such insignia *within Germany*. This raises the question whether an offender who carries out these acts through internet communications such as email, websites, or social media from abroad could be prosecuted in Germany.[19]

The territoriality principle applies regardless of the nationality of either the defendant or the victim. Under German law the principle of legality means that prosecution authorities have no discretion whether to prosecute or not—if the offence has been committed on the territory of Germany they have to prosecute.[20] However, this principle has been relaxed for crimes committed at a distance, from abroad, and for accessory liability, where the main crime was committed abroad.[21] Thus, where jurisdiction is based on *extraterritorial* grounds such as the active or passive personality principle,[22] the German prosecution authorities have discretion whether to pursue a prosecution.[23]

Application of the territoriality principle raises the question of when a crime is considered to have been committed on German territory. German law (like English law, as we will see) had to grapple with the complex question of the precise place where online crimes have been committed and localization of the criminal act in internet cases.[24]

Determination of the place where the offender physically was acting when carrying out the relevant acts may cause evidential issues. But the location of the offender as such is not difficult to determine on a conceptual level (even in the twenty-first century a person can only be physically in one place at any one time). By contrast,

[14] "Das deutsche Strafrecht gilt für Taten, die im Inland begangen werden" (Translation by the author).

[15] E Hilgendorf, "Die Neuen Medien und das Strafrecht" (2001) 113(4) Zeitschrift für die gesamte Strafrechtswissenschaft 650–80, 660.

[16] Eser in *Schönke/Schröder StGB Commentary* s 9 para 7a (29th edn, C.H. Beck 2014); K Ambos, *Internationales Strafrecht* (5th edn, C.H. Beck 2018) 32.

[17] ibid.

[18] Further detailed in s 86(1) StGB ("illegal propaganda").

[19] F Zimmermann, "NS Propaganda im Internet" (11/2015) HRRS 441–48, 442.—discussed further later.

[20] ibid para 8.

[21] *Lackner/Kühl Strafgesetzbuch Kommentar* (n 13) s 9 para 7; s 153c I No 1, II StPO.

[22] Discussed further later.

[23] Ambos (n 16) 47.

[24] Zimmermann (n 19) 441.

pinpointing the consequences and results of an act to a particular territory may be more ambiguous, and controversial, and of course, criminal results may occur in several locations at the same time. Thus, the application of the territorial principle is most uncertain where the *results of the criminal offence* are used to create the connection to the territory.[25] Moreover, sometimes, depending on the definition of the criminal offence, it may also be difficult to distinguish between the criminal act and the criminal result—for example, is *publication* a criminal act or a criminal result?[26] In a 2014 case the German Supreme Court[27] held[28] that for offences concerning internet publications or online distribution the place of the commission of the offence is solely the place where the offender was physically located when carrying out the crime.

The German Criminal Code states expressly that a criminal offence is committed at each place where the offender has acted (or, for crimes committed by omission, should have acted) or where the criminal result or consequence (the German word is "Erfolg"), as stated in the offence,[29] has occurred, or would have occurred as envisaged by the offender.[30] For omissions it is particularly difficult to define the geographical location of where the offender *should* have acted and there may be more than one location.[31]

This principle is the so-called ubiquity principle, which means that for the purposes of jurisdiction based on the territoriality principle, a single crime may be committed in several locations.[32] German law therefore makes a distinction between the place where the defendant acted, and the place where the criminal results occurred.

It has been argued in the literature that, if the place of the commission of the offence was expanded to where the offender acted virtually and remotely through the use of technology, this would blur the difference between the place of the commission of the offence ("Handlungsort") and the place of the criminal result ("Erfolgsort").[33] However, it should be noted that this argument ignores the possibility of a scenario where the offender acts at a distance through technological means to achieve a result in a third place—for example, where the offender is physically situated in country A, manipulates a computer in country B, in order to achieve a criminal result in country C.[34] Here the place of the criminal act would be country A and the place of the result would be country C, but what about country B?

It should be considered whether it can be said that the offender in this scenario in fact acted virtually in country B. However, if country B was merely the place where content was uploaded to a server for making the content available—for offences

[25] Eser (n 16) s 3 para 1.

[26] Hilgendorf (n 15) 650–80.

[27] Bundesgerichtshof, BGH.

[28] BGH 3 StR 88/14, Decision of 19 August 2014.

[29] *Lackner/Kühl Strafgesetzbuch Kommentar* (n 13) s 9 para 2, criminal result as defined in the offence: BGHSt 44, 52; 51, 29, 31.

[30] S 9(1) StGB.

[31] Rotsch (n 8) 171: here a distinction can be made between the place where the offender is physically located and the place where he or she should have been in order to prevent the criminal result.

[32] *Lackner/Kühl Strafgesetzbuch Kommentar* (n 13) s 9 para 1; Rotsch (n 8) 170; Hilgendorf (n 15) 660.

[33] Zimmermann (n 19) 444.

[34] eg uploading and processing in order to make available illegal content targeted at country C, where that content is being accessed and used.

concerned with publication and dissemination of illegal content—arguably country B may be fortuitous, as it is merely the place of processing and storing the information (as in cloud computing) and therefore arguably this is not a place where the offender acted within the meaning of s 9(1) StGB. However, in a computer misuse scenario the intermediate computer in country B may be a relevant connecting factor. For example, if the offender physically situated in country A, unlawfully accesses a computer in country B, in order to obtain access to information, which is then used to commit a fraud in country C, it may be more difficult to argue that the offender did not act in country B (since unauthorized access to a computer in country B can be classified as the criminal result).

Thus, if the "Erfolg" of a criminal offence can be located on German territory, the offender can be prosecuted under German law. If the result can be divided into different parts, it is sufficient that one part has occurred in Germany,[35] for the whole offence being committed in Germany.[36]

However, what amounts to the criminal result for different types of criminal offences is controversial among German scholars. In many internet publication cases it is difficult to distinguish between the criminal conduct and the result. Ulrich Sieber posited in 1999 that a distinction should be made between the result that immediately flows from the conduct concerned, and defined this new concept as "Tathandlungserfolg," for example, where the accused actively pushed a publication towards German users. He thus distinguished between "push" technologies (such as email) where the recipient stays passive in receiving the unlawful content and "pull" technologies (such as websites) where the recipient has to actively seek out the unlawful content.[37] The distinction between "push" and "pull" technologies, however, is no longer accurate twenty years later.[38] But the fundamental thought of making a distinction between internet publications that are targeted to a specific jurisdiction and those that are not continues to be relevant.

According to German criminal law theory, a distinction is made between different types of criminal offences. The first category is criminal action leading to a particular result ("Erfolgsdelikt"), such as murder or manslaughter leading to the death of a human being. The second category is criminal action that poses a threat to certain protected interests in a very concrete and identifiable manner, for example, in the way dangerous driving can endanger human health and property ("Konkretes Gefährdungsdelikt"). The third category is called potential endangering of an identifiable protected interest, even though this interest may be intangible, such as public order and public peace, which can be jeopardized by hate speech ("abstrakt-konkretes Gefährdungsdelikt").[39] The fourth category are criminal actions that pose a threat to protected interests that are difficult to identify and difficult to separate from the criminal action itself ("abstraktes Gefährdungsdelikt"). This fourth category concerns

[35] *Lackner/Kühl Strafgesetzbuch Kommentar* (n 13) s 9 para 2.

[36] ibid para 4.

[37] U Sieber, "Internationales Strafrecht im Internet- Das Territorialitätsprinzip" (1999) 52 (29) Neue Juristische Wochenschrift 2065–73, 2072.

[38] As in practice this technological distinction is now blurred, as web 2.0 applications consist of a mixture of "push" and "pull" technologies and are usually account based.

[39] This category has been criticized by Hilgendorf (n 15) 672.

criminal actions that are prohibited as such without reference to any particular consequence. For such crimes there would be no jurisdiction under German law unless the offender has acted in Germany.[40]

The controversy is whether for the third category of criminal offences it is sufficient that the threat was manifested in Germany, in such a manner that the territoriality principle applies to the offence.[41] One argument is that the noun "Erfolg" captures *all* consequences of a criminal action, such that, if a threat is potentially manifested on German territory, this would be sufficient for the territoriality principle to apply. In particular, it has been argued that every consequence that is part of the definition of the offence and that has been effected domestically on German territory should be sufficient to justify the application of German criminal law under the territoriality principle.[42] Thus, under this interpretation, for example, the offence of making available pornography without age-verification from abroad could be prosecuted under German law, unless the person responsible uses geo-blocking or similar technology to prevent access by German users.[43]

Under this interpretation, an offence has therefore been committed in Germany if (1) the offender was carrying out the relevant action on German territory or (2) if either the criminal result *or the threat* has manifested on German territory. An example for this interpretation is the decision by the German Federal Criminal Court, which held in the *Töben* case in 2002 that the defendant could be criminally prosecuted under para 130 for disseminating and making available Holocaust denial materials by way of a website operated from and hosted in Australia. The Court classified the Holocaust denial offence as a third category offence ("abstrakt-konkretes Gefährdungsdelikt"): the definition of the offence includes the requirement that the offence has to be carried out "in a way which is liable to disturb the *public peace*."[44] It therefore held that the result of this offence was the identifiable threat of endangering public order in Germany and that this threat would be effected by the website *in Germany*. The Court required a particular connecting factor to German territory,[45] but stopped short of requiring the actual targeting of Germany by the offender.[46]

In a more recent case of 2014, a German person travelled to the Czech Republic and while physically situated there made available propaganda entitled "Arian Music Movement," including the depiction of swastikas, by uploading this content on social media. The content was active for at least three months and the prosecution could show that it had been downloaded at least twice from Germany.[47] The question before the German Supreme Court was whether the German courts are competent to judge the defendant according to s 86(1) No 1 StGB, which, as mentioned, makes it

[40] Hilgendorf (n 15) 662–63.

[41] Eser (n 16) s 9 para 7a.

[42] "Tathandlungserfolg" Sieber (n 37) 2065–73 and T Hörnle, "Verbreitung der Auschwitzlüge im Internet" (2001) Neue Zeitschrift für Strafrecht 306–11.

[43] Disagreeing: *Lackner/Kühl Strafgesetzbuch Kommentar* (n 13) s 9 para 5.

[44] S 130(1) StGB.

[45] It is not clear whether these connecting factors relate to the offender's actions or to the consequences resulting from the offender's actions. Some authors have suggested that it should be the former (the offender's actions) see Eser (n 16) s 9 para 7a.

[46] BGH 12.12.2000-1StR 184/00, BGHSt 46, 212 (221).

[47] BGH 3 StR 88/14, Decision of 19 August 2014.

a criminal offence to disseminate insignia of prohibited associations or parties (such as the swastika) or to use publicly in publications distributed by the offender or in a public assembly such insignia *within Germany*. The Court held that this offence falls into the fourth category of offences ("abstraktes Gefährdungsdelikt") and that it was impossible to pinpoint a criminal result. It found that a criminal result has to be separable from the criminal action and has to lead to a discernible change—here no such result was part of the *actus reus* of the offence. Therefore, it was not possible to rely on s 9(1) to justify jurisdiction of the German courts purely on the ground of the location of a criminal result.[48]

In cases where a foreign person makes available illegal contents that are accessed in Germany it may be difficult to identify what this particular connecting factor to Germany is. In particular, the question arises whether the connecting factor relates to the content itself (as was the case in *Töben* where the Court argued that the Holocaust denial had an obvious link to German history) or whether it relates to the targeting of potential recipients of the content (such as targeting of German resident through factors such as language, payment means, advertising, search ranking, or the use of a .de domain name).[49] Targeting as a suitable limitation factor has also been discussed by German scholars.[50]

German scholars have suggested the following limitations[51] to prevent jurisdictional overreach:[52] (1) limiting the applicability of German criminal law to cases where the offender is German (active personality principle) or where extradition is possible,[53] (2) the requirement of dual criminality in transnational internet crimes,[54] and (3) the development of principles for allocating competences between states in transnational internet cases.[55]

However, a number of scholars in Germany have argued that the word "Erfolg" should be interpreted narrowly so that the territoriality principle only serves to justify jurisdiction if there is a *result* in Germany, but that an abstract threat being potentially manifested in Germany should not be sufficient to invoke the territoriality principle, regardless of the action being targeted at Germany.[56]

For accessory liability, the crime is committed at the place where the crime has been committed as well as at the place where the accessory acted (or in case of an omission should have acted) or where the accessory envisaged the criminal act to be committed.[57] Finally, if the accessory has acted in Germany, contributing to what is a criminal offence under German law, but which was committed abroad, then he or she may be prosecuted under German law, *even if* the act is not a crime in the place

[48] Zimmermann (n 19) 442–43.
[49] See further the discussion of targeting in Chapter 13.
[50] Hilgendorf (n 15) 670 "territorial Spezifizierung der Tat."
[51] Eser (n 16) s 9 para 8.
[52] As to the need for preventing jurisdictional overreach see Hilgendorf (n 15) 661.
[53] ibid 663.
[54] M Kienle, *Internationales Strafrecht und Straftaten im Internet* (Hartung-Gorre 1998) 173.
[55] L Wörner, "Einseitiges Strafanwendungsrecht und Entgrenztes Internet?" (2012) Zeitschrift für Internationale Strafrechtsdogmatik 458–65, 464.
[56] Eser (n 16) s 9 para 7a; *Lackner/Kühl Strafgesetzbuch Kommentar* (n 13) s 9 para 2.
[57] S 9(2) 1st Sentence StGB; *Lackner/Kühl Strafgesetzbuch Kommentar* (n 13) s 9 para 3.

where it has been committed.[58] By focusing on the place of commission of the criminal act and the accessory act this leads to a multiplication of jurisdictional connecting factors.[59]

The second conflict of law principle in German criminal law is derived from the territoriality principle, but independent from it. This is the principle that German criminal law applies on board of ships and aircraft under a German flag, before they have landed and opened their doors and regardless whether the aircraft or ship is in private or state ownership ("German criminal law applies, without prejudice to the law of the place of commission, for criminal acts, committed on board a ship or an aircraft, which are entitled to carry the German flag or other signifier of nationality"[60]). This is different from the territoriality principle since the application of German law and German jurisdiction are not exclusive and can come into conflict with the law of the place where the ship or aircraft is physically located (such as foreign territorial waters, a foreign port, or a foreign airport).[61] Furthermore, the German prosecution authorities have discretion whether to prosecute or not if jurisdiction is solely based on s 4.[62]

1.3 Protecting particular German interests, frequently combined with the active and passive personality principle for a limited number of specified offences (protective principle)

However, German law is extraterritorially applicable to certain criminal offences, which are committed outside German territory but that are directed against specific German interests ("Schutzgüter"), which are specifically listed in s 5 by reference to the relevant offences in the German Criminal Code (StGB). This is an emanation of the protective principle under international law. These interests either arise because of the position of the defendant committing the crime that imposes a duty of loyalty to German interests, or because of the crime being targeted against German state interests. Sometimes a prosecution in Germany is only possible if, additionally, the active or, more rarely, the passive personality principle apply, in addition to the specific German interests being engaged. However, significantly, these examples of the active and passive personality principle are *not* subject to the dual criminality principle and therefore manifest significant mistrust towards the legal order in the place of commission of the criminal offence and may raise questions as to their conformity with public international law, unless based on an international treaty.[63]

In the following, this rather disparate category of "German interests" is further explained by some examples.

[58] S 9(2) 2nd Sentence StGB; *Lackner/Kühl Strafgesetzbuch Kommentar* (n 13) s 9 para 3; cf the different approach of English law discussed below.

[59] Rotsch (n 8) 170.

[60] S 4 StGB translated by the author: "Das deutsche Strafrecht gilt, unabhängig vom Recht des Tatorts, für Taten, die auf einem Schiff oder in einem Luftfahrzeug begangen werden, das berechtigt ist, die Bundesflagge oder das Staatszugehörigkeitszeichen der Bundesrepublik Deutschland zu führen."

[61] Eser (n 16) s 4 paras 4, 7.; Ambos (n 16)38.

[62] ibid para 7.

[63] Ambos (n 16) 52.

These interests can be classified into three categories: (1) national state interests[64] such as protecting German national security and defence interests, (2) the public interest (crimes committed by German officials-who are not necessarily German nationals- abroad),[65] and (3) individual interests[66] (infringing trade secrets of German enterprises; certain sexual offences if the offender (and the victim in some cases) is German; abortion if the offender is both German and is permanently resident in Germany; trade in organs if the offender is German).[67]

Thus, for some limited and specific offences, individual interests are protected by applying the active personality principle focusing on the nationality of the offender to ensure these individual interests can be prosecuted in Germany based on the passive or active personality principle, in addition to and potentially conflicting with, the jurisdiction of the state at the place where these criminal acts were committed. The idea is that this extraterritoriality provides an additional layer of protection for these specific interests, as local territorial prosecution may be unlikely, in order to avoid gaps in protection of vital interests through criminalization.

In subsections 1.3.1–1.3.3, these three categories of interests, namely national state interests, public interests, and individual interests, are examined in more detail.

1.3.1 National state interests

In turn, the crimes concerning the first category, namely national state interests, fall into two subcategories—those that can be prosecuted in Germany, regardless of the nationality of the offender or the victim, and those that can be prosecuted in Germany only if the active or passive personality principle applies.

As to those that can be prosecuted in Germany regardless of the nationality of the offender, they include serious national security offences,[68] such as the use of force or threatening the use of force to endanger the existence or territorial integrity of the Federal Republic of Germany or one of its constituent Länder, or threatening the Constitutional order or preparing treason.[69] Likewise, defendants committing offences relating to state secrets and espionage, which entail the risk of a serious disadvantage for external security of the German Federal Republic, can be prosecuted in Germany, even if the offence is entirely committed abroad and the offender is not German.[70] It also includes the offence of evading national service obligations (presumably in the German or international forces) through inflicting an injury on oneself or another[71] and military sabotage[72] and military espionage.[73] In addition to these specific national security offences it also includes offences protecting against perverting the course of justice, such as perjury or falsely swearing an oath or making a statutory declaration before a German court (eg during a witness examination using

[64] S 5 Nos 15, 10, 11, 11a, 14, and 14a
[65] S 5 Nos 12 and 13.
[66] S 5 Nos 7, 8, 9, and 15.
[67] Eser (n 16) s 5 paras 3–6.
[68] S 5 No 2 StGB.
[69] Ss 81, 82, 83 StGB (approximate translation by the author).
[70] Ss 94–100a StGB and s 5 No 4.
[71] S109 StGB.
[72] S109e StGB.
[73] S 109f and g StGB.

remote video-conferencing where the witness is abroad) or before an entity exercising German official authority (such as a foreign notary).[74] This provision is particularly relevant for mutual legal assistance for German courts and authorities.[75] Moreover, certain offences relating to environmental law[76] that are committed in the German Exclusive Economic Zone,[77] to the extent that international treaties for the protection of the high seas, which enable the prosecution of such crimes, are also included in the list of offences that can be prosecuted in Germany, even if committed outside Germany on non-German territory.[78] Furthermore, it includes criminal acts committed against German public officials, someone acting for German public services, against a member of the German armed forces while they are performing their services or with reference to their services.[79]

But, finally, it also includes what are comparably more trivial offences such as the public vilification of the Federal President[80] or public vilification of state symbols such as the colours, the flag, the coat of arms, or the national anthem.[81]

For some of these national interest offences, it is necessary that the offender is German *and* permanently resident in Germany (a variant of the active personality principle), for example, systematically influencing members of the German armed forces or other public security forces, in order to undermine their willingness to defend the Constitutional order or to defend public security in Germany, with the intention of undermining public security and the Constitutional order in Germany.[82] Likewise, if a German who is permanently resident in Germany vilifies in public the Federal Republic of Germany, one of the Länder, the Constitutional Order, or one of the organs of the state (such as the government or Parliament) from abroad, the active personality principle would apply and that person could be prosecuted in Germany.[83] These offences also include fraudulently avoiding national service,[84] defamation of the German army that prevents it from carrying out its tasks,[85] or hiring Germans for foreign military service.[86] Finally, for some of the environmental crimes relating to radioactive substances, such as causing a nuclear explosion, these can be prosecuted in Germany, even if committed abroad, if the active personality principle applies (ie committed by a German national). Presumably, although this clearly contradicts the territoriality principle, offences involving radioactive substances are serious and relate to weapons that normally only states have access to and, in particular, relate to nuclear testing.[87]

[74] Ss 153–56 and 5 No 10.
[75] Eser (n 16) s 5 para 18.
[76] Ss 324, 326, 330, 330a StGB.
[77] This is a maritime law concept that extends states' influence over a zone of 200 sea miles, see Art 55 UN Convention on the Law of the Sea (UNCLOS) of 10 December 1982.
[78] S 5 No 11 StGB.
[79] S 5 No 14 StGB.
[80] S 90 StGB.
[81] S 90a(2) StGB.
[82] S 5 No 3 a and s 89 StGB.
[83] S 5 No 3a and ss 90a(1), 90b StGB.
[84] S 109a StGB.
[85] S 109d StGB.
[86] S 109h StGB.
[87] Eser (n 16) s 5 para 18b.

1.3.2 German public interests

A German public official, someone acting for German public services, or a member of the German armed forces committing a criminal act during an official stay abroad or in the context of their public duties on foreign territory can be prosecuted in Germany.[88] The application of German criminal law to such offences could be justified under international law according to the protective principle.

The criminal offence committed by an official may be unconnected to the public office (such as a sexual offence committed during a conference abroad) in the first alternative ("during an official stay abroad"). For the second alternative ("in the context of their public duties") this could be an offence committed by a public official during a private stay abroad (eg a public official accepting a bribe from a businessman while they are both on holiday together).[89] There must be a link between the offence and the offender's status as a public official.[90]

German jurisdiction also applies to criminal acts committed by a foreigner acting as a German public official or as someone acting for German public services.[91] In both these scenarios someone commits a criminal offence in connection with a German public office abroad, which therefore affects the public interest of the state in the integrity, probity, and reputation of persons acting in the name of Germany, thus affecting German public interests, which provides the link to German powers of prosecution, and is akin to the active personality principle (which is also based on the notion of loyalty obligations to the state).

Moreover, a German prosecution is also possible in the case of (online) sports betting fraud and manipulation of professional sports competitions committed abroad, if the actual competition takes place in Germany.[92] This ground of jurisdiction protects the public interest in the integrity of professional sport events taking place in Germany and is based on an extension of the territoriality principle as the territorial connecting factor is the competition itself.

Furthermore, bribery involving a member of a parliament[93] is subject to German criminal law and jurisdiction, if the offender is a German national, or a member of the German Parliament, or if the criminal act is committed towards a German member of Parliament or towards a German national, even if the act is committed abroad.[94] Both the person paying the bribe and the elected person accepting the bribe ("unlawful advantage") are committing a criminal offence, so that the active personality principle relates to either person here. The offence applies to the European Parliament, foreign parliaments, and regional elected chambers or representatives.[95] Finally, the range of corruption offences in ss 331–37 StGB, which extend to German officials, someone acting for German public services, European officials, judges of German courts or the courts of the EU, and arbitrators can be prosecuted under German law if there is one of

[88] S 5 No 12 StGB.
[89] Eser (n 16) s 5 paras 19–20.
[90] Ambos (n 16)54.
[91] S 5 Nos 12 and 13 StGB.
[92] S 5 No 10a StGB.
[93] S 108e StGB.
[94] S 5 No 16 StGB.
[95] S 108e(3) StGB.

a number of connecting factors to Germany. This can be that the offender is German, the official seat of the institution is in Germany, the corruption concerns a German official, German public service or a soldier of the German army, or a German national as European official or arbitrator.[96]

1.3.3 Protection of individual interests

Arguably, this category concerns scenarios where individual interests require protection from attacks occurring from abroad, given increased cross-border information flows on the internet and increased mobility of persons. How easily these scenarios sit with accepted jurisdiction principles under international law (and in particular the protective principle) is debatable. The first type of protection of individual interests concerns criminal acts against personal liberty, largely governed by the passive personality principle. This includes kidnapping or trafficking to expose a person to political persecution and political denunciation, where the victim is German and permanently resident/domiciled in Germany. Thus, even if the political persecution and denunciation occurs abroad, the German courts have jurisdiction.[97] Likewise, provided the victim was permanently resident/domiciled in Germany, the victim being both the child and the parents, it is a criminal act to hold a child against the will of the parent(s) in a place on foreign territory, which can be prosecuted in Germany.[98] Finally, if the offender is German or the victim was permanently resident/domiciled in Germany the criminal act of a forced marriage entered into abroad can also be prosecuted in Germany.[99] The protection of trade and business secrets are the next individual interest[100] to which the passive personality principle applies—criminal acts against trade and business secrets can be prosecuted in Germany as long as they belong to a business or company located or established in Germany or to a foreign company (such as a foreign subsidiary of a German parent) that is part of the same corporate structure and dependant on a German company.[101] Moreover, the third type of individual interest protected through the active personality principle is the right to sexual self-determination in relation to the following criminal acts committed abroad *by a German national* (active personality principle):[102] (1) sexual abuse in a relationship of trust,[103] (2) sexual abuse of children[104] and teenagers,[105] and (3) sexual assault, harassment, and rape.[106] These provisions reflect the greater mobility of people in general and of sexual offenders in particular (sexual "grooming" of children over the internet, sex tourism by German offenders arranged over the internet). The fourth type of individual interest protected relates to bodily integrity, this includes abortion (to the

[96] S 5 No 15 StGB.
[97] Ss234a and 241a and 5 No 6(a) StGB.
[98] S 235(2) No 2 and s 5 No 6(b) StGB.
[99] S 237 and s 5 No 6(c) StGB.
[100] cf Ambos (n 16) 62, who regards the protected interests to be macroeconomic interests of Germany—arguably too far-fetched an argument.
[101] S 5 No 7 StGB.
[102] S 5 No 8 StGB.
[103] S 174 (1), (2), and (4) StGB.
[104] S 176 StGB.
[105] S 182 StGB.
[106] Ss177, 178 StGB.

extent that it continues to be illegal in Germany) if the offender is German,[107] grievous bodily harm leading to sterilization if the offender is German,[108] and female genital mutilation[109] if the offender is German or the mutilation is committed against a girl or woman permanently resident/domiciled in Germany.[110] These provisions, based on the active/passive personality principle take into account that offenders/victims frequently travel abroad in the context of these particular offences to evade German jurisdiction and again remote communication has assisted the commission of these types of offences. Finally, the criminal offences of trade in human tissue or organs are justiciable in Germany, if the offender is German, even if the criminal acts take place abroad.[111]

1.4 Universality principle (Weltrechtsprinzip)

As has been discussed,[112] the universality principle applies to the most heinous offences infringing fundamental protected rights shared by the whole of humanity (crimes against international peace and humanity). Essentially, the universality principle confers jurisdiction on a state in respect of these offences, even if they were committed by foreigners against foreigners, on foreign territory.[113] The rationale behind the principle is that these offences concern universally shared rights, which need to be protected, and that it is in the mutual interests of all states that these criminal offences are effectively prosecuted. These offences therefore represent the common denominator between all states and are difficult to define. It might be more useful to focus on the mutuality of the interest of prosecution rather than the universality of shared interests and therefore, arguably, the principle should be called the "mutuality principle." These offences are frequently based on approximation of criminal law in international or European treaties.

There are two different branches of the universality principle under German law. First of all, it applies to the offences defined in the German Code on International Criminal Law, even if the crime was committed abroad and there is no domestic connection factor.[114] This first branch of the universality principle concerns the core of offences for which the universality principle is internationally recognized (eg piracy, genocide, crimes against humanity, wars of aggression).[115]

However, additionally, under the second branch of the universality principle, s 6 StGB lists a limited number of specific criminal offences. These include offences covered by international treaties to which Germany is a party.[116] However, while these

[107] S 218 StGB—there are variations in this provision, for some of which the offender also has to have his centre of life ("Lebensgrundlage") in Germany.
[108] S 226(1) No 1 StGB.
[109] S 226a StGB.
[110] S 5 Nos 9 and 9a StGB.
[111] S 5 No 17 StGB.
[112] Chapter 4.
[113] Ambos (n 16)64.
[114] S 1 VStGB.
[115] Ss6–12 VStGB, Ambos (n 16)67–68.
[116] *Lackner/Kühl Strafgesetzbuch Kommentar* (n 13) s 6 para 1, see also the catch-all clause in s 6 No 9.

offences protect important interests and reflect serious transborder harms, arguably they are based on the priorities of the German legislator rather than universally protected interests recognized by the international community of states (such as world peace and security) and s 6 has been criticized on this basis.[117] Therefore in order to make this provision compatible with international law and the principle of non-interference with the affairs of other states, the universality principle can only be applied, even in the specific instances listed in s 6, if there are no norms of public international law that prohibit the application of German criminal law and there is a connecting factor justifying German prosecution in the individual case.[118]

The first group[119] concerns offences involving nuclear energy, explosives, and radiation, namely causing an explosion by releasing nuclear energy endangering health or life of others or valuable property,[120] causing an explosion through explosives endangering health or life of others or valuable property,[121] releasing radiation that is liable to damage human health on a massive scale,[122] or producing, procuring, supplying, or storing the relevant materials or equipment for such an explosion or release of radiation.[123] The second offence for which German criminal law applies the universality principle is attacks on air and sea traffic, including piracy, violent attacks, and hijacking.[124] The third offence contains different variations of participation (eg by accommodating or transporting such a person) in the trafficking of human beings under the age of twenty-one, including forced prostitution and modern slavery.[125] Fourth, offences related to unauthorized distribution of illegal drugs (narcotics) fall under the universality principle.[126] Furthermore, the fifth group of offences to which the universality principle applies are offences concerning the distribution and dissemination (but not possession or consumption), including on the internet, of pornography[127] (violent pornography, animal pornography,[128] pornography depicting children or teenagers (below eighteen years old)[129]). The universality principle does not apply to the offence of distributing adult pornography without age-verification barriers.[130]

Distribution includes the making available online of pornography.[131] The reason that these provisions are subject to universal German jurisdiction is the nature of the dissemination of pornography online on a global basis where content is increasingly

117 Ambos (n 16) 68–69.
118 *Lackner/Kühl Strafgesetzbuch Kommentar* (n 13) s 6 para 1; BGHSt 45,68.
119 S 6 No 2.
120 S 307 StGB.
121 S 308 StGB.
122 S 309(2) StGB.
123 S 310 StGB.
124 S 6 No 3; s 316(c) StGB.
125 S 6 No 4 and s 232 StGB.
126 S 6 No 5 StGB.
127 S 6 No 6 StGB; see also T Hörnle, ss 183, 183a, 184, 184a, 184b, 184c, 184d, 184e, 184f, 184g, 184h in W Joecks & K Miebach (Eds.), Vol 3 Münchener Kommentar zum Strafgesetzbuch (3. Ed 2017 Beck München), 1672–1788, Para 49.
128 S 184a StGB.
129 S 184b and s 184c StGB.
130 S 184 StGB.
131 S 184d StGB.

violent and extreme, and without efficient age-verification at the point of consumption. Moreover, the universality principle in s 6 applies to child sex abuse content disseminated or made available online through international gangs of child sex abusers. However, some German scholars regard this provision as jurisdictional overreach and question its compatibility with public international law.[132] Ambos in particular points out that, in respect of child sex abuse materials, neither the EU Directive[133] nor the Council of Europe Convention[134] require the application of the universality principle.[135] Arguably, the effects doctrine under the territoriality principle, discussed earlier, is not sufficient to ensure that the online distribution of pornography and other illegal content can be prosecuted in Germany, as such content will not endanger public peace in Germany or be targeted at a German audience.

The sixth group of offences concerns the forgery of money and investment certificates, as well as the forgery of payment cards and Euro-based cheques.[136] The seventh group of offences concerns fraud in relation to state aid and state subsidies.[137] Finally, the universality principle applies to all criminal offences for which Germany has entered into a binding obligation in an international convention to prosecute these offences, even if committed abroad, and without the need of further connecting factors.[138] This duty may arise under any international treaty, including Council of Europe Conventions.[139] For example, Article 22(3) of the Cybercrime Convention[140] imposes a duty on Convention States to exercise representative jurisdiction in cases where State A (eg the territorial state where the offence was committed) requests State B to extradite the offender, State B being the place where the offender is present and can be apprehended, but State B refuses to extradite them on the grounds that he or she is a national of State B. In this scenario State B has a duty to exercise criminal jurisdiction over the offender.[141] Article 22(3) of the Cybercrime Convention applies to the specific cybercrime offences defined in Articles 2–9 of the Convention (illegal access, illegal interception, data interference, system interference, misuse of devices, computer-related forgery, computer-related fraud, and offences related to child pornography) if they are punishable by a year or more (unless an existing extradition treaty makes the offence an extraditable offence).[142] This duty under Article 22(3) is both an emanation of the universality principle and the representative principle.

The application of this blank obligation to assume jurisdiction, if warranted by an international obligation, is likely to have limited effect, as universal jurisdiction has

[132] Eser (n 16) s 6 para 7; Ambos in *Münchener Kommentar zum Strafgesetzbuch* Vol 1 (3rd edn, C.H. Beck 2017) s 6 para 14.

[133] Directive 2011/92/EU of 13 December 2011, Art 17.

[134] Convention for the Protection of Children from Sexual Exploitation of 25 October 2007, Arts 20 and 25.

[135] Ambos (n 132) s 6 para 14.

[136] S 6 No 7.

[137] S 6 No 8 and s 264 StGB.

[138] S 6 No 9; BGHSt 46, 292(307).

[139] Ambos (n 16) 75.

[140] 23 November 2001, Budapest, ETS No 185.

[141] According to the principle of *aut dedere, aut iudicare*.

[142] Cross-reference to Art 24(1).

been introduced in German criminal law by the specific provisions in s 6 StGB and the German International Criminal Law Code,[143] such as infringements of the Geneva Conventions,[144] apartheid,[145] and torture.[146] However, other than Article 22(3) of the Cybercrime Convention there are no specific international obligations to apply the universality principle to cybercrimes.

1.5 Passive personality principle

The German Criminal Code, furthermore, provides that German criminal law applies to *all and any offences* that were committed *against a German national* on foreign territory, but only if the offence is a criminal offence in the place of its commission or the place of commission is outside the jurisdiction of any state.[147] Thus, German criminal law has adopted the controversial passive personality principle but making it subject to dual criminality or the offence being committed outside the jurisdiction of any state.[148] The dual criminality principle heeds to criminal justice considerations and protects the offender who may be unaware that his or her victim is a German national on foreign territory and who therefore should not be guilty of an offence that does not exist in the territorial state.[149] However, additionally, the application of the passive personality principle is problematic from the viewpoint of international law because German law thus interferes with the sovereignty of the territorial state and provokes (rather than avoids) conflicts of law.[150] The basis of this extension of German sovereignty is that German citizens should be protected extraterritorially and to ensure criminal prosecution of offences committed against German citizens.[151] The principle protects the interests of individuals and therefore does not apply in the case of offences protecting general interests.[152]

However, the principle of dual criminality does not require that the offence is the same or equivalent in the foreign jurisdiction, but it must be a criminal offence in both states, so that German criminal law would not apply if the defendant would only be subject to administrative sanctions in the foreign jurisdiction.[153] The passive personality principle only applies if the victim is identified or identifiable as a German national. Furthermore, the principle does not apply to legal persons.[154]

143 Völkerstrafgesetzbuch, VStGB.
144 Ss 1, 8–10 VStGB.
145 Ss 1, 7(5) VStGB.
146 Ss 1, 7(1) No 5 VStGB.
147 S 7(1) StGB.
148 *Lackner/Kühl Strafgesetzbuch Kommentar* (n 13) s 7 para 1.
149 Ambos (n 16) 57.
150 ibid 58.
151 ibid 59.
152 ibid 59.
153 *Lackner/Kühl Strafgesetzbuch Kommentar* (n 13) s 7 para 3.
154 *Lackner/Kühl Strafgesetzbuch Kommentar* (n 13) s 7 para 4; BGHSt 18, 283.

1.6 Active personality principle

Moreover, German law is applicable to crimes committed on foreign territory *if the offender was German at the time of commission or became a German national thereafter*, and if the offence is a criminal offence in the place[155] of its commission or the place of commission is outside the jurisdiction of any state.[156] This active personality principle could apply, for example, in respect of online gambling offences, or computer fraud or misuse, as it makes the precise place of the criminal act less important, because if there are connecting factors to several territories, as long as the act is a criminal offence in each territory, the dual criminality principle is satisfied.

The active personality principle has its origins in the German Constitution,[157] which prohibits the extradition of German nationals from Germany.[158] Germans who have committed a crime abroad (outside the EU[159]) could otherwise return to Germany, invoke their right not be extradited to a foreign jurisdiction, and thereby avoid prosecution for the crime committed.[160] The active personality principle is based on the duty of loyalty of citizens to the legal order of their nationality and has been criticized on two counts: (1) being authoritarian as it imposes this duty of loyalty, but also (2) on the basis that it unduly conflicts with the sovereignty of the state where the crime was committed.[161] However, provided the active personality principle is limited by the requirement of dual criminality, it has been argued that it can also be understood as supporting international solidarity in that the prosecuting state (Germany) would protect the sovereign interests of the territorial state by punishing infringements of the criminal law, which had occurred there (or there and everywhere).[162] To the extent that the dual criminality principle applies, however, the act must be a criminal (and not merely administrative) offence there,[163] but it need not necessarily be the same type of offence, protecting the same type of legitimate interests.[164] The German courts also take into account defences applicable in the jurisdiction where the offence was committed,[165] but they ignore any barriers preventing the prosecution for a procedural reason.[166] However, as Ambos points out, certain procedural barriers may show that the state where the offence was committed declined to prosecute. As a consequence, a German prosecution may lead to a conflict of interest (eg where an amnesty[167] is in place, or limitation periods have run out).[168]

[155] "mit Strafe bedroht," subject to criminal punishment.

[156] S 7(2) StGB and *Lackner/Kühl Strafgesetzbuch Kommentar* (n 13) s 7 para 1.

[157] Art 16(2) Satz 1 Grundgesetz.

[158] *Lackner/Kühl Strafgesetzbuch Kommentar* (n 13) s 7 para 5(a); Ambos (n 16) 47.

[159] Germany had to change its Constitution with the entry into force of the European Arrest Warrant.

[160] Ambos (n 16) 43.

[161] ibid 43–44.

[162] ibid 44.

[163] ibid 48–49.

[164] ibid 49.

[165] BGHSt 2, 160(161); Ambos (n 16) 50.

[166] BGH NStZ-RR 2000, 361.

[167] Unless the amnesty itself is an infringement of general recognized human rights or international law principles.

[168] Ambos (n 16) 51.

1.7 Representation principle

This principle means that a state may try an offender *on behalf of* the state who has territorial jurisdiction if the offender cannot be tried in the state on whose territory the crime was committed. German criminal law provides that in a situation where (1) a criminal offence has been committed on foreign (non-German) territory, (2) this offence is a criminal offence in the place where it has been committed (dual criminality) or the place of commission is outside the jurisdiction of any state, (3) the offender is not a German national, but has been apprehended in Germany and (4) the offence is an extraditable offence under German law, but (5) the extradition cannot be carried out because the limitation period has expired, the request has been denied, or for some other reason.[169] This principle can only be applied under German law if it is clear that the offender will not and cannot be extradited.[170]

2. Jurisdiction under English criminal law

2.1 Prevalence of territoriality principle

Unlike German criminal jurisdiction, English[171] criminal jurisdiction has been largely[172] confined to the territoriality principle without recourse to extraterritorial jurisdiction based on the active or passive personality principle.[173] A foreigner or national committing criminal acts abroad would not be liable.[174] The only exception is treason, where the foreigner owes a duty of allegiance to the Crown.[175] Another

[169] S 7(2) No 2 and *Lackner/Kühl Strafgesetzbuch Kommentar* (n 13) s 7 para 1.

[170] *Lackner/Kühl Strafgesetzbuch Kommentar* (n 13) s 7 para 5 b); BGHSt 45, 65.

[171] This chapter focuses on the law of England and Wales, Scotland and Northern Ireland are separate criminal jurisdictions; where a statutory offence applies to the whole of the UK, each of the three jurisdictions will regards the offence as a separate English, Scottish, or Northern Irish offence within each territory, see Hirst (n 3) 5–6.

[172] Exceptions are eg s 9 Offences Against the Person Act 1861 (murder/manslaughter committed by a *British subject* anywhere) as in *R v Cheong (Micheal Andrew)* [2006] Crim L R 1088 (CA); s 4 Suppression of Terrorism Act 1978 (extending jurisdiction over certain listed, violent offences such as murder, manslaughter when committed in any of the countries being part of the Council of Europe, European Convention on the Suppression of Terrorism ETS No 090 as in *R v Venclovas (Rimas)* [2013] EWCA Crim 2182; s 57 Offences Against the Person Act 1861 (bigamy, regardless where 2nd marriage is entered into by a British subject); s 31 Criminal Justice Act 1948 (indictable offence committed by a British subject in Crown service), but this does not apply to the Prime Minister: *The Queen on the Application of Defending Christian Arabs v Tony Blair* [2020] EWHC 1850 (Admin), Para 20; s 72 Sexual Offences Act 2003 combatting "sex tourism" where offenders travel to commit a sexual offence abroad (subject to the dual criminality principle and the extended active personality principle, ie British citizenship or UK residence); s 24 Theft Act 1968 handling of stolen goods applies to theft, fraud etc committed abroad; ss 327–29, 340 Proceeds of Crime Act 2002.

[173] Mr Justice Amphlett in *R v Keyn (Ferdinand) (The Franconia)* (1876) 2 Ex D 63, 117–18; *Lord Tucker* in *Board of Trade v Owen* [1957] AC 602 (HL) 625; *Viscount Simons* in *Cox v Army Council* [1963] 48 (HL) 67; *R v Harden* [1963] 1 QB 8 see also *Archbold Criminal Pleading Evidence and Practice* (Westlaw 2019) para 2.35 and Hirst (n 3) 5.

[174] For a recent example see *The Queen on the Application of Defending Christian Arabs v Tony Blair* [2020] EWHC 1850 (Admin), paras 13, 19.

[175] *Joyce v DPP* [1946] AC 347 (HL).

narrowly crafted exception has recently been introduced by the Electronic Commerce Directive (Miscellaneous Provisions) Regulations 2018, which extended jurisdiction to certain offences committed in an EEA State by information society services providers. These offences are listed in the Regulations and are related to reporting restrictions, human trafficking, extreme pornography, and publication of intimate images.

The reason for this difference has been explained in Chapter 2 to be partly due to geographical factors (England as an island location had less reasons to deal with fugitive offenders) and partly due to differences in criminal procedure (the right to be tried by local peers in a jury trial) between the English common law and Continental legal systems.[176] Thus, the starting point is that English criminal law only applies to criminal acts which take place on English territory and that there is a strong presumption for statutory offences that Parliament intended them to only apply to the relevant UK territory.[177] However the English Courts have been prepared to apply statutory offences extraterritorially. The presumption can be rebutted by specific statutory provisions: in *R v Rogers* the Court of Appeal held that the offence of conversion of criminal property under section 327(1)(c) Proceeds of Crime Act 2002 can be applied extraterritorially. In this case, the proceeds of various advance fee fraud schemes committed in the UK were paid into a Spanish bank account (which was the place of the commission of the conversion of criminal property offence). The Court[178] interpreted the unclear wording in section 340(11)(d)[179] to make clear that the money laundering offences are offences under English law, even if done extraterritorially.[180]

The common law development of the rules on jurisdiction has, however, caused some confusion, as neatly summed up by Mr Justice La Forest in *Libman v The Queen*:

> the courts have taken different stances at different times, and the general result (…) is one of doctrinal confusion, a confusion compounded by the fact that the discussion often focuses on the specific offence charged, a discussion made more complicated by the further fact that some offences are aimed at the act committed and others at the result of that act.[181]

As we have seen, German courts had to grapple with similar confusions in the context of a Civil Law system with codified rules on jurisdiction, namely distinguishing between criminal conduct and its results.

In a similar fashion to the German legal system, in applying the territoriality principle, English courts also had to distinguish between the criminal acts themselves and the results effected by the criminal acts and have found both relevant for determining

[176] Hirst (n 3) 28–59.

[177] *Archbold* (n 173) para 2.35.

[178] Moreover, the Court of Appeal held *obiter* that even if the Act contained no express provision applying it extraterritorially, it would have nevertheless found that the English Court had jurisdiction on the basis of the substantial measure test, see the discussion in section 2.3.

[179] "Money laundering is an act which would constitute an offence specified [in the relevant parts of the Act] if done in the United Kingdom."

[180] *R v Rogers* [2015] 1 WLR 1017 (CA) 1025; followed in *Sulaiman v France* [2016] 11 WLUK 407 (Admin).

[181] *Libman v The Queen* [1985] 2 SCR 178 (SCC) 186 (Mr Justice Law Forest) Canadian case.

territorial jurisdiction.[182] Under the English common law sometimes the criminal act has been extended to include distant results of the criminal act.

At example for this is *ex parte Levin*, were the question arose in the context of extradition proceedings, which are considered to be criminal proceedings,[183] whether the US Federal Courts had jurisdiction.[184] Levin had managed to hack into Citibank's cash management system and transfer ten million US dollars to himself and various accomplices using a computer while in Russia in 1995.[185] The US charges were the equivalent of theft, forgery, false accounting, and computer misuse. As to jurisdiction, the Divisional Court held that the (false) instructions the defendant had effected from his keyboard in Russia had been transferred instantaneously and inserted in Citibank's computer in the US and that therefore the crime had been committed there, despite the fact that the defendant had acted remotely:[186]

> For the reasons we have already indicated, the operation of the keyboard by a computer operator produces a virtually instantaneous result on the magnetic disk of the computer even though it may be 10,000 miles away. It seems to us artificial to regard the act as having been done in one rather than the other place. But, in the position of having to choose on the facts of this case whether, after entering the computer in Parsipenny, the act of appropriation by inserting instructions on the disk occurred there or in St. Petersburg, we would opt for Parsipenny. The fact that the applicant was physically in St. Petersburg is of far less significance than the fact that he was looking at and operating on magnetic disks located in Parsipenny. The essence of what he was doing was done there.[187]

Thus, while traditionally English criminal law has confined jurisdiction to the territoriality principle, it has shown flexibility in situating the criminal act to a place other than the place where the defendant had physically acted, and in the *Levin* case, the Court was prepared to accept that the criminal act was carried out in the place where it instantaneously took effect. Likewise in *Perrin*,[188] in respect of publication of an obscene article,[189] the Court of Appeal found that publication on the internet in the form of making available for download within England was sufficient for jurisdiction and that therefore there was no need for the prosecution to show that the defendant had taken the major steps necessary for publication in England. Here again the English Court has relied on the immediate results of the defendant's criminal act (access as a consequence of publication), as defined by the relevant offence. Thus, publication and accessibility were the relevant connecting factors to the territory.

[182] Hirst (n 3) 118.
[183] *Ex parte Levin* [1997] AC 741 (HL) 746–47.
[184] *R v Governor of Brixton Prison and another, ex parte Levin* [1996] QB 65.
[185] https://www.nytimes.com/1995/08/19/business/citibank-fraud-case-raises-computer-security-questions.html?mcubz=3 accessed on 16/07/2020.
[186] *Ex parte Levin* [1997] QB 65 (DC) 80–84.
[187] At 81–82.
[188] *R v Perrin (Stephane Laurent)* [2002] EWCA Crim 747 (CA).
[189] S 1(1) Obscene Publications Act 1959.

It seems that, in internet cases, similar to the German rules on jurisdiction, the English courts have found territorial jurisdiction based on *both criminal acts and the criminal results* effected by the defendant's conduct, as defined in the relevant offence. The English courts in these two cases have attributed the effects to the criminal act, the latter giving rise to jurisdiction.

The English common law has had to grapple with principles of criminal jurisdiction long before the arrival of the internet, particularly in maritime cases. Traditionally, the courts had developed the principle that jurisdiction should follow the territoriality of the *conduct*, in other words, criminal jurisdiction has been based on the location of the criminal act as the relevant connecting factor for a court's authority. However, the English courts have not made the distinction between conduct offences and such offences that create a specific risk of harm in a particular location (as the notion of *Gefährdungsdelikte* mentioned in relation to the criminal jurisdiction rules in Germany mentioned earlier).[190]

However, the courts have been prepared in some cases to crystallize the criminal act at the place where the result of the conduct[191] (such as the death of a person) occurred. This has been apparent not only from the more recent "internet" cases discussed earlier, but also from some of the historical (maritime) cases.

In *R v Coombes* (1786) a person was shot while on board an English ship from a foreign shore, and the Court found (English) Admiralty jurisdiction:

> If a loaded pistol be fired from the land at a distance of one hundred yards from the sea, and a man is maliciously killed in the water one hundred yards from the shore, the offender shall be tried by the Admiralty Jurisdiction; for the offence is committed where the death happens, and not at the place from whence the cause of the death proceeds.[192]

By contrast, in *R v Keyn* (1876) the accused was a German captain of a ship sailing to a foreign port and while within three miles of the coast of England negligently caused a collision with a British ship, which sank and caused the death of a passenger. The captain was charged with manslaughter, but the majority of the Central Criminal Court found that it had no jurisdiction. The English Court held that locus of the criminal conduct was decisive and rejected that the *effects*[193] of the criminal act could be sufficient as a base for jurisdiction. It pointed out that the captain had not intended his

[190] *R v Berry* [1985] AC 246 (HL).

[191] As became apparent from the German cases already discussed, sometimes it is difficult to distinguish clearly whether an element of a criminal offence can be classified as "conduct" or as a "result" of the conduct. For example, is internet publication (or the making available of illegal content) an act or is it the result of an act?

[192] *The King v George Coombes* (1785) 1 Leach 388 (Westlaw).

[193] In contrast to the *Lotus* case where the Permanent International Court of Justice, some fifty years later, confirmed the "effects" doctrine under International Law in 1927, in a factually very similar case: "the courts of many countries (…) interpret criminal law in the sense that offences, the authors of which at the moment of the commission of the offence are in the territory of another State, are nevertheless to be regarded as having been committed in the national territory, if one of the constituent elements of the offence, and more especially its effects, have taken place there" 23, Series A, No 10 Collection of Judgments.

acts to cause effects on British territory and had not acted there.[194] Interesting to note is that if the German captain's conduct had been targeted at the British vessel the decision would have gone the other way.

2.2 The terminatory approach or last act rule

English courts adopted a very narrow territorial approach[195] to jurisdiction by the twentieth century, the so-called *terminatory or "last act" rule.*[196] Thus, English courts had jurisdiction only if the last, relevant constituent element of the conduct that leads to the criminal result had taken place in England. Thus, it was necessary to identify the last act required to complete the criminal offence and the English courts did not have jurisdiction *unless this last act had been carried out in England.*[197]

Thus, English courts have traditionally restricted their competence, even more narrowly than allowed by the territoriality principle in international law, limiting jurisdiction to the last act of the criminal conduct to produce the criminal result.[198] Earlier acts constituting criminal conduct could also not be used as a basis for jurisdiction. In respect of the obtaining of property by false pretences, Viscount Dilhorne made the following *obiter dictum* in *DPP v Stonehouse*: "I can find no authority for the proposition that the English Courts have jurisdiction in a case where the false pretences were made in this country and the obtaining of goods or money in consequence thereof occurred outside the jurisdiction."[199]

This terminatory rule included the result itself, which was seen as part of the final act of the criminal conduct. For example, Lord Diplock in *DPP v Stonehouse* found that there was "long-standing authority to the effect that in a 'result crime' the English Courts have jurisdiction to try the offence if the described *consequence of the conduct* of the accused which is part of the definition of the crime took place in England."[200]

The terminatory, last act rule was sometimes also expressed as the essence or the "gist" of the offence, for example, in *R v Harden*,[201] where it was held that the gist of the offence of obtaining by false pretences was the obtaining, it being the last act to complete the offence. The terminatory rules have been strongly criticized on the basis that it led to cases being decided on technicalities and not on a coherent policy approach, with the consequence that results frequently were bizarre or unjust.[202]

[194] *R v Keyn (Ferdinand) (The Franconia)* (1876)2 Ex D 63, 66 and 86, 149, 151 (Sir R Phillimore and Mr Justices Bramwell, Kelly, Cockburn, Pollock, and Field); but see dissent by Justices Lindley, Grove, Amphlett, and Brett (criminal law applying in coastal waters) 98–99, 109, 124, 148–49; Mr Justice Denman (offence committed on British ship where death occurred) 101, 108.

[195] With some statutory exceptions, see for example s 10 Offences Against the Person Act 1861 (murder/manslaughter—constituent element approach, jurisdiction if the either the criminal act or the death occurs within jurisdiction).

[196] *Ellis* [1899] 1 QB 230; *R v Harden* (n 173); *R v Treacy* [1971] AC 537 (CA) 545 (Lord Parker); *R v Manning* [1999] QB 980 (CA).

[197] *R v Manning* (n 196).

[198] G Williams, "Venue and the Ambit of Criminal Law" (1965) 81 Law Quarterly Review 276, 518–38.

[199] *DPP v Stonehouse* [1977] 65 Cr App R 192, 214.

[200] ibid 206.

[201] *R v Harden* (n 173) 21–22 arguing that the gist of the offence is where the last act is completed (posting of the cheques on Jersey).

[202] Hirst (n 3) 110.

2.3 Substantial measure test

The Court of Appeal widened territorial jurisdiction and complemented the terminatory rule with the so-called substantial measure test in *R v Smith (Wallace Duncan) (No 4)*[203] in 2004, thus vitiating the terminatory rule as the *sole* basis for jurisdiction. The defendant in this transnational fraud case had made dishonest arrangements to obtain a repo[204] (secured loan) with a bank in London and the resulting money was paid into a bank account in New York. He was convicted on one count under section 485 of the Companies Act 1985 (fraudulent trading) and two counts under section 15(1) of the Theft Act 1968 (obtaining property by deception).[205]

On appeal, he challenged the jurisdiction of the English courts. The Court of Appeal in *R v Smith (Wallace Duncan) (No1) (Lord Justice Rose)* held that if a substantial measure of the activities constituting a crime took place in England, the English courts had jurisdiction unless it can be "seriously argued on a reasonable view that these activities should, on the basis of comity be dealt with by another country."[206] It held that this substantial measure test, which had been established in the Privy Council Judgment of *Liangsiriprasert v US*,[207] did not only apply to inchoate offences such as attempt and conspiracy[208] but additionally to result crimes such as the dishonest obtaining of property.[209] Lord Justice Rose also held that the rules on jurisdiction had a strong procedural element, which meant that they should be developed by the courts in a common law fashion in the light of "developing and advancing communications technology."[210] Lord Justice Rose quoted Mr Justice La Forest in the Canadian Supreme Court in *Libman v The Queen*:

> The English courts have decisively begun to move away from definitional obsessions and technical formulations aimed at finding a single situs of a crime by locating where the gist of the crime occurred or where it was completed. Rather, they now appear to seek by an examination of relevant policies to apply the English criminal law where a substantial measure of the activities constituting the crime takes place in England, and restricts its application in such circumstances solely to cases where it can seriously be argued on a reasonable view that these activities should on the basis of international comity be dealt with by another country.[211]

After the Court of Appeal had expanded the substantial measure test in *R v Smith (Wallace Duncan) (No1)* to the offence of dishonest obtaining of property, a differently

[203] *R v Smith (Wallace Duncan) (No 4)* [2004] QB 1418 (CA); *R v Smith (Wallace Duncan) (No 1)* [1996] 2 Cr App R 1 (CA).

[204] Repurchase Agreement.

[205] Repealed by the Fraud Act 2006 Sch 3 para1.

[206] *R v Smith (Wallace Duncan) (No 1)* [1996] 2 Cr App R 1 (CA) 18–20.

[207] [1991] 1 AC 225 (PC) 250 (Lord Griffiths).

[208] *Sansom & Others* (1991) 92 Cr App R 115.

[209] *R v Smith (Wallace Duncan) (No4)* [2004] QB 1418 (CA)1432; *R v Smith (Wallace Duncan) (No 1)* [1996] 2 Cr App R 1 (CA) 18–20.

[210] Para 20.

[211] [1985] 2 SCR 178 (SCC) 198–99.

constituted Court of Appeal in *R v Manning*[212] reverted to the terminatory theory as the sole test for determining jurisdiction. Lord Justice Buxton held that the Court of Appeal was bound by the common law rule in *R v Harden*.[213]

The *Harden* case concerned the offence in the predecessor of section 20(2) of the Theft Act 1968 of obtaining cheques by false pretences.[214] Mr Justice Widgery held that the gist of the offence was the obtaining by false pretences and that the last act to effect the result of this offence had been the posting of cheques from Jersey—hence the English courts had no jurisdiction. The contradiction between these two Court of Appeal cases meant that the rules on jurisdiction for dishonesty offences were unsettled, which prompted the UK Parliament to pass the Criminal Justice Act 1993, in order to address the number of transborder interactions and transactions through electronic data interchanges and the internet, and the concomitant economic and financial crimes.

Thus, the terminatory approach was abolished by legislation for offences involving dishonesty. The Criminal Justice Act 1993, Part I introduced the constituent elements approach for fraud and other offences involving dishonesty. This approach essentially means that if *any* element (criminal act or criminal result) of the offence occurs in England, the English courts have jurisdiction based on the subjective and objective territoriality principle.[215] For fraud this includes the place where the gain or loss envisaged actually occurred.[216]

However, the Criminal Justice Act 1993 only widened the rules on jurisdiction for two groups of dishonesty offences, namely the specific offences listed in section 1(2) ("Group A Offences") and in section 1(3) ("Group B Offences"). Group A are offences related to theft, false accounting, blackmail, handling stolen goods, fraud, and counterfeiting.[217] Group B offences are the inchoate offences in respect of these Group A offences, namely conspiracy to defraud, conspiracy to commit a Group A offence, attempting to commit a Group A offence, and incitement to commit a Group A offence.

Looking beyond these offences, the unsettled state of the rules of jurisdiction prompted the Criminal Cases Review Commission[218] to refer the *R v Smith* case (again) to the Court of Appeal.[219] Mr Chief Justice Woolf in the latter Court of Appeal strongly endorsed the preceding judgment by Lord Justice Rose and in particular his dictum that the common law needed to adapt in the light of developing and advancing communications technology.[220]

212 [1999] QB 980 (CA) 989–90.

213 *R v Harden* (n 173).

214 Repealed by the Fraud Act 2006 Sch 3 para 1.

215 S 2(1) Criminal Justice Act 1993: "any act or omission or other event (including any result of one or more acts or omissions) proof of which is required for conviction of the offence"; *Archbold*(n 173) para 2.54.

216 S 2(1A)—albeit that under the definition of fraud in s 1 Fraud Act 2006 there is no need that the envisaged gain or loss actually occurred.

217 Listed are ss 1, 17, 19, 21, 22, 24A Theft Act 1968; ss 1, 6, 7, 9, 11 Fraud Act 2006; ss 1–5, 14–17, 20–21 Forgery and Counterfeiting Act 1981; and ss 4–6 Identity Documents Act 2010 and the common law offence of cheating in relation to the public revenue.

218 Pursuant to s 9 of the Criminal Appeal Act 1995.

219 *R v Smith (Wallace Duncan) (No4)* [2004] QB 1418 (CA).

220 Paras 1426, 1433, 1437.

For the substantial measure test, the court needs to consider all constituent elements of the criminal offence and decide whether a substantial measure of these had taken place in England, which means that the court has to weigh up all the factors pertaining to the definition of the offence.[221] In particular, the Court held that it was not necessary that the final act completing the offence should occur on English territory. If a substantial measure of the criminality has occurred within England, the court can accept jurisdiction unless it can be argued that another country is better placed to assume jurisdiction according to the principles of international comity.[222]

The substantial measure test was subsequently confirmed as the relevant test[223] and applied in a case concerning a prosecution under section 19 of the Public Order Act 1986[224] in respect of an internet publication by the Court of Appeal in *R v Sheppard v Whittle*[225] in 2009. The content in question had been written and edited in England by the accused, but was uploaded to and hosted by a server in the US. The Court examined all the circumstances pertaining to the publication and found that the accused operated in England, generated, uploaded, and controlled the content from there, and that the content was intended for the public in England and weighed against this the fact that the content was hosted on a server in the US, which was merely a stage in the transmission of the material.[226] The Court of Appeal therefore held that a substantial measure of the criminality had occurred in England and hence the English courts had jurisdiction. While the fact that the content was aimed at an English audience was only one factor in deciding where the substantial measure of criminality had taken place, the Court stopped short of adopting a targeting test.[227] Interestingly, unlike the German Supreme Court, the Court of Appeal did not find that the fact that public order in England (as one of the possible results of the criminal conduct) may be impacted by the publication is a relevant factor for determining the substantial measure. Nor did the Court of Appeal hold that actual access by the public in England must be shown—instead it found that "publication" on the internet merely means making available to the public and this was evidenced by one police officer downloading the relevant material, as the Court had previously held in *Perrin*, and that there was no need to show that anyone had in fact read or heard the content of the publication.[228]

The substantial measure test was also applied in *R v Rogers* in respect of the money laundering charge of converting criminal property, in this case the payment of the proceeds of an advanced fee fraud scheme into a bank account in Spain. Lord Justice Treacy found *obiter* that the money laundering in Spain was directly linked to the fraudulent acts that had taken place in the UK and had impacted on UK victims, including their continued deprivation of the moneys that had been taken from them and that this was the substantial measure of the criminality on which jurisdiction was based.[229] This approach is interesting as the advance fee fraud and the subsequent

[221] *Libman v The Queen* [1985] 2 SCR 178 (SCC) 179, 189; *R v Rogers* [2015] 1 WLR 1017 (CA) 1026.
[222] For a discussion of the comity doctrine see Chapter 9.
[223] [2010] 1 WLR 2779 (CA) 2784–5.
[224] Publishing etc., material intended or likely to stir up racial hatred.
[225] [2010] 1 WLR 2779 (CA).
[226] Paras 2785–6, 2788.
[227] J Hörnle, "The Internet and Criminal Jurisdiction" (April–May 2010) 21(1) Computers & Law 11–12.
[228] [2010] 1 WLR 2779 (CA) 2789.
[229] *R v Rogers* [2015] 1 WLR 1017 (CA) 1027.

money laundering are separate offences and the test here focused not on the substantial measure of a particular offence but the *substantial measure of the criminal scheme as a whole.*

The substantial measure test was heavily influenced by Lord Diplock's *obiter opinion* in *Treacy v DPP*, which now constitutes the "modern" approach to jurisdiction.[230] It could be called the "enlightened" approach to jurisdiction as it recognizes that an international legal system founded on the principle of sovereignty and allegiance to local law must be supplemented by a principle of mutuality of criminal laws in cross-border criminal cases while respecting comity. In the interconnected world of the internet and cross-border cybercrime this is even more important than in 1970.

In essence, unless the statute itself contains express provisions on its jurisdictional reach, Lord Diplock was of the opinion that the doctrine of comity[231] is the correct test *to limit* the jurisdictional reach of English criminal law. He held that the territorial principle allowed states to exercise jurisdiction if either the criminal acts or the consequences of these acts occurred in England and thus proposed (*obiter*) that the terminatory approach be abolished and that jurisdiction be widened to include any constituent element of the relevant offence.[232] As to comity, Lord Diplock held that:

> There is no rule of comity to prevent Parliament from prohibiting under pain of punishment persons who are present in the United Kingdom, and so owe local obedience to our law, from doing physical acts in England, notwithstanding that the consequences of those acts take effect outside the United Kingdom. Indeed, where the prohibited acts are of a kind calculated to cause harm to private individuals it would savour of chauvinism rather than comity to treat them as excusable merely on the ground that the victim was not in the United Kingdom itself but some other state.[233]

2.4 Inchoate offences

Inchoate offences such as conspiracy and attempt cause particular challenges in respect of jurisdiction. Essentially two polar constellations can be distinguished: (1) where the defendant(s) have acted in England with a view to causing a criminal result abroad and (2) where the defendant(s) have acted abroad with a view to causing a criminal result in England and in neither situation has the criminal result been achieved. The courts have held that in the second situation the English courts do have jurisdiction,[234] whereas in the first situation it was held in *R v Cox*[235] that the English courts do not have jurisdiction. In *R v C*[236] the English Court found jurisdiction for a

230 *Archbold* (n 173) para 2.35.
231 See Chapter 9 on the principle of comity.
232 *R v Treacy* (n 196) 563–65.
233 ibid 561–62.
234 *Liangsiriprasert v Government of the USA* [1991] 1 AC 225 (PC) followed by the Court of Appeal in *R v Sansom* [1991] 2 QB 130 (CA).
235 *R v Cox (Peter Stanley)* [1986] 1 WLR 88 (CA).
236 [2007] Crim LR 235 (CA) 236–37.

charge of incitement to distribute indecent photographs of children where the person inciting others was within the jurisdiction and the distribution would likely at least be *partly within England*, even though the actual distributors were abroad.

However, again statutory provisions have now superseded the common law rules on jurisdiction. Section 1A of the Criminal Law Act 1977[237] provides that in relation to a conspiracy within England but which relates to criminal offences abroad the English courts *do have* jurisdiction. If the agreed course of conduct involves an act by the defendants or the happening of some event intended to take place abroad, English criminal law applies (including the offence of conspiracy) provided several other conditions are met: the act or event must constitute an offence under the law of the place where it occurs (dual criminality)[238] and the defendant must have done something or omitted to do something in pursuance of the conspiracy in England, or the defendant must have become a party to the conspiracy in England (link to the jurisdiction).[239] As in Germany, the dual criminality principle is used to provide for different links to the jurisdiction, which increases the potential for conflicts with foreign states. However, this provision concerns the territoriality principle under international law, not the active or passive personality principle as in Germany: the nationalities of the offender or victim are[240] irrelevant.[241]

2.5 Computer misuse offences and jurisdiction

In respect of cybercrime the issue is particularly pertinent in relation to offences protecting the confidentiality and authenticity of computer data, the functioning of computers and the integrity of computer systems and networks. The person launching the attack over the internet may be located in State A, causing some changes to a computer in State B, and the object of the crime might again in a third State C. For this reason, specific provisions were included in the Computer Misuse Act 1990 dealing with jurisdiction, both for completed and for inchoate offences. These offences are only triable in England, Scotland, or Northern Ireland if a significant link to the relevant jurisdiction exists.[242] The Computer Misuse Act itself defines different constellations as to what constitutes that significant link.

The first significant link only applies to section 1 and this is that the offender was in the relevant country while carrying out the criminal acts concerned (place where the criminal acted).[243]

Alternatively, for the offences in sections 1, 2, 3, and 3ZA, the second significant link is that the computer, which is the object of the attack, is located in the relevant country.[244] This second significant link focuses on the result of the crime. Third, in

[237] Added by the Criminal Justice Act 1993.
[238] S 1A(3) Criminal Law Act 1977.
[239] S 1A(5) Criminal Law Act 1977.
[240] Largely see s 5(1A) .
[241] S 9 Computer Misuse Act 1990.
[242] S 4(2).
[243] S 5(2)(a), (3)(a), (3A)(a) Computer Misuse Act 1990.
[244] S 5(2)(b), (3)(b), (3A)(b).

respect of the offences concerning unauthorized acts of causing, or creating, the risk of serious damage[245] it is sufficient that the unauthorized act caused, or created, a significant *risk of serious damage of a material kind in* the relevant country.[246]

Furthermore, the Computer Misuse Act 1990 created a composite offence in section 2. This consists of unauthorized access plus another offence. Thus, if the offender either acted in the UK or the relevant computer was in the UK, the English, Scottish, or Northern Irish courts have jurisdiction even if the "other" offence was not connected to a UK territory.[247] However, the composite offence is only justiciable in the UK if the "other" offence was also a criminal offence in the place where it was committed (dual criminality).[248] Furthermore, where the further offence has been committed in the relevant country, then there is no need for a further link to England, Scotland, or Northern Ireland.[249]

Fifth, if the offender did not carry out the criminal acts required for the attack in the UK, a significant link is that the offender was a UK *national* and that the act constitutes a criminal offence under the law of the place where it occurred.[250] This jurisdictional provision applies to all computer misuse offences. Here UK law introduces the active personality principle in respect of computer misuse, coupled with the dual criminality principle.

As to inchoate offences,[251] section 6(1) of the Computer Misuse Act 1990 provides for *conspiracies* that (1) *the place where* an offender became part of a conspiracy, *and* (2) whether any act, omission, or other event occurred in England or Northern Ireland is immaterial to a conviction. For *attempts* under section 6(2)(a), the place where the attempt was made *and* section 6(2)(b) the question whether it had any effect in England or Northern Ireland are likewise immaterial for a conviction. For jurisdictional purposes, for inchoate offence in section 1 the English or Northern Irish courts are competent, if the computer, which the offender intended to produce effects on, is in the respective country.[252]

Section 3 (doing any unauthorized act in relation to a computer with intent to impair the operation of the computer or software or hinder access to data etc) is an inchoate offence itself. Again, the significant link is either that the defendant acted in England or Northern Ireland or that his or her intention was to affect a computer in these countries.[253]

Furthermore, in respect of jurisdiction for attempts or conspiracy in relation to section 3ZA, the English or Northern Irish courts are competent if the act concerned created a significant risk of serious damage of a material kind in England or Northern Ireland respectively.[254]

245 S 3ZA Computer Misuse Act 1990 as amended by the Serious Crime Act 2015.
246 S 5(3A)(c) Computer Misuse Act 1990.
247 S 4(4).
248 S 8(1).
249 S 4(3).
250 S 5(1A) Computer Misuse Act 1990, added by the Serious Crime Act 2015.
251 These provisions in the Computer Misuses Act 1990 do not apply to Scotland.
252 Ss 5(2) and 6(2).
253 S 5(3).
254 S 5(3A)(c).

In relation to attempts of the impairing offences in section 3 of the Computer Misuse Act 1990, the Act provides that if the offender acted within England and his or her criminal acting has reached the stage of an attempt, the offender may be tried in England, even if the result of the criminal offence would have occurred outside the jurisdiction.[255] This is, however, subject to the dual criminality principle.[256]

Finally, for the offence under section 3A (offering or supplying an article for computer misuse) the defendant need not necessarily be in the UK for the courts to have jurisdiction.[257]

Section 13 of the Computer Misuse Act 1990 stipulates the jurisdictional rules for Scotland—these provide for jurisdiction in the district (Sheriffdom) in which the offender acted, or the Sheriffdom in which the computer affected was located. However, if the offender acted outside Scotland and the courts have jurisdiction on the basis that the computer was in Scotland, the offender can additionally be prosecuted in any district in which he or she was apprehended, or as directed by the Lord Advocate.[258]

3. Conclusion

This comparison between the English and German rules of jurisdiction of the criminal courts has shown some fundamental differences and similarities in approaches. In Germany, in addition to the territoriality principle, jurisdiction is assumed based on the passive (German victim) and active personality (German offender) principles, provided the conduct was a criminal offence in the state where the offender acted. Furthermore, German criminal law applies the *universality* principle to the criminal offences relating to the distribution of certain forms of violent pornography and child sex abuse content. Thus, Germany relies on the full range of jurisdictional principles under international law, and in some respects exceeds them, arguably stretching the jurisdictional boundaries to their limit.

By contrast, other than some specific exceptions defined in statutory provisions, in England the territoriality principle limits jurisdiction in criminal cases. Until recently, the English common law rules on jurisdiction were even more restrictive, being limited to the last act to complete the crime. The courts have now replaced the terminatory approach with the substantial measure test, which takes into account all elements of the crime as connecting factors to the territory. While the English courts have limited jurisdiction to the territoriality principle, thus adopting a narrower approach to jurisdiction, the courts in England have been willing to accept that conduct outside the territory may reach into territory through its virtual effects on a computer within the territory. In this respect, the courts have developed a more flexible approach to the connection to the territory itself (as in *Levin* and *Perrin*).

One question scholarly debate and the courts have had to grapple with in both countries is the question whether internet access to illegal content is sufficient to

[255] S 7 Computer Misuse Act 1990.
[256] S 8(3).
[257] S 4(4A).
[258] S 13(10A).

satisfy the territoriality principle. Neither country has adopted a targeting test here in the sense that jurisdiction arises if, and only if, the illegal content was targeted at an audience in the jurisdiction. In Germany, while the courts have decided that mere internet access to illegal content was insufficient for jurisdiction if the offender has acted outside Germany, the courts have focused on identifying harm to protected interests within the jurisdiction. Thus, if an internet publication is likely to disturb the public peace and stir up racial hatred within Germany, this may be sufficient for jurisdiction. By contrast, in England, in some criminal cases the courts decided that access to illegal publications is sufficient, while in other cases the court have applied the substantial measure test to examine whether the gist of the crime has been connected to England.

Given the potential remoteness of the offender's conduct to the criminal result and the potential spread of the criminal harm, for example, in cases of illegal publication or criminal offences harming cybersecurity such as the spread of malware, narrow-tailored jurisdiction rules make it difficult to prosecute and may mean a lack of effective enforcement. By contrast, wide-tailored jurisdiction rules lead to three risks: first that offenders are prosecuted for acts that were not criminal in the place they were committed, second, that they are prosecuted for the same offence more than once, and, third, the risk of conflicts of jurisdiction between states. While the first risk can be addressed by the requirement of dual criminality, addressing the second and the third risks requires international coordination of prosecutions between states, which is currently largely missing, as discussed in Chapter 4.

6

Digital Investigations in the Cloud—Criminal Enforcement Cooperation

1. Introduction

This chapter examines in detail the jurisdictional aspects of obtaining computer data for the purposes of gathering information to find out that a crime has been committed in the first place, investigations by police authorities and similar bodies to find the relevant facts and prepare the evidence, up to the stage of prosecution and preparing a criminal case for trial. This obtaining of computer data in this pre-trial phase will be called digital investigations for the purposes of this chapter. The authorities involved are collectively and in a deliberately imprecise manner referred to as Law Enforcement Authorities (LEAs). The focus here is on the troika of *international* jurisdictional competence, extraterritoriality, and state sovereignty in respect of digital investigations. However, jurisdiction, extraterritoriality, and sovereignty in criminal investigations are directly linked to questions of safeguards for the citizens and domiciles in a nation state, and in particular the vital question as to *which state* is responsible for protecting their fundamental rights under the national criminal procedure rules. Furthermore, it should be noted that jurisdictional questions surrounding digital investigations are not limited to cybercrimes, as digital investigations and electronic evidence in the twenty-first century are involved in almost *any* criminal investigation or prosecution.[1]

The internet, modern computing technology, and, in particular, cloud computing[2] have brought about two important changes in paradigm for digital investigations.

First, in the "old" days law enforcement would have used coercive, physical search and seizure powers, usually requiring a judicial warrant as the authorization requirement,[3] in order to obtain the data residing in computers. In other words, law enforcement would force their way into a building and take away computers and data storage equipment, which would then be forensically analysed—by contrast, now computers can be remotely accessed through hacking, and searched. In the age of cloud computing, where computer data is increasingly processed and stored on servers in data centres physically remote from the computers used to access the data, this strategy is likely not to be successful, as the data is remotely stored "in the cloud."[4] Instead, law

[1] P de Hert et al, "The Cybercrime Convention Committee's 2017 Guidance Note on Production Orders" (2018) 34 Computer Law & Security Review 327–36, 328.

[2] See further I Walden, "Law Enforcement Access to Data in the Cloud" in C Millard, *Cloud Computing Law* (1st edn, Oxford University Press 2013), 285–310.

[3] For England and Wales eg ss 8 and 20 Police and Criminal Evidence Act 1984.

[4] But see s 20(1) of PACE, which extends the power of seizure to any information accessible from the computer seized, but of course it may still be inaccessible because of access restrictions; on this dilemma

Internet Jurisdiction. Julia Hörnle, Oxford University Press (2021). © Julia Hörnle.
DOI: 10.1093/oso/9780198806929.001.0001

enforcement requires remote access to the data stored in the cloud. But it is here that the territoriality principle clashes with the concept of cloud computing, since law enforcement powers are restricted to the territory of the LEA. Law enforcement access to cloud data raises issues of jurisdiction, if either the data is stored in a data centre in another jurisdiction or it is unclear in which jurisdiction the data is stored, or if the controller of data or data subject is domiciled[5] in another jurisdiction.

The second paradigm change in respect of criminal investigations concerns modern forms of communication. In the past the main means of remote communication (ie between two persons not physically in the same location) was the *national* postal service or the *national* telephone service, enabling law enforcement to use local powers in respect of interception of content (usually based on a warrant) and the obtaining of communications metadata (such as telephone numbers, subscriber data, time and duration of calls). Obviously, in the modern age much postal and telephony data has been replaced with other communication methods such as email, messaging on online social media, and internet telephony (Facebook, Twitter, WhatsApp, Skype, Snapchat, Instagram, etc). These internet service providers (ISPs) are largely headquartered in the US,[6] so that the relevant data is likely to be controlled outside the LEA's local territory. These ISPs store the data in the cloud, in remote data centres so that, again, jurisdictional issues arise in respect of law enforcement powers such as interception and the obtaining of metadata.

These two fundamental changes of paradigm hamper law enforcement investigations significantly, as even for purely domestic crimes (a crime committed on local territory by a locally domiciled citizen against a local crime victim), if some of the evidence, as is increasingly likely, is located in the cloud, LEA would have to use Mutual Legal Assistance (MLA) procedures, which are slow and cumbersome.[7] Extraterritoriality considerations notwithstanding, one could argue that digital investigations are easier than "real-world" ones, as there is no longer any need to *physically* seize computers to obtain data, instead replacing search and seizure by judicial production orders, whereby the service provider is compelled to obtain and disclose the relevant information or by remote computer searches and hacking.

The fundamental problem underlying this paradigm change is that traditionally states' enforcement authority has been based on the notion of territoriality,[8] namely that this authority is concomitant to, and strictly limited to, its territory.[9] Thus, in the context of digital investigations territoriality as a base of jurisdiction raises the question of location of data. The speed of communication online and the remote storage of data in a cloud computing environment seriously challenges jurisdiction based on the location of data.[10] In this environment Jennifer Daskal rightly questions the normative significance of the location of data as the determining factor linking jurisdiction and

more generally see D Kahvedzic, "Cybercrime Investigations of Mobile Phone Devices and the Cloud in the Light of EU Safe Harbor Rulings" (2016) 17 ERA Forum 355–67, 362.

[5] Further complication may arise from the question of the connecting factor: is it nationality, domicile, or simply location?

[6] Or increasingly also in China, such as TikTok.

[7] As discussed in section 2.1.

[8] De Hert et al (n 1) 328.

[9] See Chapter 2.

[10] J Daskal, "The Un-territoriality of Data" (2015) 125 Yale Law Journal 326–98.

territoriality.[11] She posits that computer data in the age of cloud computing has three characteristics that make location as the basis for jurisdiction meaningless: mobility, interconnectedness, and divisibility.[12] Data is mobile because it can be sent in fractions of seconds and be accessed remotely from almost anywhere and it is precisely this ubiquity of internet technology and the availability of broadband that helped cloud computing as a technological and business concept to become dominant. But data is also interconnected and intermingled as the vast quantities of data produced now make it difficult for ISPs to separate data, for example, according to citizenship or domicile. Finally, data is divisible in the sense that technologies such as sharding[13] or inline linking[14] allow different sets of data to be stored in different locations on several servers, but nevertheless be processed and presented as one composite data set. These characteristics have led to what can be described as loss of location.[15] But this loss of location does not sit easily with states' need to fight crime and their insistence on full sovereignty (including data sovereignty[16]) on their territory. The conflict between the recognition of the need for international cooperation and states' insistence on maintaining exclusive jurisdictional authority over territory has found its expression in provisions such as Article 4(2) of the League of Arab States Convention on Combatting Information Technology Offences, which expressly prohibits the exercise "in the territory of another State the jurisdiction or functions the exercising of which is the exclusively right of the authorities of that other State by virtue of its domestic law."

As we will see in this chapter, states have reacted to the loss of location in four ways: (1) by increasing international cooperation through MLA, (2) by unilateral extension of jurisdiction, extending investigatory powers beyond their territory, (3) by creating international frameworks for extending domestic investigative procedures on a mutual basis, and (4) by cross-border, voluntary cooperation with ISPs (Table 6.1). All four of these reactions have serious human rights implications, which this chapter highlights.

The big question in this field is to what extent is it possible to protect individual privacy but still allow law enforcement capability to combat illegal activities, as it seems that one comes at the expense of the other.[17] States resorting to extension of jurisdiction can lead to practices that are at best doubtful under international law, such as the sting carried out by the US in the *Gorshkov* case[18] or the creation of backdoors and remote direct access to computers using hacking techniques.[19]

As for increased international cooperation, this chapter distinguishes between specific cooperation established by international instruments (such as MLATs or the Cybercrime Convention and, potentially, the executive agreements envisaged by the US Cloud Act) and cooperation, which takes place within the framework of specific

[11] ibid 329.
[12] ibid 331.
[13] Which is a way to partition databases into smaller fragments spread over several locations.
[14] Where certain objects (such as images) on a website are stored on different servers.
[15] Walden (n 2).
[16] Discussed in section 7.
[17] Kahvedzic (n 4) 356.
[18] See text and (n 510).
[19] N Dalla Guarda, "Governing the Ungovernable: International Relations, Transnational Cybercrime Law and the Post-Westphalian Regulatory State" (2015) 6(1) Transnational Legal Theory 211–49, 237.

Table 6.1 Four ways of reacting to loss of location

	Four ways of reacting to loss of location	Basis	Power-Measure Access Point	Coercive or Voluntary?	Examples
1	International cooperation: Mutual legal assistance	MLA Treaties	Different types of enforcement measures: including search and seizure; production orders from third parties, including ISPs	Coercive	Cybercrime Convention
2a	Extension of domestic investigative powers	Arguments about extended territoriality; domestic criminal procedure rules	Production orders from third parties, including ISP	Coercive-domestic criminal procedure rules	Belgian *Yahoo* case; Guidance Note Art 18 Cybercrime Convention
2b	Extension of domestic investigative powers	Arguments about extended territoriality; domestic criminal procedure rules	Search and seizure; remote computer searches by LEA; incl. hacking and data mining techniques?	Coercive-domestic criminal procedure rules	Belgian Criminal Procedure Rules; Danish Supreme Court Case; Art 32 a Cybercrime Convention
3	Extension of domestic investigative powers, but based on international agreement/ international cooperation	International agreement	Production orders from third parties, including ISP	Coercive-domestic criminal procedural rules and international framework	US Cloud Act; EU E-Evidence Regulation (Proposal)
4	Extension of domestic powers—cooperation with private ISPs	Discretion of private party; domestic criminal procedure rules	Disclosure by third party ISPs (conflict with data protection)	Voluntary	Art 32(b) Cybercrime Convention

international and intergovernmental institutions (such as Eurojust and Europol). A further distinction is made between, on the one hand, cooperation within the EU based on the EU constitutional framework and, on the other hand, international cooperation based on bilateral and multilateral treaty-based frameworks. Until the Treaty of Lisbon, the EU institutions had no competences in the area of criminal law (other than the Council based, intergovernmental, Third Pillar framework) and EU law was considered to be completely separate from national criminal law. The Treaty of Lisbon created a new power of the EU institutions for criminal matters, although this is restricted by not allowing the EU to pass law directly applicable to individuals. In the new era of the European Area of Freedom, Security and Justice, Article 67(3) Treaty on the Functioning of the European Union (TFEU) provides for mutual recognition, operational cooperation and law approximation.

With regard to states unilaterally extending their jurisdiction, this could be termed extraterritorial. Extraterritoriality has been discussed in detail in Chapter 2. In this chapter cross-border digital investigations are examined in the context of criminal law enforcement and in particular the need of states to obtain data that is located or controlled in another state. If LEAs (or the courts) in State A order a person in State B to disclose data that is controlled from or located in State B this can be classified as *extraterritorial*. Likewise, if law enforcement in State X (under their own domestic procedure) directly access data (through remote search and seizure), which is controlled and hosted on computers in State Y, this could equally be termed *extraterritorial*. It has been universally accepted that law enforcement agents of State C would have no authority and no jurisdiction to physically travel to State D and carry out investigations there (eg seizing and searching a computer) and such an investigation would both be extraterritorial *and* illegal under international law. However, with remote data searches it is less clear what amounts to territoriality and what amounts to extraterritoriality.[20] Daskal has termed this phenomenon the *unterritoriality of data*.[21] The pertinent questions here are the following: What is the territoriality of data and in particular what are the connecting factors that make law enforcement access to data territorial or extraterritorial? Thus, while states are not allowed to take law enforcement measures outside their own territory,[22] this restriction is not entirely relevant to data access, as remote access through the internet enables access to data by law enforcement taking the actual measures while *physically staying in their own territory*, for example, accessing open source intelligence or by hacking into foreign computers. The connection between the authority to regulate and enforce and territory has been partly dissolved by cloud computing and this disconnect forces states increasingly to make use of measures with extraterritorial effect.[23] One good illustration of this disconnection between data location, territory, and jurisdiction is the almost irrational connection EU Data Protection Authorities have maintained between the *physical location of data* and the prohibition on the transfer of personal data from an EU Member State to a non-EU state without adequate data protection standards. Thus, for deciding whether such a transfer has taken place, data protection authorities are reluctant to accept that in a cloud computing environment the infrastructure owner (such as a data centre for hosting data) may have no access to or control of the data stored and that therefore, even if data is stored in the cloud outside the EU, this should not necessarily mean that a data export has actually taken place.[24] For data this raises in particular the question

[20] J Albrecht and F Jotzo, *Das Neue Datenschutzrecht der EU* (Nomos 2017) 37.
[21] Daskal (n 10).
[22] P Uecker, *Extraterritoriale Regelungshoheit im Datenschutzrecht* (Nomos 2017) 26.
[23] ibid 23, 35.
[24] K Hon, *Data Localisation Laws and Policy* (Elgar 2017) 167.

of what the relevant factor should be connecting the territory to the jurisdiction, and whether possession and control should be a dominant factor over mere location.

Following this section, the chapter proceeds in the section 2 by discussing international cooperation, examining MLA and multilateral cooperation under the Cybercrime Convention. The third section of this chapter discusses EU cooperation mechanisms in the field of digital investigations, starting off by discussing the principle of mutual recognition as the core feature of EU cooperation in criminal law and its relationship to fundamental rights more generally, including examples of case law from the area of the European Arrest Warrant.[25] Section 3 continues by focusing on the specific instruments for EU cooperation in the field of digital investigations, in particular the European Investigation Order, joint investigation teams (JITs), and intra-EU institutional cooperation, in particular Eurojust.

Since the chapter considers international cooperation agreements and these require the export of personal data from the EU to non-EU countries, the section 4 examines in detail the export requirements under the EU data protection law framework, including the Privacy Shield and the EU–US Umbrella Agreement, both negotiated with the aim of alleviating data protection concerns about US *LEAs* processing EU data.

Section 5 investigates the extraterritorial extension of jurisdiction under national laws and transnational instruments, and the recognition of such extensions of jurisdiction beyond territory. Commencing with the Cybercrime Convention, it discusses the attempt to interpret the Article 18 provision on Production Orders as authorizing an extension of jurisdiction and Article 32(a) on open source internet data and Article 32(b) on voluntary and lawful access. In this connection it discusses the *Microsoft* case in the US and the passing of the Cloud Act as an example of a national law extending jurisdiction to data located abroad but controlled within the US. In other jurisdictions we see examples going even further in terms of extraterritoriality: domestic procedure being applied to *foreign ISPs* controlling the data from a foreign location (Belgian *Yahoo!* case). Furthermore, section 5 examines "lawful" remote hacking by LEAs (also termed, euphemistically, Computer Network Exploitation) as another form of extension of jurisdiction. The second part of section 5 concentrates on new forms of transnational cooperation between the US and the EU, in particular the US proposed framework of executive agreements under the US Cloud Act, and it also discusses the Proposal for a Regulation on E-Evidence, which would allow Member States to extend their jurisdiction directly to foreign service providers within the EU. Finally, the chapter examines the common practice of LEAs to request data from foreign ISPs, on an informal, voluntary basis, without using domestic coercive powers.

Having examined how states cooperate internationally in digital investigations and how territorial jurisdiction is being reinterpreted and extended, the "elephant in the room" is states' data sovereignty, which is discussed in section 6. This examines the notion of data sovereignty, in particular discussing the data localization laws passed by Russia to counter US hegemony over internet data. Section 7 contains an examination more generally of fundamental rights (including data protection) in the sphere of

[25] Extradition procedures are not part of this chapter otherwise, focusing on digital investigations.

transnational digital investigations and what is required to achieve safeguards for data subjects and the accused under criminal investigation. This section argues that the focus on state interests and comity is not sufficient, and that any application of investigatory powers transnationally must include a fundamental rights analysis.

This chapter does not discuss (for lack of space) another two developments that could likewise be seen as reactions to the loss of location: data sharing and interoperability through shared databases (such as part of the Schengen cooperation mechanism or Europol) and bilateral or multilateral sharing of *intelligence* data (such as the so-called "Five Eyes"[26]).

2. International cooperation and digital investigations

One of the fundamental principles of international law is that states respect each other's territorial sovereignty and the principle of non-interference in the affairs of another nation state. Therefore states have the exclusive right to carry out criminal investigations or other law enforcement activities on their territory. On a practical level this means that criminal investigations conducted by a state's LEAs are limited to that state's geographical territory. If a state requires the execution of criminal investigations outside its territory it needs to cooperate transnationally with the state where the information is controlled and/or located and request legal assistance from that state. Since such legal assistance is in the mutual interests of all states, this concept is called MLA.

2.1 Ad hoc cooperation and treaty-based international cooperation: MLA

MLA in criminal matters is one state (the requested state) helping another state (the requesting state) in that state's criminal investigations without necessarily having an interest in this particular investigation itself. This type of criminal assistance through letters rogatory has been recognized in the common law for a long time.[27] The mutuality is based on the idea that the requested state in the future may need such assistance and therefore the favour will be returned. MLA can be by an ad hoc request (letters rogatory) without a treaty, or it can be based on bilateral or multilateral treaties. Since treaties create binding legal obligations on states,[28] treaty-based requests are more likely to be successful, compared to ad hoc requests.[29]

The earliest modern[30] multilateral MLA treaty and the most significant in the intra-European context is the Council of Europe Convention on Mutual Criminal

[26] https://www.theguardian.com/world/2013/dec/02/history-of-5-eyes-explainer accessed on 17/7/2020.

[27] D McClean, *International Co-operation in Civil and Commercial Matters* (3rd edn, Oxford University Press 2012) 150 referring to the House of Lords Decision *Re State of Norway's Application* [1900] 1 AC 723.

[28] Art 26 "Pacta Sunt Servanda" Vienna Convention on the Law of Treaties, Vienna 23 May 1969 UN Treaty Series 18232.

[29] T Hackner and C Schierholt, *Internationale Rechtshilfe in Strafsachen* (2nd edn, C.H. Beck 2012) 8.

[30] McClean (n 27) 153.

Assistance[31] (with two Additional Protocols[32]). This was eventually supplemented by the EU Convention on Mutual Assistance in Criminal Matters[33] (with one Additional Protocol[34]). The EU Convention only adds to its predecessors and does not constitute an independent basis for a request.[35] In the context of cybercrime and digital investigations, the Council of Europe Cybercrime Convention contains provisions on MLA.[36] To the extent that their provisions and scope of application overlap, the European Investigations Order Directive 2014/41/EU has replaced the provisions of the Council of Europe Convention and the EU Convention in respect of intra-EU MLA from 22 May 2017.[37] However, the setting up of JITs continues to be governed by Article 13 of the EU Convention.[38] A non-regional MLA agreement is the Commonwealth Scheme for MLA of 1986, the so-called Harare Scheme[39] (revised in 2011).[40] Unlike traditional MLA treaties (MLATs), the Harare scheme provides a voluntary, non-binding framework of recommendations for MLA.[41] One of the downsides of a voluntary scheme is that it leads to inertia by states when implementing the framework in domestic legislation and even some of the states that have implemented the scheme only apply it to some of the other Commonwealth countries, thus it is not fully reciprocal.[42] Arguably, the Commonwealth scheme has not been very successful as during a round of assessments in 2006–07 it was reported that many states had chosen not to rely on the provisions in the Harare Scheme for MLA and had preferred to enter into bilateral MLAT as a binding legal justification, especially for coercive measures, such as obtaining official records, tracing and seizing and confiscating the proceeds of crime, and the preservation of computer data.[43] However, the non-binding nature of the Scheme meant that its scope was wide and it was easier to negotiate and conclude such a broad-ranging instrument.[44] Additionally, there are a number of other regional conventions. These are the Association of Southeast Asian Nations (ASEAN) Convention

[31] 20 April 1959, ETS No 30, which entered into force on 12 June 1962 https://www.coe.int/en/web/conventions/full-list/-/conventions/treaty/030 ratified by the 47 Council of Europe States and Chile, Israel and Korea (status as of 17 July 2020) accessed on 17/7/2020.

[32] ETS 99 of 17 March 1978 (removes fiscal offences as a ground of refusal and other amendments) and ETS 182 of 8 November 2001 (improving channels of communication and introducing video-conferencing for witnesses and experts).

[33] EU Council Act of 29 May 2000, entered into force 23 August 2005, OJ C197 of 12 July 2000.

[34] OJ C326 of 21 November 2001.

[35] McClean (n 27) 191.

[36] ETS No 185 signed at Budapest on 23 November 2001, in force 1 July 2004 discussed separately at section 2.2.

[37] Art 34 Directive 2014/41/EU discussed in section 3.2.1.

[38] And Council Framework Decision 2002/465/JHA.

[39] Office of Civil and Criminal Justice Reform "Commonwealth Schemes for International Co-operation in Criminal Matters," 2017, 14–39, http://thecommonwealth.org/sites/default/files/key_reform_pdfs/P15370_13_ROL_Schemes_Int_Cooperation.pdf accessed on 17/7/2020.

[40] Adopted in July 2011 in Sydney Australia which included amendments on interception of telecommunications and postal items; covert electronic surveillance; the use of video-conferencing for questioning witnesses in investigations and judicial proceedings as well as asset recovery—see Commonwealth Office of Civil and Criminal Justice Reform "Commonwealth Schemes for International Co-operation in Criminal Matters," 2017, 3.

[41] V Reddi, "The Commonwealth Scheme Relating to Mutual Assistance in Criminal Matters within the Commonwealth, the Harare Scheme: an Appraisal" (2012) 38 Commonwealth Law Bulletin 119–25, 120.

[42] ibid 122.

[43] ibid 123.

[44] ibid 124.

on MLA,[45] the Inter-American Convention on Mutual Assistance in Criminal Matters,[46] the Caribbean MLA Treaty in Serious Criminal Matters,[47] Economic Community of West African States Convention on Mutual Assistance in Criminal Matters,[48] the Economic Community of Central African States (ECCAS) Mutual Assistance Pact,[49] Intergovernmental Authority on Development (IGAD) MLA Convention,[50] Southern African Development Community (SADC) Protocol on MLA in Criminal Matters,[51] and the South Asian Association for Regional Cooperation (SAARC) Convention on MLA in Criminal Matters.[52] Other multilateral conventions cover MLA as part of their remit, for example the UN Convention against Transnational Organized Crime 2004[53] or the Schengen Implementation Convention 1990,[54] both of which are not examined any further here.

On a fundamental level a distinction can be made between (1) mutual assistance in the area of criminal investigations and prosecution of offences, leading up to the criminal proceedings, on the one hand, and (2) extradition and surrender of fugitives (assistance with the person of the accused/convicted), which are normally contained in different treaties (Extradition Treaties). The scope of MLA sometimes covers a range of international cooperation measures,[55] but at its core is the provision of information, collection of evidence, and witness testimony from abroad. In addition to a general clause (mutual assistance to the widest extent possible[56]), MLAT usually contain provisions on:

(1) identifying and locating persons;[57]
(2) serving documents;[58]
(3) procuring evidence[59] through coercive measures including controversial and highly invasive measures such as covert investigation[60] (eg undercover police officers), interception of communications,[61] disclosure of documents[62]

45 Treaty on Mutual Legal Assistance in Criminal Matters, signed at Kuala Lumpur on 29 November 2004, http://agreement.asean.org/home/index/2.html accessed on 17/7/2020.
46 Adopted at Nassau, Bahamas on 23 May 1992, entered into force on 14 April 1996, OAS Treaty Series No 75, 28 ratifications.
47 6 July 2005, CARICOM.
48 29 July 1992, ECOWAS (West African States).
49 24 February 2002, ECCAS (Central African States).
50 8 December 2009, IGAD (East African States).
51 3 October 2002, SADC (South African States).
52 3 August 2008, SAARC (South Asia).
53 Art 18.
54 Convention of 19 June 1990 Implementing the Schengen Agreement OJ 2000 L 239, 19.
55 R Cryer et al, *An Introduction to International Criminal Law and Procedure* (3rd edn, Cambridge University Press 2014) 108; Hackner and Schierholt (n 29) 2.
56 See eg the Cybercrime Convention Art 25(1) in respect of computer data and electronic evidence or the 2013 bilateral MLAT between Jordan and the UK, Art 1(1), Council of Europe Convention, Art 1.
57 Art 1(2)(j) ASEAN Convention "locating and identifying witnesses and suspects"; para 1(5)(a) Commonwealth Scheme.
58 Art 7 Council of Europe Convention; Art 1(2)(c) ASEAN Convention; para 1(5)(c) Commonwealth Scheme; Art 7(g) Inter-American Convention.
59 Art 3(1) Council of Europe Convention: "procuring evidence or transmitting articles to be produced in evidence, records or documents"; Art 1(2)(a) ASEAN Convention; para 1(5)(b) Commonwealth Scheme: "taking evidence"; Art 7(h) Inter-American Convention.
60 Art 14 EU Convention.
61 Arts 17–22 EU Convention; para 1(5)(l) Commonwealth Scheme.
62 Art 1(2)(f) ASEAN Convention "providing copies of relevant documents, records, items of evidence"; para 1(5)(e) Commonwealth Scheme.

(production orders), preservation of evidence,[63] search and seizure of property;[64]
(4) examination of witnesses,[65] including persons who are already in custody in the requested state, through interviews or through personal appearance,[66] or, in modern treaties, frequently through video-conferencing;[67]
(5) production of judicial or other records;[68]
(6) tracing,[69] freezing,[70] or confiscating[71] proceeds of crime or assets;[72]
(7) the return of property;[73]
(8) information on bank accounts, banking transactions, or monitoring of banking transactions;[74]
(9) covert electronic surveillance.[75]

The 2000 EU Convention on MLA and the 2003 UK–US MLAT (bilateral) also provide for JITs.[76]

However, multilateral MLATs are far outnumbered by bilateral agreements[77] on MLA between two states on a reciprocal basis. The number of such bilateral agreements is likewise currently growing due to increased international mobility, globalization of crimes, the current fear of terrorism, and, of course, the fact that cybercrime is on the rise and even for domestic, non-cybercrime more and more criminal evidence is now stored in a cloud computing environment with the cross-border implications already discussed.

By way of illustration some statistical data may be useful here. As of 2016, the UK was a party to forty *bilateral* MLATs in addition to the EU and Council of Europe instruments.[78] In 2017 the UK received 6757 requests for mutual assistance (as the

[63] Art 29(1) Cybercrime Convention: "expedited preservation of stored computer data."

[64] Art 1(2)(d) and (e) "examining objects and sites" ASEAN Convention; para 1(5)(d) Commonwealth Scheme; Art 7(e) and (f) "examining objects and places" Inter-American Convention.

[65] Art 3(2) Council of Europe Convention; Art 1(2)(b) ASEAN Convention; para 1(5)(f) Commonwealth Scheme: "facilitating the voluntary attendance of persons in the requesting country"; Art 7(b) and (c) Inter-American Convention.

[66] Art 11 Council of Europe Convention and Art 9 of the EU Convention providing for the rules on temporary transfer of persons in custody; para 1(5)(g) Commonwealth Scheme; Art 7(i) Inter-American Convention.

[67] Art 13 Second Protocol to the Council of Europe Convention and Art 10 EU Convention raising issues such as the right against self-incrimination or witness protection measures.

[68] Art 13 Council of Europe Convention.

[69] Art 1(2)(g) ASEAN Convention.

[70] Art 1(2)(h) ASEAN Convention.

[71] Art 1(2)(i) ASEAN Convention.

[72] para 1(5)(h) Commonwealth Scheme; Art 7(d) Inter-American Convention; Art 1(2)(k) US–UK MLAT 1994.

[73] para 1(5)(i) Commonwealth Scheme.

[74] Protocol to the EU Convention on Criminal Mutual Legal Assistance of 2001; EU–US bilateral MLAT of 2003.

[75] para 1(5)(m) Commonwealth Scheme.

[76] Arts 13 and 5 respectively.

[77] Interestingly some countries such as Germany prefer multilateral MLATs, as they guarantee greater consistency of measures and more legal certainty; as of 2012 Germany only had entered four bilateral MLATs: with Canada, the US, Tunisia, and Hong Kong, Hackner and Schierholt (n 29) 9.

[78] Algeria, Antigua and Barbuda (drug trafficking only), Argentina (drug trafficking only), Australia (drug trafficking only), Bahamas (drug trafficking only), Bahrain (drug trafficking only), Barbados (drug trafficking only), Brazil, Canada, Chile (drug trafficking only), China, Colombia, Ecuador (drug trafficking only), Guyana (drug trafficking only), Grenada (drug trafficking only), Hong Kong, India, Ireland,

requested party). Just over 5 per cent, namely 355 of these, were made from other EU Member States under the European Investigation Order.[79] The EU, in turn, has entered into bilateral MLATs with third states, in particular the US[80] and Japan.[81] As of 1 January 2018, the US was party to forty-one bilateral MLATs.[82] In 2015 it received 3352 incoming requests for MLA.[83] According to a 2013 UN Office on Drugs and Crime (UNODC) survey of international cooperation mechanisms used in transnational cybercrime cases, 73 per cent of LEAs reported that formal MLA processes were used most often to obtain evidence from other jurisdictions (compared to other methods).[84]

MLATs contain varying restrictions, partly due to the current trends prevailing at the time when they have been negotiated, and partly due to the negotiation powers and the legal traditions of the states involved. However, it can equally be said that just as the range of investigative measures has become increasingly broader, the features restricting the discretion of the requested state have been reduced. The features that traditionally have restricted or slowed down international cooperation are: 91) the fixation on more or less rigid communication channels through a Central Authority, (2) the principle of reciprocity, (3) dual (or double) criminality at least for certain types of requests, (4) a list of general grounds on which refusal to cooperate is justified, and (5) a minimum level of seriousness of the offence investigated (or limitation to certain types of offences). These restrictions are of greater significance in the context of extradition, but also feature in MLATs concerning investigative measures and evidence. However, it can be equally argued that these restrictions protect individual rights (of suspects and, to an extent, of witnesses, such as witness protection).

One of the main obstacles to international cooperation is not necessarily these restrictions as such but simply different legal traditions and communications issues due to linguistic and cultural barriers.[85] It should be possible to overcome these barriers

Italy (drug trafficking only), Jordan, Kuwait, Kazakhstan, Libya, Malaysia, Mexico (drug trafficking only), Morocco, Netherlands (drug trafficking only), Nigeria (drug trafficking only), Panama (drug trafficking only), Paraguay (drug trafficking only), Philippines, Romania (drug trafficking only), Saudi Arabia (drug trafficking), Spain (drug trafficking), Sweden (drug trafficking), Thailand, United Arab Emirates, the US, Ukraine (drug trafficking only), and Vietnam—Source: UK Treaty Office list (April 2016), https://assets.publishing.service.gov.uk/government/uploads/system/uploads/attachment_data/file/516418/Treaty_List.pdfaccessed on 17/7/2020.

[79] Source: https://www.gov.uk/guidance/mutual-legal-assistance-mla-requests#obtaining-mla-from-overseas accessed on 17/7/2020.

[80] Council Decision 2009/820/CFSP of 23 October 2009, see OJ L291 of 7 November 2009.

[81] Council Decision 2010/616/EU of 7 October 2010, see OJ L271 of 15 October 2010.

[82] Argentina, Austria, UK, Belize, Brasil, China, Colombia, Czech Republic, Denmark, Estonia, France, Georgia, Grenada, Haiti, Hungary, Israel, Jamaica, Korea, Liechtenstein, Luxembourg, Malaysia, Malta, Marshall Islands, Mexico, Morocco, New Zealand, Nigeria, Palau, Panama, Philippines, Portugal, Russia, Saint Lucia, Singapore, Slovenia, Spain, Sweden, Trinidad and Tobago, Ukraine, UK, and Uruguay—Source: State Department Treaties in Force.

[83] A Keane-Woods, "Mutual Legal Assistance in the Digital Age" in D Gray and SE Henderson, *The Cambridge Handbook on Surveillance Law* (Online edn, Cambridge University Press October 2017) 659–76, 665.

[84] United Nations Office on Drugs and Crime, "Comprehensive Study on Cybercrime" (2013) https://www.unodc.org/documents/organized-crime/UNODC_CCPCJ_EG.4_2013/CYBERCRIME_STUDY_210213.pdf, 201 accessed on 17/7/2020.

[85] Cryer et al (n 55) 110.

through greater investment in technology and legal personnel without sacrificing fundamental rights safeguards and checks and balances.

Especially in older instruments, much emphasis was placed on the formality of communication channels[86] so that requests for MLA in criminal matters have to be passed from the investigating authority in the requesting state to the foreign ministry or ministry of justice, then to the central authority in the requested state (likely to be the foreign ministry or the ministry of justice), and from there to the judicial and LEAs in the requested state for authorization and execution of the request.[87] As requests are passed from desk to desk, there is a substantial time lag. The principle of reciprocity[88] adds a political "tit for tat" element to MLAT and allows states to refuse to execute a request if the requesting state has not executed a request in a previous case or has entered a derogation or reservation.[89] The principle of dual or dual criminality means that the offence investigated must be a criminal offence in both the requested and requesting state,[90] albeit not necessarily the same type of offence.[91] For example, the same criminal act could be classified in one state as computer misuse and in the other state as fraud. In *Ortmann v the United States of America* the New Zealand High Court, on appeal from the District Court,[92] held that Kim Dotcom and other executives in the *Megaupload copyright infringement* case were eligible for extradition under the US–New Zealand Extradition Treaty. The dual criminality requirement was fulfilled even though the New Zealand Copyright Act 1994 only provided for civil, not criminal, liability for the infringement of the communication to the public right. Instead, the Court relied on conspiracy to defraud offence in the New Zealand Crimes Act.[93] The problem with interpreting the dual criminality principle in such a wide manner (or doing away with it under the EU principle of mutual recognition) is that there is a risk that an accused will be investigated for an offence that does not exist in the requested state/his or her domicile and therefore may contradict the principle of *nullum crimen sine lege*.[94]

[86] See eg Art 15(1) of the Council of Europe Convention 1959: "letters rogatory (. . .) shall be addressed by the Ministry of Justice of the requesting Party to the Ministry of Justice of the requested Party and shall be returned by the same channels." By contrast, this is changed for those states which have ratified the 2nd Protocol which gives the option in the amended Art 15(1) to directly forward some requests between judicial authorities but it also gives states the right to reserve channels of communication through a Central Authority in Art 15(8).

[87] Also in the 2013 bilateral MLAT between Jordan and the UK (not yet in force), Art 2(1) requests sent through Central Authorities, likewise Art 2(3) US–UK MLAT 1994 or Art 3 Inter-American Convention etc.

[88] Hackner and Schierholt (n 29) 34.

[89] See Arts 5(2) and 23(3) Council of Europe Convention 1959; Art 3(g) ASEAN.

[90] The Inter-American Convention, for example limits the dual criminality principle to search & seizure or confiscation of property, Art 5; the Council of Europe Convention 1959 also foresees this as an option Art 5(1); Art 3(1)(e) ASEAN.

[91] Hackner and Schierholt (n 29) 35.

[92] *Ortmann v the United States of America* DC North Shore CRI-2012-092-001647, 23 December 2015.

[93] *Ortmann v the United States of America* [2017] NZHC 189

[94] A Roma Valdes, "The Mutual Recognition Principle in Criminal Matters: a Review" (2015) 16 ERA Forum 291–303, 295.

The grounds of refusal vary but usually include that the underlying offence is a fiscal (in older instruments),[95] political,[96] discriminatory[97] or military[98] offence, public policy or an infringement of a state's sovereignty,[99] that the investigation or other measure requested is not proportionate or necessary,[100] that the accused has already been acquitted or sentenced for the same offence (*ne bis idem* principle),[101] or that the requested measure is not available or authorized under the law of the requested state.[102] The offences for which MLA is possible are usually expressed either by a minimum–maximum tariff as expressed in the criminal law of the requesting and/or the requested state (such as that the maximum sentence prescribed for the offence has to be at least one year[103]). Alternatively, the range of offences could be limited to a specific type of offences such as drug trafficking or terrorism or a list of offences.[104]

Finally, another impractical but legally important limitation of MLATs is that usually the request is carried out according to the criminal procedure rules in the requested state.[105] This is impractical from the viewpoint of the prosecution in the requesting state, but legally important from the viewpoint of fundamental rights and protection of citizens in a state.[106] This limitation and focus on the procedural requirements in the requested state has two different conflict of law implications.

First, non-compliance with the procedural requirements in the requested state may simply mean that the evidence will not be available because of a blocking statute in the requested state. As for the first implication, if the requesting state asks for certain coercive measures that are associated with particular authorization requirements under the law of the requested state, the conditions for this authorization must be fulfilled. Therefore the requesting state must be aware of these conditions and effectively communicate these requirements, which frequently causes practical problems in a transnational environment. For example, if a non-US state required the contents of an email communications it would have to request the US courts to issue a warrant under

[95] Art 2(a) Council of Europe Convention 1959; amended in the Protocol of 1978; see also Art 3(5) ASEAN; but contrast this for example with the contrary provision in Art 25(4) Cybercrime Convention.

[96] Art 9(c) Inter-American Convention; Art 2(a) Council of Europe Convention 1959; Art 3(1)(a) ASEAN.

[97] Art 9(b) Inter-American Convention "The investigation has been initiated for the purpose of prosecuting, punishing, or discriminating in any way against an individual or group of persons for reason of sex, race, social status, nationality, religion, or ideology.," Art 3(1)(c) ASEAN.

[98] Art 8 Inter-American Convention; Art 1(2) Council of Europe Convention; Art 3(1)(b) ASEAN.

[99] Art 9(e) Inter-American Convention; Art 13 2003 EU–US bilateral MLAT; Art 2(b) Council of Europe Convention 1959; Art 3(f) ASEAN.

[100] Proposal on the E-Evidence Regulation discussed in section 5.2.2.

[101] Art 9(a) Inter-American Convention; Art 3(1)(d) ASEAN.

[102] Art 3(k) ASEAN.

[103] See for example Art 6 Inter-American Convention "For the purposes of this convention, the act that gives rise to the request must be punishable by one year or more of imprisonment in the requesting state."

[104] As in the European Investigation Order.

[105] Art 10 Inter-American Convention; Art 3(1) Council of Europe Convention; Art 25(4) Cybercrime Convention but cf Art 27(3).

[106] As an example of what can go wrong where the requested state (New Zealand) executes procedures in accordance with the requesting state's (US) practices, is the *Kim Dotcom* case, which led to a series of compensation claims, J Ip, "New Zealand: Megaupload's Kim Dotcom - US copyright enforcement efforts and the New Zealand legal system" (2013) Public Law 671–73.

the Stored Communications Act.[107] In practice, even if the circumstances of the investigation in the non-US state fulfil this probable cause standard, complying with this standard may slow the communication down and delay the process.[108]

But conversely, this conflict of law situation may mean that compliance with the law in the requested state may cause issues with the admissibility of evidence before the courts in the requesting, prosecuting state. It is interesting to observe that in more modern (post-1999s) MLATs the wording has changed to reflect this conflicts of law issue.[109] For example, Article 4(1) of the EU Convention on Mutual Assistance in Criminal Matter provides: "the requested Member State shall comply with the formalities and procedures expressly indicated by the requesting Member State, provided that such formalities and procedures are not contrary to the fundamental principles of law in the requested Member State." This reflects a tendency (at least within the EU) to allow more room for the domestic criminal procedures in the requesting state, a trend that has resulted in the domestic law of the investigating Member State being applied to the European Investigative Order (EIO), discussed later.[110]

In conclusion, then, the trend is clearly towards greater international cooperation (frenetic activity and increase in the number of MLATs in the last twenty years[111]), cooperation involving a greater range of investigative measures (newer instruments have included for the first time procedures for interception of communications, electronic surveillance, preservation of computer data, information on banking accounts and bank transactions, JITs, and the questioning of witnesses through video-conferencing), and procedures have been simplified and streamlined.[112] Outside the EU, MLA continues to be largely confined to the traditional principles, even if in an expanded and accelerated form.[113] However, as we will see in section3, within the EU, the Member States have advanced beyond MLA and new forms of international cooperation have developed for a number of years: for example, the cooperation within Europol went beyond the classical notion of MLA from the beginning.[114]

It seems that of these restrictions and limitations just discussed the greatest deficiency is the slow speed of the process. For example, it has been reported for the US that typically it takes ten months (or more) for a MLAT request to be executed.[115] Clearly, in many transnational criminal investigations this would mean that MLAT is pointless. The same report, however, also laments that the US Department of Justice has "severely under-resourced" the MLAT process[116] and therefore recommends that funding and resources from the US side should be increased so that MLAT requests

107 18 USC ss 2701–12.

108 Keane-Woods (n 83) 662–63.

109 See also eg Art 7(1) ASEAN: "subject to its domestic laws and practices, the requested party shall carry out the request in the manner specified by the requesting party."

110 Section 3.2.1.

111 McClean (n 27) 153–54.

112 Cryer et al (n 55) 108–09.

113 Hackner and Schierholt (n 29) 3.

114 ibid 2.

115 RA Clarke et al, "Liberty and Security in a Changing World: 2013 Report and Recommendations of the President's Review Group on Intelligence and Communications Technology" 2013, https://obamawhitehouse.archives.gov/sites/default/files/docs/2013-12-12_rg_final_report.pdf, 227 accessed on 17/7/2020, see also Keane-Woods (n 83) 667–68.

116 Clarke (n 115) 227.

are dealt with more quickly[117] and that an online e-submission system for MLAT requests should be introduced with a single point of contact and a dynamic electronic form guiding the requester through the procedural requirements, in order to make the system more efficient.[118]

The restrictions and limitations of the MLAT process just described have the dual purpose of both protecting the requested state's sovereignty and to protect the fundamental rights of persons domiciled in the requested state by introducing checks and balances at both ends.[119] Therefore, from a jurisdictional perspective, as we see in other parts of this chapter, sovereignty and the protection of rights are entwined. Given current concerns about cross-border law enforcement and the need for more efficient law enforcement this leads to a dilemma: Should the MLAT process of transnational cooperation be upheld and improved or should it be replaced (wherever possible) with more direct forms of international cooperation between states? The concern here is that, if the MLAT process is perceived to be not functioning well, states may resort to other coercive cross-border measures (which may or may not be illegal under domestic and/or international law) such as direct requests to foreign service providers for voluntary disclosure, or direct access through hacking. However, given the availability of technologies such as online communication platforms and artificial intelligence it should be possible to build an efficient and functioning system for MLATs, which is human rights compliant with the necessary safeguards. This requires substantial financial investment in the resources required to implement the required checks and balances (including legally qualified human resources) and political will to make international cooperation work.

2.2 The Cybercrime Convention: multilateral cooperation

The Council of Europe Cybercrime Convention[120] is one of the most significant instruments in the area of international cooperation in cross-border digital investigations.[121] It has been ratified by forty-three of the forty-seven Council of Europe

[117] How likely it is that the Trump administration would invest into something which directly only benefits foreign countries, is another question, though.

[118] Clarke (n 115) 228–29; see also Google Position Paper, "Digital Security and Due Process: Modernizing Cross-border Government Access Standards for the Cloud Era" (2017), 12–13 which argues for modernization of the MLAT system, https://storage.googleapis.com/gweb-uniblog-publish-prod/documents/CrossBorderLawEnforcementRequestsWhitePaper_2.pdf. accessed on 17/7/2020.

[119] See eg Statewatch's discussion of the EU-UK MLAT negotiations: http://www.statewatch.org/news/2002/jul/11Buseu.htm accessed on 17/7/2020.

[120] Kahvedzic (n 4) 356.

[121] Other regional instruments have been modelled on, or inspired by, the Cybercrime Convention: see eg the Commonwealth of Independent States (CIS) Agreement on Cooperation in Combating Offences related to Computer Information 2001; Commonwealth Model Laws on Computer and Computer-related Crime 2002 and Electronic Evidence 2002; East African Community Draft Legal Framework for Cyberlaws 2008; Draft Directive on Fighting Cybercrime within ECOWAS 2009; the Shanghai Cooperation Organization Agreement on Cooperation in the Field of International Information Security 2009; League of Arab States Convention on Combating Information Technology Offences 2010; International Telecommunication Union (ITU)/Caribbean Community (CARICOM)/Caribbean Telecommunications Union (CTU) Model Legislative Texts on Cybercrime, e-Crime and Electronic Evidence 2010; International Telecommunication Union (ITU) (Secretariat of the Pacific Community) Model Law on Cybercrime 2011; Common Market

states[122] and by Argentina, Australia, Canada, Chile, Costa Rica, Dominican Republic, Israel, Japan, Mauritius, Panama, Philippines, Senegal, Sri Lanka, Tonga, and the US, making a total of sixty-two ratifications.[123] The Cybercrime Convention consists of essentially three main parts.[124] First, it approximates cybercrime law by stipulating minimum standards for certain offences,[125] thus aiding international cooperation as states will be more willing to cooperate if their substantive law is similar. Second, it stipulates that states should have certain investigatory powers in their toolbox of investigative powers,[126] thus approximating important digital investigatory powers to enable international cooperation in the area of law enforcement, by ensuring that states have the powers most relevant for digital investigations and for the obtaining of electronic evidence. Contracting states are thereby mandated to implement these powers for digital investigation domestically, so that they can respond to a request for MLA accordingly. Third, the Cybercrime Convention then creates an obligation on Member States to provide MLA in respect of these (domestic) digital investigation powers. It is important to note that this system of international cooperation applies to the collection of evidence in electronic form for all types of crimes, not limited to cybercrime.[127] Furthermore, the Convention is based on mutual assistance and not the mutual reciprocal expansion of jurisdiction, with the exception of one provision:[128] Article 32, which will be discussed later.

The Convention contains the usual provisions on MLA already discussed, including the usual grounds for refusal of a request.[129] Mutual Assistance under the Cybercrime Convention can be based on existing treaties or, in the absence thereof, the Cybercrime Convention provides for the relevant MLA framework in Article 27.[130] It was clearly recognized that speed is of the essence for many digital investigations and the Cybercrime Convention therefore envisages expedited requests in urgent circumstances, including "by fax and email."[131] It also envisages and encourages the exchange of spontaneous information[132] and provides for the setting up of a network of twenty-four/seven contact points for informal cooperation.[133] Nevertheless, like other MLATs, the Cybercrime Convention also relies on the cumbersome use of communication channels through central authorities.[134] Disappointingly, the Cybercrime

for Eastern and Southern Africa (COMESA) Cybersecurity Draft Model Bill 2011; Southern African Development Community (SADC) Model Law on Computer Crime and Cybercrime 2012; African Union Convention on Cyberspace Security and Protection of Personal Data 2014—see United Nations Office on Drugs and Crime, "Comprehensive Study on Cybercrime" (2013) 64.

122 Not by Ireland, Russia, San Marino, and Sweden.
123 As of 14 June 2018.
124 Para 16 Explanatory Memorandum.
125 Which will not be discussed here.
126 Art 14(1).
127 Art 14(2)(c) and para 19 Explanatory Memorandum.
128 Para 20 Explanatory Memorandum.
129 Arts 25 and 27: eg dual criminality, political offences, sovereignty, and *ordre public*.
130 Dalla Guarda (n 19) 218.
131 Art 25(3).
132 Art 26.
133 Art 35.
134 Art 27(2)(a).

Convention missed the opportunity to set up an online platform, heavily armed with the latest technology to provide for the most efficient exchange of mutual assistance requests. Cleary the setting up of such a network would have raised questions of who would carry this forward institutionally and how the costs would have been shared. While the Convention is based on mutual assistance it did not implement an effective and innovative communication system for this.

Preparations are underway for a Second Additional Protocol to the Cybercrime Convention and the draft of this Protocol attempts to improve the provisions on MLA.[135] At the time of writing this included provisions for emergency mutual assistance, in situations involving a significant and imminent risk to the life or safety of any natural person, requiring the requested party to "maximally expedite" a request. Furthermore, the draft provides for time limits for MLA in respect of production orders for subscriber information and traffic data stipulating as time limits twenty days and forty-five days respectively.

In terms of international cooperation, the main focus of the Cybercrime Convention is on investigative powers and how to exercise them across a border on the basis of mutual assistance. In view of the fragile and ephemeral nature of computer data and the significance of metadata for identifying sources of communications, Articles 16 and 17 provide for powers to order the expedited preservation of computer data, regardless of the location where it is stored,[136] for a later[137] disclosure order. Articles 29 and 30 are the corresponding provisions that allow a state to request, through mutual assistance, the expedited preservation of computer data across a border. Articles 18 and 19 provide for the domestic powers for production orders in respect of specified[138] stored communications, content and subscriber data,[139] and the search and seizure of stored computer data respectively. The latter power (search and seizure) is expressly limited to the territory of the state concerned.[140] This raises the question of whether the power for production orders can be extended extraterritorially.[141] The corresponding provision, under which a state may request such stored data under MLA, is Article 31. Finally, the Convention provides that states need to create domestic powers in their domestic legal systems for the collection of real-time data through covert investigations such as real-time collection of traffic data (eg cellular data recorded in respect of a mobile phone to track the movements of a suspect, or missing victim in real time) and interception of communications content, in Articles 20 and 21. The corresponding provisions to request the application of these powers across a border are Articles 33 and 34,

[135] Council of Europe, T-CY (2018)23 of 8 November 2019, https://rm.coe.int/provisional-text-of-provisions-2nd-protocol/168098c93c accessed on 17/7/2020.

[136] Explanatory Memorandum, 26.

[137] The Explanatory Memorandum makes clear that a separate disclosure order is required, 26.

[138] This is targeted and specified data preservation not bulk data retention for the distinction see Explanatory Memorandum, 25.

[139] Discussed further in section 5.1.1.

[140] Art 19(1), Explanatory Memorandum, 33.

[141] Discussed in section 5.1.1.3.

referring to the domestic law of the requested party for the availability and extent of these powers.

The T-CY Cloud Evidence Group recommended the following measures to improve MLA and international cooperation in the context of cybercrime and digital investigations (to be laid down in a future Protocol to the Convention):

- a special, simplified regime for MLA for subscriber information,
- international production orders being sent *directly between judicial authorities*,
- direct cooperation between judicial authorities,
- JITs,
- all requests in English language,
- the use of video-conferencing for the testimony of witnesses (including victims and experts),
- the establishment of superfast emergency procedures in order to prevent loss of life,
- provisions allowing for direct cooperation with service providers, and
- stronger safeguards.[142]

As far as the last point is concerned, the Cybercrime Convention also lacks innovative models in respect of safeguards for the protection of fundamental rights, or for transparency and accountability, and thus follows the pattern of traditional, intergovernmental treaties, which have been plagued by these deficiencies and have been criticized by transnational law scholars on these grounds.[143] There is a declaratory reference in Article 15 to safeguards and international human rights standards but this in itself is ineffective and not suited to provide *actual* checks and balances on the investigative powers and their exercise, as mandated in Article 15 of the Convention, nor does it clarify which institution (judicial or otherwise) is responsible for these safeguards. The Explanatory Memorandum simply states that "as the Convention applies to Parties of many different legal systems and cultures, it is not possible to specify in detail the applicable conditions and safeguards for each power or procedure," which seems to be an easy way out. This is another example of the "crime control bias" of transnational criminal law,[144] since it may indeed be easier for states to agree on new measures to be tough on crime, and agree on urgently needed international cooperation mechanisms, than to agree on human rights safeguards and their effective implementation.[145] Again, this is a missed opportunity that could have created a truly transnational system of cybercrime cooperation and would have given the system legitimacy and durability by increasing the respect for the rule of law.

[142] T-CY Cloud Evidence Group, "Criminal Justice Access to Electronic Evidence in the Cloud" Final Report (16 September 2016), https://rm.coe.int/CoERMPublicCommonSearchServices/DisplayDCTMContent?documentId=09000016806a495e accessed on 17/7/2020.
[143] Dalla Guarda (n 19) 218.
[144] Further, see section 7.
[145] Dalla Guarda (n 19) 240.

3. Intra-EU cooperation in digital investigations

3.1 Mutual recognition and mutual trust in the EU: how does criminal enforcement jurisdiction in the EU legal order relate to fundamental rights?

The principle of mutual recognition is the "cornerstone" of European cooperation in criminal matters, first established at the Tampere European Council in 1999[146] and now expressly recognized in Article 82(1) TFEU: "Judicial cooperation in criminal matters in the Union shall be based on the principle of mutual recognition of judgments and judicial decisions."[147]

Mutual recognition essentially means, as a principle, that a judicial decision made in the court of one Member State will be recognized and given effect by the authorities in another Member State, extraterritorially.[148] Obviously, the UK, on leaving the EU, will no longer be part of the system of mutual recognition within the EU. The UK will not benefit from EU cooperation measures such as the European Investigation Order, the European Arrest Warrant, or the institutional coordination mechanisms such as Europol and Eurojust and will instead have to fall back on international mechanisms such as Interpol or bilateral third-country agreements.[149]

As Valsamis Mitsilegas has pointed out, "mutual recognition creates extraterritoriality (. . .) [as], the will of an authority in one Member State can be enforced beyond its (. . .) borders" and that the key feature of this mutual recognition of judicial decisions is a degree of "automaticity," in the sense that this mutual recognition is (almost) automatic, with (almost) no questions asked.[150] Mutual recognition is the logical consequence of the notion of the EU as a borderless area where people can move freely, and it is a fundamental aspect of the creation of an Area of Freedom,[151] Security,[152] and Justice[153] (AFSJ), since it is the means to ensure the effectiveness of legal cooperation[154] between the EU Member States.[155] Mutual recognition makes international

[146] Presidency Conclusions Tampere European Council, 15–16 October 1999, para 33: "Enhanced mutual recognition of judicial decisions and judgements and the necessary approximation of legislation would facilitate co-operation between authorities and the judicial protection of individual rights. The European Council therefore endorses the principle of mutual recognition which, in its view, should become the cornerstone of judicial co-operation in both civil and criminal matters within the Union. The principle should apply both to judgements and to other decisions of judicial authorities."

[147] Police and Criminal Evidence Act (n 3) 58.

[148] Roma Valdes (n 94) 292.

[149] https://ec.europa.eu/info/sites/info/files/factsheet_police_and_judicial_coordination_final.pdf accessed on 17/7/2020.

[150] V Mitsilegas, "Mutual Recognition, Mutual Trust, and Fundamental Rights after Lisbon" in V Mitsilegas et al, *Research Handbook on EU Criminal Law* (Edward Elgar 2016) 148–67, 149–50.

[151] Freedom of Movement.

[152] Enforcement of law, including criminal law in the sense of "law and order."

[153] Justice in the sense of legality, respect for fundamental human rights, legal redress, and access to the courts for citizens.

[154] In civil and criminal matters, although in this chapter we are focusing only on criminal enforcement jurisdiction.

[155] Daskal (n 10) 149.

cooperation between the Member States effective as it removes (most of the) grounds for refusing cooperation, it decreases the legal discretion of national authorities, and it reduces the possibilities of mounting legal challenges, thus making legal cooperation smoother, faster, and more efficient.[156] By the same token, however, this legal discretion potentially reduces fundamental rights standards to the lowest common denominator and eliminates some of the higher fundamental rights standards that Member States may grant locally to their own citizens (in domestic criminal proceedings), based on national Constitutional protections. Albeit that, since the Lisbon Treaty, the Charter of Fundamental Rights has been integrated into EU law, which is therefore now an integral part of the EU legal order, so that whenever EU law applies the EU now has its own fundamental rights standards upheld by the Member State courts, and, ultimately, by the Court of Justice of the EU (CJEU).[157] Of particular relevance in the context of intra-EU cooperation in criminal matters are the Right to Liberty and Security,[158] the Rights to Privacy and Data Protection,[159] the Right to a Fair Trial,[160] the Presumption of Innocence and the Right of Defence,[161] Legality and Proportionality of Criminal Offences,[162] and the *Ne Bis Idem* Principle (rule against double jeopardy).[163] Furthermore, all the EU Member States have all signed up to the European Charter of Human Rights (ECHR).

The ideological underpinning of mutual recognition in the EU is the notion of mutual trust between the EU Member States, trusting each other mutually to uphold the respect for the rule of law and fundamental human rights, not only for their own national citizens, but equally for citizens of other EU Member States. It is this abstract notion of mutual trust that is supposed to justify the imposition of systems of mutual recognition of judicial decisions in intra-EU cooperation in criminal matters.

Generally speaking, international cooperation in criminal investigations and law enforcement requires a degree of mutual trust in each other's legal systems (in terms of respect for the rule of law and implementation of fundamental human rights) between the participating states. This section will discuss, in the context of EU mutual recognition, what this notion of mutual trust means for the tension between, on the one hand, the need for the effectiveness of intra-EU cooperation in criminal investigation and, on the other hand, the need for the protection of fundamental rights.

It is argued here that this tension is inherently connected to the conflicting needs of states for international cooperation and the need to maintain territorial sovereignty.

This tension within the EU legal order raises *three questions*. First, whether higher fundamental rights standards can be maintained by Member States under their own, national Constitutional framework vis-à-vis their own citizens and persons *on their*

[156] See the further discussion on the European Investigation Order and the European Arrest Warrant section 3.2.1.

[157] Case C-311/18 *Data Protection Commissioner v Maximilian Schrems* ECLI:EU:C:2020:559 para 99: "the interpretation of EU law and examination of the legality of EU legislation must be undertaken in the light of the fundamental rights guaranteed by the Charter".

[158] Art 6 of the Charter of the Fundamental Rights of the EU, OJ C 364 of 18 December 2000, 1–22.

[159] Arts 7 and 8 of the Charter.

[160] Art 47 of the Charter.

[161] Art 48 of the Charter.

[162] Art 49 of the Charter.

[163] Art 50 of the Charter.

territory.[164] Second, whether mutual trust can be assessed *categorically* and a priori or, on the contrary, whether trust has to be confirmed on a case-by-case basis and measured against the common fundamental rights established in the Charter. The third question immediately flows from the answer to the second question, namely even *if* each act under an international cooperation system that has to be screened for its fundamental rights' compliance, which Member State has jurisdiction to assess fundamental rights compliance?

These three questions arise within the EU legal order (as a constitutional matter) but also, more generally, in international cooperation, for example, in the context of the operation of the bilateral MLATs, discussed earlier, or the executive agreements under the US Cloud Act, discussed later.[165]

Returning to the EU legal order, the answer should be "No" to the first question, since to maintain *national* Constitutional rights standards in the context of international cooperation under EU law would impede the effectiveness of such international cooperation, thus leading to the conclusion that the fundamental rights standards expressed in the Charter/ECHR as the common denominator must be sufficient and are exclusively applicable within the sphere of EU law under the principle of the primacy of EU law. This has been recognized expressly, for example, by the UK Supreme Court in the *Assange* decision:

> There is therefore an irreducible core of basic standards which all European systems must respect and implement. That creates a harmonising pull irrespective of the differences between systems, and reaffirms the basic principles which must be accommodated across common law and civilian traditions and induce convergence in standards to ensure due process and the rule of law.[166]

The CJEU has held in *Melloni* that Member States may not apply higher Constitutional standards (compared to the Charter rights) as a ground to refuse the surrender of a person tried in absentia (or imposing a condition of a retrial), as this would undermine the primacy of EU law.[167]

However, this realization that Member States cannot insist on their own Constitutional rights standards in intra-EU cooperation in criminal matters has met with considerable academic criticism and a realization that Member States have ceded a crucial aspect of their territorial sovereignty to the EU.[168]

The answer to the second question should likewise be "No" since the assessment of whether an infringement of the fundamental rights contained in the Charter has occurred can only be undertaken in the light of *specific facts and circumstances*. In other words, if a court or other body in a Member State takes a judicial decision, this decision should be open to challenge as to its compliance with the common fundamental

[164] Compared to the Charter of Fundamental Rights.

[165] Section 5.2.1.

[166] *Assange* [2012] 2 AC 471 (SC) 480.

[167] Case C-399/11 *Melloni* Judgment of 26 February 2013 ECLI:EU:C:2013:107.

[168] Mitsilegas (n 150) 158–59; LFM Baselink, "The Parameters of Constitutional Conflict after *Melloni*" (2004) 39(4) European Law Review 531–52; Roma Valdes (n 94) 293.

rights as expressed in the Charter or the ECHR. Thus, effectively, the Charter has replaced the national Constitutional standards in cases where EU law is applicable (such as the EU law on international cooperation).[169] However, this leads us to the third question, which is not about applicable law but about jurisdiction: Does the executing (requested) Member State have jurisdiction to assess the compliance with fundamental rights? This is the question whether the executing Member State may examine the fundamental rights compliance of a European Investigation Order, or a European Arrest Warrant and therefore refuse its execution. The CJEU has emphasized the importance of the efficiency of international cooperation and it stressed the importance of mutual recognition in Case C-396/11 *Radu*. In this case it held that there was no need for the accused (or convicted, as the case may be) to be heard in the issuing Member State *before* the European Arrest Warrant was issued.[170] Furthermore, the CJEU has insisted that mutual trust further implies that a challenge against a legal act (such as the issuing of a European Arrest Warrant) can only be brought in the Member State where that legal act *originated* (ie the *issuing* Member State) under the law of that issuing Member State.[171]

The CJEU has framed this question not in terms of jurisdiction but in terms of mutual trust and the principle of mutual recognition, which boils down to a finding of exclusive jurisdiction in the issuing Member State as to fundamental rights compliance. However, this exclusive jurisdiction would bring about two serious pitfalls. Firstly, in the context of extradition and surrender, the defendant, by necessity, is not present in the issuing Member State, which makes it difficult to challenge the decision in the *issuing* Member State. Secondly, considering that the *issuing* Member State will only apply its *own* criminal procedure rules, this may sit at odds with the application of the Charter (which only applies to EU law, not domestic criminal procedure). It is for this second reason that a degree of approximation of national criminal procedure is important, complementing the international cooperation measures.[172]

Arguably, a better approach would be to allow a fundamental rights challenge *based on the Charter and/or the ECHR* in *either* the executing *or* the issuing Member State at the claimant's choice. Thus, in international cooperation cases, it should be possible to mount a challenge in the issuing Member State in which the decision has been made, or in the Member State where the decision is recognized and executed.[173] This has now been expressly recognized (after the criticisms made in respect of the European Arrest Warrant[174]) in Directive 2014/41/EU on the European Investigation Order, discussed

[169] Art 51(1) of the Charter and Joined Cases C-402/05P and C-415/05P *Kadi* [2009] AC 1225 ECLI:EU:C:2008:11.

[170] Judgment of 29 January 2013, ECLI:EU:C:2013:39, paras 33, 31.

[171] ibid.

[172] Mitsilegas (n 150) 164; see eg Directive 2012/13 on the Right to Information and Translation of 22 May 2012; Directive 2013/48/EU on the Right to Access to a Lawyer of 22 October 2013; Directive 2016/343/EU on Presumption of Innocence of 9 March 2016; Directive 2016/800/EU on Special Safeguards for Children of 11 May 2016 etc.

[173] See eg the Directive on the European Investigation Order 2014/41/EU Arts 6(1) and 11(1)(f), which as the first post-Lisbon international cooperation instrument imposes obligations on both authorities with regard to fundamental rights (both in the issuing and the executing Member State).

[174] S Alegre and M Leaf, "Mutual Recognition in European Judicial Co-operation: A Step Too Far Too Soon? Case Study: the European Arrest Warrant" (2004) 10(2) European Law Journal 200–17.

in section 3.2.1.[175] Expressed in a different way, one could say that the need for international cooperation (arising from globalization and cybercrime) leads to a concomitant need to ensure a common human rights framework, which within the EU has now been realized in the Charter (since its incorporation in the Lisbon Treaty) and jurisdiction in each of the participating states applying that common human rights framework in a coherent fashion as the applicable law. We need a transnational human rights law approach with transnational safeguards in transnational criminal justice matters.

Concomitantly the "old" paradigm of decisions related to international cooperation in criminal matters (such as extradition and MLA) being essentially political decisions made through cumbersome administrative diplomatic channels has been switched to a "new" paradigm of more efficient direct judicial cooperation in the EU.[176]

> In the case of extradition, contact is initiated between two sovereign states, the requester and the requested, each of which acts from an independent position. One state asks for the co-operation of the other state which decides whether to provide that co-operation on a case-by-case basis, having regard to grounds which exceed the purely legal sphere and enter into the scope of international relations, where the principle of opportuneness plays an important role. Accordingly, the intervention of politicians and criteria such as reciprocity and dual criminality are justified because they have their origins in different spheres.
>
> The nature of the situation changes when assistance is requested and provided in the context of a supranational, harmonised legal system where, by partially renouncing their sovereignty, states devolve power to independent authorities with law-making powers.[177]

Under the old paradigm, individual rights were supposed to be protected by a large measure of discretion of the executive (and, ultimately, its political accountability through the media and democratic processes). Under the new paradigm the protection of individual rights is supposed to be ensured through the rule of law and human rights framework implemented in all Member States. But this raises the interesting question of what amounts to a judicial decision, in particular whether a decision by a public prosecutor is a judicial decision. Article 6(1) of the Framework Decision on the European Arrest Warrant[178] leaves the determination of the competent judicial authority for issuing the arrest warrant to the issuing Member State. Clearly, a prosecutor lacks the independence and impartiality of a judge, as effectively the prosecutor is a party in a criminal trial.[179] But some Member States have given this task to their public prosecutors, which then raises the question whether these prosecutors are the

[175] Daskal (n 10) 152.

[176] *Assange* [2012] 2 AC 471 (SC) 497 (Lord Phillips).

[177] Advocate Ruiz-Jarabo Colomer's Opinion in Case C-303/05 *Advocaten voor de Wereld* [2007] ECR I-3633, 3651–52, paras 42–43.

[178] Council Framework Decision 2002/584/JHA of 13 June 2002, OJ L190 of 18 July 2002, 1.

[179] *Assange* [2012] 2 AC 471 (SC) 480.

"competent judicial authority" for the purposes of issuing a European Arrest Warrant. In *Assange* the UK Supreme Court held in 2012 that under the intergovernmental measure of the European Arrest Warrant, there is a common practice among Member States to recognize a decision issued by a public prosecutor as "judicial" as a matter of international law.[180] Under Directive 2014/41/EU[181] it is now expressly stated that the authority issuing the European Investigation Order need not necessarily be a judge.[182] This again is an expression of the trust between the criminal justice systems in the Member States and shows how the paradigm has been changed.

In its zealousness to ensure the principle of mutual recognition, emphasizing effectiveness of international cooperation and, in order to emphasize that Member States no longer can maintain their own Constitutional standards in EU law cross-border enforcement cases, the Court has sometimes only given cursory regard to assessing compliance with fundamental Charter rights or the interface between the criminal legal systems of the Member States involved. For example, Case C-367/16 *David Piotrowski*[183] is exemplary for this proposition: Belgium had a minimum age from which minors were presumed to be criminally responsible but this was supplemented by other tests assessing whether the accused minor should be tried in the juvenile courts (focus on care, protection, education) or the ordinary criminal courts. Under Belgian law minors younger than sixteen years old are tried in the juvenile courts, adults above the age of eighteen are tried in the criminal courts, but there is a set of "in-between" rules for the age group sixteen–eighteen who can be tried in either court, depending on a number of factors pertaining to the accused and the circumstances of the criminal offence, which are there to achieve a balance between protecting minors and facilitating their rehabilitation under the criminal justice system and protecting society from the most serious criminals. On the issuing of a European Arrest Warrant by Poland for surrender of the accused, who was seventeen years of age at the time of the commission of the offence, the Belgian courts had to grapple with the interpretation of the ground for refusal in Article 3(3) of the Framework Decision on the European Arrest Warrant, which allows Member States to refuse surrender if the person cannot be held criminally responsible under the law of the executing Member State because of his or her (minor) age.[184] It should, however, also be pointed out that the Framework Decision on the European Arrest Warrant has been supplemented by Directive 2016/800 on Procedural Safeguards Protecting Minors.[185] The overarching principle of this Directive, in accordance with Article 24(1) of the Charter,

[180] ibid 508–10 (Lord Philipps) 514 (Lord Walker) 514–15 (Lord Brown) 517–18 (Lord Kerr), 524–29 (Lord Dyson), Baroness Hale and Lord Mance dissenting.

[181] OJ L130 1 May 2014, 1.

[182] Art 2(c)(ii) of the 2014 Directive refers to any competent authority in the issuing Member State; however, if the decision is not made by a judge or public prosecutor under Art 2(c)(i), it needs validation by a judicial or prosecutorial authority (thus the police could not issue a EIO on its own).

[183] 23 January 2018 ECLI:EU:C:2018:27.

[184] Council Framework Decision (n 178) Art 3(3): "if the person who is the subject of the European arrest warrant may not, owing to his age, be held criminally responsible for the acts on which the arrest warrant is based under the law of the executing State."

[185] 11 May 2016, OJ L132 of 21 May 2016, 1.

is that the child's best interests are always a primary consideration.[186] However, the Directive does not as such establish an obligation of the Member States to introduce specific juvenile courts for the protection of minors. The CJEU held in *Piotrowski* that the Belgian authorities must *not* make the individual case-by-case assessment that the juvenile courts make in order to establish whether the accused should not be tried before the ordinary criminal courts and instead just focus on the age of criminal responsibility.[187] If the minor has an age where he or she can in certain circumstances be tried in the criminal courts, then the executing Member State has to surrender the accused, even if in the *specific* circumstances the minor would have been dealt with the juvenile courts. As in several other judgments[188] on the European Arrest Warrant, the CJEU again places much emphasis on the principle of mutual recognition, and the smooth and timely functioning of cooperation as an *overriding* principle.[189] It held that it is the primary responsibility of the issuing Member State to implement the rights of minors, "which must be *presumed* to be complying with EU law."[190] The court did not enter into an assessment of whether the refusal to have regard to the specific circumstances of the case would lead to child protection falling "between the cracks" of both legal systems (in this case the interface between the Belgian and the Polish criminal justice systems) and therefore constitute an infringement of Article 24(2) of the Charter. In particular, the assessment of whether a minor should be dealt with in the juvenile courts depends on facts and information that is likely to be partly located in the issuing and partly located in the executing Member State and, as the Court pointed out, the European Arrest Warrant procedure is deliberately based on a very limited range of facts contained in a form, in order to speed up the process.[191] Despite the fact that Article 15(2) of the Framework Decision provides for the exchange of supplementary information, the court prioritized the *speed and efficiency* of the procedure. This is highly concerning from a fundamental rights perspective, in view of the fact that the European Arrest Warrant enables the extradition and surrender of a country's own, under-age nationals (who may have never left the country, when eg committing a computer misuse offence that has effect in another country).

Thus, the main concern with EU cooperation is the discrepancy between the presumed mutual trust and insistence on mutual recognition while EU secondary legislation in creating approximated criminal justice rules for cross-border cases, protecting the rights of the accused and other persons involved in a criminal trial (such as victims and witnesses), has not been sufficiently advanced with the consequence that there is a gap in protection of fundamental rights.[192]

[186] Recital 9, Art 24(2) of the Charter: "In all actions relating to children, whether taken by public authorities or private institutions, the child's best interests must be a primary consideration."

[187] Paras 42–44.

[188] Case C-261/09 *Mantello* 16 November 2010, ECLI:EU:C:2010:683, para 35; Joined Cases C-404/15 and C-659/15 PPU *Aranyosi* and *Căldăraru* 5 April 2016, ECLI:EU:C:2016:198, para75; Case C-477/16 PPU *Kovalkovas* 10 November 2016, ECLI:EU:C:2016:861, para 25; Case C-571/17 PPU *Samet Ardic* 22 December 2017 ECLI:EU:C:2017:1026, para 87.

[189] Paras 46, 52–53.

[190] Para 50.

[191] Paras 57–61.

[192] Roma Valdes (n 94) 291.

3.2 Specific instruments for EU cooperation in the field of digital investigations

Article 82(1) TFEU contains a wide-ranging power to approximate the laws of Member States for the purposes of judicial cooperation, and this goes beyond cooperation in the strict legal sense and includes, for example, training of the judiciary. In the context of investigatory powers, the most pertinent powers are contained in Article 82(1)(a): to "lay down rules and procedures for ensuring recognition throughout the Union of all forms of judgments and judicial decisions" and (d): to "facilitate cooperation between judicial or equivalent authorities of the Member States in relation to proceedings in criminal matters and the enforcement of decisions." The European Agenda on Security 2015–20[193] establishes the goals of increased exchange of information and better intra-EU cooperation[194] as well as overcoming the limitations of jurisdiction in respect of criminal investigations online, in particular access to evidence on the internet.[195]

3.2.1 European Investigation Order

Article 82 enabled the passing of the European Investigation Order in Criminal Matters Directive 2014/41/EU[196] (EIO).[197] The EIO enables the judicial organs of one Member State, Member State A, to *order* investigative measures to be carried out in another Member State, Member State B. How the mutual recognition of EIOs (and indeed within the system of European Arrest Warrants) will play out after the EU's withdrawal from the EU was not clear at the time of writing and will depend on the outcome of the negotiations on the future relationship.

Article 1(1) of the Directive defines an EIO as "a judicial decision[198] which has been issued or validated by a judicial authority of a Member State (. . .) to have one or several specific investigative measures carried out in another Member State to obtain evidence." An EIO may be instigated not only by the prosecution but also the defence according to the applicable national criminal procedure, it may thus benefit the prosecuting authorities, or the defendant, in a criminal case.[199] The EIO not only applies to

[193] EU Commission Communication "The European Agenda on Security" COM(2015) 185 final of 28 April 2018.

[194] ibid 2.

[195] ibid 19.

[196] OJ L130 1 May 2014, 1; Ireland and Denmark have not opted into this Directive, Recitals 44 and 45. The Directive had to be implemented since 22 May 2017 (Art 36(1)).

[197] This was preceded by Council Framework Decision 2003/577/JHA (expedited evidence preservation) and Council Framework Decision 2008/978/JHA (European Evidence Warrant) relating to evidence already in existence such as disclosure of objects, documents, and data for the use in criminal proceedings—both had a much more limited scope.

[198] This need not necessarily be a judge, Art 2(c)(ii) of the 2014 Directive refers to any competent authority in the issuing Member State; however, if the decision is not made by a judge or public prosecutor under Art 2(c)(i), it needs validation by a judicial or prosecutorial authority (thus the police could not issue a EIO on its own). In *Assange*, the UK Supreme Court had held in 2012 that under the Third Pillar (intergovernmental) measure of the European Arrest Warrant, there is a common practice among Member States to recognize a decision issued by a public prosecutor as "judicial," see [2012] 2 AC 471 paras 10, 67–71, 76, 92, 95, 106–09, 127–41, 151, 153–54.

[199] Art 1(3).

criminal offences in the strict sense (proceedings brought under the criminal law, including corporate criminal liability) but also administrative and other offences, if they are brought before a *criminal court*—therefore, whether an EIO can be issued depends on the jurisdiction of the criminal courts, not the applicability of the criminal law.[200] The issuing authority in Member State A may only issue and EIO if the investigative measure is necessary and proportionate and it would have been available in a similar domestic case in Member State A, under the same conditions.[201]

But provided this is the case, the effect of an EIO is that Member State A may use its *own domestic criminal procedure* to order investigative measure to be carried out, across a border, extraterritorially[202] in Member State B (the "executing" Member State[203]). This is a clear change to traditional MLA procedures: as a matter of fully protecting national sovereignty, normally the criminal procedure rules of the place where the evidence was gathered apply.[204] By contrast, for the EIO, the executing authority in Member State B has to comply with the procedures and formalities indicated by the issuing authority.[205] This may be less protective of territorial sovereignty, but has the distinct advantage that this ensures that the procedure produces evidence definitively admissible before the courts of the issuing Member State A, without having to argue about the "equivalence" of the foreign procedural rules in Member State B. A concern expressed in the literature is that in balancing human rights considerations and the efficiency of complex cross-border cooperation, human rights may lose out as they are likely to slow down and complicate cross-border cooperation in criminal investigations.[206]

The EIO is revolutionary in that it covers the *whole range of investigative measures*[207] from interception of live communications,[208] production orders and disclosure of stored content, traffic, location or subscriber data from ISPs or any other person, search and seizure, preservation of computer data, covert investigations,[209] obtaining information about a bank account or monitoring a bank account,[210] appearance of witnesses (who may be in custody in Member State B) by video-conferencing[211] or temporary transfer, or, indeed, any other investigative measure available and recognized

[200] Art 4.

[201] Art 6(1).

[202] In the sense that it applies its own *domestic procedure* to instigate procedures carried out in another Member State.

[203] Notice the difference in terminology: under traditional MLAT terminology the recipient state is called "requested" state (which implies an element of discretion whether or not to carry out the request) whereas under the terminology of the Directive, the recipient Member State is called the "executing" Member State which implies that this state normally has no choice but to execute the EIO. Likewise the "issuing" Member State no longer "requests" mutual assistance, but issues an order—Arts 1 and 2(a) and (b) (definitions) Directive 2014/41/EU.

[204] eg Art 3(1) of the 1959 Council of Europe Convention on Mutual Legal Assistance in Criminal Matters; see further M Daniele, "Evidence Gathering in the Realm of the European Investigation Order" (2015) 6(2) New Journal of European Criminal Law 179–94, 181.

[205] Art 9(2).

[206] Daniele (n 204) 186.

[207] Contrast with the European Evidence Warrant.

[208] Art 30.

[209] Art 29.

[210] Arts 27, 28.

[211] Art 24.

under both Member States' criminal procedure. It encompasses both evidence already in existence and evidence that needs to be gathered.[212] Provided the investigatory measure exists in its arsenal of procedural weapons, and would be available in a similar domestic case,[213] the executing Member State B must recognize an EIO issued in the other Member State A, without further formalities, and must execute it unless it invokes one of the specific grounds for refusing immediate cooperation.[214]

In contrast to traditional mutual assistance procedures, the Directive contains time limits for enforcement.[215] The standard time limit for reaching a decision is thirty days plus a further ninety days for executing the EIO, which makes the standard time frame a total of just under four months.

More importantly, it limits further the usual grounds for refusing cooperation (see the earlier discussion on MLATs). By contrast the Directive focuses on more specific grounds for refusal and does not require prima facie evidence as such. However, it still does contain a list of grounds for refusal and considering limited resources of Member States for crime investigation generally a Member State may look at this list twice to see whether a ground for refusal applies.[216] The grounds for refusal relate, on the one hand, to criminal justice and, on the other hand, to state sovereignty.

With regard to the criminal justice grounds, first of all, the executing Member State B may refuse to follow the order where the executing authorities have substantial grounds to believe that the execution of the order may lead to an infringement of the defendant's rights under the Charter of Fundamental Rights.[217] Mutual recognition in the EU, based on the establishment of an EU wide area of freedom, security, and justice, equally emphasizes *justice* that implies mutual trust in the protection of fundamental rights, but this is a rebuttable presumption.[218] Therefore Member State B *may* not only refuse its execution, it must do so.[219] The Charter as primary law[220] takes priority over the obligations under the Directive (as secondary law). The Directive makes clear that the (relevant) rights in the Charter of Fundamental Rights are applicable to the EIO by reference to Article 6(1) of the Treaty on European Union, which reaffirms the incorporation of Charter rights into primary EU Law.[221] Secondly, the executing Member State may refuse to comply with the Order if to do so would infringe on an immunity or privilege granted under national law, such as, for example, legal privilege (pertaining to legal advice given in a lawyer-client relationship), medical or banking privileges, or the privilege given to the media of not having to disclose their sources of information.[222] Thirdly, there is also a specific ground for refusal if the principle of *ne bis idem* would be breached by the execution of the EIO. Since *ne bis*

212 Recital 7.
213 Art 10(1).
214 Art 9(1).
215 Art 12.
216 R Zaharieva, "The European Investigation Order and the Joint Investigation Team—Which Road to Take?" (2017) 18(3) ERA Forum 397–408, 407.
217 Art 11(1)(f).
218 Expressly referred to in Art 1(2).
219 Recital 19.
220 Art 6 Treaty on European Union.
221 Art 1(4) Directive 2014/41/EU.
222 Art 11(1)(a) of the Directive.

idem it is a Charter right,[223] it must be considered by the national courts.[224] Arguably, this ground of refusal would already be covered by the general reference to Charter rights and Article 50 thereof, but clearly it was felt that this principle should be emphasized as a separate ground. Thus, if the defendant is being prosecuted, has been prosecuted, or has been convicted elsewhere (including the executing Member State B), this ground may be applicable to an investigative measure, which could lead to his or her conviction for the same offence in Member State A. However, the difficult question here is the question as to what amounts to the *same offence* and what amounts to a different offence. In addition to the lack of consensus under international law as to the precise *legal* definition of what amounts to the same offence, before the completion of the investigations, the factual evidence may also not be clear.[225] However, as Recital 17 of the Directive points out, this uncertainty could be solved by the issuing Member State A undertaking not to use any information obtained in evidence for prosecution of the defendant in respect of the same facts. The legality of the EIO can be challenged before the courts of the issuing Member State A (whose domestic criminal procedure largely governs the investigative matter), however, where infringement of one of the Fundamental Rights of the Charter is alleged an action for judicial review can also be brought in the executing Member State B.[226]

As for the grounds related to state sovereignty, one of the most intractable issues in international cooperation in the investigation of offences arises where the defendant's conduct amounts to an offence in the investigating state but not *in* the state requested to cooperate, as here the clash of legal cultures, the conflicts of interests, and conflicts of laws are most acute. The Directive uses a combination of the dual criminality principle *and* a long list of types of criminality where the obligation to cooperate is imposed on the executing Member State B, even in the absence of dual criminality.[227] Annex D contains thirty-two different types of criminality, ranging from computer-related offences, terrorism, sexual exploitation of children and child pornography, drug trafficking, murder and grievous bodily harm (GBH), racism and xenophobia, counterfeiting and piracy, to fraud.

Thus, if the criminal offence, under the definition of the legal system of the issuing Member State A, falls into one or several of the categories listed in Annex D to the Directive *and* the maximum custodial sentence under the criminal law of Member State A is three years (or more), the obligation to cooperate applies, regardless of dual criminality. If the offence does not fall into the category of offences listed or is of a less serious nature *in the Issuing Member State A*, attracting a maximum penalty of less than three years, the obligation to comply with a EIO nevertheless applies, if there is

223 Art 50 of the Charter.

224 Case C-617/10 *Åklagaren v Hans Åkerberg Fransson* 26 February 2013 ECLI:EU:C:2013:280.

225 See further Chapter 4.

226 Art 14(2); see also Case C-324/17 *Criminal Proceedings Against Ivan Gavanozov* where the Bulgarian court has issued an EIO for a search and seizure but does not provide for judicial review of this under its domestic law and has asked the CJEU whether this would be a breach of Art 14(2). The CJEU held that there is no requirement for the issuing Member State to provide for the availability of judicial review, which again demonstrates the lack of provision for legal redress in a Member State, see ECLI:EU:C:2019:892 Judgment of 24 October 2019, paras 23–38.

227 Art 11(g).

dual criminality. Thus, the ground for refusal based on differences in the national laws alone has been considerably narrowed compared to MLA.

Furthermore, an additional ground for refusal based on non-criminality in the executing Member State B was created by combining it with the principle of territoriality. This has created effectively three conditions for this additional ground of refusal. The Executing Member State B is allowed to refuse execution of the EIO if (1) the conduct amounts to a criminal offence in Member State A, and was not carried out in Member State A, but (2) it was at least partially carried out on the territory of the executing Member State B, and (3) such conduct is lawful in the executing Member State B.[228]

A second exception, related to state sovereignty, exists where execution of the EIO would harm essential national security interests, or jeopardize the sources of information, or involves classified information from intelligence operations.[229] It is notable that this national security exception is tightly formulated, unlike similar national security provisions in mutual assistance treaties.

If the investigative measure is not available under the law of the executing Member State B or if they would not be available in a similar domestic case (eg because it is only available for more serious offences under domestic law),[230] then the executing authority should consider having recourse to an alternative investigative measure,[231] or inform the issuing authority that it has not been possible to comply with the order.[232] Furthermore, an executing authority may consider using an alternative investigative measure, if this alternative measure would achieve the same result while being less intrusive.[233] Finally the executing authority may postpone the transfer of the evidence to Member State A if the execution of the EIO would prejudice its own ongoing criminal investigation or prosecution.[234]

The Directive also stipulates in Article 10(2) five investigative measures that should *always* be at the disposal of an issuing Member State A, unless the specific grounds for refusal listed in Article 11 apply to the measure. These are:

(a) information or evidence already in the possession of the executing authority and that would be available in a criminal case there;
(b) information contained in directly accessible databases held by police or judicial authorities;
(c) the hearing of witnesses, experts, victims, suspects, or accused on the territory of the executing authority;
(d) non-coercive measures;
(e) the identity data relating to a subscriber of a mobile phone or IP address.

It is important to note that the EIO respects Member States' territorial sovereignty. It does not allow the issuing authority of Member State A to directly carry out the investigative order through its own agencies on the territory of Member State B—it

228 Art 11(e).
229 Art 11(1)(b).
230 Art 11(1)(c) and 11(1)(h).
231 Art 10(1).
232 Art 10(5).
233 Art 10(3).
234 Art 15.

requires the cooperation of the executing police and judicial authorities in Member State B.[235] In other words, the EIO is addressed to the relevant authorities in Member State B and is thus more akin to a form of accelerated "turbo" mutual assistance, rather than a carte blanche to act extraterritorially. Where an investigative measure has to be implemented by a private communications service provider in State B (such as interception or the disclosure of data), the issuing Member State A is not allowed to address its order directly to that private ISP, unlike the provisions foreseen in the US Cloud Act or the E-Evidence Proposal discussed in section 5.2. The Directive is careful not to encroach on the territorial sovereignty of Member States; for example, in relation to interception, it provides that if interception is implemented in a Member State other than the Member State where the suspect is located, then that (third) Member State of the suspect's location has to be notified, even if no technical assistance is required from that (third) Member State.[236] This third Member State may prohibit the interception if it would not have allowed interception in similar domestic circumstances.[237]

Related to the question of territorial sovereignty are questions of responsibility of states and immunity. The traditional paradigm is that a state official is not allowed to take any investigative measures on foreign territory and in fact can only act in official capacity abroad in a diplomatic mission, for which he or she is then immune from liability. However the Directive goes beyond this traditional paradigm by expressly providing for officials from the issuing Member State A assisting and cooperating with the executing authorities of Member State B, if Member State A requests this.[238] This then raises the question of to what extent these co-operating officials from Member State A are liable for acts in Member State B. The Directive stipulates in Articles 17 and 18 that with respect to criminal and civil law, officials from Member State A are placed in the same position as officials from Member State B and that the law of Member State B applies, albeit that, as regards civil liability, any damages paid to claimants would have to be borne by Member State A. Thus, the active involvement of officials from another Member State removes any immunity under public international law and therefore establishes a different paradigm as regards state responsibility.

3.2.2 Joint investigation teams (JITs)

JITs are used where the crime affects the countries involved mutually so they have a joint interest in investigating and prosecuting and frequently are a form of multilateral cooperation.[239] This difference reflects a difference in the issue of jurisdiction: for MLA the question arises whether the state investigating has jurisdiction, whereas for JITs the issue of which state(s) will end up prosecuting only arises at a much *later* juncture.[240]

235 Art 9(4) and (5): "The authorities of the issuing State present in the executing State shall be bound by the law of the executing State during the execution of the EIO. *They shall not have any law enforcement powers* in the territory of the executing State, unless the execution of such powers in the territory of the executing State is in accordance with the law of the executing State and to the extent agreed between the issuing authority and the executing authority."

236 Recital 31 and Art 31.

237 Art 31(3).

238 Art 9(4).

239 Zaharieva (n 216) 398.

240 ibid 399.

Europol defines a JIT as an "international co-operation tool based on an agreement between competent authorities, both judicial (judges, prosecutors, investigative judges) and law enforcement, of two or more states, established for a limited duration and a specific purpose, to carry out criminal investigations in one or more of the involved states."[241] The European Council has developed a Model Agreement for EU authorities to use when setting up JITs in order to facilitate their set up.[242] JITs under EU law rest on a double basis:[243] Article 13 of the 2000 EU Convention on MLA in Criminal Matters and a Framework Decision.[244] Both the Convention and the Framework Decision pre-date the Lisbon Treaty and implementation in the EU Member States has been very slow as the Commission has no oversight role here (unlike Directives). JITs may also be set up between EU and non-EU partners and bilateral or multilateral agreements usually form the basis for such joint teams with non-EU countries—for example, the Agreement on MLA between the EU and the US[245] or the Second Protocol to the European Convention on Mutual Assistance in Criminal Matters.[246] JITs have become more common in recent years. Eurojust reports in its Annual Report of 2017 that "JITs are progressively recognised as an effective cooperation tool in cross border cases, with 200 JITs supported by Eurojust, representing an increase of 35% in comparison to 2016."[247] The number of JITs with non-EU partners was twenty-one in 2017, with ten new ones having been formed in 2017.[248] The non-EU partners in these JITs were: Albania, Australia, Bosnia and Herzegovina, Malaysia, Moldova, Norway, Serbia, Switzerland, and Ukraine.[249] JITs frequently involve seconded members from other Member States' authorities that are part of the JIT and most Member States allow them to cooperate with local team members in carrying out investigations.[250] This gives them more opportunities to act in the foreign territory than the EIO, which only allows officials from the issuing authority to be "observers."[251] Another interesting difference to the EIO is that the legal framework for JITs is silent on grounds for refusing cooperation. From a prosecutor's point of view, JITs have definitive advantages over EIOs, in that all participating states have a common interest in the investigation and therefore do not regard the substantial resources required for a cross-border investigation as "wasted" on a foreign investigation. Furthermore, since not each investigative measure has to be formally ordered and recognized JITs are more flexible and dynamic in the face of an evolving investigation.[252] Ultimately, it is the definition of the common interest and cooperation that

[241] Available on their website https://www.europol.europa.eu/activities-services/joint-investigation-teams accessed on 17/7/2020.

[242] Council Resolution on a Model Agreement for Setting Up A Joint Investigation Team 2017 OJ C 18 of 19 January 2017, 1.

[243] See Zaharieva (n 216) 398.

[244] Framework Decision 2002/465/JHA on Joint Investigation Teams.

[245] OJ L181 of 19 July 2003, 34.

[246] Council of Europe [2001], ETS No 182.

[247] Eurojust Annual Report 2017, 19.

[248] ibid.

[249] ibid.

[250] Zaharieva (n 216) 402.

[251] ibid 401.

[252] ibid 404–06.

are the foundation of a JIT and a reflection of the mutual recognition principle within the EU.

Each authority in the JIT essentially uses its own domestic powers for the gathering of evidence on its territory for its part of the investigation and therefore avoids the cross-border conflict of investigatory jurisdiction—such conflicts, however, may surface at the point when the evidence is shared within the team and used for prosecution. At that point differences in criminal procedure and conflicts regarding the use of foreign obtained information as evidence may arise.

3.2.3 Intra-EU institutional cooperation

EU institutional cooperation plays a crucial role in the fight against cross-border crime and consists of information and data sharing, coordinated actions, as well as strategic assessments and action plans. However, one concern here is including civil society and the European Parliament in the developments concerning cross-border digital evidence and cybercrime.[253]

3.2.3.1 Europol and Europol's Cybercrime Centre

The European Cybercrime Centre (EC3)[254] is a specialized agency for cybercrime information gathering and intelligence sharing within Europol, which was established in 2013.[255] Since its launch, EC3 has become the focal point in the EU for fighting cross-border cybercrime and in particular large-scale online fraud, large-scale cyberattacks against critical infrastructure and information systems, and tackling online child sex abuse content by sharing expertise, providing operational support, and giving strategic[256] guidance.[257]

3.2.3.2 Eurojust

Eurojust[258] is in practice the main actor in respect of cooperation in criminal matters and coordination between different criminal justice systems.[259] Eurojust was envisaged by the Council Meeting in Tampere in 1999[260] and was officially established by Council Framework Decision 2002/187/JHA[261] as amended by Council Decision

[253] L Buono, "Fighting Cybercrime Between Legal Challenges and Practical Difficulties: EU and National Approaches" (2016) 17 ERA Forum 343–53.

[254] European Commission Communication, "Tackling Crime in our Digital Age: Establishing a European Cybercrime Centre" COM(2012) 140 final of 28 March 2012.

[255] Buono (n 253) 344.

[256] See eg the Internet Organised Crime Threat Assessment, published by EC3/Europol in 2015.

[257] Buono (n 253) 346.

[258] The UK's role in Eurojust after the end of the transition period 31 December 2020 was unclear at the time of writing. The UK's withdrawal from the EU may mean that it no longer participates in Eurojust.

[259] (n 3) 56, governed by Art 85 TFEU.

[260] Presidency Conclusions Tampere European Council, 15–16 October 1999, para 46: "To reinforce the fight against serious organised crime, the European Council has agreed that a unit (Eurojust) should be set up composed of national prosecutors, magistrates, or police officers of equivalent competence, detached from each Member State according to its legal system. Eurojust should have the task of facilitating the proper coordination of national prosecuting authorities and of supporting criminal investigations in organised crime cases, notably based on Europol's analysis, as well as of co-operating closely with the European Judicial Network, in particular in order to simplify the execution of letters rogatory."

[261] 28 February 2002 OJ L136 of 6 March 2002, 1.

2009/426/JHA,[262] which strengthened its the power. It consists of a college of national prosecutors or members of the judiciary, paid and seconded by the emitting Member State. Each of the twenty-eight EU Member States is represented by one member plus liaison prosecutors from Montenegro, Norway, Switzerland, and the US who are also seconded to Eurojust.[263] Eurojust is supported by an Administrative Director, has its seat in The Hague in the Netherlands, and in 2017 had a budget of Euro 48.7 million.[264] Core to its work is the tool of coordination meetings, between the twenty-eight National Members, the National Members concerned in a particular investigation, or the National Members concerned in a particular investigation plus members of other authorities in these concerned Member States (such as judicial authorities and police),[265] and it held 302 such coordination meetings in 2017. Its close cooperation with Europol is shown by the fact that Europol was present in over a third (108) of these coordination meetings.[266]

Member States have an obligation to transmit to Eurojust information on certain cross-border investigations and prosecutions and of cases in which a conflict of jurisdiction has arisen or is likely to arise.[267] The role of the National Members is to encourage and facilitate international cooperation in criminal matters, in particular mutual assistance (now the EIO) and the European Arrest Warrant.[268] It acts where Member States are reluctant to cooperate and mediates solutions in conflict situations (eg where several Member States wish to obtain extradition of the same person in order to prosecute).[269] In this vain Eurojust also has a mandate to coordinate questions of investigation and prosecution jurisdiction through mediating between the Member States and coordinates parallel investigations and prosecutions as well as the transfer of proceedings. It has the mandate to ask a Member State to undertake a particular investigation or prosecution or in the reverse suggest to a Member State that another Member State may be better placed to investigate and prosecute.[270] The College can also issue non-binding Opinions to prevent or solve conflicts of Jurisdiction between the Member States.[271]

It can ask for specific information to carry out its tasks[272] or request the Member States to carry out particular investigative measures or other measures justified for investigation and prosecution.[273] All these cooperation and coordination measures are implemented through the National Members representing their respective Member State. It also facilitates the set-up of JITs through providing expertise and funding as well as coordinating the network of national experts on JITs.[274] It hosts the secretariats for

262 16 December 2008 OJ L138 of 4 June 2009, 14.
263 Eurojust Annual Report 2017, 7.
264 ibid 9.
265 M Coninsx, "Eurojust" in V Mitsilegas et al, *Research Handbook on EU Criminal Law* (Edward Elgar 2016) 441–56, 449.
266 Eurojust Annual Report 2017, 9.
267 Art 13 Decision 2009/426/JHA.
268 It was involved in the execution of 320 European Arrest Warrant cases in 2017, Eurojust Annual Report 2017, 9.
269 Coninsx (n 265) 444–45.
270 Art 6(1)(a) and Art 7(1)(a) Decision 2009/426/JHA.
271 Art 7(2).
272 Arts 6(1)(a)(v) and 7(1)(a)(v) Decision 2009/426/JHA.
273 Art 6(1)(a)(vi) and (vii).
274 Arts 6(1)(a)(iii) and 7(1)(a)(iii) Decision 2009/426/JHA.

the European Judicial Network (the network of judicial contact points in the EU), the Network of Experts on JITs, and the "Genocide Network" (connecting various stakeholders aiming at the investigation and prosecution of the international crime of genocide).[275] One important aspect of its work are also real-time data sharing and the setting up of coordination centres for the joint execution of arrests, and searches and seizure.[276]

The self-stated priority areas for Eurojust are: terrorism, cybercrime, migrant smuggling, and trafficking in human beings and it supported 4400 judicial and police authorities in 2017.[277] The caseload increased by 10.6 per cent in 2017 (compared to 2016) to 2550 cases, involving non-EU Member States in just over 10 per cent of all cases (258 cases). In terms of number of cases the highest caseload was in the area of fraud (700), followed by drug trafficking (324), money laundering (315), mobile organized crime groups (208), trafficking of human beings (132), terrorism (87), cybercrime (70), migrant smuggling (64), crimes against the financial interests of the EU (61), corruption (61), and environmental crime (9).[278]

4. Export of data from the EU

European data protection law can function as a defence or blocking mechanism, as it may restrict private entities disclosing data to foreign law enforcement or could restrict public entities' data sharing with non-EU entities,[279] at least in theory. As is shown in this section, the principles on the prohibition of data exports from the EU may in theory function as such a defence mechanism, but in reality, because of the data hegemony of US service providers, that defence mechanism has become unworkable, as workarounds had to be found to allow for inevitable international data flows.

4.1 The EU legal framework and its workarounds

In order to explain how the export of personal data to non-EU states is governed by EU data protection law one has to keep in mind three legal concepts, which are like filters placed one after the other: (1) adequacy, (2) safeguard mechanisms where there is no adequacy, or (3) derogations (exceptions to the principle) where there is no adequacy and safeguard mechanisms cannot be achieved. For each of these concepts it is necessary to examine the provisions applying to private data exporters (General Data Protection Regulation—GDPR[280]) and the provisions applying to public authorities as data exporters (Law Enforcement Data Protection Directive[281]). The UK has implemented the new EU data protection regime through the Data Protection Act 2018, but at the time of writing it was not clear whether it would achieve adequacy status as

275 Eurojust Annual Report 2017, 7.
276 ibid 12.
277 ibid 7.
278 ibid 23.
279 Uecker (n 22) 68.
280 General Data Protection Regulation EU/2016/679; OJ 2016 L119/1.
281 Directive on Data Protection by LEAs 2016/680/EU; OJ 2016 L119/89.

a third country after the withdrawal from the EU and what the future coordination mechanisms with the EU would look like.

4.1.1 Adequacy

The fundamental principle in EU data protection laws[282] is that no personal data must be transferred from the territory of the EU to a country outside the EU or EEA, unless the Commission[283] has found that that non-EU country provides an "adequate" standard of data protection.[284]

The terminology of EU data protection law uses the concept of "transfer," which as such is not defined in the legislation but focuses on the physical movement of personal data from an EU state to a non-EU state.[285] Arguably, it is highly questionable whether the concept of a transfer continues to make sense in the cloud computing age where the physical location of data in a data centre may be different from the location of the person(s) who can control the data. Therefore there is a conceptual problem here with the data export prohibition. Data protection authorities in the EU have focused too much on the actual physical location of the data, making an unspoken assumption that the location of the data centre is congruent with control over data.[286] Arguably a more sensible approach would be to focus on regulating the person who has *control* over the data in defining what data exports mean, that is, transferring control over data (including copying the data or granting access) from a person domiciled in an EU state to a person domiciled outside the EU.

This conceptual criticism apart, this "prohibition on data export principle" includes transfers of personal data in the context of criminal investigations or criminal litigation, albeit, as we will see, there are numerous exceptions to this principle, such that not much is left of the principle. The Law Enforcement Data Protection Directive applies to data processing by public authorities[287] for "the protection of natural persons with regard to the processing of personal data by competent authorities for the purposes of the prevention, investigation, detection or prosecution of criminal offences or the execution of criminal penalties, including the safeguarding against and the prevention of threats to public security."[288] If a transfer to a non-EU state has to be made by a public authority for such purposes the data transfer additionally has to be necessary and proportionate for the objective pursued.[289]

The adequacy principle raises the question of what amounts to an adequate standard of data protection in the destination, non-EU country. In Case C-362/14 *Schrems v Data Protection Commissioner* the CJEU pointed out[290] that the then Directive did not

[282] This structure already existed in Arts 25–26 Data Protection Directive 1995/46/EC.

[283] Art 45(3) through the Committee procedure mentioned in Arts 93(2) and 5 Regulation EU/182/2011.

[284] Art 25(1) EU Data Protection Directive 1995/46/EC now replaced by Art 45(1) General Data Protection Regulation EU/2016/679 (n 280) and Arts 35(1) and 36(1) Directive on Data Protection by LEAs 2016/680/EU (n 281) repealing Council Framework Decision 2008/977/JHA.

[285] Hon (n 24) 320.

[286] Hon (n 24) 91.

[287] See Art 3(7) for definitions of the competent authorities; processing for intelligence purposes is excluded, Arts 2(3)(a) and 4(2) TEU.

[288] Art 1(1) Law Enforcement Data Protection Directive (n 282).

[289] Art 35(1)(a) , otherwise, there could be a breach of Art 8(2) of the ECHR or Art 8 of the Charter.

[290] 6 October 2016, ECLI:EU:C:2015:650.

define the concept of an adequate level of protection but that the third country had to "ensure" an adequate level of "protection of the private lives and basic rights and freedoms of individuals."[291] The Court held that "adequate" should not be taken to mean "identical" but that is should mean "equivalent." Thus, the third country had to ensure "a level of protection of fundamental rights and freedoms that is *essentially equivalent*[292] to that guaranteed within the EU," even though that third country's means of implementing these standards could be different.[293] In the second *Max Schrems* decision the CJEU held that the "measuring stick" for assessing this essential equivalence are the protections in the GDPR read in the light of the Charter and it emphasized that this protection must include appropriate safeguards,

enforceable rights and effective legal remedies.[294] In particular, the Commission must carry out regular adequacy checks and adapt the test according to changes in technology, business practices, and other circumstances that have arisen since the original adequacy decision.[295] The Commission must withdraw an adequacy decision where this is no longer warranted or put pressure on a non-EU country to change laws or practices by threatening to withdraw an adequacy decision.[296] Whereas Directive 95/46/EC only focused on whether the third *country* provided an adequate level protection, the GDPR has provided for the extended possibility that a particular sector or territory within a country could be given an "adequate" data protection status.[297] Article 45(2) of the GDPR and Article 36(2) of the Law Enforcement Data Protection Directive list the criteria taken into account for the adequacy decision, which pivot around three themes: (1) the rule of law and protection of human rights in the destination country, (2) the existence of effective enforcement and a regulator, and (3) international obligations and commitments entered into with respect to data protection. It seems that countries who wish to apply for adequacy status have to enter into bilateral negotiations with the European Commission[298]—the decision is made by a Committee under Article 45(3) of the GDPR or Article 36(3) of the Law Enforcement Data Protection Directive. The prohibition on data export established in these provisions encourages other states to adopt higher data protection standards.[299] The effect of the data export prohibition is that states that do not provide adequate data protection standards risk that they will be partially excluded from international data exchange and economic opportunities.[300] As a consequence

[291] Para 69.

[292] See also (n 159) para 105.

[293] Paras 73–77.

[294] (n 159) para 105.

[295] Para 77; this is now expressly contained in Art 45(3) GDPR and Art 36(3) Law Enforcement Data Protection Directive which provide for a periodic review every four years.

[296] Art 45(5) and (6) GDPR, Art 36(5) and (6) Law Enforcement Data Protection Directive.

[297] Art 45(1): "Commission has decided that the third country, a territory or one or more specified sectors within that third country, or the international organization in question ensures an adequate level of protection."; see also Art 36(1) Law Enforcement Data Protection Directive.

[298] Email on file with author from senior diplomat involved in the former Art 31 Committee for determining adequacy decisions.

[299] Y Poullet, "Transborder Data Flows and Extraterritoriality: The European Position" (2007) 2 Journal of International Commercial Law & Technology 141–53.

[300] M Cunningham, "Diminishing Sovereignty: How European Privacy Law Became International Norm" (2013) 11 Santa Clara Journal of International Law 421–53.

(and intended effect[301]) many countries have adopted data protection laws modelled on the EU data protection framework and the EU has punched above its economic weight in its influence on data protection laws across the world.[302] This influence on the global data protection dialogue notwithstanding, the EU data protection framework has not been successful in ensuring data protection for data generated in the EU as the data export prohibition is unrealistic in view of the data flows in an interconnected world and therefore workarounds had to be found. These workarounds by necessity compromise the standard of protection, particularly in view of the data hegemony of the US combined with very different cultural and political approaches to privacy in the US and many other non-EU countries.[303]

4.1.2 Other safeguard mechanisms

This raises the question of what happens for non-EU states who do not provide an adequate level of data protection. Given that vast quantities of data cross territorial borders across the internet every second, it is inevitable that in the course of international communication, business life, and trade personal data *have to be* transferred to non-EU states who *do not* provide for an adequate data protection standard. Under EU data protection law there are other safeguard mechanisms crafted around specific transfers and this potentially includes transfers in the context of criminal investigations and litigation.[304]

The safeguard mechanisms in the GDPR, which only applies to private entities (businesses and individuals acting as data controllers), must create "enforceable data subject rights" and "effective legal remedies for data subjects."[305] Article 46(2) lists these mechanisms as: instruments between public bodies, binding corporate rules, standard data protection rules, approved codes of conduct, and certification mechanism. These are standard schemes, which are pre-approved by the Commission and can then be "picked off the shelf" by EU data exporters and their non-EU data importers. Furthermore, parties to a transaction, for example, can create their own tailor-made contractual scheme that also has to be approved by the relevant competent supervisory authorities,[306] which is likely to be more expensive.[307] These contractual schemes for private entities are less likely to be relevant in the criminal context. However, they are relevant where a transfer is made from an EU entity to a private non-EU entity, who then has to share data under foreign law with that foreign government.[308] One of

[301] Uecker (n 22) 105.

[302] L Bygrave, *Data Privacy Laws* (Oxford University Press 2014) 208.

[303] For a description of how states use data protection to increase their data sovereignty see the discussion on Russia's data localization laws in section 6.

[304] Arts 35(1)(d), 37 Law Enforcement Data Protection Directive.

[305] Art 46(1) GDPR.

[306] Unfortunately the decision as to whether a particular scheme should be approved is not made centrally and data protection authorities may disagree, in which case the consistency mechanism provides a coordination process for solving the disagreement between the authorities—but this is likely to be cumbersome, slow, and expensive.

[307] Art 46(3) GDPR.

[308] Case C-311/18 (Schrems II) n 158 upheld the validity of Decision 2010/87/EU approving the Standard Contractual Clauses transfer mechanism; Advocate General Opinion of 19 December 2019 ECLI:EU:C:2019:1145 recommended that the Court finds that the Decision 2010/87/EU is valid as the Data Protection Authorities have the duty to suspend data transfers to inadequate countries, see paras 124–29, 140 and the Court agreed see paras 121, 149.

the big open questions after Brexit is how these mechanisms, which rely on cooperation with the European Data Protection Board and the European Commission, work for the UK.

By contrast to private entities, public LEAs, who transfer data to a non-EU country without adequacy status, must either rely on a specific law and comply with the safeguard mechanisms established therein[309] or the authority itself must undertake an assessment that appropriate safeguards apply to the transfer in question.[310] These provisions give public LEAs in the Member States a large amount of discretion as to data sharing in the criminal context (as long as it is necessary and proportionate[311]), a discretion the EU Directive was not able to fetter in respect of data protection *in the public sector*. Notably absent are the following safeguards: some form of requirement that data subjects should be notified of the transfer (where this is possible without prejudicing a criminal investigation), that data subjects have enforceable data subject rights, and any form of effective legal remedies for data subjects, as was provided for the transfers by *private entities* in the GDPR. This flexibility and discretion of course completely hollows out the general starting principle that data transfers should only be made to non-EU states with an adequate standard of data protection. However, Recital 71 also states that data requests should be specific, and mentions the right to obtain effective administrative or judicial redress. Moreover, Recital 71 expressly refers to specific cooperation agreements made in the context of *Europol* and *Eurojust*, for example, in the context of the setting up of JITs. More concerning in this connection is the prospect that the US–EU Framework Umbrella Agreement could be used generally to justify law enforcement transfers to the US, see the discussion in section 4.4. However, Recital 71 adds one slight gloss of protection obliging data controllers in Member States' LEAs to take into consideration when assessing the safeguards that data should "not be used to request, hand down or execute a death penalty or any form of cruel and inhuman treatment."

4.1.3 Derogations

In addition to these specific mechanisms crafted in advance to ensure adequate data protection in the third country, there are also certain exceptions (called derogations) to the adequacy standard.[312] For private entities, these include, for example, where the data subject has explicitly consented to the transfer,[313] necessity for the performance of a contract either by the data subject[314] or in the interests of the data subject[315] by another person (such as an e-commerce consumer disclosing the name and postal address for delivery of ordered goods). Other derogations exist in respect of protecting the vital interests of a person incapable of giving consent[316] (such as a medical emergency or a disappeared person), entries in a public register[317] and limited,

[309] Art 37(1)(a) Law Enforcement Data Protection Directive.
[310] Art 37 (1)(b) Law Enforcement Data Protection Directive.
[311] Art 35(1)(a) Law Enforcement Data Protection Directive.
[312] Derogations for specific situations, Art 49.
[313] Art 49(1)(a).
[314] Art 49(1)(b).
[315] Art 49(1)(c).
[316] Art 49(1)(f).
[317] Art 49(1)(g).

non-repetitive transfers, concerning only a limited number of data subjects for compelling legitimate interest of the data controller.[318]

For private entities, these derogations also provide that data transfers to third countries, not providing an adequate standard of data protection, are allowed, if they are *necessary for important reasons of public interest*.[319] Could this *public interest* exception be used in the context of criminal investigations and criminal litigation? Is *public interest* akin to state interest and, if so, does it include the *interests of a non-EU state*? These questions raise the question of the meaning of the phrase "public interest" with which the GDPR is spiked.[320] The term "public interest" is mentioned in connection with archiving purposes, scientific or historical research purposes or statistical purposes,[321] exercise of official authority vested in the controller,[322] public health, quality and safety of health care,[323] national security, defence, public security, *prevention, investigation, detection or prosecution of criminal offences or the execution of criminal penalties, including the safeguarding against and the prevention of threats to public security, economic or financial interests of the Union or a Member State, including monetary, budgetary and taxation matters*, public health, and social security[324] and social protection.[325] As may be clear from this long list of public policy objectives, the term *public interest* is used in a wide sense, more akin to legitimate *interests of society* or *state interest*.

Thus, the question arises whether in a situation, where a private entity in the EU (such as a subsidiary of a foreign company) is compelled by a foreign, non-EU law promoting the public interest to transfer data to that non-EU state without any adequacy status, it may be justified in doing so by the public interest derogation. More specifically, would an EU subsidiary of a US company be able to use this derogation from the "no transfers out principle" when faced with a subpoena or warrant from a US court to disclose electronic data such as the content of emails in the context of criminal proceedings?

The public interest derogation may be particularly important in a conflicts of law situation, where the (foreign) law of non-EU states requires disclosure and transfer of EU based or controlled personal data to this non-EU state. In particular, frequent conflicts have arisen in respect of US subpoenas or discovery, where US courts have ordered a third party to disclose documents in civil or criminal litigation, if they have personal jurisdiction over this third party (or its parent company). Such orders have been made against subsidiaries of US companies that are established in the EU.[326] Similar conflicts have also arisen in respect of financial disclosure laws such as the US Gramm-Leach-Bliley Act. However, it is not clear whether the *public interest* referred to in Article 49(1)(d) of the GDPR only refers to *public interests of the Member*

318 Art 49(1).
319 Art 49(1)(d).
320 It uses the phrase no less than seventy times in recitals and articles.
321 Art 5(1)(b).
322 Art 6(1)(e).
323 Art 9(2)(i).
324 Art 23(1).
325 Art 36(5).
326 For a detailed discussion of the jurisdictional conflicts with subpoenas, see Chapter 9 and also Albrecht and Jotzo (n 20) 111–12.

States or whether it would include a *non-EU state's public interests*. Taking a contextual interpretation of the new wording in the GDPR, it would appear that it includes non-EU public interests as long as the reasons of public interest are recognized under EU law and/or the law of the Member State concerned.[327] This provision in Article 49(4) would be unnecessary if the *public interest* only encompassed EU or Member States' public interests. Moreover, Article 49(5) provides that EU law or Member States' law may pre-emptively prohibit certain types of public interest disclosure to a non-EU state without adequacy status. Again, this would not be necessary if *public interest* was limited to EU or Member States' public interest. Thus, the GDPR has adopted a more pragmatic *comity* approach,[328] a concept of the US common law, to the inevitable conflicts of law arising under EU data protection laws, probably as a result of US lobbying,[329] but also in recognition of the problems that have arisen in practice and striving to avoid conflicts of law by this compromise. The fundamental conflict between two states here is between different norms of protection: crime prosecution and national security are fundamental protection functions of the state, but so is the protection of fundamental rights, such as data protection[330]. Both are difficult to balance by a general principle approach (such as the vague notion of *comity*). These values, fighting crime and data protection, need to be balanced on a case-by-case basis. Therefore, a general reference to public interests of other states and the notion of comity do not solve this conflict on their own.

This is also made clear by Article 48, which restricts the direct recognition and enforceability of non-EU court or administrative orders as non-authorized transfers. It provides:

> any judgment of a court or tribunal and any decision of an administrative authority of a third country requiring a controller or processor to transfer or disclose personal data may only be recognised or enforceable in any manner if based on an international agreement, such as a mutual legal assistance treaty, in force between the requesting third country and the Union or a Member State (…)

Article 48 therefore provides that, for example, a subpoena by a US court (or warrants under the Stored Communications Act as amended by the Cloud Act) that is not enforced through a mutual assistance procedure or an executive agreement[331] would not give an EU private entity a legitimate reason *in and of itself* to transfer personal data to a non-EU country without an adequacy status or safeguard mechanism.[332] However, Article 49(1)(d) would give this private entity *discretion to decide* whether disclosure is justified in the public interest nevertheless. Moreover, Article 49(1)(e) permits transfers for the establishment, exercise of defence of legal claims, which

[327] Art 49(4)—for a different interpretation of the provision see Albrecht and Jotzo (n 20) 110, who state that this excludes foreign public interests.

[328] For a detailed discussion of comity see Chapter 9.

[329] As to US lobbying generally, Bygrave (n 302) 107 states, "US actors have also lobbied aggressively for outcomes favourable to their interests during the EU legislative process."

[330] Uecker (n 22) 193.

[331] Discussed further in section 5.2.1.

[332] Albrecht and Jotzo (n 20) 111–12.

likewise could justify such a transfer. The combination of Articles 48 and 49(1)(d) and (e) establishes a delicate balance between giving recognition to non-EU *public interests*, on the one hand, and not allowing the *automatic* recognition of foreign court orders without mutual assistance, on the other hand. But this throws the responsibility of making that balance on a case-by-case basis back onto the private company, who is left without clear guidance and uncertainty in a conflict of law situation.[333] This situation insufficiently protects the interests of data subjects.

Moving on to public entities, some of the derogations are the same, for example, protecting the vital interests of the data subject or another person[334] or establishment, exercise or defence of legal claims.[335] Most of the derogations relate of course to the specific functions of public authorities such as guarding the legitimate interests of the data subject (eg in connection with diplomatic cooperation between countries in the case of a disaster or emergency),[336] or for the prevention of an immediate and serious threat to public security.[337] But there are additionally much broader derogations, for example, data export in individual cases simply for the purposes set out in Article 1(1).[338] This ground for derogation is therefore wide and general and, gives EU public authorities full discretion to transfer personal data to countries not providing an adequate standard of protection. Both for the safeguard mechanisms and the derogations the public authority must document its data protection analysis and transmit these to its national data protection authority.[339]

As a general principle (subject to the exceptions set out in Article 39) public authorities are only allowed to transfer personal data to other competent *public* authorities, according to Article 35(1)(b) Law Enforcement Data Protection Directive. As will be discussed in section 4.2, data exchanges in the internet-enabled twenty-first century take place between the public and the private sector in both directions. Article 39 allows *public authorities* to make a transfer of personal data to a *private entity* in a non-EU state in specific (meaning targeted?) cases subject to a number of conditions. These conditions are that the transfer is strictly necessary for a task that the public authority has to perform as part of its statutory functions,[340] the public interest overrides any fundamental rights concerns of the data subject,[341] the relevant public authorities in the destination country are informed,[342] and the transferring authority binds the recipient of the personal data to use these data only for the specified purpose.[343]

[333] J Daskal, "Microsoft Ireland, the Cloud Act, and International Lawmaking 2.0" (2018) 71 Stanford Law Review Online 9–16.

[334] Law Enforcement Data Protection Regulation Art 38(1)(a).

[335] In the criminal context Art 38(1)(e), subject to a balancing test with the fundamental rights and freedoms of the data subject, Art 38(2).

[336] But only if the law of the transferring Member State allows for this, Art 38(1)(b).

[337] Art 38(1)(c).

[338] "prevention, investigation, detection or prosecution of criminal offences or the execution of criminal penalties, including the safeguarding against and the prevention of threats to public security," but this is subject to a balancing test with the fundamental rights and freedoms of the data subject, Art 38(2).

[339] Art 38(3).

[340] Art 39(1)(a).

[341] Art 39(1)(b).

[342] Art 39(1)(d).

[343] Art 39(1)(e).

This raises the question why and in what circumstances does an EU public authority need to exchange personal data with a *private entity* in a non-EU state. This concerns EU public authorities making direct requests for subscriber, communications, or content data extraterritorially to foreign, non-EU (most likely US) service providers—clearly, when making such a request, the public authority has to exchange personal data (such as an IP address or a username) with the private entity in the first place. Effectively Article 39 sanctions such extraterritorial requests bypassing MLA. Although Article 39(1) states that these provisions are without prejudice to "bilateral or multilateral international agreement in force between Member States (…) in the field of judicial cooperation in criminal matters and police cooperation,"[344] it expressly acknowledges that public authorities may circumvent such mutual assistance treaties by directing requests for data to private entities such as communication services providers "in particular because the transfer cannot be achieved in good time."[345] It seems strange that a Directive whose very purpose is the safeguarding of the fundamental right of data protection expressly acknowledges the circumvention by *public authorities* of the restrictions and safeguards provided for in the system of MLA. By sanctioning this circumvention, it could even be argued that the Directive contributes to the change of the norm that, under international law extraterritorial direct requests are illegal. This provision[346] demonstrates two realizations that are highly uncomfortable from a rule of law point of view: (1) that Member States regard the system of MLA as not working (why otherwise introduce this provision *here*) and (2) given that most ISPs are headquartered in the US, the US would have to make MLA work, but does not necessarily have an interest to do so, or put in another way, that mutuality has gone out of MLA, at least to the extent that internet and ISP data are concerned.

In summary it can be said that the Law Enforcement Data Protection Directive steers clear from approximating Member States' criminal justice procedures by stipulating minimum standards.[347] Instead it leaves the Member States a large scope of discretion and does not attempt to provide minimum safeguards required by the jurisprudence of the CJEU.[348] Since Member States were unable to agree such minimum safeguards it is likely that ultimately the Court will have to pronounce what these minimum standards under the Charter will be. However, this a slow process and clouded in uncertainty. Moreover, is it noteworthy that private entities are under stricter obligations to maintain data protection standards as they are under stricter obligations as regards safeguards and derogations compared to public entities.

[344] Art 39(2).

[345] Art 39(1)(c).

[346] Art 39(1)(c).

[347] C Jasserand, "Law Enforcement Access to Personal Data Originally Collected by Private Parties: Missing Data Subjects' Safeguards in Directive 2016/680?" (2018) 34 Computer Law & Security Review 154–65, 164–65.

[348] Joined Cases C-293/12 and C-594/12, *Digital Rights Ireland* and *Seitlinger* [2014] ECLI:EU:C:2014:238; Joined Cases C-203/15 and C-698/15 *Tele2 Sverige AB* and *Secretary of State for the Home Department v Tom Watson and others* [2016] ECLI:EU:C:2016:970.

4.2 The different permutations of the dilemma

In respect of data protection, in the EU, as we have just seen, a fundamental distinction is made between, on the one hand, data processing by a private sector entity[349] and, on the other hand, data processing by public LEAs for the purposes of crime investigation, detection, prevention, and prosecution[350] as encapsulated in the two different legal frameworks just discussed. Data processing and data sharing by national security intelligence agencies are not covered by the EU data protection framework, as this is outside the remit of EU law.[351] At a conceptual level, this strict separation between a private sector framework and a public sector framework assumes that there is no cross-over between the private sector and the public sector. However, this is of course not the case. In the internet age, the private sector is collecting, processing, aggregating, and mining personal data on a massive scale never seen before and enabled by technology. This phenomenon started in the area of data processing for advertising and marketing purposes, through tracking, online profiling, and online behavioural advertising.[352] Since personal data has become such a goldmine in the private sector[353] a whole data economy based on the exploitation of "big data" has been built on this phenomenon with data brokers aggregating individual profiles and monetizing personal data in a variety of ways involving complex data intelligence systems, which are not transparent and not necessarily easily explained or penetrated.[354] While the public sector was perhaps initially lagging behind (not having the commercial funding and innovation drive of the private sector) it was unavoidable that LEAs and intelligence agencies wanted to tap into this data treasure trove.[355] While a detailed examination of how this has happened would go beyond the confines of this book, a few examples should suffice by way of illustration.[356] For example, in the US, there are specific data mining programs developed by LEAs (and intelligence agencies) as revealed by Edward Snowden in 2013,[357] including the PRISM program, which allowed the National Security Agency (NSA) direct access to individuals' information on the servers of nine ISPs, including Google/YouTube, Yahoo!, Microsoft/Skype, and Facebook.[358] Related to that is the increase of powers LEAs are obtaining to achieve

[349] General Data Protection Regulation EU/2016/679 (n 280).

[350] Directive on Data Protection by LEAs 2016/680/EU (n 281).

[351] Art 4(2) TEU.

[352] See further on the topic of profiling: L Edwards and J Hatcher, "Consumer Privacy Law 2: Data Collection, Profiling and Targeting" in L Edwards and C Waelde, *Law and the Internet* (3rd edn, Hart Oxford 2009) 511–44; CJ Hoofnagle, "Behavioural Advertising: The Offer You Cannot Refuse" (2012) 6 Harvard Policy & Law Review 273–96; O Tene et al, "To Track or Do Not Track" (2012) 13 Minnesota Journal of Law, Science and Technology 281–357.

[353] J Taplin, *Move Fast and Break Things* (Pan Books 2017) 6.

[354] B Marr, "Who Are the Biggest Consumer Data Brokers and Where Can You Buy Big Data?" Huffpost (12 October 2017).

[355] An early example of this was the Total Information Awareness program 2002–03, https://epic.org/privacy/profiling/tia/ Accessed on 17/7/2020.

[356] Jasserand (n 347) 154–55.

[357] On a summary of the Snowden leaks see eg https://www.bbc.com/news/world-us-canada-23123964 or his website at https://edwardsnowden.com/revelations/ accessed on 17/7/2020.

[358] https://www.bbc.com/news/technology-23051248 accessed on 17/7/2020.

bulk access and bulk data mining of content and communications data from ISPs and access to data streams on transatlantic cables.[359] Another example is open source intelligence (OSINT) whereby law enforcement gain access and extract information from publicly accessible internet and social media sources.[360] Moreover, there are a number of specific obligations on private sector entities such as airlines[361] to share data sets with LEAs or the EU–US Terrorist Finance Tracking Program.[362] Finally, the increasing development and use of technology based on artificial intelligence and algorithmic data mining should be mentioned in this context.[363] Therefore, broadly speaking, the end result of these developments is that the private sector ecosystem (including communication services providers, ISPs, social media companies, data brokers, e-commerce businesses, etc) collect and aggregate vast data sets and profiles on individuals, which can then be mined for law enforcement purposes. It is this interconnection between data collection for commercial purposes and state surveillance that is the major concern, as illustrated also in the second *Max Schrems* judgment.[364]

The international, cross-border sharing of personal data between private and public sector entities, however, means that there are different permutations to the cross-border transfers of personal data, and therefore it may be helpful to unpack these different permutations (Table 6.2).

First of all,[365] where individuals *directly disclose their own personal data* to a private service provider in the US, the GDPR[366] only applies to the US service provider, if the jurisdictional tests in Article 3 are fulfilled, otherwise, such a data transfer would not be protected by EU data protection legislation.[367]

Secondly, in the context of personal data transfers from the EU to the US, which data protection framework applies depends on the nature of the entity making the transfer. Private entities[368] are governed by the GDPR[369] and public law enforcement entities[370] are governed by the LEAs and Data Protection Directive[371] and, as already discussed, both frameworks prohibit the transfer of personal data outside the EU unless the destination country (such as the US) has been found to provide an adequate

[359] PM Schwartz, "Regulating Governmental Data Mining in the US and Germany" (2011) 53 William and Mary Law Review 351–87; in the UK in recent times through the Investigatory Powers Act 2016.

[360] See further the discussion regarding Art 32a of the Cybercrime Convention in section 5.1.2.2.

[361] Agreement between the USA and the EU on the Use and Transfer of Passenger Name Records to the US Department of Homeland Security OJ L215 of 11 August 2012, 5; Council Decision 2012/380/EU Agreement between the European Union and Australia on the processing and transfer of Passenger Name Record (PNR) data by air carriers to the Australian Customs and Border Protection Service OJ 2012 L186 14 July 2012, 3; Directive (EU) 2016/681 Passenger Name Records, OJ 2016 L119 4 May 2016, 132

[362] Agreement between the EU and the USA on the Processing and Transfer of Financial Messaging Data from the EU to the US OJ L 8 of 13 January 2010, 11.

[363] See eg H Hodson, "Inside China's Plan to Give Every Citizen a Character Score" New Scientist (9 October 2015); F Lee, "Die AAA Bürger" Zeit Online (30 November 2017); A Ma, "China Ranks Citizens with a Social Credit System" The Independent Online (10 April 2018).

[364] Kahvedzic (n 4) 356 and (n 159).

[365] See right-hand column of Table 6.2.

[366] (n 280).

[367] See the discussion in Chapter 7.

[368] See left-hand column.

[369] (n 280).

[370] See middle column.

[371] (n 281).

Table 6.2 Possible permutations of data transfers from within the EU to the US

<table>
<tr><td colspan="2">Foreign Law Enforcement (US) Post Schrems Privacy Shield Ombudsman?</td><td colspan="2">Foreign Law Enforcement (US) Compliance with domestic US law</td><td colspan="2">Foreign Law Enforcement (US) Compliance with domestic US law</td></tr>
<tr><td>US Private Entity (Data Import under the Privacy Shield- formerly the Safe Harbor Agreement, Art 45 or Arts 46-49 GDPR)</td><td>Foreign Law Enforcement (US) (Extraterritorial- uses domestic US procedure?- under future Cloud Act Executive Agreement (?) or sector specific agreement such as EU-US PNR Agreement[367] or US extraterritorial procedures such as subpoenas or warrants under the Stored Communications Act as amended by the Cloud Act)
Art 48 and Art 49 (1) (d) public interest?</td><td>US Private Entity Extraterritorial data requests and co- operation with service providers</td><td>Foreign Law Enforcement (US): for example joint investigation team</td><td>US Private Entity (No restrictions on transfer out; but GDPR may be applicable or may not be applicable to US Private Entity, see Art 3- jurisdictional limitations of GDPR)</td><td>Foreign Law Enforcement (US) (Extraterritorial- territorial limitations to warrants, depending on where data is stored and US procedural restrictions)</td></tr>
<tr><td colspan="6">EU BORDER</td></tr>
<tr><td colspan="2">EU Private Entity (GDPR-Transfer Out Arts)</td><td colspan="2">EU Law Enforcement (LE-DP Directive-Transfer Out)
(compliance obligations-Arts 36, 37, 38, 39 LE-DP Directive)</td><td colspan="2">Individual Direct Transfer (Individual's own data-GDPR- Consent)
GDPR-applicable?</td></tr>
</table>

Black arrow is transfers out, white arrows show onward transfers—read this table from bottom to top.

[1] Agreement between the USA and the EU on the Use and Transfer of Passenger Name Records to the US Department of Homeland Security OJ L215 of 11 August 2012, 5.

standard of data protection. This provides for a very limited protection in two respects: first there is the risk that adequacy decisions (such as the Privacy Shield[372]) are influenced by political and practical considerations (the fact that, given that most ISPs are headquartered in the US, EU Member States need data disclosure in the other direction, namely from the US to the EU, even more urgently). Secondly, there is the risk of onward transfer—while the first data export from the EU to the US is governed

[372] Now declared in valid in the 2nd Max Schrems Judgment No 159 para 199.

by the restrictions contained in the EU instruments, this may be difficult to ensure for further onward transfers, for example, from a private US entity (such as Facebook Inc) to US LEAs (which would be governed by the arguably lower data protection standards under the US Fourth Amendment jurisprudence).[373] This was the issue that gave rise to the Court of Justice[374] declaring the Safe Harbor arrangement invalid in Case C-362/14 *Schrems v Data Protection Commissioner*.[375] Safe Harbor was a self-regulatory regime that provided an adequate data protection status to those US companies who had signed up to this self-regulatory standard.

4.3 Safe Harbor, the Privacy shield and *Schrems I* and *II*

The lethal blow to the Safe Harbor Agreement, which provided for EU–US data transfers between private companies to ensure adequate data protection in the US, came on 6 October 2015 when the CJEU found in Case C-362/14 *Schrems v Data Protection Commissioner* that it was invalid in its entirety.[376] The declaration of invalidity by the highest court of the EU raises serious questions about the feasibility of personal data transfers from the EU to the US that comply with EU data protection law and the fundamental right to privacy, enshrined in Article 8 of the ECHR and Articles 7 (privacy) and 8 (data protection) of the EU Charter,[377] including for crime investigation and international cooperation purposes. The *Schrems* ruling is symptomatic of a new paradigm: the data exchange between the private and public sector and the privacy concerns arising from dataveillance instigated by the private sector but completed by the state.

Max Schrems, an Austrian citizen and domicile had been a Facebook user since 2008. He complained to the Irish Data Protection Commissioner about the transfer of his personal data from Austria to the US and, in particular, potential disclosure of that data to the NSA under the PRISM program (or other programs).[378] The reason that the Safe Harbor Agreement had not provided an adequate level of protection was that it mainly focused on data protection concerns arising from the data processing of private entities in the US (such as in the context of employment relations or marketing) but *did not effectively address the onward transfer to US law enforcement agencies*.

The case raised the question whether a transborder data flow, although compliant with an adequacy decision under the then applicable Directive could nevertheless be a breach of a fundamental right under the Charter (Arts 7 and 8 and the right to a fair trial in Art 47).[379]

The CJEU held in its judgment that the national data protection authorities were bound by an adequacy decision made by the EU Commission. In other words, national data protection authorities did not have the competency to review a Commission

373 See eg Schwartz (n 359).
374 See also (n 306).
375 6 October 2016, ECLI:EU:C:2015:650.
376 (n 308) para 106.
377 Charter of the Fundamental Rights of the EU, OJ C 364 of 18 December 2000, 1–22.
378 Para 28.
379 Para 38.

adequacy decision and declare it or treat it as invalid.[380] Thus, for the sake of the consistency and uniformity of EU law, data protection authorities have to accept Commission adequacy decisions..

But the Court additionally held that the national data protection authorities had to hear complaints about data transfers even in circumstances where an adequacy finding applies. Furthermore, under the regime set up by the then in force Data Protection Directive 95/46/EC, both the national data protection authorities and the Commission had the power to declare adequacy findings. However, once the Commission has made an adequacy finding the Member States are bound by it.[381]

Only the CJEU had jurisdiction to declare a Commission's adequacy decision invalid, which the Court then proceeded to do in this case. The Court stated that the provisions of the Directive had to necessarily be interpreted in the light of the fundamental rights guaranteed by the Charter, which meant that a complaint that the transfer of personal data to a third country did not provide for adequate protection should be examined in the light of that person's fundamental rights to data protection, privacy, and a right to a fair trial.

The referring Irish Court had held that the Safe Harbor Agreement only imposed obligations on Facebook Ireland Ltd as transferor and Facebook Inc as transferee, and does not apply to the data processing by the US government (as the onward transferee in the line). The Safe Harbor Decision itself provided for broad exceptions for US organizations disclosing or transferring data to the US government:

> Adherence to these Principles may be limited: (a) to the extent necessary to meet national security, public interest, or law enforcement requirements; (b) by statute, government regulation, or case-law that create conflicting obligations or explicit authorisations, provided that, in exercising any such authorisation, an organisation can demonstrate that its non-compliance with the Principles is limited to the extent necessary to meet the overriding legitimate interests furthered by such authorisation; or (c) if the effect of the Directive [or] Member State law is to allow exceptions or derogations, provided such exceptions or derogations are applied in comparable contexts.

The Court held that it is clear that the level of protection must *continue* after the transfer of the personal data to the third country (implicitly: *even after a further onward transfers*).[382] This means that a US–EU arrangement on transfers of personal data such as Privacy Shield must make provision to guarantee protection additionally for later, onward transfers, according to the CJEU in *Schrems*.

These rules for US government, including law enforcement and national security agencies did not stipulate that they had to comply with necessity and proportionality requirements, or that there had to be safeguards, or effective recourse to redress for EU citizens or that any interference had to be targeted. This makes it clear that there was a fundamental clash between the rights to data protection and privacy under the

[380] Para 51.
[381] Paras 52–61.
[382] Para 82.

Charter and the ECHR, on the one hand, and US law on US government interference with the personal data of foreigners, and the lack of redress for EU citizens, on the other hand.[383]

After the EU–US Safe Harbor Agreement had been struck out the EU and the US agreed the Privacy Shield to replace the previous Agreement.[384] The Privacy Shield was announced by the EU Commission in February 2016[385] and approved as providing an "adequate standard" by the decision of the European Commission on 12 July 2016.[386] As of 2 December 2017, 2555 US organizations had self-certified as complying with the Privacy Shield.[387]

However, the Privacy Shield has not overcome the deficiencies identified by the Court and has been declared invalid in the second *Max Schrems* judgment on 16. July 2020.[388] The Civil Liberties Committee of the European Parliament, in the wake of the *Facebook–Cambridge Analytica* scandal has urged for a suspension of the Privacy Shield if it was not fully implemented by 1 September 2018 on the basis that it did not provide an adequate standard for the protection of data protection as a fundamental right under the Charter, since the US has not yet implemented it. The Chair of the Civil Liberties Committee, Claude Moraes, stated that:

> while progress has been made to improve on the Safe Harbor agreement, the Privacy Shield in its current form does not provide the adequate level of protection required by EU data protection law and the EU Charter. It is therefore up to the US authorities to effectively follow the terms of the Agreement and for the Commission to take measures to ensure that it will fully comply with the GDPR.[389]

The then Article 29 Data Protection Working Party (now the European Data Protection Board) made several criticisms in its first annual review of the Privacy Shield in October 2017.[390]

In academic literature, too it has been argued that the Privacy Shield does not comply with the principles enunciated in *Schrems*.[391] The Safe Harbour Agreement scheme was declared insufficient because it was found lacking in terms of (1) substantive protection, (2) clear limitations to data processing by US LEAs and intelligence, (3) safeguards and oversight mechanisms for US government surveillance, and

[383] Paras 90–95; see also referring Irish High Court's findings in Advocate -General's Opinion in Case C-311/18 Schrems II (n 308) paras 71–72.

[384] P Fischer, "From the Safe Harbour to the Privacy Shield" (2018) International Business Law Journal 143–53.

[385] http://ec.europa.eu/newsroom/just/item-detail.cfm?item_id=30375 accessed on 17/7/20.

[386] Commission Implementing Decision (EU) 2016/1250 of 12 July 2016 on the Adequacy of Protection Provided by the EU–US Privacy Shield OJ 2016 L207 of 1 August 2016, 1.

[387] ibid.

[388] (n 159).

[389] European Parliament Press Release dated 12 June 2018; Draft Resolution at http://www.europarl.europa.eu/meetdocs/2014_2019/plmrep/COMMITTEES/LIBE/RE/2018/06-11/1149002EN.pdf accessed on 17/7/2020.

[390] Art 29 WP 55 of 28 November 2017.

[391] A Butler, "Whither Privacy Shield in the Trump Era?"(2017) 3 European Data Protection Law Review 111–13; A-L Philouze, "The EU–US Privacy Shield: Has Trust Been Restored?" (2017) 3 European Data Protection Law Review 463–72.

most importantly (4) avenues for judicial review and redress for EU citizens.[392] As for substantive protection, the Privacy Shield has improved protection but continues to contain serious gaps—for example, in respect of the right of EU citizens to object to processing, automated processing and bulk collection.[393] With regard to clear limitations, one of the main defects of Safe Harbour was precisely that US legislation allowed access to personal data on far more extensive grounds than would be deemed justified by EU law.[394] Not much has changed in this respect, other than the Freedom Act 2015, which amended section 215 of the Patriot Act and prohibited the bulk collection of telephone metadata without specific selectors and other changes limiting government surveillance. Presidential Policy Directive 28 (PPD 28) also introduced some legitimate objectives limiting counter-terrorism intelligence activities, and data minimization principles. The then Article 29 Working Party criticized as too extensive the collection and access of personal data for national security purposes under both section 702 of FISA[395] and Executive Order 12333.[396] As for oversight mechanisms and safeguards, the Privacy Shield is supported by PPD 28, which envisages an Ombudsperson, not for individual complaints, but as a contact point for foreign (EU and other selected) governments. The Ombudsperson's envisaged function was to respond to queries and confirm that it has investigated the matter and either that remedial measures have been taken or that no violation of US law has been found. However, it was not clear how the Ombudsperson's independence was assured, what powers of investigation the institution possessed, how it ensured compliance by US agencies with any findings, and its findings were not subject to any form of judicial review.[397] More than two years after the Privacy Shield had been agreed, the Ombudsperson's position continued to be formally vacant[398] The biggest doubt, however, on whether the Privacy Shield provided an adequate standard of data protection related to the redress mechanisms for EU citizens. There were multifarious, out-of-court redress mechanisms that were complex and likely to prove unworkable.[399] First of all, EU citizens had to address any complaint to the US private entity who has signed up to the Privacy Shield. At the second stage Privacy Shield companies had a choice[400] whether to use a dispute resolution scheme offered by the EU Data Protection Authorities or a private ADR body. Only the third stage guaranteed binding legal review to EU data subjects in the form of an arbitration procedure (Privacy Shield Panel) paid by the Privacy Shield companies (through their membership fees), but no damages could be paid under this procedure. However, this three-stage dispute resolution procedure only applied to private sector data processing. For data processing by US law enforcement and

[392] (n 324) 14.

[393] See (n 324) 12 and Philouze (n 391) 466–67.

[394] Paras 91, 93–94.

[395] Which has been renewed.

[396] (n 324) 3.

[397] Philouze (n 391) 469 and (n 324) 19; see also the findings of the referring Irish High Court in Case C-311/18 *Data Protection Commissioner v Facebook Ireland Ltd and Max Schrems* (Schrems II) (n 308), Advocate General's Opinion para 73.

[398] (n 324) 4.

[399] Philouze (n 391) 467, 472.

[400] Unless the data relates to an employment relationship in which case they have to use the EU Data Protection Authority as dispute resolver.

intelligence authorities EU subjects did not have any avenues of redress or judicial review. While the Judicial Redress Act 2015 on the face of it seemed to give certain rights to EU citizens under the Privacy Act 1974, this avenue of redress was subject to discretion by the relevant authorities in respect of the countries covered and in respect of the agencies covered. President Trump's Executive Order 13768 limits the ability of US officials to designate their agencies as covered agencies under the Judicial Redress Act.[401] Therefore the only avenue of complaint in respect of US government surveillance was for EU citizens to complain to their data protection authority, who in turn could take up the matter with the European Data Protection Board, who then in turn could liaise with the US Ombudsperson, but without a clear decision or even compensation to be expected. It is precisely for these deficiencies that the CJEU, in the second *Max Schrems* judgment, held that the Commission's Implementing Decision regarding the Privacy Shield was invalid.[402] The CJEU found that "The Ombudsperson mechanism to which the Privacy Shield Decision refers does not provide any cause of action before a body which offers the persons whose data is transferred to the United States guarantees essentially equivalent to those required by Article 47 of the Charter."[403]

4.4 US–EU Umbrella Framework Agreement

The US and the EU have signed an "Umbrella" Agreement[404] applying to all data exchanges between LEAs in June 2016 and the Agreement entered into force on 1 February 2017.[405] The Agreement itself provides that, if the terms of the Agreement are complied with, the processing shall be deemed to comply with the "respective data protection legislation restricting or conditioning international transfers of personal information, and no further authorisation under such legislation shall be required."[406] Although this provision does not make direct reference to the adequacy provisions in the Law Enforcement Data Protection Directive, its wording implies that neither an adequacy decision nor further safeguards is required for such data exchanges from the EU side. The Agreement is therefore designed to overcome the EU data protection legislation as a "blocking statute" and its prohibition on data exports.

Jan Albrecht and Florian Jotzo state in their book that the Agreement does *not* imply adequacy, but without further support from the Agreement itself.[407] However, what is clear is that the agreement does not provide the legal basis authorizing the transfer[408] so that another legal basis (such as another agreement—an executive agreement under the Cloud Act) would have to be found. The stated aim of the Agreement is to provide for minimum data protection standards when law enforcement agencies in the EU

401 Butler (n 391) 112.
402 (n 159) at para 199.
403 Para 197.
404 Agreement between the US and the EU on the Protection of Personal Information Relating to the Prevention, Investigation, Detection and Prosecution of Criminal Offences, OJ L336 of 10 December 2016, 3.
405 OJ L 25, 31 January 2017, 1.
406 Art 5(3) of the Agreement.
407 Albrecht and Jotzo (n 20) 112.
408 Art 1(3) of the Agreement.

and the US exchange information for the purpose of prevention, investigation, detection, and prosecution of criminal offences, including terrorism.[409] Arguably, it fails to fulfil this aim, as the Agreement is poorly and incompletely drafted.[410] The Umbrella Agreement itself[411] is not limited to "serious crime," but could cover any crime, however minor. Furthermore, it expressly excludes from its scope intelligence agencies—thus any cooperation between the intelligence agencies between a EU Member State and US intelligence agencies would be unfettered ("without prejudice") by EU data protection law.[412] The minimum data protection standards are, *inter alia*, purpose and use limitations,[413] the need to obtain authorization from EU agencies for any onwards transfer to third countries[414] (onward transfers to other entities within the EU or the US is permitted[415]), giving EU residents a qualified right to access personal data held about them[416] and the right to correct inaccuracies in their personal data,[417] and the need to define the periods of data retention.[418] The problem with this Umbrella Agreement is that in many places when establishing data protection standards it leaves the relevant provisions "to be agreed" and it therefore constitutes more of an Agreement to Agree.[419] The access right for citizens is also unlikely to constitute much of a barrier as in the law enforcement context there will be many good reasons not to grant such a right and the Agreement contains a long list of exceptions in Article 16(2). Furthermore, the Agreement stipulates that automated decisions (eg by data mining) are permissible, as long as they are authorized under domestic law.[420] The right to correct inaccuracies is also a limited right, as it is limited to *factual* inaccuracies, but does not encompass prejudicial effects of data presentation, data processing, data mining, and the ensuing discrimination. Moreover, the Agreement does not specify judicial redress procedures and limits redress to breaches of the subject access request (riddled with exceptions in any case), the right to have factual inaccuracies corrected or unlawful disclosure of data (which includes a right of compensation). There is no judicial redress for breaching domestic evidential rules causing prejudice or unreliability of evidence, or misuses of personal information, or data breaches, or unauthorized onward transfers. Arguably, the Agreement does not really establish minimum standards for data protection in the context of law enforcement—instead it refers back to the provisions of the domestic law of the processing LEA.[421] It would be really difficult to

[409] Arts 1(1) and 2(5).

[410] One wonders whether the negotiators wanted this Agreement safe and dry before the incoming Trump administration in January 2017.

[411] The Agreement forming the basis of the data exchange might be so limited.

[412] Art 3(2).

[413] Art 6—this refers to the legal basis for the exchange.

[414] Art 7—but such authorization may be contained in the underlying Agreement.

[415] Art 7(4).

[416] Art 16.

[417] Art 17.

[418] Art 12.

[419] Data retention periods in Art 12(2) or processing of sensitive data in Art 13(2) (principle that data should be kept no longer than necessary).

[420] Art 15, this will provide absolutely zero protection for EU residents who might be affected by data mining of US LEAs, cf Art 22 GDPR.

[421] eg Arts 6(4), 15, 16(2), 18(2), 19(2), and 20.

argue that this Agreement provides sufficient safeguards or a functionally equivalent standard of data protection as was required by the Court of Justice in *Schrems*.[422]

5. Cross-border access to data for digital investigations—extending jurisdiction under international law?

The legal complexity surrounding data exchanges raises the question if, and under what circumstances, law enforcement can obtain direct access to remotely stored cloud data by extending their jurisdiction under international law. There are essentially four potential avenues for such direct access (avoiding MLA):

(1) LEAs using coercive powers under domestic criminal procedures achieving direct disclosure of foreign stored data by ISPs extraterritorially;[423]
(2) direct access through lawful remote search and seizure (hacking by law enforcement), or the use of OSINT authorized under domestic criminal procedures applied extraterritorially;[424]
(3) extending jurisdiction through international agreement for disclosure of data (production orders);[425]
(4) voluntary, informal cooperation with private, foreign ISPs without the use of formal coercive powers.[426]

This section examines extraterritorial coercive powers under domestic criminal procedures first, then moves on to the extension of jurisdiction through international agreements and finishes with voluntary cooperation with ISPs.

5.1 Using coercive powers under domestic criminal procedures

This method essentially means that LEAs use coercive powers authorized under their domestic criminal procedure extraterritorially, potentially in breach of the territoriality principle and hence the principle under international law that law enforcements can only act within their own territory. It essentially expands the jurisdiction of LEAs beyond their territory.

5.1.1 Domestic criminal procedures achieving direct disclosure of foreign stored data by ISPs

This section examines extraterritorial production orders under domestic criminal procedures. It looks at the US cases, in particular *the Microsoft* case, the

[422] See criticism by *Meijer Committee*, Statewatch, http://www.statewatch.org/news/2016/nov/meijers-committee-umbrella-agreement-note.pdf accessed on 17/7/2020.
[423] See Table No 2a and Belgian *Yahoo!* case discussed in section 5.1 and Guidance Note Art 18 Cybercrime Convention discussed in section 5.1.1.3.
[424] See Table No 2b and Belgian Criminal Procedure Rules discussed in section 5.1.1.2; Danish Supreme Court Case discussed in section 5.1.2.1; Art 32a Cybercrime Convention discussed in section 5.1.2.2.
[425] See Table No 3 and US Cloud Act discussed in section 5.2; EU E-Evidence Regulation (Proposal) discussed in section 5.2.2.
[426] See Table No 4 and Art 32(b) Cybercrime Convention discussed in section 5.3.

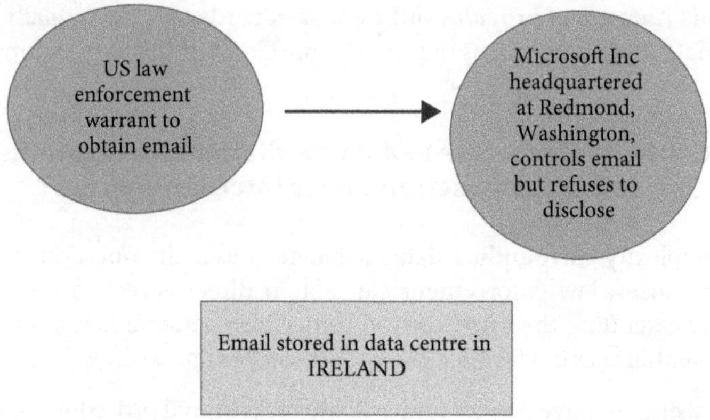

Figure 6.1 Microsoft Ireland case

extension of the reach of warrants under the amendments of the Cloud Act to the Stored Communications Act, the Belgian *Yahoo!* case, and the Guidance to Article 18 of the Cybercrime Convention.

5.1.1.1 Domestic ISP controls data, but not data in foreign locations, US Microsoft *case and the Cloud Act*

In this first scenario, law enforcement of State A requires access to the contents of an email controlled by service provider X, which is also headquartered in State A, but the email itself is stored in a data centre in State B.

This was the scenario underlying the *Microsoft Ireland* case (Figure 6.1).

In *Re Warrant to Search a Certain Email Account Controlled and Maintained by Microsoft Corp*[427] the Magistrate ordered by way of a warrant under the Stored Communications Act[428] that Microsoft disclose the content of emails in connection with a criminal investigation into drug trafficking, even though the emails were stored in a data centre in Ireland by Microsoft's wholly owned subsidiary.[429] The court order was affirmed by the Federal District Court for Southern District of New York. Microsoft had already disclosed metadata stored on its servers in the US but had refused to disclose content data physically stored in a data centre located in Ireland, citing presumption against extraterritorial reach of US laws and the warrant requirement in the Stored Communications Act.[430] The Federal District Court did not accept this argument and held that this was *not* an extraterritorial application of the law,[431] as it was sufficient that Microsoft had (remote) control over the data in

[427] 15 F Supp 3d 466 (SDNY 2014).

[428] 18 USC ss 2701–12.

[429] 15 F Supp 3d 466, 477 (SDNY 2014).

[430] S 2703(a) and s 2703 (b)(1)(A) and (B).

[431] Other District Courts have also come to this conclusion: *In re Search Warrant Issued to Google* 264 F Supp 3d 1268, 1279–80 (ND Ala 2017); *In re Search Warrant No. 16-960-M-1 to Google*, 275 F Supp 3d 605, 619 (ED Pa 2017), aff'g 232 F Supp 3d 708, 725 (ED Pa).

the US.[432] A distinction was made between a "normal" search and seizure warrant, which was limited by its nature to US territory,[433] and a warrant under the Stored Communications Act, which allows for electronic disclosure and is therefore more akin to a subpoena for the disclosure of documents,[434] and as this does not require physical access by US law enforcement personnel, it is not limited to US territory.[435] Subpoenas under US law impose a broad obligation to disclose documents regardless of the location of the document.[436] Microsoft then appealed to the 2nd Circuit Court of Appeals, which reversed the District Court's decision:[437] The Circuit Judge, Susan Carney held that the Stored Communications Act of 1986 "neither explicitly nor implicitly" envisions the application of its warrant provisions in a foreign territory and that the Act maintained both the Constitutional privacy protections (in the form of the warrant requirement) and the territorial limitations thereof.[438] She referred to the recent case law of the US Supreme Court emphasizing the presumption of extraterritoriality in *Morrison* and *Nabisco*[439] and therefore held that the warrant infringed the presumption against extraterritorial application of US law[440] and as a consequence ordered the District Court to quash the finding of civil contempt against Microsoft.[441] She referred to the entirely different technological context of 1986.[442] In a concurring but separate Opinion, Circuit Judge Gerald E Lynch found that updating the law to such fundamental new technologies has to be made by a balance struck by Congress in a legislative act.[443] Essentially the 2nd Circuit held that a warrant is a warrant and a subpoena is a different instrument.[444]

Looking on the *Microsoft* case under the lens of jurisdiction, it seems that there are several theoretical connecting factors to locate investigatory jurisdiction: (1) the place where the person controlling access to the data (here Microsoft Inc) is located, (2) the place where the data is in fact stored (the data centre in Dublin), and (3) the place where the data subject is located.[445] Each of these three options are unsatisfactory as a ground for jurisdiction. The first option (place where the person controlling the information is located) is unsatisfactory as it allows law enforcement to order disclosure of data on the thin ground that a service provider or its subsidiary has factual access to and control over the data. This in many ways resembles the wide-ranging civil and criminal subpoena powers that US courts have exercised over their subsidiaries and

[432] 15 F Supp 3d 466, 472 (SDNY 2014).

[433] Rule 41 Federal Rules of Criminal Procedure: United States law enforcement officers may be directed by a court-issued warrant to seize items at locations in the United States and in United States-controlled areas, but their authority does not go any further.

[434] A production order.

[435] 15 F Supp 3d 466, 471 (SDNY 2014); see also Case Review in 128 Harv L *Rev 1019*.

[436] *Marc Rich & Co., A.G. v United States*, 707 F 2d 663 (2d Cir 1983), see also the discussion in Chapter 9.

[437] 829 F 3d 197 (2d Cir 2016).

[438] ibid 201, 218.

[439] See the discussion in Chapter 2.

[440] 829 F 3d 197 (2d Cir 2016) 201, 210–13, 217–19.

[441] ibid 202, 222.

[442] ibid 206.

[443] ibid 222–23.

[444] ibid 215–16.

[445] J Hörnle, C Velasco, AM Osula, and D Svantesson, "Global Views on Internet Jurisdiction and Trans-Border Access" in S Gutwirth, S Leenes, and P De Hert, *Data Protection on the Move* (Springer 2016) 465–76.

that has caused so many jurisdictional conflicts with EU data protection law.[446] The second option is too limited as data frequently will be stored in another jurisdiction. As for the third option, in the *Microsoft* case, Microsoft stored the data geographically close to the data subject for technical reasons, but the decision where to store data in the cloud was made based on the data subject's (the email user's) provided information, so that a user could easily provide false information to achieve data storage outside the US.

But the ruling in the case largely focuses on the statutory interpretations of the US Stored Communications Act and did not pronounce that extraterritorial data access is a breach of the Fourth Amendment. The Court's focus on extraterritoriality shows that the Court was more concerned about jurisdiction and the notion of comity in the relations between the US and foreign states than about privacy. In any case, the 2nd Circuit Decision sent a clear signal to the US government to change the legislation, as otherwise US law enforcement would be left in the impossible position of having to seek cumbersome mutual assistance each time data controlled by US service providers was stored in the cloud outside the US (including cases where the location of the data was not known), even if that data related to a crime committed on US territory by a US citizen.[447] The response of the US Government was the Cloud Act, which was signed into law by President Trump on 23 March 2018, at the time the *Microsoft* case was pending before the US Supreme Court. As a new warrant had already been issued under this new legislation the US Supreme Court finally dismissed the *Microsoft* case as moot when it finally came to hand down its Decision on 17 April 2018.[448]

The Cloud Act changed the Stored Communication Services Act by expressly stipulating that service providers are required to preserve and disclose all content or subscriber data in their possession, custody, or control, regardless of whether the data is located in or outside the US.[449] Therefore, now that the Cloud Act is in force, it is clear that the warrant provisions in the Stored Communications Act are expressly made to apply extraterritorially, and hence the general presumption against extraterritoriality of US law does not apply as such. However, a warrant under the Act can be quashed on the grounds of comity, but *only* if the data relates to a non-US person and there is a risk of conflict with the law of a qualifying foreign government.[450] Both these terms need further explanation: a non-US person is essentially a non-US domiciled person (including legal persons) *and* a non-US citizen[451] and a qualifying foreign government

[446] On subpoenas see the discussion in Chapter 9 and on Arts 48–49 GDPR see section 4.

[447] Daskal (n 333) 10: "from the government perspective, the Second Circuit's ruling was a significant security blow: It meant that any time sought-after data happened to be held outside of the United States, it had to request access via a foreign government."

[448] *US v Microsoft Corporation* 138 SCt 1186 (2018) 1188: "no live issue remains between the parties."

[449] 18 USC s 2713, in force 23 March 2018: "A provider of electronic communication service or remote computing service shall comply with the obligations of this chapter to preserve, backup, or disclose the contents of a wire or electronic communication and any record or other information pertaining to a customer or subscriber within such provider's possession, custody, or control, regardless of whether such communication, record, or other information is located within or outside of the United States."

[450] 18 USC s 2703(h)(2).

[451] 18 USC s 2523(a)(2): "the term 'United States person' means a citizen or national of the United States, an alien lawfully admitted for permanent residence, an unincorporated association a substantial number of members of which are citizens of the United States or aliens lawfully admitted for permanent residence, or a corporation that is incorporated in the United States."

is a foreign government,[452] which has entered into a reciprocal "executive agreement" with the US to allow US law enforcement mutual access to metadata and content data of foreign-based service providers.[453] The disclosure order can only be quashed if three conditions are fulfilled: (1) the disclosure would violate the law of the foreign government, (2) this would be in the interests of justice, and (3) the data subject is a non-US person and does not (even temporarily) reside in the US.[454] Finally, the Act allows service providers to disclose to "qualifying governments" only the fact that a warrant for disclosure of data in respect of one of their citizens has been made, but not to other governments.[455]

Thus, effectively, the US limits the doctrine of comity to those "friendly" states who allow the US "mutual" direct access to the data of *their* ISPs. The message is, "if you co-operate with us, we respect your comity, if you don't, we don't." But considering how much of the world's data is located or controlled in the US and that non-US law enforcement requires access to such data from time-to-time, it is likely that the executive agreements will be one-sided, in favour of the US. As a consequence, the US is wielding its power over the world's electronic data, to gain access to the—relatively speaking—little data held by other states. The US nods to laws such as the EU GDPR, but this hides the reality of superior "data power" when negotiating mutual international cooperation in criminal matters. In the context of our discussion on jurisdiction, this means that the US extended the jurisdiction of its law enforcement to data stored abroad (which considering the realities of cloud computing was a necessity), but the Cloud Act did this in a way that limits the notion of comity (which is supposed to protect the sovereignty of other states) and uses the superior "data power" of the US in order to achieve concessions from other states concerning their sovereignty. The statute could have been drafted in a manner, which would have both meant less aggressive expansion of jurisdiction and a more respectful approach to the sovereignty of other states by requiring connecting factors to territory other than the mere location of the data needed for investigation. Such connecting factors include the nationality of the data subject, a showing that the US courts have jurisdiction over the crime investigated, and a demonstration that investigations are reasonable and furthering essential interests of the US (such as investigating *serious* crime connected to the US).[456]

5.1.1.2 Foreign ISP controls data in foreign locations

In this second scenario the ISP is established and controls the data in a foreign jurisdiction. An example for this second scenario is the Belgian *Yahoo!* case.[457]

The Belgian *Yahoo!* case has been widely discussed and criticized.[458] This case concerned a criminal prosecution of fraud committed through the use of Yahoo! email

452 18 USC s 2703(h)(1)(A)(ii) and s 2523 (Executive Agreements).

453 Section 5.2.1.

454 18 USC s 2703(h)(2)(B).

455 18 USC s 2703(h)(B).

456 These comity factors are applied additionally (in respect of the "friendly" states): 18 USC s 2703(h)(3).

457 See also the discussion of the case in A-M Osula "Remote Search and Seizure of Extraterritorial Data" PhD Dissertation, University of Tartu, University of Tartu Press 2017, 25–26.

458 See P de Hert and M Kopcheva, "International Mutual Legal Assistance in Criminal Law Made Redundant" (2011) 27 Computer Law & Security Review 291–97.

accounts. The Public Prosecutor requested *subscriber information* from Yahoo! under Article 46bis of the Belgian Code of Criminal Procedure to identify the perpetrators of the fraud. Yahoo! refused to comply with the request, arguing that the request must be served by *US* authorities[459] under the Stored Communications Act and that it could not accept the extraterritorial application of Belgian criminal procedure.[460] Yahoo! did not have an office or establishment in Belgium. At first instance, the Dendermonde Court in 2009 ordered Yahoo! to disclose the information requested and resolved to levy a fine of Euro 55,000 and a Euro 10,000 penalty for each day of non-compliance. The Belgian Court found jurisdiction on the basis of commercial presence: Yahoo! was commercially present in Belgium through the provision of internet services to persons located in Belgian territory.[461] Yahoo! appealed the case and in its first Decision, the Belgian Court of Cassation[462] found on 4 September 2012 that the direct order requesting subscriber information sent by the Belgian Public Prosecutor had been validly made to Yahoo! (upholding the original decision of 2009).[463] The case was relegated to the Court of Appeals of Antwerp, who in November 2013 again confirmed the opinion of the Court of First Instance of Dendermonde and found: (1) that Yahoo! had a territorial presence in Belgium, (2) that Yahoo! is and should be considered a provider of electronic communications services within the meaning of Article 46bis of the Code of Criminal Procedure, and therefore (3) that Yahoo! should collaborate with investigative authorities in the facilitation of the information requested and (4) levied a penalty of Euro 44,000 against the company. Yahoo! then appealed again against the penalty imposed on it on the basis that the extraterritorial enforcement of a Belgian order to disclose data was a breach of international law, but the Court of Cassation rejected the appeal on 1 December 2015.[464] The Court of Cassation acknowledged that the disclosure order for subscriber data was a coercive measure, but it adopted a proportionality analysis by arguing that it was a coercive measure with limited reach: the measure was only to obtain identification data, the service provider was active on Belgian territory, the Belgian authorities had jurisdiction to investigate the crimes to which the order related, and the measure did not require the physical presence of investigation officers in another jurisdiction, nor was there any physical intervention outside the territory of Belgium.[465] The Court denied that the Belgian order was an extraterritorial exercise of authority because of these connecting factors to Belgian territory.[466]

[459] Using Mutual Legal Assistance under the MLAT between the US and Belgium of 28 January 1988.

[460] For a synthesis of the scope of *ECPA*, see the website of the United states Department of Justice, Office of Justice Programs, https://it.ojp.gov/default.aspx?area=privacy&page=1285 accessed on 17/7/2020.

[461] The Belgian position on subscriber data is similar to the position taken in the T-CY Guidance Note to Art 18(1)(b) of the Cybercrime Convention, including the definition of the jurisdictional link (providing services on the territory), but Art 18(1)(b) would not oblige the service provider or the US authorities to recognize the Belgian order, see the discussion in sections 2.2 and 5.1.1.

[462] Supreme Court, 4 September 2012, AR P.11.1906.N/2.

[463] There was also an issue as to whether Yahoo! was an electronic ISP, but this is not relevant for purposes of this chapter.

[464] Supreme Court, 1 December 2015, Nr P.13.2082.N, Case Translation at (2016) 13 *Digital Evidence and Electronic Signature Law Review* 156–58.

[465] ibid para 6.

[466] ibid para 8.

This logic of denying extraterritoriality was applied again by a Belgian court again in 2016 in the *Skype Belgium* case. An Investigating Judge in Belgium addressed an order directly to the Luxembourg establishment of Skype to set up interception capabilities in a specific investigation of organized crime in Belgium. Skype countered that it cannot intercept communications because of end-to-end encryption and refused to comply with the order. At first instance the Correctional Court in Mechelen[467] held that it had jurisdiction to directly order a Luxembourg entity to carry out such interception under the Belgian criminal procedure code[468] without having to go through judicial cooperation mechanisms or MLA. It argued that the order was not extraterritorial as it should have been complied with in Belgium where the intercepts would have to be provided. Microsoft appealed, but the Appeal Court confirmed the ruling in November 2017 holding that Skype has a sufficient connection to Belgian territory as it provides its services there and targets advertising at the Belgian market.[469]

5.1.1.3 Guidance Note interpretation of Article 18 Production Orders

The Cybercrime Convention proceeds from the realization of the urgent need for cross-border cooperation for digital investigations. As has been discussed, it attempts to achieve this purpose by three different mechanisms: (1) approximating a number of criminal offences in the cybercrime area, (2) setting out the *minimum* investigative tools and powers that ratifying states should have, in order to deal with digital investigations, and (3) providing for cross-border cooperation through MLA. Article 18 of the Cybercrime Convention falls into the second category of mechanisms, that is, its purpose is to ensure that states have production orders in their investigative toolkit. We will come back to why this position of Article 18 in the "powers" section[470] is important at the end of this section.

This toolkit of digital investigative powers in Article 18 includes two types of orders. First, State B's LEAs must be empowered by their domestic law, to order a *person in their territory* (in State B) to disclose specified[471] computer data in that service provider's possession *or control*.[472] This raises the interesting question (from a jurisdictional perspective) whether there is a requirement that the *computer data itself* has to be physically hosted in State B before this power can be exercised, or whether it can be located at an unknown location in the cloud or at a known location, in a data centre in another State C. If it is the latter this would help to overcome the scenario where law enforcement issues a production order against a local person, but the data is likely to be physically located abroad, as in the *Microsoft* case. However, if the LEA is located in

[467] ME20.F1.105151-12, Judgment of 27 October 2016, available from http://www.wolterskluwer.be/files/communities/legalworld/rechtspraak/2016/Corr.%20Mechelen%2027%20oktober%202016%20(Skype).pdf accessed on 17/7/2020.

[468] Arts 88 and 90.

[469] https://www.technologyslegaledge.com/2018/03/lawful-intercept-on-voip-services-skype-in-belgium/ accessed on 17/7/2020.

[470] Cybercrime Convention Committee (T-CY), T-CY Guidance Note #10 "Production Orders for Subscriber Information," 28 February 2017, adopted on 1 March 2017 and available from https://www.coe.int/en/web/cybercrime/cegaccessed on 17/7/2020 (quoted as Guidance Note), p 3 acknowledges that this section is a "domestic power."

[471] Not bulk data.

[472] Art 18(1)(a).

a different state than the person controlling the data, mutual assistance under Articles 23 and 25 of the Cybercrime Convention must be used. Thus, if State A requires disclosure of data from a person located in State B controlling data, and that data is physically stored in a data centre in State C, State B should have the power under Article 18 to order disclosure of the data to its LEAs, notwithstanding the data's location in State C, but State A would still have to go through legal mutual assistance to obtain disclosure of the data from the authorities in State B.

The Cybercrime Convention Committee of the Council of Europe adopted a Guidance Note on Production Orders in respect of Article 18(1)(b) in March 2017. This Guidance Note is clearly a soft law instrument, but signifies the common understanding of the states in respect of the interpretation of the Cybercrime Convention and will therefore be influential.[473] According to the Guidance Note there is no need for the data to be stored in the same State B, thus State B should implement this power of ordering production of data from persons on its territory, regardless of where the data is hosted.[474] This has been criticized as extraterritorial,[475] namely an "exercise of State power in the territory of another State."[476]

The second tool in the kit in Article 18(1)(b) is that State X should be able to request *subscriber information*[477] from a service provider under two conditions: (1) that the service provider offers its services on the territory of State X[478] and (2) that the service provider has possession or control of subscriber information, regardless of whether this service provider is established on the territory of State X. This is essentially the Belgian *Yahoo!* scenario.

Thus, the Cybercrime Convention seems to envisage a direct *disclosure order* for subscriber information (but not any other stored data, such as traffic and content data[479]) against a *foreign* service provider located in State Y, as long as that service provider operates in State X (and the order relates to such services[480]), without the need to go through MLA.[481] The Guidance Note clarifies the phrase "offering its services in the territory" by stating that the service provider need not be "legally or physically present in the territory"[482] and also states that a service provider offers its services in

473 De Hert et al (n 1) 329.

474 Guidance Note, 6—this is already stated in the Explanatory Memorandum to the Cybercrime Convention, para 173.

475 The Guidance Note itself acknowledges that "concerns regarding privacy and the protection of personal data, the legal basis for jurisdiction pertaining to services offered in the territory of a Party without the service provider being established in that territory, as well as access to data stored in foreign jurisdictions or in unknown or multiple locations 'within the cloud' need to be addressed," p 3.

476 De Hert et al (n 1) 334.

477 Subscriber information is the most commonly requested type of data in investigations (which is not surprising, given the difficulties of identifying internet users, and their location, online), Guidance Note, 3; it is defined in Art 18(3). On the interesting question of the overlap between subscriber and traffic data (such as IP addresses) which is outside the scope of this discussion on jurisdiction, see de Hert et al (n 1).

478 De Hert et al (n 1) 331–32, see also the Belgian *Yahoo!* case discussed at section 5.1.1.2.

479 For the definition see Art 18(3).

480 De Hert et al make the important point that if a service provider were to collect data related to a user's religious denomination (unrelated to the services provided) as part of the subscriber data, this would not have to be disclosed, see de Hert et al (n 1) 331–32.

481 ibid 332.

482 Guidance Note 6.

the territory if two conditions are fulfilled: (1) the service provider enables persons on the territory to subscribe to its services and (2) it has a real and substantial connection to that state.[483] The Guidance Note clarifies the meaning of "real and substantial connection," which is essentially a targeting test—"the extent to which a service provider orients its activities towards such subscribers"—and is based on multiple factors: local advertising, the language of the advertising, the use of subscriber data in the course of its activities (for example for profiling), and the degree of interaction with users in the relevant state.[484] The extension of jurisdiction to foreign service providers without a physical establishment or presence has again been criticized as unwarranted extraterritoriality and not necessarily clear from the text of the Cybercrime Convention.[485]

The problem of extraterritoriality in this literal interpretation of Article 18(1)(a) and (b) is acknowledged by the T-CY itself[486] and is largely self-evident, but nevertheless a matter of concern. However, the impact of this recognition of extraterritorial power in the interpretative Guidance Note is limited if one considers the systematic position of Article 18 in the Cybercrime Convention as a whole. As has been emphasized at the beginning of this section, Article 18 is a provision that requires the ratifying state parties to create a power under its *domestic* criminal law procedures for the disclosure of data in the form of a production order. Thus, it creates a tool for the state in *its* investigative toolkit from a *domestic* law perspective. The fact that we are considering here a *domestic* criminal procedure cannot be overstated: the Cybercrime Convention is not forcing the receiving State (on whose territory the power creates effect) to recognize or approve of this power.[487] In other words, it does not force the receiving state to cede sovereignty to the investigating state and this is the important distinction to instruments such as the executive agreements envisaged in the US Cloud Act or the European E-Evidence Proposal. This is not just a theoretical distinction: for example, if State X issued a production order for subscriber data to a foreign service provider in State Y and that provider simply refused to comply, State Y has no obligation to enforce the order and is free to protest against State X's production order on the grounds of extraterritoriality and comity. There is no obligation to recognize or enforce the request outside MLA. However, this would mean that the protection of civil liberties of data subjects depends on the discretion of service providers to refuse to comply with such an order and on the non-enforcement by State Y. This clearly is far from satisfactory. In this vain, what is more concerning is that it is immediately obvious from the wording that the Guidance Note has been influenced by the EU doctrines of mutual trust and mutual recognition in that some of the phrases are practically identical to those used in the Proposal for the E-Evidence Regulation.[488] The Guidance Notes state that "the Parties to the Convention are expected to form a community of trust" in the context of the safeguards referred to in Article 15 of the Cybercrime Convention. This sounds suspiciously like the insistence on "mutual trust" between

[483] Guidance Note 8–9.
[484] Guidance Note 8–9.
[485] De Hert et al (n 1) 333–34.
[486] Guidance Note 3, 6.
[487] This is expressly stated in the Guidance Note itself, 3, 6, 7.
[488] Discussed in section 5.2.2.

the EU Member States in the context of their adherence to fundamental rights safeguards. Furthermore, in the context of production orders served on foreign service providers under Article 18(1)(b), the test for deciding when a provider provides its services in the investigating Member State is an almost identical targeting test to the draft E-Evidence Regulation both referring to a substantial connection to the investigating Member State.[489] This is highly concerning as the Cybercrime Convention, other than the reference in Article 15, does not harmonize procedural safeguards or provide for a system of cross-border remedies in respect of breaches of fundamental rights. The reference to mutual trust and respect for fundamental rights is nothing but lip service and does not contribute to cross-border justice or practical remedies in cases of breach, the possibility of a referral to the European Court of Human Rights is too remote;[490] instead practical access to a first instance court is required in these cross-border cases. Again, we see the need for effective remedies for data subjects and effective transnational rights. Arguably, one could even say that the Guidance Note itself is in breach of Article 13 of the ECHR as it does not provide for effective remedies in these cross-border cases.

5.1.2 Remote search and seizure and the use of OSINT authorized under domestic criminal procedures

This section examines remote search and seizure (hacking by law enforcement, network exploitation) and the use of open source data. The reason why these two techniques are grouped together is that they both involve access to data and the use of sophisticated analytical tools, including artificial intelligence.

5.1.2.1 Remote search and seizure—hacking by law enforcement

One option for LEAs is to simply gain access to stored data remotely, by hacking into foreign controlled and hosted data. As Kahvedzic has put it, "the hacking community and the forensics community have a lot in common."[491]

One way to achieve such direct access would be for the police or other investigating authorities to obtain the credentials of the user whose account they are seeking to secretly access, for example, by installing malware on the user's computer. Both the initial act of installing malware on a suspect's computer and the subsequent access to data would have to be authorized by domestic criminal procedure. The question of jurisdiction arises if the data that the LEAs are accessing is physically located in another jurisdiction.

Belgium has extended the jurisdictional reach of remote computer searches (content) in its domestic criminal procedure. The Belgian Code of Criminal Procedure[492] gives power to the Investigating Judge to extend computer searches to other computer systems located elsewhere, if this is necessary and proportionate in the specific criminal investigation at hand (the search must be targeted and based on suspicion) and if there are no less invasive investigatory measures available or there is a real risk that the

489 See the discussion in sections 5.1.1.3 and 5.2.2.
490 Say under Arts 6 and 13 of the ECHR.
491 Kahvedzic (n 4) 356, 360.
492 Art 88 of the Belgian Criminal Code.

evidence may disappear otherwise, given the fragile and volatile nature of computer and network evidence. But the search may only be extended to those parts of other computer systems to which the users of the original computer would have had access (such as access to remote storage systems) and are controlled by the users. The procedure foresees that the person responsible for the remote computer system will be informed of the access. If possible, the country on whose territory the data is stored will be informed after the event through diplomatic channels. The infringement of sovereignty of the foreign country is minimized by the notion that the data taken from the remote computer storage is only copied, the data at source is not removed or changed in any way, so data privacy, but not data integrity, is affected. Data obtained in this way would be admissible as evidence in criminal proceedings in Belgium.

Another example is Denmark. Here, the Danish Supreme Court decided that such remote searches are not extraterritorial as long as the underlying offence, which is being investigated is within the jurisdiction of the Danish courts.[493] The police gained access to a suspect's Facebook and Messenger profiles in the context of a drug trafficking investigation by using the relevant credentials, which they had obtained through (one assumes) authorized telephone intercepts. They used these credentials to covertly access the suspect's Facebook and Messenger profiles at a time when the suspect was outside Denmark. However, the Danish Supreme Court held that these remote repeated searches are made on the basis of Danish Criminal Procedure Law[494] and found that they were permitted on the basis that the suspect is subject to Danish jurisdiction and on the basis that these remote searches can be made without the involvement of foreign authorities. As pointed out by Lars Bo Longsted:

> the Danish police were able to carry out the search from their own office in Denmark since they were in possession of the necessary username and password and because the content of the computer in question was linked to the internet (...) it seem as if the Supreme Court has simply stated that the search was legal because it was possible.[495]

Remote computer searches where the location of the computer is not known raise difficult jurisdictional issues, as warrant authorization should be limited to searches in the territory of the country concerned. In the US it used to be the case that these warrants were even more local: they used to be limited to the territory of the district in which the warrant was authorized. In *In re Warrant to Search a Target Computer at Premises Unknown*,[496] the US District Court rejected the Government's argument that data surreptitiously seized from a computer at an unknown location would be "located" within the district where the agents would first *view* it for purposes of conforming to the territorial limitations of US search and seizure warrants, which are

[493] U 2012.2614 H, Danish Supreme Court, 10 May 2012, reported and translated in (2013) 10 *Digital Evidence and Electronic Signature Law Review* 162–65.
[494] Administration of Justice Act ss 793.1 (1) and 799.
[495] At 165.
[496] 958 F Supp 2d 753 (SD Tex 2013).

required for repeated surreptitious searches.[497] Thus, the strict territoriality requirements for search warrants meant that the US government could not seek a warrant to hack a computer suspected of criminal use but whose location was unknown.[498]

In a large-scale criminal investigation concerning a dark net website for the sharing of illegal child sex abuse materials (PlayPen) the FBI had used network investigation techniques (NITs). This allows the tracking of users accessing a website using the Onion Router (TOR) for anonymization purposes, which works by infecting the target computers with a type of malware and collecting identifying information on the targeted computers remotely. The FBI used NIT after they had seized the operation of the PlayPen website, which led to thousands of computers being implanted with malware and 137 arrests in the US alone.[499] The NIT remote computer searches were authorized by one single warrant and related to "the server operating the Tor network child pornography website," which by then was located at a government facility in Eastern Virginia.[500] This warrant caused a spate of litigation challenging the validity of the warrant and its territorial reach.[501]

In *US v Robert MacLamb*[502] the 4th Circuit cast a critical light on territorially limiting remote computer searches where the location of the target computers are unknown. The 4th Circuit confirmed that the authorization was not void because the location of the suspects' computers was not known and a single warrant was used for multiple remote computer searches. However, other Circuit courts found otherwise and held that the warrant was void ab initio because it exceeded the jurisdiction of the authorizing magistrate.[503] This caused the Supreme Court to change Rule 41 of the Federal Rules of Criminal Procedure in 2016. Rule 41(b)(6) gives a magistrate in a district "where activities related to a crime may have occurred" the power to authorize remote searches of electronic storage media and to seize or copy information stored within or outside that district. However, these extended search warrants may only be issued if either the location of the information has been concealed (as in the case of TOR) or in investigations of certain computer fraud and abused cases[504] if the computers are spread over at least five different locations (to avoid the delay and complication of multiple warrants having to be issued). This would extend to remote searches on computers whose location is unknown, but which might be on foreign territory. In fact, it seems that the PlayPen investigation caught information on computers around the world (as would be expected) and led to investigations and arrests globally (through police cooperation eg with Europol).[505] It should, however, also

[497] See Rule 41 "allows a "magistrate judge with authority in the district . . . to issue a warrant to search for and seize a person or property located *within the district*," 958 F Supp 2d 753 (SD Tex 2013) 756–57.

[498] At 761.

[499] https://www.eff.org/pages/playpen-cases-frequently-asked-questions#whathappened accessed on 17/7/2020.

[500] https://www.eff.org/files/2016/08/25/nit_warrant.pdf accessed on 17/7/2020.

[501] See K Widenhouse, "Playpen, the Nit, and Rule 41 (b): Electronic Searches for Those Who Do Not Wish to Be Found" (2017) 13 Journal of Business Technology Law 143–69.

[502] 880 F 3d 685 (4th Cir 2018).

[503] *US v Horton* 863 F 3d 1041, 1047–48 (8th Cir 2017); *US v Workman* 863 F 3d 1313, 1321 (10th Cir 2017); *US v Levin* 874 F 3d 316 (1st Cir 2017)—but the evidence was not suppressed.

[504] S 1030(5) USCA.

[505] https://motherboard.vice.com/en_us/article/qkj8q3/child-porn-sting-goes-global-fbi-hacked-computers-in-denmark-greece-chile accessed on 17/7/2020.

be noted that in respect of computers that are known to be outside the US, the Rule Amendment has not abandoned the presumption against extraterritoriality, meaning that such remote searches would not be permissible. In this connection it is important to emphasize the US Constitution and in particular that the 4th Amendment (privacy) does not apply to aliens outside US territory.[506] This also raises the point that as states extend their criminal investigations to have extraterritorial effect such extension should not take place without a corresponding extension of human rights safeguards and effective remedies.[507]

In *Gorshkov*[508] the warrant was found to be properly authorized, even though the computers hacked into by the FBI were *located in Russia*. In that case the FBI had traced criminal computer abuse activities harming businesses in the US to two Russian individuals (Gorshkov and Ivanov). Subsequently, the FBI set up a sting operation (a fake computer security firm, Invita) under the pretence of an intention to hire the Russian hackers as employees. As part of the fake interview, Gorshkov accessed their computers in Russia and the FBI used keyboard loggers to capture passwords, subsequently accessed the computers located in Russia, and downloaded incriminating evidence. However, jurisdiction was not argued in this case and the court did not regard this search as extraterritorial even though the evidence was located and seized from a foreign computer.

5.1.2.2 Access to open source materials: Article 32(a) of the Cybercrime Convention

The Cybercrime Convention focuses on international cooperation through mutual assistance, not the extension of jurisdiction by states. However, there are two exceptions to this. The Convention defines the limits of states' investigative jurisdiction in terms of territoriality. But it has made clear that two types of extraterritorial investigation are permissible under international law by extending jurisdiction. This issue was first discussed by the former G8 High Tech Subgroup of Senior Experts on Transnational Organised Crime and approved under the heading "Principles on Transborder Access" in a document at a Ministerial Conference in Moscow in November 1999.[509] Before that date there was scant evidence on practice and recognition of cross-border internet access to computer data in the course of digital investigations.[510]

The first example is Article 32(a), which allows the LEAs of a state without the authorization of another state to "access *publicly available* (*open source*) stored computer data, regardless of where the data is located geographically." This is an exception to the general principle that network searches should not be carried out across national borders.[511] Thus, the Cybercrime Convention clarifies that LEAs may

[506] *US v Verdugo-Urquidez* 494 US 259, 260 (1990) but cf *Boumedienne v Bush* 553 US 723 (2008), which probably only applies to Habeas Corpus—for a detailed examination see also Daskal (n 10) 336–442.

[507] S Brenner, "Fourth Amendment Future: Remote Computer Searches and the Use of Virtual Force" (2012) 81 Mississippi Law Journal 1229–62, 1257: "U.S. courts may well find it necessary to revise the interpretation that limits the applicability of the Fourth Amendment to extraterritorial actions, at least when those actions involve the use of cyberspace."

[508] United States District Court, WD Washington, 23 May 2001, Unreported, 2001 WL 1024026.

[509] (1999) 9(6) Statewatch Bulletin (November–December 1999) http://www.statewatch.org/eufbi/eufbi08.htmaccessed on 17/7/2020.

[510] C Velasco, "Cybercrime Jurisdiction: Past, Present and Future" (2015) 16 ERA Forum 331–47.

[511] See eg Art 19, which expressly limits domestic search seizure powers to the state's territory.

extend their jurisdiction to access such data even if this data is hosted by a foreign service provider and/or data centre located abroad/in the cloud. However, as several academics have pointed out, law enforcement access to such data may infringe the data subjects' privacy.[512] Publicly available open source data on the internet can take various forms, ranging from social media interaction to blogging, from tweeting to e-commerce websites and intuitively one may indeed ask the question: If the public can freely access such websites, why should the police not be able to? But on reflection it becomes clear that the answer to this question is complex—users may have legitimate expectations of privacy in relation to how their public online communications are used (and exploited in ways not necessarily foreseen by users). In this regard, as police are likely to use more and more invasive and extensive data mining techniques powered by artificial intelligence, for intelligence led policing[513] (eg finding crime hotspots and concentrating police resources there) as well as for crime investigation, this may engage both data protection laws and privacy rights of data subjects. While a detailed discussion of this area is outside the scope of this book, it should be pointed out that the engagement of data protection and privacy means that states should pass legislation on what the police can and cannot do in the open source space.[514] From a jurisdictional point of view, the fact that this balance between, on the one hand, police powers and data protection and privacy rights, on the other, varies between states with the consequence that conflicts of law and jurisdiction will probably arise. The accessing state is likely to base its access on its own domestic procedural laws, ignoring any higher standards (if any) in the state where the data is accessed. Although the Cybercrime Convention only seems to allow "access," in the literature it has been expressed that this includes copying and recording the data.[515] Since the Cybercrime Convention has now been ratified by a large number of states and this provision seems to reflect international practice, it may well be that it reflects a consensus that has become part of international law.[516] The Explanatory Memorandum makes clear that all states involved in drafting the Convention unanimously agreed that unilateral action in the case of open-source data and publicly available data is permissible.[517] Nevertheless, the scope of the provision is not entirely clear as the Convention uses two different phrases, *publicly available* and *open source*. The discussion centres around the questions of (1) whether this includes commercial data behind a paywall, (2) whether it includes sources for which one has to register, and (3) whether this reflects the characteristics of the data as private data or public data.[518] With regard to the first question there seems to be consensus

[512] B-J Koops, "Police Investigations in Internet Open Sources: Procedural-law Issues" 29 (2013) Computer Law & Security Review 654–65, 655–56; L Edwards and L Urquhart, "Privacy in Public Spaces: What Expectations of Privacy Do We Have in Social Media Intelligence?" (2016) 24(3) International Journal of Law and Information Technology 279–310.

[513] M O'Floinn and D Ormerod, "Social Networking Sites, RIPA and Criminal Investigations" [2011] 10 Criminal Law Review 766–89, 770.

[514] B-J Koops (n 512) 655.

[515] ibid 658.

[516] ibid.

[517] Explanatory Memorandum, 53.

[518] B-J Koops (n 512) 659–61.

that law enforcement may acquire commercial data in a foreign jurisdiction—there is not obvious good reason why the provision should not extend to this type of data. However, the second type of data where there is a registration requirement raises more interesting issues. The point of a registration requirement surely is that the user has to disclose his or her identity and become part of a user group—if LEAs do not disclose their true identity this may mean that they are engaging in a form of covert, undercover investigation,[519] which arguably should not be covered by Article 32(a). Finally, it would also make sense to limit this extension of jurisdiction to data that is of a public nature, but this is not part of the wording of Article 32(a), so it would be difficult to argue that the drafters had limited cross-border access to data of a public nature.[520]

5.2 Extending jurisdiction through international agreement for disclosure of data

5.2.1 The Cloud Act and executive agreements

Any form of effective bilateral transnational cooperation in the field of digital investigations requires a degree of mutual recognition of laws and procedures. As we have seen with respect to the EU, mutual recognition in turn requires some sort of understanding that legal standards are roughly equivalent or at least "adequate" so that states can cede a degree of sovereignty to each other. This section discusses the Cloud Act and how this proposes to deal with the dilemma by distinguishing on a general basis between states that respect due process and privacy rights, and those states that do not. It argues that this notion of "general trust" creates a dangerous precedent as compliance with fundamental rights needs to be checked on a case-by-case basis and not only a priori. This section examines the dilemma in the context of data transfers.

The US passed the Cloud[521] Act on 23 March 2018. It establishes a regime whereby the US government may enter into bilateral "executive agreements" with non-US governments.[522] If these executive agreements are implemented by both sides, this would allow the LEAs of each state (US/non-US) to order investigative measures[523] under its own national *domestic criminal procedure directly to a service provider in the other state* (non-US/US) who would then have to comply with such a request, according to the law of the issuing state (Figures 6.2 and 6.3).[524]

519 O'Floinn and Ormerod (n 513) 771.

520 But interestingly, the Romanian legislation implementing this provision does limit the power of foreign authorities to "public Romanian sources of public computer data," Art 65 Law No 161/2003.

521 Clarifying Lawful Overseas Use of Data.

522 18 USC s 2523.

523 Which investigative measures will depend on the terms of each bilateral executive agreement, but the provisions in the Cloud Act are wide-ranging and may include not just access to existing communications data (both metadata and content data) but also interception see 18 USC s 2523(b)(4)(D)(vi).

524 Arts 3(2) and 5(1) US–UK Executive Agreement of 3 October 2019.

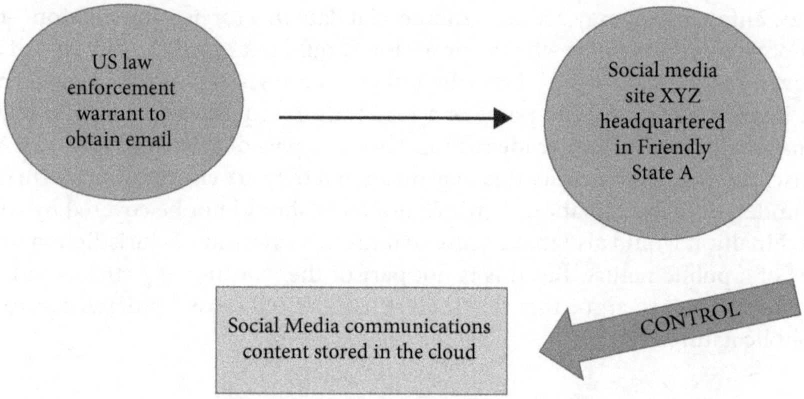

Figure 6.2 US law enforcement requesting data from non-US service providers

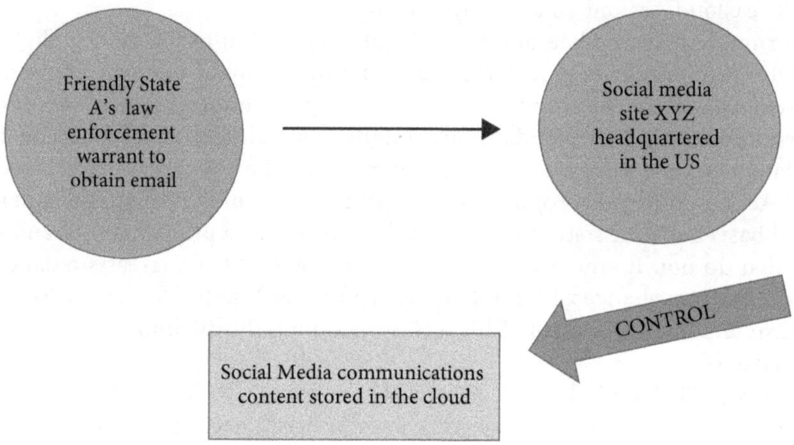

Figure 6.3 Non-US law enforcement requesting data from US service providers

This regime is therefore a kind of bilateral, international cooperation based on mutual cessation of sovereignty and, for the other party, extension of sovereignty. As such it is a novel way of constructing international cooperation through a series of bilateral agreements,[525] providing for minimum procedural safeguards and a form of mutual recognition.[526]

[525] Daskal (n 333) 15.

[526] See further K Walker (SVP & General Counsel), "Digital Security and Due Process" Google Blog (22 June 2017). https://www.blog.google/topics/public-policy/digital-security-and-due-process-new-legal-framework-cloud-era/ and the Framework itself: https://storage.googleapis.com/gweb-uniblog-publish-prod/documents/CrossBorderLawEnforcementRequestsWhitePaper_2.pdf accessed on 17/7/2020.

As to procedural safeguards, any requests for data by non-US government must be targeted since it must identify "a specific person, account, address, or personal device, or any other specific identifier"[527] and must be necessary[528] and subject to judicial oversight or review.[529] Therefore the Cloud Act does not provide for bulk disclosure of data. Furthermore, it limits the potential privacy risks posed by the executive agreements by stating expressly that decryption obligations may not be part of it[530] and that the system of direct data access must not be used to infringe freedom of speech.[531]

It also imposes certain data minimization obligations on the investigative measures *ordered by the non-US government*.[532] Further safeguards are imposed on interception measures, in particular in respect of their limited duration.[533] As to mutual recognition, the framework under the Cloud Act provides that only governments that respect fundamental rights, have adequate privacy protections, fair trial rights, prohibition of arbitrary detention and torture, a procedural framework for digital investigations with appropriate safeguards, the minimum powers outlined in the Cybercrime Convention, and respect the rule of law may enter into such an executive agreement. This qualifying status must be certified by the US Attorney General with the concurrence of the Secretary of State.[534] These qualifying criteria for admission to the system of bilateral cooperation are different to, but reminiscent of the concept of mutual recognition built on mutual trust in the intra-EU framework of law enforcement cooperation, discussed in section 3. It is built on a shaky foundation of bilateral, intergovernmental agreements without the institutional framework of a supranational organization such as the EU or a common human rights charter. On the one hand, the minimum standards as to procedural safeguards might incentivize some countries without clear procedural safeguards for digital investigations to update their laws and include such safeguards in their national laws.[535] On the other hand, it may also lead to a lowering of safeguards, as countries with higher safeguards (compared to US legislation and 4th Amendment jurisprudence) in their domestic criminal procedure might have to tolerate US law enforcement carrying out investigative measures without recourse to national, non-US law. However, much will depend on what countries negotiate in the executive agreement, but countries may have insufficient bargaining strength. Given the US power over the world's electronic data many countries will start from a lower bargaining position. An international version of presumed "mutual trust" is highly problematic also for the reason that the legal situation in a country may change and it

527 18 USC s 2523(b)(4)(D)(ii); N Brown, "The CLOUD Act: Cross-border Law Enforcement and the Internet" (2018 April/May) Computers & Law 5–6; Art 4(5) US–UK Executive Agreement of 3 October 2019.

528 18 USC s 2523(b)(4)(D)(iv): "shall be based on requirements for a reasonable justification based on articulable and credible facts, particularity, legality, and severity regarding the conduct under investigation"; Art 5(3) US–UK Executive Agreement of 3 October 2019.

529 18 USC s 2523(b)(4)(D)(v); Art 5(2) US–UK Executive Agreement of 3 October 2019.

530 18 USC s 2523(b)(3).

531 18 USC s 2523(b)(4)(E), see Art 8(4)(a) US–UK Executive Agreement—UK providers may refuse to comply with a US order if the data requested is used to prosecute for an offence for which the death penalty is used.

532 18 USC s 2523(b)(4)(F) and (G); Art 7(3)—(5) US—UK Executive Agreement.

533 18 USC s 2523(b)(4)(D)(vi).

534 18 USC s 2523(b).

535 Daskal (n 333) 15.

may be proven that the trust is no longer warranted. Furthermore, a general notion of general compliance is of no solace to an individual whose rights have been infringed. A system of mutual recognition requires mutually agreed privacy standards and enforceable remedies in courts that are accessible to the data subject. The system of bilateral executive agreements under the Cloud Act does not guarantee such mutually agreed privacy standards nor accessible judicial review.

Considering that many of the internet communications companies are headquartered in the US (Microsoft/Skype, Facebook/Instagram, Snapchat, Twitter) and that non-US governments and LEAs have grappled with the difficulties of obtaining disclosure of metadata and content data from such providers, this possibility of using coercive powers under domestic criminal procedure[536] directly against US service providers is likely to be attractive for qualifying governments. This may make them less inclined to negotiate for high privacy rights and remedies for their citizens/domiciles, which is a highly disconcerting prospect. No doubt the proposed legal framework would give communication service providers more legal certainty and therefore has been supported, for example, by Google.[537] However, these executive agreements are mutual in the sense that the US likewise is seeking direct access to data held by foreign service providers.[538]

The legislative framework in the Cloud Act further suggests that the obligations are asymmetric in the sense that non-US law enforcement may only request data about non-US persons[539] (not domiciled or resident in the US and non-US citizens[540]), whereas US law enforcement may obtain data about non-US persons. Furthermore, non-US governments may obtain data only for the prevention, detection, investigation, or prosecution of *serious crime, including terrorism*,[541] whereas no such limitation exists in the Cloud Act in respect of the US government. However, whether these limitations will remain one-sided depends, of course, on the terms of the executive agreements and the safeguards, which the non-US governments will be able to negotiate and in particular whether non-US governments will publicly discuss the executive agreement and present it to their parliament for debate and approval. It is vital that a public debate of this issue occurs now, not after the executive agreements have been signed behind closed doors.

The US has entered the First Executive Agreement with the UK on 3 October 2019. It comprehensively covers content data, computer data, traffic, and other metadata and subscriber information.[542] It only applies to "serious" crime defined as crime

[536] 18 USC s 2523(b)(4)(D)(iii): "shall be in compliance with the domestic law of that country, and any obligation for a provider of an electronic communications service or a remote computing service to produce data shall derive solely from that law."

[537] Walker (n 526) and the Framework itself: https://storage.googleapis.com/gweb-uniblog-publish-prod/documents/CrossBorderLawEnforcementRequestsWhitePaper_2.pdf accessed on 17/7/2020.

[538] 18 USC s 2523(b)(4)(I); Brown (n 528).

[539] 18 USC s 2523(b)(4)(A) "the foreign government may not intentionally target a United States person or a person located in the United States, and shall adopt targeting procedures designed to meet this requirement."

[540] For the definition see 18 USC s 2523(a)(2).

[541] 18 USC s 2523(b)(4)(D)(i).

[542] Art 1(3).

subject to a maximum custodian penalty of three years or more.[543] The UK may not request data in respect of US citizens, government authorities, US permanent residents, a person located in the US, or a US company.[544] The US may not request data in respect of UK government authorities, UK companies, or a person located in the UK.[545] However, this targeting limitation is asymmetrical in that the US *may* target UK citizens and permanent residents who are not located in the UK at the time of the request. The targeting, however, is only a good faith effort on both sides, as it may not be clear in a case at hand where the target is or who runs an account.[546] Moreover, the Executive Agreement is biased towards the US in that the data minimization requirements in the Cloud Act are implemented in favour of the US, but not in favour of the UK. The UK has a duty to "segregate, seal, or delete, and not disseminate material" that is not necessary[547] and to minimize the acquisition, retention, and dissemination of data related to US persons collected incidentally.[548] No such obligation is imposed on the US.

The communication service provider's obligation to disclose data arises under the law of the issuing state. If a communication service provider refuses to disclose the data, the issuing state must enforce the legal obligation across a foreign border. The Agreement does not say explicitly that the receiving state must assist in such enforcement. However, communication service providers risk extraterritorial enforcement by the issuing state. Judicial review of the order likewise has to take place in the issuing state across a border. The US–UK Agreement therefore arguably lacks precisely the possibility of a case-by-case judicial review at the place of its execution, in the receiving state (in the UK for US issued orders), which is the concern expressed in respect of the Executive Agreements above. A distinction must be made between the interests of communication services providers and data subjects whose data is sought. Communication services providers need legal certainty as to when they are obliged to comply with a request by a foreign law enforcement authority and the Cloud Act satisfies that need. However, the Cloud Act does not satisfy the needs of data subjects as the system does not allow for sufficient safeguards or accessible judicial review. It purely relies on the safeguards in the issuing state, which may not cover the privacy interests of the data subjects targeted.

Finally, the draft for a 2nd Additional Protocol to the Cybercrime Convention envisages direct disclosure orders from contracting states to foreign service providers, but only in respect of subscriber data, where this is needed for the issuing state's specific criminal investigation.[549]

5.2.2 The EU E-Evidence Regulation (Proposal)

In parallel with the US Cloud Act, the EU Commission has presented a Proposal for a Regulation on European Production and Preservation Orders for Electronic

543 Art 1(14).
544 Arts 1(6) and (12) and 4(3).
545 ibid.
546 Art 7(1).
547 Art 7(3).
548 Art 7(2).
549 See (n 137).

Evidence in Criminal Matters on 17 April 2018.[550] This draft Regulation is yet another EU measure based on the principle of mutual recognition and mutual trust in criminal matters in Article 82(1) TFEU.[551] If passed, it would establish a procedure whereby Member State A could directly serve a preservation order ("European Preservation Order Certificate" EPOC-PR) and/or a production order ("European Production Order Certificate" EPOC) on a service provider in another Member State B without having to go through the judicial (or for that matter any other official) authorities in Member State B, thus directly issuing a judicial order to a private entity in Member State B. This provides an alternative to the EIO for the LEAs in Member State A, thus giving them another tool in their kit of cross-border investigative measures. In the context of a discussion on jurisdiction, more importantly, the EPOC goes far beyond the EIO (which is communicated between the judicial authorities of the Member States) in that it exceeds "mere" international cooperation. It effectively extends a Member State's jurisdiction into the territory of another Member State and, like the system of executive agreements envisaged by the US Cloud Act, involves a mutual cessation of sovereignty between the states involved.

The EPOC-PR and the EPOC essentially are coercive measures, which oblige the service provider to disclose or preserve certain subscriber, access, transactional, or content data for the LEA in the issuing Member State A.[552] As drafted, it would only apply to existing data that is stored somewhere, usually in a cloud computing environment ("data at rest"), but it would not apply to covert measures such as interception or data not yet in existence. It is furthermore limited[553] in that is allows the disclosure of *transactional and content data* only for criminal offences with a maximum tariff of at least three years according to the law of the issuing Member State A *and*, regardless of the degree of seriousness of the offence, for those (cyber-) crimes that have been approximated at EU-level, namely fraud, child sex abuse offences, computer misuse, and terrorism-related offences.[554]

By contrast, the coverage of service providers is wide: it would apply to a wide range of service providers, namely electronic ISPs, information society service providers, domain name services (such as domain name registrars), and proxy services.[555] The obligation would in principle[556] arise notwithstanding of whether the data is *controlled* by the EU-based service provider.

For example, a Belgian issued EPOC-PR and/or EPOC could be served on the Irish EU subsidiary (eg in Dublin) of a US headquartered social media company (such as Facebook, Instagram, WhatsApp), regardless of *who* controls or physically hosts the data, *where the data* is controlled or hosted, and *where the data subject* is geographically located.

550 COM(2018) 225 final.

551 Explanatory Memorandum, 5 and Recital 1.

552 Art 2.

553 Art 5(4).

554 The Draft refers to the following four legal instruments establishing EU offences: Council Framework Decision 2001/413/JHA; Directive 2011/93/EU; Directive 2013/40/EU; Directive 2017/541/EU.

555 Art 2(3).

556 But see the concession to the notion of comity in Arts 15 and 16.

As drafted, the Regulation is not entirely clear on whether and how it applies to service providers not having any form of establishment in an EU Member State.[557] The jurisdictional link is quite vaguely formulated as "a substantial connection" to the Union,[558] which determines "the ambit of application of the present Regulation."[559] This substantial connection is present if the service provider has an establishment in or targets users in the EU, or where the service provider has a significant number of users in one or more Member States.[560] Targeting is defined by the multi-factor test[561] established in the jurisprudence of the CJEU in respect of "directing" of services to a Member State under Articles 17–19 of the Brussels Regulation (consumer jurisdiction in civil and commercial matters), to which Recital 28 explicitly refers.[562] This means that *only if* a service provider is *not* established within the EU, does *not* target its services at EU domiciled persons, or does *not* have a substantial numbers of users within the EU will it escape being the addressee of an EPOC-PR or an EPOC. It is not clear how an EPOC will be enforced if the service provider has no establishment in the EU, especially since the Member State of the establishment of the service provider will be tasked with enforcement.[563] Maybe the answer to this question depends on whether the EU will enter into executive agreements or similar bilateral agreements with the US.

In any case, it is clear that the Regulation, as drafted, extends jurisdiction far beyond the territory of the issuing Member State A and, potentially, beyond the territory of the EU. However, the Draft also emphasizes that it does not wish to harm the economic interests of EU domiciled service providers or the interests of states by causing conflicting legal obligations. As will be shown, however, the Draft is less concerned about fundamental rights protection and is in potential conflict with data protection (despite lip service to the GDPR and Data Protection in Law Enforcement Directive).

The Draft provides for direct channels of communication between the issuing Member State A and the service provider in Member State B to address practical issues such as incompleteness of the EPOC-PR or EPOC.[564] Furthermore, the Proposal has included the US notion of comity, so that, if the service provider (such as a US subsidiary) claims that compliance with the EPOC would be infringing the laws of a third country *and* fundamental interests *of that country* (such as human rights principles or national security of defence in the US), the *issuing* authority may either withdraw the

557 Art 2(4) and (5).

558 Art 2(4)(a) and (b) "enabling legal or natural persons in one or more Member State(s) to use the services (. . .) and having a substantial connection" to this/these Member State(s).

559 Recital 28.

560 ibid.

561 "The targeting of activities towards one or more Member States can be determined on the basis of all relevant circumstances, including factors such as the use of a language or a currency generally used in that Member State, or the possibility of ordering goods or services. The targeting of activities towards a Member State could also be derived from the availability of an application ('app') in the relevant national app store, from providing local advertising or advertising in the language used in that Member State, or from the handling of customer relations such as by providing customer service in the language generally used in that Member State." (Recital 28).

562 Regulation EU/1215/2012 see discussion in Chapter 10.

563 Art 14.

564 Arts 9 and 10.

EPOC or refer the matter to its local court (in Member State A) to assess the conflict of law situation, based on legal evidence from that country.[565]

In addition to extending jurisdiction in this way, the Proposal for the E-Evidence Regulation additionally provides for intra-EU cooperation by obliging Member State B to enforce the EPOC-PR and EPOC in case of non-compliance[566] through effective sanctions subject to a limited number of recognized objections.[567] If the service provider objects to carrying out the EPOC or the EPOC-PR, and the authorities in Member State B (which is the place of establishment of the service provider) impose sanctions, the service provider should have an effective local judicial remedy against these sanctions.[568]

The Regulation acknowledges fundamental rights concerns, in particular the right to privacy and the right to a fair trial, by referring[569] to the rights and remedies provided under the Data Protection Law Enforcement Directive[570] and the GDPR,[571] the rights of the defence and the fairness of proceedings,[572] and the necessity of the intra-EU cross-border investigative measure.[573] However, the *data subject* (who may be domiciled anywhere[574]) must bring any legal review in respect of the EPOC in the issuing Member State[575] so may have to resort to cross-border litigation, which is difficult and expensive for individuals. It is interesting that in respect of civil litigation and data protection litigation in consumer cases the EU deems it too burdensome for consumers to litigate in another Member State,[576] whereas it does not allow the data subject to litigate in respect of an infringement of his or her fundamental rights before the courts in his or her own country. If the data subject is the accused in criminal proceedings the challenge of the EPOC would be likely to take place in the framework of these proceedings within the criminal justice system of the issuing Member State. If the data subject is a third party then the legal challenge would have to be an action for judicial review, or potentially a special tribunal in Member State A. Arguably, more emphasis should be placed on ensuring access to justice in these scenarios involving cross-border investigative measures and cross-border, transnational litigation for data subjects.

Moreover, the tricky issue with investigative measures in general is that the data subject may not be aware of such measures being taken, as by their very nature they are secret, and service providers are placed under confidentiality obligations, so as to not defeat the object of a criminal investigation.[577] However, Member States have different

565 Arts 15 and 16.
566 Arts 13 and 14.
567 Art 14(4) and (5).
568 Art 14(10).
569 Art 17. (1) in relation to the suspect/accused and Art 17. (2) regarding a third party.
570 Directive 2016/680/EU.
571 Regulation EU/2016/679.
572 Art 17(6) implicitly nodding to Arts 47 and 48 of the EU Charter of Fundamental Rights (n 14)
573 Proportionality test, Art 17(3).
574 But who may be near (not necessarily in the same country) the service provider or the hosting provider because of latency issues overcome through the use of (regional) content delivery networks.
575 Art 17(3).
576 Arts 17–19 Brussels Regulation EU/1215/2012 see Chapter 10; and Art 79(1) GDPR see Chapter 11.
577 Art 11.

measures to counterbalance this need for secrecy such as, for example, obligations to inform the data subject after the event, or parliamentary or executive review procedures, and it would be essential that similar measures are taken for EPOCs. Here the Proposal refers to the law of the issuing Member State A: "(...) the issuing authority shall take the appropriate measures to ensure that information is provided about the possibilities under national law for seeking remedies and ensure that they can be exercised effectively."[578] Again, the principles of mutual recognition and mutual trust mean that the Commission entirely relies on the law of the issuing Member State, without counter-balancing the disconnection that arises from the cross-border nature of the EPOC with stronger rights for data subjects. A much better approach would be to include *specific and harmonized* procedural safeguards for data subjects whose data has been requested through an EPOC (such as a duty to inform the data subject after the event or a review by a special committee of the European Parliament or a committee of the European Commission or Eurojust). As we are moving (and forced to do so by globalization and technological innovation) towards EU transnational investigative powers in criminal matters it is vital to counterbalance these powers with EU transnational procedural safeguards instead of relying on the law of the issuing Member State and court procedures in the issuing Member State to which the data subject may not have access, given practical reasons such as costs and complexity of cross-border litigation.

Finally, the Proposal for the Regulation also recognizes that, under the law of many Member States, immunities and privileges mean that certain data cannot be disclosed to law enforcement in the context of a criminal investigation.[579] These immunities and privileges vary between the Member States and hence the question arises as to which Member State's law should apply in this respect. The Proposal pivots around the law of Member State B (which is where the service provider is located).[580] However, in order to make these privileges effective in protecting, for example, the lawyer–client or the journalist–informant relationship, the applicable law should be that of the locations of the *data subject*, that is, the location of the person(s) to whom the data relates. This again illustrates that the Regulation is more concerned with the interests of the states involved[581] than the fundamental rights of the data subject. In fact, it becomes clear from the proposed wording of Article 18 that the Commission confuses the fundamental interests of the Member State where the service provider is located with the rights of the accused/data subject.[582]

[578] Art 17(4).

[579] Such as legal privilege (ie concerning legal advice given by lawyers to their clients) or medical privileges (concerning the doctor-patient relationship) or journalists not having to disclose their sources.

[580] Art 18.

[581] See p 6 of the Explanatory Memorandum: "The rights under the law of the enforcing State are fully respected by ensuring that immunities and privileges which protect the data sought in the Member State of the service provider are taken into account in the issuing State."

[582] "If transactional or content data obtained by the European Production Order is protected by immunities or privileges granted under the law of the Member State of the addressee, or it impacts fundamental interests of that Member State such as national security and defence, the court in the issuing State shall ensure during the criminal proceedings for which the Order was issued that these grounds are taken into account in the same way as if they were provided for under their national law when assessing the relevance and admissibility of the evidence concerned."

In conclusion, the necessity for extending jurisdiction and international cooperation envisaged by the Proposal is palpable for the reasons explained here. This section has shown how the draft Proposal for a Regulation on E-Evidence attempts to achieve both these goals (extending jurisdiction and international cooperation). Given the contemporaneous and parallel developments in the US in the shape of the Cloud Act, one can speculate to what extent the Proposal was a reaction of the EU to these developments. In this speculative mode one could say that the EU potentially send two signals. The first is that EU Member States are not solely dependent on international cooperation with the US in being given access to US-established ISPs by the grace of the US—it can simply extend its jurisdiction to reach beyond its territory and force service providers to cooperate (provided they have an EU subsidiary).[583] This signal would serve to increase the EU's negotiation power in the context of the cooperation agreements with the US, such as the executive agreements envisaged by the Cloud Act or the EU–US Framework Agreement. Secondly, the EU is signalling its willingness to cooperate with the US in the area of law enforcement access to cloud data, notwithstanding its strong EU data protection framework, and the Proposal demonstrates through its emphasis on comity (a US law concept in any case) the willingness to accept (to a degree) US fundamental interests. Given the EU's political emphasis on data protection in the years leading up to the two new data protection instruments, this is a shift change.

Regardless of the political dimensions of the Proposal and the need for effectiveness of law enforcement it should, however, also be noted that more emphasis must be placed on fundamental rights protection of data subjects and cross-border redress, as has been discussed. Ultimately this can only be achieved through the establishment and greater harmonization of transnational (intra-EU and EU–US) procedural safeguards.

5.3 Voluntary disclosure by ISPs

5.3.1 Direct, "voluntary" informal cooperation with foreign service providers

US service providers cooperate on a voluntary and discretionary basis with LEAs. As a result of the revelations by *Edward Snowdon* about large-scale access by the NSA and its allies to data held by private service providers the practice by ISPs of quietly complying with government requests has becomes more controversial,[584] but it nevertheless continues.[585] The transparency reports of service providers reveal how many requests for user information (unspecified) were made and the percentage of disclosure: in Table 6.3 the UK and Germany are used as an example.

However, it is not clear from these figures whether they are based on voluntary cooperation or the service of legal process. For example, Facebook states in its privacy

[583] This is vaguely similar to the US issuing subpoenas to US based companies for execution by EU subsidiaries see the discussion in Chapter 9 or the logic of the reasoning of the CJEU in its *Google Spain* Judgment see Chapter 7.

[584] Kahvedzic (n 4)356, 363.

[585] ibid 356, 363.

Table 6.3 Transparency reports from Germany and the UK

2017	Google (all products)	Facebook	Twitter
Germany	21,057 (57%)	12,744 (60%)	718 (34%)
UK	11,021 (72%)	17,886 (91%)	1,579 (72%)

policy addressed to users: "we access, preserve and share your information with regulators, law enforcement or others (. . .) when we have a good-faith belief that the response is required by law in that jurisdiction, affects users in that jurisdiction, and is consistent with internationally recognized standards."[586] In its "Information for LEAs" it states: "We disclose account records solely in accordance with our terms of service and applicable law. A Mutual Legal Assistance Treaty request (. . .) *may* be required to compel the disclosure of the contents of an account."[587] These policy statements do not reveal clear guidelines and seem to leave cooperation up to Facebook's discretion and weighing up of commercial interests.

In any case, US-based service providers are prohibited from disclosing the *contents* of an electronic communication or remote computing service without a warrant (which would have to be obtained via MLA) unless made under an executive agreement entered into and certified under the Cloud Act.[588]

However, even if US service providers are not barred from disclosing certain non-content data to foreign law enforcement, there is nevertheless the question whether they could be liable if foreign law enforcement use this data in a way that (potentially) breaches a data subject's fundamental rights. Moreover, voluntary cooperation with foreign law enforcement places service providers in a difficult position, potentially involving a conflict of laws (such as data protection laws, privacy laws, or laws protecting whistle-blowers or journalistic sources). Thus, if service providers (as private entities) comply with *foreign* law enforcement requests for information stored on their servers the question arises whether this compliance with these *extraterritorial* law enforcement requests on a voluntary basis gives rise to liability on the part of the service provider. It is for this reason that service providers prefer clear, international legal frameworks that avoid such conflicts of law.[589]

A US district court ruled in 2008 that US service providers were not liable under the Electronic Communications Act to individuals whose personal information has been handed to foreign law enforcement.[590] There, the plaintiffs sought damages against an ISP on the ground that it had provided user information about them to the People's Republic of China (PRC). The Court found that "the alleged interceptions and disclosures *occurred* in the PRC."[591] The claim was dismissed on the basis of the

[586] https://www.facebook.com/about/privacy#legal-requests-prevent-harm accessed on 17/7/2020.
[587] https://en-gb.facebook.com/safety/groups/law/guidelines/ accessed on 17/7/2020.
[588] 18 USC s 2702(a) and (b)(9), s 2703.
[589] See the Framework Proposal by Google: https://www.blog.google/topics/public-policy/digital-security-and-due-process-new-legal-framework-cloud-era/ accessed on 17/7/2020.
[590] *Cunzhu Zheng v Yahoo! Inc.*, No. C–08–1068, 2009 WL 4430297 (ND Cal 2 December 2008).
[591] ibid at 4.

presumption against extraterritoriality of the Electronic Communications Act, which was here used to prevent a non-US citizen from obtaining redress for an act done by his government.[592] Again, it is wrong that in cases of extraterritorial searches, which cross-international borders but originate in the US by a decision of a US service provider, the law refuses to protect individuals and offers no legal safeguards under the US Constitution.[593]

5.3.2 Access—voluntary and lawful: Article 32(b) Cybercrime Convention

The second deviation of the principle that MLA is the only method of international cooperation in the Cybercrime Convention can be found in Article 32(b) and has been controversial. It relates to voluntary cooperation with a person who has lawful access (control) over computer data *stored in a foreign* jurisdiction and who can lawfully disclose such data. A state may, without authorization from another state, "access or receive, through a computer system in its territory, stored computer data located in another Party, if the Party obtains the *lawful and voluntary consent of the person who has the lawful authority to disclose* the data to the Party through that computer system."[594] This person can either be a private person (the suspect, a third party) or a service provider who voluntarily cooperates with law enforcement.[595] The provision is uncertain as it is far from clear what amounts to *lawful and voluntary consent* (eg where a suspect is tricked into disclosing data as in the *Gorshkov*[596] sting operation or data is being accessed while the suspect is arrested having been caught red-handed as Ross Ulbricht was during the successful Silk Road FBI investigation[597]). Equally unclear is the meaning of *lawful authority to disclose*—for example, if a social media service provider reserves the right to comply with law enforcement requests for users' personal data in the terms and conditions of service, would that be sufficient? The answer probably depends on the data protection and privacy laws applicable to the user's data and the relevant notion of consent thereunder.[598] The Guidance Note on Transborder Access states that the person providing access must not be deceived or forced to do so, which would exclude the two aforementioned scenarios (sting operation and police coercion when arresting a suspect).[599] The Explanatory Memorandum states that the Cybercrime Convention neither permits nor precludes states accessing computer data in foreign jurisdictions outside the scenarios recognized in Article 32.[600] Furthermore, the Guidance Note on

592 "[p]laintiffs point to no language in the ECPA itself, nor to any statement in the legislative history of the ECPA, indicating Congress intended that the ECPA ... apply to activities occurring outside the United States," at 3.

593 But contrast this with a 9th Circuit decision which found that emails are protected by the ECPA if they are stored in the US even if the sender/recipient are foreign: *Suzlon v Microsoft* 671 F 3d 726 (9th Cir 2011).

594 Art 32(b) Cybercrime Convention.

595 Although the Guidance Note seems to indicate that service providers cannot lawfully disclose data, see T-CY Guidance Note 3 "Transborder Access to Data" Adopted December 2014, 7.

596 (n 510).

597 https://arstechnica.com/tech-policy/2013/10/how-the-feds-took-down-the-dread-pirate-roberts/ accessed on 17/7/2020; a similar situation is mentioned in T-CY Guidance Note #3 "Transborder Access to Data" Adopted December 2014, 5.

598 In the EU this would fail because the notion of express and informed consent and in the US content data could not be disclosed under the Electronic Communications Privacy Act.

599 (n 598) 6.

600 ibid 53.

Transborder Access states that Article 32(b) does not apply if it is uncertain where the data is located—for example, if the data is stored in the cloud.[601] Thus, Article 32(b)'s remit is limited, it does not apply to coercive, non-voluntary measures and does not overcome the fact that in many situations it will be unlawful for service providers to disclose data to law enforcement. Again, the major barrier here is that many countries do not have adequate safeguards and data protection laws, or provide for checks and balances for LEAs, all of which might help dispel the reluctance for states to agree to transborder access.[602] Interestingly, the survey carried out by UNODC showed that of the twenty European LEAs returning a response 50 per cent replied that they use transborder access to computers, but the survey did not allow for more details, in particular whether this was within the Article 32(b) framework or whether it went beyond (eg direct access by hacking).[603]

6. Data sovereignty and data localization

Cloud computing has led to some states enacting data localization laws, which mandate that data must be stored on computers and servers *on their own territory*. Data localization laws can be understood as a claw-back reaction of states to a loss of sovereignty over data stored (at an unknown location) in the cloud. While they are frequently passed under the banner of data protection, it is important to place data localization laws in the wider context of sovereignty over information and censorship. This chapter has shown how states find it difficult to obtain access to data stored and controlled in another jurisdiction, access that is needed for the purposes of law enforcement. Data localization laws seem to solve this dilemma by keeping the data within the jurisdiction so that states maintain their data sovereignty. They are a reaction of states to a period of global instability and division, as manifested in a resurgence of terrorism, mass migration, the Arab spring, the revelations of *Edward Snowden* about mass US surveillance, and the destructive processes of the digital revolution. This reassertion of sovereignty in the shape of sovereignty over data did not start with concerns over law enforcement and national security. The first prominent form of data localization laws was the EU Data Protection Directive 95/46/EC and its prohibition on transfers of personal data to non-EU countries without adequate data protection standards.[604] There may be other examples for data localization laws in specific sectors to ensure enforcement of regulation, for example, some gambling regulatory authorities insist that some of the servers, on which player data is stored, are within the jurisdiction.[605] But data localization laws, additionally, may also have non-legal reasons and have more to do with the assertion of state power and state authority. Having data controlled by ISPs within their own jurisdiction confers power

601 ibid 6.
602 Velasco (n 510).
603 United Nations Office on Drugs and Crime, "Comprehensive Study on Cybercrime" (2013) 219, available from https://www.unodc.org/documents/organized-crime/UNODC_CCPCJ_EG.4_2013/CYBERCRIME_STUDY_210213.pdf. accessed on 17/7/2020
604 See the discussion in section 4.1.
605 eg France.

on states. First, it means that states can data-mine huge reserves of information and use the insight gained for purposes of law enforcement, national security, and regulatory control. Second, sitting on such a large data trove means that other states are likely to want their share of information, which in turn puts the state who has easiest access to the data in a strong bargaining position vis-à-vis the states who have less access to data. Third, given the value of big data exploitation, controlling data also means increasing economic opportunities. Therefore linked to data localization laws are data retention laws whose function is also to enrich states and their capacity for data access and data mining for the purposes of law enforcement and national security.

A distinction can be made between three different types of data localization laws:

(1) data localization laws, which require back-ups being stored locally, but data may otherwise freely be transferred to other countries (which clearly have no relevance to data protection);
(2) data localization laws, which require that the primary database is stored within the same country, but secondary data may be stored in other countries—such as back-ups, mirroring sites, or segments of a database (these may also not do much to increase data protection in the country concerned);
(3) data localization laws, which prohibit transfers to other countries.

As for the last category, such laws may theoretically enhance data protection but might in practice be infeasible, as the country concerned would be cut-off from international communications and have limited access to new technologies involving big data, the internet of things, and cloud computing.

Russia has recently passed a number of laws, both on data localization and data retention, in several waves. The earliest wave was a law forcing financial institutions acting under a licence from the Russian Central Bank to retain electronic records of all financial transactions in a back-up database in Russia for five years.[606] In response to the terrorist attacks in the Russian city of Volgograd at the end of 2013 Russia passed legislation in 2014 applying a whole host of obligations[607] to Organizers of Information Dissemination on the internet, which is a category of internet services provider defined as "any person, facilitating the functioning of information systems and computer programs, which may be used and/or are used for receipt, transfer, delivery and/or processing electronic messages of internet users." This is a very wide definition that has been described as "almost anyone associated with an internet service" and has been narrowed through legal guidance to internet communication services such as social networks, providers of public email, providers of collaboration/storage cloud services, and providers of fora and other discussion groups. These service

[606] Federal Law "On Banks and Banking Activities" (2013) and s 3.6 Regulation of Central Bank of Russia No 397-п of 21 February 2013 discussed in A Savelyev, "Russia's New Personal Data Localization Regulations: a Step Forward or a Self-imposed Sanction?" (2016) 32 Computer Law & Security Review 128–45, 129.

[607] Including notification requirements, co-operating with Russian law enforcement by giving them access to stored data on request, blocking illegal content; see the discussion in ibid 129 and M Zhuravlev, "Russian Data Retention Requirements: Obligation to Store the Content of Communications" (2018) 34 Computer Law & Security Review 496–507.

providers have to retain user data, metadata about electronic communications, and data about electronic payment transactions for six months and at least a copy of that data must be stored locally in Russia.[608] This was extended in 2016 to oblige telecoms operators and internet communications service providers to store the *content* of communications from 1 July 2018.[609] The main purpose of this combined data retention and data localization law is to facilitate "investigatory activities without jurisdictional complications."[610]

In a third wave of data localization legislation Russia passed a specific law on personal data protection in 2014, which imposes an obligation on "data controllers when collecting personal data of Russian citizens online or offline, to (…) [process and store[611]] such data in databases located in Russia."[612] The Russian regulator Roskomnadzor has provided that a primary database of personal data (the master copy) must be maintained in Russia (including updates and later additions) but secondary data may be exported if the importing country provides adequate standards of data protection or the data subject has consented. There are four exceptions to the data export prohibition, namely international agreements, law enforcement, provision of public services and processing for mass media, and scientific and creative purposes.[613] Sanctions for non-compliance are a low administrative fine[614] and internet access blocking of the website concerned.[615] It has been widely reported in 2016 that LinkedIn was blocked as a consequence of these data localization laws.[616]

Alexander Savelyev discusses the reasons for the adoption of the data localization legislation in Russia and finds that since it does not prevent transborder transfers of personal data it may not achieve the stated goal of data protection. While it may have some effect as a means to reduce US (and other foreign) surveillance, it could also be argued that it creates information on Russian citizens in fewer places, thus increasing the risk of direct access/hacking by foreign intelligence and law enforcement. Kuan Hon also argues in the context of her discussions of the EU–US Privacy Shield that data localization does not necessarily protect EU residents' data against US government surveillance, as EU residents transfer their own data directly to US based websites and cloud providers.[617]

Savelyev also reports that at the time the 2014 data localization law was passed there was much speculation on whether this was a retaliation of the US/EU sanctions over Russia's actions in Ukraine.[618] Like with any data localization laws IT industry protectionism and support for local data centres and local (regional) cloud services may be part of the motivation, but of course data localization laws may also have negative

608 Federal Law No 97-FZ; Zhuravlev (n 607)130.
609 Federal Law No 374-FZ; Zhuravlev (n 607) 497.
610 ibid 130.
611 My simplification.
612 Federal Law No 242-FZ, s 18(5) discussed in Savelyev (n 606) 131.
613 ibid 133–34.
614 In 2016 RUB 10,000, approx 175 US dollars.
615 Savelyev (n 606) 135.
616 https://www.bbc.com/news/technology-38014501 and https://www.theguardian.com/world/2016/nov/17/russia-blocks-access-to-linkedin-over-foreign-held-data accessed on 17/7/2020.
617 Hon (n 24) 170.
618 ibid.

effects on the local IT industry as it may limit innovation and investment in the fields of big data, cloud computing, and the internet of things.[619] He concludes that "something bigger than purely economic interests was at stake here" and in particular connects the Russian data localization laws with an agenda of the Russian government to claw back on digital sovereignty. He defines this as national governments exercising "control over information processes within the country without external interference."[620] This motivation also explains the distinction between primary and secondary databases. The obligation to keep the primary database in Russia has the purpose of ensuring access to data even in times of conflict (eg if Russia was somehow disconnected from the global internet), it means law enforcement and national security agents can avoid having to deal with jurisdictional complications, it means takedown requests for illegal content can be enforced at source, in Russia (censorship in its purest form), and taxation of virtual activities may be made more efficient.[621] Thus, data localization in Russia is at best marginally about data protection: it is an assertion of digital sovereignty with the goal of implementing censorship, national security, and taxation measures.[622]

However, there are concerns about data sovereignty in most states in the cloud computing age where data from one country is stored on servers and/or controlled from other countries.[623] Thus, the impact of cloud computing on the control of data by cloud providers in foreign jurisdictions and unknown location of cloud storage has effects on state's data sovereignty with immediate impact for digital investigations and crime fighting as discussed in this chapter.

7. Digital investigations, jurisdiction, and fundamental rights of citizens

Planning this book, and in particular this chapter I asked myself repeatedly the following question: Why *does* jurisdiction matter? If we have reached a stage in the development of human history where legal relationships are transforming into a complex web governed both by national and transnational law with spheres of overlapping jurisdiction and international cooperation one could simply argue that this is the new way of doing things. Answering this question, I think jurisdiction matters since four important legal institutions are tied up with jurisdiction: (1) the rule of law, (2) checks and balances for executive power, (3) fundamental rights guaranteed by the nation state, and (4) citizenship. In this section, drawing on my preceding discussion of digital investigations and jurisdiction, I explain why this is so. As has been explained at the outset of this chapter, increasing globalization, online cross-border activity, and increasing information flows are concomitant with growing levels of transnational crime—in particular, cybercrime and fears related

[619] ibid 140, 143.
[620] ibid 140.
[621] ibid 140–41, 144.
[622] ibid 145.
[623] Bygrave (n 302) 124–25.

to information security. This coupled with security threats transcending traditional crime, such as state-sponsored cyberattacks and mis-information campaigns, as well as the fear of terrorism, have heightened calls for greater law enforcement powers. At the same time, the "unterritoriality of data" and loss of location have caused a change of paradigm in the cloud computing age. This change of paradigm is that traditional *territorial* law enforcement powers such as search and seizure of computers and interception of telecommunications on a nation state's territory do no longer give law enforcement access to data. Hence LEAs demand access to data controlled remotely and stored in the cloud. As we have seen, states have reacted to these changed circumstances in three ways: (1) calling for more transnational law enforcement powers, (2) extending jurisdiction beyond the territory (extraterritoriality), and (3) engaging increasingly in international cooperation at an intergovernmental and executive (LEAs) level.

In this context a new concept, namely that of transnational criminal law, has entered the stage. This concerns the legal frameworks establishing the structures necessary to fight transnational crime in an interconnected world and encompasses a debate, which has been shaped by the scholarship of the last few decades.[624] Scholars have criticized that transnational criminal law focuses too much on the agenda of states and their interests to expand their crime-fighting capacity (which Sabine Gless terms the "Bird's Eye View") and not sufficiently on the position of individuals and their human rights "in the possibly overlapping normative orders" (which she terms the "Worm's Eye View").[625] The conclusion is that what is required is a "set of general principles necessary to determine the relevant rules," which are self-contained and developed from the existing national legal frameworks[626]—moving from a Westphalian nation state model to a transnational model of international Constitutional rights. Gless refers to the case law of the CJEU who has derived a common human rights framework from the common traditions of the constitutions of the EU Member States and the European Court of Human Rights[627] and points out that "this is the point where constitutionalism and Transnational Criminal Law intersect, and the states that pierce through sovereignty by way of co-operation must provide a functional equivalent to protect all exposed citizens."[628]

However, fundamental rights pertaining to digital investigations are sacrificed in this new way of doing things. As we have seen in this chapter in the discussion about the US–EU Umbrella Agreement, the Law Enforcement Data Protection Directive and the Privacy Shield, data protection, and privacy rights are undermined through direct access to data by foreign government and through data exchanges between LEAs. Intergovernmental agreements have omitted effective rights to judicial review and redress, as, for example, US Constitutional Fourth Amendment rights and

[624] N Boister, *An Introduction to Transnational Criminal Law* (Oxford University Press 2012) 3–23.

[625] S Gless, "Bird's-Eye View and Worm's-Eye View: towards a Defendant-Based Approach in Transnational Criminal Law" (2015) 6(1) Transnational Legal Theory 117–40, 117; NI Thorhauer, "Conflicts of Jurisdiction in Cross-border Criminal Cases in the Area of Freedom, Security and Justice" (2015) 6(1) New Journal of European Criminal Law 78–101.

[626] Gless (n 625) 138–40.

[627] ibid 135.

[628] ibid 130.

the Privacy Act 1974 do not apply to non-US citizens[629] and attempts in the Judicial Redress Act to change this have so far failed. Furthermore, as discussed in relation to the E-Evidence Proposal and the concept of mutual recognition in the EU, transborder access to the courts (in another state, applying foreign law) is frequently not possible for data subjects or the accused in criminal proceedings. Just as in the sphere of Private International Law where the EU has introduced rules allowing consumers suing in their domestic courts,[630] the costs of transborder access to the courts are likely to be prohibitive (need to engage foreign lawyers, translation costs) and the evidence spread over several jurisdictions may not be available to an accused. Thus, transborder digital investigations raise questions of pre-trial criminal procedure and due process, which are there to protect the accused against injustice. As the discussion of international cooperation and MLATs has shown, there is frequently confusion about which state's criminal procedure rules apply, which may be prejudicial to the accused and furthermore jeopardize a successful prosecution. As the discussion of the Cybercrime Convention and the EU Mutual Recognition principle have shown, instruments for international cooperation frequently rely on vague notions of "mutual trust" and "mutual recognition" that are used to paper over any conflicts in domestic criminal procedure. Furthermore, to the extent that states have extended their own investigation jurisdiction beyond their national territory and apply their domestic criminal procedures, this subjects the accused or a third party to foreign criminal procedure that may not contain the same level of fundamental rights protection. Another concern is the lack of checks and balances of executive power, for example, through judicial or parliamentary controls of investigative powers. Intergovernmental processes conducted behind closed doors lack transparency and political debate. Informal direct requests by law enforcement to obtain data from private ISPs likewise do not provide for safeguards other than the discretion of these private entities (eg by publishing transparency reports). These disclosures by private service providers largely occur in a legal void and endanger the rule of law.

Moreover, the new paradigm of transnational criminal law ultimately will endanger the notion of citizenship in modern democracies, which is based on the executive being accountable to its citizens and on the notion of the rule of law and fundamental rights protection. The core notion of citizenship is threatened, as citizens cannot influence law-making and legislation in other states, which leads to a lack of democratic influence and lack of accountability.[631]

These concerns could be tackled by two different approaches. First, transnational criminal law must be complemented by transnational human rights law and transnational constitutionalism, not just in terms of substantive rights, but also in terms of safeguards, checks and balances, realistic access to the courts, judicial redress, and accountability mechanisms.[632] Second, states must agree rules on how to deal

[629] *US v Verdugo-Urquidez* 494 US 259, 265 (1990).

[630] See Chapter 10.

[631] S Glaser et al, "Mutual Recognition and its Implications for the Gathering of Evidence in Criminal Proceedings: a Critical Analysis of the Initiative for a European Investigative Order" (2011) 1(1) European Criminal Law Review 56–79, 63; Thorhauer (n 625) 96–97.

[632] Thorhauer points to the differing standards even within the EU: Thorhauer (n 625), 90.

with conflicts of jurisdiction and applicable law, ensuring clear protection under the accused's or data subject's national law in international cooperation mechanisms. This means, for example, in a criminal case, defendants and their legal representatives must have access to international cooperation mechanisms in the context of digital investigations and the collection of transborder evidence. The current risk of international cooperation is that intergovernmental agreements are based on the respective bargaining power and might of states concerned, including their data sovereignty, which governs international relations and politics. Transnational criminal law must move from this sphere to one where the rule of law is central to transnational constructs (both bilateral and multilateral agreements and understandings of jurisdiction, sovereignty, and territory). It is for this very reason that jurisdiction does matter.

For cross-border digital investigations *within the EU* there exists a common human rights framework in the shape of the ECHR and the Charter of Fundamental Rights and secondary data protection laws, which are in the process of development.[633] Additionally, within the EU there is a criminal justice framework, which albeit in its infancy is slowly developing, in the shape of secondary laws providing protections and safeguards for defendants in criminal trials. These frameworks provide *some* minimum standards within the EU that may at least paper over some of the intergovernmental cracks in regulating digital investigations as they enable judicial review of procedural powers in the area of digital investigations[634] (and other powers arising under criminal procedures such as the European Arrest Warrant with even greater implications for individual liberty). These frameworks notwithstanding, there is a legitimate concern that too much focus is placed on extended crime-fighting powers and transnational cooperation and that this is not counter-balanced with equal attention to constructing safeguards for individuals affected and whose privacy is intruded upon and data protection infringed by these powers. Such rights continue to fall through these intergovernmental cracks. Furthermore, the bitter pill to swallow for those Member States who provide higher standards of criminal protection[635] is that a common framework inevitably means that protection will be provided as a common denominator, which for some Member States equates to a lowering of protection standards. Since individual citizens are "always influenced by the legal values of the country [they] substantially and regularly belong to,"[636] this raises interesting questions as to citizenship within the EU. If EU citizens regard themselves primarily as citizens of the nation state (rather than EU citizens), but human rights protection is lowered to some common but incomprehensible EU standard, this may give further impetus to opposition against the EU and questions regarding citizenship and identity.

Moreover, more attention should be given to institutional controls and safeguards (a surveillance committee in the European Parliament?) as well as judicial review and redress in individual cases. For this latter point there are two deficiencies that need to be overcome. First, remote cross-border litigation in foreign courts is expensive

633 Thorhauer points to the differing standards even within the EU: Thorhauer (n 625) 88.
634 *Schrems, Digital Rights Ireland, Tele2, Canada PNR Agreement, Google Spain.*
635 Thorhauer (n 625) 84.
636 ibid. 91.

and raises access to justice issues. Second, jurisdictional rules on the competence of investigative and prosecution authorities as well as the criminal courts should be harmonized to avoid *double jeopardy* and implement effective and clear protections against *ne bis idem*.[637] As Thorhauer states: "the intergovernmental state-oriented and security-focused approach, excluding the individual as a subject of rights, is no longer compatible with an AFSJ [Area of Freedom Security and Justice] that (...) places the individual at the heart of its activities."[638] Currently too much emphasis is placed on state interests, comity, and sovereignty and insufficient emphasis is placed on citizens' rights and remedies.

As for cross-border digital investigations involving non-EU countries and in particular the US, it should be noted that the cultural and legal human rights standards are different. Furthermore, states such as the US limit Constitutional protections to US domiciles and US citizens and, as has been already discussed in the context of the Judicial Redress Act, the US are loath to extent these protections to non-resident foreigners. Furthermore, recent US Supreme Court decisions have limited the protection of US laws for foreigners through the doctrine of extraterritoriality.[639] And in addition cross-border investigations in the EU–US context raise all the challenges discussed in this chapter in the respect of intra-EU cross-border digital investigations ranging from inadequate safeguards, to questions of *ne bis idem* and accessible judicial review.

8. Conclusion

Paradigms in respect of communications have changed in the last fifteen years: fixed line telephony has been replaced or supplemented by mobile telephony, and telephony itself has been replaced by over-the-top internet communication, such as internet voice telephony and instant messaging. More and more people are using social media platforms for sharing and storing content, and more and more data is communicated, processed, and stored in cloud computing environments, where these data are remote and the location is frequently not known, or even if known, is in another jurisdiction. Increasingly, data is encrypted, frequently by the devices used, with the result that end-to-end encryption is integrated to protect users' privacy and the confidentiality of communication. Since, unfortunately, some internet users pursue criminal ends, a fraction of this data will be urgently needed in the context of criminal investigations and prosecution of crime, in order to obtain the electronic evidence for successful convictions. A society that does not enforce its criminal laws does not respect the rule of law and guarantee individual liberty and security, which are a precondition for a "free" society. As a consequence, it is strikingly obvious that the traditional law enforcement powers of interception of telephony, search and seizure of computers on national territory, and production orders for stored computer data are outdated to the extent that they are jurisdictionally limited to the territory of the LEA. In the main, states have reacted to this need for electronic data in criminal investigations and prosecutions in

[637] ibid 98–99.
[638] ibid 99.
[639] Discussion in Chapter 2.

four different ways. First, they have increased the scope of international cooperation and this chapter has discussed MLATs, the Cybercrime Convention, the European mutual recognition initiatives, and the US Cloud Act as examples for this. Second, since international cooperation is difficult to achieve given its political nature and the reluctance to cede sovereignty, states have simply extended their jurisdiction to the cloud, by using *domestic* criminal procedures to coerce ISPs to carry out digital investigations, regardless of the location of the data, and regardless of the establishment of the ISP. Third, states have attempted to avoid having to rely on the (voluntary or coerced) cooperation of ISPs by directly accessing data through investigatory tools based on hacking, authorized under their domestic criminal procedure. Fourth, they have relied on voluntary direct disclosures from service providers.

All four approaches are problematic and need further safeguards in order not to jeopardize fundamental rights such as privacy, the rule of law, and, even more fundamentally, the notion of citizenship in the digital age. The scary prospect of these technological developments is that we could be doomed if we do and we could be doomed if we do not (do it right). On the one hand, if we do not somehow extend law enforcement powers into the cloud, liberty and security are threatened by the lack of law enforcement. On the other hand, if we do not build adequate safeguards, rights, and remedies into effective cross-border investigative techniques, we also undermine the important foundations of democratic societies.

Here is an explanation of why these four reactions to the cross-border nature of cloud computing are problematic and require new ways of thinking about cross-border safeguards. First, international cooperation based on such vague notions as "mutual recognition" and "mutual trust" in each other's protection of fundamental rights and these notions are woefully inadequate to secure the protection of human rights. If we move away from the current system of treaty-based MLA where both the issuing and the requested state (at least in theory) check the investigative measure for its compliance with fundamental rights and the relevant safeguards, then we need to reinvent another method for guaranteeing these fundamental rights. What is required is an approximation of the rights themselves coupled with a dispute resolution procedure that allows affected persons to obtain remedies. Second, extending jurisdiction to foreign established ISPs is problematic as it may place the ISPs in a conflict of law situation where they cannot comply with two conflicting sets of law both applicable to them.[640] Hence international negotiation is required to formalize the notion of comity so that ISPs have legal certainty and know which law they need to comply with. Third, the problem with hacking is that it constitutes an extremely invasive but also powerful tool, as it is likely to reveal not only one specific dataset but would open up a user's entire life to law enforcement leading to perfect surveillance without limits (stored data, interception of contemporary data, content, subscriber, access, and traffic data). Hence it is important that international cooperation and extension of jurisdiction under domestic law is done in a workable way, as otherwise, in an "all or nothing" game, states will hack into suspect's computers, which is, potentially, the most invasive investigation method and could lead to total dataveillance. Protection of fundamental

[640] See Walker (n 526).

rights of citizens is required on three levels. First, organizational safeguards such as documentation and reporting requirements, oversight by the judiciary or parliament and reporting requirements have to be implemented. Second, clear principles of criminal justice and fundamental rights must be formulated on the transnational level. Third, individuals affected must have access to judicial review, which is affordable and transparent.

Thus, the debate should increasingly focus on transnational criminal law and citizenship rights, and redress and move away from a debate that is largely focused purely on sovereignty and state interests.

7

Data Protection Regulation and Jurisdiction

1. Introduction

The main focus of this chapter[1] is the intriguing question of *when* EU law is applied to, and enforced against, foreign data controllers by data protection authorities situated in a Member State of the EU. The chapter examines jurisdiction and applicable law in the area of data protection enforcement in the light of recent jurisprudence of the Court of Justice of the EU (CJEU) and Member States' courts. Given that this case law relates to the "old" data protection instrument, namely the Data Protection Directive 1995/46/EC (DPD), this is contrasted with the "new" General Data Protection Regulation (GDPR),[2] which entered into force in 2018. The comparison with the now superseded DPD is also important as it sketches the background and development of EU data protection law, which is important for the wider context and in particular for showing how difficult a coordination of national competences in this field has been. The chapter does not examine jurisdiction in civil litigation before the courts,[3] but instead focuses exclusively on administrative and regulatory competence under public law.

The UK left the EU on 31 January 2020 with a transition period until 31 December 2020, after which period the UK itself will become a third state. While the UK has implemented the GDPR in the Data Protection Act 2018, whether it would achieve adequacy status (and how quickly) and the UK's relationship with the European Data Protection Supervisory Board was not clear at the time of writing.

The chapter analyses the vexed relationship between the jurisdictional competence of data protection authorities and the law they apply. It makes two main arguments: (1) that the rules on applicable law effectively have become jurisdictional rules in that they determine the competent enforcement authority and (2) that a distinction should be made between internal and external conflicts of data protection law, both on a doctrinal, conceptual level and in the application of the conflict rules.

Internal conflicts of law are conflicts between the data protection authorities of each of the EU Member States in their application and enforcement of EU data protection

[1] The author gratefully acknowledges the feedback and comments by Prof Marise Cremona and the helpful comments and suggestions of the two peer reviewers from International Journal of Law and Information Technology. Any errors or mistakes are, of course, solely my responsibility. An earlier version of this chapter has been published as J Hörnle, "Juggling More Than Three Balls at Once: Multi-level Jurisdictional Challenges in EU Data Protection Regulation" (2019) 27(2) International Journal of Law and Information Technology 142–70.

[2] Regulation (EU) 2016/679 of the European Parliament and of the Council of 27 April 2016 on the protection of natural persons with regard to the processing of personal data and on the free movement of such data, and repealing Directive 95/46/EC (General Data Protection Regulation) (Text with EEA relevance) Citation: OJ 2016 L119/1.

[3] But see Chapter 11.

Internet Jurisdiction. Julia Hörnle, Oxford University Press (2021). © Julia Hörnle.
DOI: 10.1093/oso/9780198806929.001.0001

law(s), despite the fact that EU data protection law is largely[4] harmonized. Thus, internal conflicts are essentially intra-EU conflicts. These conflicts arise because data protection authorities are independent from each other and can interpret data protection law independently from each other.[5] External conflicts of law are conflicts between the harmonized data protection law(s) of the EU, on the one hand, and the law of third countries (such as the US or China or India), on the other hand. For the many third countries that generally have lower standards of data protection than the EU,[6] safeguarding fundamental data protection standards in the EU arguably should mean interpreting the jurisdictional criteria more expansively. It is precisely this variation in standards of data protection that means that mutual recognition cannot be assured. Thus, there are good policy reasons protecting data subjects in the EU, which lead to a more expansive interpretation of jurisdiction rules for external conflicts (as the CJEU has done in *Google Spain* as discussed in section 4.1), compared to internal conflicts.

Equally it is argued here that, for internal conflicts of law, EU Member States (other than the Member State where the main establishment is located) *should* refrain from exercising their jurisdiction and from applying their national data protection rules or interpretation of harmonized rules, in order to avoid multiple national laws applying, thereby fragmenting the effectiveness of data protection law, unless exceptional circumstances apply. Since the fundamental right to data protection in the EU Charter of Fundamental Rights applies everywhere in the EU, Member States should be prepared to trust each other's standard of regulation, at least as far as any jurisdictional rules are concerned. Any differences in approaches to data protection law should not be dealt with through the mechanism of jurisdiction, but through enforcement cooperation mechanisms (now contained in the GDPR) and at the political level.

The chapter proceeds by first examining the concepts of jurisdiction and applicable law and the differences between these two concepts. For someone who is not a conflicts of law scholar it may not seem obvious how the concept of jurisdiction (competence to rule and adjudicate) relates to the concept of applicable law (the set of national rules governing a particular *act of data processing* or *the obligations of a particular data controller*/processor). The doctrinal differences between jurisdiction and applicable law will be examined in section 2. The chapter then examines which national authority has regulatory competence and which data protection authority the data subject can

[4] Some variations will continue to exist, see Arts 6(2), 9(4), and 23 GDPR, for example. Under Art 6(2) Member States can introduce more specific requirements to processing in compliance with a legal obligation or in the public interest, Art 9(4) allows for further conditions and limitations in respect of the processing of genetic, biometric, or health data, and Art 23 allows Member States to maintain or introduce restrictions to data protection rights.

[5] Art 29 Working Party WP 225 Guidelines, 8; Case C-230/14 *Weltimmo v Nemzeti* Judgment of 1 October 2015, ECLI:EU:C:2015:639, para 28; Advocate General Bot in Case C-210/16 *Unabhängiges Landeszentrum für Datenschutz Schleswig-Holstein v Wirtschaftsakademie Schleswig-Holstein GmbH* Advocate General Opinion of 24 October 2017, paras 96–97; Case C-210/16 *Unabhängiges Landeszentrum für Datenschutz Schleswig-Holstein v Wirtschaftsakademie Schleswig-Holstein GmbH* Judgment of 5 June 2018, ECLI:EU:C:2018:388, paras 69–74.

[6] Which may not be the case for countries who have adequacy status or have higher standards than the EU in particular subject areas, such as the US Child Online Privacy Protection Act (1999), which imposed higher standards of protection than the Directive. However, certainly the great majority of countries in the world have, generally speaking, lower data protection standards than the EU. Only the EU has elevated data protection to fundamental rights status in Art 8 of the EU Charter of Fundamental Rights.

turn to for filing his or her complaint (section 3) and which law this authority must apply (section 4). Section 5 places the rules on jurisdiction and applicable law in the wider context of international law and sets out some of the principles used in the discussion of international jurisdiction (without going into too much doctrinal detail for lack of space in this chapter) and how the data protection jurisdictional principles fit into that wider discussion, before the chapter concludes in section 6.

2. Applicable law versus jurisdiction

The distinction between jurisdiction and applicable law in the area of data protection has remained obscure for a long time and it is only in the recent jurisprudence of the CJEU that a clearer picture of the relationship has emerged. No international principles, rules, or consensus exists on jurisdiction and applicable law in data protection matters. The drafting processes of the 1981 OECD Privacy Guidelines, the 1999 Hague Conference on Private International Law, and the 2009 Madrid Resolution all considered including provisions on data protection conflicts of law rules, but omitted including them.[7] As a matter of general principle, there are two types of conflict of law rules: jurisdiction and applicable law.

The rules on jurisdiction determine the competence of the national data protection authorities to exercise their decision and enforcement powers,[8] whereas the rules on applicable law determine which state's laws apply to an act of data processing.[9] Doctrinally, therefore, jurisdiction and applicable law are two separate stages in the law enforcement process: first, a national data protection authority needs to decide whether it can deal with the matter at hand, and second, it must decide which law governs its decision-making power.[10]

As to which Member State's law applies, to the chagrin of many online businesses, the DPD did not fully harmonize data protection laws across the EU, since it is in the nature of a directive that Member States have some discretion in the detailed implementation of its provisions. Therefore there were considerable differences between the data protection laws of the Member States before the GDPR came into force. Now the Data Protection Regulation EU/2016/679 is in full force (since 25 May 2018), data protection laws in the EU have been further harmonized, thus providing for fewer conflicts between internal laws of the EU. Some internal conflicts continue to persist because of differing interpretations of the GDPR between the Member States, albeit that only time will tell how significant these divergences will be. By contrast, external conflicts will persist. These external conflicts are about whether or not EU data protection laws apply to non-EU established companies (including US online service

[7] C Kuner, "Data Protection and International Jurisdiction on the Internet" Part I (2010) 18(2) International Journal of Law and Information Technology 176–93, 186–87.

[8] Jurisdiction of the courts and civil litigation are covered in Chapter 11.

[9] Kuner (n 7) 179referring to the seminal work FA Mann, "The Doctrine of Jurisdiction in International Law" (1964) 111 Recueil des Cours de L'Académie de Droit International 9–158, 13.

[10] Case C-230/14 *Weltimmo v Nemzeti* Judgment of 1 October 2015, ECLI:EU:C:2015:639, paras 21–23; see also the Opinion of Advocate General Pedro Cruz Villalon in Case C-230/14 *Weltimmo v Nemzeti* of 25 June 2015, ECLI:EU:C:2015:426, para 17 and Kuner (n 7) 179 referring to FA Mann's (n 9) seminal work. 13

providers such as Google and Facebook). Some may argue that such application is extraterritorial.[11] However, in this book the approach is taken that connecting factors *other than* domicile or presence in the jurisdiction to the jurisdiction do not mean that the application of law is extraterritorial.[12] From the point of view of *protecting* EU residents' personal data, arguably this is a more important issue than internal conflicts.[13] One of the main reasons for the broad formulation and interpretation of the provisions in the DPD and GDPR on when EU data protection law applies is to prevent that EU residents are being deprived of the protection standards enshrined in EU law (such as the DPD, GDPR, and the Charter).[14] This is important for external conflicts, but to a lesser degree for internal conflicts.

The layers of competences in EU data protection law in the shape of national jurisdictional competence combined with pan-EU harmonization and coordination make data protection law very complex, uncertain, and difficult to comply with and this will be discussed in more detail later.

In public law, traditionally an administrative authority only applies its *own* national law and never that of another state, which would be inimical to the notion of sovereignty of the state. Thus, the paradigm in *public law* is that the applicable law is that of the state to which the administrative authority belongs.

However, the "old" DPD in Article 28(6) provided that "each supervisory authority is competent, *whatever the national law applicable to the processing in question*, (...)" to exercise the powers of enforcement on its territory. This phrasing suggested that, under the now superseded DPD, a data protection authority had the power to apply the data protection law of another Member State in some instances. This would have been a novel concept in International Law—the idea that a public authority applied the administrative law of another state would be totally against the grain of the concept of national sovereignty.[15] Indeed, the CJEU has made clear in *Weltimmo* that this power to act on the basis of foreign data protection law was limited to the initial investigative powers, mutual assistance, and cooperation, but did not extend to enforcement action per se, namely the imposition of penalties.[16] This will be discussed in greater detail, but it should be pointed out already in this section that essentially the CJEU has maintained the status quo, that competence follows the applicable law, that is, only the national data protection authority/authorities whose law applies to a specific infringement is/are in fact competent to enforce the data protection law *on their territory*. Advocate Bot stated in the *ULD v Wirtschaftsakademie* case that "given that the law of the Member State to which the German supervisory authority belongs is applicable to the processing of personal data (...), that authority is in a position to exercise all its powers of intervention in order to ensure that German law is applied and observed by Facebook on German territory." Effectively, this means that under

[11] D Svantesson, *Extraterritoriality in Data Privacy Law* (Ex Tuto Publishing 2013) 85.

[12] See discussion in Chapter 2.

[13] Art 29 Working Party WP 179 Update of Opinion 8/2010 on applicable law in light of the CJEU Judgment in Google Spain, 6.

[14] ibid and Case C-131/12 *Google Spain*, ECLI:EU:C:2014:317, paras 53–55.

[15] J Crawford, *Brownlie's Principles of Public International Law* (8th edn, Oxford University Press 2012) 204, 472; Kuner (n 7) 181.

[16] Discussed in section 3.

the old DPD the rules on applicable law determined both jurisdiction *and* applicable law.[17] This then raises the question of how the specific rules on the competence of the supervisory authorities[18] relate to this determination of jurisdiction through the applicable law. As will be discussed in section 3, the GDPR provides for much wider jurisdictional competences than just establishment of the controller, but limits the jurisdictional competences at the same time by the consistency mechanism.

3. Specific rules on the competence of the supervisory authorities in EU data protection law

3.1 Data Protection Directive 1995/46/EC

In a situation where the data controller is established in one Member State and the data subject is resident in another the following question arises: Which state's data protection authority is competent/has jurisdiction to hear complaints, make use of investigatory powers, and take enforcement action? The question of competency of the national data protection authorities used to be addressed by Article 28(6) of the DPD: "is competent (…) to exercise on the territory of its own Member State the powers conferred on it (…)."

In Case C-230/14 *Weltimmo v Nemzeti*[19] a business—*formally registered* and established in Slovakia[20]—allowed owners of holiday properties in Hungary to advertise on its real estate website. It operated a freemium business model with the first month of advertising being free, but a fee was payable thereafter. However, several property owners complained to the local data protection authority in Hungary. Weltimmo had omitted to delete advertisements and personal data of these Hungarian property owners even though they had withdrawn from the transaction within the first month. Instead, Weltimmo demanded payment of a fee and passed on the property owners' details to debt collection agencies. The question was whether the Hungarian data protection authority had jurisdiction to take enforcement action against the business formally established in Slovakia. The Hungarian data protection authority imposed a fine of approximately Euro 32,000 on the business established in Slovakia in accordance with Hungarian law (the Slovakian data protection authority did not have the power under its own law to impose any fine). The case was referred to the CJEU on appeal by Weltimmo who argued that the Hungarian data protection authority was not competent and therefore should not have imposed a fine under Hungarian law.[21]

[17] Case C-210/16 *Unabhängiges Landeszentrum für Datenschutz Schleswig-Holstein v Wirtschaftsakademie Schleswig-Holstein GmbH* Advocate General Opinion of 24 October 2017, para 111; Case C-210/16 *Unabhängiges Landeszentrum für Datenschutz Schleswig-Holstein v Wirtschaftsakademie Schleswig-Holstein GmbH* Judgment of 5 June 2018, ECLI:EU:C:2018:388, para 52.

[18] Art 28(6) DPD previously and now Art 56 GDPR.

[19] Judgment of 1 October 2015, ECLI:EU:C:2015:639.

[20] Though the CJEU thought it likely that, on the facts (to be determined by the national court) it was established in Hungary as well, paras 32–33.

[21] Paras 9–12.

The CJEU held in *Weltimmo* that a data protection authority has to follow its own national procedural law when exercising its investigative and enforcement powers, but that these powers are *limited to its territory*.[22] A data protection authority in one Member State (eg Hungary) may not impose a penalty on a data controller in another Member State (eg Slovakia), if the data protection law of the first Member State (Hungary) is not applicable under Article 4 of the DPD (eg where the data controller is *not* established in the first Member State (Hungary) and does not use equipment there). Therefore in the case that Hungarian law did *not* apply to *Weltimmo*,[23] the Hungarian data protection authority may investigate according to its own procedural law, however, it must not apply fines and other penalties, but should cooperate with the Slovakian data protection authority in respect of enforcement.[24] Otherwise the principle of national sovereignty and the rule of law would be infringed. Therefore, as a consequence of this CJEU ruling it is now clear that the rules on applicable law effectively determine both applicable law *and jurisdiction*, for external conflicts of law situations as well as internal conflicts of law situations.[25]

Thus, since data protection authorities are independent, and independent from each other, they may exercise jurisdiction for their territory and may equally apply the law independently from each other. This was certainly the case under the DPD, as confirmed by *Wirtschaftsakademie*, where the CJEU held that data protection authorities do not need to take into account a countervailing decision of another data protection authority who has come to a different conclusion and that there was no priority for the data protection authority at the place of the (main) data controller's main establishment.[26] The GDPR maintains that in principle each independent data protection authority remains jurisdictionally competent, but introduces a mandatory coordination procedure, the so-called consistency mechanism. The GDPR is discussed in section 3.2.

Thus, it is now clear that if a data controller is not established in the Member State whose data protection authority is examining the case (and no other ground for applying its laws exist), then the data protection authority should investigate and use its power to cooperate with other data protection authorities, but it may *not* impose penalties under its own law, according to *Weltimmo*. While national data protection authorities have a duty to cooperate, for example, by exchanging information and granting each other mutual assistance,[27] they cannot apply the enforcement powers of

[22] Case C-230/14 *Weltimmo v Nemzeti* Judgment of 1 October 2015, ECLI:EU:C:2015:639, paras 50, 52; see also Case C-210/16 *Unabhängiges Landeszentrum für Datenschutz Schleswig-Holstein v Wirtschaftsakademie Schleswig-Holstein GmbH* Judgment of 5 June 2018, ECLI:EU:C:2018:388, para 50.

[23] Although the fact-finding is ultimately a question for the national courts, the CJEU indicated that Weltimmo is likely to be established in Hungary with a relevant establishment and that therefore Hungarian law applies, paras 32–33,38. So the prohibition on applying fines under Hungarian law is *only* relevant if the national court was to find on the facts that Weltimmo is *not* established in Hungary at all: paras 42, 55, 57.

[24] ibid paras 57, 59 and Opinion of Advocate General Pedro Cruz Villalon in Case C-230/14 *Weltimmo v Nemzeti* of 25 June 2015, ECLI:EU:C:2015:426, paras 60–66.

[25] Case C-210/16 *Unabhängiges Landeszentrum für Datenschutz Schleswig-Holstein v Wirtschaftsakademie Schleswig-Holstein GmbH* Judgment of 5 June 2018, ECLI:EU:C:2018:388, paras 50–52.

[26] Case C-210/16 *Unabhängiges Landeszentrum für Datenschutz Schleswig-Holstein v Wirtschaftsakademie Schleswig-Holstein GmbH* Judgment of 5 June 2018, ECLI:EU:C:2018:388, paras 69–74.

[27] Case C-210/16 *Unabhängiges Landeszentrum für Datenschutz Schleswig-Holstein v Wirtschaftsakademie Schleswig-Holstein GmbH* Judgment of 5 June 2018, ECLI:EU:C:2018:388, para 68; coordination now further enhanced by the consistency mechanism discussed later.

another Member State. So, for example, the data protection authority of one Member State (eg Greece) may ask a data protection authority of another (eg a German Data Protection Authority) to exercise *its* enforcement powers against a data controller established in that country (eg a German trader) on behalf of data subjects in the former Member State (eg consumers in Greece). But the Greek authority may not impose these measures itself. Such cross-border enforcement is likely to be coordinated by the European Data Protection Board (EDPB). How this will work in situations where the UK is one of the countries concerned is not an open question after the UK's withdrawal from the EU.

One example for a coordinated approach between the different data protection authorities of the Member States are the common criteria for handling of complaints in respect of search engines' refusal to delist search results after the *Google Spain* case.[28] This approach ensures some consistency between the enforcement actions different national data protection authorities may take in response to delisting requests that have been refused by search engines.

Furthermore, Article 29 Working Party has made clear in its Guidelines that data subjects are entitled to contact their local establishment (eg subsidiary) of the search engine with their delisting request and may complain to their local, domestic data protection authority. In other words, the data protection authority at the place of residence of the data subject is competent to hear a complaint and must act on it. This is mandated by the principle of effective protection.[29] In turn, a national data protection authority may contact the local establishment/subsidiary of the data controller who has to deal with and/or coordinate any requests for information and cooperate in respect of complaints.[30] Moreover, it is equally clear that a national data protection authority's power is limited in that it cannot declare invalid an *EU* legal act such as the Safe Harbour Adequacy Decision, which only the CJEU has jurisdiction to declare invalid (as it has done in Case C-362/14 *Max Schrems*) in order to guarantee the uniform application of EU law.[31] However, national data protection authorities have the power, in exceptional circumstances, to prevent the transfer of personal data under standard contractual clauses (SCC) approved by the Commission, if this is necessary to guarantee effective and enforceable data protection.[32] In fact it is this power which provides data subjects with avenue of redress and therefore the Commission's decision approving the SCC was valid.[33]

As this discussion illustrates, the duties to cooperate and coordinate between data protection authorities in the EU/EEA Member States had been limited and it is in this context that the improvements in the GDPR have to be examined. From the viewpoint of the operation of the DPD it was clear that a better-defined system of enforcement

[28] See Art 29 Working Party WP 225 Guidelines, 5, 12–20.

[29] Art 29 Working Party WP 225 Guidelines, 8; see also Case C-362/14 *Max Schrems* of 6 October 2015, ECLI:EU:C:2015:650, paras 56–58.

[30] ibid paras 56–58.

[31] ibid para 61, see also the second Schrems judgment Case C-311/18 *Data Protection Commissioner v Maximilian Schrems* ECLI:EU:C:2020:559 paras 116, 118–20.

[32] Second Schrems judgment (n 31), paras 115, 119, 121.

[33] ibid paras 129–49.

cooperation was required and this deficit has now been addressed (but not solved) in the new GDPR, which will be discussed next.

3.2 GDPR EU/2016/679

The approach in the DPD with potentially several data protection authorities being competent to enforce data protection laws simultaneously and independently of each other against the same data controller, with only a minimum and vague duty to cooperate their enforcement actions has created an unsatisfactory situation, which is both ineffective from a law enforcement point of view and creating legal uncertainty for data controllers and processors, and leads to conflicts of law. This section shows the importance of coordination through the EDPB, which the UK is likely to be no longer a member of following its withdrawal from the EU.

This situation has been addressed by the GDPR by providing for a lead data protection authority at the place of the main establishment of a data controller or processor for cross-border data processing ("one stop shop"), greater obligations of data protection authorities to cooperate, and a mechanism to coordinate conflicts between data protection authorities ("consistency mechanism"), an EU body with enhanced powers, including the making of binding decisions (EDPB) and clearer and more comprehensive rules on national competency.[34] These innovations of the GDPR are seriously threatened by Brexit, as the cooperation mechanisms with the UK will cease until a new arrangement has been agreed.

3.2.1 One stop shop

If a data controller has several establishments across the EU, the data protection authority in the state of the *main* establishment will be the lead data protection authority for cross-border[35] processing.[36] This overcomes the deficiencies discussed earlier in relation to internal conflicts, at least partially. The lead authority is essentially the data protection authority who has the primary responsibility for enforcement.[37] This is only a partial solution, however, as it only applies where there is a main establishment within the EU—it does not apply where the data controller has no establishment and EU law applies because of the targeting provisions in Article 3(2).[38]

However, if the subject matter of enforcement relates only to the establishment in one Member State other than the main establishment, and/or if only persons in one Member State are affected, then the local data protection authority of that Member State remains competent and not the lead authority.[39] Therefore enforcement

[34] See also the EDPB Guidelines on the Lead Supervisory Authority WP244rev.01 of 31 October 2017.

[35] Cross-border data processing is defined as two alternatives: (1) where a data controller has several establishments in the Member States and carries out data processing in the context of its activities and (2) where a data controller has only one establishment, but the data processing substantially affects persons in several Member States, Art 4(23); see also the 2017 EDPB Guidelines (n 34).

[36] Art 56(1) GDPR.

[37] 2017 EDPB Guidelines (n 34) 4.

[38] 2017 EDPB Guidelines (n 34) 10.

[39] Art 56(2) GDPR.

continues to be fragmented to deal with local issues. In that case, the local supervisory authority must inform the lead authority and give it an opportunity to take on the lead of any enforcement action.[40] Even if the lead authority takes on the case, the local supervisory authority may pass a draft decision, which should be taken into account by the lead authority.[41] But in any case, all communications, decisions, orders, and so on to the data controller in cross-border cases must come from the lead data protection authority.[42]

The main establishment is defined as the place of central administration in the EU, or, for data controllers, the establishment where the decisions on purposes and means of data protection are taken,[43] or, for data processors who do not have one central administration in the EU, the establishment where the main processing in the context of the activities of that establishment *actually* take place[44] (such as the location of a data centre used in cloud computing). This is largely determined by the companies themselves (eg through designation), but the data protection authorities will look at the factual reality of where decisions are made.[45] Also, in some cases, for example, where data processing decisions are made outside the EU and EU establishments are not involved in these decisions and no central administration exists within the EU, no lead authority may exist and several national data protection authorities may be equally competent, according to the 2017 Guidelines.[46]

This provision is more compliance friendly (compared to the Directive) for data controllers such as Amazon or Facebook whose corporate structure has designated one of their EU establishments as the EU headquarters (including for data protection compliance and policy purposes), but the GDPR has created a complicated, almost byzantine coordination structure, which may prove slow and cumbersome but it does at least encourage cooperation between the Member States.

3.2.2 Competence of data protection authorities—jurisdiction

Additionally, the GDPR provides much more detailed rules on the competence of the data protection authorities in the Member States. First, it makes clear that the national data protection authority in the Member State where the data subject is habitually resident has jurisdiction to hear complaints, in other words data subjects can make complaints to their local data protection authority.[47] Furthermore, data subjects may also lodge a complaint in their place of work or the place of the alleged infringement.[48] The Regulation also imposes an obligation on Member States to provide data subjects with a judicial remedy[49] and stipulates that the courts at the place of establishment of

40 Art 56(3) GDPR.

41 Art 56(4).

42 Arts 56(6) and 60.

43 Art 4(16)(a) GDPR—if decisions in respect of different acts of processing are made by different main establishments this could mean that there will be more than one lead authority, 2017 EDPB Guidelines (n 34) 5–6.

44 Art 4(16)(b) GDPR.

45 2017 EDPB Guidelines (n 34) 6, 8.

46 2017 EDPB Guidelines (n 34) 7.

47 Art 77(1) on the right to lodge a complaint with a supervisory authority.

48 ibid.

49 Further discussed in Chapter 11.

the controller (or processor) *and* the courts in the place of habitual residence of the data subject have concurrent jurisdiction,[50] unless the data controller is a public body acting in the exercise of official authority.[51] The GDPR also provides for *lis pendens* rules whereby any court other than the court first seized must suspend proceedings to prevent irreconcilable judgments.[52]

Each authority's acts are expressly limited to its territory in a similar provision to Article 28(6) of the DPD as interpreted in *Weltimmo*. Article 55(1) of the GDPR states: "each supervisory authority shall be competent for (...) the exercise of the powers conferred on it in accordance with this Regulation *on the territory of its own Member State*."

Furthermore, the GDPR sets out which data protection authorities are (in principle jointly, but subject to the hierarchy of the lead authority and the cooperation mechanism[53]) competent to act, thereby setting out the required jurisdictional links by defining the concept of "the supervisory authority concerned." This has evolved from the case law under the DPD discussed earlier. The supervisory authority concerned can be the data protection authorities in the following Member States: (1) the Member State where the controller/processor is established, (2) a Member State in which data subjects are or are likely to be substantially affected, and (3) a Member State before whose supervisory authority a complaint has been lodged.[54] These grounds of jurisdictional competence of data protection authorities are extremely wide in that from this wording it seems that a data protection authority cannot refuse to initially investigate based on jurisdiction and that, if a particular practice impacts on consumers in all Member States, potentially all authorities are competent to investigate. However, this wide competency is tempered by the mechanisms examined in section 3.2.3. Therefore competency is no longer limited to the rules on applicable law[55] and national data protection authorities other than the lead authority have jurisdiction.[56]

3.2.3 Cooperation obligation of the Member States, the consistency mechanism and the EDPB

Under the new cooperation provisions in the GDPR, national data protection authorities, even if competent, can only act under the consistency mechanism and are thereby forced to cooperate. However, it remains to be seen how well this cooperation mechanism will work in practice and the UK is likely to be excluded from the cooperation mechanism in any case. The express obligation of the supervisory authorities to cooperate with each other and the European Commission is contained in Article 51(2) and its purpose is to contribute to the consistent application of the Regulation. This cooperation includes the sharing of information, mutual assistance, and conducting joint operations.[57] Given the different approaches to data protection

[50] Art 79(2).

[51] ibid—in which case presumably the courts in that Member State have jurisdiction according to national law, but the Regulation leaves this open.

[52] Art 81(2).

[53] Described in section 3.2.

[54] Art 4(22).

[55] Art 4 DPD and Art 3 GDPR.

[56] 2017 EDPB Guidelines (n 34) 9.

[57] Arts 57(g) 60(2) and 61–62.

in different Member States it is, however, probable that some Member States are more likely to cooperate than others.

In cross-border cases there is an obligation for supervisory authorities to cooperate with each other with a view to reaching a consensus decision and the GDPR contains detailed procedural rules for achieving this.[58] In particular, the lead authority should circulate any draft decisions and, if any other authority expresses a "relevant and reasoned" objection,[59] which the lead authority does not wish to follow, the EDPB[60] will decide any disputes between the authorities ("consistency mechanism" in Article 63).[61] In urgent cases[62] a local supervisory authority has the power to take provisional measures for a maximum period of three months[63] or if final measures are required in such urgent cases it can request a decision from the Board.[64] The EDPB will also have an advisory role, giving guidance and issuing Opinions (similar to the Article 29 Working Party).[65] This procedure is likely to be cumbersome and will lead to the usual political entanglements in international state cooperation. The inability of the Member States to fully empower the EDPB with the responsibility for enforcement measures is regrettable as a missed opportunity. However, given the existing differences between Member States, this could be an intermediate step to the ultimate creation of a full EU enforcement body.[66] However, given the current centrifugal tendencies in (some) EU Member States (the strongest of which is of course the UK's Brexit), further integration in the EU data protection area may not be quickly forthcoming. Furthermore, even if the UK has implemented the GDPR, it may or may not be able to join these cooperation mechanisms. This will cause problems not only for UK–EU data transfers, but also for data transfers between the UK and other non-EU countries, as the UK export mechanisms (to the US, China, and India) will be separate, and independent of the EU countries' data export mechanisms (to the US, China, and India). Thus, a pan-EU data controller such as a large multinational company will have to get separate mechanisms approved, hindering trade and disadvantaging the UK as a place of doing business.

4. Rules on applicable law

Article 3 of the GDPR[67] contains the provisions on applicable law. The rules on applicable law were contained in Article 4 DPD, which determined conflicts of law between different national laws in the EU Member States. However, since a public regulatory authority only applies its own law, it became clear that these provisions additionally,

[58] Art 60.
[59] Art 60(3)–(4).
[60] Consisting of representatives of all data protection authorities, having replaced the Art 29 Working Party.
[61] Arts 60(4) and 65(1)(a).
[62] "urgent need to act in order to protect the rights and freedoms of data subjects," Art 66(1).
[63] Art 66(1).
[64] Art 66(2).
[65] Art 70.
[66] This is just speculation on the author's part.
[67] OJ L119/1 of 4 May 2016.

by necessity, determined regulatory competence under the old DPD[68] and therefore indirectly stipulated when an EU data protection authority was able to apply *its* data protection law. As has already been explained, Article 4 of the old DPD therefore effectively determined *both* the applicable law and which EU data protection authority was competent to enforce it. This has now changed as the GDPR has set out separate provisions on regulatory competence in Article 4(22) by defining the "supervisory authority concerned." This was possible as the GDPR works on the basis that EU data protection law has now been completely harmonized and that therefore all Member States apply the same law (the GDPR).

4.1 Establishment link in the Directive and the Regulation

There are two basic principles for determining the data protection law applicable to a particular act of processing. The main basis for deciding which state's law applies to an act of data processing is the concept of establishment, originally contained in Article 4(1)(a) of the DPD[69] but now contained in Article 3(1) of the GDPR.[70]

The Directive provided and the Regulation now continues to provide that if the processing is carried out in the context of the activities of an establishment of the controller (and, in the case of the GDPR, additionally, the processor) the law at the place of that establishment applies.[71] In order to provide for effective protection, the CJEU has interpreted the concept of establishment broadly and this broad application refers to both the Directive and the Regulation.[72]

The main distinction[73] between the establishment provision in the "old" Directive and the "new" Regulation is that the Directive referred to establishment in a Member State and the Regulation now refers to establishment in the EU. The reason behind this difference is that since the aim of the Regulation is to harmonize data protection law, there is no need to provide for any internal conflicts of applicable laws between the Member States. However, since in practice (some) gaps are likely to remain (see the derogation in Article 6(2) and the exceptions in Article 23) there is uncertainty about how these remaining internal conflicts are solved under the GDPR.

It is important to emphasize here that the location of the processing as such is irrelevant for determining the applicable law.[74] For example, if a French-established business (who is responsible for the data processing and the data controller) uses a

[68] More generally with respect to regulatory law: C Ryngaert, *Jurisdiction in International Law* (2nd edn, Oxford University Press 2015) 17.

[69] OJ L281/31 of 23 November 1995.

[70] OJ L119/1 of 4 May 2016.

[71] Art 4(1)(a) of the DPD and Art 3(1) of GDPR: "This Regulation applies to the processing of personal data in the context of the activities of an establishment of a controller or a processor in the Union, regardless of whether the processing takes place in the Union or not."

[72] Case C-131/12 *Google Spain*, ECLI:EU:C:2014:317, paras 53–54; Case C-230/14 *Weltimmo v Nemzeti* Judgment of 1 October 2015, ECLI:EU:C:2015:639, para 25.

[73] The other distinction is that the GDPR now only refers to the processor's establishment for actions taken against processors.

[74] Recital 20 DPD; Recital 22 and Art 3(1) GDPR; but see potential argument that the place of processing could be a link under public international law in section 4.6.

Canadian cloud company who uses a data centre in the US (where the processing physically takes place), French data protection laws would nevertheless apply.[75] Likewise, if the data centre is located in Belgium, only French data protection law applies, as the data controller (French company) has an establishment in the EU. The nationality of the data subject complaining about a data protection infringement is irrelevant.[76]

In order to apply this jurisdictional link it is necessary to determine (1) what amounts to "establishment" and (2) what amounts to processing in the context of the activities of the controller (or processor). The first element was clarified and at issue in Case C-230/14 *Weltimmo v Nemzeti* in 2016 and the second element was clarified in Case C-131/12 *Google Spain v AEPD/Mario Costeja Gonzalez* in 2014 and both have been further refined in *Wirtschaftsakademie* in 2018.

4.1.1 The concept of establishment in the jurisprudence of the CJEU

The concept of establishment has been interpreted in an extensive jurisprudence of the CJEU, for example, in connection with the distinction between two of the four elementary freedoms guaranteed by the Internal Market: the freedom to provide services in Article 49 TFEU and the freedom of establishment in Article 56 TFEU.[77]

The case law of the CJEU in essence held that establishment means "the effective and real exercise of activity through stable arrangements" in the Member State concerned, irrespective of the legal form this establishment takes (branch or subsidiary with its own legal personality).[78] In *Factortame* the CJEU defined establishment as "the actual pursuit of an economic activity through a fixed establishment in another member state for an indefinite period."[79] The time element means that the pursuit of the economic activity must not be only temporary, but must be on a stable and continuous basis, taking into account the regularity, periodicity, or continuity of the activity, which is what distinguishes it from the provision of services.[80] The CJEU has taken a broad and flexible approach to establishment, so that, for example, an undertaking maintaining a permanent presence in a Member State even if that permanent presence does not amount to a branch or agency but consists only of an office managed by a person who acts on behalf of that undertaking would count as "establishment."[81] Thus, the concept of establishment provides a relatively low threshold. While

[75] K Hon, J Hörnle, and C Millard, "Which Law(s) Apply to Personal Data in Clouds?" in C Millard (ed), *Cloud Computing Law* (Oxford University Press 2013) 220–53, 222.

[76] Case C-230/14 *Weltimmo v Nemzeti* Judgment of 1 October 2015, ECLI:EU:C:2015:639, para 40.

[77] Advocate General Pedro Cruz Villalon in his Opinion Case C-230/14 *Weltimmo v Nemzeti* refers to the case law on freedom of establishment, permanent establishment for VAT purposes, and the Rome and Brussels Conventions, paras 29–30.

[78] Regulation Recital 22; Case C-230/14 *Weltimmo v Nemzeti* Judgment of 1 October 2015, paras 28, 30, 41 and Case C-131/12 *Google Spain & Google* para 48; Advocate General Bot in Case C-210/16 *Unabhängiges Landeszentrum für Datenschutz Schleswig-Holstein v Wirtschaftsakademie Schleswig-Holstein GmbH* Advocate General Opinion of 24 October 2017, para 88 and Case C-210/16 *Unabhängiges Landeszentrum für Datenschutz Schleswig-Holstein v Wirtschaftsakademie Schleswig-Holstein GmbH* Judgment of 8 June 2018, para 54.

[79] Case C-221/89 *Factortame* [1991] ECR I-3905, [1991] CMLR 589 (CJEU) 627; Case C-81/87 *Daily Mail* [1988] ECR 5500, [1988] 3 CMLR 713 (CJEU)716 (Advocate General Darmon).

[80] Case C-55/94 *Gebhard* [1995] ECR I-4165 (CJEU) paras 25–26; Case 2/74 *Reyners v Belgium* [1974] ECR 631, (CJEU) para 21.

[81] Case C-316/07 *Markus Stoß* [2010] ECR I-8069 para 59.

a mere website or server would not count as establishment,[82] a continuing presence of a physical nature (office, staff, representative, etc) would be sufficient. A data centre may well count as an establishment if it is run by the data controller. Furthermore, the CJEU has held that the concept is a flexible one, particularly for internet businesses, and that the concept of establishment must be interpreted in the light of the specific nature of the economic activities and the provision of services concerned.[83] Therefore a subsidiary, branch or agent, or a dedicated data centre in the EU count as establishment, regardless of its legal form or whether it has legal personality.[84] In fact the presence of a single business representative/agent on the territory of a Member State may indeed count as establishment, if the arrangement has sufficient stability and the representative has the relevant business equipment for specific services.[85] In *Weltimmo* the fact that the business representative of the Slovakian company was running two websites from Hungary, directed at Hungarian customers, had opened a bank account and maintained a post box address was held to be sufficient for the purposes of establishment.[86] Against the wording of the DPD the CJEU (but not the Advocate General[87]) in *Weltimmo* makes much of the fact that the websites were targeted at the Hungarian market, introducing a targeting test (language of the website, context) not dissimilar to the test established in *Pammer/Alpenhof* in the context of determining jurisdiction and the law applicable to consumer contracts.[88] However, in *Verein für Konsumenteninformation v Amazon* the CJEU held that for the data protection law of a Member State (in this case Austria) to apply, it is not sufficient that the business (established with its EU headquarters in Luxembourg) directs its activities to that Member State. For Article 4(1)(a) to apply there must be a physical establishment, at least a minimal one, exercised through stable arrangements.[89] The accessibility of a website is not sufficient to count as establishment.[90]

4.1.2 In the context of the activities of an establishment of the controller

The second factor, namely that the data processing must be carried out in the context of an establishment of the controller has given rise to more uncertainty.[91] As a starting point, the different language versions of the DPD used different terms: "context" (English) but "framework" (German and French versions).[92] In an early case *Google Italy*, both Italian courts came to the conclusion that they had jurisdiction

[82] See also E-commerce Directive 2000/31/EC, Recital 19.

[83] Case C-230/14 *Weltimmo v Nemzeti* Judgment of 1 October 2015, ECLI:EU:C:2015:639, para 29.

[84] See also the discussion in Hon, Hörnle, and Millard (n 75) 2.1; Recital 19 DPD and 22 GDPR; Case C-131/12 *Google Spain*, ECLI:EU:C:2014:317, para 48.

[85] Case C-230/14 *Weltimmo v Nemzeti* Judgment of 1 October 2015, ECLI:EU:C:2015:639 para 30; see also Opinion of Advocate General Pedro Cruz Villalon in Case C-230/14 *Weltimmo v Nemzeti* of 25 June 2015, ECLI:EU:C:2015:426, para 33.

[86] Case C-230/14 *Weltimmo v Nemzeti* Judgment of 1 October 2015, ECLI:EU:C:2015:639, para 33.

[87] Opinion of Advocate General Pedro Cruz Villalon in Case C-230/14 *Weltimmo v Nemzeti* of 25 June 2015, ECLI:EU:C:2015:426, para 42.

[88] Joined Cases C-585/08 and C-144/09 Judgment of 7 December 2010, ECLI:EU:C:2010:740.

[89] Judgment of 28 July 2016, ECLI:EU:C:2016:612, para 75.

[90] ibid para 76.

[91] D Svantesson, "Article 4(1)(a) 'Establishment of the Controller' in EU Data Privacy Law—Time to Rein in this Expanding Concept?" (2016) 6(3) International Data Privacy Law 210–21, 210.

[92] Hon, Hörnle, and Millard (n 75) 222.

based on Article 4(1)(a) DPD. The Google establishment in Italy, namely the Italian-incorporated subsidiary Google Italy SRL, was held to perform more than mere marketing or advertising functions—for example, it had responsibility for compliance with Italian data protection laws and was processing personal data, ultimately finding that the two entities (Google Inc and Google Italy SRL) were closely linked.[93]

The meaning of this phrase has been clarified by the CJEU in a similar vein in *Google Spain v AEPD/Mario Costeja Gonzalez* in 2014.[94] Most online service providers such as search engines and social media services finance their content delivery activities through advertising. The relevant scenario is this: The main establishment (in the US) is responsible for all aspects of the content, but has one or more agents/subsidiaries in an EU Member State (eg Spain) who is/are placing advertisements locally but has/have no control over the online service. The question that arises in this scenario is whether the data processing for the online service is in the context of the activity of advertising. The CJEU in *Google Spain* tackled the question of whether EU data protection applied, given that the search engine activities of Google are controlled by Google Inc, the parent company with its seat in the US and Google Spain merely is responsible for placing advertisements and carrying out other ancillary and supporting activities. Google Spain did not carry out in Spain any activities directly linked to the indexing or storage of information contained on third parties' websites (ie the search function).[95] The Court found that the advertising activities were inextricably linked with the free search engine activities, in other words without the search engine activities carried out by Google there would be no advertising revenues: "since the activities relating to the advertising space constitute the means of rendering the search engine at issue economically profitable and that engine is, at the same time, the means enabling those activities to be performed."[96] The Court also pointed out that on the same search results page there would be results appearing on the basis of Google Inc search activities and commercially paid for sponsored ads that appear as a result of the activities of Google Spain, so the search activities took place in the context of the commercial activities of advertising without which the search could not be financed.[97] The Court looked at the business model of the data controller (in this case Google Inc) and the relationship and connection between the EU establishment and the data controller. The Court found that Google Inc was indeed acting in the context of the advertising activities of its subsidiaries (including Google Spain) and that Spanish data protection law and the then EU Directive 1995/46/EC applied (and the same would apply to the GDPR).[98] This interpretation was clearly motivated by the need to protect fundamental rights in the EU.[99] Thus, for *external* conflicts (in this case with the US) the

93 Sentenza n 1972/2010, Tribunal of Milan and Sentenza 8611/12 del 21-12-2012, Corte di Appello di Milano, discussed in Hon, Hörnle, and Millard (n 75) 223.

94 Judgment of 13 May 2014, ECLI:EU:C:2014:317.

95 Para 46.

96 Para 56.

97 Para 57.

98 Paras 55–60; see also Opinion of Advocate General Jääskinen of 25 June 2013; Case C-131/12 *Google Spain* ECLI:EU:C:2013:424, paras 64–67; see also Case C-210/16 *Unabhängiges Landeszentrum für Datenschutz Schleswig-Holstein v Wirtschaftsakademie Schleswig-Holstein GmbH* Judgment of 5 June 2018, ECLI:EU:C:2018:388, para 64.

99 Paras 53–54, see also O Lynskey, "Control over Personal Data in a Digital Age: Google Spain v AEPD and Mario Costeja Gonzalez" (2015) 78 The Modern Law Review 522–48, 526.

CJEU has interpreted the framework of activities widely in order to ensure the application of EU data protection law against non-EU data controllers with establishments in the EU. The judgment is not limited to the specific business model of search engines and will equally apply to other "free" online services such as social media services, which are financed by advertising.[100]

Before the entry into force of the GDPR multiple national data protection laws still applied where the business activities at different EU places of establishment were inextricably linked with data processing.[101] The GDPR has now further harmonized EU data protection law and, as a Regulation, is of course directly applicable, but differences between Member States' practices in respect of data protection law enforcement are likely to continue and some differences in the law will probably persist. These differences mean that even after the GDPR is in force there will be some conflicts of law and the question of which data protection authority is competent to apply its law will continue to be relevant.

A good example for internal conflicts of law and the application of the establishment ground is the *Amazon* case. Amazon has its European headquarters in Luxembourg, but no other subsidiary or branches, for example, in Austria and the question arose whether Austrian data protection law applies to some of its selling methods targeted at Austria. The Opinion of Advocate General Henrik Saugmandsgaard Øe pointed clearly in the direction of accepting the European headquarters as the most logical place to pinpoint the establishment to whom the data processing should be allocated (in the sense of the "in the context of the activities" test in Article 4(1)(a)).[102] The Opinion states that it is unlikely that the data processing in respect of credit reference checks of potential buyers paying invoices after delivery was carried out in the context of the activities of the customer services in Austria (fulfilling orders, dealing with complaints about non-delivery, and other after sales matters) and that it is more likely that the processing was carried out in the context of the activities of the *EU headquarters* in Luxembourg. The Opinion thereby (in my view correctly) indicates that an *internal* conflict of law situation (finding the most relevant EU establishment) is treated differently from an external conflict of law situation, such as *Google Spain* where there was no EU main establishment to anchor conflicts of laws.[103] Comparing *Verein für Konsumenteninformation* and *Google Spain* one could argue that stricter standards *should* be applied to external conflicts.[104] However, the Court itself did not go into such detail and ultimately treated the question of whether an establishment in Austria existed and whether the activities were carried out in the context of that establishment as a matter of fact, not a matter of law, for the Austrian Court to decide.[105]

[100] Art 29 Working Party WP 179 Update of Opinion 8/2010 on applicable law in light of the CJEU Judgment in *Google Spain*, 5.

[101] See also Art 29 Working Party WP 225 Guidelines, 8 and also Case C-230/14 *Weltimmo v Nemzeti* Judgment of 1 October 2015, ECLI:EU:C:2015:639, para 28.

[102] Case C-191/15 *Verein für Konsumenteninformation v Amazon* paras 119, 121.

[103] ibid paras 122–25.

[104] Svantesson "Article 4(1)(a)" (n 91) 221.

[105] R Bond, "VKI v Amazon: Governing Law" (Oct/Nov 2016) Computers & Law 20–21.

By contrast, the CJEU,[106] following the Opinion of Advocate General Bot[107] in *ULD v Wirtschaftsakademie* stated that *Google Spain* equally applied to *internal conflicts*. This case, still under the DPD, concerned a German private college using a Facebook fan page as a marketing tool. A German data protection authority (ULD) found the college in breach of its data protection obligations, as those users who did not have a Facebook account were not told about the tracking technology employed by Facebook and the ULD ordered the college not to use Facebook. The Court[108] (and the Opinion of Advocate General Bot[109]) stated that Facebook Inc, Facebook Ireland, and the Wirtschaftsakademie were (joint) data controllers. Thus, applying *Google Spain*, both Facebook and the Wirtschaftsakademie had relevant establishments in Germany in accordance with Article 4(1)(a) DPD, so that German data protection law could be applied, and hence the ULD was one of the competent German data protection authorities and could apply and enforce its laws there.[110] This was despite the fact that Facebook had its *main* establishment in Ireland (the data controller).[111] The Court therefore effectively held that no distinction should be made between *internal* and *external* conflicts of law.

By contrast, the German courts had previously held that, for internal conflicts, *only* the law of the *main establishment* should apply. The German data protection authority had held that Facebook's "real names" policy of blocking the accounts of users who had registered using false personal data or pseudonyms, was against German data protection law, which provides a right to pseudonymous or anonymous use.[112] On Facebook's appeal, the German court held that (1) the *contractual* choice of law between Facebook Ireland and German users did not affect whether German data protection law did or did not apply and (2) based on German law and Article 4(1)(a) DPD Irish, not German, data protection law applied, so the German authority was not competent to issue its order. The activities of Facebook's German subsidiary were limited to advertising and marketing, and no personal data of German users were processed in the context of activities of the German establishment. While the *result* is another indication that internal conflicts of law should be treated differently than external conflicts, it is doubtful whether the *reasoning* of the German court is compatible with the latter case of *Google Spain*. These German cases[113] predated *Google Spain*.

[106] Case C-210/16 *Unabhängiges Landeszentrum für Datenschutz Schleswig-Holstein v Wirtschaftsakademie Schleswig-Holstein GmbH* Judgment of 8 June 2018, para 52.
[107] Case C-210/16 *Unabhängiges Landeszentrum für Datenschutz Schleswig-Holstein v Wirtschaftsakademie Schleswig-Holstein GmbH* Advocate General Opinion of 24 October 2017.
[108] Case C-210/16 *Unabhängiges Landeszentrum für Datenschutz Schleswig-Holstein v Wirtschaftsakademie Schleswig-Holstein GmbH* Judgment of 8 June 2018, paras 42–44
[109] Paras 42–52.
[110] Advocate General Opinion para 111; Judgment paras 52, 62.
[111] Advocate General Opinion paras 96–97, 125; Judgment paras 62–64.
[112] Telemediengesetz para 13(6).
[113] *Facebook Ireland, Facebook Inc v Unabhängiges Landeszentrum für Datenschutz Schleswig-Holstein*, Az 8B 60/12, Judgment of 14 February 2013 (Case against Facebook Ireland) and Az B8 61/12, Judgment of 14 February 2013 (Case against Facebook Inc). These judgments have been confirmed on appeal to the Administrative Appeal Court of Schleswig-Holstein on 24 April 2013, Az 4 MB 10/13, 4 MB 11/13, https://www.datenschutzzentrum.de/artikel/743-OVG-Schleswig-Holstein-Fuer-Facebook-gilt-kein-deutsches-Datenschutzrecht.html#extended accessed on 25 July 2020.

Summarizing the position on external and internal conflicts, it seems clear that for external conflicts, as in *Google Spain* Article 4(1)(a) DPD, the establishment link is interpreted widely, in such a way that the local EU data protection authority is competent to apply its law if there is a sufficiently close link between the activities of the local establishment and those of the non-EU data controller. The Court did not need to address the issue of internal conflicts in *Amazon* (there was no clear local establishment of Amazon in Austria in *Amazon*). However, as discussed in this section, in *Wirtschaftsakademie* the Advocate General and then the Court adopted the same wide interpretation and application of local national law for *internal* conflicts. As has been argued here, as a matter of policy, this is the wrong approach, in the opinion of the author.[114] However, this problem of *internal conflicts of law* has been lessened by the GDPR, as this now only refers to EU law, on the basis that data protection law is now (almost) fully harmonized, and as far as regulatory competence is concerned, the GDPR has adopted a procedure to coordinate regulatory responses.

4.2 Equipment as a territorial link

Furthermore, a Member State's data protection law used to be applicable under Article 4(1)(c) if the data controller is not established on EU territory but makes use of equipment or means for the purpose of data processing in the Member State concerned. The question of what amounts to equipment had been controversial[115]—in particular the question of whether cookies or executable code (such as Dynamic Java Script) downloaded on an EU user's computer while interacting with a non-EU website could constitute "equipment," thereby triggering the application of EU data protection law.[116] The problem with data in networked and cloud computing environments is that such data is intangible, mobile, or even volatile, which may make it difficult or impossible to determine its geographical location and therefore the jurisdictional link to a territory.[117] Thus, the location of data or data processing is an unsuitable connecting factor, and hence the "equipment ground" has been abandoned in the GDPR and is no longer relevant.

[114] See the reasons given in section 1.

[115] C Kuner, "Data Protection and International Jurisdiction on the Internet" Part II (2010) 18(3) International Journal of Law and Information Technology 227–47, 242.

[116] Article 29 Working Party Opinions WP 148, 163, 179; see further Hon, Hörnle, and Millard (n 75) 227, 230.

[117] V Krishnamurthy, "Cloudy with a Conflict of Laws" Berkman Research Publication No 2016-3, describing how multi-national cloud service providers operate and data sharding, p 4; J Daskal, "The Unterritoriality of Data" (2015) 125 Yale Law Journal 326–98, 329, 365; D Svantesson *Extraterritoriality in Data Privacy Law* (n 11) 46–50 identifying seven factors: (1) large data collections, (2) interconnectivity between networks, (3) the border-disregarding nature of the internet, (4) the ease of data distribution, (5) the difficulty of data deletion, (6) the ease of data searches, and (7) the security difficulties; W Kuan Hon and C Millard, "Cloud Technologies and Services" in C Millard (ed), *Cloud Computing Law* (Oxford University Press 2013) 1–18; for the opposite view, ie that data in the cloud is not conceptually different see AK Woods, "Against Data Exceptionalism" (2016) 68(4) Stanford Law Review 729–89, 734–35.

4.3 Domain names as a jurisdictional link and geo-blocking

After the *Google Spain* judgment, search engines were obliged to implement the ruling by providing for a policy dealing with the removal of search result links on notification. One of the crucial questions in this respect was the territorial scope of such removals and in particular the question of whether the obligation only relates to the country code domain name of the complainant's Member State concerned (eg google.es)[118] or whether the take-down also applies to the .com domain. Initially, Google limited the removal of links to the country code *sub-domains* of EU Member States and refused to implement the policy in relation to google.com. In other words, a user resident in France who searched under a person's name on google.fr would be informed that some research results may be blocked and could then find the search result unblocked on google.com.

The French data protection authority, Commission Nationale de l'Informatique et des Libertés (CNIL), threatened to fine Google in September 2015 after having formally decided that Google had only partially complied.[119] The Article 29 Working Party also stated in its Guidelines that "limiting de-listing to EU domains on the grounds that users tend to access search engines via their national domains cannot be considered a sufficient means to satisfactorily guarantee the rights of data subjects according to the judgment (…) de-listing should also be effective on all relevant domains, including.com."[120]

Google amended its policy in February 2016. If it finds a delisting request justified under EU law it will remove the search result from all EU country code sub-domains *and* using geo-location tools to identify the IP address of the browser of the search engine user, it will remove search results accessed from the relevant EU Member State on google.com, but will leave google.com unaltered for users outside that particular EU Member State.[121] This change acknowledges that the country code domain name is not the only appropriate territorial link to the EU, considering that .com is in fact used by users across the EU. Google now directs internet users to the national version of the search engine corresponding to the location of the user, thereby moving from an approach that focused purely on the domain name to a geo-blocking approach.[122]

However, even the amended policy does not apply EU law to all users accessing google.com from the EU, as it only delists results on google.com if google.com is

[118] The Spanish data protection authorities who had to deal with hundreds of delisting requests before and after the *Google Spain* case did not stipulate in their orders whether delisting only in the country code domain is sufficient compliance: M Peguera, "In the Aftermath of Google Spain: How the 'Right to be Forgotten' is Being Shaped in Spain by the Courts and the Data Protection Authority" (2015) 23(4) International Journal of Law and Information Technology 325–47, 329.

[119] https://www.theguardian.com/technology/2015/sep/21/french-google-right-to-be-forgotten-appeal accessed on 25/7/2010.

[120] Art 29 Working Party WP 225 Guidelines on the Implementation of the CJEU Judgment on Google Spain of 26 November 2014, 3, 9.

[121] https://www.google.com/transparencyreport/removals/europeprivacy/faq/?hl=en#how_does_googles_process accessed on 20/7/2020.

[122] Case C-507/17 *Google LLC v CNIL* ECLI:EU:C:2019:772, Judgment of 24 September 2019 paras 32, 42.

accessed from the particular Member State from which the request originates, not from any other Member State. For example, if an Irish resident wants a link to inaccurate information delisted it will be removed from google.com search results accessed from Ireland, but would still be available for google.com users in Germany (so effectively the implementation does not cover the whole of the EU territory). The dispute between Google and CNIL eventually wound its way up to the CJEU in *Google LLC v CNIL*[123] and the Court had to examine how a search engine operator should give effect to the right to dereferencing both in the light of the Directive and the GDPR.[124,125] In particular, the question was whether the dereferencing has to take place (1) only in the version of the search engine displayed in the complaining data subject's Member State, or (2) in the versions of the search engine in all EU Member States (the territory of the EU), or (3) in all the versions of the search engine, globally.[126]

The CJEU referred to the immediate and substantial effects on data subjects of breaches of the right to be forgotten and that this impact at the place where the data subject has his or her centre of interests[127]would justify the jurisdictional competence of an authority in the EU to apply EU law and order dereferencing in all versions of the search engine, globally.[128] However, the Court then went on to recognize that "numerous third States do not recognise the right to de-referencing (...)" and that the right to data protection had to be balanced against other fundamental rights, including freedom of information.[129] Therefore the CJEU held that the scope of a dereferencing order under EU law is limited to the territory of the EU and that there was no obligation under EU law to carry out the dereferencing in all the versions of the search engine on a global basis.[130] Having knocked out number 3 as the scope, the CJEU proceeded to say that a dereferencing order is, in principle, "supposed to be carried out in all the Member States," in other words the scope of a dereferencing order should be the whole of the EU (number 2), at least as a rule of thumb.[131] However, after that the judgment loses its clarity, as the CJEU refers to the continuing differences in EU data protection law, the Regulation notwithstanding, and in particular the exemptions in respect of processing undertaken for journalistic purposes, or for the purpose of artistic or literary expression.[132] The Court felt that because of these differences, national authorities or courts ultimately have to make the decision whether the measures adopted by the search engine meet the requirements of the balance between data protection *and other* fundamental rights.[133] The CJEU also refers to the duty to cooperate to achieve consistency across the EU.[134] Thus, the Court does not mandate that a national dereferencing order under the GDPR always has to cover the whole of the

123 ibid.
124 The CJEU referred to the "right to be forgotten" in Art 17(1) GDPR.
125 Paras 40–41.
126 Para 43.
127 This wording comes from the Court's privacy jurisdiction cases, see Chapter 11.
128 Paras 57–58.
129 Para 60.
130 Paras 62–64.
131 Para 66.
132 Para 67.
133 Para 71.
134 Para 68.

EU, that is, all versions of the search engine displayed in the EU. Additionally, while the Court repeated that EU law does not mandate global dereferencing in all versions of the search engine (number 3), a national authority *may choose* to order such global dereferencing under the requirements of its national law and its balancing of data protection rights with other rights.[135] Therefore the Court left the decision of the scope to the national authorities and courts to make the balance, thereby fragmenting the territorial scope of dereferencing orders between different Member States. The UK in any case would not be bound by the CJEU's interpretation of the GDPR.

4.4 Residency as a further requirement before EU data protection law applies

If EU data protection law applies to a particular act of data processing, the question arises whether EU data protection law only applies to the personal data of EU residents or persons present in the EU, that is, persons who are located in the EU (at the time of processing). In theory, this could be a further limiting requirement and territorial link to prevent extraterritorial overreach but was not included in the DPD or GDPR. The Guidelines of the Article 29 Working Party indicate that, in practice, data protection authorities in the EU will only take action if there is a clear link with the EU (such as EU residency): "Under EU law, everyone has a right to data protection. In practice, DPAs[136] will focus on claims where there is a clear link between the data subject and the EU, for instance where the data subject is a citizen or resident of an EU Member State."[137] This Guidance, however, assumes that it is always possible to make a clear distinction between the data of EU residents and those of non-EU residents. As has been discussed, Google found a solution by using geo-location blocking based on the IP address of the search engine user at the point of access (focusing on momentary presence). However, such a neat solution may or may not be available in all scenarios. For example, if a US data controller uses a data centre in the EU for data storage, this data centre may well count as an establishment under Article 3(1), especially if the data processing (controlled from the US) may indeed be inextricably linked to a data centre in the EU, in the sense that there would be no need for a data centre without the data processing operations. But the data may well relate to both EU and non-EU residents and it might be difficult for the US data controller to distinguish between the two. In practice, this may mean that US data controllers may be reluctant to use EU data centres or, conversely, in certain situations it may give data controllers a competitive advantage to comply with higher EU data protection standards.

[135] Para 72.

[136] On appeal, the Spanish Data Protection authority refused to delist a Google search result against a complainant's name on the basis that the complainant was a citizen and resident of Chile and his personal and business interests were located in that country: AEPD decision of 20 March 2014 (TD-01094-2014). By contrast it did allow the delisting in a case where a Colombian citizen requested removal of a link showing a students' admission list to a Colombian university, on the basis that the complainant was resident in Spain and had a permanent residence card, thus real links with Spain: AEPD decision of 31 March 2015 (TD-01848-2014). See Peguera (n 118) 341.

[137] Art 29 Working Party WP 225 Guidance, 3, 8.

4.5 Targeting link in the Regulation

The GDPR introduced a new ground for providing a link between EU data protection law and the processing of personal data in Article 3(2). The GDPR applies to the processing of personal data of persons who are physically in the EU (if the data controller/processor is not established in the EU) if at least one of two conditions is fulfilled: (1) the processing is related to the offering of goods or services to such persons in the EU[138] or (2) the processing relates to the monitoring of these persons' behaviour in the EU (such as online tracking and online profiling).[139]

This link is based on the concept of targeting, that is, here the minimum contacts with the EU are established by business contacts. For the GDPR to apply, the data controller (or processor) must envisage to offer their services to and/or profile persons in the EU.[140] As the Recitals make clear, mere accessibility of a website is not sufficient for this purpose, nor is the fact that a website is soliciting enquiries by providing contact details. Moreover, the fact that the website is in a language spoken in a Member State if the data controller is established in a non-EU state in which this language is also spoken (eg Portuguese in Brazil) is irrelevant (at least as a single factor).[141] The targeting test is likely to involve several factors, including language, currency, contextual information (such as tax), endorsements or customer ratings from persons in the EU, and so on.[142]

Of interest here is the concept of "being in the EU," as this is a much looser territorial link compared to residency. However, as just discussed in relation to *Google Spain*, in the online world it is easier to establish a person's location at the time of the internet connection (through geo-location technologies mapping IP addresses etc) than determining a person's habitual residence (especially if there is no card payment). Clearly, not everyone's IP address can be accurately mapped to that person's location, as he or she may access the internet using proxy servers or virtual private networks. But such geo-location mapping may be the closest approximation there can be to solving data protection conflicts of law.

Furthermore, the wording of the article ("offering") suggests that EU data protection law may apply even before there is a contract between the parties, including the processing of personal data for advertising purposes or for the purposes of service improvement or security (and online tracking is expressly mentioned in Article 3(2)(b)). The online tracking link makes EU data protection law applicable whenever personal data is processed for the purpose of monitoring behaviour in the EU. This includes online tracking by way of cookies, flash cookies, digital fingerprinting and associated technologies, and the subsequent profiling activities, no matter for what purpose these tracking activities are carried out (targeted marketing, security, user convenience,

[138] Irrespective of whether the data subject has to pay (money), ie this provision applies to "free" services that are paid by advertisers such as search engines, price comparison, and social media.

[139] Recital 24 GDPR.

[140] Recital 23 GDPR.

[141] ibid.

[142] ibid see also *Pammer/Alpenhof* Joined Cases C-585/08 and C-144/09 Judgment of 7 December 2010, ECLI:EU:C:2010:740.

national security, taking decisions, credit risk, insurance risks, employment context).[143] The limiting factor here for the application of the GDPR is the complex legal question of whether the tracking/profiling includes *personal* data.[144]

If it does include the processing of personal data, the data controller must appoint an EU representative in one of the targeted Member States as a liaison point unless the processing is only occasional, and does not include sensitive data on a large scale and "is unlikely to result in a risk to the rights and freedoms" of individuals.[145] How workable the application of EU data protection law to online profiling activities will be remains to be seen. Real, practical enforcement issues arise where the controller or processor has no establishment in the EU.

4.6 Application of EU law/Member States' law by virtue of public international law

Of less practical relevance, but for the sake of completeness, it should be mentioned that the third ground for applying EU data protection law is that the data controller is established "in a place where Member State law applies by virtue of public international law."[146] This refers to places such as foreign embassies[147] and ships and aircraft where the law of the place where that ship or aircraft is registered and whose flag it flies applies. Google has obtained a US patent for floating data centres on the high seas, using seawater to generate power and cool equipment.[148] So, in future such data centres may be deployed, using flags of convenience for data protection law purposes, thus avoiding the application of the obligations under the GDPR.[149] In a very wide interpretation of this provision, it could capture the law of the place where the processing physically takes place, since, of course, the territoriality principle, as a principle of public international law, states that the law of that territory applies in that place.

5. General principles

The discussion in this section places the rules on regulatory jurisdiction and applicable law in the area of data protection in the wider context of the jurisdiction principles under international law.[150] However, the general principles of jurisdiction under

143 Recital 24 GDPR.

144 Not further discussed here.

145 Art 27 GDPR.

146 Art 4(1)(b) DPD and Art 3(3) GDPR.

147 Recital 25 GDPR.

148 L Dignan, "Google Wins Floating Data Center Patent' Between the Lines, ZDNet 2009, http://www.zdnet.com/blog/btl/google-wins-floating-data-center-patent/17266 accessed on 20/7/2020.

149 Although other factors may influence server location eg tax. For a discussion see SR Swanson, "Google Sets Sail: Ocean-Based Server Farms and International Law" (2011) 43(3) University of Connecticut Law Review 709–51, 739 (analogy of pirate radio stations), 745, 749 outlining the importance of the freedom of the high seas.

150 For lack of space these are not discussed here in detail, but readers may refer to Crawford (n 15) 457–65 and Ryngaert (n 68) 49–144, see also Chapters 2 and 4.

international law, although ultimately imposing the outer limit of states asserting regulatory competence vis-à-vis other states,[151] are in practice highly malleable rules and, as long as there is a strong nexus between the situation to be regulated and a state's territorial sovereignty, they are unlikely to be a real barrier to the assumption of regulatory jurisdiction.[152]

The most relevant international law principles in the data protection context are:

- the territoriality principle (states governing matters occurring on their territory);[153]
- the effects doctrine (jurisdiction based on foreseeable effects within the territory);[154]
- the protective principle (states being obliged to protect citizens/persons present or resident on their territory);[155]
- the "country of origin" principle;[156]
- the targeting principle,[157] first developed in the internet context.[158]

As will be shown, these principles are not mutually exclusive and do overlap.

5.1 The territoriality principle and the effects test

Essentially, before applying their law, states have to find a suitable connecting factor to their territory.[159] It is this link to the territory that makes the exercise of state authority legitimate vis-à-vis other states.[160] The connecting factor can relate to the place where the subject in a criminal or regulatory case is acting (subjective territoriality principle) or to the place where the object or any constituent element of the subject matter to be regulated is located (objective territoriality principle).[161] The territoriality principle is inherently wide and allows states to assume jurisdiction widely, based on a whole array of connecting factors, depending on the elements set out in *national* law (or EU law, in the case of data protection). Since these connecting factors as such are not limited by international law, the territoriality principle does not provide a litmus test for jurisdiction—arguably, the connecting

[151] It is not clear whether public international law makes inadmissible principles of jurisdiction that are not generally well-recognized: Council of Europe, European Committee on Crime Problems "Extraterritorial Criminal Jurisdiction," Report Strasbourg (1990) 25–26.

[152] Ryngaert (n 68) 19.

[153] Crawford (n 15) 458.

[154] U Kohl, *Jurisdiction and the Internet* (Cambridge University Press 2007) 91–96.

[155] Crawford (n 15) 462.

[156] J Hörnle, "Country of Origin Regulation in Cross-Border Media: One Step Beyond the Freedom to Provide Services?" (2005) 54 International Comparative Law Quarterly 89–126, 90–91.

[157] DJB Svantesson, "Extraterritoriality and targeting in EU data privacy law: the weak spot undermining the regulation" (2015) 5(4) International Data Privacy Law 226–34.

[158] See eg M Geist, "Is There a There There? Towards Greater Certainty for Internet Jurisdiction" (2001) 16 Berkeley Technology Law Journal 1345–406.

[159] C Reed, *Internet Law* (2nd edn, Cambridge University Press 2004) 218–19.

[160] Kohl (n 154) 89.

[161] Crawford (n 15) 458–59.

factors discussed earlier[162] contained in Article 4 of the DPD and Article 3 of the GDPR would easily fall within the territoriality principle: establishment,[163] equipment,[164] and data processing on ships and aircraft[165] are obvious connecting factors to tangible, physical elements situated on territory. More problematic in this respect is the new targeting test established in Article 3(2) of the GDPR,[166] which provides as connecting factors the activity of offering goods or services to data subjects in the EU and the monitoring of the behaviour of data subjects in the EU. Under the lens of the territoriality principle, this could be categorized as an example of the effects test,[167] which originated from competition law[168] and allows states to assume jurisdiction where the regulated conduct produces significant and demonstrable negative effects on their territory/market, which need to be counter-acted in order to protect their citizens and residents. As such, it is closely aligned to the protective principle and the country of destination approach, examined in section 5.2. But, importantly for this section, the effects test is also closely related to the objective territoriality principle, since for that principle it is sufficient that one constituent element of the subject matter to be regulated is within the territory.[169] Since the (EU or national) legislator determines and defines what are the constituent elements of the conduct to be regulated, this leaves wide scope to bring the effects of conduct within the territoriality principle. Thus, arguably, protective laws such as data protection or consumer protection laws, which aim at preventing harmful effects of conduct targeted to citizens or residents on a particular territory or market, easily fall within the objective territoriality principle. Therefore it can also be argued that Article 3(2) of the GDPR falls within the objective territoriality principle in that it regulates the objects of conduct (offering of goods or services or monitoring of behaviour) within the territory of the EU. For those arguing that internet jurisdiction should be limited to avoid conflicts of jurisdiction, the territoriality principle therefore does not offer a convincing argument to limit jurisdiction.[170] However, the territoriality principle has been supplemented by other jurisdictional principles,[171] which are beginning to crystallize in the internet regulatory context and, to the extent that they are relevant, are discussed in sections 5.2–5.4.

[162] Section 4.

[163] Section 4.1.

[164] Section 4.2.

[165] Section 4.6.

[166] See discussion in section 4.5.

[167] First formulated as such in the criminal (shipping) case before the Permanent Court of International Justice, *The Case of SS "Lotus"* (1927) PCIJ Reports, Series A No 10: territorial jurisdiction is proper "if one of the constituent elements of the offence, and more especially its effects, have taken place there," p 23.

[168] See eg Case C-89/85 *A Ahlstrom Osakeyhtio v Commission of the European Communities* [1988] ECR 5193 (Wood Pulp); case T-102/96 *Gencor Ltd v Commission of the European Communities* [1999] ECR II-753; case T-286/09 *Intel Corp v European* Commission EU:T:2014:547; [2014] 5 CMLR 9 and *United States v Aluminium Co of America* 149 F 2d 416, 443 (2nd Cir 1945).

[169] Kohl (n 154) 90–94.

[170] Kohl (n 154) 104.

[171] Svantesson "Extraterrritoriality and targeting" (n 157) 226–28 arguing that the distinction between territoriality and extraterritoriality is not helpful.

5.2 The protective principle under international law

The protective principle is another recognized principle for jurisdiction under international law. It has had a restricted application limited to the fundamental interests of a state jeopardizing its sovereignty or political independence (such as protecting its currency, protecting against treason, fundamental national security interests).[172] Any expansion of the protective principle increases jurisdictional uncertainty and opens up abuse of the principle for political interests.[173] By the same token the categories of what may be considered to be a fundamental interest of the state are also not closed and states argue that grave injuries of fundamental interests may fall under it.[174]

In respect of data protection, it may be argued that the fact that the EU has elevated data protection from a mere secondary law principle (ie Directive 95/46/EC) to a fundamental right (Primary/Treaty law) in Article 8 of the Charter[175] is evidence that, for EU Member States, data protection law is a central concern of public policy, for which the protective principle may be claimed.[176]

The referring Court in *Google Spain* asked the CJEU whether, if none of the specific territorial links mentioned in Article 4(1) of the DPD[177] applied, EU data protection law may nevertheless apply to protect the fundamental right of data protection in Article 8 of the Charter of Fundamental Rights[178] if the centre of gravity of the dispute is located in a Member State.[179] This would have been an assertion of applying EU law in order to protect fundamental rights of the EU outside the express jurisdictional rules contained in secondary legislation. The CJEU did not answer the question as it found jurisdiction based on the Article 4(1)(a) link. Advocate General Jääskinen found in his Opinion that the interpretation of the DPD in accordance with the Charter could *not* add any new jurisdictional grounds that might give rise to the territorial applicability of the national legislation implementing the DPD, and that therefore the geographical centre of gravity of the dispute is irrelevant for the applicable data protection law[180] (but would be relevant for the jurisdiction of the courts in privacy related civil tort actions[181]). This was based on the principle that the Charter did not extend the field of application of EU law.[182]

172 Ryngaert (n 68) 114–19; Crawford (n 15) 462.
173 ibid.
174 ibid.
175 Charter of Fundamental Rights of the EU published in OJ C364/1 of 18 December 2000.
176 Case C-362/14 *Max Schrems* of 6 October 2015, ECLI:EU:C:2015:650 and J Hörnle, "The EU–US Safe Harbour Decision is Dead—Long Live its Successor?" (2015) SCL Online see http://www.scl.org/site.aspx?i=ed44927, also see also O Lynskey, *The Foundations of EU Data Protection Law* (Oxford University Press 2015) 56.
177 Discussed in section 4.
178 Charter of Fundamental Rights of the EU published in OJ C364/1 of 18 December 2000.
179 The centre of interest test or the centre of gravity test is discussed in the context of jurisdiction of the civil courts in Chapter 11.
180 Opinion of Advocate General Jääskinen paras 54–59.
181 The "centre of gravity" test was applied by the CJEU to determine the jurisdiction of the civil courts in privacy-related tort cases in Joined Cases C-509/09 and C-161/10 *e-Date Advertising* and *Martinez* [2011] ECR I-10269.
182 Art 51(2) of the Charter: "The Charter does not extend the field of application of Union law beyond the powers of the Union," see para 54.

Based on this principle it is extremely unlikely that the protective principle under international law could be used *on its own* to expand the jurisdictional reach of EU data protection law, despite its incorporation into the canon of fundamental rights in the Charter. In the opinion of this author this is correct, as the rules contained in secondary legislation provide the *lex specialis* for regulatory jurisdiction in data protection cases.

However, regarding the question of to what extent the jurisdictional grounds laid down in EU secondary legislation, namely Article 4 of the DPD and Article 3 of the GDPR, are *themselves* justified by international law, the use of the protective principle as a well-established principle may be helpful. Even if the targeting approach under Article 3(2) of the GDPR could not be justified under the *territoriality* principle,[183] it would certainly fall under the protective principle because data protection is now a fundamental human rights interest. The "protective" nature of that provision is also indicated in Recital 23 of the GDPR:

> in order to ensure that natural persons are not deprived of the protection to which they are entitled under this Regulation, the processing of personal data of data subjects who are in the Union by a controller or a processor not established in the Union should be subject to this Regulation where the processing activities are related to the offering of goods or services to such data subjects (. . .).

5.3 The "country of origin" regulation principle

Country of origin regulation is an emanation of international (regulatory) jurisdiction based on establishment[184] or the presence of physical business equipment or assets in a jurisdiction.[185] In cross-border business regulation more generally, principles have been established to deal with the mobility and potential remoteness of business in determining the competent state to regulate. In the EU context, one principle for regulatory competence in media and internet regulation is the place of establishment of the business— this gives the state of the place where the business is established exclusive regulatory jurisdiction and is sometimes called the "country of origin."[186] So, for example, in the E-Commerce Directive,[187] Article 3(1) mandates for information society services within the coordinated field[188] regulatory compliance with the law

[183] It is argued in section 5.1 that it falls under the territoriality principle.

[184] Arts 7(5) and 17(2).

[185] S 26(3) UK Gambling Act 2005 (in its original version); para 23 of the German Civil Procedure Rules allowing personal jurisdiction to be exercised over a non-resident defendant, if that defendant has substantial assets in the jurisdiction.

[186] Art 3 E-commerce Directive 2000/31/EC of 8 June 2000 on certain legal aspects of information society services, in particular electronic commerce, OJ 2000 L178/1C; Art 3 Directive 2010/13/EU of 10 March 2010 on the coordination of certain provisions laid down by law, regulation, or administrative action in Member States concerning the provision of audiovisual media services (Audiovisual Media Services Directive), OJ 2010 L95/1.

[187] E-commerce Directive (n 186).

[188] Art 2(h): requirements regarding the taking up of the activity in question, such as licensing, qualifications, notification and authorization requirements and requirements concerning the pursuit of the activity

in the country where the service provider is established.[189] Article 3(2) consequently provides that Member States other than the country of origin must not apply their laws and regulate the service provider in such a way that its freedom to provide services is restricted.[190] This is an example for a wider trend of media regulation in the EU, which as part of the establishment of an Internal Market, especially for services that can be delivered electronically, adopts a twin strategy of "country of origin" regulation and law approximation, the latter in turn enabling the mutual recognition on which "country of origin" regulation relies.[191] While the "country of origin" principle for information society services does not apply to data protection matters,[192] it is used here as an illustration of a more general trend in media regulation of business conduct and advertising. The rules on establishment in the DPD and the GDPR[193] are an example of "country of origin" approach.

5.4 The "country of destination" regulation principle, consumer protection law, and the targeting principle

The "country of destination" regulation is the opposite of "country of origin" regulation as a principle for cross-border business regulation. The principle establishes the concept that the regulators of the place where consumer goods or services are consumed should be competent and the law of that country should apply to protect consumers. An example of this "country of destination" principle is the exception in respect of consumer protection in Annex I of the E-Commerce Directive. However, a pure "country of destination" approach is rarely found in regulatory jurisdiction. A more common approach is that of "targeting" or "directing," which focuses on the question of whether the business actively and/or foreseeably[194] directs its activities to the consumers' jurisdiction.[195] An example of this are the special rules on consumer jurisdiction and the law applicable to consumer contracts[196] and the "centre of interest" test in respect of personality rights infringements[197] in the harmonized private international law rules of the EU, and the "effects doctrine" under US conflicts of law.[198] The "targeting" principle originated from US conflict of law rules, especially as

such as conduct, quality of content of the information society service, advertising and contractual requirements, and liability. However, not coordinated are requirements concerning goods, the delivery of goods, or rules on services not provided by electronic means.

189 Country of origin regulation is also discussed in Chapters 8 and 11.

190 Subject to the exceptions in the Annexes and the possibility to derogate in Art 3 (4).

191 See further Hörnle "The EU–US Safe Harbour Decision is Dead" (n 176).

192 Art 1(5)(b) E-Commerce Directive.

193 Section 4.1.

194 On targeting and foreseeability see Chapters 9, 10, and 13.

195 Joined Cases C-585/08 and C-144/09 *Pammer/Alpenhof* ECLI:EU:C:2010:740.

196 Art 6 Rome I Regulation 593/2008/EU and Arts 17 and 18 Brussels I Regulation (Recast) 215/2012/EU or in relation to competition law (place where the competitive relations or collective interests of consumers are affected) Art 6(1) Rome II Regulation EC/864/2007, see further Chapter 10.

197 See Chapter 11.

198 *Calder v Jones* see Chapter 9.

applied in media and internet cases[199] and has been applied subsequently in the regulatory context.[200] Targeting is further discussed in the final chapter.[201]

As has been pointed out,[202] Article 3(2) can be explained as a version of the "targeting approach" now incorporated in the GDPR. It becomes clear from the wording of Recital 23 ("envisages") that the provision only applies if the business *intends or foresees* that EU residents would take up the offer.[203]

However, whether a "country of origin" or the "country of destination" principle is applied to data protection regulation it is important to consider not only the assumption of jurisdiction by states but also the practicalities and realities of enforcement. Two points can be made here. First, "country of origin" regulation may work among a homogenous group of states with similar laws, which after having approximated their laws share a degree of trust and mutual recognition. But it cannot work among heterogeneous states with differing legal standards and regulatory approaches, which preclude mutual recognition. Second, no matter which law is applied, effective enforcement can only be achieved if Member States cooperate in enforcement, as the state where data subjects suffer detriment may differ from the state where penalties can be enforced, as enforcement requires some sort of presence and/or assets against which penalties can be enforced.

6. Conclusion

From a *protective* point of view, external conflicts are more significant since the law on data protection has now been very closely approximated by the GDPR, so that similar standards exist within the EU and the real difference in standards are only laid bare in external conflicts of law with (some) non-EU Member States. For this reason, it has been argued that Member States should recognize the place of the main EU establishment as the place of jurisdiction and applicable law. Unfortunately, the jurisprudence of the CJEU (based on the DPD) is not clear on this point and even the GDPR has left open the multi-jurisdictional approach of the DPD even though the GDPR imposes a clearer duty on Member States to cooperate.

Nevertheless, now that the GDPR is in force, EU law does not fully recognize internal conflicts of laws between the Member States, as, legally, the Regulation proceeds on the basis that it fully harmonizes data protection law, even though the GDPR itself recognizes a number of derogations, where Member States may maintain different rules and different interpretations of the same provisions of the GDPR. As far as external conflicts are concerned, they will be represented as conflicts between EU

[199] Geist (n 158); see also M Sableman and M Nepple, "Will the Zippo Sliding Scale for Internet Jurisdiction Slide into Oblivion?" (2016) 20(1) Journal of Internet Law 3–6; *Calder v Jones* 465 US 783, 104 SCt 1482 (1984).

[200] eg s 36(3A) Gambling Act 2005, introduced by the Gambling (Licensing and Advertising) Act 2014 and s 21(3) of the Financial Services and Markets Act 2000.

[201] Section 5.4.

[202] Section 4.5.

[203] See also in Recital 23: "whereas the mere accessibility of the controller's, processor's or an intermediary's website in the Union, of an email address or of other contact details, or the use of a language generally used in the third country where the controller is established, is insufficient."

law and the third country law for the first time. Therefore jurisdictional competence will become more important than applicable law for internal conflicts, whereas for external conflicts the question of whether the GDPR applies in the first place is more important for the outcome and the shaping of legal obligations.

Comparing the interpretation of the existing DPD in internal and external cases, in the external conflict in *Google Spain* the CJEU bent over backwards to interpret the phrase of "in the context of the activities of the establishment" expansively. The CJEU should apply a different jurisdictional test, if the conflict is between two Member States (say Ireland and Germany) and recognize the existence of a main EU establishment. However, as we have seen in *Wirtschaftsakademie*, the CJEU has adopted the same approach and found that the German data protection authority was competent to apply German data protection law on the same principles as in *Google Spain*.

It is argued here that, for internal conflicts of law, EU Member States *should* recognize the jurisdiction of the Member State of the main establishment and refrain from exercising their jurisdiction and applying their national data protection rules, so as to avoid multiple national laws applying, thereby fragmenting the effectiveness of data protection law. Since the fundamental right to data protection in the EU Charter of Fundamental Rights applies everywhere in the EU, Member States should be prepared to trust each other's standard of regulation, at least as far as any jurisdictional rules are concerned. Any differences in approaches to data protection law *should not* be dealt with through the mechanism of jurisdiction, but through the coordination mechanism envisaged in the GDPR.

With the GDPR in force, the lead authority is in fact the data protection authority at the controller's main establishment in the EU, and while other data protection authorities may make decisions concerning the processing of local data subjects' personal data this has to be coordinated within the procedures established by the GDPR. So, for internal conflicts, the GDPR establishes one set of EU law (with slight national variations) and a lead data protection authority.

More generally, in terms of justifying jurisdiction based on connecting factors to the territory it has been shown that the DPD had used a number of different links to the territory. The advantage of the establishment connecting factor is that it is a recognized link for justifying business regulation ("country of origin regulation") and that the location of the actual data processing is irrelevant. But as has been discussed, it has been difficult to decide in what circumstances the processing takes place in the context of the activities of the establishment. This ground of jurisdiction continues to exist in Article 3 of the GDPR.

Finally, the DPD contained an equipment ground, which had given rise to controversy over how physical this equipment has to be (eg whether a cookie constituted "equipment"). Thankfully, the new GDPR has scrapped the equipment ground and relies instead on a targeting test, so that EU data protection law applies if persons in the EU have been targeted for the collection of personal data (or other data processing). This test relates more to the targeting principle used in business regulation where a state uses its regulatory law to protect citizens from harm and is also used in other consumer protection cases or competition law cases. Therefore, arguably, the jurisdictional tests in the Regulation are clearer for the digital age, albeit how workable the profiling jurisdictional link turns out to be, in terms of practical enforcement, is another question.

Furthermore, as we have seen in this chapter, although the rules on applicable law and jurisdiction are conceptually separate, they are also related, especially in the sphere of public (administrative) law, including data protection. Since a public authority normally *only* applies its own law, the rules of applicable law in Article 4 DPD automatically determined the authority that was fully competent to enforce the law. Although Article 28(6) of the DPD indicated that data protection authorities may apply the law of another EU Member State, the CJEU has clarified that this applied only to the initial power of examining complaints, powers of investigation, and mutual cooperation, but *not to law enforcement* powers such as sanctions and fines. The CJEU thereby has recognized the territorial sovereignty of the Member States in respect of enforcement powers, for internal and external conflicts alike. This limitation of enforcement powers to the territory of the Member State will remain in place even after the GDPR.

But the improvement the GDPR has introduced, as discussed in this chapter, is that there are clearer lines defining *which* authority is competent internally to act. This is achieved by imposing greater and stricter obligations on data protection authorities to cooperate and coordinate their activities in the shape of the consistency mechanism and an override mechanism for the lead data protection authority and ultimate decision by the EDPB. However, the goal of a "one stop shop" has not been fully achieved, as the coordination procedure may well prove to be slow and cumbersome in practice, so there will be a "shop" but it potentially has several stops. It is disappointing that the Member States were not able to agree on giving up more of their own powers and confer greater decision-making powers on a fully operational European Data Protection Authority.

Arguably, the changes in the Regulation will lead to a levelling out of the data protection standards *within the EU* so that Member States will have less sovereignty in respect of these protective standards. But it will also mean that Member States as a group will be able to more effectively protect these standards vis-à-vis the rest of the world. This is not just good news for those believing in data protection and privacy as fundamental values, it also enhances national sovereignty (even if this national sovereignty is based on an EU compromise and embedded within EU institutions) *globally*. Arguably therefore, overall, in this interconnected, globalized world, sovereignty (with respect to data protection) is enhanced.

This chapter has shown how important the coordination of the implementation of data protection law is between the EU Member States. This coordination takes place through the EDPB and the interpretation of the GDPR via the CJEU. Since, following Brexit, the UK will no longer be part of either mechanism, this is likely to lead to further disruptions and additional cost for businesses. Ultimately this means less sovereignty, not more.

8

Civil and Commercial Cases in the EU: Jurisdiction, Recognition, and Enforcement, Applicable Law—Brussels Regulation, Rome I and II Regulations

Julia Hörnle and Ioannis Revolidis

1. Introduction

1.1 The internet challenge and EU private international law

It is not more than a commonality that the commercialization of the internet has not only unlocked completely new dimensions of entrepreneurship and creativity,[1] beyond and across geographical borders,[2] but that it has also maximized the scale and multiplied the stakeholders of private law conflicts with international elements. Simply put, it is barely surprising that by allowing a wider range of stakeholders to assume the role of both the provider and the consumer of information goods (produced, created, and distributed from all possible jurisdictions across the world), the internet has created legal disputes that ignore geographical borders.

The EU has displayed some interesting institutional and regulatory reflexes in its effort to cope with the problem of internet regulation, that are not limited to the sector specific agendas that dominate its regulatory strategies.[3] Regarding the creation of a common area of freedom, security, and justice that lies at the centre of this chapter,[4] one can monitor a continuity of key institutional changes that have been running in parallel with the gradual transformations of the internet economy and the subsequent challenges that have flowed from this transformation.

The first major institutional step towards the creation of a more efficient civil justice cooperation between the Member States was achieved around the same period as the

[1] For the disruptive effect of internet applications to the traditional media industry see T Wu, *The Master Switch* (Vintage Books 2011) 269.

[2] For a detailed account of the new economy built around information society technologies see M Castels, *The Rise of the Network Society* (2nd edn, Wiley-Blackwell 2010) 77.

[3] Digital Single Market Strategy for Europe, COM(2015) 192 final.

[4] The long tradition of EU involvement in cross-border facilitation of private rights dates back to the very early years of the existence of the European Economic Community. Art 220 of the Rome Treaty establishing the European Economic Community provided that: "... Member States shall, so far as is necessary, enter into negotiations with each other with a view to securing for the benefit of their nationals: ... the simplification of formalities governing the reciprocal recognition and enforcement of judgments of courts or tribunals and of arbitration awards ..."

Internet Jurisdiction. Julia Hörnle, Oxford University Press (2021). © Julia Hörnle.
DOI: 10.1093/oso/9780198806929.001.0001

emergence of the first phase of internet commercialization across Europe. The Treaty of Amsterdam,[5] signed in 1997 and enacted in 1999, signalled a major turning point in the EU's involvement in the area of judicial cooperation in civil matters, by granting the EU the power to issue secondary legislation aiming at the approximation of Member States' civil procedural laws in cross-border cases. The second major turning point towards a stronger cross-border cooperation in the area of judicial enforcement of civil judgments was the Lisbon Treaty.[6] By awarding primary EU law status to the Charter of Fundamental Rights, the Lisbon Treaty offered a complete new dimension and meaning in the political mandate to abolish all intermediary inter-state recognition and enforcement mechanisms. The Stockholm programme[7] set the tone of the new EU ambitions. Enhanced cooperation in the area of recognition and enforcement of civil judgments was no longer seen as a mere technical mechanism for the sake of a closer economic cooperation amongst the Member States, and the facilitation of a common market. Instead the swift circulation of civil judgments across EU Member States has been seen as an existential guarantee for the enforcement of fundamental rights within the EU.[8] By acquiring such a strong political and institutional mandate, the EU legislator was generally in a better position to cope with the challenges created by the internet.

While the institutional transformations recorded here might have justified the enactment of internet specific legislative acts coping with the internet challenge and have, in any case, paved the way for the creation of a stronger civil justice union, the EU legislator did not choose to address internet-related disputes per se. The core of the EU's system of cross-border enforcement of civil law judgments on internet-related cases has remained technologically neutral.

1.2 Some core principles of EU private international law

The task of adapting the traditional EU private international law instruments to the specific problems of online communications fell upon the Court of Justice of the EU (CJEU), whose role in that transformation process must not be underestimated. In doing so, the CJEU had to combine the integrity of the traditional EU private international law values with the pressing need to create access to justice while protecting defendants in the context of internet-related violations. The Court has not been afraid to stretch the limits of EU intervention or even dismantle previously unquestioned private international law principles.[9]

Eliminating the barriers of cross-border recognition and enforcement of civil judgments is the first major principle of EU private international law. By offering a privileged regime for the circulation of civil judgments across the EU the procedural position of the claimants is strengthened, as they are the potential beneficiaries

[5] Treaty of Amsterdam [1997] OJ C340/1.

[6] Treaty of Lisbon [2007] OJ C306/1.

[7] A five-year programme in the area of justice and home affairs from 2010–14: "The Stockholm Programme-An Open and Secure Europe Serving and Protecting Citizens" [2010] OJ C115/1.

[8] See the political priorities of the Stockholm programme.

[9] For a summary of such innovative CJEU approaches see U Maunsbach, "The CJEU as an Innovator-A New Perspective on the Development of Internet Related Case-law" (2017) MUJLT 77.

of cross-border recognition and enforcement of judgments.[10] Nevertheless, EU private international law is balanced between the legal protection of claimants and defendants. The second principle of EU private international law is the protection of the rights of the defence.[11] The principle of protecting the defendant aims to secure that the free circulation of civil judgments across the EU will not entail a severe distortion of the basic fair trial guarantees that defendants enjoy. There are three basic mechanisms installed within the Brussels system of jurisdiction, recognition, and enforcement that guarantee particularly the legal protection of defendants. The first one refers to the rules of international jurisdiction,[12] which shall function as a counterpoise to the simplified recognition and enforcement system established in chapter three of the Brussels Ibis Regulation.[13] Secondly, the jurisdictional system of the Brussels Ibis Regulation centres around the basic rule that the defendant shall, in principle, be sued at his or her domicile.[14] By securing that the defendant shall be brought before his or her native courts, the Brussels Ibis Regulation acknowledges the vulnerability of the defendant's procedural position, especially in cases of international litigation.[15] From the fact that the defendant's domicile shall be the basic jurisdictional rule stems yet another protective function, namely the strict and narrow interpretation of the jurisdictional rules that deviate from the *actor sequitur forum rei* principle.[16] The CJEU has highlighted that the interpretation of the (exceptional) jurisdictional rules deviating from the basic rule of the defendant's domicile, shall not lead to the creation of claimant jurisdictions (forum actoris),[17] albeit more recently the case law of the Court, especially in internet-related cases, has not been entirely consistent.[18] The third mechanism to protect the defendant relates to the grounds for refusing recognition and enforcement of judgments, namely that the claimant did not effect proper service of the documents instituting the proceedings to the defendant.[19]

Legal certainty is another basic trait of EU private international law with three distinct dimensions. At a general level, the CJEU has confirmed that it is its mission to secure an equal and uniform application of the rights and obligations that stem from EU private international law.[20] To serve this purpose, the Court has introduced

[10] JA Pontier and E Burg, *EU Principles on Jurisdiction and Recognition and Enforcement of Judgments in Civil and Commercial Matters* (TMC Asser Press 2004) 27.

[11] A Dickinson and E Lein (eds), *The Brussels I Regulation Recast* (Oxford University Press 2015) 21.

[12] In the words of the CJEU in Case C-166/80 *Klomps v Michel* [1981] ECR 1593, para 7: "... it must be recalled that Title II of the Brussels Convention contains provisions regulating directly and in detail the jurisdiction of the courts of the state in which judgment was given, and also provisions concerning the verification of that jurisdiction and of admissibility. *These provisions, which are binding on the court in which judgment was given, are of such a nature as to protect the interests of defendants ...*"

[13] See Case C-220/84 *Autoteile v Malhé* ECLI:EU:C:1985:302, para 15.

[14] Art 4 Brussels Ibis Regulation. This rule is also described under the "actor sequitur forum rei" axiom, see H Schack, *Internationales Zivilverfahrensrecht* (6th edn, C.H. Beck 2014) 90.

[15] See Jenard Report [1979] OJ C59/1, p 18. See also Case C-412/98 *Group Josi Reinsurance Company SA and Universal General Insurance Company (UGIC)* ECLI:EU:C:2000:399, para 35.

[16] Case C-189/87 *Athanasios Kalfelis v Bankhaus Schröder* [1988], ECLI:EU:C:1988:459, paras 8, 19; Case C-26/91 *Jakob Handte v TMCS* ECLI:EU:C:1992:268, para 14.

[17] Case C-220/88 *Dumez v Hessische Landesbank* ECLI:EU:C:1990:8, para 16 where the Court explicitly stated that the Brussels Ibis Regulation is hostile towards forum actoris.

[18] See section 4.1.

[19] See Art 45(1)(b) Brussels Ibis Regulation.

[20] See Case C-7/98 *Krombach v Bamberski* ECLI:EU:C:2000:164, para 20.

the concept of autonomous interpretation of the terms found in secondary EU private international law legislation,[21] although important deviations from that concept have also been observed.[22] Predictability of EU private international law rules is another trait derived from the principle of legal certainty.[23] For example, the rules shall offer the opportunity to both the claimant and defendant to easily identify the court where litigation will take place[24] as well as the law that will be applicable. It is this need for predictability that paved the way for the rejection of the forum non-conveniens doctrine in the *Owusu v Jackson* case.[25] The avoidance of multiplication of the jurisdictional heads found within the Brussels Ibis Regulation is another important characteristic to be derived from the principle of legal certainty.[26]

Adjudicating a given dispute before the most appropriate court, which shall at the same time apply the most appropriate law, is another basic goal of EU private international law. The notion of most appropriate court and most appropriate law is viewed from different perspectives. Where socioeconomically unequal parties are involved, EU private international law functions as a medium that shall ameliorate such inequalities.[27] Where no inequalities are involved, EU private international law affords a rather generous space to the contractual autonomy of the parties. It contains a general assumption that rational litigants know better which forum and which law are appropriate to secure a smooth resolution of their disputes.[28] Where, finally, the will of the parties is absent, EU private international law sees as appropriate the forum and the law that have the closest relationship with a given dispute.[29] At a jurisdictional level, the close connection of a forum to a dispute is generally considered as offering better terms of justice administration and therefore a deviation from the "actor sequitur forum rei principle" is justified, albeit in narrow terms. Regarding the law applicable, the close connection of a legal order to a certain case offers the necessary amount of predictability and provides for better justice in individual cases.[30]

The above-mentioned principles apply to internet-related cases, although one shall be ready to accept necessary modifications that meet the special needs attached to the uniqueness of the internet.[31] The main corpus of this chapter is dedicated to this interaction between the traditional EU private international law rules and principles and how they are interpreted in respect of the internet.

[21] For the concept of autonomous interpretation in general see I Scholz, *Das Problem der autonomen Auslegung des EuGVÜ* (Mohr Siebeck 1998).

[22] The most important being the non-autonomous interpretation of the term "place of performance" in Art 7(1)(a) of the Brussels Ibis Regulation in Case C-12/76 *Tesili v Dunlop* ECLI:EU:C:1976:133, para 14.

[23] See Recital 15 Brussels Ibis Regulation, Recital 16 Rome I Regulation and Recital 14 Rome II Regulation.

[24] Among others see Case C-269/95 *Benincasa v Dentalkit* ECLI:EU:C:1997:337, para 26; Case C-334/00 *Tacconi v Sinto Maschinenfabrik* ECLI:EU:C:2002:499, para 20.

[25] Case C-281/02 *Owusu v Jackson* ECLI:EU:C:2005:120.

[26] J Schmidt, *Rechtssicherheit im europäischen Zivilverfahrensrecht* (Mohr Siebeck 2015) 157.

[27] V Lasic, "Procedural Justice for 'Weaker Parties' in Cross-Border Litigation under the EU Regulatory Scheme" (2014) Utrecht Law Review 100.

[28] For the foundation of this idea from a law and economics perspective see G Rühl, *Statut und Effizienz* (Mohr Siebeck 2011) 435.

[29] Recital 16 Brussels Ibis Regulation, Recital 21 Rome I Regulation, Recital 14 Rome II Regulation.

[30] S Geisler, *Die engste Verbindung im Internationalen Privatrecht* (Duncker & Humbolt 2001) 71.

[31] For a neat summary of the reasons that make the internet a unique challenge for private international law see D Jerker and B Svantesson, *Private International Law and the Internet* (3rd edn, Wolters Kluwer 2016) 51.

1.3 The UK's position after Brexit

EC/EU law has had a strong influence on the private international law rules under English and Scottish law from the Brussels Convention 1968 onwards. At the time of writing, it was unclear whether the Brussels Recast Regulation would be replaced by a treaty—in any case, it is unlikely that the CJEU's interpretation of EU private international law will be binding for the development of English and Scottish law. Potentially, this might mean that, after the transition period is over,[32] English law may further diverge from EU law in this area. The European Union (Withdrawal) Act 2018 stipulates that direct EU legislations such as a Regulation are converted into English law and form part of the body of retained EU law.[33] However, the UK government has largely repealed the implementation of the Brussels Regulation in the UK—the common law rules (including *forum non conveniens*) will apply to determine jurisdiction of the courts in England, Scotland, and Northern Ireland from 1 January 2020. The Regulations have maintained, however, the special protection rules for consumers and employees.[34] Furthermore, the recognition and enforcement of judgments can only occur on a reciprocal basis, therefore the EU Member States individually are under no obligation to continue the current mutual recognition and enforcement. Therefore the harmonization and coordination mechanisms in the field of private international law will have to be renegotiated. This is one of the highly problematic areas of Brexit, as it means that the automatic cross-border recognition and enforcement of judgments in civil and commercial matters is in jeopardy. In order to reduce the blow, the UK has submitted an instrument of accession to the Hague Convention on Choice of Court Agreements.[35] During the transition period, the EU Withdrawal Agreement[36] in Article 67(1)(a) provides for the application of the Brussels (Recast) Regulation (No 1215/2012) for legal proceedings "instituted before the end of the transition period," including the rules on *lis pendens*. Proceedings started before the 31 December 2020 will be recognized and enforced in the UK (or the EU Member States) under the provisions of the Brussels Recast Regulation, according to Article 67(2)(a). For the same reason the UK may also accede quickly and ratify the Hague Convention[37] on the Recognition and Enforcement of Judgments in Civil and Commercial Matters.[38]

[32] Unless extended: 31 December 2020.

[33] S 3.

[34] Civil Jurisdiction and Judgments (Amendment) (EU Exit) Regulations 2019/479.

[35] Hague Convention on Choice of Court Agreements 2005) (EU Exit) Regulations 2018, SI 2018/1124.

[36] 19 October 2019, https://assets.publishing.service.gov.uk/government/uploads/system/uploads/attachment_data/file/840655/Agreement_on_the_withdrawal_of_the_United_Kingdom_of_Great_Britain_and_Northern_Ireland_from_the_European_Union_and_the_European_Atomic_Energy_Community.pdf accessed 27/7/2020.

[37] This will not be further discussed in this book as it is too early to tell at this point whether the Hague Convention will be a success because this depends on a significant number of states ratifying the Convention.

[38] Hague Convention 41 of 2 July 2019 will enter into force when ratified by three states; available from https://www.hcch.net/en/instruments/conventions/full-text/?cid=137 accessed 25 July 2020.

2. Scope of application and general rules of jurisdiction and law applicable

2.1 Civil and commercial matters

The material scope of application of the Brussels Ibis, Rome I and Rome II Regulations is captured by the term "civil and commercial matters."[39] What "civil and commercial matters" means has been a problem that has regularly appeared in the case law of the CJEU, which has opted for an autonomous interpretation of the term.[40] In its essence "civil and commercial matters" is meant to draw a line between private law and public law matters. Only private law matters fall within the scope of Brussels Ibis, Rome I and Rome II. To make the distinction between private law and public law matters the CJEU has developed the criterion of the exercise of public powers,[41] namely the ability of one of the parties to use legal powers that are not afforded to private persons.[42] If public power is exercised by one of the litigation parties, then there is a public law matter that falls outside of the scope of the Regulations. In the reverse, where no public power is exercised there is, in principle, a private law matter that falls within the scope of the Regulations. The involvement of a Member State or a public authority in a transaction does not necessarily mean that there is a public law matter.[43] Not all civil and commercial matters fall within the material scope of the Regulations. All three Regulations provide for a substantial number of exceptions.[44] For example, the Brussels Ibis Regulation retains the exception of arbitration from its material scope,[45] while conflicts of laws related to privacy and personality rights (which consist a very significant body of internet-related cases) are exempted expressly from the scope of the Rome II Regulation[46] and, according to CJEU case law, it seems that they also fall outside of the material scope of the Rome I Regulation.[47]

2.2 The cross-border character of a case

The application of the Brussels Ibis, Rome I and Rome II Regulations also presupposes the existence of a cross-border case.[48] The cross-border character of a case is evident

[39] Art 1 Brussels Ibis Regulation, Art 1 Rome I Regulation and Art 1 Rome II Regulation.

[40] See Case C-29/76 *LTU v Eurocontrol* ECLI:EU:C:1976:137, para 3.

[41] Case C-814/79 *Netherlands v Rüffer* ECLI:EU:C:1980:291, para 8.

[42] D Czernich, G Kodek, and P Mayr (eds), *Europäisches Gerichtsstands- und Vollstreckungsrecht* (4th edn, LexisNexis 2015) 69.

[43] Case C-167/00 *VKI v Henkel* ECLI:EU:C:2002:555, para 29; Case C-49/12 *The Commissioners for Her Majesty's Revenue & Customs v Sunico* ECLI:EU:C:2013:545, para 34; Case C-302/13 *flyLAL-Lithuanian Airlines AS v Starptautiskā lidosta Rīga VAS* ECLI:EU:C:2014:2319, para 30.

[44] See Art 1(2) Brussels Ibis, Rome I and Rome II Regulations.

[45] See Art 1(2)(d) Brussels Ibis Regulation.

[46] See Art 1(g) Rome II Regulation.

[47] Outcome in Case C-191/15 *VKI v Amazon EU* ECLI:EU:C:2016:612.

[48] See Recital 3 Brussels Ibis Regulation ("... For the gradual establishment of such an area, the Union is to adopt measures relating to judicial cooperation in civil matters having cross-border implications, particularly when necessary for the proper functioning of the internal market ...") Art 1 Rome I Regulation

where parties domiciled in different Member States are involved in the litigation process. More difficult is the classification of a case where parties or subject matters connected to a single Member State are involved. Regarding the Brussels Ibis Regulation, the CJEU has afforded a rather wide interpretation to the notion of a cross-border case, not limiting this to domiciles of the parties in different Member States.[49] Many commentators have also given an equally wide meaning to the notion of "situations involving a conflict of laws" found in Rome I and Rome II Regulations, submitting that any objective or subjective elements that link a case to a foreign legal order shall deem a legal relationship as international and justify the application of the Rome I and Rome II Regulations.[50]

2.3 Scope of application

The scope of the three Regulations is not completely identical. The Rome I and Rome II Regulations enjoy, in general, a "universal application,"[51] namely they are applicable to any conflict of laws issues that fall within their material scope of application irrespective of the nationality or domicile or any other circumstances that might affect a legal relationship.[52] The Brussels Ibis Regulation is applicable if one of the defendants has his or her domicile in a Member State.[53] The nationality of the parties or the domicile of the claimant do not influence the personal scope of the Brussels Ibis Regulation. Despite the ambitious plan of the Commission to expand the personal scope of the Regulation also to defendants domiciled outside the EU,[54] the Member States have resisted such an extension.[55] The Brussels regime may apply even if the defendant(s) are domiciled outside the EU in consumer cases,[56] employment cases,[57] *in rem* cases,[58] and for express jurisdiction agreements, stipulating a court in the EU.[59] For a jurisdiction agreement to fall within the Brussels regime, the designation of an EU court in a

("... situations involving conflict of laws ... ") and Art 1 Rome II Regulation ("... situation involving conflict of laws ...").

[49] Case C-281/02 *Owusu v Jackson* ECLI:EU:C:2005:120, paras 25–26; Case C-478/12 *Maletic v lastminute.com* ECLI:EU:C:2013:735, para 26; cf D Paulus in R Geimer and R Schütze (eds), *Internationaler Rechtsverkehr in Zivil- und Handelssachen* (C.H. Beck 2017) 70, who supports a more restrictive interpretation of the cross-border character of a case.

[50] See D Martiny in C Reithmann and D Martiny (eds), *Internationales Vertragsrecht* (8th edn, Otto Schmidt 2015) 56 as well as A-L Calvo Caravaca and J Carracosa Conzalléz in U Magnus and P Mankowski (eds), *Rome I Regulation-Commentary* (Otto Schmidt 2016) 74.

[51] See Art 2 Rome I Regulation and Art 3 Rome II Regulation.

[52] See on the Rome I Regulation Calvo Caravaca and Carracosa Conzalléz (n 50) 84 and for the Rome II Regulation see A Halfmeier in Galliess (ed), *Rome Regulations* (2nd edn, Wolters Kluwer 2015) 493.

[53] See Art 4 Brussels Ibis Regulation; subject to exceptions.

[54] COM(2010) 748 final.

[55] European Parliament, Session document, A7-0219/2010, 3–15.

[56] Art 18(1).

[57] Art 21(1).

[58] Art 24.

[59] Art 25.

jurisdictional agreement is enough, irrespective of the domicile or nationality of the parties.[60]

2.4 The contractual or non-contractual character of a case

The legal nature of the dispute plays a significant role in identifying which set of EU rules on applicable law are applied to a case. While the Brussels Ibis Regulation covers both contractual and non-contractual obligations, there are two separate instruments, *viz* Rome I and Rome II Regulations for either type of relationship. Rome I covers only contractual obligations[61] and Rome II covers only torts and other non-contractual legal relationships.[62] The terms "contractual" and "non-contractual" obligations are interpreted autonomously[63] and in conformity with one another and with the similar terms that appear in Article 7(1) and (2) of the Brussels Ibis Regulation.[64] Disparities within the concepts of "contractual" and "non-contractual" obligations between the Brussels Ibis and Rome I and Rome II Regulations might nonetheless be justified because of their different subject matter and purpose. Brussels Ibis Regulation provides for rules of international jurisdiction, while the Rome I and Rome II Regulations cover the applicable law and EU private international law does not seem to endorse an absolute parallelism between jurisdiction and applicable law.[65]

According to the case law of the CJEU on Article 7 Brussels Ibis Regulation, the answer to the question whether the contested obligation is contractual or non-contractual depends on whether the parties have or have not assumed the obligation freely.[66] Freely assumed obligations are of a contractual nature.[67] Every obligation that has not been freely assumed, will, in principle, be of a non-contractual nature.[68]

[60] See A Staudinger and B Steinrotter, "Das neue Zuständigkeitsregime bei zivilrechtlichen Auslandssachverhalten" [2015] JuS 1, 2. The parallel application of the Lugano Convention as well as the Hague Convention on choice of courts agreements shall nonetheless be taken into account. On that see T Hartley, *Choice-of-Court Agreements under the European and the International Instruments* (Oxford University Press 2013) 105–26.

[61] Art 1 Rome I Regulation.

[62] Art 1 Rome II Regulation.

[63] Regarding the term "non-contractual obligations" see in particular Recital 11 Rome II Regulation.

[64] There must be a conformity in the interpretation of the terms and concepts that appear in the Brussels Ibis, Rome I and Rome II Regulations see Recital 7 Rome I and Rome II Regulation.

[65] M Würdinger, "Das Prinzip der Einheit der Schuldrechtsverordnungen im Europäischen Internationalen Privat- und Verfahrensrecht - Eine methodologische Untersuchung über die praktische Konkordanz zwischen Brüssel I-VO, Rom I-VO und Rom II-VO" (2011) RabelsZ 102; M Köck, *Die Einheitliche Auslegung der Rom I, Rome II- und Brüssel I-Verordnung im europäischen internationalen Privat- und Verfahrensrecht* (Duncker & Humbolt 2014) 141.

[66] Case C-26/91 *Jakob Handte v TMCS* ECLI:EU:C:1992:268, para 15.

[67] Case C-51/97 *Réunion Européenne SA and Others v Spliethoff's Bevrachtingskantoor BV, and the Master of the vessel Alblasgracht V002* ECLI:EU:C:1998:509, para 17; Case C-265/02 *Frahuil SA v Assitalia SpA* ECLI:EU:C:2004:77, para 24.

[68] Case C-189/87 *Athanasios Kalfelis v Bankhaus Schröder* ECLI:EU:C:1988:459, para 18; Case C-334/00 *Tacconi v Sinto Maschinenfabrik* ECLI:EU:C:2002:499, para 21; Case C-572/14 *Austro-Mechana Gesellschaft zur Wahrnehmung mechanisch-musikalischer Urheberrechte GmbH v Amazon EU* ECLI:EU:C:2016:286, para 32.

2.5 The relationship of EU private international law with the "principle of country of origin" established in Article 3 E-Commerce Directive

Before presenting the general EU rules on international jurisdiction and applicable law, the relationship between EU private international law and the "principle of country of origin" established in the E-Commerce Directive[69] should be mentioned. According to Article 3 of the E-Commerce Directive, information service society providers shall in general comply only with the stipulations of the law of the country where they are established, when offering their services within the coordinated field established by the E-Commerce Directive, save for the exceptions listed in Article 3(4) of the same.[70] It has long been debated whether Article 3 of the E-Commerce Directive shall be interpreted as a rule of private international law that renders, in all internet-related cases, the law of the country where an information service provider is established as applicable. The prevailing view denies such a role to Article 3 of the E-Commerce Directive,[71] but recognizes that it can function as a corrective mechanism that shall secure that an internet service provider could claim the applicability of the law of his or her country of establishment, if the law applicable pursuant to traditional private international law rules, would entail stricter requirements in offering information society services within the coordinated field established by the E-Commerce Directive.[72] The CJEU has adopted this view in *eDate*.[73] The law applicable in internet-related cases is determined by the Rome I and Rome II Regulations while Article 3 of the E-Commerce Directive shall operate on the substantive level and ensure that an internet service provider will not be subject to stricter requirements.[74]

2.6 General rule of jurisdiction under the Brussels Ibis Regulation

If a case falls within the material and personal scope of the Brussels Ibis Regulation, the general jurisdictional rule is found in Article 4(1). The *actor sequitur forum rei* principle is the starting point of the jurisdictional system of the Regulation, and therefore the claimant must sue at the courts of the country of domicile of the defendant.

[69] Directive (EC) 2000/31 on certain legal aspects of information society services, in particular electronic commerce, in the Internal Market (Directive on electronic commerce) [2000] OJ L178/1.

[70] For the principle of country of origin in the E-Commerce Directive see also A Savin, *EU Internet Law* (Edward Elgar 2014) 45.

[71] J Hörnle, "The UK Perspective on the Country of Origin Rule in the E-commerce Directive—A Rule of Administrative Law Applicable to Private Law Disputes?" (2004) 12(3) International Journal of Law and Information Technology 333–63.

[72] See among others M Wilderspin, "The Rome II Regulation: Some Policy Observations" (2008) NIPR 408, 409.

[73] Joined Cases C-509/09 and C-161/10 *eDate Advertising GmbH v X* and *Olivier Martinez v MGN Limited* ECLI:EU:C:2011:685.

[74] ibid, paras 53–68.

Article 4 is a general jurisdictional rule, namely—save for the cases that an exclusive jurisdiction in Article 24—one of the special grounds of jurisdiction in Article 7, or a prorogation of jurisdiction in Articles 25–26, or some protective rule in Articles 10, 17, or 20 are involved. It affords to the courts of the defendant's domicile the power to decide any dispute between the litigating parties.

Despite the strong criticism to the *actor sequitur forum rei* principle, which is usually considered inflexible and therefore not particularly fair or adaptive to new challenges,[75] the existence of such a general and easily identifiable ground of jurisdiction might be very important especially in internet cases. Apart from offering a better balance of the litigation risks involved to an international dispute by affording a counterpoise to the claimant's privileges in terms of recognition and enforcement of judgments within the EU, the defendant's domicile provides for an important level of legal certainty in the sense that it is a basis of jurisdiction easily identified by both litigants. The domicile of the defendant is also a jurisdictional ground immune to the borderless and ubiquitous nature of internet transactions. No matter how unconnected to real-world geography the elements of an internet case might be, the defendant's domicile points to a clearly identified litigation venue.

Moreover, by suing at the courts of the defendant's Member State, the claimant can usually secure better chances of obtaining a remedy, not only because there is a considerable possibility that the evidence is located there, and that the defendant retains his or her assets in the country of his or her domicile, but also because it makes it highly probable that the documents instituting the proceedings are served on the defendant without errors.

However, the courts of the defendant's domicile might not be the most appropriate forum for every internet-related litigation scenario, especially in terms of the proximity of the court to the dispute. For this reason, the strong proximity of the court to a case, that the Brussels Ibis Regulation opens alternative jurisdictional fora, which are discussed in the next chapters.

2.7 Choice as a conflict of laws rule for contractual obligations under the Rome I Regulation

Turning to the law applicable, choice as a conflict of laws rule for contractual obligations is contained in Article 3 Rome I Regulation. Article 3 gives precedence to the will of the parties and renders applicable the law that the parties have chosen. The agreement on the law applicable might be express or even tacit: "the choice shall be made expressly or clearly demonstrated by the terms of the contract or the *circumstances of the case*."[76] Article 11 contains the rules as to the formal validity of

[75] For a critique to the actor sequitur forum rei principle from a European perspective see B Buchner, *Kläger- und Beklagtenschutz im Recht der internationalen Zuständigkeit* (Mohr Siebeck 1998) 50, while for a critical comparison to the more flexible US approach see A Lowenfeld, *International Litigation and the Quest for Reasonableness. General Course on Private International Law* (RCADI, Martinus Nijhoff Publishers 1995) 81.

[76] Art 3(1), 2nd Sentence.

contracts, but does not contain any specific rules on electronic contracts. These are contained in Article 9(1) of the E-Commerce Directive 2000/31/EC, which stipulates that electronic contracts are valid.[77] Defining the law applicable to an internet contract via a choice of law agreement is beneficial for the parties, as it can provide for legal certainty and allows the parties to tailor the law applicable to their individual needs, without risking any unexpected outcomes due to the ubiquitous nature of the internet. Depending on the wording of the choice of law clause, it might cover not only the contractual obligations arising out of a contractual relationship but additionally may include non-contractual obligations that arise in the contractual relationship.[78] The choice of the law applicable to non-contractual obligations must additionally comply with the stipulations of Article 14 Rome II Regulation, mirroring the provisions in Article 3 Rome I Regulation.

The freedom of the parties to choose the law applicable to their contractual obligations is not limitless. Article 3(3) and (4) provide for a limitation in respect of mandatory laws. According to Article 3(3), the parties cannot deviate via a choice of law agreement from mandatory law, if another country has a *closer connection to a contract* in comparison to the country, whose law has been chosen in the contract. Mandatory laws are the provisions of the law of a country that cannot be derogated from, such as consumer protection law or employment law. The same applies, according to Article 3(4) for EU mandatory law. If a contract has a closer connection to any Member State, the choice of a law of a non-EU Member State only applies to non-mandatory provisions of EU law. The determination of such a closer connection must be factual and take into account all the circumstances surrounding the contract.[79] The internet might make such an assessment challenging, however, as contracts can be largely delocalized and the connecting factors spread over several countries. The wording in Article 3(3) and (4) refers to "all other elements relevant to the situation at the time of the choice" and such elements include the domicile or location of the parties, the place of performance of the contract and other factors. It has been submitted that even in internet contracts such a factual assessment of whether there is a close connection of a contract to a certain country is possible.[80] If such a closer connection to a country other than the one whose law has designated by the parties is established, the choice of law is, nevertheless, as such, valid. The contract follows the law designated by the parties, albeit that the provisions of the law of the country that has a closer connection and cannot be derogated from will displace, within their material scope of application, the choice of law made by the parties. Furthermore, the Rome I Regulation makes provision for the mandatory law of the forum adjudicating a dispute, and the mandatory provisions of the place of the forum, both of which apply irrespective of the law chosen by the

[77] OJ L178/12, p 1.

[78] P Mankowski in U Magnus and P Mankowski (eds), *Rome I Regulation-Commentary* (Otto Schmidt 2016) 135–37.

[79] P Mankowski in U Magnus and P Mankowski (eds), *Rome I Regulation-Commentary* (Otto Schmidt 2016) 230, 236.

[80] D Martiny (n 50) 144.

parties.[81] However, these mandatory provisions are limited to those provisions, the respect for which is regarded as crucial by a country for safeguarding its public interests, such as its political, social, or economic organization, to such an extent that they are applicable to any situation falling within their scope.[82] Finally, Article 21 contains a public policy derogation and permits a complete refusal of the law designated by the parties, if such a choice is incompatible with the public order of the forum.

2.8 General conflict of laws rule for non-contractual obligations under the Rome II Regulation

If the subject matter of the disputed case refers to a non-contractual obligation, as it is often the case in internet transactions, the general rule for determining the law applicable is Article 4 of the Rome II Regulation. It is important to note that several important internet-related subject matters are not covered Article 4. In particular, the rules on applicable law concerning privacy and personality rights are excluded from the scope of the Rome II Regulation by virtue of Article 1(g). Furthermore, for certain types of non-contractual obligations special rules apply such as, for example, intellectual property (Article 8[83]), product liability (Article 5), or infringements of competition and unfair competition law (Article 6). Internet-related torts that fall within Article 4 are, for example, negligent misstatement or other forms of negligence or computer misuse in the context of cybersecurity. As a general rule for torts, Article 4(1) provides that the law of the place of the direct damage is the applicable law. Thus, the place where the tort was committed or any further consequences flowing from the tort are not taken into account. Since the damage flowing from a wrongful act online can be widely spread over several countries, a multitude of laws may be applicable.

This means applying the "mosaic principle" according to the *Shevill* case on jurisdiction regarding ubiquitous personality infringements.[84] On the negative side, the mosaic approach complicates the administration of justice, as it endorses the application of multiple different laws for the same legal relationship and considers the same wrongful act under a multitude of laws. The application of different Member State tort laws for the same case also jeopardizes legal certainty (especially because the tort laws that shall be applicable might present important deviations from one another and lead to completely different outcomes for the same case). If both the tortfeasor and the victim are habitually resident in the same country, then the law of that country applies, by way of exception, according to Article 4(2). Finally, if a case is more closely connected with yet another country, the law of that country will apply as stipulated by Article 4(3), giving the court discretion to take into account all the circumstances of the case (escape clause).

[81] Art 9(2) and (3).
[82] Art 9(1).
[83] See Chapter 12.
[84] See Case C-68/93 *Fiona Shevill v Presse Alliance SA* ECLI:EU:C:1995:61, para 33 further discussed in Chapter 11.

3. Special EU rules of jurisdiction and law applicable for contractual obligations

3.1 Overview

Contractual disputes enjoy a detailed treatment from the Brussels Ibis jurisdictional regime. Following the fundamental principles of legal certainty, foreseeability, proximity, and the creation of better terms for the administration of justice, as well as respect for the contractual freedom of the parties, the Brussels I Regulation opens alternatives to the courts of the domicile of the defendant.[85] The alternative rules of jurisdiction on contractual issues do not always operate in parallel, as some of them claim exclusive application over the others (even over Article 4 Brussels Ibis). That is the case for the protective regime for insurance policy holders (Article 10 Brussels Ibis), consumers (Article 17 Brussels Ibis),[86] and employees (Article 20 Brussels Ibis). The jurisdictional rules of these protective regimes take precedence over all jurisdictional rules referring to contractual issues. If no protective regime is applicable, one must turn to the rules referring to prorogation of jurisdiction: Article 25 Brussels Ibis recognizes the parties' express choice of jurisdiction. A valid express jurisdiction clause, if agreed as exclusive,[87] renders Articles 4 and 7(1) Brussels Ibis inapplicable.

Finally, if no protective regime is applicable and no exclusive jurisdiction agreement is present, then Articles 4 and 7(1) of the Brussels Ibis Regulation regulate jurisdiction for contracts. The courts of the domicile of the defendant are available along with the courts of the country where the contractual obligations are performed or should have been performed, which is the additional special ground of jurisdiction contained in Article 7(1).

It should be pointed out here that some internet contracts are concluded online but performed physically, and for these contracts the rules of special jurisdiction in Article 7(1) do not present any specific challenges.[88] Contracts concluded and performed online involve more complex jurisdictional issues.[89]

3.2 Prorogation under Article 25 Brussels Ibis

Article 25 of the Brussels Ibis Regulation is the central provision regulating the express prorogation of jurisdiction. Allowing the parties to designate the court or courts that shall adjudicate over their contractual disputes is not only a realization of their

[85] See Arts 7, 24–25, 10, 17, and 20 Brussels Ibis Regulation.

[86] See further Chapter 10.

[87] Art 25 allows the parties to decide whether the jurisdictional agreement shall have exclusive or non-exclusive character.

[88] eg if a professional painter buys brushes, colours, and further painting materials from an online retailer, no specific jurisdictional issues will occur due to the use of the internet. Although the contract has been concluded via the website of the retailer, the purchased physical products are delivered to the painter. Such a contract has strong territorial links and the localization of the place of performance is not difficult.

[89] For that assessment see D Jerker and Svantesson (n 31) 438.

contractual autonomy but also a mechanism that shall provide legal certainty and predictability, especially in internet-related contracts.

The essence of Article 25 Brussels Ibis lies with the stipulations that regulate the formal validity of the jurisdictional agreements. Although the form requirements of Article 25 Brussels Ibis seem technical in their nature, they perform a very substantive role, namely that of establishing the existence of a consensus between the parties for the jurisdictional clause, which is the most important material requirement that justifies their strong procedural effect.[90] Article 25 Brussels Ibis covers the formal requirements of the jurisdictional agreements exclusively,[91] so that no recourse to national law is either necessary or permissible. Four main formal types meet the standards of Article 25 Brussels Ibis:

(1) a jurisdictional agreement in writing (Article 25(1)(a));
(2) a jurisdictional agreement evidenced in writing (Article 25(1)(a));
(3) a jurisdictional agreement in a form which accords with the practices which the parties have established between themselves (Article 25(1)(b);
(4) a jurisdictional agreement that comes in a form that accords with the norms that are habitually used in international trade or commerce (Article 25(1)(c)).

The most interesting formal type for internet-related contracts is the one that requires an agreement in writing or evidenced in writing, as the lack of physical documentation in electronic contracts might create several challenges. To afford an equal treatment to electronic contracts,[92] Article 25(2) provides that any communication by electronic means that provides a durable record shall be equivalent to "writing." The ruling of the CJEU in *Jaouad El Majdoub v CarsOnTheWeb.Deutschland GmbH*,[93] where the Court was asked whether a jurisdictional agreement included in an online click wrap contract was valid, is an illustrative example of how this equivalency of electronic communications to the written form can operate. The case referred to the purchase of a car online, where the buyer has accepted the general terms and conditions of the seller, by clicking on the respective button of the seller's website. The general terms and conditions of the seller that contained, inter alia, the disputed jurisdictional agreement, were not displayed directly on a website but they were available

[90] The CJEU has as early as the 1970's highlighted the existential meaning of the form requirements for the establishment of the consensus of the parties in a jurisdictional agreement. See eg Case C-24/76 *Estasis Salotti v RÜWA* ECLI:EU:C:1976:177, para 7, Case C-25/76 *Segoura v Bonakdarian* ECLI:EU:C:1976:178, para 6. See also Recital 11 Brussels Ibis Regulation.

[91] On the contrary, it is still open to debate how the material requirements of a jurisdictional agreement shall be treated. Inserting a new conflict of laws rule that shall define which law shall be applicable to the material validity of a jurisdictional agreement has been a major innovation of Art 25 Brussels Ibis Regulation. Recital 20 Brussels Ibis Regulation explains that the law applicable to a jurisdictional agreement shall be determined according to the conflict of laws rules of the forum prorogatum. For a more detailed overview see P Mankowski, "The Role of Party Autonomy in the Allocation of Jurisdiction in Contractual Matters" in F Ferrari and F Ragno (eds), *Cross-Border Litigation in Europe: the Brussels I Recast Regulation as a Panacea?* (Wolters Kluwer, CEDAM 2015) 97.

[92] The equal treatment of electronic contracts from the Member States is a general ambition of the EU legislator, established already in Art 9 of the E-Commerce Directive. See A Lodder, "Directive 2000/31/EC on Certain Legal Aspects of Information Society Services, in Particular Electronic Commerce, in the Internal Market" in Arno Lodder and Andrew Murray (eds), *EU Regulation of E-Commerce-A Commentary* (Edward Elgar 2017) 41.

[93] Case C-322/14 *Jaouad El Majdoub v CarsOnTheWeb.Deutschland* GmbH ECLI:EU:C:2015:334.

on a hyperlink that allowed their separate storing or printing, prior or after the conclusion of the contract. The Court ruled that such an electronic jurisdictional agreement meets the formal requirements of Article 25 Brussels Ibis.[94] Drawing inspiration from the wording of Article 25 as well as the Pocar Report on the Lugano Convention[95] and the historical background of the provision,[96] the Court ruled that the creation of a durable record is not a prerequisite for the equivalency of electronic communications with the written form. It suffices if the electronic mode of concluding a contract (click wrap) offers the possibility of the creation of a durable record, irrespective of whether such a record was indeed created.[97] The fact that both Article 25(2) and the CJEU adopted a rather wide, open and technologically neutral wording on which electronic communications shall be deemed equivalent to writing form, allows the conclusion that the provision shall cover the majority of electronic modes of concluding contracts and will most likely survive the invention of more complicated electronic modes of contracting in the future, as long as they provide the possibility of the creation of a durable record.

If the formal requirements of Article 25 are met, the parties enjoy a rather wide freedom in determining the court that shall have international jurisdiction. In fact, the designated court might not even present any connection to the dispute.[98] Agreements on the place of performance of the contractual obligations of the parties, must be distinguished from jurisdictional agreements. The parties are free to choose the place where an obligation shall be performed, without observing the formal stipulations of Article 25, if the designated place of performance displays some connection with the dispute. If the designated place of performance is arbitrary and does not present any connection to the dispute, then, according to the case law of the CJEU, the formal requirements of Article 25 shall be observed.[99]

3.3 Jurisdiction—special rule of Article 7(1) Brussels Ibis

Article 7(1) of the Brussels Ibis Regulation is one of the most important jurisdictional provisions, as it covers all contractual disputes for which no (express or tacit) prorogation of jurisdiction is present and no protective regime is involved. In sum, Article 7(1) opens an additional forum to that of the domicile of the defendant, by allowing contractual disputes to be litigated before the courts of the Member where the contractual obligations are performed or should have been performed.[100] Article 7(1)

[94] ibid para 40.

[95] See Pocar Report [2009] OJ C319/1, 29.

[96] *Jaouad El Majdoub* (n 93) para 35.

[97] For the application of Art 25 Brussels Ibis Regulation in online contracts see also AS de Sousa Concalves, "Choice of Court Agreements in the E-Commerce international contracts" (2017) MUJLT 63–76.

[98] U Magnus in Ulrich Magnus and Peter Mankowksi (eds), *Brussels Ibis Regulation-Commentary* (3rd edn, Otto Schimdt 2016), 613–14.

[99] Case C-106/95 *MSG v Les Gravières Rhénanes SARL* ECLI:EU:C:1997:70, paras 31–35.

[100] The place where the contract was formed plays no role within the jurisdictional regime of Art 7(1). On the discussion about why the place of performance prevailed over the place of the contact formation see H Schack, *Der Erfüllungsort im deutschen, ausländischen und internationalen Privat- und Zivilprozeßrecht* (Alfred Metzner Verlag 1985) 103–10.

inserts a differentiation between contracts for the sales of goods and provision of services on the one hand and all other contracts on the other.[101] According to Article 7(1)(b), contracts for the sales of goods or contracts for the provision of services enjoy, in absence of a contractual agreement on the place of performance, an autonomous definition of the place of performance of the characteristic obligation, which shall cover all the disputed obligations. Article 7(1)(a) does not provide for an autonomous definition of the place of performance, which is accordingly decided based on the law applicable to the contract.[102] Moreover, Article 7(1)(a) leads to a jurisdictional division of the obligations that stem from the same contract, as it affords jurisdiction to the place of performance of each individual obligation that forms the basis of litigation.[103]

Applying Article 7(1) therefore requires two basic steps. The first step shall be the legal classification of the disputed contract, which will decide whether 7(1)(a) or 7(1)(b) is applicable. The second is the identification of the place of performance that will indicate the forum that shall have the power to adjudicate over a contractual dispute, in addition to the defendant's domicile. Internet contracts might create some interesting problems that refer both to the legal classification of the disputed contracts and the localization of the place of performance.

Starting with the legal classification of internet contracts for digitized goods or services, one might encounter problems in trying to fit them within the scope of sales contracts or contracts for the provision of services that enable the application of Article 7(1)(b). According to the case law of the CJEU, sales contracts cover contractual relationships where one party is obliged to supply goods to the other.[104] More precisely, contracts for the sales of goods entail the *transferring of ownership* of the purchased goods from one party to the other against remuneration.[105] Contracts for the provision of services, on the other hand, are contracts where one of the parties carries out a particular activity in return for remuneration.[106]

It has long been disputed whether the supply of software and other digitized goods (eg music, movies, and books in digital form) falls within the sales contracts covered in Article 7(1)(b). Some commentators support the view that sales contracts in Article 7(1)(b) refer only to the transfer of ownership over tangible goods and not over intangible ones,[107] unless they are somehow incorporated to a tangible medium.[108] A distinction can also be made between standardized and customizable software products. Standard software shall be treated equally to tangible goods and therefore contracts that refer to the transferring of standardized software shall be treated as sales contracts

[101] For the structure of Art 7(1) Brussels Ibis see P Rogerson, *Collier's Conflict of Laws* (4th edn, Cambridge University Press 2013) 79.

[102] Case C-12/76 *Tesili v Dunlop* ECLI:EU:C:1976:133, para 14.

[103] Case C-14/76 *De Bloos v Bouyer* ECLI:EU:C:1976:134, para 11.

[104] Case C-381/08 *Car Trim GmbH v KeySafety Systems Srl* [2010], para 32.

[105] J Kropholler and J von Hein, *Europäisches Zivilprozessrecht* (9th edn, Verlag Recht und Wirtschaft 2011) 168.

[106] Case C-533/07 *Falco Privatstiftung v Gisela Weller-Lindhorst* [2009], para 29; Case C-469/12 *Krejci Lager v Olbrich Transport und Logistik GmbH* [2013], para 26. See also H Wais, *Der Europäische Erfüllungsgerichtstand für Dienstleistungsverträge* (Mohr Siebeck 2013) 81.

[107] eg P Stone, *EU Private International Law* (3rd edn, Edward Elgar 2014) 84.

[108] See J Schrammen, *Grenzüberschreitende Verträge im Internet: Internationale Gerichtszuständigkeit und anwendbares Recht* (Cuvillier Verlag Göttingen 2005) 37.

within Article 7(1)(b), irrespective of whether the digitized products are incorporated to a tangible medium or transferred online.[109] Customizable software products, on the other hand, are covered under the contracts for the provision of services, as the main obligation of the software provider is no longer the mere transfer of digitized goods, but the creation as well the modification of the digital products so that they meet the individual needs and specifications of the recipient.[110] This view shall in general be preferred, as it seems to be having a solid foundation in international contract law,[111] albeit a further refinement shall be made. Only the digital transfer of standardized software for an unlimited period shall be classified as a sales contract, while allowing the use of standardized software for a limited period of time resembles more a lease contract and shall thus not be classified as a sales contract under Article 7(1)(b) Brussels Ibis.[112]

Under CJEU case law, licensing agreements are not contracts for the provision of services, as the rightsholder does not display any active conduct while allowing the lawful acquirer to perform certain exploitation acts on the protected work or simply use it.[113] Such contracts fall within Article 7(1)(a) and the place of performance of each disputed obligation shall be decided individually according to the law applicable to the contract. The same shall apply to software licensing agreements as well as alternative licensing schemes between the author of the software and the end user (eg open source, creative commons, shareware licences).[114] More complicated is the situation when the rightsholder, apart from allowing the use or exploitation of the protected work, undertakes the obligation to perform particular activities towards the end user (eg delivery of user manuals and updates, software and server maintenance, etc). In that case the contract will have a mixed nature, namely it will present elements of a licence agreement as well as of a contract for the provision of services. While one could argue that such mixed contracts shall automatically fall within Article 7(1)(a), it could also be equally valid to claim that one should classify them according to their

[109] P Mankowski in U Magnus and P Mankowksi (eds), *Brussels Ibis Regulation-Commentary* (3rd edn, Otto Schimdt 2016) 196.

[110] In that line see Kropholler and von Hein (n 105) 169, S Leible in T Rauscher (ed), *Europäisches Zivilprozess- und Kollisionsrecht vol I* (4th end, Otto Schmidt 2016) 303.

[111] Most prominently the CISG, within the premises of which contracts for the supply of standardized software are usually classified as sales contracts. For the argumentation that the CISG shall inspire the interpretation of Art 7(1)(b) in terms of contracts for the supply of software see T Lynker, *Der besondere Gerichtsstand am Erfüllungsort in der Brüssel I-Verordnung* (Peter Lang 2005) 57; K Mumelter, *Der Gerichtsstand des Erfüllungsortes im Europäischen Zivilprozessrecht* (Neuer Wissenschaftlicher Verlag 2007) 139. The CJEU has already draw inspiration from the CISG while interpreting Art 7(1)(b) in general. See Case C-381/08 *Car Trim GmbH v KeySafety Systems Srl* [2010], paras 36–37. Further support for this view might be deduced by the ruling of the CJEU in Case C-128/11 *UsedSoft GmbH v Oracle Intenational Corp.* [2012], paras 45–48. Although the case was not one of private international law, the CJEU has nonetheless provided a legal classification of a software contract, where the software acquirer downloads an electronic copy of standardized software over the internet and retains the right to use it for an unlimited period of time. The CJEU ruled that in such contracts there is, in essence, a transfer of property of the downloadable software copies and, therefore, the relevant contracts shall be viewed as sales contracts.

[112] J Marly, *Praxishandbuch Softwarerecht* (6th edn, C.H. Beck 2014) 342, who notes: "... Entscheidend für die Zuordnung zu einem Vertragstyp ist dementsprechend wie bei den allgemeinen Ausführungen zur Rechtsnatur der Softwareüberlassungsverträge dargelegt, ob Standar- oder Individualsoftware auf Dauer oder auf Zeit überlassen wird ...."

[113] *Falco Privatstiftung* (n 106) paras 30–31.

[114] Marly (n 112), 391, 408.

predominant obligation. If that is the display of a particular activity, then the contract shall fall within Article 7(1)(b) as a contract for the provision of services.[115]

The problems that refer to the classification of internet contracts within Article 7(1) Brussels Ibis go beyond the traditional standardized and customizable software products divide or even the traditional or alternative licensing schemes. Cloud computing contracts present a good example. Cloud computing refers, in general, to the delivery of scalable computing services via the internet and despite its limitless technological potential, cloud computing is usually specified in three basic models: (1) Infrastructure as a Service ("IaaS"), where the availability of storage and processing power is the predominant element, (2) Platform as a Service ("PaaS"), which refers to platforms enabling the development of software applications, and, finally, (3) Software as a Service ("SaaS"), where end-user applications become relevant.[116] The legal classification of cloud computing programmes is as complicated as its different models. A first approach submits that all cloud computing contracts irrespective whether they follow the IaaS, PaaS, or SaaS model shall be classified as lease contracts and therefore fall within Article 7(1)(a), as the predominant element in all cloud computing contracts is the continuous and uninterrupted availability of computing services.[117]

A second approach focuses more on the services that accompany the offering of computing services and therefore suggests that all cloud computing contracts shall be classified as contracts for the provision of services under Article 7(1)(b), as the predominant element in those contracts refers to the particular activities of the cloud provider in making the computer services available.[118] The third approach proposes a differentiated classification according to the nature of each cloud computing model. According to this opinion, IaaS (and possibly PaaS) is closer to the contracts for the provision of services and therefore subject to Article 7(1)(b), as the cloud provider shall undertake certain activities in making the offering of computer services available, while SaaS shall be classified as a lease contract, subject to Article 7(1)(a), considering that the cloud provider shall only make the services available to the end user for a limited period.[119] The second opinion that classifies all cloud computing contracts as contracts for the provision of services shall be preferred, as it seems better suited to the flexible nature of cloud computing models (which usually go beyond the mere availability of computing services for a limited period) and comes with the extra benefit of offering a unified solution for all cloud computing models.

The problems related to the localization of the place of performance can be equally thorny, albeit an agreement of the parties on the place of performance, especially for the contracts that fall in Article 7(1)(b), might simplify matters. In absence of such a contractual designation of the place of performance and if the disputed internet contract is either a sales contract or a contract for the provision of services, the definition

[115] Leible (n 110) 308.

[116] For a definition of cloud computing and its different models see W Kuan Hon and C Millard, "Cloud Technologies and Services" in C Millard (ed), *Cloud Computing Law* (Oxford University Press 2013) 1–5.

[117] B Kian, *Cloud Computing-Herausforderung für das Rechtsystem* (Nomos 2016) 35–45.

[118] B Barnitzke, *Rechtliche Rahmenbedingungen des Cloud Computing* (Nomos 2014) 76–77.

[119] In favour of the differentiated approach, C Thole "Die internationale Zuständigkeit bei grenzüberschreitenden Rechts- streitigkeiten über Cloud Computing" in G Borges and JG Meents (eds), *Cloud Computing Rechtshandbuch* (C.H. Beck 2016) 482.

of the place of performance is autonomous and founded on pragmatic considerations.[120] The main purpose of defining the place of performance autonomously in Article 7(1)(b) Brussels Ibis was to secure predictability and proximity,[121] but internet contracts might put these objectives in serious question.

For sales contracts, the CJEU ruled that the requirements of predictability and proximity are better satisfied when the place of performance is located at the Member State where the purchased goods were physically transferred or should have been transferred to the buyer.[122] That such a factual definition of the place of performance can be really challenging in internet-related contracts shall be no surprise. If one takes the example of the supply of digitized products and under the presumption that such contracts could be classified as sales of goods within Article 7(1)(a?), identifying the place where the digitized goods where physically transferred might turn out to be a riddle. It could first be disputed whether a physical transfer is possible, considering the intangible nature of digitized products. Downloading of the digital products to a tangible medium could be a functional equivalent to the physical transfer, but it is not particularly prone to serve the main purposes of the autonomous definition of the place of performance, namely predictability and proximity. By its very nature, downloading of digitized products can occur anywhere. This might lead to unpredictable jurisdictional outcomes, tie the adjudication of contractual disputes with courts that have only trivial connections to the case and nurture excessive forum shopping.[123] Moreover, downloading might not even be possible or necessary as, in many contractual constellations referring to the supply of digital goods, streaming might be a frequent alternative to downloading. If the place of downloading is excluded there are two main possibilities. The first one would be to remain within the premises of Article 7(1)(b) Brussels Ibis and look for an alternative that meets the requirements of predictability and proximity. In that sense, it has been submitted that in contracts related to the supply of digitized goods, the place of performance shall be the domicile of the buyer.[124] Even though such a definition might not be factual, but rather normative, it seems to meet the requirements of predictability and proximity. In online purchases buyers usually share their place of domicile with the seller, so the later will in general be able to predict being litigated before the courts of the Member State of the buyer's domicile. In addition, the localization of the place of performance at the domicile of the buyer offers a certain amount of proximity, albeit not a strictly territorial one. The second possibility would be to render Article 7(1)(b) inapplicable and return to Article 7(1)(a), in which case one shall inquire for a definition of the place of

[120] See the proposal of the Brussels I Regulation COM(1999) 348 final, 14.

[121] See eg Case C-386/05 *Color Drack GmbH v Lexx International Vertriebs GmbH* [2007], paras 24, 26.

[122] Case C-381/08 *Car Trim GmbH v KeySafety Systems Srl* [2010], paras 60–61.

[123] eg if a UK lawyer buys an e-book on IT law from a Dutch online retailer and downloads it in an airport in Cyprus, while waiting a flight to Malta, a strict application of Art 7(1)(b) would afford jurisdiction to the courts of Cyprus, which in that factual circumstance will be neither predictable by the Dutch retailer nor will be closely related to the case, whose main procedural elements will be located mostly in the UK and the Netherlands.

[124] FF Wang, *Internet Jurisdiction and Choice of Law* (Cambridge University Press 2010) 56.

performance according to the law applicable to the contract. Article 7(1)(a) should be inapplicable to the downloading or streaming of digital content or software as the original rationale for the close proximity between the place of performance in sales contracts, that is, the place of delivery, was the fact that this is the place where the risk and ownership passes from the seller to the buyer. The same is not true for digital content and software.

Problems of localizing the place of performance might also occur for contracts that refer to the online provision of services. If one accepts, for example, that cloud computing contracts fall within Article 7(1)(b) as contracts for the provision of services, the actual place of performance of these services, due to the delocalized, shifting nature of cloud computing, might be open to debate, especially because they might be divided between numerous possible countries. Nonetheless, the case law of the CJEU is rather promising. In *Wood Floor* the Court provided for a flexible cascade of possible places of performance of the services, shall they be offered in a multitude of countries.[125] After reiterating the importance of a contractual designation of the place of performance, the Court submitted that, in the absence of such an agreement on the place of performance, focus shall be shifted to the place where the service provider has mainly performed the relevant activities. The Court allowed a flexible assessment of all the circumstances of the case for the place of the main delivery of services to be localized. Finally, if the circumstances of the case do not offer a clear assessment on where the service provider has mainly acted, the Court affords the power to adjudicate to the courts of the domicile of the service provider. Despite the criticism expressed in legal literature,[126] the solution of the Court is rather flexible, fair, and tied to the factual circumstances of each individual case. Under this ruling, proximity is defined in a wider context and Member State judges can go beyond strictly factual territorial links in assessing where the service provider mainly acted,[127] making thus the analysis of internet-related cases easier. Moreover, the domicile of the service provider as the ultimate jurisdictional alternative offers a high level of legal certainty, without necessarily neglecting proximity, as the courts of the provider's domicile will almost always be somehow connected to a dispute in procedural terms, considering that the service provider is the party that affects the characteristic obligation and therefore his or her centre of interests, territorially manifested in his or her domicile, might provide for crucial procedural modalities (eg existence of evidence, better chances of enforcement).

[125] Case C-19/09 *Wood Floor Solutions Andreas Domberger GmbH v Silva Trade SA* [2010], paras 38–42.

[126] See eg M Lehmann, "Exclusive Jurisdiction (Art. 24)" in A Dickinson and E Lein (n 11) 155.

[127] The flexibility of the Court in assessing the place where the service provider has mainly performed the relevant activities must also be methodologically praised. By defining the proximity of the designated court to the disputed case in wider and not strictly territorial terms, the Court went beyond the grammatical interpretation of Art 7(1)(b), but it did so justifiably, in the sense that the solution adopted is more loyal to the purpose of the provision, even if its grammatical limits would, in this case, be narrower. Instead of insisting in a formalistic approach, the Court decided to secure the realization of the objectives of Art 7(1)(b). That such judicial flexibility can and shall be the case in continental private international law see J Esser, *Grundsatz und Norm* (Mohr Siebeck 1990) 242–66. It is this kind of judicial flexibility that can offer valuable adaptations of the traditional EU private international law patterns to the challenges of the internet.

3.4 Choice of law—Article 4 Rome I

The designation of the law applicable to internet contracts in absence of a choice of law agreement is generally less troublesome than the designation of the jurisdictional venue. Article 4 of the Rome I Regulation provides for adequate solutions that are immune to the particularities of internet transactions.[128] Article 4(1) will in general tie the law applicable to internet-related contracts to the habitual residence of the party affecting the characteristic performance, for all contracts that can be classified within the contractual types listed there. If, for example, contracts for the supply of digital products are considered as contracts for the sale of goods, the law applicable will be the law of the country where the online seller is habitually resident. Article 4(2) establishes the same principle for mixed contracts or contracts that do not fall in one of the contractual types listed in Article 4(1), minimizing thus the problems of legal characterization. Finally, the escape rules of Article 4(3) and (4) secure the reassessment of the necessary amount of proximity of the law applicable to each individual internet contract, if necessary, through a flexible assessment of all the circumstances of the case.

4. Special EU rules for jurisdiction and law Applicable for non-contractual obligations

Article 7(2) Brussels Ibis contains the special jurisdictional rule regarding non-contractual obligations and due to its wide scope of application it will frequently be employed in internet-related tortious activities. According to Article 7(2) actions related to torts can, in addition to the defendant's domicile, be brought before the Courts of the place where the harmful event occurred or might occur. The underlying principle that justifies the adoption of this rule is fostering better terms of administration of justice,[129] as the courts of the place of the harmful event display a very strong connection to the tortious dispute at hand.[130]

In interpreting the term "place where the harmful event occurred," the CJEU has consistently declared that the place of the harmful event has a dual nature, and encompasses both the place where the unlawful conduct took place and the place where the primary damage was sustained.[131] The ubiquitous nature of the internet can create serious challenges to this traditional scheme, as it not only leads to the dislocation of

[128] See on that S Leible in R Hüßtege and H-P Mansel, *BGB Rom-Verordnungen* (2nd edn, Nomos 2015) 113.

[129] See section 9.1.2.

[130] Contributing to the realization of the legitimate expectations of the parties for the adjudication of their dispute from a court that can, due to its proximity to the case, provide better terms of administration of justice. See H Dehnert, *Der deliktische Erfolgsort bei reinen Vermögensschäden und Persönlichkeitsrechtsverl etzungen* (Peter Lang 2011) 63.

[131] A solution adopted already in Case C-21/76 *Handelskwekerij G. J. Bier BV v Mines de potasse d'Alsace SA* [1976], paras 15–18.

the two basic prongs of Article 7(2) but also because it makes a multitude of possible jurisdictional venues relevant.[132]

There is already a corpus of CJEU case law that deals with the application of Article 7(2) Brussels Ibis in internet-related contracts. The first general point is that in dealing with internet-related torts, the CJEU has, in general, remained loyal to its classic case law on ubiquitous torts first developed in the *Shevill* case.[133] The case referred to ubiquitous personality infringements via printed media and the Court retained the validity of both prongs of Article 7(2) Brussels Ibis, by allocating jurisdiction both at the place where the infringing material was published (place where the alleged unlawful conduct took place) and at each individual place where the infringing material has been circulated (place where the damage occurred), albeit in the latter case only for the extent of the damage suffered within the respective Member State.[134] The justification for this so-called "mosaic approach" is tied to the proximity of the courts of the Member States where the infringing material has been distributed to the subject matter of the case, as well as the fact that the place of publication will usually (but not always) coincide with the defendant's domicile, thus minimizing the significance of that jurisdictional prong.[135] The CJEU has retained this basic pattern for copyright[136] and national trademark[137] infringements over the internet, declaring that jurisdiction shall be afforded both to the courts of the Member State where the infringing material was made available and to the courts of the Member States where the infringing material caused direct damage, provided that the rightsholder enjoys protection in these Member States.[138] Quite remarkably, the only subject matter that raised heated discussions on the validity of the *Shevill* case law in internet-related situations is that of personality rights,[139] namely the very same subject matter that gave rise to the basic jurisdictional CJEU case law for ubiquitous torts.[140] In *eDate and Olivier Martinez*,[141] the Court decided to modify the *Shevill* case law by adding an additional venue of litigation for the entire damage suffered at the courts of the Member State where the victim of personality infringements has his or her "centre of interests." The CJEU considered that internet publications are easier, faster, and directly accessible to a much wider audience than those of printed media and therefore the victims of personality rights must be privileged with a claimant jurisdiction. Not surprisingly the decision

[132] See R Pichler, *Internationale Zuständigkeit im Zeitalter globaler Vernetzung* (C.H. Beck 2008) 502, who makes special reference to the ubiquitous nature of the internet as the real challenge in terms of allocating international jurisdiction for non-contractual relationships.

[133] First adopted in Case C-68/93 *Fiona Shevill v Presse Alliance SA* ECLI:EU:C:1995:61.

[134] ibid para 33.

[135] ibid paras 29–32.

[136] Case C-170/12 *Peter Pinckney v KDG Mediatech AG* [2013], para 47; Case C-441/13 *Pez Hejduk v EnergieAgentur NRW GmbH* [2015], para 38.

[137] Case C-523/10 *Wintersteiger AG v Products 4U Sondermaschinenbau GmbH* [2012], para 39.

[138] See further Chapter 12.

[139] See further Chapter 11.

[140] In legal literature, all possible opinions have been represented. For a detailed account of the discussions and proposals on how to treat online privacy violations from a jurisdictional point of view see E Márton, *Violations of Personality Rights through the Internet: Jurisdictional Issues under European Law* (Nomos, Hart Publishing 2016) 201–31.

[141] Joined Cases C-509/09 and C-161/10 *eDate Advertising GmbH v X* and *Olivier Martinez v MGN* Limited [2011], paras 48–52.

has caused diametrically opposite reactions. While some commentators considered the *eDate and Olivier Martinez* case law a positive development, which offers a better balance between the victims of personality infringements and proves the adaptiveness of the Court to the particularities of the internet,[142] others expressed a series of valid criticisms.[143]

The second general point refers to the usefulness of internet infrastructure in localizing the first prong of Article 7(2) Brussels Ibis, namely the place where the unlawful conduct has been displayed. In *Wintersteiger*, the CJEU was offered the chance to decide whether the server through which AdWords, infringing national trademarks, are displayed shall be considered the place where the event giving rise to the damage occurs. The CJEU denied that line of thinking by highlighting that the location of a server does not meet the requirement of predictability, as the localization of the server can be difficult to determine. One could add that apart from lacking predictability the place where a server or other internet-related hardware is located might be random and does not possess an adequate amount of proximity to the dispute. Therefore, the rejection of the place of internet equipment as a potential jurisdictional ground on ubiquitous internet torts is in line with the basic principles underlying the function of Article 7(2) Brussels Ibis.

5. *Lis pendens* and related actions

The ubiquitous nature of internet transactions usually allows the allocation of jurisdiction in the courts of different Member States, and will therefore give rise to the institution of parallel legal proceedings for the same subject matter in a multitude of Member States. Such an uncontrollable multiplication of the jurisdictional bases would endanger both procedural economy[144] and decisional harmony within the common justice area. The more Member State Courts involved in the adjudication of a case, the more possible it would be to end up with irreconcilable decisions, a situation that would reduce the trust of the citizens in the common justice area and cause severe difficulties in the circulation of civil judgments across the EU. Defending decision harmony, securing legal certainty, and therefore enhancing the free movement of civil judgments is the general aim of the *lis pendens* and related actions regime established in Articles 29–34 Brussels Ibis Regulation. Article 29(1) Brussels Ibis requires the court second seized to stay its proceedings in favour of the court first seized.

[142] See B Hess, "Der Schutz der Privatsphäre im Europäischen Zivilverfahrensrecht" (2012) JZ 189–93; M Bogdan, "Website Accessibility as Basis for Jurisdiction Under the Brussels I Regulation in View of New Case Law of the ECJ" in D Jerker, B Svantesson, and Stan Greenstein (eds) *Internationalisation of Law in the Digital Information Society* (Ex Tuto Publishing 2013) 167.

[143] C Heinze, "Surf global, sue local! Der europäische Klägergerichtsstand bei Persönlichkeitsrechtsver letzungen im Internet" (2011) EuZW 947–50; A Dickinson, "By Royal Appointment: No Closer to an EU Private International Law Settlement?" (Conflict Of Laws.net, 24 October 2012), <http://conflictoflaws.net/2012/by-royal-appointment-no-closer-to-an-eu-private-international-law-settlement/> accessed 25 July 2020.

[144] See HD Jarass, *Charta der Grundrechte der Europäischen Union-Kommentar* (2nd edn, C.H. Beck 2013), 408.

The Brussels Ibis Regulation has improved the *lis pendens* regime by introducing two major innovations. The first innovation targeted the torpedo actions nurtured by the ruling of the CJEU in *Gasser*.[145] Article 31(3) Brussels Ibis Regulation has modified the *lis pendens* rule, by affording priority to Member States courts that claim jurisdiction based on a jurisdiction agreement. As soon as a Member State court claiming jurisdiction based on prorogation of jurisdiction is seized of a case, all other Member State courts seized of the same case in parallel shall stay their proceedings, irrespective of whether they were seized of the case before or after the forum prorogatum.[146]

The second innovation is established in Article 33 Brussels Ibis Regulation, which introduces a *lis pendens* system that allows Member State courts to consider the pendency of a case before the courts of third state countries (including the UK after Brexit). That rule is very interesting in cases of internet litigation, as the strong international character of internet disputes might lead to parallel proceedings on the same case before Member State and third state courts. The rule of Article 33 Brussels Ibis Regulation allows Member States courts to stay their proceedings in favour of third state courts, if third state courts are expected to give a judgment capable of enforcement in the relevant Member State and if proper administration of justice requires so, echoing to a certain extend the common law *forum non conveniens* mechanism.[147]

6. Recognition and enforcement

The free movement of civil law judgments across different Member States lies at the very centre of the EU private international law ecosystem and penetrates both the legislative initiatives of the EU[148] and the case law of the CJEU.[149] This principle shall be understood as including two separate mandates aiming towards the same direction, that of the creation of a true common civil justice area. The first mandate refers to the axiom of mutual trust between the civil justice systems of the Member States.[150] The creation of a simplified and effective procedure for the recognition and enforcement of another Member State's judgments is the second mandate originating from the principle of free movement of civil law judgments. In conformity with these mandates the Brussels Ibis Regulations has abolished the exequatur procedure,[151] simplifying thus the stipulations of cross-border judgment circulation across the EU, albeit not in the

[145] Case C-116/02 *Erich Gasser GmbH v MISAT Srl* [2003], paras 50–54.

[146] That leaves the door of a reversed torpedo action open. On this issue see C Heinze and B Steinrotter, "The Revised Lis Pendens Rules in the Brussels Ibis Regulation" in V Lasic´and S Stuij (eds), *Brussels Ibis Regulation-Changes and Challenges of the Renewed Procedural Scheme* (Asser Press, Springer 2017) 17–21.

[147] See P Rogerson, P Garcimartin, and M Lehmann, "Lis Pendens and Related Actions (Arts. 29–34)" in A Dickinson and E Lein (n 11) 350.

[148] See eg Recitals 4, 6, 26, 27 of the Brussels Ibis Regulation. For an overview of the current EU models of simplified cross-border recognition and enforcement of civil judgments see M Hazelhorst, *Free Movement of Civil Judgments in the European Union and the Right to a Fair Trial* (Asser Press, Springer 2017) 43–59.

[149] See eg Case C-258/83 *Brennero v Wendel* [1984], para 10.

[150] On Mutual Trust within EU private international law see M Weller, "Mutual Trust: in Search of the Future of European Union Private International Law" [2015] JPIL 64–102.

[151] D Schramm, "Enforcement and the Abolition of Exequatur under the 2012 Brussels I Regulation" (2013) Yearbook of Private International Law 143–74.

revolutionary manner suggested by the original Commission Proposal.[152] Although the procedure for the declaration of enforceability has been removed, Article 45 of the Brussels Ibis Regulation has retained the traditional refusal grounds, shifting the burden of proof to the judgment debtor, making use of the legal remedies of the Member State of enforcement introduced for that reason.

The European Payment Order Regulation[153] as well as the European Small Claims Procedure Regulation[154] prescribe a more simplified recognition and enforcement system. Both Regulations introduce pure EU civil procedural remedies, operating on common standards that render the exequatur procedure as well as the existence of traditional refusal grounds unnecessary. The European Payment Order Regulation establishes a procedure tailored to provide for rapid debt collection for *uncontested* claims.[155] Due to the prima facia uncontested nature of the claims, the first stage of the procedure is mandatory, standardized, and allows only one party, the claimant, to be involved, by submitting the necessary forms before the competent Member State courts. The debtor can take part in a second stage, by lodging a statement of opposition. If no such statement is lodged within the prescribed time limit, the payment order becomes enforceable, without any procedure for declaration and without any possibility of opposing its recognition. Enforcement can be refused only on the basis of the limited grounds provided for in Article 22 of the European Payment Order Regulation.

The European Small Claims Procedure Regulation establishes a genuine EU civil procedural system for claims that do not exceed the amount of Euro 5000. The Procedure is designed to minimize the litigation costs that are usually involved in cross-border cases, as it operates through standardized forms, is usually only written, and if an oral hearing is deemed necessary, the court can make use of modern technologies in conducting the proceedings. No legal representation is required. Like in the European Payment Order, the decision issued under the European Small Claims Procedure is immediately enforceable[156] without any procedure for declaration of enforceability and without any possibility of opposing its recognition. Refusal of enforcement can be invoked for a very limited number of reasons before the courts of the Member State of enforcement.[157]

[152] COM(2010) 748 final.

[153] Regulation (EC) 1896/2006 creating a European order for payment procedure [2006] OJ L399/1.

[154] Regulation (EC) 861/2007 establishing a European Small Claims Procedure [2007] OJ L199/1.

[155] For a more detailed account of the procedure established by the European Payment Order Regulation see X Kramer, "Enhancing Enforcement in the European Union. The European Order for Payment Procedure and Its Implementation in the Member States, Particularly in Germany, the Netherlands, and England" in CH van Rhee and A Ucelac (eds), *Enforcement and Enforceability. Tradition and Reform* (Intersentia 2010) 17–39.

[156] Art 20 European Small Claims Procedure Regulation.

[157] Art 22 European Small Claims Procedure Regulation.

9
Conflicts of Law and Internet Jurisdiction in the US

1. Introduction

US adjudicative jurisdiction operates on the basis of general, common law principles under the focal lens of the Constitutional due process requirement. The interface between US common law and the laws of other countries is governed by the concept of *comity* and this interface includes *both* the scope of the applicability and effect of foreign law within the US legal systems *and* the applicability of US law and US law enforcement vis-à-vis foreign entities (whether defendants or "innocent" third parties). From a US doctrinal point of view, conflicts of law are approached from a bilateral as opposed to multilateral point of view, which focuses on the relationship of the relevant US state or federal legal system with the respective foreign legal system, as opposed to a multilateral approach under international law. This bilateral approach means that reciprocity is an important ingredient in this interface.[1] Furthermore, the common law does not make a sharp distinction between private and public law, or between substantive and procedural law in adjudicative matters, and applies the forum's law to the matter, unless the doctrine of comity, contract, or the presumption against extraterritoriality[2] dictates otherwise. Adjudicative jurisdictional competence is based on the defendant's "minimum contacts" with the forum state and contacts not connected to the dispute in hand are relevant for assessing whether it is "fair" to force the out-of-state defendant to defend an action in the forum court. This is a type of targeting test for jurisdiction as the defendant must have purposefully directed her action to the forum state. While this "minimum contacts" test is inherently flexible and malleable and therefore uncertain, the US rules on adjudicative jurisdiction contain a number of "neutralizers" with the aim of preventing excessive assumption of jurisdiction, and in particular the notion of fair play and substantial justice, the reasonableness doctrine, the test of forum non-conveniens, the comity analysis, and the presumption[3] against the extraterritorial effect of US law. While many aspects of the US principles of jurisdiction have a common origin[4] with principles prevalent in European jurisdictions (such as the doctrine of comity, or the distinction between personal and *in rem*

[1] However, reciprocity as a condition for the enforcement of civil judgments can also be found in civil law countries, see eg s 328 (1) No 5 ZPO (German civil procedure rules).
[2] See discussion in Chapter 1.
[3] See Chapter 1.
[4] See further the discussion in section 2.

Internet Jurisdiction. Julia Hörnle, Oxford University Press (2021). © Julia Hörnle.
DOI: 10.1093/oso/9780198806929.001.0001

jurisdiction, or the recognition of the parties' contractual choice under the doctrine of party autonomy), the US approach is fundamentally different. It is different in its preference for principle-based flexibility and bilateralism, contrasted with a preference for certainty and clear treaty-based rules and a multilateral approach to international law in the EU[5]. What both regions have in common in respect of jurisdiction over conflicts arising online is the continuing trend towards the development of a targeting test. While the US has developed this specifically in respect of internet torts, by contrast, this approach has influenced jurisdiction in respect of consumers,[6] personality rights,[7] and, in a more limited fashion, intellectual property[8] in the EU. Finally, the third marked difference between the rules in the US and the EU is that the EU has far-reaching consumer protection provisions embedded within the harmonized private international law rules, whereas in the US this depends on the application of the unconscionability test under state contract law which varies significantly between states.

This chapter proceeds by way of examining jurisdictional due process and minimum contacts jurisprudence in general, the distinction between general and specific personal jurisdiction and the application of the jurisdictional principles to internet cases. It then continues by looking at specific doctrines and how they have evolved in respect of internet disputes such as the effects doctrine, stream of commerce cases, and e-commerce contracts. The chapter analyses the doctrines tempering the assumption of jurisdiction and governing the interface with foreign law and specifically *forum non-conveniens*, comity and reasonableness.[9] Finally, it examines procedural jurisdiction in the context of adjudications and conflicts of law with regard to (civil litigation) evidence and draws conclusions from the subject matters examined.

2. Adjudicative jurisdiction and US principles

2.1 The Constitutional due process clauses and long-arm statues

The US is a federal state with state and federal jurisdiction, so the different states have varying rules on the jurisdictional competence of their courts (laid down in so-called "long-arm" statutes, named after the image of a long-arm reaching out and pulling the defendant from his state to the court chosen by the plaintiff (the forum)). Each state's long-arm statute determines the jurisdictional reach of the courts located in that state (both state and *federal* courts).[10] The federal courts are part of a unitary federal system as well as the state court system (diversity jurisdiction), thus conflicts of jurisdiction between federal courts are not a pure administrative question of allocating competence.[11]

[5] See Chapter 8.
[6] Chapter 10.
[7] Chapter 11.
[8] Chapter 12.
[9] The rule against extraterritoriality is examined in Chapter 1, as it relates to prescriptive jurisdiction.
[10] *Daimler AG v Bauman* 571 US 117; 134 SCt 746, 771–72 (2014) (Justice Ginsburg).
[11] AT von Mehren and DT Trautman, "Jurisdiction to Adjudicate: A Suggested Analysis" (1966) 79 Harvard Law Review 1121–79, 1123.

The ultimate framework for jurisdictional competence of the courts is the Due Process Clause in the US Constitution, which applies to both intra-US and foreign conflicts.

Thus, US law does not make a distinction between conflicts of jurisdiction between two sister states and conflicts of jurisdiction between a US state or federal court, and a foreign state.[12] Recognition and enforcement of judgments between two US states is ensured by the Full Faith and Credit Clause of the US Constitution,[13] whereas in relation to foreign judgments this is governed by the doctrine of comity discussed in section 5.

The general approach to jurisdiction in the US has two arms, one is to ensure fairness to a defendant in view of the inconvenience of defending an action in a foreign court, the other is to respect the sovereignty of other states (principle of non-interference under international law). While the internet has exacerbated these concerns, they are by no means new. The US Supreme Court found already in 1958:[14]

> As technological progress has increased the flow of commerce between States, the need for jurisdiction over non-residents has undergone a similar increase (. . .) But it is a mistake to assume that this trend heralds the eventual demise of all restrictions on the personal jurisdiction of state courts. Those restrictions are more than a guarantee of immunity from inconvenient or distant litigation. They are a consequence of territorial limitations on the power of the respective States.

Pollack has pointed out that increasing cross-jurisdictional mobility in the late nineteenth and twentieth century has led to an extension of the jurisdictional doctrine and that current internet challenges are an accelerated continuation of this trend, which originally abandoned purely territorial standards such as domicile or presence for the serving of process in favour of the more flexible minimum contacts doctrine.[15] The minimum contacts doctrine is now, in turn, challenged by the increasingly complex commercial arrangements enabled by the internet, which means that a person does not have to move across a border in order to communicate with a person in another state (whether by distributing products or by accessing them). A further evolution arises from cloud computing technologies, which mean that files are hosted and processed in (frequently unknown, domestic, or foreign) locations, with the consequence that files and communications are accessed online but no longer downloaded to a specific user's computer, which would have had a foreseeable location. One of the main advantages of cloud computing is precisely that files can be accessed from many locations and are not controlled locally. Moreover, businesses do not always specifically target a jurisdiction to transact business and obtain commercially valuable benefits.[16] For many digital content products—for example, in the gaming sector—businesses rely on online targeting based on profiling of individual customers instead of a geographically based marketing strategy.

[12] ibid 1122.

[13] Art IV s 1.

[14] *Hanson v Denckla* 357 US 235, 250–51 (1958).

[15] RM Pollack, "'Not of Any Particular State' *J McIntyre Machinery Ltd v Nicastro* and Non-specific Purposeful Availment" [June 2014) 89 *New* York University Law Review 1088–16, 1095–96.

[16] ibid 1099.

The primary concern in the case law is to ensure due process to the defendant, if he has to defend a claim in a foreign forum, that is, not in his state of domicile or residence.[17] The US courts apply the same due process principles in intra-state (ie between two US states) and international (ie concerning a non-US defendant) conflicts of jurisdiction. The Due Process Clause is contained in the Fifth Amendment[18] and Fourteenth Amendment[19] to the US Constitution: "no-one shall be deprived of life, liberty or property without due process of law."[20]

A plaintiff can always sue a defendant in the defendant's domicile or place of residence and in *Pennoyer* the US courts have added mere presence of the defendant in a state for service of process as another ground for assuming jurisdiction over an out of state defendant ("tag jurisdiction").[21] This principle does not apply to the service of process on an executive officer of a company who is temporarily present in a state—it only applies to real persons.[22]

Moreover, a court is also competent if the defendant voluntarily consents to the court's assumption of jurisdiction, for example, by participating in the process. However, outside these four straightforward grounds[23] for assuming jurisdiction over a defendant, residence/domicile, presence, nationality, and consent, there are specific federal statutes that provide for the jurisdiction of the US federal courts based on the (US) nationality of the plaintiff.[24] If none of these bases for jurisdiction apply, the courts will engage in a due process analysis to decide on jurisdiction.

The due process analysis is based on the test formulated in *International Shoe* where the US Supreme held that a plaintiff had to show that the defendant had "minimum contacts" to the forum state such that the assumption of jurisdiction would not offend "notions of fair play and substantial justice."[25] In this case the US Supreme Court found that a Delaware incorporated company with principal place of business in Missouri, which employed around twelve salesmen residing in the State of Washington who regularly solicited business in that state, using samples (only one shoe of a pair) and entertaining some salesrooms there, and who were paid a commission, was present and doing business in Washington so that it was liable to pay contributions to the Washington State unemployment fund. The Court, both the majority Opinion[26] and the concurring Opinion,[27] found that International Shoe was essentially carrying on

[17] *Walden v Fiore* 134 SCt 1115, 1125 (2014).

[18] Federal courts.

[19] State courts.

[20] US Constitution.

[21] *Pennoyer v Neff* 95 US 714, 733; 24 LEd 565 (1878): requiring personal service of process in the forum state; *Burnham v Superior Court* 495 US 604 (1990).

[22] *Martinez v Aero Caribbean* 764 F 3d 1062, 1067–69 (9th Cir 2014); *James-Dickinson Farm Mortgage Co v Harry* 273 US 119, 122 (1927).

[23] See also s 421(2)(a)-(e), (g), (3) American Law Institute, Restatement of the Law Third "Foreign Relations Law of the US, Jurisdiction" (1987); von Mehren and Trautman (n 11) 1137–38.

[24] eg in a civil claim arising on the basis of "international terrorism," see Antiterrorism Act 18 USC ss 2333 and 2334(a).

[25] *International Shoe Co. v State of Washington* 326 US 310, 316; 66 SCt154 (1945).

[26] Mr Chief Justice Stone para 320.

[27] Mr Justice Black para 324.

business in the State of Washington, which made it reasonable for the courts to assume jurisdiction to determine its contributions to the unemployment fund, despite the fact that its business model was constructed in such a way that the contracts were concluded and orders fulfilled from Missouri. The due process doctrine established in *International Shoe* establishing the minimum contacts and notions of fair play and substantial justice standards are now the standard basis[28] for the jurisdictional analysis, including in internet cases.

2.2 "Minimum contacts" and notions of fair play and substantial justice

The meaning of minimum contacts has been examined in the case law of US courts as the first leg of the due process analysis. The courts examine the defendant's contacts with the forum to assess whether he purposefully availed himself of the privilege of doing business in that state to such an extent that he should anticipate being sued there ("purposeful availment").[29] The courts assess whether the defendant does business in the forum state by examining whether he has business contacts there[30] or whether he intended to transact with customers in that location.[31]

Furthermore, the courts have found jurisdiction in the so-called "stream of commerce" cases where a manufacturer or distributor of a product or component of a product was held to be able to foresee that the product might end up in the forum state and cause actionable harm there, especially in the case of famous, globally distributed products in product liability cases.[32]

Finally, the courts have found jurisdiction under the minimum contacts doctrine on the basis that the defendant intentionally targeted a tortious action into the forum state, in cases where the defendant could foresee that his intentional conduct would have actionable harmful effects in the forum ("effects doctrine").[33]

All three doctrines for assessing jurisdiction, purposeful availment, stream of commerce, and the effects doctrine are emanations of the minimum contacts test and their implications for internet cases will be discussed in greater detailin section 4. At this point it is interesting to note that, unlike the EU doctrine, the US minimum contacts

[28] The minimum contacts ruling in the Headnote of Westlaw had been cited 16,786 times on 18 March 2017.

[29] *International Shoe Co. v State of Washington* 326 US 310, 321; 66 SCt 154 (1945); *Hanson v Denckla* 357 US 235, 253 (1958); *World Wide Volkswagen v Woodson* 444 US 286, 297; 100 SCt 559 (1980); *Burger King Corp. v Rudzewicz* 471 US 462, 474–475, 105 SCt 2174 (1985).

[30] *Hanson v Denckla* 357 US 235, 251 (1958): "We fail to find such contacts in the circumstances of this case. The defendant trust company has no office in Florida, and transacts no business there. None of the trust assets has ever been held or administered in Florida, and the record discloses no solicitation of business in that State either in person or by mail."

[31] *McGee v International Life Ins. Co.* 355 US 220, 223; 78 SCt 199 (1957) "It is sufficient for purposes of due process that the suit was based on a contract which had substantial connection with that State" (Mr Justice Black).

[32] S Emanuel, *Emanuel Law Outlines: Civil Procedure* (25th edn, Wolters Kluwer 2015) 9; see *Asahi Metal Industry Co. v Superior Court* 480 US 102, 107 SCt 1026 (1987)—further discussed later.

[33] *Calder v Jones* 465 US 783 (1984).

approach makes no principled distinction between different types of bases of claim, it applies equally to breach of contract cases and non-contractual, tort claims (such as privacy infringements, defamation, trade mark infringement, unfair competition, and copyright infringement). Furthermore, unlike EU doctrine, US jurisdictional analysis places heavy emphasis on an intentional element of the defendant's conduct—the defendant must, in some way, have targeted their conduct to the forum state,[34] albeit that different courts have put different emphasis on whether foreseeability per se is sufficient or whether something else is required (such as deliberately *aiming* his or her conduct or activities at the forum).[35]

Thus, an element of directing or targeting is part and parcel of the minimum contacts doctrine—this is important in particular for internet cases as it limits (but not eliminates) the possibility that a completely fortuitous connection to the forum leads to a finding of jurisdiction.[36] But as we will see in the following sections, the minimum contacts doctrine is flexible and has thus led to confusing and inconsistent case law in respect of internet cases, which in some cases has led to wide jurisdictional reach of the courts and in some cases a denial of access to justice and uncertainty.[37]

However, the potentially wide aspects of targeting can be compensated for and counterbalanced by the second leg of the due process analysis. This second leg is an examination of whether the assumption of specific jurisdiction would comport with notions of fair play and substantial justice ("fairness test"). The fairness test is not always applied in the jurisdictional assessment; in fact it is not always explicitly discussed and in most cases the courts seem to assume that the assertion of jurisdiction complies with notions of fair play and substantial justice.[38]

The purpose of the fairness test is to temper the heat of the jurisdictional analysis—in a metaphorical sense one could think of this test as a kind of "garam masala," the beautiful mix of spices added at the end of cooking in some Indian dishes to rebalance the flavours to the right balance before serving the dish.

In a similar vein, the fairness test has the purpose of finding the right balance between conflicting jurisdictional interests. It weighs up (1) the plaintiff's interest of having justice done[39] and obtain redress, (2) the inconvenience to the defendant of being hauled into a foreign court,[40] (3) the interests of the forum state in adjudicating

[34] *World Wide Volkswagen v Woodson* (n 29) 286, 295–97, 100 SCt 559 (1980); Emanuel (n 32); M Geist, 'Is There a There There? Towards Greater Certainty for Internet Jurisdiction' (2001) 16 Berkeley Technology Law Journal 1345–406, 1385: describes foreseeability as the "core jurisdictional principle."

[35] *Burdick* 233 Cal App 4th 8 (2015); (2016) 43 Western State Law Review 291–95.

[36] M Sableman and M Nepple, "Will the Zippo Sliding Scale for Internet Jurisdiction Slide into Oblivion?" (2016) 20(1) Journal of Internet Law 3–6; Geist (n 34) 1381–85.

[37] A Soo Yeon Anh, "Clarifying the Standards for Personal Jurisdiction in Light of Growing Transactions on the Internet" (2015) 99 Minnesota Law Review 2325–62.

[38] Emanuel (n 32) 9.

[39] *Mac Dermid Inc v Deiter* 702 F 3d 725, 731 (2nd Cir 2012) citing *Chloe v Queen Bee of Beverly Hills* 616 F 3d 158, 173 (2nd Cir 2010).

[40] However, the burden to the defendant is only one of several factors, see eg *Mac Dermid Inc v Deiter* 702 F 3d 725, 731 (2nd Cir 2012): "the conveniences of modern communication and transportation ease what would have been a serious burden only a few decades ago," citing *Kernan v Kurz-Hastings, Inc* 175 F 3d 236, 244 (2d Cir 1999).

the dispute,[41] (4) any conflict with the state in which the defendant is resident, and (5) the practicality of hearing the dispute in the forum state, for example, the location of witnesses[42] and the evidence,[43] or the expertise of the court to deal with disputes of this kind.[44,45]

In some cases the courts have applied a seven-actor test:

(1) the extent of a defendant's purposeful targeting of the forum;
(2) the burden on the defendant in defending in the forum;
(3) the extent of conflict with the sovereignty of the defendant's state;
(4) the forum state's interest in adjudicating the dispute;
(5) the most efficient judicial resolution of the controversy;
(6) the importance of the forum to the plaintiff's interest in convenient and effective relief;
(7) the existence of an alternative forum.[46]

It is interesting to note here that the fairness test balances the interests of the parties with the suitability of the forum[47] (akin to elements of the *forum non-conveniens* analysis) and with state interests (which is similar to the *comity* or *reasonableness* analysis). Its purpose therefore is to blend together, as in the "garam masala" metaphor, a variety of interests of different stakeholders to achieve the most harmonious balance. Frequently, however, the courts have drawn an inference that if the minimum contacts test is passed, that the suit is also reasonable and the courts tend to find that the forum state has an interest in applying its law to foreign defendants.[48]

The relevance of this second element of the due process analysis to internet disputes is that it fits with the argument of those who are concerned that the borderless nature of the internet leads to wide and conflicting assertions of jurisdiction, which should be tempered by a reasonableness analysis. This fairness test could play a role in achieving this reasonableness analysis.[49] It examines the positions of both parties and their respective ability to obtain justice, if they have to cross a border, and the relevant state interests. However, in many cases these interests will pull in opposite directions so that the fairness test does not add much to deal with the uncertainty of the jurisdictional analysis and how to weigh these opposing interests.

[41] See eg *McGee v International Life Ins. Co.*355 US 220, 223; 78 SCt 199 (1957): "It cannot be denied that California has a manifest interest in providing effective means of redress for its residents when their insurers refuse to pay claims" (Mr Justice Black).

[42] See eg *McGee v International Life Ins. Co.*355 US 220, 223; 78 SCt 199 (1957): "Often the crucial witnesses—as here on the company's defense of suicide—will be found in the insured's locality" (Mr Justice Black) and *Mac Dermid Inc v Deiter* 702 F 3d 725, 731 (2nd Cir 2012).

[43] *Feldman v Google, Inc* 513 F Supp 2d 229, 247 (ED Pa 2007).

[44] *Feldman v Google, Inc* 513 F Supp 2d 229, 248 (ED Pa 2007).

[45] *Asahi Metal Industry Co. v Superior Court* 480 US 102, 114–16; 107 SCt 1026 (1987).

[46] *Burger King Corp. v Rudzewicz*, 471, 476-7 US 479, 105 SCt 2185; *Panavision v Toeppen* 141 F 3d 1316, 1323 (9th Cir 1998).

[47] See also 28 USC s 1404(a): For the convenience of parties and witnesses, in the interest of justice, a district court may transfer any civil action to any other district or division where it might have been brought or to any district or division to which all parties have consented.

[48] See eg *CompuServe, Inc. v Patterson*, 89 F 3d 1257, 1268 (6th Cir1996) or *Keeton v Hustler Magazine, Inc* 465 US 770, 776; 104 SCt 1473 (1984).

[49] Pollack (n 15)1112–16.

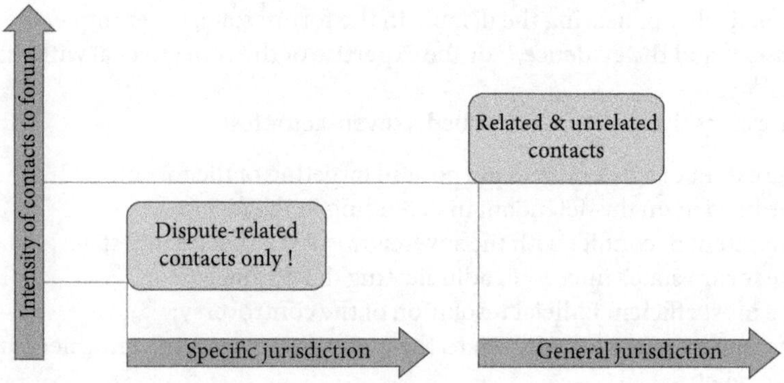

Figure 9.1 Specific and General Jurisdiction before Goodyear and Daimler

2.3 Personal jurisdiction: general and specific

In analysing minimum contacts, the courts in the US make a distinction between two types of personal jurisdiction over an out of state defendant: general and specific.

General jurisdiction gives the court power to rule on any dispute involving the defendant, even if his or her minimum contacts with and business conduct in the forum are completely unrelated to the dispute before the court. For general jurisdiction the claim need not arise from the defendant's contacts with the forum state.[50] This makes his or her minimum contacts to the forum almost akin to establishment or residence or domicile.[51] By contrast, specific jurisdiction gives the court competence to decide only a specific dispute where the defendant's contacts with the forum relate to this specific dispute. For a finding of specific jurisdiction the claim on which the action is based must arise from the defendant's contacts with the forum state.[52] Thus, for a finding of general jurisdiction the court examines all contacts of the defendant with the state, whereas for a finding of personal jurisdiction the court only takes into account the contacts and conduct which are directly relevant to the dispute in which the defendant has to defend himself.

At the same time the hurdle to find general jurisdiction is much higher—both quantitatively and qualitatively. The defendant's contacts to the forum must be more intensive, compared to a finding of specific, personal jurisdiction.

Before two Supreme Court cases decided in 2011 and 2014, discussed later, it was generally thought that the difference between specific and general jurisdiction is a question of degree and depends on the intensity of the defendant's contacts with the forum (Figure 9.1). The rule was, that, for a finding of general jurisdiction the defendant had to have *substantial, continuous and systematic* contacts.[53] Thus, if a

[50] Emanuel (n 32) 51.

[51] F Fangfei Wang, *Internet Jurisdiction and Choice of Law* (Cambridge University Press 2010) 65.

[52] Emanuel (n 32) 51.

[53] *Perkins v Benguet* 342 US 437, 448 72 SCt 413 (1952); *Helicopteros Nacionales de Colombia, SA v Hall* 466 US 408, 415–16; 104 SCt 1868 (1984).

corporation had substantial, continuous, and systematic business connections with the forum state, even if these connections had nothing to do with the dispute before the court, the lower courts did find that this could be sufficient for general jurisdiction over the defendant. However, it is clear that the US Supreme Court has always set the bar for a finding of general jurisdiction fairly high.

For example, *Helicopteros Nacionales de Colombia* concerned claims brought by the family of US citizens killed in a helicopter crash against the Columbian company who had provided services to a Texas-based joint venture. The contacts of the Columbian company, all unrelated to the claim, were three-fold: (1) the chief executive had travelled to Texas to negotiate the transportation services contract, (2) the Columbian company had accepted cheques drawn on a Texan bank, and (3) it had bought some helicopters, equipment, and training services in previous years in Texas. However, these limited contacts were held by the US Supreme Court not to be sufficiently continuous and substantial to justify a finding of general jurisdiction.[54]

The jurisdictional bar has been raised even higher by two US Supreme Court decisions in *Goodyear Dunlop Tires Operations v Brown*[55] and *Daimler AG v Bauman*.[56] In *Goodyear* the Supreme Court held unanimously that a corporation normally only has continuous and systematic contacts in the place where it is "essentially at home."[57] *Goodyear* was a product liability claim concerning the death of two minors in a coach accident in France, which was blamed on a defective tyre. The question was whether the parents could bring an action in the courts of North Carolina. The defendants were three foreign Goodyear subsidiaries domiciled in France, Turkey, and Luxemburg who were responsible for producing tyres for the European and Asian markets and the evidence showed that a certain number of tyres manufactured in Turkey found their way to the market in North Carolina, however, none of these tyres were of the same kind as that which deflated in the accident. The US Supreme Court held that this connection is too limited to justify general jurisdiction.[58] Additionally, it limited the application of general jurisdiction by finding that, "for an individual, the paradigm(atic) forum for the exercise of general jurisdiction was the individual's domicile, and for a corporation, it was an equivalent place, namely one in which the corporation is fairly regarded as at home."[59] Although Justice Ginsburg did not state what amounted to a corporation being fairly regarded as at home, she indicated that this may mean a corporation's domicile, place of incorporation, or principal place of business.[60]

In *Daimler* the US Supreme Court outlined further the meaning of the place where a corporation was essentially at home, and limited this as a matter of principle to the place of incorporation of a company or its principle place of business.[61]

[54] *Helicopteros Nacionales de Colombia, SA v Hall* 466 US 408, 415–16; 104 SCt 1868 (1984).

[55] *Goodyear v Brown* 564 US 915, 131 SCt 2846 (2011).

[56] 134 SCt 746 (2014).

[57] Paras 919, 924 (Justice Ginsburg delivering the Opinion of the Court).

[58] Para 920; para 929 on different facts, if the bus accident had occurred in North Carolina and the subsidiaries had actively distributed the tire there, a finding of specific jurisdiction under the stream of commerce doctrine would have been likely.

[59] Para 919.

[60] Para 924, referring to L Brilmayer et al, "A General Look at General Jurisdiction" (1988) 66 Texas Law Review 721–83, 781.

[61] *Daimler* (n 10) 760–61.

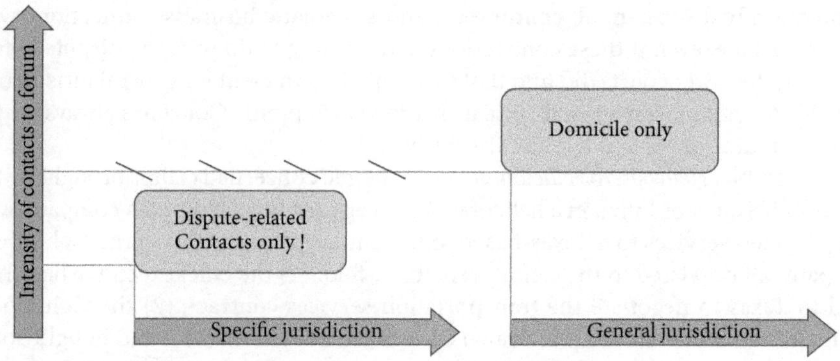

Figure 9.2 Specific and General Jurisdiction after Goodyear and Daimler

Before *Goodyear* and *Daimler* the scope of general jurisdiction was not approached consistently by the lower courts and some courts did find jurisdiction based on minimum contacts. It seems that since these two US Supreme Court cases, general jurisdiction requires domicile (in the case of individual defendants) or establishment (in the sense of place of incorporation or principal place of business). Although it should be noted that the US Supreme Court left open the possibility of a finding of general jurisdiction outside these parameters in exceptional cases. In such an exceptional case a company may be subject to general jurisdiction in a forum other than its principal place of business or its place of incorporation if its connections are so substantial and of such a nature as to render the company virtually at home in that forum state (Figure 9.2).[62]

For internet cases this means that contacts established through a website are unlikely to give rise to general jurisdiction.

Before *Goodyear* and *Daimler* some of the lower courts had established minimum contacts sufficient for general jurisdiction based on internet contacts. For example, in *Gator.com Corp v L.L.Bean, Inc* the 9th Circuit[63] based general jurisdiction on substantial or continuous and systematic contacts with California in the form of extensive marketing and sales.[64] L.L. Bean had no presence or establishment in the state, in the sense that it had no shops, no office, no agents for serving process, was not licensed to do business, was not incorporated, and did not pay tax there, but conducted extensive marketing and resulting sales there. Six per cent of its e-commerce sales worth millions of dollars took place in California and the Court of Appeals found that these contacts "approximate" physical presence and, based on the economic reality of the contacts, held that the Californian courts may assert jurisdiction.[65] The Court concluded that

[62] Restatement of the Law Fourth—the Foreign Relations Law of the US Jurisdiction, Tentative Draft No 2 (22 March 2016) s 302 Reporters Notes, 114 and *Daimler* (n 10) 761.

[63] *Gator.ComCorp. v L.L. Bean, Inc.* 341 F 3d 1072 (9th Cir 2003).

[64] The case concerned *Gator* seeking a declaratory relief that its practice of subjecting e-commerce websites to pop-up advertising by a competitor of that e-commerce website (paid, presumably by that competitor) is not a trademark infringement or act of unfair competition.

[65] Paras 1077–79.

"its website is clearly and deliberately structured to operate as a sophisticated virtual store in California"[66] and that "even under the heightened standard applied to general jurisdiction, the consistent and substantial pattern of business relations represented by these facts is sufficient to confer general jurisdiction."[67] Finally, the Court also found that this assertion of jurisdiction is reasonable, finding that the inconvenience to L.L. Bean was not disproportionate given that it regularly visits vendors in California and is a multi-million dollar turnover business.[68] However, this ruling was subsequently overturned when the 9th Circuit granted an *en Banc* rehearing (which cancelled out the precedent character of the previous Decision).[69] Another example is the case of *Gorman v Ameritrade* where the District of Columbia Circuit held that general jurisdiction may arise from Ameritrade (a securities broker) doing business via the internet (selling of securities through an online account) in the District.[70] The dispute was entirely unrelated to the selling of securities, but concerned an agreement to allow *Gorman* established in Virginia to set up a hyperlink from Ameritrade's homepage to his estate agency business website. He brought suit in DC and, on appeal, Circuit Judge Garland held that the DC courts can base general jurisdiction on the fact that Ameritrade may have extensive business contacts with DC residents and that therefore jurisdictional discovery should have been allowed as a matter of jurisdiction.[71]

Generally speaking, however, the lower courts, because of the high threshold of the general jurisdiction test, have been reluctant to find general jurisdiction on the basis of the operation of a website.[72] Now, after *Daimler*, this will be even more unlikely absent any truly exceptional circumstances.

3. *In rem* and *quasi in rem* jurisdiction

US courts also assume jurisdiction in the forum in which the defendant's property is located.[73] If the dispute is connected to the property this type of jurisdiction is called *in rem* jurisdiction.[74] However, courts have also assumed jurisdiction where the dispute is unrelated to the property and the dispute is merely based on the courts' power over the property for enforcing a judgment debt—*quasi in rem* jurisdiction.[75] For the latter type of jurisdiction the due process principles apply requiring minimum contacts and reasonableness as for personal jurisdiction.[76] Furthermore, *in rem* and *quasi*

[66] Para 1078.
[67] Para 1078.
[68] Para 1081.
[69] *Gator.ComCorp. v L.L. Bean, Inc.* 366 F 3d 789 (9th Cir 2004) the case settled which rendered the jurisdiction question moot: 398 F 3d 1125.
[70] 293 F 3d 506, 512–13 (2002).
[71] Para 513.
[72] WF Patry, "Section 17:185 The Internet and Personal Jurisdiction Generally" Patry on Copyright (March 2017 Update Westlaw)," and *Revell v Lidov* 317 F 3d 467 (5th Cir 2002); *Lakin v Prudential Securities Inc* 348 F 3d 704,712 (8th Cir 2003); *ALS Scan Inc v Digital Service Consultants, Inc* 293 F 3d 707, 715 (4th Cir 2002).
[73] *Shaffer v Heitner* 433 US 186, 199; 97 SCt 2569 (1977).
[74] Domain names and *in rem* jurisdiction is examined in Chapter 12.
[75] von Mehren and Trautman (n 11)1121–79.
[76] ibid 209 and Restatement of the Law Fourth (n 62) s 302 Reporters Notes, 117.

in rem jurisdiction is limited to the value of the property concerned.[77] *In rem* jurisdiction has been used in domain name disputes to find jurisdiction in the state where the domain name registry is located. The Anti-cybersquatting Consumer Protection Act allows the owner of a trademark to sue in the place of the domain name registry.

4. Internet cases: jurisprudence

4.1 Specific personal jurisdiction

The courts, when applying the "minimum contacts" test, have almost consistently found that mere access to a website is not sufficient as a basis for finding personal jurisdiction, but that "something more" is required.[78] This something more is the targeting approach under the minimum contacts doctrine discussed earlier, the defendant must have purposefully directed conduct towards the forum residents in such a way that it can be said that "the defendant makes the choice to dive into a particular forum."[79] Defining this "something more" has proved to be highly elusive and has resulted in different, overlapping jurisdictional tests being applied to internet jurisdiction cases.

In tort cases concerning data "theft," privacy invasion, and computer misuse (illegal access to and misuse of personal information) the question arises whether the location of the data, that is, the place where the data is physically stored, is relevant for the jurisdictional analysis.[80] The courts have found jurisdiction on the basis that the defendant knew that the email servers she used and the confidential files she misappropriated were centrally hosted at her former employer's place in Connecticut.[81] However, as data are increasingly stored on remote cloud computing servers it is unlikely that defendants know where data are located, so that the courts are more likely to focus on location of the plaintiff as the location of the injury, especially where the defendant was in direct contact with the plaintiff.[82] Thus, server location is unlikely to be determinative of jurisdiction.

The common approach of the courts is to insist on a degree of foreseeability and deliberate conduct to provide the connection with the forum state. One of the first US Supreme Court cases that elucidated this approach was *World-Wide Volkswagen Corp. v Woodson*.[83] This was a personal injury case where the defendants had driven

[77] ibid 199 and 117.

[78] *Cybersell, Inc. v Cybersell, Inc.* 130 F 3d 414 (9th Cir 1997).

[79] Patry (n 72), ," see also *Qwest Communications Intern., Inc v Sonny Corp* 2006 WL 1319451 (WD Wash 2006).

[80] For the discussion of the same question in relation to criminal jurisdiction see Chapter 4.

[81] *Mac Dermid Inc v Deiter* 702 F 3d 725, 730 (2nd Cir 2012) (computer misuse and misappropriation of trade secrets): "Deiter purposefully availed herself of the privilege of conducting activities within Connecticut" because she was aware "of the centralization and housing of the companies' e-mail system and the storage of confidential, proprietary information and trade secrets" in Waterbury, Connecticut, and she used that email system and its Connecticut servers in retrieving and emailing confidential files."

[82] *Microsoft Corp v Mountain West Computers Inc* 2015 WL 4479490 (US District Court WD Washington 2015) 7: "Regardless of whether Defendants knew where Plaintiff's servers were located, Defendants admit that they knew Microsoft is located in Washington. Even though Defendants' contacts with Plaintiff were made remotely, they knew Plaintiff to be located in and operating out of the State of Washington." (Copyright infringement action concerning allegations of the use of unlicensed software.)

[83] 444 US 286 (1980); 100 SCt 559.

a car across the US and had an accident in Oklahoma, allegedly due to a defect in the car. The defendants, that is, the distributor and the retailer of the Audi car, had sold the car in New York state and had no business contacts as such with Oklahoma. The plaintiffs, nevertheless, filed their claim in Oklahoma and the US Supreme Court held by a majority[84] that theoretical foreseeability on the part of the defendants that someone might drive a car to Oklahoma and have an accident there, cars being inherently highly mobile consumer goods, was not sufficient for a finding of minimum contacts, and that the defendant's contacts with the forum must be more than fortuitous. The adjective "fortuitous" is meant here in the sense that this was where the harm happened. Under the US doctrine, the driving to Oklahoma would be regarded as a unilateral act of the plaintiffs, which cannot be imputed to the defendants.[85]

However, the US Supreme Court has held that for jurisdiction over a defendant to exist, the defendant need not have physically entered the forum state at any point—mere regular dealing and contractual relationships, including an express jurisdiction clause in a franchising contract, are sufficient:[86]

> It is an inescapable fact of modern commercial life that a substantial amount of commercial business is transacted solely by mail and wire communications across state lines, thus obviating the need for physical presence within a State in which business is conducted.

A much cited first instance, 1997 US District Court case *Zippo*[87] established the parameters for internet cases by defining what intentional conduct and business contacts sufficient for the establishment of jurisdiction means. The case is a domain name dispute alleging trademark infringement and dilution brought by the manufacturer of *Zippo* lighters (based in Pennsylvania) against an internet news portal (based in California). *Zippo* set out a test distinguishing between merely passive websites, which do no more than host information that can be accessed online at one end of the spectrum (no jurisdiction[88]), and fully interactive, fully e-commerce enabled websites, which are virtual shopfronts allowing transactions to take place at a distance. For the latter, jurisdiction would be proper if the defendant actively conducts business over the internet, thus establishing electronic contacts.[89] For the websites in the middle of the continuum, the degree of interactivity is decisive. Thus, the Court developed the so-called sliding scale, which requires the court to assess the degree of interactivity of a website in order to see where on the scale the website is situated, based on the notion that "the likelihood that personal jurisdiction can be constitutionally exercised is directly proportionate to the nature and quality of commercial activity that an entity conducts over the Internet."[90] In the actual *Zippo* case the Pennsylvanian court found that it had jurisdiction, since the defendant was doing business over the internet,

[84] With a strong dissent by three judges: Justices Marshall, Blackmun, Brennan.
[85] Paras 295–98.
[86] *Burger King Corp. v Rudzewicz*, 471, 476 US 479, 105 SCt 2185.
[87] *Zippo Mfg Co v Zippo Dot Com, Inc* 952 F Supp 1119 (US District Court WD Pennsylvania).
[88] See also *Bensusan Restaurant Corp. v King*, 937 F Supp 295 (SDNY 1996).
[89] See also *CompuServe, Inc. v Patterson*, 89 F 3d 1257 (6th Cir 1996).
[90] Paras 1124–25.

allowing people to subscribe to its newsgroup services over the internet, and 2 per cent of its customers were resident in the forum state.[91]

Zippo has been preceded by cases where the courts had found *specific* personal jurisdiction grounded on (1) the defendant doing business in the forum over the internet and (2) repeated electronic contacts with the forum as the "minimum" contacts required. For example, in *CompuServe, Inc v Patterson*,[92] Mr Patterson, a lawyer based in Texas, distributed a software developed by him as shareware through CompuServe's platform. The contract with CompuServe stipulated Ohio law as being applicable to the contract, but had no express jurisdiction clause. When he alleged that CompuServe infringe his trademark/engaged in unfair competition, CompuServe quickly filed for a declaration that their product does not infringe Mr Patterson's rights, in their local courts in Ohio. The Court found jurisdiction on the basis that Mr Patterson had repeatedly uploaded his software to the platform of an Ohio based company, he must have known that this company was in Ohio, it was an ongoing business relationship that had lasted for three years, and that these repeated electronic contacts are sufficient for a finding that he purposefully availed himself of the privilege of doing business in Ohio.[93] It is peculiar that one of the supporting grounds for jurisdiction was that Mr Patterson had addressed email and correspondence to CompuServe in Ohio concerning his trademark/unfair competition infringement claims.[94] This is peculiar because it raises the question of how else would any plaintiff send a letter before action to the other party, so that this ground always exists in *any* dispute.

The sliding scale test established in *Zippo* has been applied in a number of cases following it, which examined the degree of interactivity of a website and depending on where on the scale a case was held to sit, jurisdiction was either found[95] or denied.[96] Indications for a high degree of interactivity were held to be a website were users could effect an initial loan application, chat online with an employee of the bank, and send an email where a response rate of an hour was guaranteed,[97] or where customers could buy a fitness shirt (a fitness app) through the website, allowing for communication and inviting potential customers to contact the company,[98] or where customers could select "Utah" from a dropdown menu, indicating that the website was interacting with customers from that state.[99]

Insufficient interactivity was held to be a website that merely posts information about the defendant's products and contains a printable mail-order form, telephone

[91] Para 1126.

[92] *CompuServe, Inc. v Patterson*, 89 F 3d 1257 (6th Cir 1996).

[93] Paras 1263–64, quoting *Burger King Corp. v Rudzewicz* 471 US 462, 474–75, 105 SCt 2174 (1985).

[94] Para 1266.

[95] *Citigroup Inc v City Holding Company* 97 F Supp 2d 549 (US District Court SDNY 2000); *Sarvint Technologies, Inc. v Omsignal, Inc.* 161 F Supp 3d 1250 (US District Court ND Georgia 2015); *Zing Bros., LLC v Bevstar, LLC* 2011 WL 4901321 (US District Court Utah 2011).

[96] *Mink v AAAA Development LLC* 190 F 3d 333 (5th Cir 1999); *Best Van Lines v Tim Walker* 490 F 3d 239 (2nd Cir 2007); *Oldfield v Pueblo De Bahia Lora, SA* 558 F 3d 1210 (11th Cir 2009); *Millenium Enterprises Inc v Millenium Music LP* 33 F Supp 2d 907 (United District Court Oregon 1999).

[97] *Citigroup Inc v City Holding Company* 97 F Supp 2d 549, 565 (US District Court SDNY 2000).

[98] *Sarvint Technologies, Inc. v Omsignal, Inc.* 161 F Supp 3d 1250, 1259 (US District Court ND Georgia 2015).

[99] *Zing Bros., LLC v Bevstar, LLC* 2011 WL 4901321, at *3 (US District Court Utah 2011).

number, and email address, when orders were not taken through that website and there was no sign that the defendant conducts business through the internet[100] and the posting of allegedly defamatory comments on a feedback website about home removal businesses.[101]

Even though the 1997 *Zippo* has been described[102] as "seminal authority regarding personal jurisdiction based upon the operation of an Internet web site," in recent cases[103] and literature[104] it has also been described as obsolete. Contemporary websites are unlikely to be purely passive websites, only hosting information, but most websites allow for highly interactive communications and allow the defendant to conduct business transactions remotely:

> Virtually all websites, even those created with only minimal expense, are now interactive in nature. It is an extraordinarily rare website that does not allow users to do at least some of the following: place orders, share content, "like" content, "retweet," submit feedback, contact representatives, send messages, "follow," receive notifications, subscribe to content, or post comments. And those are only interactions immediately visible to the user. In fact, most websites also interact with the user "behind the scenes" through the use of "cookies."[105]

It is no understatement to say that the very essence of the internet is interactivity in communications, marketing, and business conduct—which makes this an unsuitable factor for determining specific jurisdiction. It is also not very sensible to merely focus on the nature of the website in "internet cases" and ignore the nature of the underlying dispute and basis of the claim (breach of contract, misleading online advertising, trademark infringement, privacy, defamation, etc).[106] Moreover, it is not necessarily clear why the degree of interactivity of a website is supposed to be decisive and not an assessment of the defendant's conduct as a whole. Furthermore, if the defendant actively aims harm into the forum through the publication of defamatory contents, that is, the publication of information classified as passive under the *Zippo* sliding scale, it does not make sense to focus on the degree of interactivity of the website. Conversely,

[100] *Mink v AAAA Development LLC* 190 F 3d 333, 337 (5th Cir 1999).

[101] *Best Van Lines v Tim Walker* 490 F 3d 239 (2nd Cir 2007).

[102] *Toys "R" Us, Inc. v Step Two SA* 318 F 3d 446, 452 (3rd Cir 2003).

[103] *Toys "R" Us, Inc. v Step Two SA* 318 F 3d 446, 452 (3d Cir 2003); *Kindig It Design, Inc v Creative Controls, Inc* 157 F Supp 3d 1167, 1173–75 (US District Court Utah 2016); *Caiazzo v American Royal Arts Corp.* 73 So 3d 245 (District Court of Appeal of Florida 2011); *Hy Cite Corp. v Badbusinessbureau.com, L.L.C.* 297 F Supp 2d 1154, 1160 (WD Wis 2004); *Carlson v Fidelity Motor Group LLC* 860 NW 2d 299, 305 (Wis Ct App 2015).

[104] KA Meehan, "The Continuing Conundrum of International Internet Jurisdiction" (2008) Boston College International and Comparative Law Review 345–369; H Hestermeyer, "Personal Jurisdiction for Internet Torts" (2006) 26 Northwestern Journal for International Law & Business 266–288; Fangfei Wang (n 51) 70; Geist (n 34) 1371; Pollack (n 15)1101; Sableman and Nepple (n 36) 3; BD Boone, "Bullseye Why a Targeting Approach to Personal Jurisdiction in the E-commerce Context Makes Sense Internationally" (2006) 20 Emory International Law Review 241–78, 257–58.

[105] *Kindig It Design, Inc v Creative Controls, Inc* 157 F Supp 3d 1167, 1174 (US District Court Utah 2016) US (District Court Judge Jill N Parrish).

[106] Sableman and Nepple (n 36) 4.

a website can be highly interactive but target only local residents (eg such as the website of a local take-away restaurant).[107]

Therefore *Zippo* has not clarified what the "something more" is, which is required to subject a defendant whose website can be accessed in the forum state. This means it is essential to fall back on the multi-factor calculus in the minimum contacts doctrine described above.[108]

Irrespective of *Zippo*, the flexibility of the minimum contacts test is likely to lead to inconsistency between court decisions and a high degree of unpredictability. Pollack[109] cites a number of US court decisions in which purchasers of vintage cars and paintings acquired on eBay sued sellers in their local jurisdiction—the courts came to different conclusions about whether the buyers' courts had jurisdiction[110] or not.[111]

In particular, the courts have decided the question whether the defendant has minimum contacts in the sense of transacting business in manifold ways.[112] For example, some courts have held that a single negotiation process or entering into a single contract is sufficient where the communication was targeted at a particular state.[113] In *Deutsche Bank Securities, Inc v Montana Board of Investments*[114] the New York Court of Appeals, for example, honed in on the fact that the defendant (based in Montana) had initiated a new set of negotiations with the plaintiff (whose principal place of business in New York was known to the defendant) through instant messaging. Thus, the fact that the Montana Board of Investments had reached out to a New York investment bank was seen as sufficient for jurisdiction in New York. By contrast, in other cases the courts have held that there must be a course of business transactions targeted at a particular state and a single transaction is not sufficient.[115] Sometimes the courts examine fairness arguments in addition to the nature and quality of the contacts, considering the nature of the parties involved (protecting consumers and individual investors) as part of the minimum contacts analysis.[116]

[107] *Kindig It Design, Inc v Creative Controls, Inc* 157 F Supp 3d 1167, 1173–75 (US District Court Utah 2016).

[108] Section 2.2.

[109] Pollack (n 15).

[110] *Erwin v Piscitello* 627 F Supp 2d 855, 856 (ED Tenn 2007): jurisdiction based on telephone calls and making use of the internet for business contacts directed at Tennessee; *Dedvukaj v Maloney* 447 F Supp 2d 813, 816–17 (ED Mich 2006); jurisdiction based on transaction of business in Michigan through email messages and telephone calls, accepting the winning bids in the eBay auction, confirming shipping charges to Michigan and accepting payment and the degree of interactivity of the eBay auction website.

[111] *Boschetto v Hansing* 539 F 3d 1011, 1014 (9th Cir 2008): single eBay sale with buyer in California insufficient to establish jurisdiction over Wisconsin seller: "once the car was sold the parties were to go their separate ways"; *Hinners v Robey* 336 SW 3d 891, 893 (Ky 2011).

[112] KD Johnson, "Measuring Minimum Contacts over the Internet: How Courts Analyze Internet Communications to Acquire Personal Jurisdiction over the Out-of-state Person" (2007) University of Louisville Law Review 313–33, 325–31.

[113] *Chloe v Queen Bee of Beverly Hills* 616 F 3d 158, 165–67 (2nd Cir 2010) (one shipping of a counterfeit bag to plaintiff's lawyers in New York sufficient—as part of other contacts with New York which demonstrated a larger business plan directed at customers in New York).

[114] 850 NE 2d 1140 (NY 2006).

[115] *Rothschild, Unterberg, Torbin v McTamney* 449 NE 2d 1275 (NY 1983): call by an individual investor to a New York stockbroker not sufficient for jurisdiction in New York; *Boschetto v Hansing* 539 F 3d 1011, 1014 (9th Cir 2008).

[116] *Dedvukaj v Maloney* 447 F Supp 2d 813, 822-3 (ED Mich 2006); *Rothschild, Unterberg, Torbin v McTamney* 449 NE 2d 1275 (NY 1983).

4.2 *Calder v Jones* and "effects doctrine"

In the seminal defamation case *Calder v Jones* the US Supreme Court[117] established the so-called effects test. In this case a Californian entertainer brought an action for libel in California against the writer and the editor of a Florida based magazine, the *National Enquirer*.

In some ways the label given to the *Calder v Jones* test is a misnomer, as jurisdiction under this test is not grounded on harmful "effects" within the forum state alone but on the defendant purposefully targeting their tortious conduct to the forum state, in such a way that the brunt of the harmful effects were caused there and this was foreseeable for the defendant, as the plaintiff lived and worked there and the magazine had its largest circulation in California.[118] The Court concluded:

> the allegedly libelous story concerned the California activities of a California resident. It impugned the professionalism of an entertainer whose television career was centered in California. The article was drawn from California sources, and the brunt of the harm, in terms both of respondent's emotional distress and the injury to her professional reputation, was suffered in California. In sum, California is the focal point both of the story and of the harm suffered.[119]

Interestingly, in *Calder v Jones* the US Supreme Court held that First Amendment considerations should not influence the jurisdictional analysis but that questions of free speech should only be dealt with in the substantive law analysis.[120]

This analysis was applied in an early internet case, concerning cybersquatting, *Panavision v Toeppen*.[121] Mr Toeppen registered multiple trademark protected brands of well-known businesses such as Panavision as generic top-level domain names, then allocated them on a first-come, first-serve basis, with the intention of selling them to the trademark owner. The Court found that Mr Toeppen's acts were aimed at Panavision with its principal place of business in California and caused it to suffer injury there (trademark dilution)[122]—the defendant did not merely register a domain name (while never leaving Illinois) he actively pursued a strategy to sell the domain name to the Californian company and this was sufficient for the Californian courts having jurisdiction.[123]

The *Calder v Jones* analysis, however, leaves open the question whether it is sufficient that the defendant foresees where the plaintiff will suffer the brunt of the harm[124] (so in a defamation case this would be, for most people, the place where they have the focus of their life, ie where they have a reputation) or whether the defendant needs to

[117] 465 US 783, 104 SCt 1482 (1984).
[118] Para 1486.
[119] Para 1486.
[120] Para 1487.
[121] 141 F 3d 1316 (9th Cir 1998).
[122] Para 1321.
[123] Para 1322.
[124] Similar to the centre of interest test developed by the CJEU, see Chapter 10.

actively target the forum state as such,[125] not just the defendant. This distinction becomes apparent in two internet defamation cases where jurisdiction was at issue.

In the first, *Young v New Haven Advocate*,[126] two Connecticut regional newspapers, some of whose articles were published online on their respective websites, had reported on a controversial and much debated prisoner transfer programme, which led to mostly black prisoners being sent south to Virginia. Mr Young was a prison warden in a Virginia prison and he claimed that he had been defamed in these newspaper articles as a racist. Based on *Calder v Jones*, one would have expected the courts in Virginia to have jurisdiction as Mr Young lived and worked in Virginia and this was where he would have felt the brunt of the harm to his reputation—and the plaintiffs were aware of both these factors. However, the US Court of Appeals for the 4th Circuit established a new "audience targeting" test.[127] It declined jurisdiction on the basis that the articles were published in two regional newspapers targeted only at local readers in Connecticut and were therefore not aimed at an audience in Virginia, and hence not at the forum. The Court held that in internet defamation cases it was necessary to "manifest an intent to aim the websites or the posted articles at" the forum's "audience,"[128] even though the reporters had made some calls and interviewed people on the phone in Virginia—one of the newspapers had two handful of subscribers in Virginia—and even though the story was centred around prisons in that state. The Court, on the facts, however, decided that the article focused *more* on Connecticut than Virginia as it discussed the implementation of the policy there and its negative effect on the prisoners and their families.[129] Arguably, this argument is deeply flawed, as readers in Virginia, in a state likewise affected by the prison policy, would also have been interested in this debate and, even though the articles were published in regional newspapers,[130] they would have found these articles through search engines and republication on other internet sources.

The second case, *Burdick v Superior Court*,[131] concerns a claim for defamation made on the defendant's Facebook wall. The Californian plaintiffs are medical scientists who ran a blog "Barefacedtruth.com" in which they exposed a skin care product as unsafe and defective. The representatives of the skin care company reacted with a campaign of harassment including allegedly defamatory statements on Facebook that associated the plaintiffs with fraud and domestic violence. The Californian courts declined to assert jurisdiction and found that the plaintiffs had failed to show that the Facebook post had been aimed or targeted at California, in particular there was no evidence that the Facebook posts had been accessed in California.

[125] See also *Shrader v Biddinger* 633 F 3d 1235, 1240 (10th Cir 2011).

[126] 313 F 3d 256 (4th Cir 2002).

[127] See also SH Ludington, "Aiming at the Wrong Target: the 'Audience Targeting' Test for Personal Jurisdiction in Internet Defamation Cases" (2011–12) Ohio State Law Journal 541–74, 552.

[128] 313 F 3d 256, 258–59 (4th Cir 2002).

[129] 313 F 3d 256, 263–64 (4th Cir 2002).

[130] From the case report, though it is not entirely clear whether there was evidence that the two articles complained of were in fact published online. Circuit Judge Michael states in his Opinion that the plaintiff "alleged" that they were so published, but the evidence he adduces relate to print outs from the websites which do not contain the offending articles at para 258.

[131] 233 Cal App 4th 8 (2015); (2016) 43 Western State Law Review 291–95.

The Californian Court in particular referred to the US Supreme Court decision in *Walden v Fiore*.[132] The context of *Walden v Fiore* is not internet related, the case concerns the seizure of cash from the plaintiffs in Puerto Rico and later action by a Georgia-domiciled US drug enforcement official at Atlanta airport suspecting the money to be the proceeds of crime. The plaintiffs then travelled to their destination in Las Vegas, Nevada, the money was eventually returned and they brought proceedings against the immigration official in Nevada. The US Supreme Court held that it was not sufficient for jurisdiction over a defendant that the defendant could foresee where the injury would fall (here the immigration official knew that the plaintiff were Nevada residents when conducting the search, and seizure of the money). The US Supreme Court held that the *tort itself* must be *aimed* at the forum *state* and declined jurisdiction.[133] Therefore the minimum contact analysis must focus on the defendant's contacts with the forum state itself, not the defendant's contacts with persons who reside in the forum state.[134] However, in *Walden* the US Supreme Court distinguishes the case before it from defamation cases in that defamation requires publication of the libel to third parties and hence it is the publication in the forum state that may provide the link between the defendant and the forum state.[135] By contrast, none of the defendant's conduct at the airport in Atlanta linked him with Nevada: "the effects of [defendant's] conduct on [plaintiffs] are not connected to the forum State in a way that makes those effects a proper basis for jurisdiction."[136]

These three cases show a trend to find that the defendant being able to foresee that the defendant would suffer the, direct or indirect, effects of the harm in their state of residence is not sufficient to fulfil the purposeful availment test under the minimum contacts doctrine. In addition, the plaintiff must have actively aimed the tort into the forum state, for example, by targeting a communication or publication there, such that it can be said that jurisdiction is based on the defendant's conduct (and not merely linking him to a plaintiff resident in the forum).[137] However, it should also be noted that *Walden* has not overruled *Calder v Jones*, but distinguished it for publication/communication torts. Furthermore, the narrowing of the doctrine in *Calder v Jones* in *Burdick* (in a state court) does not as such change federal law—thus it can be said that *Calder v Jones* is good law and can be applied to internet communication torts.

In *Keeton*,[138] decided in the same year as *Calder v* Jones (1984), the plaintiff was a New York resident who claimed to have been defamed in a nationally circulated magazine by the defendant, an Ohio corporation. She brought proceedings in New Hampshire where 10–15,000 copies, a small proportion of the overall circulation numbers of the magazine, had been distributed, for the reason that this state had a

132 *Walden v Fiore* 134 SCt 1115 (2014).

133 Paras 1123–24.

134 Paras 1122–23.

135 Para 1124.

136 Para 1125; although one could argue that the harm of the tort had effects in Nevada when the plaintiffs were unable to access their money. Under EU law, a similar distinction has been made between direct harmful effects and indirect harmful effects, which are more remote: see *Marinari* and *Dumez v Hessische Landesbank*.

137 W Schildknecht, "Justice for J-Law? Specific Personal Jurisdiction Over Internet Torts in the Wake of *Walden v Fiore*" (2016) 56 Santa Clara Law Review 1–32, 10–11.

138 *Keeton v Hustler Magazine, Inc* 465 US 770, 104 SCt 1473 (1984).

particular long limitation period, whereas the limitation period had run out in other states. Even though neither the plaintiff[139] nor the defendant had any contacts with New Hampshire other than the publication of the magazine, the US Supreme Court found, nevertheless, that New Hampshire may assert jurisdiction since the defendant corporation had established minimum contacts through its publication of a substantial number of copies:

> Such regular monthly sales of thousands of magazines cannot by any stretch of the imagination be characterized as random, isolated, or fortuitous. It is, therefore, unquestionable that New Hampshire jurisdiction over a complaint based on those contacts would ordinarily satisfy the requirement of the Due Process Clause that a State's assertion of personal jurisdiction over a non-resident defendant be predicated on 'minimum contacts' between the defendant and the State."[140]

This decision has to be seen in the light of the "single publication rule" for mass media in the US,[141] a doctrine that allows a plaintiff to sue for defamation in respect of the same publication (eg the same edition) only once,[142] but may recover damages for the whole harm to reputation in this one action, not just the harm to reputation suffered in that state, but the harm to reputation suffered in all states.[143] The single publication rule applies to defamation on the internet.[144]

This stands in contrast to the "mosaic" doctrine adopted, for example, by the Court of Justice of the EU (CJEU) in *Shevill*,[145] which allows the plaintiff to sue in each and every jurisdiction where she has suffered harm, but in relation to each proceedings only for the damage to reputation suffered in that particular state. It has sometimes been argued that the mosaic theory is more burdensome for the protection of freedom of expression, as multiple actions against the same defendant potentially have an intimidating effect on the publisher, editor, and author of the statement.[146] However, it can be equally argued that the single publication rule (to the extent that it is a rule of jurisdiction) is likewise burdensome to the defendant (and hence for freedom of expression), as it makes it much easier for the plaintiff to recover substantial damages and shop for an opportunistic forum, as happen in *Keeton*. This is of particular relevance to defamatory publications on the internet whose publication and impact may be spread over several states. For internet defamations this means that if a plaintiff can prove that the statement has been "published" in a jurisdiction, the plaintiff may be able to recover the whole loss there, which is likely to mean that she can pick and choose the forum among several states, and thus engage in forum shopping.

139 The Court found that the plaintiff did not have to have a reputation (before the publication) in the forum state at para 777.

140 Para 774.

141 Said so expressly by the Supreme Court, para 778.

142 Once in time and once in place (only in one forum court).

143 Restatement (Second) of Torts s 577A (1977).

144 *Firth v State*, 98 NY 2d 365, 370, 747 NYS 2d 69 (2002).

145 Case C-68/93 *Fiona Shevill v Presse Alliance SA* discussed in Chapter 10.

146 See the discussion Chapter 10 and LA Wood, "Cyber-defamation and the Single Publication Rule" (2001) 81 Boston University Law Review 895–915, 897–98.

4.3 Stream of commerce cases

The stream of commerce cases is an interpretation of the minimum contacts doctrine in product liability (and other tort) cases where a manufacturer or distributer of widely spread, well-known products can foresee that a substantial number of them would end up in the forum state through the normal distribution process (and not as an isolated, fortuitous, and unexpected incident). As in many other sectors of the economy, globalized production and distribution systems fuelled by technology make this basis for asserting jurisdiction more relevant, as products cross national borders more frequently in the twenty-first century than ever before.

The leading authority in this field is the US Supreme Court case of *Asahi*[147] concerning product liability litigation over an allegedly defective valve between a Japanese defendant and a Taiwanese claimant. A valve stem manufactured by a Japanese company was incorporated into a tyre assembled by a Taiwanese company, which in turn was used for a Honda motorcycle. The tyre suddenly deflated, thus causing serious injuries to a Californian resident. The US Supreme Court (four votes to four) had no majority on the question of minimum contacts.[148]

However, half the Justices held that the Japanese company *had minimum contacts* to California, as it knew that its valve would ultimately be incorporated in a product distributed worldwide, and therefore it was entirely foreseeable that a significant number of the products would end up in California:[149]

> The stream of commerce refers not to unpredictable currents or eddies, but to the regular and anticipated flow of products from manufacture to distribution to retail sale. As long as a participant in this process is aware that the final product is being marketed in the forum State, the possibility of a lawsuit there cannot come as a surprise.[150]

However, the majority also held that in this instance it would be unreasonable for the Californian courts to assume jurisdiction since it would not comply with the notion of fair play and substantial justice. The main claim concerning damages for injuries sustained had been settled and the US courts had no interest in determining liability in an indemnity dispute between two foreign companies and the pieces of evidence concerning the litigation would also be abroad.[151]

The stream of commerce doctrine was applied in the internet copyright infringement litigation concerning the Grokster peer-to-peer file sharing technology.[152] Grokster, Kazaa, and Streamcast distributed software which facilitated the free exchange of digital media files (including copyrighted music and films) via a peer-to-peer transfer network. The software had been provided to approximately two million

147 *Asahi Metal Industry Co v Superior Court of California* 480 US 102, 107 SCt 1026 (1987).

148 Justice Stevens finding that it was not necessary to decide the issue.

149 Paras 117–21.

150 Para 117.

151 Paras 114–16.

152 *Metro-Goldwyn-Mayer Studios Inc v Grokster Ltd* 243 F Supp 2d 1073 (United States District Court CD California 2003).

California resident users (compared to 143 million downloads worldwide) and they executed the relevant end-user licence agreements. In addition the defendant, Sharman Networks, engaged in some limited commercial contacts such as those with advertising vendors, and public relations and legal representatives.[153] However, the Court held that these contacts were unrelated to the copyright infringement claim and therefore not relevant for a finding of specific jurisdiction.[154] The Californian courts found specific, personal jurisdiction on the basis that the sheer number of downloads of the software made it foreseeable that a substantial number would have occurred in California.[155]

The stream of commerce doctrine has been significantly narrowed in the 2014 US Supreme Court plurality decision in *J McIntyre Machinery Ltd v Nicastro*[156] where the court denied a finding of specific personal jurisdiction.

In this case an English manufacturer of metal shearing machinery had appointed and used a general distributor of its specialist equipment in Ohio for the whole of the US, and only one machine (possibly four of them) ended up in New Jersey. This machine was alleged to have been defective and injured an employee in New Jersey. Since the manufacturer had not specifically marketed their equipment to New Jersey, the Court found there was no personal jurisdiction, so that the liability question could not be heard.[157] It held that mere foreseeability is insufficient[158] and that "it is the defendant's actions, not his expectations that empower a State's courts to subject him to judgment."[159] First of all, a significant minority (four to nine) of the total Court based this finding on a new principle that a finding of jurisdiction in stream of commerce cases is proper only if the defendant has targeted the specific forum *state* (New Jersey) and that the appointment of a distributor in *Ohio* for the whole of the US was not sufficient for a finding of jurisdiction of the New Jersey state courts. By contrast, a federal court may exercise personal jurisdiction based on sufficient contacts with the US as a whole (in accordance with the Due Process Clause of the Fifth Amendment).[160]

The Court in *McIntyre* focused on sovereignty and the state's authority over a defendant and less on due process for the defendant. This case has clear implications for internet cases and e-commerce. While some online conduct may be targeted at a specific state of the US, much conduct will not be so targeted at all. This ruling suggests that unless a putative defendant's tortious conduct is specifically targeted at a particular US state (and absent any other deliberate and related business conduct in that state) there is no specific jurisdiction over that defendant. This is even though the defendant deliberately did not exclude his product from any state and intended

[153] Paras 1083–84.

[154] Para 1085.

[155] Para 1087; as an alternative the Court also considered the *Calder v Jones* effects test as a ground for showing minimum contacts.

[156] *J. McIntyre Machinery, Ltd. v Nicastro* 564 US 873, 131 SCt 2780 (2011).

[157] Paras 877, 882: "The defendant's transmission of goods permits the exercise of jurisdiction only where the defendant can be said to have targeted the forum; as a general rule, it is not enough that the defendant might have predicted that its goods will reach the forum State."

[158] Para 883.

[159] Para 883 (Justice Kennedy).

[160] *Holland v America Line Inc v Wartsila North America Inc* 485 F 3d 450,462 (9th Cir 2007); *Pinker v Roche Holdings Ltd* 292 F 3d 361, 369 (3rd Cir 2002); Restatement of the Law Fourth (n 62) s 302 Reporters Notes, 112.

and expected to sell to the whole of the US.[161] Should a seller, who deliberately targets the market of the whole of the US, benefiting from market entry in a large territory, not also expect to be sued in any of the fifty states of the US? It is not clear why a producer or distributor who deliberately does not target his product only to particular states and therefore benefits from a much larger market and larger economies of scale should escape being sued in any state that is part of that larger market.[162] This ruling is a blow in the face of product liability plaintiffs (be they employees or consumers) and is another example of the trend to favour the efficiency of transnational commerce (or e-commerce) over access to justice for plaintiffs in product liability cases. It is precisely the nature of many internet transactions (although McIntyre was not an "internet case") that the defendant will have purposefully directed their actions at a large geographical area, transcending any specific jurisdiction. It is the deliberate and purposeful, but non-specific targeting of a larger geographical area that makes it difficult to apply the minimum contacts doctrine.[163] Such cases (and internet disputes will frequently be paradigmatic) involve a stark "all or nothing" choice between finding that the defendant has targeted more than one state or none at all. As an alternative approach the courts should consider to what extent it was possible for the defendant to avoid a particular market (eg through geolocation tools) and question whether or not the defendant should have the burden of defending itself in a foreign forum on the basis that it did not take measures to avoid a particular market.[164]

4.4 Jurisdiction clauses in contracts

US law recognizes and enforces express jurisdiction (forum selection) clauses in contracts[165] as the choice of the parties in the absence of some compelling and countervailing reason making enforcement unreasonable.[166] Consent is one of the traditional bases for a finding of jurisdiction over a defendant.[167] The jurisdiction clause is either

[161] This is what distinguishes this case from *Woodson*—here it was the efforts of *McIntyre* and their US distributor that caused the sale and installation of the defective machine in New Jersey, not a unilateral act of the plaintiff (as in *Woodson*).

[162] Justice Ginsburg delivered the powerful minority opinion, see paras 905, 904: "On what measure of reason and fairness can it be considered undue to require McIntyre UK to defend in New Jersey as an incident of its efforts to develop a market for its industrial machines anywhere and everywhere in the United States?"

[163] Further discussion in Pollack (n 15).

[164] TE Wandell, "Geolocation and Jurisdiction: From Purposeful Availment to Avoidance and Targeting on the Internet" (2011) 16 Journal of Technology Law & Policy 275–305, 287.

[165] Before the US Court ruled in *M/S Bremen* in 1972 it was disputed in the different Circuits whether forum selection clauses in advance of the dispute were against public policy, see eg *Carbon Black Export Inc. v The Monrosa* 254 F 2d 297 (CA5 1958), cert dismissed, 359 US 180, 79 SCt 710 (1959); see also Restatement of the Law Third (n 23) 308; Restatement of the Law Fourth (n 62) s 302 Reporters Notes, 112; *National Equipment Rental Ltd v Szukhent* 375 US 311, 316 (1964): "parties to a contract may agree in advance to submit to the jurisdiction of a given court."

[166] *M/S Bremen v Zapata Off-Shore Co.* 407 US 1, 12–13; 92 SCt 1907 (1972); see also *TradeComet.com LLC v Google Inc* 647 F 3d 472 (2nd Cir 2011); Art 5(1) Hague Convention on the Choice of Court Agreements of 30 June 2005, this has not been ratified by the US.

[167] Emanuel (n 32) 15.

enforced by transfer between different US District Courts[168] or alternatively by dismissal under the Federal Rules of Civil Procedure.[169]

Thus, a "freely negotiated private international agreement, unaffected by fraud, undue influence or overweening bargaining power should be given full effect."[170] The clause can only be set aside if it contravenes the strong public policy of the forum[171] and the party who applies to have the clause set aside has a heavy burden of proof showing such countervailing strong public policy or that the clause is contained in an unenforceable adhesion contract or that the particular dispute is outside the contract.[172] The US Supreme Court held in *M/S Bremen*: "The expansion of American business and industry will hardly be encouraged if, notwithstanding solemn contracts, we insist on a parochial concept that all disputes must be resolved under our laws and in our courts"[173] and that "the choice of that forum was made in an arm's-length negotiation by experienced and sophisticated businessmen, and absent some compelling and countervailing reason it should be honored by the parties and enforced by the courts."[174] Before the US Supreme Court ruling in *M/S Bremen*, it was disputed in the different Circuits whether forum selection clauses in advance of the dispute were against public policy even in business-to-business contracts, as was held, for example, in *Carbon Black Export Inc. v The Monrosa*.[175] But it should also be noted that even after *M/S Bremen* not all Circuits have been following the *M/S Bremen* decision consistently. In particular, a small minority of Circuits had decided not to automatically enforce an express jurisdiction clause where the jurisdictional conflict is between two US federal courts.[176] The US Supreme Court decision of *Atlantic Marine* confirmed that the transfer provision can be used to decide on the enforcement of a forum selection clause, but it limited the discretion previously allowed to the District Courts in deciding whether to enforce a forum selection clause. The US Supreme Court made clear that normally such a forum selection clause *should be upheld*. The Court stated that "when parties have agreed to a valid forum-selection clause, that clause should be given controlling weight in all but the most exceptional cases, and a district court should ordinarily transfer case to the forum specified in [the] clause."[177]

Unlike under EU law,[178] a jurisdiction clause in a contract with a significant power imbalance between the parties, such as a business-to-consumer contract[179]

[168] 28 USC s 1404(a) and *Jumara v State Farm Ins Co* 55 F 3d 873, 877 (3d Cir 1995); *Salovaara v Jackson Nat'l Life Ins Co* 246 F 3d 289, 298–99 (3d Cir 2001).

[169] FRCP Rule 12(b)(3) improper venue.

[170] *M/S Bremen v Zapata Off-Shore Co.* 407 US 1, 12–13; 92 SCt 1907 (1972).

[171] See also Art 6(c) Hague Convention on the Choice of Court Agreements of 30 June 2005.

[172] Paras 15–19.

[173] Para 9.

[174] Para 12.

[175] 254 F 2d 297, 301 (5th Cir 1958), cert dismissed, 359 US 180, 79 SCt 710 (1959): "universally accepted rule that agreements in advance of controversy whose object is to oust the jurisdiction of the courts are contrary to public policy and will not be enforced," see also *Insurance Co of North America v N. Stoomvaart-Maatschappij* 201 F Supp 76, 78 (ED La 1961).

[176] 28 USC s 1404(a).

[177] *Atlantic Marine Const Co Inc v US Dist. Court for Western Dist. of Texas* 571 US 49; 134 SCt 568, 579 (2013).

[178] See Brussels Regulation (Recast) 1215/2012/EU Arts 17–19 (consumers); Arts 20–23 and the Hague Convention on the Choice of Court Agreements of 30 June 2005 Art 2(1).

[179] *Carnival Cruise Lines v Shute* 499 US 585, 111 SCt 1522 (1991) discussed further in Chapter 10.

is, in principle at least, valid and enforceable. In *Burger King v Rudzewicz*[180] the US Supreme Court upheld jurisdiction in favour of *Burger King's* local courts in Florida against a Michigan established franchisee[181] who clearly had no negotiation power in this respect.[182] The franchise agreement did not provide for an express jurisdiction clause but provided that the franchise relationship was based in Miami, that the contract was governed by Florida law, and that all payments had to be made to, and all notices given to, *Burger King's* headquarters in Miami. The US Supreme Court held that an individual's contract with a party in another state *alone* may not be sufficient to establish minimum contacts with that other state, but that the antecedent negotiations, anticipated consequences, the contract terms, and the course of dealing between the parties may. The US Supreme Court in particular considered that "Upon approval [of the contract], he [*Rudzewicz*] entered into a carefully structured 20-year relationship that envisioned continuing and wide-reaching contacts with Burger King in Florida. In light of *Rudzewicz'* voluntary acceptance of the long-term and exacting regulation of his business from Burger King's Miami headquarters" he was taken to have minimum contacts with that state.[183] Hence even where a contract has no express jurisdiction clause, other provisions of the contract are taken into account to establish minimum contacts and due process.

Jurisdiction in business-to-consumer contracts and the control of adhesion contracts through the doctrine of unconscionability is further discussed in Chapter 10.

5. Additional principles: forum non-convenience, comity, and reasonableness

Like English law, US law also recognizes the common law doctrine of *forum non-conveniens*: s 304 of the draft (2016) *Restatement* Fourth states that "a court in the US may dismiss a case if there is an available and adequate alternative forum and (. . .) the balance of private and public interests favor dismissal."[184] Private interest considerations include convenience to the litigants such as access to sources of evidence, including witnesses, and also the enforceability of any judgments resulting.[185] The public considerations relate to interests such as the courts' workload, the need to apply foreign laws to the dispute, and how localized the dispute is.[186] For a transfer between two

[180] 471 US 462, 105 SCt 2174 (1985).

[181] The Florida long-arm statute provided that courts in Florida have jurisdiction in disputes about a contractual obligation that should have been performed in Florida and here the contractual obligation was payment, which the contract located at the Miami headquarters. Hence the examination of under what circumstances a contract can establish minimum contacts is to ensure Constitutional due process.

[182] However ,the US Supreme Court did point out that the two franchisees were experienced business people and were legally advised throughout their negotiations with Burger King—I would argue though that there probably was no room for any negotiation on the terms of the franchise agreement, which is borne out by the facts described by the Court, the franchisees negotiated for five months and managed to obtain only some very minor concessions. It seemed that the Court would only consider the proposing party's bargaining advantage as relevant if it amounted to fraud or economic duress, see para 2189.

[183] Paras 2185–86.

[184] Restatement of the Law Fourth (n 62) s 304.

[185] *Gulf Oil Corporation v Gilbert* 330 US 501, 508 (1947).

[186] ibid para 509.

US federal courts *forum non-conveniens* has been codified.[187] However, the doctrine has continuing application to cases where the alternative forum is foreign and allows US courts to dismiss a case over which it has jurisdiction otherwise, even before it has decided on the issue of jurisdiction,[188] "when considerations of convenience, fairness and judicial economy so warrant."[189] Under federal law there is a requirement that the plaintiff has access to an available and adequate forum, where the parties will not be deprived of a remedy or treated unfairly.[190] Expiry of the limitation period in the alternative forum means that this condition is not fulfilled and *forum non-conveniens* does not apply in such a case.[191] The US Supreme Court has also held on several occasions that ordinarily if a US court has jurisdiction, the plaintiff's choice of forum should not be disturbed and that the defendant has a strong burden to rebut the presumption that the chosen forum should hear the case.[192] This deference to the plaintiff's choice of forum was never accorded to the same extent to non-US residents—in fact the US Supreme Court has held in *Piper* that "a foreign plaintiff's choice of [a US court] deserves less deference."[193] But since the doctrine only applies if there is an alternative available foreign court whose decision will be enforced in the US, it is less concerning than the doctrine of extraterritoriality[194] in relation to its impact on foreign plaintiffs seeking redress before the US courts.

The doctrine of comity is unique to the US understanding of private international law. It is not practised in other states, and it is not part of customary international law.[195] It concerns the interface between US law and foreign law and has been described as a bridge between US law and foreign law.[196] It provides a practical framework for the interfaces between private litigation, public policy, and the public functions of the courts.[197]

The doctrine has been stated in the much cited 1895 case of *Hilton v Guyot*:[198]

> Comity in the legal sense, is neither a matter of absolute obligation on the one hand nor of mere courtesy and good will upon the other. But it is the recognition which one nation allows within its territory to the legislative, executive or judicial acts of another nation, having due regard both to international duty and convenience, and

[187] 28 USC s 1404(a) see *Atlantic Marine Const Co Inc v US Dist. Court for Western Dist. of Texas* 134 SCt 568, 580 (2013).

[188] Restatement of the Law Fourth (n 62) s 304 Reporters' Notes, 127.

[189] *Sinochem Intern Co Ltd v Malaysia International Shipping Corp* 549 US 422, 432; 127 SCt 1184 (2007).

[190] *Piper Aircraft Co. v Reyno* 454 US 235, 254; 102 SCt 252 (1981); *Gulf Oil Corporation* (n 185) 501, 506–07.

[191] Restatement of the Law Fourth (n 62) s 304 Reporters' Notes, 130 citing *Bank of Credit and Commerce International v State Bank of Pakistan* 273 F 3d 241, 246 (2nd Cir 2001); *DiFederico v Marriott Intern.* 714 F 3d 796, 801–02 (4th Cir 2013); *Fireman's Fund Ins. Co. v Thyssen* 703 F 3d 488 (10th Cir 2012); *Chang v Baxter* Healthcare 599 F 3d 728, 736 (7th Cir 2010).

[192] *Piper Aircraft Co. v Reyno* 454 US 235, 255; 102 SCt 252 (1981); *Sinochem Intern Co Ltd v Malaysia International Shipping Corp* 549 US 422, 430; 127 SCt 1184 (2007); *Gulf Oil Corporation v Gilbert* (n 185).

[193] *Piper Aircraft Co. v Reyno* 454 US 235, 256; 102 SCt 252 (1981), see also the discussion in Restatement of the Law Fourth (n 62) s 304 Reporters' Notes, 131.

[194] Discussed in Chapter 2.

[195] JR Paul, "Comity in International Law" (1991) 32(1) Harvard International Law Journal 1–78.

[196] ibid 5.

[197] ibid.

[198] 159 US 113, 164 (1895) (Justice Horace Gray).

to the rights of its own citizens or of other persons who are under the protection of its laws.

US courts use the doctrine of comity for three purposes in cases with a foreign element. It enables the US courts to make a decision (1) to refrain from applying US law or to decline jurisdiction (in favour of another state court or arbitration),[199] (2) to apply foreign law ("prescriptive comity"),[200] and (3) to aid or prevent the enforcement of a foreign judgment or arbitral award in civil and commercial matters.[201]

As is apparent from the formulation in *Hilton v Guyot* quoted above, it is unclear to what extent the principle contains a legal obligation, binding on US courts, subject to exceptions or to what extent it simply gives the court a discretionary power to make the decisions enumerated above. This uncertainty includes the question of whether the principle of comity only applies if the *foreign* law gives effect to *US law* on a reciprocal basis or whether reciprocity is assumed as a matter of good international relations, in the sense that, if US courts show a willingness to accommodate foreign law and a foreign legal system in this way, it is hoped that foreign courts will do the same (in the future). In any case, the formulation confer on the courts a significant discretion in their treatment of foreign law.[202]

Interestingly, in *Hilton v Guyot* itself the US Supreme Court ultimately applied reciprocity and declined to recognize ("give full faith and credit" to) and enforce a French executory judgment in which a French liquidator sought to recover a debt against a US defendant for the reason that the French courts did not allow for the enforcement of foreign debts. But it should also be noted that the Court did *not* include reciprocity in the formulation of the principle.

In the *Yahoo! v LICRA* case the US Court of Appeals used the doctrine of comity to explain why it would not enforce the French courts' prohibitive injunction ordering *Yahoo!* to filter out access from French internet protocol (IP) addresses to Nazi memorabilia content on the Yahoo! auction site and subjecting Yahoo! to a fine for non-compliance on a daily basis. This injunction was *potentially* not enforceable for two separate reasons. First, that the enforcement would be unconstitutional as an infringement of the First Amendment of the US Constitution. A plurality of the Court found that the standard under the principle of comity according to which a judgment would not be enforced is that it must be *repugnant* to public policy (which is a higher bar than just being merely *inconsistent* with US law[203]).[204] Second, and the plurality of the US Court found this the more likely alternative, according to the doctrine of comity, US courts would simply not enforce a foreign public sanction such as a monetary penalty or fine against a US company.[205] But in the end, the Court found that effectively

[199] WS Dodge, "International Comity in American Law" (2015) 115 Columbia Law Review 2071–141, 2103.

[200] ibid 2100.

[201] ibid 2101, 2105.

[202] Paul (n 195) 11.

[203] However, the minority found that First Amendment rights could well be engaged: para 1235.

[204] Para 1215.

[205] *Yahoo! Inc. v La Ligue Contre Le Racisme Et L'Antisemitisme* 433 F 3d 1199, 1210, 1218–19 (9th Cir 2006).

it did not have to rely on the principle of comity in the case before it, since *Yahoo!* had voluntarily complied with the order (subject to some exceptions) or it did not have jurisdiction.[206] With a narrow (six to five) majority the Court therefore refused to grant *Yahoo!* a declaration that the French courts' judgment should not be enforced and dismissed the case.[207]

The justifications for the doctrine of comity can be explained as protecting the legitimate interests and expectations of private parties in litigation, thereby facilitating international trade and commerce, respecting the sovereignty of other states in the hope of reciprocity and in the spirit of bilateral, mutual cooperation and the division of power between the executive and judicial arms of US government, with the judiciary deferring in matters of foreign policy to the executive.[208]

Comity can also be understood by the metaphor of a wall,[209] and like most walls its function is twofold: keeping domestic laws in (ie restricting the application of US law in cases with a foreign element) and at the same time keeping foreign laws out (ie providing the justification for when the courts refuse to apply or enforce foreign law to protect US public interests/public policy by way of exception).

These two functions become clear when one looks at the historical origins of the doctrine of comity and how it has been used by its three main proponents, the Dutch seventeenth century scholar Ulrich Huber, Lord Mansfield in the 1772 English case on slavery in *Somerset v Stewart*,[210]and the nineteenth century US international law scholar, Joseph Story.

Ulrich Huber's use of the doctrine has to be seen in the context of the Netherlands' newly won independence from Catholic Spain—his approach was informed by the aim to cut the ties with the Catholic Church and Spain and at the same time to deal with conflicts of laws (and religion) in the provinces of the Netherlands, thus reinforcing the union of these provinces. His approach to international law and conflicts of law was firmly rooted in the notion of territoriality[211] and the principle that each state has sovereign power over any person within its territory. However, he sought to give the courts discretion to allow for the application of foreign law to the extent that this is necessary to avoid infringing on the sovereignty or rights of another state or its subject. He solved the apparent paradox between the principle of territoriality and the desirability that sometimes foreign law should apply beyond the territory by the notion of comity.[212] He thought that comity was about mutual assistance between states and described this power of the courts to apply foreign law as "comity." However, in his view comity was not an obligation under international law, but merely an exception to the dominant principle of territoriality, which he regarded as the victory of the independent nation state over the doctrine of universality of the Roman Catholic Church.[213]

206 Para 1224.
207 Para 1224.
208 Paul (n 195) 6, 44.
209 ibid 1–78 uses that metaphor, but only focuses on the first function of the "wall," see 71ff.
210 98 Eng Rep 499 (1772).
211 D McClean et al, *Morris: the Conflict of Laws* (8th edn, Sweet & Maxwell 2012) 19-005.
212 ibid.
213 Paul (n 195) 15–17 contains a summary of the discussion of comity in U Huber's *De Conflictu Legum*.

Consequently, he developed three principles[214] reconciling the doctrine of territoriality and the exceptional recognition of foreign law:

> First, the laws of each state have force within the limits of that government, and bind all subject to it, but not beyond. All persons within the limits of a government, whether they live there permanently or temporarily, are deemed to be subjects thereof. Sovereigns will so act by way of Comity that rights acquired within the limits of a government retain their force everywhere so far as they do not cause prejudice to the power or rights of such government or of its subjects.

Lord Mansfield was familiar with Huber's writing and relied on his conflicts of law theory to develop English law in aid of the growth of international commerce in the eighteenth century. He used the notion of comity to justify, by way of exception, the situation in which states should *not* apply foreign laws for reasons of the forum state's public policy[215] and held that despite the general recognition of foreign property under English law that an English court would not recognize property rights in slaves, disregarding the applicable law.[216]

The influential US scholar of International Law Joseph Story[217] used the doctrine of comity to the opposite end, to justify why the anti-slavery states must recognize the federal law that captured fugitive slaves who had fled from Confederate states must be returned to their former "owner," no matter how repugnant that law may be to the courts of the Union states.[218] He used it as a wall to localize and isolate different laws from each other. Story was strongly against slavery, but felt that the mutual recognition of laws was necessary to preserve the Republic and that these same federal laws also imposed obstacles on slave "owners" to recapture slaves who had escaped their tormenters to the North.[219] However, Story also did not perceive comity as an absolute obligation to recognize foreign laws, but rather a discretion guided by mutual interest and utility.[220] He recognized that states can refuse to apply foreign laws that are repugnant to their own fundamental public policy. The doctrine of comity never took hold in Europe in the same way as it did in the US. The influential nineteenth-century theorist Savigny believed that each legal relationship and dispute had its proper seat, thus European private international law scholars developed a number of "recognized" connecting factors that linked a conflicts of law situation to a particular territory to determine jurisdiction and/or applicable law.[221] His thinking therefore supported a multilateral approach and sought to harmonize private international law among states

[214] Quoted from McClean (n 211) 19-004.
[215] Paul (n 195) 19.
[216] *Somerset v Stewart* 98 Eng Rep 499 (1772).
[217] J Story *Commentaries on the Conflict of Laws, Foreign and Domestic* (Hilliard Grey 1834).
[218] *Prigg v Pennsylvania* 6 Peters 539 (1842) concerning the compatibility of the federal Fugitive Slave Act with the US Constitution.
[219] Paul (n 195) 22–23.
[220] McClean (n 211) 19-009.
[221] Paul (n 195) 30; McClean (n 211) 19-007.

to achieve legal certainty, consistency, and minimize opportunistic forum shopping, although his idealistic vision was never achieved in full.[222]

Thus, conceptually, there is a fundamental difference between the US and the European approach to the forum court desisting from applying its own law and instead applying foreign law and to the recognition and enforcement of foreign judgments. US courts adopt a bilateral approach making the decision on a case-by-case basis, giving judges discretion to balance the interests of the parties and the state interests involved.[223] By contrast, European rules adopt a multilateral approach with general rules on the proper connecting factors between the dispute and the competent court and/or the applicable law. The English common law, like the rest of Europe, does not recognize the doctrine of comity in the context of private international law,[224] but finds jurisdiction on the grounds of specific connection factors.[225] However, unlike the EU harmonized rules,[226] English law also applies the doctrine of *forum non-conveniens*,[227] which, like the doctrine of comity, gives the courts discretion to balance the interests of the parties (but not the interests of the states) to see whether it should decline jurisdiction in favour of a more appropriate court to better serve the interests of justice.[228]

However, European states do not automatically and statically apply these connection factors, but recognize a doctrine of public policy (ordre public) that gives them the power to refuse to recognize and enforce a foreign judgment or arbitration award if this contradicts the fundamental public policy values of the legal system of the enforcement court.[229] Thus, they may refuse, on a discretionary basis, to apply foreign law if this foreign law infringes on the fundamental public policy of the forum state. For example, German law stipulates that a court will not apply foreign law or enforce a foreign judgment if this is manifestly incompatible with essential principles of German law or if this is manifestly irreconcilable with fundamental principles of German law and basic Constitutional rights.[230]

This is broadly similar to the approach in the US, where courts also have a public policy exception and the right to refuse the recognition and enforcement of foreign judgments where the basis for the foreign court's assertion of jurisdiction was exorbitant or extravagant or ignoring a valid and enforceable choice of court agreement by the parties.[231]

[222] Even the Brussels Regulation EU/1215/2012 does not fully harmonize the rules on jurisdiction in the EU.

[223] Paul (n 195) 32.

[224] Referred to in English cases, eg *H v H* [2016] 4 WLR 102 (Fam) 102; *Ecobank Transnational Inc v Tanoh* [2016] 1 WLR 2231 (CA) 2262 in the context of anti-suit injunction; *Regina (Khan) v Secretary of State for Foreign and Commonwealth Affairs* [2014] 1 WLR 872 (CA) 883–84 acts of foreign states and state immunity.

[225] McClean (n 211) 1-011.

[226] Case C-281/02 *Owusu v Jackson* ECLI:EU:C:2002:499.

[227] Restatement of the Law Fourth (n 62) s 304.

[228] *Spiliada Maritime Corp v Cansulex Ltd* [1987] AC 460 HL 476–78.

[229] See eg the English case of *Kuwait Airways Corp v Iraqi Airways Corp (No 6)* [2002] 2 AC 883 (HL) 1078: "exceptionally and rarely, a provision of foreign law will be disregarded when it would lead to a result wholly alien to fundamental requirements of justice as administered by an English court."

[230] Zivilprozessordnung s 328.

[231] Restatement of the Law Third (n 23) 304–05: eg based on the nationality of the plaintiff see also s 421.

Thus, the reasons for *not* applying foreign law or recognizing and enforcing a foreign judgment or arbitration award are broadly similar between European states and the US. Comity gives US courts likewise the discretion to refuse to give effect to foreign law or a foreign judgment for reasons of fundamental public policy. Thus, one could conclude in a nutshell that the reasons for *not applying* foreign law/not enforcing a foreign court's decision are similar, but the reasons for doing so are different (bilateralism vs multilateralism).

Comity can be criticized for the reason that it gives US courts discretion to disapply US public regulation (eg safety standards, employment law, or environmental regulation) in cases with a foreign element. Comity acts as a wall pushing back developed states' regulatory efforts by protecting the freedom of private parties to opt out of public law. According to *Paul*, the application of the doctrine by US courts has in effect lowered regulatory standards by sending plaintiffs away to arbitration or to sue in a foreign court where they would be unlikely to obtain redress.[232] This allows US businesses to circumvent health and safety, employment, and environmental standards by transferring production to countries where such standards are low—for example, through exploiting special export processing zones, free trade agreements, and intra-company trade in global value chains. An example for this is *In Re Union Carbide*, an action brought by some of the victims of the disaster of the Bhopal chemical accident where the court declined to assert jurisdiction on the basis of *forum non-conveniens* and comity.[233] Some courts have dismissed cases even in the absence of pending proceedings abroad,[234] but these are exceptional circumstances.[235] *Paul* argues that these political and economic consequences of applying comity to international cases on regulatory policy should be recognized.[236] The law thereby creates economic externalities by encouraging economic investment decisions, which are made for the "wrong" reasons: non-economic incentives are thus used to create "value" for businesses but at the expense of foreign workers, consumers, and the environment. He therefore criticizes the doctrine of comity and finds that an international harmonization of conflicts principles (multilateral approach) and coordination of regulatory policy is required.[237]

The comity doctrine is similar[238] to and overlaps significantly with the presumption against the extraterritorial application of US law,[239] the reasonableness analysis to be conducted as part of the test to be conducted under the *Shoe* minimum contacts analysis whether the assertion of jurisdiction comports with "notions of fair

[232] Paul (n 195) 72.

[233] *In re Union Carbide Corp Gas Plant Disaster at Bhopal* 809 F 2d 195; 89 ALR Fed 217 (2d Cir 1987): although in this case the defendant had to agree to submit to the jurisdiction of the Indian courts and waive the statute of limitation applicable there. Most of the witnesses and evidence was located in India (including evidence related to the construction of the plant which caused the disaster).

[234] *Mujica v AirScan Inc* 771 F 3d 580, 596–615 (9th Cir 2014) and *Ungaro-Benages v Dresdner Bank AG* 379 F 3d 1227, 1237–40 (11th Cir 2014).

[235] Dodge (n 199) 2112–114.

[236] Paul (n 195) 73–74.

[237] Paul (n 195) 74–75.

[238] Restatement of the Law Third (n 23) 306 states that the reasonableness test for jurisdiction to prescribe has to be distinguished from the reasonableness test for jurisdiction to adjudicate. The former is wider and based on the considerations discussed in the Restatement (Chapter 4), whereas the latter is based on the due process clause in the US Constitution (section 2.1).

[239] See the discussion in Chapter 2.

play and substantial justice" (jurisdiction to adjudicate),[240] and the reasonableness test in s 403 of the Restatement of the Law Third in respect of jurisdiction to prescribe (applicable law).[241] The reasonableness test in s 403 states that even if the US has jurisdiction to prescribe it should exercise restraint by applying this test before applying US law to cases with a foreign element. Unlike the comity test, this is formulated as a legal obligation and an obligation that does not depend on reciprocity.[242] So the basic rule is that a state may not exercise jurisdiction to prescribe law "with respect to a person or activity having connections with another state when the exercise of such jurisdiction is unreasonable."[243] To determine whether such prescription is unreasonable a multi-factor test is applied balancing eight (non-exclusive, exemplary) factors. The first factor to be taken into account is the connection between the activity and the regulating state—this can either be that the activity takes place on the territory or that it has substantial, direct, and foreseeable effect on the territory.[244] The second factor is the link between the person principally responsible for the activity to be regulated, those who the regulation is intended to protect, and the regulating state, and it is here that nationality, residence, establishment, and economic activity in the regulating state are taken into account.[245] The third factor is the character of the activity to be regulated, the importance of regulation to the regulating state, the extent to which other states regulate the activity, and the degree to which the desirability of such regulation is generally accepted.[246] The fourth factor is the justified expectations (of the parties?) that may be protected or impinged on by the regulation.[247] The next two balancing factors are how important the regulation is for the international political, legal, or economic system and the extent to which regulation of this area is "consistent with the traditions of the international system."[248] The final two factors take into account the extent to which another state may have an interest in regulating the activity and the likelihood of conflict with regulation by another state.[249] If the regulation of two states conflicts in such a way that entities subject to regulation by both states cannot comply with both sets of regulation (eg one proscribes the other requires a particular activity) the Restatement provides that the state with the weaker interest in regulation should defer to the state with the clearly greater interest.[250] It is submitted that usually both states will assert that they have a great interest in regulation because the relative interests cannot be objectively or neutrally assessed, as they depend on cultural, political, and social factors that differ between nations significantly. For example, in France there was a

[240] See the discussion in section 2.2.
[241] Restatement of the Law Third (n 23).
[242] ibid 246, 251.
[243] S 403(1).
[244] S 403(2)(a).
[245] S 403(2)(b).
[246] S 403(c).
[247] S 403(d).
[248] S 403(e) and (f).
[249] S 403(g) and (h).
[250] S 403(3) and p 247.

potential[251] conflict for EU companies listed on a US stock exchange or a subsidiary of a listed US company in complying with the whistleblowing procedures concerning fraudulent accounting practices under the Sarbanes-Oxley Act 2002 and the provisions of the French legislation implementing the Data Protection Act 1995/46/EC. This was addressed by Guidance from the Commission Nationale de L'Informatique et des Libertés[252] and a series of exchange of letters between the EU Article 29 Working Party and the US Securities and Exchange Commission, reconciling the application of both sets of laws, rather than by one state not applying its law.[253]

Moreover, in some ways the reasonableness doctrine as interpreted in the 1987 Restatement makes an assumption that some laws regulate what are, by their very nature, more internal affairs (eg labour law, social security), whereas others regulate what are more external-facing aspects (eg safety standards in modes of transport, trade).[254] This distinction does not work logically for laws regulating internet communications and content in the twenty-first century: although the internet is a cross-border communication medium, thus external-facing restraint may be called for to avoid a plethora of conflicts due to this cross-border nature. By the same token, states cannot afford to not regulate communications media and content in the twenty-first century, because of the internal repercussions. Thus, the internet severely challenges the conceptual distinction between internal-facing and external-facing regulation. The Restatement cautions in particular that, where jurisdiction is based on the harmful effects doctrine (as will be the case for internet cases), states should use the reasonableness doctrine and exercise restraint.[255] Given the *Megaupload* case saga discussed in Chapter 4 and the prosecution in the US of officers of online gambling companies,[256] it is interesting that the 1987 Restatement advocates even more restraint in respect of criminal proceedings stating that "no case is known of a criminal prosecution in the United States for an economic offense (not involving fraud) carried out by an alien wholly outside the United States."[257]

Notably, s 403 of the 1987 Restatement of the Law Third has not been included in the Tentative Draft of the Restatement of the Law Fourth and has been replaced with s 204 "to avoid unreasonable interference with the legitimate sovereign authority of other states, US courts may interpret federal statutory provisions to include other limitations on their applicability as a matter or prescriptive Comity."[258]

251 Depending on how companies implemented these whistleblower hotlines and procedures, see eg the French Supreme Court Decision of 8 December 2009 Judgment No 2524 of 8 December 2009 (08-17.191).

252 https://www.cnil.fr/sites/default/files/typo/document/CNIL-recommandations-whistleblowing-VA.pdf accessed on 25 July 2020—later Guidelines were issued in 2010.

253 See exchange of letters between the Chairman of the Art 29 Working Party and the Director of the Office of International Affairs of the Securities and Exchange Commission in 2006, http://ec.europa.eu/justice/data-protection/article-29/documentation/other-document/index_en.htm#maincontentSec12accessed on 25 July 2020.

254 Restatement of the Law Third (n 23) 246, 250.

255 ibid 250.

256 See eg https://www.theguardian.com/business/2007/may/25/gambling.uknews accessed on 25 July 2020.

257 Restatement of the Law Third (n 23) 253.

258 Restatement of the Law Fourth (n 62) s 204, p 35; *F. Hoffmann-La Roche v Empagran SA* 542 US 155 (2004).

6. Procedural jurisdiction from a US perspective

In international litigation, where some of the evidence is located in a different jurisdiction (ie either physically stored or controlled from a foreign country), the question arises as to which set of civil procedure rules govern the disclosure and production of that foreign evidence. The internet obviously allows for the seamless transmission of data across national borders and in a modern cloud computing environment relevant electronic evidence may be stored in a foreign jurisdiction, moved between jurisdictions, or the physical location of the evidence may be unknown.[259]

In the US, courts (and some administrative and other bodies) have legal powers[260] to order a person, either a party to litigation or a third party, to produce a document, including an electronic document, or other (electronic) evidence and to submit to depositions and other forms of compulsory interviews regardless of where the evidence or interviewee is physically located, namely by way of a subpoena.[261] This subpoena power is available as long as the court has personal jurisdiction over the person to whom the order is addressed and this person has control over the material to be produced or has knowledge of the facts relevant to the litigation.[262] Clearly, the US court has jurisdiction over the parties themselves and can apply the Federal Rules of Civil Procedure directly, even if the evidence is abroad. As far as third parties (not involved in litigation) are concerned, US courts apply the rules on personal jurisdiction and the minimum contacts doctrine, as discussed earlier, for example, based on a person doing business in a US state.

Thus, a court can order a foreign subsidiary of a US corporation, or a US subsidiary of a foreign corporation, to produce electronic evidence located in another country without the need to resort to international treaty-based procedures. For nationals and residents of the US who are temporarily outside the US, 28 USC s 1782 provides this personal jurisdiction. Thus, US law focuses on personal jurisdiction over the person whose evidence is sought, rather than the location of the evidence per se.

Thus, if electronic evidence relevant to US civil litigation is stored in a data centre by a cloud provider in Ireland but controlled by a person over whom the US court has personal jurisdiction, a subpoena could order the controller to produce the data physically stored in Ireland, unless one of the exceptions apply, for example, under the Stored Communications Act 1986.[263]

In addition, the US is a signatory of the Hague Convention on the Taking of Evidence Abroad in Civil and Commercial Matters,[264] which it ratified on 8 August

[259] In the criminal law context, see Chapter 4.

[260] eg under the Federal Rules of Civil Procedure.

[261] Restatement of the Law Fourth (n 62) s 306(1).

[262] *Société Internationale pour Participations Industrielles et Comerciales SA v Rogers* 357 US 197 (1958); *Matter of Marc Rich* 707 F 2d 663, 667 (2nd Cir 1983).

[263] For a discussion of criminal and administrative subpoenas see Chapter 4.

[264] Convention of 18 March 1970 on the Taking of Evidence Abroad in Civil or Commercial Matters, entered into force on 7 October 1972, 845 UNTS 245, see https://www.hcch.net/en/instruments/conventions/status-table/?cid=82accessed on 25 July 2020.

1972. If US courts do not have personal jurisdiction then the Convention procedure must be used.[265]

The Convention essentially provides for a system of letters of request for evidence that are transmitted through governmental or diplomatic channels[266] and that may only be refused if the execution of the evidence request does not fall in the competency of the judiciary in the state requested or if that state considers that its sovereignty or security would be prejudiced.[267] However, the Convention allows countries to derogate by a declaration not accepting to execute requests for pre-trial discovery from common law countries (the US) and most states have done so without limitations.[268]

If the courts in the US *do* have personal jurisdiction over the person who must produce foreign evidence a direct subpoena *may* be used without having to go through the Convention procedure. In such cases the US courts have regarded the use of Convention procedures as optional, not mandatory.[269] The US applies its own domestic rules on the basis of its wide understanding of personal jurisdiction even for countries who have declared under the Convention that they do not recognize requests for pre-trial discovery.[270] US courts tend to prefer the direct application of their domestic subpoena powers since international procedures are more cumbersome and slow and in order to circumvent the derogations declared by most signatory states.

This direct application has attracted international criticism as a form of exorbitant jurisdiction[271] and several European states have passed blocking statutes that make it an offence for the party who has been made subject to a subpoena to comply with it.[272] Furthermore, compliance with the US subpoena conflicts with other laws of foreign states—in particular, EU data protection legislation.

[265] ibid.

[266] They cannot be sent directly from one court to another 28 USC s 1781.

[267] Art 12 and Chapter II.

[268] Arts 23 and 35(c) and the majority of signatories (thirty-two of sixty-one) have in fact a wide derogation in place: Albania (2010), Armenia (2012), Australia (1992), Brazil (2014), Bulgaria (2000), Croatia (2009), Cyprus (1983), Czech Republic (1993), Denmark (1972), Finland (1976), Macedonia (2009), Germany (1979), Greece (2005), Hungary (2004), Iceland (2009), Italy (1982), Korea (2010), Lithuania (2000), Luxembourg (1977), Monaco (1986), Montenegro (2012), Norway (1972), Poland (1996), Portugal (1975), Romania (2003), Singapore (1978), South Africa (1997), Spain (1987), Sri Lanka (2000), Sweden (1975), Turkey (2004), Ukraine (2001)—many states limit pre-trial discovery to documents listed in the request (eg UK 1976).

[269] Restatement of the Law Fourth (n 62) s 306, p 146; *Societe Nationale Industrielle Aerospatiale v US Dist. Court for Southern Dist. of Iowa* 482 US 522; 107 SCt 2542, 2548–53 (1987): "The Convention does not deprive the District Court of its jurisdiction to order, under the Federal Rules, a foreign national party to produce evidence physically located within a signatory nation." (2546)

[270] *Societe Nationale Industrielle Aerospatiale v US Dist. Court for Southern Dist. of Iowa* 482 US 522; 107 SCt 2542, 2545 (1987).

[271] C Ryngaert, *Jurisdiction in International Law* (Oxford University Press 2015) 89–93; see also SI Strong, "Jurisdictional Discovery in Transnational Litigation: Extraterritorial Effects of US Federal Practice" (2011) 7 Journal of Private International Law 1–31, 23.

[272] eg France and Germany, in response to what they consider as intrusive evidence requests made to French/German companies, frequently by their US competitors—V Grosswald Curran, "United States Discovery and Foreign Blocking Statutes" (2016) 76 Louisiana Law Review 1141–49, 1143; a 2007 French Cour de Cassation Decision has upheld the French Blocking Statute by fining a French lawyer with Euro 10,000 for disclosing evidence in breach of the Statute, 12 December 2007, Bull Crim, No 7168; France is in the process of limiting its blocking statutes to business secrets http://www.assemblee-nationale.fr/13/ta/ta0826.aspaccessed on 25 July 2020.

The subpoena powers under US procedures are extraordinarily broad and far reaching, compared to civil law countries. The process is driven by the parties' counsel (unlike civil law countries where evidence disclosures are ordered by an investigatory, judge-led process) and requests are not specific (instead based on wide notions of relevancy), which imposes an enormous burden on parties to the litigation and third parties alike, which foreign lawyers are unaccustomed to.[273] In addition, US courts may conduct jurisdictional pre-trial discovery that imposes these significant burdens even before the court has determined jurisdiction.[274]

From a US perspective, pre-trial discovery is regarded as part and parcel of the justice process, an essential ingredient of the fact-finding process and fairness, as without it a party may simply not know which evidence relevant to the litigation is in the possession of the other party or third parties with almost Constitutional rank.[275] For this reason US courts insist on conducting pre-trial discovery. These different perceptions of the nature of pre-trial discovery have led to international resistance, insistence by the US, and conflict.[276]

The US regards this power under US federal procedure rules as being within the territoriality principle, as the *production* of the evidence (supplying evidence) takes place within the US.[277] By contrast, non-US states regard this power as extraterritorial, since the evidence itself or the person is not physically located in the US.[278]

The person ordered to produce the foreign evidence may be subject to procedural sanctions,[279] such as their own evidence being inadmissible or dismissal of the case, or contempt of court proceedings in the US in case of non-compliance with the US subpoena, even if compliance means that the person infringes their own domestic law, such as privacy provisions (eg bank secrecy statutes or a blocking statute[280]).[281] It should, however, also be pointed out that the subpoena must be reasonable and proportionate in the light of international comity and the court must take into account a number of factors such as the significance of the evidence to the investigation or litigation, how specific the request for evidence is, whether the evidence originated in the US or abroad, whether there are other alternative means of obtaining the evidence, the

273 P Grosdidier, "The French Blocking Statute, the Hague Evidence Convention, and the Case Law: Lessons for French Parties Responding to American Discovery" (2014) Texas International Law Journal Forum 11–56, 15.

274 Ryngaert (n 271) 89–93; see also Strong (n 271) 21–22.

275 Grosswald Curran (n 272) 1141.

276 ibid.

277 *Adidas (Can) Ltd v SS Seatrain Bennington*, 1984 WL 423, at *2 (US District Court SDNY 1984).

278 Ryngaert (n 271) 91; Grosswald Curran (n 272) 1144.

279 Grosdidier (n 273) 45.

280 ibid 32—he identifies thirty-three cases where US Courts have dismissed the French Blocking Statute as a defence, at 34.

281 Restatement of the Law Fourth (n 62) s 306(3): "a court in the United States may impose sanctions on a person who fails to comply with an order to produce evidence or submit to a compulsory interview, even if complying with the order would subject the person to punishment under foreign law"—however, in contempt of court proceedings the court will take into account (1) the significance of the evidence to the proceedings, (2) the good faith efforts of the person to comply with the subpoena, and (3) the legitimate interests of the foreign jurisdiction in enforcing its law, s 306 (3); *Société Internationale pour Participations Industrielles et Comerciales SA v Rogers* 357 US 197, 204–06 (1958); *Richmark Corp. v Timber Falling Consultants, Inc* 937 F 2d 1444, 1478 (9th Cir 1991).

interests of the US, and the interests of the foreign state.[282] The US courts, however, frequently find that US interests trump those of the foreign state.[283]

In the reverse situation the subpoena power is also available: a court in the US may subpoena a person over whom is has personal jurisdiction to produce evidence *located in the US* for use in a *foreign* (ie non-US) or international court or tribunal procedure, including foreign administrative procedures.[284] This subpoena power is available in foreign proceedings, regardless of whether the foreign state is a signatory of the Hague Convention and regardless of the admissibility of the evidence under the procedural rules of the foreign court.[285] For example, in *Kulzer v Biomet* a German company suing a US company in a theft of trade secrets action in Germany obtained documents by way of subpoena, which it could not have done under the forum court's rules, in this case the German civil procedure.[286] The forum state may also regard this as a breach of its powers to conduct the evidence process and it may cause an imbalance in the procedural weapons of the parties, as the non-US party may obtain US-style discovery against its opponent, but not the other way round.

However, in the US, there are certain limitations on when *electronic* evidence (such as the *content* of email or that contained on social media sites) is not available for pre-trial discovery for reasons of specific US privacy laws for electronic communications.[287] For example, the Stored Communications Act 1986 may prevent certain providers having to disclose communications stored on their services in civil litigation discovery depending on the circumstances.[288] This would equally apply to electronic data stored abroad.

Electronic communications are only protected if they fall within the scope of the communications protected under the Act. It makes a distinction between two types of services, namely electronic communications services (ECS), defined as "any service which provides to users thereof the ability to send or receive wire or electronic communications,"[289] and remote computing services (RCS), defined as "provision to the public of computer storage or processing services by means of an electronic communications system."[290]

Technology has developed so rapidly, which makes it difficult to apply these definitions from more than thirty years ago. In the meantime, not only has email moved

[282] Restatement of the Law Fourth (n 62) s 306 Comment a and Reporters Notes, 147 quoting *Argentina v NML* 134 SCt 2250, 2258 FN 6 (2014): In an enforcement action the District Court had discretion to order third-party banks to disclose judgment debtors assets held outside the US; *Societe Nationale Industrielle Aerospatiale v US Dist. Court for Southern Dist. of Iowa* 482 US 522; 107 SCt 2542, 2556–57 (1987): "American courts, in supervising pretrial proceedings, should exercise special vigilance to protect foreign litigants from the danger that unnecessary, or unduly burdensome, discovery may place them in a disadvantageous position."

[283] Grosdidier (n 273) 35.

[284] eg procedures before the European Commission *Intel Corp v Advanced Micro Devices* 542 US 241, 257–58 (2004).

[285] Restatement of the Law Fourth (n 62) s 306(2); 28 USC s 1782.

[286] 633 F 3d 591, 593-4 (7th Cir 2011).

[287] 18 USC 2702 (a).

[288] Subjecting the communication service provider to potential civil action and the party who obtained the subpoena to sanctions in the litigation: *Theofel v Farey-Jones* 359 F 3d 1066, 107177 (9th Cir 2004).

[289] 18 USC 2510 (15).

[290] 18 USC 2711 (2).

from locally run applications to web-based email, many service providers now offer a sophisticated and integrated blend of communication and storage facilities, and users in the age of always on, reliable broadband are more likely to store *all* their communications permanently and remotely in the cloud (by contrast, the Act was drafted in the age of dial-up internet access services and only temporary remote storage). A further complication in this age of cloud computing is that services are provided by a chain of providers, such as a social media provider giving access to third party applications and processing facilities, and contracting out their storage requirements to other hosting providers, but users will only deal with, and be in a contractual relationship with, the social media provider, who determines the communication infrastructure and value-added functions, such as search, and usually has access to the content itself. Nor is the phenomenon of cloud computing limited to email and social media. More and more data are now stored, and software services hosted, remotely by a chain of cloud service providers. If such a service provider is then issued with a subpoena to disclose content of communications (eg in the social media context, wall posts, or photos), the question arises whether they are an ECS or RCS, or both, or neither.

The reason why this matters is that under the Act ECS are protected as private (subject to exceptions,[291] none of which apply here), but for RCS the content of communications is only protected if the communication is maintained "solely for the purpose of providing storage or computer processing services" and "the provider is not authorized to access the contents of any such communications for purposes of providing any services other than storage or computer processing."[292] Thus, it is unclear to what extent communications in the context of a RCS are protected. Doubts have been raised due to the fact that the content stored and processed remotely is frequently mined by the RCS provider for purposes of online profiling, advertising, and search functionality. For some pure storage and processing services this may not apply (eg Dropbox), but it will apply to most social media providers. It seems, however, that some courts have categorized social media providers as ECS and private, even though data mining is applied by the provider.

In *Crispin v Audigier Inc* the defendant sought to obtain, by way of *civil* subpoena to social media providers, communications of the plaintiff on various social media and communication applications (including Facebook and MySpace). The Court ultimately held that the social media did not have to produce the plaintiff's communications, as long as public access to them was restricted through privacy settings, for the reason that the Act does not contain an explicit exception to its privacy protections in respect of civil subpoenas for electronic communications.[293] As to the distinction between ECS and RCS, the Court held that the social media provide both at different

[291] 18 USC 2702(b), (c), (d).

[292] 18 USC 2703(b)(2).

[293] *Crispin v Audigier Inc* 717 F Supp 2d 965, 975–76 (US District Court CD California 2010), copyright infringement case. The Stored Communications Act 1986 provides expressly for several exceptions, including disclosure by *criminal warrant* of communications stored less than 180 days, s 2703(a) and by *criminal subpoena* (administrative subpoena or grand jury or trial subpoena) if stored for more than 180 days in s 2703(b), but omits to provide for disclosure of stored communications through civil subpoenas; see also *Viacom International Inc. v YouTube Inc.* 253 FRD 256, 264 (US District Court SDNY 2008); *In re Subpoena Duces Tecum to AOL* 550 F Supp 2d 606, 611 (US District Court ED Va 2008); *O'Grady v Superior Court*, 139 Cal App 4th 1423, 44 Cal Rptr 3d 72 (2006).

times. While private, direct messages (akin to email or instant messages) that have not yet been read are more like ECS, those that have been opened and retained on the services are more like RCS. By contrast, comments and postings that are instantly shared (within the group) are different from email, as they are not opened to be read (unlike email and similar messages). But the Court found that this should not matter, and whether a message deserves privacy protection or not should depend instead on whether or not the message is private in the sense of not being posted on a public-facing website, which depends on the privacy settings of the service, or the specific user account, as the case may be.[294]

However, it should also be pointed out that in other cases the courts have completely ignored the provisions of the Stored Communications Act and issued subpoenas to social media providers.[295] A further limitation of this privacy protection is that service providers to whom the Act applies may disclose content if the user of the service consents.[296] Hence it is possible to issue a subpoena directed not at the service provider, but the user of the service.[297] Since the user has control over communications on remotely stored services he or she may well be obligated to produce the evidence.[298]

Furthermore, in *Recording Industry Association of America Inc v Verizon Internet Services Inc* the US Court of Appeals for the DC Circuit held that an internet access provider could not be ordered by a civil subpoena[299] to disclose the subscriber details identifying anonymous internet users engaging in copyright infringing file sharing activities.[300] The case turned on an interpretation of the wording of s 512(h), which requires identification of the works claimed to have been infringed. Chief Justice Ginsburg held that under the Digital Millennium Copyright Act (DMCA) copyright infringement provisions, a subpoena may only be served on an internet service provider that *stores* infringing content, not on an *access* provider. The Court of Appeals never reached the question of whether a subpoena to find out the identities of the subscribers would be unconstitutional under the First Amendment.[301] However, the *Verizon* case should not be read as meaning that copyright owners cannot obtain subscriber information from internet access providers through a subpoena in copyright infringement cases. In *West Bay One v Does 1-1,1653*[302] a US District Court refused to quash a motion for a subpoena[303] as the users had no recognized claim to privacy.[304]

[294] Para 980: "not strictly public."

[295] *Ledbetter v Wal-Mart Stores* 2009 WL 1067018 (US District Court D Colo 2009); *Romano v Steelcase* 907 NYS 2d 650 (Sup Ct NY 2010) current and deleted Facebook material.

[296] S 2702(b)(3).

[297] *Flagg v City of Detroit* 252 FRD 346, 363, 366 (US District Court ED Mich 2008).

[298] See Federal Rules of Civil Procedure 34 or equivalent state rules.

[299] Subpoena provision of the Digital Millennium Copyright Act, 17 USC s 512(h).

[300] *Recording Industry Association of America v Verizon Internet Services* 351 F 3d 1229, 1237 (DC Cir 2003): We agree that the presence in s 512(h) of three separate references to s 512(c) and the absence of any reference to s 512(a) suggests the subpoena power of s 512(h) applies only to ISPs engaged in storing copyrighted material and not to those engaged solely in transmitting it on behalf of others.

[301] Paras 1231, 1237.

[302] 270 FRD 13 (US District Court, DC 2010).

[303] Which was not based on s 512(h) DMCA, but on the Federal Rule of Civil Procedure 45.

[304] Para 16: individuals generally lose their reasonable expectations of privacy once they disclose information such as subscriber information to a service provider, citing *Guest v Leis* 255 F 3d 325, 335–36 (6th Cir2001); *US v Hambrick* Civ No 99-4793, 2000 WL 1062039, at *4 (4th Cir 2000); *US v Kennedy* 81 F Supp 2d 1103, 1110 (D Kan 2000).

It held that the subpoena was not oppressive and did not impose an undue burden.[305] Similarly, in *Signature Management Team v Auttomatic*[306] a US District Court held that a subpoena issued under s 512(h) DMCA against a hosting provider to disclose account information should not be quashed to protect a defendant's First Amendment right to anonymous speech, which is not absolute, thus distinguishing *Verizon* (where the subpoena was issued against the internet access provider not the hosting provider).[307] Thus, subpoena powers are available to procure the production of subscriber details and electronic information, subject only to very narrow privacy and freedom of speech protections.

7. Conclusion

The US jurisdictional tests are very flexible and malleable based on general principles that can be interpreted to suit new factual scenarios. On the one hand, this adaptability accommodates new business models and new communication technologies. On the other hand, it also means that the tests can be applied to achieve political aims (both by asserting jurisdiction and by refraining from asserting jurisdiction). One extreme example of this is the US asserting jurisdiction over US companies' foreign subsidiaries and foreign-based branches on the basis of an analogy to the nationality of persons. This has proved to be extremely controversial where the US expanded economic sanctions programmes to such branches and subsidiaries.[308] An example where the flexibility test serves political agendas of deregulation is where the principle of comity is used to disapply US regulation to US companies deliberately acting abroad to avoid US regulatory standards.[309]

The internet has created a further dimension to the complexity of jurisdiction—in many cases internet communications or interactions are directed nowhere and everywhere at the same time. This is encapsulated in the paraphrase[310] of Gertrude Stein's suggestion that there is "no there, there" on the internet—the jurisdictional analysis frequently does not result in an obvious "there." Operators on the internet may in certain instances not target a particular US state for business but at the same time target the whole of the US in an effort to maximize their reach and/or the numbers of sales.

In some instances, this has led courts to assert jurisdiction widely and broadly, finding minimum contacts merely based on remote, internet mediated contacts (*Patterson*, *Zippo*, *Panavision*). In other cases the courts have latched on to the fact that the defendant's conduct was not actively directed at a specific forum, hence denying jurisdiction for this reason (*Young*, *Burdick*). The latest trend examined is a higher test—for minimum contacts—where plaintiffs must show that they targeted a

305 Para 15.

306 941 F Supp 2d 1145 (US District Court, ND California 2013).

307 Para 1154.

308 Restatement of the Law Third (n 23) s 414(2)(b).

309 Section 5.

310 *Digital Equipment Corp v Altavista Technology, Inc* 960 F Supp 456, 462 (D Mass 1997) quoted in Geist's seminal article (n 34) 1346: "the "there" is everywhere there is internet access. The quote stems from G Stein, *Everybody's Autobiography* (Exact Change 1993) 298.

particular state, not just knowing that the defendant is located in a particular state as in *Burdick* and *McIntyre*. In product liability cases a manufacturer may purposefully target a geographical area larger than a particular jurisdiction in an effort to maximize sales, but without being specific *ex ante* where these sales should be fulfilled. This scenario has been labelled as "non-specific purposeful availment."[311] The US Supreme Court in *McIntyre* limited access to redress in such product liability cases even where the product was targeted at the US as a whole. This encourages distribution and communication models that maximize access to a large audience or market while at the same time avoiding direct contacts and thus exposure to legal liability.[312]

Arguably, the burden should be the other way round: if businesses target a wider geographic area the burden should be on them to prove that they did not have contacts with a specific state within that wider geographic area.[313] As the Court in *Dedvukaj v Maloney* pointed out:

> Internet forums such as eBay expand the seller's market literally to the world and sellers know that, and avail themselves of the benefits of this greatly expanded marketplace. It should, in the context of these commercial relationships, be no great surprise to sellers—and certainly no unfair burden to them—if, when a commercial transaction formed over and through the internet does not meet a buyer's expectations, they might be called upon to respond in a legal forum in the buyer's home state. Sellers cannot expect to avail themselves of the benefits of the internet-created world market that they purposefully exploit and profit from without accepting the concomitant legal responsibilities that such an expanded market may bring with it.[314]

The targeting test that seems to be the standard test for assessing jurisdiction in internet cases, both in EU law[315] and US law, has originated in the minimum contacts analysis to ensure due process for out-of-state defendants. It is based on the idea that it is the defendant's purposeful availment of conducting business in the forum state or directing tortious activities at residents in the forum state that subjects him or her to the power of the courts there. As we have seen in Chapter 8 on EU jurisdiction, this has become a legal transplant that influenced jurisdictional thinking there.[316]

The targeting test is counterbalanced by the fairness test (second leg of the *Shoe* analysis) and subject to the notion of comity examined in this chapter. This test has the potential "to protect small-scale and part-time sellers from an over-inclusive doctrine of personal jurisdiction"[317] or in turn protect the interests of consumers or employees as claimants (or defendants) by balancing the ability of the parties to cross a jurisdictional border and defending the state's interest to ensure public policy interests such as

311 Pollack (n 15) 1090–91.

312 ibid 1092; J Reidenberg, "Technology and Internet Jurisdiction" (2005) 153 University of Pennsylvania Law Review 1951–74, 1956.

313 eg based on the availability of geo-location technology, ibid: "In effect, the technological choice either to filter or not to filter becomes a normative decision to 'purposefully avail' of the user's forum state."

314 *Dedvukaj v Maloney* 447 F Supp 2d 813, 820 (ED Mich 2006).

315 Chapters 10, 12, and 13.

316 Geist (n 34) 1381.

317 Pollack (n 15) 1115.

product safety or consumer protection legislation. However, as we have seen, the "fairness test" is rarely used or only to further justify the outcome of the minimum contact analysis. Instead, courts have limited the scope of the minimum contact analysis to prevent overbroad assertion of jurisdiction in internet cases to protect economic efficiency and to shield businesses transacting or communicating using the internet. Arguably, a more active use of the multi-factor fairness analysis would yield better results.

10

Consumer Protection and Jurisdiction

1. Introduction

E-commerce contracts are known for their presentation of standard terms on a "take it or leave it" basis.[1] The terms are generally long and full of legal jargon, usually drafted by one party and containing choice of law and forum selection clauses among others. In US law, these standard form contracts are often referred to as contracts of adhesion, a term "introduced into the legal vocabulary of the United States in the early 20th Century."[2] These adhesion contracts were brought about by companies' need for uniformity, especially for companies that deal with the same mass products, and in order to reduce the risk of litigation under multiple laws in multiple courts.[3] Thus, in order to keep up with the rapid pace of globalization, the incorporation of arbitration, choice of law, and choice of forum clauses have become increasingly an important strategy for businesses. However, these clauses have been seen to detrimentally affect consumers, and may give cause for concern in states that "wish to maintain local control" over certain aspects of consumer protection.[4] In addition, as standard terms are usually drafted by the business party, consumers are unable to negotiate the terms as webpages do not allow for interaction with a human being, and the consumer has to accept the fact that reading the terms and conditions is unlikely to bring them any benefit. Thus, they are lulled into a false sense of security or display a fatalist attitude that there is no point even reading the terms.

This chapter examines the validity and enforceability of forum selection (jurisdiction) and choice of law (applicable law) clauses in the US and the EU, comparing two differing approaches to finding a balance between business' interests and consumer protection in e-commerce.

In a globalized world with an increase of transnational commercial relationships, the benefits of express jurisdiction and choice of law clauses[5] are risk management[6] (from the viewpoint of the person using the clauses), legal certainty,[7] and economic

[1] My thanks go to Asma Al Abbarova, who has provided invaluable research assistance for this chapter. For the general rules of jurisdiction in the EU see Chapter 8 and in the US see Chapter 9.

[2] M Zhang, "Contractual Choice of Law in Contracts of Adhesion and Party Autonomy" (2008) 41 Akron Law Review 123–73, 123.

[3] ibid 124.

[4] WJ Woodward, "Finding the Contract in Contracts for Law, Forum and Arbitration" (2006) 2(1) Hastings Business Law Journal 1–46, 5.

[5] See further NJ Davis, "Presumed Assent the Judicial Acceptance of Clickwrap" (2007) 22 Berkeley Technology Law Journal 577–98, 578.

[6] See *Carnival Cruise Lines v Shute* 499 US 585, 593–94; 111 SCt 1522 (1991).

[7] ibid.

Internet Jurisdiction. Julia Hörnle, Oxford University Press (2021). © Julia Hörnle.
DOI: 10.1093/oso/9780198806929.001.0001

efficiency, thus encouraging transnational commerce and trade. Their purpose is to enable the parties to foresee in which jurisdiction they will be sued and which law applies to a dispute, facilitating transnational transactions. Legal certainty and transactional efficiency are achieved by lowering transactional cost through the reduction of litigation processes necessary to establish the relevant court and the applicable law with the associated costs and delay entailed by such processes.

The downsides of express jurisdiction and applicable law clauses are that the parties' interests as to the preferred forum are likely to diverge and therefore it is difficult to find a meaningful "choice" common to all parties. In many situations one party may be in a much stronger, if not overwhelming, bargaining position compared to the other. Furthermore, the party with the stronger bargaining position is likely to contract using its own standard terms, so frequently the stronger party dictates the choice of forum and the choice of law. Cross-border litigation is more costly, requires the appointment of foreign lawyers, and may necessitate translation, the travelling of witnesses, and transfer of evidence, but most importantly may subject the weaker party to a foreign law, potentially avoiding the protection of consumer and privacy rights arising in the weaker party's local jurisdiction, and avoiding consumer litigation tools such as class action. This means that the weaker party will find it harder, if not impossible, to access justice.

An unfavourable choice of law clause can bind consumers to a law of a state that has no connection to the dispute, which may offer less protection to the consumer than another state's laws, and could potentially bar any or all of the consumer's claims and procedural advantages, including class actions.[8] This is *not* to advocate that the law should be reformed to achieve that such clauses should only be valid if the parties are of equal bargaining power. But it is equally clear that in many online transactional relationships there may exist an access to justice issue that needs to be addressed, for example, through the creation of fair online dispute resolution systems.[9]

This power imbalance situation is not limited to business-to-consumer (B2C) contracts, but may encompass many business-to-business (B2B) contracts, where increasingly there might be a similar imbalance of power where a small-to-medium sized enterprise (SME) contracts with a large multinational corporation. For example, a franchisee will not be able to negotiate jurisdiction or choice of law with Burger King; or an AdWords advertiser on Google search,[10] likewise, will not be able to change the provisions put forward by Google. However, the law in many jurisdictions mainly makes a binary distinction between B2C and B2B contracts assuming that for B2C contracts there is a natural imbalance of negotiation power, which may lead to the assessment that forum selection and choice of law clauses are unfair.[11]

The internet has exacerbated these power imbalances: because of potentially large-scale exposure to being sued in courts near and far, internet companies have even more of an incentive to include jurisdiction and choice of law clauses in their lengthy

[8] JR Camarote, "A Little More Contract Law with my Contracts Please: The Need to Apply Unconscionability Directly to Choice-Of-Law Clauses" (2009) 39 Seton Hall Law Review 605–33, 606.

[9] J Hörnle, *Cross-border Internet Dispute Resolution* (Cambridge University Press 2009).

[10] *TradeComet.com LLC v Google Inc.* 647 F 3d 472 (2nd Cir 2011).

[11] *Adams Reload Co Inc. v International Profit Associates* 143 P 3d 1056 (Colo Ct App 2005).

terms and conditions. However, if the parties are established in different jurisdictions the weaker party may find it even more difficult to obtain cross-border redress if the dominant party fails to fulfil the contract or commits a tort (such as privacy-related torts[12]). Powerful e-commerce giants and social media companies are frequently in an overwhelming bargaining position because of network effects and their dominant position on the market.

2. The approach to forum selection and consumer protection in the US

2.1 The contractual analysis: party autonomy and mutuality in the US

Originally the status of jurisdiction and choice of law clauses in US litigation was not clear,[13] but after the landmark case of *M/S Bremen*,[14] US law recognizes and enforces express jurisdiction (forum selection) clauses in contracts[15] as an expression of the choice of the parties in the absence of some compelling and countervailing reason making enforcement unreasonable.[16] Thus, a "freely negotiated private international agreement, *unaffected by fraud, undue influence or overweening bargaining power* should be given full effect."[17]

US law now even recognizes and enforces jurisdiction and choice of law clauses in contracts with a significant power imbalance between the parties, including B2C contracts.[18] These are, in principle at least, valid and enforceable. In *Burger King v Rudzewicz*[19] the US Supreme Court found: "a defendant who has purposefully derived commercial benefit from his affiliations in a forum may not defeat jurisdiction there simply because of his adversary's greater net wealth."[20]

This raises the question of how these principles apply to express jurisdiction clauses in consumer contracts. *M/S Bremen* was applied in a B2C dispute in *Carnival Cruise Lines v Shute*.[21] This case concerned a cruise customer suing in tort for personal injuries sustained on a cruise ship because of the alleged negligence of staff.

[12] Examples include Case C-498/16 *Schrems v Facebook* 25 January 2018 ECLI:EU:C:2018:37; *Douez v Facebook Inc.* 2017 SCC 33, Supreme Court of Canada Judgment of 23 June 2017; *Vidal-Hall v Google* [2016] QB 1003 (CA).

[13] See discussion in Chapter 9.

[14] *M/S Bremen v Zapata Off-Shore Co.* 407 US 1, 12–13; 92 SCt 1907 (1972).

[15] American Law Institute, Restatement of the Law Third "Foreign Relations Law of the US, Jurisdiction" (1987) 308; Restatement of the Law Fourth "Foreign Relations Law of the US Jurisdiction," Tentative Draft No 2 (22 March 2016) §302 Reporters Notes, 112; *National Equipment Rental Ltd v Szukhent* 375 US 311, 316; 84 SCt 411 (1964): "parties to a contract may agree in advance to submit to the jurisdiction of a given court."

[16] *M/S Bremen* (n 14) 12–13; see also *TradeComet.com LLC* (n 10); Art 5(1) Hague Convention on the Choice of Court Agreements of 30 June 2005, this has not (yet) been ratified by the US.

[17] *M/S Bremen* (n 14) 12–13.

[18] *Carnival Cruise Lines* (n 6).

[19] *Burger King v Rudzewicz* 471 US 462, 105 SCt 2174 (1985).

[20] ibid 484.

[21] *Carnival Cruise Lines* (n 6).

The US Supreme Court held[22] that the forum selection clause in favour of Florida contained in the consumer contract for the cruise was valid and enforceable, even though the clause was non-negotiated and may have made access to the courts for the consumer, who was domiciled in Washington, impossible. The Court focused on the transactional efficiency of such clauses and in particular risk management[23] and legal certainty[24] stating that consumers ultimately benefit from this transactional efficiency through lower prices.[25] Essentially the US Supreme Court only focused on the contractual analysis (applying a law and economics perspective) and refused to recognize why such a clause should be invalid and unenforceable as a matter of *public policy* embodying consumer protection. The Court ignored the fact that forum selection clauses constitute a "powerful litigation weapon for large-scale corporate defendants or the extent to which such clauses impact materially, adversely, and unfairly on the merits of consumers' substantive claims."[26] It is also questionable whether transactional efficiency translates into economic efficiency and greater wealth, as the inability of consumers to litigate may well mean that companies perform less well.[27] This could have serious detrimental effect on the consumer as by limiting litigation to the forum chosen by the stronger party can eliminate a consumer's legal claim entirely, which can result in consumer detriment through low quality products and low levels of care that could have been avoided, if the incentives created by the law had been optimal in the form of recourse to the courts and higher consumer protection standards.[28]

In summary therefore, US law recognizes and enforces express exclusive jurisdiction (forum selection) and choice of law clauses in contracts[29] in the absence of some compelling and countervailing reason making enforcement unreasonable.[30] The jurisdiction clause is either enforced by transfer between different US District Courts[31] or alternatively by dismissal under the Federal Rules of Civil Procedure.[32]

[22] In a majority Opinion of Justices Blackmun, Rehnquist, White, O'Connor, Scalia, Kennedy, Souter with Justices Stevens and Marshall dissenting.

[23] "a cruise line has a special interest in limiting the fora in which it potentially could be subject to suit. Because a cruise ship typically carries passengers from many locales, it is not unlikely that a mishap on a cruise could subject the cruise line to litigation in several different for a" p 593.

[24] A forum selection clause "has the salutary effect of dispelling any confusion about where suits arising from the contract must be brought and defended, sparing litigants the time and expense of pre-trial motions to determine the correct forum and conserving judicial resources (. . .)" p 594.

[25] ibid.

[26] EA Purcell, "Geography as a Litigation Weapon: Consumers, Forum-Selection Clauses, and the Rehnquist Court" (1992) 40 UCLA Law Review 423–515, 425.

[27] ibid 432.

[28] Woodward (n 4) 17.

[29] Before the US Court ruled in *M/S Bremen* (n 14) in 1972 it was disputed in the different Circuits whether forum selection clauses in advance of the dispute were against public policy, see eg *Carbon Black Export Inc. v The Monrosa* 254 F 2d 297 (CA5 1958), cert dismissed, 359 US 180, 79 SCt 710 (1959); see also Restatement of the Law Third (n 15) 308; Restatement of the Law Fourth (n 15) 112; *National Equipment Rental Ltd* (n 15) 316.

[30] *M/S Bremen* (n 14) 12–13; see also *TradeComet.com* (n 10); Art 5(1) Hague Convention on the Choice of Court Agreements of 30 June 2005, which has not been ratified by the US.

[31] 28 USC § 1404(a) and *Jumara v State Farm Ins Co* 55 F 3d 873, 877 (3d Cir 1995); *Salovaara v Jackson Nat'l Life Ins Co* 246 F 3d 289, 298–99 (3d Cir 2001).

[32] FRCP Rule 12(b)(3) improper venue.

This restrictive approach is also reflected in the Restatement: The starting point of the Restatement is the adoption of the party autonomy doctrine[33] as it states generally "the law of the state chosen by the parties to govern their contractual rights and duties will be applied ..."[34] According to the US Restatement (Second) of Conflicts of Law, in order to invalidate a choice of law clause on the basis that it is contrary to the forum state's public policy, the court in question must make four findings:

> (1) the chosen law has neither a "substantial relationship" to the parties nor some other reasonable basis; (2) application of the choice-of-law clause would be in contravention to the forum state's fundamental policy; (3) the forum state's fundamental policy is materially greater than the policy of the state chosen; and (4) the forum state's law would govern absent the choice by the parties.[35]

Theoretically, section 187(2) could protect the weaker party to the adhesion contract, due to the substantial relationship requirement towards the parties' choice, if the stronger party choosing the applicable law chooses a law with no connection to either party simply to avoid otherwise applicable consumer protection or privacy laws. In addition, there needs to be evidence of a materially greater interest than that of the state chosen by the parties in the contract, as well as it having to be the state whose law would apply if the choice of law clause was absent in the contract.

The reason for the recognition of jurisdiction and choice of law clauses is the principle of party autonomy and freedom of the parties to have the bargain they have reached legally recognized (freedom to contract). This freedom to contract in turn is an expression of the internationally accepted principle of party autonomy, which allows the parties to choose the applicable law and choose the forum.[36] This also enables the parties to both determine the contractual obligations and to foresee what the resulting obligations are. However, the principle of party autonomy is complemented by the principle of mutuality, meaning that the parties must have agreed a contract before it becomes binding on them, so that the principle of autonomy and mutuality are interrelated.[37] The principle of mutuality has been described as "the foundation underlying the bargain whilst also specifying the status of the parties as a result of this bargain"[38] and a lack of a mutually agreed bargain renders the contract itself voidable. These principles apply in respect of clauses stipulating a choice of forum and a choice of law in the same way as they apply to other contractual clauses: it is important that the parties exercise their autonomous choice on a mutual basis in order to determine which law shall govern the contract in question. Mo Zhang has developed a theory whereby four requirements are stipulated to ensure the principles of party autonomy and mutuality are fulfilled. Firstly, the parties must have been brought together voluntarily and each party is able to negotiate the contract without coercion. Secondly, the bargain must be fair and negotiated freely. Thirdly, there needs to be a mutual agreement between the

[33] Camarote (n 8) 606.
[34] Restatement Second of Conflict of Laws §187(1) (1971).
[35] ibid, see further Camarote (n 8) 607.
[36] Zhang (n 2) 127.
[37] ibid 130.
[38] ibid 133.

parties and assent towards all the proposed terms of the contract. Finally, the fourth test is whether the parties intended to have a certain law governing the contract so that the resulting obligations are within the reasonable expectation of both parties.[39] If the parties are of fairly equal bargaining power, the principle of party autonomy and mutuality support each other. However, if there is a large difference in the bargaining power between the parties, the principle of party autonomy (the law recognizing the bargain reached in the contract) and the principle of mutuality (ensuring that the bargain reflects the parties' mutual agreement) may well be in conflict with each other.

Adhesion contracts are defined by three shared characteristics. First, these contracts are not entered into as a result of free negotiation between the parties involved. Second, these contracts are drafted by one party and presented to the other on a "take it or leave it" format. This in turn inhibits the consumer from picking out the terms or clauses they do not agree to, therefore the party's assent to all the terms is ambiguous. Moreover, it creates an imbalance of power among the parties.[40]

The legal consequences of such adhesion contracts for the weaker party are fairly unpredictable or unknown in particular if these agreements contain a choice of law provision, which means that the rights of both parties will be governed by a specified legal system, and the weaker party does not have a chance to opt out of this clause.[41] Furthermore, the weaker (consumer) party may have no access to litigation in a distant forum stipulated by the jurisdiction clause.

For these reasons, jurisdiction clauses and choice of forum clause are not always enforced under US law. US law has now reached a position whereby a jurisdiction or choice of law clause in a consumer contract can be set aside in one of two scenarios: (1) if the clause is contained in an unenforceable adhesion contract and the clause is procedurally or substantively unconscionable, or (2) if it contravenes the *strong* public policy of the forum,[42] and for this the party who applies to have the clause set aside has a heavy burden of proof showing such countervailing strong public policy.[43]

2.2 Unconscionable clauses in adhesion contracts: procedural and substantive unconscionability (incorporation and fairness)

The rise of the doctrine of unconscionability resulted in the courts striking unfair terms out of such contracts. The Restatement (Second) of Contracts (the Restatement) summarizes the position in section 208: if a term in the contract is unconscionable at the time it is made, there is a discretion with regards to the enforceability of the term.[44] Courts may enforce the rest of a contract without the unconscionable term, or may apply the term in such a way so as to avoid any potential unconscionable results.[45]

[39] ibid 136.
[40] ibid 126.
[41] ibid 126.
[42] See also Art 6 (c) Hague Convention on the Choice of Court Agreements of 30 June 2005.
[43] *M/S Bremen* (n 14) 15–19, see also Restatement Second (n 34) Comment (b).
[44] Camarote (n 8) 617.
[45] *Higgins v Superior Court of Los Angeles County* Cal Ct App, 140 Cal App 4th 1238; 45 Cal Rptr 3d 293 (2006).

While the concept of unconscionability has existed in US common law for a long time, the doctrine was recognized, in section 2-302 of the Uniform Commercial Code (UCC):

(1) If the court as a matter of law finds the contract or any clause of the contract to have been unconscionable at the time it was made the court may refuse to enforce the contract, or it may enforce the remainder of the contract without the unconscionable clause, or it may so limit the application of any unconscionable clause as to avoid any unconscionable result.
(2) When it is claimed or appears to the court that the contract or any clause thereof may be unconscionable the parties shall be afforded a reasonable opportunity to present evidence as to its commercial setting, purpose and effect to aid the court in making the determination.[46]

The Official Comments provide some guidance on the concept of unconscionability, by explaining that a contractual provision is unconscionable if it is "so one-sided as to be unconscionable under the circumstances existing at the time of the making of the contract. The principle is one of the preventions of oppression and unfair surprise and not of disturbance of allocation of risks because of superior bargaining power."

A clause is generally required to be both procedurally and substantively unconscionable before it may be held to be unenforceable.[47] The leading case that illustrated this two-prong test is that of *Williams v Walker-Thomas Furniture Co*,[48] where the majority opinion of Judge Wright on this subject has been highly influential. His opinion sets forth the two-limb test to determine unconscionability by examining whether there was an absence of meaningful choice and whether the contract terms unreasonably favoured one party. Substantive unconscionability refers to the substance of the contract, that is, the terms within the contract itself and the question as to which party is most favoured by these terms.

2.2.1 Procedural unconscionability

Procedural unconscionability, on the other hand, makes reference to the way the consent to the terms was obtained.[49] In the 1976 case of *Johnson v Mobil Oil Corp*[50] the Court provided a non-exhaustive range of factors when considering whether a term falls under the procedural prong of unconscionability such as "age, education, intelligence, business acumen and experience, relative bargaining power, who drafted the contract, whether the terms were explained to the weaker party, whether alterations in the printed terms were possible, whether there were alternative sources of supply for the goods in question."[51] These may be some of the factors the courts take into account

[46] UCC §2–302 (2011).
[47] *Armendariz v Foundation Health Psychcare Services, Inc* 24 Cal 4th 83, 6 P.3d 669, 99 Cal Rptr 2d 745, 2000 Cal.
[48] 350 F 2d 445 (DC Cir 1965).
[49] MN Browne and L Biksacky, "Unconscionability and Contingent Assumptions of Contract Theory" (2013) Michigan State Law Review 211–55, 219–23.
[50] 415 F Supp 264, 268 (ED Mich 1976).
[51] See further discussion in Browne and Bicksacky (n 49) 223.

when assessing whether meaningful consent to a contract was obtained and the clause incorporated. This wide range of factors can be explained by the mutuality doctrine.

As a minimum, the party imposing standard terms and conditions must ensure that the terms have been brought to the reasonable attention of the other party—otherwise the terms have not been incorporated in the contract and are not part of it. This is a question of contract law, which will largely be governed by applicable state law with variations in the requirements imposed. The standard has been described in respect of electronic contracts in Californian law by Judge (as he then was) Sotomayor: "*[r]easonably conspicuous notice of the existence of contract terms and unambiguous manifestation of assent to those terms by consumers are essential if electronic bargaining is to have integrity and credibility*."[52]

On a fundamental level, a distinction can be made between online contracting processes that require affirmative action (more likely to lead to successful incorporation[53]) and those that do not. Thus, it could be said that what is required for incorporation of online terms is notice and affirmative action.

The most common contract forms that are used in e-commerce are known as click-wrap agreements and browse-wrap agreements. Click-wrap and browse-wrap agreements have evolved out of shrink-wrap agreements, wherein the first paragraph of a shrink-wrap agreement stated that the opening of the package would indicate agreement and acceptance of the licence terms, as in the early years of the software industry, publishers boxed software with shrink-wrap surrounding the package with the licence being inside the box.[54] Similar to the shrink-wrap, click-wrap and browse-wrap agreements assume blanket assent to the terms.

For click-wrap agreements, the terms may appear as a pop-up window or are integrated in the contracting interface, encouraging the party to scroll through the terms. In addition, before the contract is concluded the party has to click on a button or check a tick box "I agree," thus indicating by affirmative action that he or she agrees to terms ("click-wrap").[55] Browse-wrap agreements do not even require the consumer to click "I Agree," in these circumstances simply the action of browsing the website indicates assent to the terms. The notice that binds the consumer may take the form of a hyperlink at the bottom of a webpage or a disclaimer that gives notice to the consumer that his or her use of the website is conditional on agreeing to the terms.[56]

Courts have held both click-wrap[57] and, less so,[58] browse-wrap[59] forum selection clauses regularly valid and enforceable, sometimes on the basis that otherwise the

[52] *Specht v Netscape Commc'ns Corp* 306 F 3d 17, 35 (2d Cir NY 2002).

[53] *Hancock v American Tel and Tel Co* 701 F 3d 1248, 1257 (10th Cir 2012); *In Re Facebook Biometric Information Privacy Litigation* 185 F Supp 3d 1155, 1166 (US District Court ND California 2016); *Nguyen v Barnes & Noble Inc.* 763 F 3d 1171, 1176–77 (9th Cir 2014).

[54] ML Rustad and MV Onufrio, "Reconceptualizing Consumer Terms Of Use For A Globalized Knowledge Economy" (2012) 14 University of Pennsylvania Journal of Business Law 1085–190, 1102.

[55] As to the distinction between the two see RL Dickens, "Finding Common Ground in the World of Electronic Contracts" (2007) 11 Marquette Intellectual Property Law Review 307–410, 386–87.

[56] Rustad and Onufrio (n 54) 1107.

[57] *Caspi v Microsoft Network* 323 NJ Super 118, 125–26; 732 A 2d 528 (Superior Court of New Jersey, Appellate Division 1999) Cert Denied: 162 NJ 199,743 A 2d 851 (Supreme Court of New Jersey 1999); *Feldman v Google, Inc.* 513 F Supp 2d 229, 233, 237 (ED Pa 2007); *Forrest v Verizon Communications Inc.* 805 A 2d 1007, 1010–11 (DC 2002); *Scherillo v Dun & Bradstreet, Inc.* 684 F Supp 2d 313, 320-1 (ED NY 2010).

[58] *Nguyen* (n 53) 1176 (9th Cir 2014): "[c]ourts have (…) been more willing to find the requisite notice for constructive assent where the browse wrap agreement resembles a click wrap agreement."

[59] *Kilgallen v Network Solutions, Inc.* 99 F Supp 2d 125, 129–30 (D Mass 2000); *In Re Facebook* (n 53) 1166.

online provider using the clause could be sued in many different locations, such that the forum selection clause is required as a risk management tool.[60] As with other contracts, not reading the terms and conditions is not a defence for asserting that a jurisdiction clause is not incorporated in the online contract.[61] A few courts have held forum selection clauses in the internet context unenforceable[62] on the basis that the clause could not easily be found. This is due to the structure of the webpage (eg where it was not obvious that the customer has to scroll through lengthy text to find the jurisdiction clause).[63]

Thus, provided the party on whom terms and conditions are imposed has clear notice of terms and has access to them, the law provides for the fiction that the terms have been incorporated. While the expression of "small print" has become proverbial to mean terms and conditions ever since mass consumer contracts have become common, e-commerce has exacerbated the problem in that the length of the terms is not now restricted to what can be fitted in small print on the back of an A4 page. Regardless of the form of incorporation of terms in online contracts their sheer length and complexity makes it extremely unlikely that customers do in fact notice them. For example, Facebook's terms contain a jurisdiction clause for exclusive jurisdiction in the "U.S. District Court for the Northern District of California or a state court located in San Mateo County" and counts 3402 words.[64] Apple iTunes store's terms contain 6712 words, which is twelve pages of small print, and there is an exclusive jurisdiction clause in favour of the courts located within the county of Santa Clara, California (with an exception for EU/EEA citizens).[65] Google's terms contain 1893 words, about five pages, and contain the same exclusive jurisdiction clause with no exceptions.[66] YouTube's terms count 3730 words, again with exclusive jurisdiction of the courts in Santa Clara, California.[67]

In addition to the terms of service, users have to take notice of the privacy policies, acceptable use policies, end-user licence agreements, and other statements.[68] Thus, each user would have to spend four hours or more reading the documentation before signing on to these or similar online media services. This raises the question whether the principle that customers are nevertheless bound by terms even if they have not read them is correct in the modern age.

[60] *Feldman* (n 57) 242–43.

[61] *Barnett v Network Solutions, Inc.* 38 S W 3d 200, 204 (Tex App 2001); *Feldman* (n 57) 238.

[62] *Janson v LegalZoom.com*, Inc., 727 F Supp 2d 782 (WD Mo 2010).

[63] *Hoffman v Supplements Togo Management, LLC* 419 NJ Super 596, 598, 610–11; 18 A 3d 210 (Superior Court New Jersey Appellate Division 2011) "website was evidently structured in an unfair manner"; *Specht v Netscape* (n 52) 31–32 (in respect of an online arbitration clause, which was contained in scroll-down text on the screen submerged far below the download button and therefore easy to overlook); *Pollstar v Gigmania Ltd* 170 F Supp 2d 974, 981 (ED Cal2000) (hyperlink in small grey print on a grey background).

[64] Version 30 January 2015, Statement of Rights and Responsibilities, https://www.facebook.com/policies?ref=pf accessed on 26/7/2020.

[65] Apple Media Services Terms and Conditions, Version 13 September 2016, https://www.apple.com/legal/internet-services/itunes/us/terms.html accessed on 26/7/2020.

[66] Google Terms of Service, Version 14 April 2014, https://www.google.com/intl/en/policies/terms/ accessed on 26/7/2020.

[67] YouTube Terms of Service, Version 10. December 2019, https://www.youtube.com/static?gl=US&template=terms accessed on 26/07/2020.

[68] See also Which? The UK Consumer Association, https://conversation.which.co.uk/technology/length-of-website-terms-and-conditions accessed on 26/7/2020.

These one-sided clauses will in turn have a chilling effect on a consumer's ability to file claims against e-commerce platforms. A study of standard contract terms of use was conducted by Professor Marotta-Wurgler at NYU School of law.[69] This study tracked the online browsing behaviour of more than 48,000 monthly visitors to the websites of ninety online software companies, and concluded that only "one or two consumers in a thousand"[70] actually accessed the terms. Moreover, the research also found that the average time spent "reading" these contracts was twenty-nine seconds, where the average length of a sample click-wrap agreement was 2,277 words, meaning the consumers "read" the contract in less than a minute. Either consumers have the ability to read at record breaking speed, or they have merely scrolled through the agreement and blindly assumed they were entering into a risk-free environment and/or that they had no real choice. It is quite obvious that it is more likely the latter.

Given the incredible information overload and the sheer quantity and complexity of terms and policies it is questionable whether customers are given reasonable notice on which to base their consent in a legally meaningful way. The incorporation of terms and conditions always laboured on a degree of legal fiction, in the sense that even at an age when terms were printed on the back of an invoice (one page of A4), many customers did not in fact read them, but they had a realistic option to do so. By contrast, now the reality may be so far detached from legal assumptions that it is time to consider whether new obligations should be placed on those using standard terms online. For example, terms could be classified according to certain models (and dispute resolution clauses would be one aspect of this model) and customers contract on the basis of these models. For an early example of what these models might look like see the "Terms of Service; Didn't Read" project.[71] Here further research in (digital) legal design will bring more clarity.[72]

2.2.2 Substantive unconscionability

A few courts have held forum selection clauses in the internet context unenforceable[73] if the chosen court is entirely inaccessible to the party challenging the forum selection clause[74] (such that it would deprive the party of her day in court[75]—a high burden of proof) or that it would deprive the plaintiff(s) of the benefit of class action.[76]

However, courts have been divided on the class action issue. Following *Carnival Cruise Lines*, a Florida court applied the *Shute/Bremen* analysis to the case of *America Online v Booker*[77]—resulting, in what some say was, an "even harsher outcome than Shute itself."[78] The plaintiff's class action was destroyed through the Court's

[69] Y Bakos, F Marotta-Wurgler, and DR Trossen, "Does Anyone Read the Fine Print? Consumer Attention to Standard Form Contracts" (2014) 43(1) Journal of Legal Studies 1–33.

[70] ibid 1.

[71] https://tosdr.org/ accessed on 26/7/2020.

[72] http://www.lawbydesign.co/en/legal-design/ accessed on 26/7/2020.

[73] *Janson* (n 62).

[74] *Carfax, Inc v Browning* 982 So 2d 491, 492–94 (Ala 2007).

[75] *M/S Bremen* (n 14) 18.

[76] *Dix v ICT Group, Inc* 160 Wash 2d 826, 841; 161 P 3d 1016 (2007) 842–43: "If a forum selection clause precludes class actions and thereby significantly impairs Washington citizens' ability to seek relief under the CPA for small-value claims, the clause violates the public policy."

[77] *America Online v Booker*, 781 So 2d 423 (Fla Dist Ct App 2001).

[78] Camarote (n 8) 616.

enforcement of the choice of forum clause. The chosen forum was the state of Virginia, a state with no class action procedure. The Court found that the plaintiff was unable to show that the selection was unjust or unfair. This is a prime example of the subtle effects a choice of forum clause may have, as it is used for defeating class action as a procedural tool for consumers, an important device for "vindicating consumer rights," without even mentioning this effect.[79]

In contrast to the approach set out in the *Booker* case, the Californian Court in *America Online*[80] refused to enforce a choice of forum contract provision. This case involved a California class action brought by AOL customers under the California Consumers Legal Remedies Act. The Court allowed the consumers to seek class action relief, even though the contract drafted by AOL contained a choice of forum clause designating Virginia as the applicable law and exclusive forum for litigating disputes. The Court refused to enforce the provision, reasoning that the enforcement of such a provision would amount to "a waiver prohibited by California policy and because enforcement would substantially diminish the consumers' rights in violation of California policy."[81]

2.3 Contravening strong public policy in the forum

In recent privacy class action cases the Californian courts have used *public policy* arguments to apply the law of the consumers' domicile as mandatory law over and above the law chosen by the social media provider or to oust a choice of forum clause if it deprives claimants of the availability of class actions.

In Re Facebook Biometric Information Privacy Litigation[82] the Californian courts are examining the compatibility of Facebook's facial recognition and tagging practices with the Illinois Biometric Information Privacy Act (BIPA) in a putative class action by Facebook users from Illinois. The plaintiffs agreed to the transfer of their case to California, but the question arose whether they were bound by the choice of law in Facebook's terms in favour of Californian law. The three plaintiffs had all joined Facebook at different points in time, but all of them had notice during the contracting process of terms through a hyperlink to these terms and they had to take affirmative action to sign up.[83] While the Court was critical of this approach, stating that it was more on the unenforceable "browse-wrap" scale it decided that the notice that terms are being agreed to close to the button to sign up was sufficient for the choice of law to be *incorporated* to the contract.[84] However, it applied the Illinois BIPA nevertheless, as it represented *fundamental public policy* and the Court refused to enforce the Californian choice of law provision for that reason.[85]

[79] Woodward (n 4) 18.
[80] *America Online, Inc. v Superior Court of Alameda County (Mendoza)*, 90 CalApp 4th 1, 108 Cal Rptr 2d 699 (2001).
[81] Woodward (n 4) 23.
[82] *In Re Facebook* (n 53). .
[83] ibid 1162–63.
[84] ibid 1166–67.
[85] ibid 1169–70.

In *Doe 1, Doe 2 and Kasadore Ramkisson v AOL* the 9th Circuit Court held that a forum selection clause in favour of the courts of Virginia was unenforceable for the reason that this would have deprived the plaintiffs of the availability of a class action in California.[86] This case arose from the publication of the AOL search records of 650,000 AOL subscribers in 2006. The claimants alleged infringements of federal privacy laws and Californian law. The Court held that California *public policy* would be violated if the plaintiffs were forced to waive their rights to a class action and remedies under California consumer law by having to litigate in Virginia. For this reason, the Court held that the forum selection clause was unenforceable for public policy reasons.[87]

The Canadian Supreme Court in *Douez v Facebook* has reached a similar conclusion concerning consumer adhesion contracts and public policy.[88] This case concerned a privacy class action[89] against Facebook by British Columbia residents under a statutory tort contained in the Privacy Act of British Colombia.[90] The alleged privacy infringement related to "sponsored stories advertising"; whereby Facebook had used the profile picture and name of Facebook account holders who had "liked" a product to advertise this fact to other users without consent. The Privacy Act confers jurisdiction to claims under the Act to the (Canadian) Supreme Court.[91] Facebook sought dismissal of the claim on the basis that its terms with its Canadian users contained an exclusive jurisdiction clause in favour of the Californian Courts and a choice of law clause in favour of Californian law.

The Canadian Supreme Court held that the jurisdiction clause in the Privacy Act did not apply to international conflicts of law,[92] but was merely a domestic jurisdiction rule. It furthermore held that although the Court Jurisdiction and Proceedings Transfer Act[93] had codified the common law of *forum non conveniens*, this doctrine did not apply to the question of whether the Canadian courts should decline jurisdiction to give effect to an exclusive jurisdiction clause in favour of a foreign court contained in the contract between Facebook and its users.[94] Instead, the Court relied on the common law doctrine[95] concerning forum selection clauses in *Pompey Industrie v ECU Line NV*, a commercial shipping case.[96] The Court held by a narrow majority of four to three that the forum selection clause could not be used to stop the class action in the courts of British Columbia and refused to order a stay. The outcome was that the

[86] *Doe 1, Doe 2 and Kasadore Ramkisson v AOL* 552 F 3d 1077 (2009).

[87] ibid 1084; see also (n 94).

[88] [2017] SCC 33, Judgment of 23 June 2017, available from CanLII https://www.canlii.org/en/ca/scc/doc/2017/2017scc33/2017scc33.html accessed on 26/7/2020.

[89] The proposed class comprising all British Columbia residents who had their name and picture used in sponsored stories advertising, about 1.8 million people.

[90] Privacy Act, RSBC 1996, c 373, s 3(2) "It is a tort, actionable without proof of damage, for a person to use the name or portrait of another for the purpose of advertising or promoting the sale of, or other trading in, property or services, unless that other, or a person entitled to consent on his or her behalf, consents to the use for that purpose."

[91] S 4.

[92] Paras 4, 44 (Majority), 142 (Dissent) but see dissent in the Concurring Opinion of Justice Abella at paras 107–10.

[93] Court Jurisdiction and Proceedings Transfer Act, SBC 2003, c 28, s 11.

[94] Paras 17–22 (Plurality), 108 (Dissenting Opinion).

[95] Paras 17–22 (Plurality), 88–94 (Concurring).

[96] *Pompey Industrie v ECU Line NV* [2003] 1 SCR 450.

forum selection clause was unenforceable. A minority of three dissenting Justices held that the Canadian class action should be stayed, as the plaintiff had *not* shown the required "strong cause."[97]

Pompey had set out a two-step test for assessing whether or not a forum selection clause was enforced under Canadian law. First the party relying on the clause had to prove that the clause was valid and clear and applied to the dispute,[98] then the burden of proof shifted to the party who claimed the clause was unenforceable, who had to show "strong cause" why the clause should not be enforced.[99]

A plurality of three judges[100] found that the plaintiff succeeded at this *second* step, saying that here the convenience of the parties, the fairness between the parties, and the interests of justice as well as public policy had to be taken into account.[101] This plurality found that while the "strong cause" had been applied very restrictively in commercial cases[102] this was very different in consumer cases.[103] Significantly, the plurality held that the traditional consumer "fairness" considerations had to be supplemented *by public policy* considerations. The emphasis on public policy is interesting in that the Court clearly acknowledged that adjudication is not (always) only about the private interests of the parties to the dispute but also a "public good": "Courts are not merely "law-making and applying venues"; they are institutions of "public norm generation and legitimation."[104] The plurality opinion also pointed to the market power of Facebook and its ubiquitous reach: "access to Facebook and social media platforms, including the online communities they make possible, has become increasingly important for the exercise of free speech, freedom of association and for full participation in democracy. Having the choice to remain 'offline' may not be a real choice in the Internet era."[105]

Here the fact that an individual consumer contracted with a large multinational corporation with overwhelming bargaining power *and* the fact that privacy was a fundamental right with quasi-constitutional rank implicating strong public policy considerations came together to oust the express jurisdiction clause.[106] The plurality held that Canadian courts had a strong public interest in adjudicating cases of constitutional rights such as privacy.[107] Furthermore, the Court found two secondary reasons. First, that not staying proceedings was in the interests of justice as the British Columbia courts were better placed than the Californian courts to decide privacy rights interpreting British Columbia legislation.[108] This is similar to a *forum*

[97] Para 125 per McLachlin CJ and Moldaver and Côté JJ.

[98] This involves applying contract law principles such as incorporation, unconscionability, undue influence, and fraud, see para 28.

[99] Paras 28–29.

[100] Justices Karakatsanis, Wagner, and Gascon.

[101] Paras 29, 49.

[102] Forum selection clauses are "generally encouraged by the courts as they create certainty and security in transaction, derivatives of order and fairness, which are critical components of private international law," citing *Pompey* (n 96) paras 20, 31.

[103] Paras 1, 33.

[104] Paras 25, 26.

[105] Para 56 omitting internal references.

[106] Paras 4, 51–63 (Plurality), 104–05 (Concurring).

[107] ibid.

[108] Paras 4, 64.

non-conveniens analysis, but puts the burden of proof on the person who opposes the foreign forum selection clause.[109] The choice of law clause in the *Facebook* contract was relevant here as Californian law might deprive the plaintiff of his or her rights under the fundamental rights under the laws of British Columbia.[110] Second, the plurality also pointed to the expense and inconvenience of British Columbia residents litigating in California relative to the expense and inconvenience caused to Facebook in defending this action in British Columbia.[111]

The concurring fourth Justice,[112] by contrast, found that the *Facebook* forum selection clause is already invalid under the first step of the *Pompey*[113] analysis (where the burden rests on the party relying on the clause, here Facebook).[114] Like the plurality, the concurring Justice held that the grossly uneven bargaining power of the parties combined with public policy considerations tilts the balance in favour of not enforcing the clause.[115] Furthermore, unlike the plurality, she found the clause also unconscionable because of its unfairness and the inequality of bargaining power.[116]

2.4 Conclusion: US law

Under US common law the starting point is that forum selection clauses in consumer contracts are enforceable because of the emphasis on party autonomy in the jurisprudence following the US Supreme Court Decision in *Carnival Cruise Lines*. However, for non-negotiated consumer contracts, so-called adhesion contracts the common law has mitigated the effect of the party autonomy doctrine by the principle of procedural and substantive unconscionability, whereby the courts have set aside forum selection clauses that have not come to the attention of consumers or are substantively unconscionable, for example, on the basis that the forum was chosen in order to defeat consumers' class action rights. The case law on unconscionability, however, has been inconsistent and the law therefore varies between different US states and different courts.

In particular in respect of privacy litigation some courts, both in the US and in Canada, have voided jurisdiction and choice of law clauses in standard terms used by Facebook on the basis that such a term infringes the *public policy* of the forum, coming to this conclusion on the basis of the importance of privacy rights and the overwhelming bargaining power of companies such as Facebook.

As the preceding discussion has shown, there are two distinct aspects to how private international law controls the enforceability of forum selection clauses. First, a contractual analysis based on unconscionability and, second, privacy and consumer rights as an aspect of the application of public policy. While in practice both doctrines

109 Para 65.
110 Paras 68–69, 71–72.
111 Paras 4, 73.
112 Justice Abella.
113 *Pompey* (n 96).
114 Para 96.
115 Para 111.
116 Paras 114–16.

may overlap in the argumentation of the courts, conceptually it is important to make a distinction between them, for the reason that contract law is based on the free will of the parties (party autonomy) and a respect for their negotiated agreement, which is only restricted to the extent that adhesion contracts do not give sufficient notice and/or contain unconscionable clauses (mutuality).

By contrast, public policy and the protection of privacy as a fundamental right override the free will of the parties in the public interest. While public policy has receded in the background for a number of years, the most recent case law in the area of privacy protection is based on strong public policy arguments. It is argued here that both aspects (contractual and public policy doctrines) are paramount for not only achieving justice between the parties of a dispute but also ensuring good administration of justice in the public interest. In particular, in cases where fundamental rights such as the right to privacy are engaged, public policy should play a role in upholding *local* values and protecting consumers from having to litigate in distant courts under unfamiliar laws. Thus, public policy has a role to play both in respect of court jurisdiction and in respect of applying local (privacy) laws as mandatory laws.

Purely focusing on transactional efficiency and a contractual analysis misses two distinct points, namely that justice is about local rights and courts have a role in not merely adjudicating on the dispute before them but also upholding the administration of justice. It is for this reason that both the contractual analysis and the public policy analysis should be part of the test for examining the enforceability of forum selection and choice of law clauses. This is all the more important in respect of social media providers such as Facebook who have a significant share of the world's population as users on their platform and whose vast resources puts them at a significant advantage to litigate in a foreign place vis-à-vis the individual user.

3. EU consumer jurisdiction

3.1 A brief history of the harmonization of the rules on private international law and special consumer protection in the EU

In the EU, the rules on private international law are split into the rules on applicable law for contractual obligations (Rome I Regulation[117]), rules on applicable law for non-contractual obligations (Rome II Regulation[118]), rules on jurisdiction, and the recognition and enforcement of civil and commercial judgments (Brussels (Recast) Regulation[119]).

The first instrument harmonizing the rules on applicable law for contracts was the Rome Convention of 1980.[120] It contained a consumer protection clause applicable to

117 Regulation EC/593/2008 on the Law Applicable to Contractual Obligations (Rome I) of 17 June 2008, OJ L177/6.

118 Regulation EC/864/2007 on the Law Applicable to Non-contractual Obligations (Rome II) of 11 July 2007, OJ L199/40.

119 Brussels Jurisdiction Regulation EU/1215/2012 of 12 December 2012, OJ L351/1.

120 1980 Rome Convention on the Law Applicable to Contractual Obligations of 19 June 1980, which entered into force on 1 April 1991; consolidated version in OJ C27/34 of 26 January 1998.

e-commerce consumer contracts, which applied if in the country of the habitual residence of the consumer the conclusion of the contract had been preceded by a specific invitation addressed to him or her, and the consumer had taken all the steps necessary to conclude the contract on his or her part in that country. If these conditions applied, the consumer could not be deprived of the mandatory (consumer protection) provisions in the law of his or her habitual residence,[121] or if the contract did not contain a choice of law, the law of the consumer's habitual residence applied.[122] However, this provision was difficult to apply to e-commerce as the concept of a "specific invitation addressed to him" was not meaningful in that context,[123] and it is difficult to determine the state where the consumer undertook "the steps necessary for the conclusion of the contract."[124] These difficulties lead to the reform in the Rome I Regulation.

The first instrument harmonizing the rules on jurisdiction was the Brussels Convention of 1968.[125] In its original version, Article 13 did not mention consumers specifically but only provided for special rules for the sale of goods on instalment credit terms and loans expressly made to finance the sale of goods and repayable by instalments.[126] It was amended in 1978 to include specific consumer protection provisions in Article 13.[127] It contained similar wording as Article 5(2) of the Rome Convention and was likewise deemed out of date specifically for e-commerce. The reform came in the shape of the Jurisdiction ("Brussels") Regulation,[128] which updated the provisions on consumer jurisdiction[129] by rewording its scope of application.[130]

[121] Art 5(2).

[122] Art 5(3).

[123] See further R Schu, "The Applicable Law to Consumer Contracts Made Over the Internet: Consumer Protection Through Private International Law?" (1997) 5(2) International Journal of Law and Information Technology 192–229, 209–11.

[124] ibid. 224.

[125] Regulation EU/1215/2012 on Jurisdiction and the Recognition and Enforcement of Judgments in Civil and Commercial Matters of 12 December 2012, OJ L351/1.

[126] See (n 127).

[127] Accession Convention of 9 October 1978 of the Kingdom of Denmark, of Ireland and of the United Kingdom to the Jurisdiction Convention (which added the consumer provisions to the Brussels Convention). The wording of Art 13 was then as follows: "In proceedings concerning a contract concluded by a person for a purpose which can be regarded as being outside his trade or profession, hereinafter called the consumer, jurisdiction shall be determined by this section (. . .) if it is:

(1) a contract for the sale of goods on instalment credit terms; or
(2) a contract for a loan repayable by instalments, or for any other form of credit, made to finance the sale of goods; or
(3) any other contract for the supply of goods or a contract for the supply of services, and
 (a) in the State of the consumer's domicile the conclusion of the contract was preceded by a specific invitation addressed to him or by advertising; and
 (b) the consumer took in that State the steps necessary for the conclusion of the contract.

[128] The EU having competence in the area of civil justice since the Treaty of Amsterdam could create an EU legal instrument instead of a new Convention, see further Explanatory Memorandum to Brussels Regulation Proposal 1999 COM(1999) 348; Arts 61(c) and 65 of the EC Treaty.

[129] The 1988 Lugano Convention concluded between the EC Member States and the then EFTA states had the same consumer protection provisions as the Brussels Convention of 1968. This Lugano Convention was also updated/recast in 2007 and now contains the same wording on consumer jurisdiction as the 2001 Brussels Regulation (Switzerland, Norway, and Iceland): Convention on Jurisdiction and the Recognition and Enforcement of Judgments in Civil and Commercial Matters 8, signed at Lugano on 30 October 2007.

[130] Arts 15–17 of Council Regulation (EC) No 44/2001 of 22 December 2000 on Jurisdiction and the Recognition and Enforcement of Judgments in Civil and Commercial Matters Official Journal L12/1.

The jurisprudence of the Court of Justice of the EU (CJEU) interpreting the provisions of the Brussels Convention continues to be relevant to the interpretation of the Jurisdiction Regulation.[131] Further reform came in 2012 in the current Jurisdiction ("Brussels Bis" or "Brussels Recast") Regulation with identical wording as far as the consumer protection provisions are concerned (but which have been moved from Articles 15–17 to Articles 17–19).[132] The aim of the 2012 revision was to "further facilitate the free circulation of judgments and to further enhance access to justice."[133] One important innovation is that the consumer protection provisions have been extended to all disputes, even if the defendant is not domiciled in an EU Member State, thus harmonizing EU law in this respect and creating uniform jurisdiction rules for consumers.[134]

3.2 Consumer protection rules in private international law in the EU

The main difference between the US/Canadian approach to jurisdiction of the courts in consumer cases and that of the EU is that consumer protection law forms a *fixed* part of the rules on private international law in the EU. In the EU, there is no need to find a breach of fundamental rights or public policy on a case-by-case basis, as the consumer protection rules are hardwired into the rules on jurisdiction and applicable law. The consumer is protected because he or she is regarded a priori as the weaker party (vis-à-vis the business) in a transaction, with less legal resources and legal experience, and therefore that it would be unfair for this weaker party to have the burden of crossing a border to sue in a foreign state and that greater legal certainty is achieved by codifying the rules.[135] By the same token, the consumer protection rules[136] only apply to certain *relevant consumer contracts*. Furthermore, the Brussels (Recast) Regulation explicitly refers to the concept of party autonomy,[137] and the CJEU has constantly emphasized that the consumer protection provisions must be narrowly interpreted.[138]

Relevant consumer contracts are contracts concluded by a consumer who is defined as a person who makes the contract "for a purpose which can be regarded as being

[131] Case C-180/06 *Renate Ilsinger v Martin Dreschers* 14 May 2009 ECLI:EU:C:2009:303, para 41 and Recital 34 of the current Brussels Regulation EU/1215/2012.

[132] Brussels Jurisdiction Regulation EU/1215/2012 of 12 December 2012, OJ L351/1 effective from 10 January 2015 (Art 81), applicable to court proceedings and judgments where proceedings were instituted on or after this date (Art 66). The Regulation has been implemented in the English courts by The Civil Procedure (Amendment No 7) Rules 2014 (SI 2014/2948).

[133] Recital 1.

[134] Arts 6(1) and 18(1) and Recital 14.

[135] Case C-89/91 *Shearson Lehmann Hutton v TVB*, 19 January 1993 ECLI:EU:C:1993:15, para 18; Case C-150/77 *Bertrand v Paul Ott KG* 21 June 1978 ECLI:EU:C:1978:137, paras 21–22; Recital 18 to Brussels Jurisdiction Regulation EU/1215/2012; Explanatory Memorandum to Brussels Regulation Proposal 1999 COM(1999) 348; see also JST Øren, "International Jurisdiction Over Consumer Contracts in e-Europe" (2003) 52 International Comparative Law Quarterly 666–95, 669.

[136] The rules used to be contained in Arts 15–17 of the Brussels Jurisdiction Regulation 44/2001/EC, which has been recast as Regulation 1215/2012/EU Arts 17–19 (identical wording); Rome I Regulation EC/593/2008 Art 6.

[137] Recital 19.

[138] Discussed further later.

outside his trade or profession."[139] Additionally, the contract must be (1) a contract for the sale of goods on instalment credit terms,[140] (2) a contract for a loan repayable in instalments or for any type of loan financing the sale of goods,[141] (3) a contract "concluded with a person who pursues commercial or professional activities[142] in the Member State of the consumer's domicile," or (4) "by any means, directs such activities to that Member State or to several States including that Member State, and the contract falls within the scope of such activities."[143] Thus, for the special consumer protection provisions in private international law[144] to apply three conditions must be satisfied: the contract must be a business-to-consumer contract, the contract must be of a particular nature, and the contract must have been concluded.[145]

In the context of e-commerce consumer contracts the condition of "directing" is the most relevant, as this was specifically introduced to cover distance selling and e-commerce.

If the contract concluded is a relevant consumer contract and the special consumer protection rules in the Regulation apply, the consequence for jurisdiction is that an EU domiciled consumer (as claimant) has a choice according to Article 18(1): they can sue the business party either at the place of *their own domicile* (home court privilege) or in the EU Member State of that *business' domicile* (foreign court, which the claimant may choose since enforcement may be easier there or the consumer protection rules may be more opportune).[146] Obviously, if the business is domiciled outside the EU and the consumer wishes to sue at the defendant's domicile, the courts in that non-EU jurisdiction will apply their own rules on jurisdiction, which are not governed by the Brussels Regulation.

In the reverse situation, where a business wishes to sue the EU-domiciled consumer (consumer as the defendant), the business can only sue the consumer in the EU Member State of the consumer's domicile and the courts of all other EU Member States have to decline jurisdiction according to Article 18(2). This provision is a strong consumer protection provision as it means that the *consumer as defendant* always has the home court privilege of being sued only in his or her local court. If the dispute arises sometime after the contract has been concluded and the business does not know the current domicile of the consumer it wishes to sue, the business can use the last known domicile and issue proceedings there.[147]

[139] Art 17 (1) Brussels Jurisdiction Regulation EU/1215/2012 of 12 December 2012, OJ L351 20/12/2012, p 1; Art 6(1) Rome Regulation on the Law Applicable to Contractual Obligations (Rome I) EU/593/2008 of 4 July 2008, OJ L177 4/7/2008, p 6.

[140] Art 17(1)(a) Brussels Recast Regulation.

[141] Art 17(1)(b).

[142] The term "pursues" can be seen in contradistinction to the term "direct" and is likely to refer to systematic and continuous business arrangements and require some physical presence in the relevant Member State and hence is likely not to apply to e-commerce; see further Øren (n 135) 677.

[143] Art 17(1)(c) Brussels Jurisdiction Regulation, Art 6(1)(a) and (b) Rome I Regulation—the provisions on contracts for the sale of goods on instalment credit terms and a contract for a loan repayable in instalments or for any type of loan financing the sale of goods are missing from the Rome Regulation.

[144] Brussels Jurisdiction Regulation and the Rome I Regulation.

[145] Case C-296/14 *Rüdiger Hobohm v Benedikt Kampik Ltd*, 23 December 2015 ECLI:EU:C:2015:844, para 24.

[146] Art 18(1).

[147] Case C-327/10 *Hypoteční Banka v Udo Lindner* 17 November 2011 ECLI:EU:C:2011:745, paras 42–46, 55: "for the purpose of applying Article 16(2) of Regulation No 44/2001, the criterion of the consumer's

This can be termed a form of "asymmetric" consumer protection jurisdiction: consumers are privileged in that the business can only sue them in their "home" court, whereas the consumer has the choice of two options as a claimant: suing "at home or abroad."[148] These are provisions of mandatory consumer protection in the sense that they cannot be deviated from by express contractual provisions or jurisdiction clauses.[149] Article 19 contains three narrowly crafted exceptions providing for *valid* jurisdiction agreements in a relevant consumer contract. The first exception is jurisdiction agreed between the parties *after* the dispute has arisen (post dispute jurisdiction agreement).[150] The second exception is an agreement between the parties that gives the consumer as claimant *additional* options where to bring a claim.[151] Thirdly, if the business and the consumer are both domiciled or habitually resident in the same EU Member State at the time of the conclusion of the contract, the agreement may validly provide that the courts of that particular, joint domicile Member State have jurisdiction[152] (as at the time of the conclusion of the contract the relationship is domestic-lacking an international element). Presumably this is to allow a business to reduce the jurisdictional risk arising from the consumer later moving away.

Furthermore, the Brussels Regulation in Article 17(2) contains a non-rebuttable presumption that if a consumer contracts with a business who is *not* domiciled or headquartered in a EU Member State, but has a *branch, agency or other establishment* in any EU Member State, the business is deemed to be domiciled in that EU Member State *if* the dispute arose out of the operation of that branch, agency or other establishment.[153]

As a general rule the Brussels Regulation only applies if (at least one of) the defendants are domiciled in the EU.[154] If none of the defendants are domiciled in the EU, the non-harmonized, domestic law (civil procedure rules) of the Member States whose courts have been called upon decides jurisdictional points. However, there are specific exceptions in the Brussels Regulation that have extended the EU harmonization of the private international law rules, even in instances where none of the defendants are domiciled in the EU. These exceptions include consumer contracts[155] and contractual choice of jurisdiction (prorogation).[156] Thus, if a consumer based in an EU Member State (eg a French-domiciled consumer) wishes to sue a business who is not domiciled in the EU (eg a US business), then that French consumer can nevertheless rely on the special consumer protection rules in the Brussels Regulation before the French courts.

last known domicile ensures a fair balance between the rights of the applicant and those of the defendant precisely in a case such as that in the main proceedings, in which the defendant was under an obligation to inform the other party to the contract of any change of address occurring after the long-term mortgage loan contract had been signed."

[148] See further J Hörnle, "The Jurisdictional Challenge of the Internet" in L Edwards and C Waelde *Law and the Internet* (3rd edn, Hart Oxford 2009) 121–59, 127.
[149] Art 19.
[150] Art 19(1).
[151] Art 19(2).
[152] Art 19(3).
[153] Art 17(2).
[154] Art 6(1).
[155] Arts 6(1) and 18(1).
[156] Arts 6(1) and 25.

If the French consumer in our example does not wish to sue the business in France (eg because the business has no presence nor assets in France or the applicable law is inopportune), then the French consumer may benefit if that US business has a branch, agency or other establishment in another EU Member State (eg Ireland). The French consumer could then sue the US business in Ireland, according to Articles 17(2) and 4(1) (the general rule that a defendant can be sued at the place of his (deemed) domicile). Furthermore, according to Article 7(5), even where the business is domiciled in an EU Member State, the consumer could sue the business in yet another EU Member State where this business has a branch, agency, or other establishment and provided the services or goods were supplied from this branch.[157] In *ZX v Ryanair* the CJEU held that the branch must have an appearance of permanence, a local management, and must be "materially equipped to negotiate business with third parties."[158] Furthermore, it is only possible to rely on Article 7(5) if the dispute concerns acts attributed or related to the operations to that branch, or contractual obligations entered into by this branch, which have to be carried out in the Member State where the branch is situated.[159] Thus, jurisdiction in the Member State of the branch only applies if the dispute is "local" to the branch itself and it was for this reason that the Spanish courts in *ZX v Ryanair* did not have jurisdiction, as the customer had booked the flight online, the entity responsible for carrying out the flight was established in Ireland and the Spanish branch was merely dealing with tax issues, not flight operations.[160]

The consequence as to *applicable law* of the consumer protection provisions is that the law of the place where the consumer is habitually resident applies, in other words the law local to the consumer applies to the contract.[161] However, if the contract contains a different choice of applicable law, that different choice of law applies, but only to the extent that it does not contradict mandatory provisions of the law of the place where the consumer is habitually resident.[162] In other words, the consumer can nevertheless rely on the consumer protection provisions of his or her local law, which cannot be deviated from by contract. However, the Rome I Regulation also contains certain exceptions to the consumer protection provisions: they do not apply to service contracts where these services are exclusively supplied in a country other than that of the consumer's residence.[163] Thus, if a consumer travels to a different Member State, for example, to have dental work done or to stay in a hotel, the law of the country of the dentist or that of the hotel will be applicable in the absence of a choice of law.[164] This applies even if the dentist or the hotel marketed their services directly to the consumer's Member State, for example, through the use of campaigns on social media or websites.

An exception, which is important for e-commerce and internet transactions, is that the consumer protection rules do *not* apply to contracts for transport, *unless* it is a

[157] Art 7(5) and see also Case C-464/18 *ZX v Ryanair DAC* of 11 April 2019 ECLI:EU:C:2019:311.
[158] ibid para 33.
[159] ibid para 33.
[160] ibid para 34.
[161] Art 6(1) Rome I Regulation.
[162] Art 6(2) Rome I Regulation.
[163] Art 6(4)(a) Rome I Regulation
[164] Art 4(1)(b) Rome I Regulation.

package travel contract—to which the consumer protection rules *do* apply. A package travel contract is essentially a contract combining travel, accommodation, and other collateral tourist services not incidental to transport.[165] Thus, an English-domiciled consumer buying an airline, ferry, or train ticket or car hire[166] on a website direct could not rely on the consumer protection rules in private international law,[167] but could do so if they bought a flight and hotel for a combined price from an online travel agent. There is a slight inconsistency here between the wording of the Rome I Regulation, which cross-refers to the *definition of package travel in the Package Travel Directive*,[168] and the Brussels Regulation, which contains the following definition: a "contract which, for an inclusive price, provides for a combination of travel and accommodation."[169] In Joined Cases *Pammer/Alpenhof* the CJEU held that a voyage on a freight ship including passage and accommodation was such a package travel contract and therefore the consumer protection provisions applied.[170] Furthermore, it found that it was necessary to interpret both Regulations consistently and that, consequently, for questions of jurisdiction this included "package travel" as defined in the Directive.[171]

However, the delineation between transport and package travel can be unclear online: if an airline offers, as part of the online booking process, hotels for the consumer to stay in, and if the consumer pays on inclusive price for the transaction, it may not be clear to the consumer whether the airline acts as an online travel agent or simply links to the hotel's booking system internally. Arguably, such a booking should fall under the Package Travel Directive, whose purpose is precisely to prevent agents avoiding liability for third party bookings, from which they benefit through commercial arrangements.[172]

Also excluded is the rental of property (whether short-term tenancies of holiday properties or longer-term tenancies of houses or flats).[173] In respect of jurisdiction, Article 24(1) of the Brussels Regulation provides that "in proceedings which have as their object rights in rem in immovable property or tenancies of immovable property, the courts of the Member State in which the property is situated" have exclusive jurisdiction, unless both the landlord and the tenant are domiciled in the same Member State and the tenancy is for no longer than six months. This *in rem* jurisdiction (jurisdiction at the place where the property is situated) does not apply to time-share contracts. Jurisdiction and applicable law in respect of time-share contracts is governed

[165] Art 6(4)(b) Rome I Regulation and Art 17(3) Brussels Regulation.

[166] Presumably this includes car hire—the Distance Selling Directive 97/7/EC also excluded certain rights such as the withdrawal right from transport services, which the CJEU in Case C-336/03 *EasyCar Ltd v OFT* 10 March 2005 ECLI:EU:C:2005:150 held to include car hire.

[167] *ZX* (n 157) para 29: "an airline passenger, who has simply purchased a ticket for a flight, rather than a travel package, cannot rely on the rules."

[168] Art 2(1) Directive 90/314/EC.

[169] Art 17(3) Brussels Regulation.

[170] Joined Cases C-585/08 *Peter Pammer v Reederei Karl Schlüter GmbH & Co. KG* and C-144/09 *Hotel Alpenhof v Oliver Heller* 7 December 2010 ECLI:EU:C:2010:740, paras 41–44.

[171] ibid.

[172] But arguing to the contrary, on the basis that the consumer is likely to contract with the hotel direct, R Steenot, "Rules of Jurisdiction and Conflict Rules Relating to Online Cross-Border Contracts Concerning Touristic Services Provided to Consumers" (2016) 32 Computer Law & Security Review 482–94, 486.

[173] Art 6(4)(c) Rome I Regulation and Art 24 Brussels Regulation.

by the consumer protection provisions in private international law.[174] In respect of applicable law the consumer protection provisions also do not apply to certain financial instruments as defined in Article 6(4)(d) and (e) of Rome I Regulation.

Moreover, the consumer protection rules in the Brussels Recast and Rome I Regulations are supplemented by the controls against unfair contract terms in the Unfair Contract Terms Directive 1993/13/EC, which blacklists in its Annex clauses, which exclude or hinder "the consumer's right to take legal action or exercise any other legal remedy,"[175] which depending on the particular circumstances may include jurisdiction clauses.[176]

As has been shown in the discussion in this section, the EU private international law rules are not limited to an analysis of the contractual relationship between the parties. They protect consumers by establishing a legally privileged position of consumers. In turn, the concept of a consumer has been narrowly defined. Section 3.3 discusses how the consumer protection rules in Articles 17–19 of the Brussels Regulation have been further refined and how the CJEU has extended the consumer protection privilege of these rules in certain circumstances.

3.3 Interpretation by the CJEU

First, this section will examine the jurisprudence on who is a consumer and the definition of a consumer contract. This examination will show that the CJEU treats the consumer privilege as an exception to the general jurisdiction rules and has therefore insisted on a very narrow interpretation.[177] However, once a person is recognized as a consumer the CJEU has interpreted the consumer protection rules in private international law expansively. The Court has interpreted these rules expansively by:

(1) allowing consumers to sue in *one single court* where different courts would have been competent under the domestic civil procedure rules;[178]
(2) applying the privileged jurisdiction rules to contracts to which they do not apply based on a purely contractual analysis, where these contracts are *closely linked to* a relevant consumer contract;[179]
(3) widening the concept of *directing*, by focusing on the *market targeted* not on the *specific* contract with the individual consumer.[180]

[174] Explanatory Memorandum to Brussels Regulation Proposal 1999 COM(1999) 348 and Rome I Regulation Art 6(4)(c) where express reference is made to the Timeshare Directive 94/47/EC.

[175] No (q).

[176] See further the discussion of Case C-240/98 *Océano Grupo Editorial SA v Roció Murciano Quintero* 27 June 2000 ECLI:EU:C:2000:346 in section 3.3.3.

[177] *Bertrand* (n 135) para 17; *Shearson* (n 135) para 19.

[178] Case C-478/12 *Maletic v lastminute.com* 14 November 2013 ECLI:EU:C:2013:735; Case C-567/13 *Baczo v Raiffeisen Bank* 12 February 2015 ECLI:EU:C:2015:88; *Océano* (n 176) but cf Case C-375/13 *Harald Kolassa v Barclays Bank* 28 January 2015 ECLI:EU:C:2015:37.

[179] *Maletic* (n 178); Case C-297/14 *Hobohm v Benedikt Kampik Ltd* 23 December 2015 ECLI:EU:C:2015:844; but cf *Harald Kolassa* (n 178) and *Shearson* (n 135).

[180] *Pammer/Alpenhof* (n 170); Case C-218/12 *Lokman Emrek v Vlado Sabranovic* 17 October 2013 ECLI:EU:C:2013:666.

Finally, the EU rules on private international law have additionally been strengthened by interpreting the Directive on Unfair Terms in Consumer Contracts to render void any jurisdiction, applicable law, or arbitration clause in standard terms of a relevant consumer contract, if they are prejudicial to consumers.[181]

3.3.1 Who is a consumer and when is a contract concluded?

As has been mentioned earlier, a consumer is a person who contracts for a purpose that can be regarded as being outside his or her trade or profession. In consistent jurisprudence the CJEU has emphasized that this legal concept of the consumer is harmonized at EU level and therefore independent of the concept of a consumer under national laws.[182] This is especially important as the definition of who is a consumer varies between Member States. As has already been mentioned, the CJEU has opted for a narrow interpretation of the consumer concept at EU level on the basis that this is an exception to the general rule on jurisdiction (defendant's court) and an exception to the special contract rules on jurisdiction.[183]

This raises the question of whether a mixed or dual-purpose contract (entered partly for consumer, partly for business purposes) falls under the notion of consumer contract. In *Johann Gruber v BayWa AG*[184] Mr Gruber was a farmer domiciled in Austria who went over the border to Germany to buy tiles for the roof of his farm, which was used for both consumer use (private residential purposes—60 per cent of the floor area) and his business (the farm—40 per cent of the floor area), and the tiles turned out to be defective. As a starting point the CJEU held that the consumer protection rules as an exception to the general jurisdiction rule (defendant's court) must be narrowly interpreted[185] and that special protective rules are unwarranted for trade or professional supplies.[186] Even though in this case the private use was dominant (more than 50 per cent) the Court agreed with the Advocate General that the purpose of the consumer protection rules was to protect the weaker party who had no business experience in relation to the contract at issue. As this was not the case here, even though the business use only amounted to 40 per cent of the floor space, the claimant was held to have the necessary business acumen, which meant he did not need the protection of the consumer rules.[187] Furthermore, the Court held that it was undesirable to split the contract into a B2C and a B2B contract, as the same legal relationship should have only one basis of jurisdiction (avoidance of multiple bases of jurisdiction).[188] Thus, unless the business use is negligible, a mixed contract does not benefit from the special consumer protection rules.[189] However, even if the business use is negligible, a consumer only benefits from the protective rules, if he or she has not given the business

[181] *Océano* (n 176).
[182] *Shearson* (n 135) para 13; *Bertrand* n 135) paras 14–15.
[183] *Bertrand* (n 135) para 17; *Shearson* (n 135) para 19.
[184] Case C-464/01 *Johann Gruber v BayWa AG* 20 January 2005 ECLI:EU:C:2005:32.
[185] Para 32 of the Judgment.
[186] Para 36.
[187] Para 39 of the Judgment; paras 41–42 of the Advocate General's Opinion 16 September 2004 ECLI:EU:C:2004:529: "he must be deemed to be on an equal footing with the supplier."
[188] Para 44.
[189] Para 47.

(the other party to the contract) the impression that he or she is acting as a business (eg by using business stationery or mentioning the possibility of recovering VAT).[190]

The Court has also refused to apply the consumer protection rules to individuals acting in connection with a business activity, who are not consumers in the strict sense because they are not acting outside their trade or professional capacity.[191] Even if there is a substantial difference in bargaining power between, for example, a sole trader and a multinational corporation, this would not justify the application of the consumer protection rules in private international law. This is even though a person may be acting in an individual capacity and there is a substantial power imbalance (such as a director giving a guarantee for the performance of an obligation of a company), or the claim is derived from a consumer contract but made by a business, as the following sections will explain.

In *Gerald Feichter*[192] the CJEU refused to apply the consumer protection provisions to a defendant who had given a *guarantee as an individual* to back up an overdraft facility given to a company in which he had a substantial business interest (managing director and majority shareholder) holding that this was not a contract concluded by a consumer.[193] It repeated its consistent jurisprudence that "only contracts concluded outside and independently of any trade or professional activity or purpose, solely for the purpose of satisfying an individual's own needs in terms of private consumption, are covered by the special rules."[194] The CJEU had already held in *Shearson Lehmann Hutton v TVB* that the assignee of a consumer claim cannot benefit from the jurisdiction rules for consumers, as they are a business and the consumer privilege was not designed for commercial entities.[195] This was the case even though the claim that had been assigned was based on a consumer contract and the claim therefore derived from a consumer contract.

Conversely, however, the CJEU has also held that the legal knowledge and sophistication of the party claiming to be a consumer is irrelevant to the assessment of whether a person is in fact a consumer.[196] Thus, EU law does not focus on the question of whether the individual as such "needs" protection. Thus, if a person who is trained as a lawyer acts in a private, non-business capacity when concluding a contract, this person would not be deprived of his status as a consumer.[197] In *Max Schrems v Facebook Ireland*[198] the CJEU held that the fact that Mr Schrems was publishing books, lecturing, operating websites, engaging in fundraising, and acting on behalf of other consumers who had assigned their claims to him for enforcement did not deprive him of his status as a consumer. However, the Court held that the

190 Paras 51–52.
191 *Bertrand* (n 135) paras 21–22; *Shearson* (n 135) para 22.
192 C-419/11 *Gerald Feichter* 14 March 2013.
193 Paras 35, 40.
194 Para 34.
195 *Shearson* (n 135) paras 16–24.
196 Steenot (n 172) 484.
197 In the context of Directive 93/13/EC: Case C-110/14 *Horatiu Ovidu Costea v SC Volksbank Romania SA* 3 September 2015 ECLI:EU:C:2015:538, para 21; see also Steennot (n 172) 484; see also Case C-208/18 *Petruchova v FIBO Group Holdings Ltd* Opinion of Advocate General Tanchev ECLI:EU:C:2019:314, para 44; CJEU Judgment ECLI:EU:C:2019:825, para 78.
198 *Schrems* (n 12).

privilege of allowing the consumer to choose between the courts of his own domicile (Austria) and that of the defendant (Ireland) did not apply to representative or group actions where the consumer claimed not only on his own behalf but also on behalf of *other consumers* domiciled in Austria, other EU Member States, and non-Member States.[199] The CJEU held that the concentration of several claims by assignment to the defendant means that the claimant has lost his jurisdictional privilege of suing in the courts of his own domicile.[200] The privilege only applied to an action of a consumer against the other party of a specific contract[201] and it was not possible to bring "those assigned claims also within the jurisdiction of that court" (in this case the Austrian Court in Max Schrems' domicile).[202] In summary therefore, it can be said that in order to qualify for the jurisdictional protection, the litigant must act in a personal capacity as a consumer (as the *Shearson Lehmann Hutton v TVB* case shows, not merely deriving their claim from a consumer, or as the *Max Schrems* case indicates, not representing another consumer, or acting in a representative capacity).

Moreover, the consumer must have *concluded* a contract that forms the basis of the claim in the litigation concerned. In three cases, the CJEU had to grapple with this requirement in respect of *unilateral* contracts, where a business makes a unilateral promise "to the world at large" and the consumer acts in reliance of such a *unilateral* promise and wishes to enforce it.[203] A number of misleading direct marketing cases, where Austrian consumers were sent "prize" notifications by German mail order companies, have given rise to three requests for preliminary rulings concerning the jurisdiction of the Austrian courts and in particular whether in such cases there was a relevant consumer contract.

In the first case, *Gabriel*,[204] a consumer received a personalized letter at his home address stating that he had won a large "cash" prize, which he would obtain if he ordered goods from the mail order company. This was contradicted by the small print on the reverse that stated that he would only be entered for a prize draw if he ordered the goods from the mail order company, with no obligation on the part of the business. The consumer filled in the relevant coupon and placed an order for goods according to the instructions given by the business. He duly received the goods ordered, but was not paid the promised cash prize. He sued the mail order company before the Austrian courts under (the then applicable) Article 13 of the Brussels Convention 1968. The CJEU held that Article 13(1) is applicable to this situation[205] and in particular that the consumer had concluded a contract with "reciprocal and interdependent" obligations[206] and was entitled to sue the German company at the courts of his domicile in Austria.

[199] Para 49.
[200] Para 48.
[201] Para 45.
[202] Para 47.
[203] Under English law such a promise can amount to a consumer contract, already recognized under the famous *Carlill v Carbolic Smoke Ball Company* [1893] 1 QB 256.
[204] Case C-96/00 *Rudolf Gabriel* 11 July 2002 ECLI:EU:C:2002:436.
[205] Para 46.
[206] Para 49.

In the second case, *Engler*,[207] an Austrian consumer was sent a notification by the same German mail order company that she had won a prize, but again, when she claimed her prize she did not obtain it. The factual difference in this case was that the consumer had not made an order as the prize was expressed not to depend on an actual order. The Court held that, since the consumer had not taken any steps in Austria to *conclude* the contract, that there were no reciprocal obligations and that therefore Article 13(1) Point 3(b) was not applicable and that she was not protected by the specific consumer protection provisions of private international law. This reasoning was based on the wording of Article 13(1) *then* in force.[208] Nevertheless, the Court held that the claim was related to a contract as it was essentially based on a pre-contractual obligation, which the defendant had voluntary assumed (by intentionally giving misleading statements), and that therefore the special rules on jurisdiction relating to contracts apply[209] in addition to the general jurisdiction rule.[210,211] Thus provided, the Austrian Court could find that the payment of the prize should have been performed in Austria, the Austrian court had jurisdiction (without relying on the consumer protection provisions).

In *Ilsinger*,[212] the third case with almost identical facts, the Court came to the opposite conclusion, namely that the consumer protection provisions *do* apply, as the wording had changed from the Brussels Convention to the Brussels Regulation.[213] It found that the wording in the Regulation was broader and included not only contracts for goods and services but contracts of any type, and in particular including *contracts that are unilaterally binding promises*.[214] However, the Court still insisted that a contract must have been concluded before the consumer can benefit from the jurisdiction privilege.[215] The Court also reiterated that the scope of the special contract jurisdiction rules is wider (as it includes pre-contractual obligations) than the scope of the special consumer protection provisions (which only applies to contracts that have been concluded and not to pre-contractual obligations).[216] Thus, it was necessary for the national court to examine whether the defendant in offering the prize to the consumer had made a binding, contractual promise (a unilateral contract) or whether the "prize" was merely advertising puffery or a non-binding contractual offer, which had not been accepted by the consumer (which may merely give rise to pre-contractual obligations). In the result therefore, the consumer protection rules in the Brussels Regulation are applicable to unilateral contracts.

[207] Case C-27/02 *Petra Engler v Janus Versand GmbH* 20 January 2005 ECLI:EU:C:2005:33.

[208] Paras 37–38.

[209] Jurisdiction at the place of the performance of the obligation (here the payment of the prize), Art 5(1) Brussels Convention and Art 7(1) Brussels (Recast) Regulation, see further Chapter 8.

[210] Defendant's local court Art 2(1) Brussels Convention and Art 4 (1) Brussels (Recast) Regulation.

[211] Paras 54–58, 60.

[212] *Renate Ilsinger* (n 131).

[213] *Gabriel* (n 204) para 48.

[214] Paras 50–51.

[215] Para 52: based on the opening wording of Art 15(1)(c) Brussels Regulation 2001/44/EC.

[216] Para 57.

3.3.2 Closely linked contracts

In a number of cases the CJEU has developed the concept of "closely linked" contracts, which extends the jurisdictional protection given to consumers even further. In these cases the CJEU has allowed consumers to sue in their local courts, even though under a strict analysis of the contract giving rise to the claim a *different* court, *less convenient or less accessible* for the consumer would have had jurisdiction.

In *Maletic v Lastminute.com GmbH and TUI Austria*[217] the claimants, an Austrian-domiciled couple, had entered into a contract for package travel to Egypt with Lastminute.com (Germany) as the travel agent, but were booked in the wrong hotel and, on return, sued for compensation for breach of contract. The tour was operated by TUI Austria established in Austria who was a co-defendant and the claimants wished to sue both defendants before their local court under Article 16(1) Brussels Regulation 2001/44/EC, which allows consumers to sue "the other party" in the courts of their domicile. It was not disputed that the consumer protection provisions in the Brussels Regulation allowed the claimants to sue Lastminute.com established in Germany in their local court in Austria, but since the second defendant was domiciled in Austria, in a purely domestic scenario, the Austrian civil procedure rules stipulated a different Austrian court, further away from the claimants. On reference from the Austrian court, the CJEU held that the two disputes were inextricably linked and that therefore the concept of "the other party" in Article 16(1) also included the second defendant, even though that defendant was domiciled in the same Member State as the claimants.[218] This made it more convenient for the claimant consumers, as they could sue both parties jointly in the same Austrian court (their local (nearest) court).

In *Hobohm v Kampik*[219] the CJEU took the concept of closely linked contracts even further to bring a *second*, later contract between the same parties within the consumer protection rules in Articles 15(1)(c) and 16 of the Regulation. While it seems logical that it should be possible to sue defendants in a joined action in the same court (*Maletic*), it is not necessarily obvious that a sequence of contracts *between the same parties* should be treated in the same manner. In *Hobohm* Mr Kampik ran a property marketing business brokering apartments in tourist complexes to be built for German consumers and entered into a brokerage contract with the claimant, Mr Hobohm. Unfortunately for Mr Hobohm, the property developer in Spain ran into financial difficulties and building on the apartment complex came to a halt. The CJEU held that this initial brokerage contract between the Spanish developer and Mr Hobohm was directed at Germany in accordance with Article 15(1)(c) as the prospectus was written in German, the website was in German, the telephone number for further enquiries was a Berlin number, and the email address mentioned on the website used the top-level domain.de.[220] Mr Hobohm then went to Spain and was persuaded there to enter into a second contract, the transaction management contract, under which he invested several more tranches of money to achieve completion of his unfinished apartment. The claimant wished to recover the tranches of money invested under this

[217] *Maletic* (n 178).
[218] Para 32.
[219] *Rüdiger Hobohm* (n 145).
[220] Paras 19, 28.

second contract. The German courts had held on the facts that this second transaction management contract was not directed at Germany and that therefore Article 15(1)(c) was not applicable to this subsequent contract, looking at this second contract on its own. However, the German Court pointed out that this second transaction management contract was closely linked to the first brokerage contract in that its purpose was to ensure that the economic purpose of the initial transaction was fulfilled (completion of the apartment so that Mr Hobohm could enjoy the benefits of the completed development). The CJEU followed this argument of the referring Court and held that where a first contract fell into the scope of Article 15(1)(c) and was then followed by a second contract between the same parties, which was *de facto* an extension of the first contract and had the sole purpose of fulfilling the economic objectives of the first contract, then the contracts were so closely linked that the consumer could sue in the courts of his domicile even under the second contract.[221]

However, the Court has not expanded the concept of closely linked contracts to widen the *class of litigants* who benefit from the special consumer protection rules. For example, in *Shearson Lehmann Hutton v TVB* it has refused to allow a commercial assignee of a consumer claim (a business) to sue in the local court, in which the consumer could have sued before the assignment.[222] In other words, the consumer privilege is personal to the consumer and cannot be transferred to an assignee of a claim under a contract.

The CJEU also has limited the concept to disallow a consumer claimant to rely on the consumer protection provisions in Article 15(1)(c) in order to bring an action for wrongful information in an investment prospectus for which a third party is responsible in his domestic court, as this is an action in tort, falling under the special jurisdiction rules for tort cases, and not a consumer contract. In *Kolossa v Barclays Bank*[223] the CJEU held that the issuer of a bearer bond held by an institutional investor, with whom the consumer had contracted, was not liable in *contract* to the consumer and that therefore Article 15(1)(c) of the Brussels Regulation was not applicable.[224] The fact that the investor was not holding the securities himself meant that there was no contract between the issuer and the investor (as is the case under securities law if the investor holds the certificates himself). Furthermore, the Court refused to adopt an "economic" analysis approach going beyond the strictly contractual analysis.[225] The CJEU pointed to its constant ruling that the consumer protection rules were an exception to the general rules of jurisdiction and refused to hold that they were applicable to a chain of contracts where there was *no contractual relationship* between the consumer and the prospectus issuer.[226]

The distinction made in these closely linked contracts cases shows again that the CJEU limited the consumer protection privilege to *consumer contracts* in the strict

[221] Paras 34–35.
[222] *Shearson* (n 135) paras 23–24.
[223] *Harald Kolassa* (n 178).
[224] Paras 24–26, 28, 30, 34–35.
[225] See the discussion in M Lehmann, "Prospectus Liability and Private International Law—Assessing the Landscape After the CJEU Kolassa Ruling" (2016) 11(2) Journal of Private International Law 318–43, 319–21.
[226] ibid.

sense of the word. Consumers are covered only if they are acting in a personal capacity and if there is a contract between the consumer and the trader. But if someone is a consumer having concluded a contract that is outside a trade or professional purpose, it is prepared to extend the privilege beyond a strict analysis of the contractual situation to include secondary, "closely linked" contracts within the scope of protection.

3.3.3 Interaction of the consumer jurisdiction rules and the national civil procedure rules in determining the venue

It is important to note that Article 18(1) states that consumer protection is not just limited to giving the consumer an option to sue in *the country of his or her domicile* but goes further by allowing the consumer to bring an action in *the place of his or her domicile*, thus determining the court local to the consumer as an optional venue.[227] This raises the interesting question of the interplay between national civil procedure rules and the consumer protection provisions in the Brussels Regulation and more particularly, Article 18(1). With the consumer as claimant, Article 18(1) determines both international and internal jurisdiction in a Member State[228] and the Brussels Regulation has therefore extended the jurisdictional protection to the micro-level. As we have seen already in *Maletic*,[229] the CJEU extended the internal, local jurisdiction not just to the "other party" in Article 18(1) but also any other connected party in closely linked contracts, such as the principal who was bound by the contracts between the consumer and the intermediary (travel agent). In fact, the consumer protection jurisprudence of the CJEU has emphasized the importance of consumers being able to sue in a court local to, and therefore accessible to, the consumer. In *Océano Grupo Editorial v Murciano Quintero*[230] the standard terms contained an exclusive jurisdiction clause, which favoured the seller of encyclopaedias on instalment credit terms, directly sold to consumers, by allowing the publishers to sue consumers centrally at their place of business in Barcelona. The Court held that this clause made access to justice more difficult for consumers who lived a far distance from the seller's place of business.[231] This was a purely domestic situation: both the seller and the consumer were domiciled in Spain. The Court found, however, that this exclusive jurisdiction clause was an *unfair contract term* under Article 3 Unfair Contract Terms Directive 1993/13/EC, since it caused "contrary to the requirement of good faith, a significant imbalance in the parties' rights and obligations arising under the contract, to the detriment of the consumer"[232] and under the Annex listing contractual clauses, which were likely to be unfair and specifically in (q) "excluding or hindering the consumer's right to take legal action or exercise any other legal remedy." Thus, when a national court rules on its jurisdiction it must apply the provisions on unfair contract terms to

[227] By contrast if the consumer is the defendant the protection is limited in Art 18(2) to the trader having to sue the consumer in the courts *of the Member State in which the consumer is domiciled*—this need not necessarily be the consumer's local venue.

[228] See further Lehmann (n 225) 318–43.

[229] See (n 210).

[230] Joined Cases C-240/98, C-241/98, C-242/98, C-243/98, and C-244/98 27 June 2000 ECLI:EU:C:2000:346.

[231] Para 22.

[232] Para 24.

an exclusive jurisdiction clause contained in a consumer contract on its own motion and determine whether it is an unfair term.[233]

A similar constellation arose in two cases referred to the CJEU by the Hungarian courts, on a domestic provision in the national Hungarian civil procedure rules, which conferred jurisdiction with respect to claims for the invalidity of contract terms to the consumer's local courts, whereas jurisdiction for invalidity of an unfair contract term under the Unfair Contract Terms Directive 1993/13/EC was conferred to the more centralized, more senior country court, which was likely to be at a greater geographical distance to the consumer, required legal representation, and involved greater costs for consumers. In *Jőrös*[234] the CJEU held that the lender's local court, which adjudicated on the invalidity of contract terms generally, should also consider on its own motion the question of unfairness under Article 3(1) of the Unfair Contract Terms Directive in order to prevent the continued use of unfair terms in accordance with Article 7(1) of that Directive, regardless of the fact that another court had jurisdiction to rule on unfairness under the Directive.[235] This is another example where the CJEU held that national procedure rules must not disadvantage consumers as to the competent court.

However, in *Nora Baczo v Raiffeisen Bank*[236] the CJEU has adopted a more cautious approach. In that case consumers had taken out a mortgage and claimed that an arbitration clause in a mortgage contract was invalid based on several heads of contract law (Hungarian national provisions and the Unfair Contract Terms Directive 1993/13/EC). They were again faced with the problem that two different courts were competent: the local court for the claims of invalidity under national Hungarian law and the County Court in Budapest for the claims as to unfairness under the Directive. Here the CJEU slightly back-tracked on its earlier ruling in *Jőrös* and found that it is not necessarily incompatible with the Directive that a local court has jurisdiction in respect of claims of invalidity of contracts and a more distant court (such as the County Court) has jurisdiction in respect of claims of invalidity under the Directive. The Court referred to its settled case law and stated that according to the principle of procedural autonomy it is for the national civil procedure rules to determine the competent court,[237] *as long as* these rules did not make it practically impossible or excessively difficult to claim rights conferred by EU law.[238] The CJEU held that there may be good reasons for the designation of the County Courts, which are hierarchical superior and may lead to a more consistent application of the Directive.[239]

There are therefore two observable trends. In conflict of law situations where the consumer wishes to litigate in the court local to him or her the CJEU has interpreted the "the place of the consumer's domicile" and the "other party to the contract" widely to enable consumers' access not just to a national court, but also to *the local court*, and it has held that an exclusive jurisdiction clause at the business' place of business may be void under the Unfair Contract Terms Directive 1993/13/EC, even in a domestic

233 Para 25.
234 Case C-397/11 30 May 2013 ECLI EU:C:2013:340.
235 Para 38.
236 Case C-567/13 12 February 2015.
237 Para 41.
238 Para 42.
239 Para 46.

situation where the Brussels Regulation would not have been applicable. But likewise, the Court has also emphasized the procedural autonomy of national courts that it only interferes with if the efficacy of EU consumer protection law is jeopardized.

3.3.4 The directing/targeting rule and e-commerce

In the late 1990s during the discussions on the reform of the Brussels (and Rome) Conventions, much controversy surrounded the question of whether or not the consumer protection provisions should apply to intra-EU cross-border e-commerce.[240] The debate centred on the question of whether a consumer buying goods or services on the internet virtually travelled to the Member State of the business (and should therefore not be protected, assuming a risk by crossing a border),[241] or whether in this scenario the business virtually opens its shop "coming" to foreign consumers based in another Member State and should therefore assume the jurisdictional risk, akin to direct sales marketing (such as traditional mail order businesses, based on catalogues sent to the consumer).[242] The business side of the debate argued that the internal market opportunities offered by e-commerce would be lost if businesses (especially SMEs) were obliged to take on the risk of having to sue, or be sued, in all other EU Member States[243] and to comply with the relevant mandatory consumer protection laws of all Member States, as this would force businesses to select carefully in which states they wished to market their products to and to select states to deliberately avoid[244] (thus depriving consumers of the opportunities brought by cross-border e-commerce). The consumer protection side argued that in the age of cross-border B2C e-commerce it was even more important to protect the "weaker" party to a transaction, as cross-border litigation is more complex, more expensive, and time-consuming—and these factors would therefore frequently mean that consumers have no access to judicial redress or an adequate remedy.[245] The consumer side also argued that if consumers could not enforce their consumer rights, there was a danger that consumer protection standards decreased generally, and the quality of goods and service provision would diminish and fraudulent transactions would be on the rise. The text finally adopted in the Brussels and Rome Regulations represented a compromise between these two positions.

The phrase "by any means, directs such activities to that Member State or to several States including that Member State, and the contract falls within the scope of such activities"[246] is capable of being interpreted in many ways.[247]

[240] See also Chapter 13on directing and targeting and geo-location.

[241] See also further Øren (n 135) 670–72.

[242] See also the discussion in P Cachia, "Consumer Contracts in European Private International Law" (2009) 34(3) European Law Review 476–90, 487–88.

[243] M Pullen, "EU's Dangerous Threat to E-commerce," Legal Week (September 1999).

[244] Explanatory Memorandum to Brussels Regulation Proposal 1999 COM(1999) 348; International Chamber of Commerce, Electronic Commerce Project (ECP)'s Ad hoc Task Force, Press Release, "Jurisdiction and applicable law in electronic commerce" of 6 June 2001; see also L Gillies, "Addressing the "Cyberspace Fallacy": Targeting the Jurisdiction of an Electronic Consumer Contract" (2008) 16(3) International Journal of Law and Information Technology 242–69, 257.

[245] BEUC position paper, BEUC 193/99, 'Consumer Rights in electronic commerce: Jurisdiction and applicable law on cross-border consumer contracts' of 8 October 1999.

[246] Art 15(1)(c) Brussels Regulation 2001/44/EC; Art 6(1)(b) Rome Regulation EC/593/2008.

[247] L Gillies, "Jurisdiction For Consumer Contracts—European Union: Modified Rules Of Jurisdiction For Electronic Consumer Contracts" (2001) 17(6) Computer Law & Security Review 395–98, 397.

It is now clear that the mere fact that a website is accessible and an order can be placed through interactive e-commerce is not in itself sufficient to argue that the business directs its activities to the consumer's state.[248] Initially, the European Commission's Explanatory Memorandum made the classic "sliding-scale"[249] distinction between "interactive" and "passive" websites derived from US jurisprudence, stating that the test is satisfied in respect of the former, but not the latter.[250] This distinction seems to be largely redundant now as most websites are highly interactive, and not much can be gained from focusing on the degree of interactivity in light of modern technology.[251] Furthermore, this distinction, developed in a different context, is ill-fitting and not supported by the wording of the consumer provision in the Jurisdiction Regulation, as a *passive* website *can* be directed at a certain Member State and the directing can occur "by any means."[252] In *Pammer/Alpenhof* the CJEU has effectively rejected the active/passive distinction as not being sufficient to establish "directing."[253]

One consumer-friendly test would be to focus on the (actual or constructive) knowledge of the e-commerce supplier and determine whether or not that business directed its activities to the consumer's Member State on the basis of whether or not they were in a position to localize the consumer's likely domicile (eg through the billing address or through using geo-location technology[254] to map the consumer's location[255] when accessing the website or using an app). The rationale behind such an interpretation is that (actual or constructive) knowledge gives the business the opportunity to decline a transaction if it does not wish to deal with consumers from certain jurisdictions.[256] If businesses knowingly transact with consumers from a particular Member State nevertheless, arguably they can be taken to direct their activities to that Member State (by not excluding consumers from that Member State).[257]

Moreover, this does mean that if a business adopts a "scattergun" approach, marketing widely and indiscriminately (without any particular Member State in mind), under this interpretation there is a presumption that it has "directed" its activities to all states reached, as long as it can localize consumers.[258] This interpretation is also supported by the wording of Article 15(1)(c): "*directs* such activities to *that* Member State or to *several* States," which clearly includes a marketing approach targeting multiple states. However, this first interpretation would force businesses to adopt costly

[248] Statement of the European Commission on Arts 15 and 73 of the Brussels Regulation 2001/44/EC of 14 Dec 2000; *Pammer/Alpenhof* (n 170) paras 71–72.

[249] *Zippo Manufacturing v Zippo Dot Com, Inc* 952 F Supp 1119.

[250] Explanatory Memorandum to Brussels Regulation Proposal 1999 COM(1999) 348.

[251] See also the discussion in Chapter X on *Zippo* and GI Zekos, "State Cyberspace Jurisdiction and Personal Cyberspace Jurisdiction" (2007) 15(1) International Journal of Law and Information Technology 1–37, 27–28.

[252] Øren (n 135) 685.

[253] *Pammer/Alpenhof* (n 170).ECLI:EU:C:2010:740, paras 68, 72, 79.

[254] See further Chapter 13.

[255] B Tedeschi, "E-commerce- Borderless is Out" New York Times (2 April 2001); The Economist "Putting It in its Place- Geography and the Net" (9 August 2001).

[256] Cachia (n 242) 484–85.

[257] S Dutson, "E-commerce-EU- Transnational E-commerce" (2000) 16(2) Computer Law & Security Review 105–07.

[258] ibid.

steps to partition their website into national segments to prevent directing where this is inappropriate.[259]

Therefore, by contrast, a more business-friendly interpretation would be to say that a business only "directed" its activities to the consumer if it intended to do so and undertook positive, active, and conclusive marketing steps to do so[260] (eg expressly stating on its website which states a business delivered to or, having different apps for different states etc). However, it is also clear that the "directing" test is a relative concept—and it is unclear what *degree* of targeting is required, before the privileged consumer jurisdiction rules apply in any case.[261] *Gillies* calls this "different degrees or spectra of web site activity."[262] Furthermore, it is not clear whether the test should be applied on a subjective basis (the business operator's actual intention) or objective basis (taking into account all objectively and externally observable facts and circumstances).[263] In view of the importance of legal certainty as to the competent court(s)[264] it is highly regrettable that the Brussels Regulation was not drafted in such a way as to obtain more guidance on how to interpret the meaning of "directing."[265]

The CJEU has now had the opportunity to rule on the interpretation of the "directing" rule and has in fact steered a middle route in terms of the extent of targeting required and has clearly applied an objective test based on multiple facts and circumstances. As will be shown, however, the jurisprudence has not removed the legal uncertainty in respect of the applicability of the consumer jurisdiction rules to e-commerce, especially in cases where there are no clearly ascertainable facts and circumstances.

In *Pammer/Alpenhof*[266] the CJEU developed a multiple factor test to assess whether the business has targeted the consumer's jurisdiction on an objective basis. In *Pammer* an Austrian consumer booked a transatlantic voyage on a freight ship with a German intermediary with a shipping line who offered passenger accommodation through a website—when arriving at the point of embarkation in Trieste he refused to travel alleging false representations about the facilities on board and claimed for the return of his deposit. He brought the action in his local Austrian court. In *Alpenhof* a German consumer booked hotel accommodation in Austria on the hotel's website from Germany, then travelled and stayed in the hotel, but refused to pay his bill. The hotel brought proceedings against the German consumer in the local court in Austria. In both cases, the question arose whether each business had directed its services to the consumer. In the framework of the preliminary reference procedure from the Austrian courts, the CJEU established a multi-factor test for determining whether the business was directing its e-commerce activities to Austria (*Pammer*) or Germany (*Alpenhof*).

[259] C Reed, *Internet Law* (2nd edn, Cambridge 2004) 228–29.
[260] Gillies "Addressing the 'Cyberspace Fallacy' (n 244) 254.
[261] ibid 253.
[262] ibid 253.
[263] Øren (n 135) 686–87.
[264] Avoiding wasted costs, delay, and access to justice, particularly in the consumer e-commerce context.
[265] Øren (n 135) 690.
[266] *Pammer/Alpenhof* (n 170); J Hörnle, "Websites and Jurisdiction: Pammer and Alpenhof" (April/May 2011) 22(2) Computers & Law 4-5.

The Court emphasized[267] that the mere use of a website was insufficient to satisfy the "directing" test. The Court found that the business must have *objectively* manifested its intention to establish commercial relationships with customers from the consumer's domicile and that such an intention was implicit in certain forms of marketing.[268] It held that it was necessary to consider all evidence, which showed that the business was envisaging doing business with consumers domiciled in the forum.[269]

The national court had to make an overall assessment looking at all relevant facts and circumstances including, but by no means limited to:[270]

- an express statement that the business was offering its goods or services in the consumer's Member State;
- the international nature of the activity itself, such as tourism services;
- the language of the website or app (if different from that of the trader);
- the currency used for payment (if different from that of the trader);
- international dialling codes or directions for travelling;
- any consumer feedback from previous customers from the consumer's Member State;
- whether the business had placed keyword advertising on search engines or other forms of online advertising, which were clearly directed at the consumer's Member State;
- whether the business was using a country-specific top-level domain name (such as .de to attract German customers).

The CJEU judgment in *Pammer/Alpenhof* is not very clear on the question as to what should happen in cases where *no* such circumstantial indicators of the business' intention to target consumer in a Member State exist. If the multi-factor test remains neutral, since there are no clear indications as to which Member States the business intends to target and/or in effect the business targets each and every Member State (everywhere and nowhere in particular), then the question arises whether the directing test can be relied upon to protect consumers in a Member State. The Court hints at this in paragraph 82 by saying, slightly cryptically: "However, a finding that an activity is 'directed to' other Member States does not depend solely on the existence of such patent evidence." It argued that if the EU legislature would have meant that consumers should not be protected in the case of websites that were not directed at any particular EU Member State, it would have adopted wording such as that the trader had "purposefully directed his activity in a substantial way" to other Member States.[271] The Court seems to indicate here that if a website is directed at everywhere and nowhere in particular, this may mean that the courts of the consumers' domicile potentially have jurisdiction under the consumer protection rules, but this remains unclear.

[267] Paras 71–72.
[268] Paras 63–65, 75.
[269] Para 76.
[270] Paras 81–84.
[271] Para 82.

Furthermore, the question arises whether there must be a causal link between the business directing its activities to the consumer's Member State and the conclusion of the contract before the consumer can benefit from the jurisdictional privilege. Such a causal link is not mentioned in Article 15(1)(c) of the Brussels Regulation. However, without a causal link the jurisdiction privilege would be extended to cases where such protection seems unwarranted going beyond distance cross-border selling. Consider a situation where a consumer from Sweden travels to Italy and, while there, buys luxury items from a shop without being aware that the trader actively markets and sells these luxury goods also in Sweden through separate e-commerce marketing and sales channels. Abandoning the causal link would mean that the Swedish consumer can sue the Italian supplier in the Swedish court, relying on the consumer privilege in Article 15(1)(c).

In a first step, the Court in *Mühlleitner v Yusufi* has extended the consumer protection rules beyond distance selling.[272] This was a preliminary reference from the Austrian Supreme Court (Oberste Gerichtshof) in a claim for rescission of a contract and damages for breach of contract by the claimant Ms Mühlleitner after the sale of an allegedly defective car. Ms Mühlleitner, domiciled in Austria, had seen a car advertised on a third-party website and telephoned the seller-defendants (a car seller in Hamburg, Germany) who offered her a different car that also met her specifications. She subsequently travelled from Austria to Germany to look at the car and concluded a contract with the defendants then and there at their garage in Hamburg before driving the car back to Austria. When the car turned out to be defective after her return with it to Austria she sued the defendants in the Austrian courts. On appeal, the Austrian Supreme Court referred a single question to the CJEU, namely whether Article 15(1)(c) of the Brussels Regulation *only* applied *if the consumer contract had been concluded at a distance*. The Court held that Article 15(1)(c) did not explicitly state that it only applied to distance contracts.[273] The CJEU compared the wording of the "old" Article 13 of the Brussels Convention with Article 15(1)(c) and noted in particular that the condition that the consumer concluded the steps necessary for the conclusion of the contract *in his or her domicile* had been dropped[274] and that the conditions in the reformed provision all referred to the trader's activities and not to where the consumer acted to conclude the contract.[275] Furthermore, the CJEU held that the purpose of the reworded provision was to provide better, wider protection for consumers and that therefore the teleological interpretation of the Article also pointed to interpreting Article 15(1)(c) as not requiring that the contract itself having been concluded at a distance.[276] It therefore concluded that the scope of Article 15(1)(c) was not limited to distance selling.

Since Article 15(1)(c) reformed the consumer protection provisions specifically with e-commerce contracts in mind and because, for e-commerce contracts, it is difficult to pin down the physical location of where the consumer concluded the contract,

[272] Case C-190/11 *Daniela Mühlleitner v Ahmad Yusufi and Wadat Yusufi* 6 September 2012 ECLI:EU:C:2012:542.

[273] Para 35.

[274] See also the discussion in Øren (n 135)673–74and Cachia (n 242) 481.

[275] Paras 38–40.

[276] Para 45.

this conclusion makes sense.[277] The CJEU did not have to rule on the question of whether there also had to be a causal link between the e-commerce marketing activities and the claimant consumer's decision to enter into a contract.

Arguably in *Mühlleitner*, on the facts, there was a causal link between the consumer seeing the car of the defendant online and the conclusion of the contract at the garage, and the contract clearly fell within the scope of the trader's activities. However, the CJEU took a further step in *Emrek v Sabranovic*[278]—again a case concerning the cross-border sale of a defective car, however, based on different facts. Mr Emrek, domiciled in Saarbrücken, Germany, heard from acquaintances about the defendant car seller's business and travelled to the defendant's garage and bought a car there. Although the seller had an interactive website, the buyer, Mr Emrek, had not been aware of this and there was no causal link between the seller's e-commerce activities and the buyer's purchase of the car. The CJEU held that such a causal link between the consumer accessing the trader's website and the conclusion of the contract at the trader's establishment was not necessary.[279] The CJEU pointed out that such a causal link would be very difficult to prove as a matter of evidence before the court.[280] The causal link between the consumer engaging with a website and the conclusion of a contract may constitute evidence of the business directing its activities to the consumer's domicile, but it was not a condition for Article 15(1)(c) to apply.[281] In other words, there is no requirement that the consumer is induced by the trader's e-commerce activities into concluding a contract with the trader.

By abandoning the causal link between, on the one hand, the trader's e-commerce activities directed at the consumer's domicile and, on the other hand, the consumer's entering into the contract, the CJEU has significantly widened the reach of Article 15(1)(c). Applying *Emrek* to the earlier example concerning the Swedish tourist would mean that the fact that the Italian seller of luxury goods maintains an e-commerce website selling to Swedish consumers is sufficient to bring a dispute between the Swedish consumer-tourist who travelled to Italy into the Swedish courts. Arguably this may mean consumer protection has gone too far: if the consumer physically travels across a border would they not assume a conscious risk that having bought products in a foreign country that they may have to litigate in a foreign country?[282] The Court has switched from focusing on the individual consumer transaction to concentrating on the market that the trader has targeted. Presumably the rationale here is that a trader who actively markets to a foreign country should be in a position to assume the jurisdictional risk. But, arguably, this risk should also depend on the marketing channel used. The Rapporteur of the Committee of the European Parliament examining the Proposal for the Brussels Regulation recommended that there should

277 Øren (n 135) 673–74.
278 *Lokman Emrek* (n 180).
279 Para 32.
280 Para 25.
281 Para 26.
282 M Foss and LA Bygrave, "International Consumer Purchases through the Internet: Jurisdictional Issues pursuant to European Law" (2000) 8(2) International Journal of Law and Information Technology 99–138, 137.

be a condition that the consumer enters into the contract from his domicile, but this amendment was unfortunately not carried into the Regulation.[283]

4. Conclusion

Under US law the question of validity of choice of forum clauses presents itself as a question of validity of unconscionable contract terms in (non-negotiated) adhesion contracts and is largely based on common law jurisprudence (codified to some extent in the Uniform Commercial Code, which has been adopted in states' contract law). The case law has been inherently flexible and inconsistent, with differences between the states, which leads to a large degree of legal uncertainty. Choice of forum and choice of law clauses in adhesion contracts have been held invalid, because of procedural unconscionability, lack of incorporation or notice, or substantive unconscionability on the basis that the forum was chosen to defeat a class action or deprived the consumer of her day in court. Furthermore, in some recent cases the courts (in California, but see also the Canadian Supreme Court) have focused on public policy considerations in the forum, which goes beyond the contractual analysis in cases involving Facebook's terms and conditions, given the overwhelming bargaining position of the social media company and given the importance of privacy protections in certain states. But these cases may be isolated and the US Supreme Court Decision in *Carnival Cruise* continues to loom large in ignoring power imbalances between the parties, focusing on party autonomy, and treating consumer contracts just like any other form of contract. By contrast, consumer protection as a matter of public policy is hardwired into the private international law rules of the EU (in the shape of the Brussels and Rome Regulations). The application of the EU rules on private international law in B2C e-commerce contracts depends on whether the business directed its services to the consumer's Member State. If these rules apply, jurisdiction of the courts in B2C contract cases is asymmetric: consumers may only be sued in the jurisdiction of their domicile, but have an option to sue the business in their domicile or that of the business. Furthermore, consumers are protected by mandatory rules of consumer protection law in their domicile, regardless of the law stipulated in the B2C contract. As we have seen in this chapter, the CJEU has interpreted the notion of who qualifies as a consumer restrictively but otherwise adopted an expansive interpretation, protecting consumer's access to justice in cross-border cases. In e-commerce cases the Brussels and Rome Regulations provide for a multi-factor directing or targeting test, but leave open what should apply, if no targeting factors are discernible. If a website is directed to everywhere but nowhere in particular it is not clear how the directing test applies. However, if all the facts and circumstances indicate that the business has an e-commerce marketing channel directed to the consumer's domicile, it is likely that the consumer's local courts have jurisdiction and the mandatory provisions of applicable law apply. The protective rules apply even if the contract was concluded at the

[283] See Report from Rapporteur Diana Wallis "Report on the Proposal for a Council Regulation on Jurisdiction and the Recognition and Enforcement of Judgements in Civil and Commercial Matters," Committee on Legal Affairs in the Internal Market, COM (1999) 348-C5-0169/1999–1999/0154 (CNS).

business' domicile and even if the consumer never used an online marketing channel. The CJEU's interpretation of the consumer protection rules therefore do not require a causal connection between the business' marketing activities and the conclusion of the consumer contract. Thus, the approaches adopted vary significantly between the US and EU: In the US there is a presumption of validity of forum selection clauses that can only be displaced by a showing of unconscionability, whereas in the EU provided the contract is a qualifying consumer contract, a jurisdiction clause is invalid and offers the consumer a choice of fora or restricts litigation against the consumer to his or her domicile.

11

Conflicts of Law in Privacy, Data Protection, and Defamation Disputes: German and English Law

1. Introduction

This chapter covers private international law (jurisdiction and applicable law) with regard to disputes based on torts between private parties arising from infringements of privacy and data protection rights, and defamation committed by internet communication, a fast-developing and changing area in England.[1] It compares the private international law rules in Germany and England and Wales.[2] The proceedings examined in this chapter are civil litigation, as opposed to judicial review of administrative action.[3] Causes of action in respect of these tort claims are loosely grouped together, for the purposes of this examination, as "personality rights" infringement raising similar issues in respect of private international law. The choice of one party's local court as the competent forum, and one party's domestic law as the applicable law, may favour one party's case over that of the other, and in that sense, pitch privacy and reputational rights against freedom of expression for online communications. Jurisdiction and applicable law thus affect constitutionally sensitive issues of freedom of expression in the media, and cultural and political notions of the limits of privacy and reputation protection, which differ from jurisdiction to jurisdiction. The UK being an island, its conflict of law rules and applicable law in respect of torts developed later than on the Continent,[4] particularly in France and Germany,[5] and later than in the US, Canada, and Australia, where more state borders could be crossed more easily. Early cases in the UK are about Colonial governors using excess violence in suppressing rebellion[6] or shipping.[7] As in so many areas of law, technology has been

[1] This chapter examines private law relationships, eg between a data controller, data processor, and a data subject—for administrative enforcement see Chapter 7, in the UK see eg the tort of misuse of private information *Vidal-Hall v Google* [2016] QB 1003 (CA) para 21; *NT1 and NT2 v Google* [2019] QB 344 (QBD) para 64; *Gulati v MGN Ltd* [2017] QB 149 (CA) para 30; *Callaghan v Independent News and Media Ltd* [2009] NIQB 1 (QBD) para 22.

[2] For the sake of brevity referred to "England" only.

[3] M Brkan, "Data Protection and European Private International Law: Observing a Bull in a China Shop" (2015) 5(4) International Data Privacy Law 257–78, 260.

[4] P Handford, "Edward John Eyre and the Conflict of Laws" (2008) 32 Melbourne University Law Review 822–60, 853.

[5] FK von Savigny, *Private International Law and the Retrospective Operation of Statutes: A Treatise on the Conflicts of Laws, and the Limits of Their Operation in Respect of Place and Time* (Lawbook Exchange Ltd 2003); original CL von Bar *Das Internationale Privat-und Strafrecht* (1862).

[6] *Mostyn v Fabrigas* (1775) 1 Cowp 161, 173; 98 ER 1021, 1028; *Phillips v Eyre* (1870) LR 6 QB 1.

[7] *The Halley* (1867) LR 2 Adm & Eccl 3 (PC).

Internet Jurisdiction. Julia Hörnle, Oxford University Press (2021). © Julia Hörnle.
DOI: 10.1093/oso/9780198806929.001.0001

a driver for increasing cross-border tort cases and hence the development of a private international law for tort cases, first the widespread use of cars in the mid-twentieth century and, now, modern information and communications technology, the internet and online dissemination of content by everyone blogging and using social media. By the same token, the defendant is more likely to be a non-professional individual than a few years ago when cross-border media activities were confined to large media organizations, which makes conflicts of law even more acute in the twenty-first century.

2. Jurisdiction

2.1 Harmonized rules on jurisdiction in the Brussels (Recast) Regulation

As has been discussed more generally in Chapter 8, the rules on jurisdiction in civil and commercial matters have been partially harmonized by the Brussels Regulation[8] in the EU and, provided a court is competent, its judgment is recognized and enforced across the EU.[9] The harmonized rules apply only if one of the defendants is domiciled within an EU Member State[10] and provides, as a general rule of jurisdiction, that the claimant can always sue the defendant in the defendant's domicile.[11] National rules of jurisdiction continue to apply only[12] if none of the defendants are domiciled in an EU Member State[13]—however, the protective rules for consumers[14] and the contractually agreed court[15] apply regardless of the domicile of the defendant.[16]

Alternatively, at the choice of the party instigating proceedings, a *special* rule of jurisdiction in Article 7(2) applies to tort cases, including privacy, data protection, and defamation. Article 7(1) provides a special rule of jurisdiction in respect of contractual claims at the place of contractual performance,[17] which is mutually exclusive to tort claims in the sense that EU law[18] categories a dispute as either contractual or non-contractual[19] and the court competent under the contractual limb may not rule on matters related to tort and vice versa.[20] In order to determine whether a dispute arises

8 "Recast" Regulation 1215/2012 on Jurisdiction and the Recognition and Enforcement of Judgments in Civil and Commercial Matters of 12 December 2012.

9 Arts 36, 39.

10 Art 6(1); Recital 13—this provides the connection factor to the EU.

11 Art 4(1).

12 Art 5.

13 Art 6(3) Recital 14.

14 Art 18, Recital 14—see further discussion in Chapter 10.

15 Art 25(1).

16 Art 6(1).

17 Jurisdiction at the place of performance, Art 7(1)(a), for contracts of sale the place where the goods should have been delivered and for service contracts the place where the services should have been provided: Art 7(1)(b).

18 The distinction is not made according to national law, Case C-189/87 *Kalfelis v Bankhaus Schröder, Münchmeyer, Hengst and Co* [1988] ECR 5579, paras 15–16: as a concept of autonomous EU law, also Case C-548/12 *Brogsitter* [2014] ECLI:EU:C:2014:148, para 18.

19 If it is not a contract, then it is tort or other non-contractual claim (such as a claim of unjust enrichment).

20 A Dickinson and E Lein, *The Brussels I Regulation Recast* (Oxford University Press 2015) 4.71, 4.18; *Kalfelis* (n 18) paras 17–21.

from contract, and not from tort, the courts have to consider whether it is necessary to interpret the contractual provisions in order to determine liability.[21] This delineation between contract and tort could be relevant in personality rights infringement cases, where a data protection breach, misuse of personal information, or breach of confidence occurs in the context of a contractual relationship and liability arises from the contractual provisions (such as a privacy policy or a non-disclosure agreement).[22]

In tort cases, "the courts for the place where the harmful event occurred or may occur" have jurisdiction.[23] The phrase "harmful event" has been interpreted in a well-established line of cases starting with *Bier* as either the place where the event giving rise to the damage occurred or the place where the *direct* damage to the defendant's interests fell.[24] The first limb in *Bier*, the event giving rise to the damage normally is the place where the tort was committed and therefore the evidence on liability is located, whereas the evidence on harm may well be situated in the place where the damage occurred (second limb of *Bier*), so that either place is sufficiently connected to the tort in question. It is likely that in many cases it is more advantageous for the claimant to rely on the second limb (where the damage occurred), and an additional bonus may be that the applicable law is also that at the place of the damage.[25]

This jurisdictional rule additionally applies to threatened harmful events in action to prevent that harm[26] and to a negative declaration that no tort has been committed.[27] Furthermore, Article 7(2) determines both international (between countries) and territorial jurisdiction (the local court within a jurisdiction).[28]

In tort cases the event giving rise to the damage is the commission of the tort. Depending on the definition of the tort under national law, this may be (1) the place where the conduct took place, (2) the place were publication or dissemination occurred, or (3) the place where any of the elements of the tort took place. The location of the server hosting the infringing content was discussed as a possible location of the tort in earlier academic writings, but has now been dismissed as arbitrary and unconnected to the tort, as especially in the era of cloud computing, content may be constantly moved between data centres or may be shared between different hosts ("sharding"), and layers of cloud service providers makes it difficult to identify which entity is the relevant host.[29]

[21] *Brogsitter* (n 18) para 25.

[22] For a decision categorizing an implied non-disclosure term in a contract as "contractual" see the House of Lords Judgment in *Agnew v Lansförsäkringsbolagens* [2000] 1 AllER 73.

[23] Relating to past and future infringements, ie Art 7(2) covers the prevention of future infringements through interlocutory injunctions.

[24] Case 21/76 *Handelswekerij GJ Bier BV v Mines de Potasse d'Alsace SA* [1976] ECR-1735, paras 24–25; Case C-364/93 *Antonio Marinari v Lloyds Bank plc and Zubaidi Trading Company*, paras 11, 14; Case C-220/88 *Dumez France SA v Hessische Landesbank* [1990] ECR-49, para 20; Case C-68/93 *Shevill v Press Alliance* [1995] ECR I- 415 paras 20–21; Joined Cases C-509/09 *eDate Advertising GmbH v X* and C-161/10 *Oliver Martinez v MGN Ltd* [2011] ECR I-10269, ECLI:EU:C:2011:685 para 41.

[25] Dickinson and Lein (n 20) 4.91; Art 4 (1) Rome II Regulation.

[26] Lord Collins et al (eds), *Dicey, Morris, and Collins on The Conflict of Laws* (15th edn, Sweet & Maxwell 2012) Vol I, 371–532, 11-291; *Bonnier Media Ltd v Greg Lloyd Smith* [2002] SCLR 977 (OH).

[27] ibid 371–532, 11-285; Dickinson and Lein (n 20) 4.84; *Equitas Ltd v Wave City Shipping Co Ltd* [2005] EWHC 923 (Comm); *Folien Fischer AG* [2012] ECLI:EU:C:2012:664, paras 50–51.

[28] Dickinson and Lein (n 20) 4.72.

[29] See for a discussion of cloud computing and jurisdiction, Chapter 1 ; F Banholzer, "Teil 5 Internationale Gerichtszuständigkeit im Online Bereich" in Hoeren, Sieber, and Holznagel (eds), *Handbuch Multimedia*

In personality rights cases the Court of Justice of the EU (CJEU) held that, under EU law, the tort is committed at the place where the publisher is established.[30] Hence the first limb of Article 7(2) the location of the event giving rise to the damage is the place of establishment of the publisher.[31] This is likely to coincide with the defendant publisher's domicile. The event giving rise to the damage is usually located in the defendant's domicile so that the jurisdictional gateway under that limb of special jurisdiction coincides with the general jurisdiction under Article 4 in many cases.[32]

As to the second limb, the place where the damage occurs, in personality rights cases, this is frequently, but not inevitably, the claimant's domicile or a place where the claimant has substantial family or business connections, constituting the place where he or she suffers reputational or privacy damage.

However, the CJEU has also made clear that the second limb does not equate to *forum actoris*, as it only connects to the immediate, direct impact of the damage, not any secondary, indirect damage at the place of the claimant's domicile. In a line of cases concerning financial harm the CJEU has made clear that the indirect consequences of a financial loss at the claimant's domicile do not constitute a sufficient link to be considered a jurisdictional gateway.[33]

However, the problem with this two-limb rule is that, in personality rights cases committed by online communication, the place where the material is accessed and/or downloaded may not always be foreseeable to the defendant, as the extent of online distribution frequently is outside his or her control. Albeit that in personality rights infringement cases the defendant frequently knows where the claimant has his or her centre of interests and suffers harm to reputation or privacy. Therefore by their inherent nature personality rights infringement are targeted, not necessarily in terms of dissemination, but in terms of where the harm occurs. However, the damage resulting from a defamatory or privacy infringing internet publication can be widely spread across several states[34] leading to multiple possible venues, from which the claimant can pick, which in turn leads to uncertainty and forum shopping.[35] This contrasts with the intention of the Brussels Regulation which states in Recital 16:

> The existence of a close connection should ensure legal certainty and avoid the possibility of the defendant being sued in a court of a Member State which he could not reasonable have foreseen. This is important, particularly in disputes concerning

Recht (C.H. Beck January 2017) para 64; Case C-523/10 *Wintersteiger v Products 4u*, ECLI:EU:C:2012:220, para 36: "by reason of its uncertain location."

[30] *Shevill* (n 24) para 24.

[31] Contrast this with the approach of the English common law, which situates the commission of the tort in the place of actual publication, ie on the internet: accessing and downloading.

[32] Dickinson and Lein (n 20) 4.90.

[33] Dickinson and Lein (n 20) 4.73; *Antonio Marinari* (n 24) para 15; *Dumez* (n 24), paras 21–22.

[34] For claimants who have an EU-wide reputation.

[35] T Lutzi, "Internet Cases in EU Private International Law- Developing a Coherent Approach" (2017) 66 International Comparative Law Quarterly 687–721, 689–90.

non-contractual obligations arising out of violations of privacy and rights relating to personality, including defamation.

Thus, the foreseeability of the potential forum/-a has been included as a limiting factor for jurisdiction with special reference to violation of personality rights in the Recast Brussels Regulation.[36] The wording of Recital 16, has been included to address some of the criticism voiced in respect of the *mosaic* rule established in *Shevill*, which, this Recital notwithstanding, is still good law.

In *Shevill*[37] the CJEU affirmed *Bier*[38] for defamation actions and established the so-called *mosaic* rule: first, the claimant can sue in each and every jurisdiction where she has suffered damage under the second limb of Article 7(2) with the proviso that she can only claim for the loss suffered in the jurisdiction concerned.[39] This rule for determining jurisdiction at the preliminary stage applies even before the court assesses whether any damage has been caused to the claimant, which is part of the substantive part of the proceedings, governed by national law.[40] The risk of multiple suits is reduced by the second aspect of the *mosaic* rule: if the claimant wishes to recover *all* losses suffered in one venue, she has to sue in the place of the event giving rise to the damage (first limb of Article 7(2)),[41] or she has to sue in the place of the defendant's domicile (Article 4 (1)).[42] For torts committed by publication the place of the event giving rise to the damage is the establishment of the publisher.[43]

The mosaic rule gives rise to two different concerns, first where the damage is indeed widespread, for example where a famous person has a reputation in several EU Member States, it is technically difficult to quantify the amount of damage to reputation for one particular territory.[44] Secondly the defendant may be subjected to multiple claims in different jurisdictions which may, at least theoretically, be an issue for freedom of expression.[45] This second criticism has been voiced by scholars, but in practice it is rare indeed for claimants to commence multiple, parallel suits in different EU countries.

In *eDate Advertising*[46] questions from the German and French courts were referred in respect of information and photographs published on the internet. The CJEU pointed to the differences in dissemination between print media and online media, whereas the former were published on a regional basis, the latter are ubiquitous: "That content may be consulted instantly by an unlimited number of internet users throughout the world, irrespective of any intention on the part of the person who placed it in regard to its consultation beyond that person's Member State of

[36] Brussels Regulation (EC) 44/2001 contained a reference to predictability in Recital 11- but no specific reference to personality rights infringements.
[37] *Shevill* (n 24).
[38] Paras 20, 27.
[39] Para 33; *eDate/Oliver Martinez* (n 24) para 42.
[40] Para 40.
[41] Para 25; *eDate/Oliver Martinez* (n 24) para 43.
[42] Para 26; *eDate /Oliver Martinez* (n 24) para 43.
[43] Para 24.
[44] Lord Collins et al (n 26) 371–532, 11–290.
[45] Lutzi (n 35) 691–92.
[46] *eDateOliver Martinez* (n 24).

establishment and outside of that person's control."[47] The CJEU, furthermore, acknowledged that the damage caused in one particular Member State was frequently difficult to quantify[48] and that it was particularly challenging to square this difficulty with the potentially serious damage suffered by a claimant in respect of personality rights infringements, made available on a worldwide basis.[49]

The CJEU proceeded to add a third place of jurisdiction where the claimant is allowed to sue for the whole loss under a new test formulated for personality infringement claims, the "centre of interests test."[50] Under this test, the claimant can sue for her whole loss at the place where she has the centre of gravity of her protected interests, such as a claimant's habitual residence or place of work or other professional activity.[51] The CJEU held that the place of the claimant's centre of interests was reasonably foreseeable for the defendant and was therefore predictable[52] and arguably, the centre of interest test is a type of targeting test.[53]

The centre of interests test also applies to companies, but for legal persons, the courts must carefully determine where a business has the centre of its interest, which is normally the place where the business' goodwill is located and the place to which its products are targeted to. One factor to assess this place is the language used on a website.[54]

The basis for the centre of interest test is not entirely clear:[55] under the two-limb rule, is this the place where the damage was felt or the place where the event giving raise to the damage occurred?[56] Given the significant impact an online personality infringement can have on a claimant the CJEU found it necessary to add an additional forum (potentially more than one) where the claimant can sue for the whole loss, not just a fraction of it.[57] Thus, the centre of interest test was added to protect claimants to sue for the whole loss locally (to their centre of interests).

Once the question of jurisdiction has been settled according to the rules harmonized in the Brussels Regulation there is no scope for common law courts applying *forum non conveniens* to decline jurisdiction in favour of a more suitable, or most appropriate, forum.[58]

The harmonized rules on jurisdiction in the Brussels Regulation 1215/2012 additionally apply to determine the competent court to issue an injunction, including

[47] Para 45.
[48] Para 46.
[49] Para 47.
[50] Para 48.
[51] Para 49.
[52] Para 50; agreeing see Dickinson and Lein (n 20) 4.120.
[53] See Chapter 13.
[54] Case C-194/16 *Bolagsupplysningen v Svensk Handel* Judgment of 17 October 2018, ECLI:EU:C:2017:766 paras 42–44.
[55] It is not really derived from the wording of the Regulation: A Mills, "The Law Applicable to Cross-border Defamation on Social Media: Whose Law Governs Free Speech in Facebookistan" (2015) 7(1) Journal of Media Law 1–35, 21.
[56] Lutzi (n 35) 696.
[57] Dickinson and Lein (n 20) 4.118.
[58] Case C-281/02 *Owusu v Jackson* [2005] ECR I-1383; however, *forum non conveniens* does apply if the conflict of jurisdiction is between Scotland and England (where otherwise the harmonized EU rules apply): *Kennedy v National Trust for Scotland* [2019] EMLR 19 (CA).

provisional and protective orders.[59] Even a court in an EU Member State that does not have jurisdiction to hear the substance of the claim may order provisional or protective measures as long as these measures are limited to the territory of *that particular Member State*.[60] This is the same as the jurisdictional rule under English law.[61]

Broad jurisdictional rules allowing the claimant to engage in forum shopping are problematic in respect of injunctions to stop online dissemination or publication of personality rights infringements, as this may lead to the lowest common denominator for freedom of expression within the EU.[62] For some online publications an injunction to take content down cannot easily be restricted to access from one country (but kept online for access from all other countries). While Facebook, for example, may easily distinguish its content dissemination according to the country from which the website is accessed, based on geo-location tools, the same may not be true for a small business selling widgets online. Because of the potentially ubiquitous reach of injunctions the CJEU in *Bolagsupplysningen* held that in respect of injunctions for suppression or removal of online information allegedly infringing personality rights can *only* be brought in the courts that have jurisdiction to adjudicate on the *totality* of loss.[63] This creates an exception from Article 35 of the Brussels Regulation for online information torts in respect of injunctions to take down content or alter information.

However, the reverse question also arises, whether, if the court is competent to rule on the totality of the loss, it may impose an injunction with extraterritorial effect. In *Eva Glawischnig-Piesczek v Facebook* the Austrian court had imposed a universal injunction with worldwide effect against Facebook to remove insulting comments against an Austrian politician.[64] Arguably, since the territorial scope of injunctions have not been harmonized at EU level, the scope of such injunctions are governed by national procedural rules.[65] Attorney General Szpunar pointed out that the principle of comity under international law imposes an obligation on the court to exercise self-restraint by limiting the territorial scope to whatever is *necessary* to protect the personality rights of the claimant.[66] The CJEU has held that there is no territorial limit on the scope of an injunction, which is governed by national law, but must respect principles of international law.[67]

Multiple infringements of personality rights such as threats, insults, defamation, misuse of private information, and so on frequently occur online when several defendants repeat the original infringement through trolling, repeating, and reposting. These defendants may be based in different jurisdictions, which raises the question whether they can be sued in the same court in a joined action. Joinder of actions depends on

[59] Art 2(a): provided the defendant is summoned or served before enforcement; Recital 33.

[60] Art 35 and Recital 33; this goes back to Case C-125/79 *Denilauler v SNC Couchet Frères* [1980] ECR 1055, see further Lord Collins et al (n 26) 371–532, 11-049.

[61] See the discussion in section 2.4 and (n 163).

[62] See discussion in Chapter 3.

[63] *Bolagsupplysningen* (n 54) para 48.

[64] Case C-18/18 *Eva Glawischnig-Piesczek v Facebook* Judgment of 3 October 2019, ECLI:EU:C:2019:821. See further the discussion in Chapter 3.

[65] See also Case C -507/17 *Google LLC v CNIL* ECLI:EU:C:2019:772, Judgment of 24 September 2019 para 72—global dereferencing injunctions *may* be imposed on search engines by national authorities.

[66] Opinion of Advocate General Szpunar of 4 June 2018, see paras 78, 86, 88, 93, 96, 100.

[67] *Eva Glawischnig-Piesczek* (n 64) paras 48–52.

national procedural rules, but in terms of jurisdiction Article 8(1) of the Brussels Recast Regulation provides that the claimant can sue all defendants in the courts of a Member State where any one of them is domiciled ("the anchor defendant"), provided that "the claims are so closely connected that it is expedient to hear and determine them together to avoid the risk of irreconcilable judgments resulting from separate proceedings."[68] This provision must not be used with the sole objective of ousting the jurisdiction of the Court where a defendant is domiciled.[69] Since the laws on privacy infringements and defamation vary widely between different EU Member States, the question arises whether for Article 8(1) to apply the claims must have the same legal basis, or whether they can be based on differently defined torts. The CJEU has held that there is no requirement that the legal basis for the joined claims is identical, but where the legal bases are identical there is a presumption that the risk of irreconcilable judgments is much higher.[70] However, the CJEU has also held that for there to be a risk of irreconcilable judgments the factual and legal situation must be similar, and that the defendants must be able to foresee that they may be sued in a court where one of the defendants is domiciled.[71] Therefore another factor is whether or not the defendants acted independently of each other.[72] If there is no connection between the defendants and they act independently of each other the likelihood that any one of them is able to foresee that they may be sued in a country where any one of them is based is much lower, compared to if they have acted in concert.

Moreover, Article 7(5) of the Brussels Regulation (Recast) may be relevant to personality rights infringements, and in particular those arising from data protection breaches[73] by a business vis-à-vis a customer (whether consumer or non-consumer). Article 7(5) provides for a forum for disputes arising "out of the operation of a branch, agency or other establishment"[74] at the place where that branch, agency, or other establishment is physically situated, and this head of jurisdiction applies to both contractual and non-contractual claims.[75] The legal relationship between the main business and the branch (eg parent company-subsidiary) is only one factor relevant in deciding whether this head of jurisdiction applies. Additionally, the courts assess the *appearance* of whether a business operates as a branch of the main business in a different jurisdiction vis-à- vis the other party.[76] In *ZX v Ryanair* the CJEU held that the branch must have been involved in the legal relationship between the passenger and the branch. In this case an air passenger could not sue Ryanair for compensation for delay in Spain only for the reason that Ryanair maintained an establishment there, as the ticket had been bought online and the branch was not directly involved in the flight provided.[77] Thus, this ground of jurisdiction can only be used if a personality

[68] Case C-98/06 *Freeport Plc v Arnoldsson* [2007] ECR I-839.

[69] Case C-189/87 *Kafelis v Schröder* [1988] ECR 5565, 5583; Case C-145/10 *Painer v Standard Verlag* EU:C:2011:798 [2012] ECDR 6, para 78.

[70] ibid paras 76, 80, 82.

[71] ibid paras 79, 81; Banholzer (n 29) para 78.

[72] ibid para 83.

[73] Framed as a claim for misuse of personal information, or breach of statutory duty under data protection legislation.

[74] As to the meaning of "establishment" see Case C-33/78 *Somafer SA v Saar-Ferngas AB* [1978] ECR 2184.

[75] Dickinson and Lein (n 20) 4.133.

[76] ibid 4.136.

[77] Case C-464/18 *ZX v Ryanair* ECLI:EU:C:2019:311 Judgment of 11 April 2019, paras 34–36.

rights dispute is directly connected to the activities of the branch. This could mean that a contract was made through the branch (or a website operated by a branch) or that the personality rights infringement itself was committed through the branch.

Online personality rights infringements additionally raise the tricky question of the relationship between the *country of origin rule* in Article 3 of the E-commerce Directive 2000/31/EC and private international law.[78] The country of origin rule provides that *information society services* should be governed by the laws applicable in the Member State at the place of establishment of the service provider[79] and that other Member States must not apply their laws to this service provider in such a way that it *restricts the service provider's freedom to provide these services.*[80] Information society services are defined as "any service normally provided for remuneration at a distance by electronic means and at the individual request of a recipient of services."[81] Thus, for commercial online publishers, whether financed through subscription or through advertising, the question arises whether the application of a more restrictive foreign law in respect of personality rights-related torts constitutes a restriction of their freedom to provide services. Tort law naturally varies between the different EU Member States with different legal values and cultures prevailing in different Member States. For example, English common law has known extensive private law rights in respect of defamation or German law has developed more exacting standards with regard to personality rights and the protection of individual honour, privacy, and dignity.[82] The country of origin principle applies to the taking up of the activity of an information society service, such as requirements concerning the service, qualifications, authorization or notification, and business conduct, requirements regarding quality or content of the service, requirements as to advertising or contracts, and liability of the service provider.[83] It may be questionable to what extent tort laws governing private relationships rather than administrative regulations are a barrier to the freedom to provide services.[84] In any case it is clear that the country of origin rule in the E-commerce Directive is not a rule of private international law and therefore does not displace rules on applicable law.[85] Consequently the CJEU held in *eDate Advertising* that the courts of Member States should apply the rules on applicable law that are part of their national procedural laws and then double-check, as a corrective, whether the application

[78] See further Chapter 8.

[79] Art 3(1).

[80] Art 3(2): note that the Directive does not state that other Member States must not apply their laws to that foreign service provider—they may merely not do this in such a way that the freedom to provide services is impaired.

[81] Art 2(a) refers to the definitions in Art 1(2) of Directives 98/34/EC and 98/84/EC; now see Art 1(1) of Directive (EU) 2015/1535.

[82] An examination of these differences would be outside the scope of this book, but readers may refer to C Coors, "Headwind from Europe: The New Position of the German Courts on Personality Rights" [2010] 11(5) German Law Journal 527–37; G Black, *Publicity Rights & Image: Exploitation and Legal Control* (Hart 2011).

[83] Art 2(h)(i) E-commerce Directive 2000/31/EC.

[84] J Hörnle, "The UK Perspective on the Country of Origin Rule in the E-commerce Directive- A Rule of Administrative Law Applicable to Private Law Disputes?" (2004) 12(3) International Journal of Law and Information Technology 333–63, but contrast *eDate/Oliver Martinez* (n 24) para 58 where the Court held that the country of origin principle may override private law obligations.

[85] Recitals 23, 25 and *eDate/Oliver Martinez* (n 24) 61; Klöpfer, "Persönlichkeitsrechtsverletzungen über das Internet" (2013) Juristische Arbeitsblätter 165–71, 170.

of *this* law constitutes a restriction of the freedom to provide services in the circumstances of each individual case. Effectively this means that the national court must not apply any stricter requirements imposed by the applicable law than those imposed by the law of the country of origin.[86] This is despite the fact that the country of origin rule is not a rule of applicable law, but only services to correct the applicable law to prevent a non-EU law compliant restriction of the freedom to provide services.[87] In practice the application of this corrective may be difficult as the court has to compare the regulatory burden imposed by the applicable law to the regulatory burden at the country of origin and this comparison may have no clear outcomes when assessing whether there is an unjustified restriction of the freedom to provide services.[88] If national courts deny jurisdiction for the reason that an information services provider is regulated by its country of origin, this is a breach of the right to due process under Article 6 of the European Convention on Human Rights (ECHR), as the European Court of Human Rights found in relation to a defamation claim brought by a Swedish domicile in respect of a broadcast from the UK, which had been produced in Sweden and in the Swedish language.[89]

2.2 Jurisdictional rules in the General Data Protection Regulation

The General Data Protection Regulation (GDPR) (EU) 2016/679 has introduced express provisions on the rights of data subjects to have an effective judicial remedy in tort against a data controller or a data processor where personal data have been processed in breach of the Regulation.[90] The rules in the GDPR can be regarded as *lex specialis* taking priority over the general Brussels Jurisdiction Regulation (EU) 1215/2012.[91] However, the GDPR is silent on the enforceability of a judgment resulting from the assumption of jurisdiction under its rules.[92]

Under the GDPR the claimant (data subject) has a choice between the courts at the place of an establishment of the data controller or data processor, and the courts at the data subject's habitual residence, provided the data controller is not a public authority acting in a public law capacity.[93] It provides for a discretionary *lis pendens* if there is more than one action pending before the courts of several Member States: where a court has information that proceedings before another Member State court are pending concerning the same subject matter and processing by the same data controller or data processor, the Regulation provides that the court *may* suspend or withdraw the action on the application of one party in favour of the court first seized or

[86] *eDate/ Oliver Martinez* (n 24) paras 62, 66–68; Klöpfer (n 85) 170.
[87] Lutzi (n 35) 715.
[88] Lutzi (n 35) 707.
[89] *Arlewin v Sweden* App No 22302/10 ECtHR, Judgment of 1 March 2016, (2016) 41 BHRC 571, paras 72–73.
[90] Art 79(1).
[91] I Revolidis, "Judicial Jurisdiction over Internet Privacy Violations and the GDPR: a Case of 'Privacy Tourism?'" 11(1) Masaryk University Journal of Law and Technology 7–38, 21.
[92] Brkan (n 3) 274.
[93] Art 79(2).

consolidate the actions.[94] Unfortunately, the GDPR has missed the opportunity here to create for a collective action encompassing different claimants in the case of systematic and large-scale infringements of data protection rights.[95]

By allowing data subjects to sue in their habitual place of residence the GDPR mirrors the rules on consumer protection[96] in Articles 17–19 of the Brussels (Recast) Jurisdiction Regulation (EU) 1215/2012 giving the data subject[97] a (privileged[98]) choice between the local courts at his or her place of residence and the courts at the place of establishment of the data controller(s) and data processor(s). Since (joint) data controllers and data processors who cause the damage are jointly liable for the whole loss,[99] claimants are likely to be able to choose between several fora. The substantive law of the GDPR[100] applies if one of the conditions on territorial scope in Article 3 GDPR is fulfilled:[101] first, it applies if the relevant data controller or processor is *established* with the EU and the processing takes place in the context of the activities of this establishment;[102] second, it applies where the data processing activities are related to the offering of goods or services to data subjects who are in the EU;[103] third, it applies where the behaviour of data subjects in the EU is monitored.[104] Scope of application of the GDPR in these three criteria can be neatly summarized as establishment of data controllers/processors and *targeting* of EU data subjects.[105] As far as the targeting criteria are concerned the application of the GDPR is not limited to EU citizens or to persons who are habitually resident in the EU. The application of the GDPR for the offering of goods and services and in respect of monitoring is triggered by mere presence of the data subject on the territory of any EU Member State at that moment (ie when the offering of goods and services or the monitoring takes place).[106]

The targeting test[107] itself is informed by *Pammer/Alpenhof*,[108] which established the CJEU's jurisprudence on consumer jurisdiction under Articles 17–19 of the Brussels (Recast) Jurisdiction Regulation (EU) 1215/2012 and found that a multi-factor assessment must be used to establish targeting. Language, currency, feedback on the website, advertising, country-specific search engines, top-level domains, directions, and

[94] Art 81.

[95] Brkan (n 3) 273; *Schrems v Facebook Ireland Ltd* EU:C:2017:863, EU:C:2018:37, [2018] 1 WLR 4343 (CJEU) paras 44–49: collective actions cannot be brought under the consumer protection provisions of the Brussels Jurisdiction Regulation.

[96] Brkan (n 3) 265—see further Chapter 10.

[97] Who is not necessarily a consumer, but may be acting in a professional capacity; Brkan 267.

[98] Criticizing this privilege as being contrary to the logic of private international law: Revolidis (n 91) 18–19.

[99] Art 82(3) and (4).

[100] Directly applicable in all EU Member States.

[101] See discussion in Chapter 7.

[102] Art 3(1).

[103] Art 3(2)(a).

[104] Art 3(2)(b) mere collection of personal data does not equate to monitoring—to establish whether monitoring takes place there as to be some data analytics, behavioural analysis, or surveillance, which amounts to monitoring: European Data Protection Board "Guidelines 3/2018 on the Territorial Scope of the GDPR (Article 3)" (16 November 2018) p 18.

[105] ibid p 3; see Recital 23 of the GDPR.

[106] Guidelines 3/2018 (n 104) p 13.

[107] Joined Cases C-585/08 *Peter Pammer v Reederei Karl Schlüter GmbH & Co. KG* and C-144/09 *Hotel Alpenhof v Oliver Heller* 7 December 2010 ECLI:EU:C:2010:740. See discussion in Chapter 10.

[108] 7 December 2010 ECLI:EU:C:2010:740; further discussed in Chapter 10.

the international nature of the offering can all indicate that a website is targeted to the EU. In other words, the offer must manifest an intention of doing business with data subjects in the EU.[109]

Finally, it applies to data processing in a place where the law of an EU Member State applies by virtue of public international law, such as a ship or aircraft operating under the flag of an EU Member State or a diplomatic mission.[110] As for the last condition for applying EU data protection law, the wording of Article 3(3) leaves open the question whether the GDPR also applies where the *data processing takes place* on the territory of an EU Member State, as arguably EU Member State law applies on the *territory of that EU Member State by virtue of public international law*.

If the GDPR does not apply to the data processing according to Article 3, for example, in the context of a non-commercial relationship involving a controller outside the EU, which does not involve monitoring or behavioural advertising, the competent court would then apply its private international law rules in respect of tort liability to ascertain the applicable law. If the national rules on applicable law indicate that the law of an EU Member State is applicable, and a breach of data protection is a tort under *that* EU Member State's private law,[111] the question arises whether the GDPR would then be indirectly applicable to ascertain a remedy under tort law. Arguably, this is currently an open question and may extend the scope of the GDPR into private international law. Thus, in private disputes the GDPR may be indirectly incorporated into national tort law, even though the GDPR does not apply directly.

2.3 Jurisdiction under German law

German civil procedure law[112] recognizes several grounds for jurisdiction, some of them do not have an equivalent under English law[113] and apply only to monetary claims.[114] As has been pointed out in Chapter 2, the reason for this may well be geopolitical and connected to the fact that the UK is an island, so that greater emphasis has been placed on the territoriality principle here than in continental European jurisdictions. Furthermore, Germany being a federal state with regional court systems, questions of jurisdictional competence arise within the national and international context and have done so for a long time.[115]

The purpose guiding the teleological interpretation of the German rules of jurisdiction is to avoid a limitless extension of jurisdiction, avoiding jurisdiction if there are only weak connections to the dispute, avoiding jurisdictional conflicts, and ensuring

[109] Recital 23 GDPR and Guidelines 3/2018 (n 104) pp 15–16, see also further Chapter 7.

[110] Art 3(3), Recital 25.

[111] Member States have to provide tort liability, see Art 82 GDPR.

[112] Contained in the ZPO, Zivilprozessordnung, or Civil Procedure Code, available from https://www.gesetze-im-internet.de/zpo/ accessed on 26/7/2020.

[113] S 23 ZPO.

[114] Banholzer (n 29) 84–85.

[115] Double functionality of the rules on jurisdiction, I Roth, *Die Internationale Zuständigkeit deutscher Gerichte bei Persönlichkeitsrechtsverletzungen im Internet* (Peter Lang 2007) 60.

foreseeability of the competent court(s) concomitantly allowing defendants to adjust their conduct accordingly.[116]

According to German civil procedure rules[117] the general ground for jurisdiction is the domicile of the defendant (*actor sequitur forum rei*), with several variations.[118] Like the Brussels Regulation,[119] German procedural rules recognize jurisdiction for claims arising from the operation of a branch of other establishment.[120]

For claims in tort a special ground of jurisdiction exists, which is the court of the district in which the tort has been committed.[121] Thus, the "tort" ground of jurisdiction is the place of commission and this applies to personality rights infringements and the infringement of image rights.[122] Like for the Brussels Regulation and English law,[123] this special ground of jurisdiction for tort claims has been interpreted to mean *both* the place where the tort has been committed and the place where the tort has been completed, that is, where the direct[124] damage has occurred.[125] Thus, the connection factors are such that they may connect to several jurisdictions simultaneously allowing the claimant a choice between the courts in different countries and allowing for a degree of forum shopping.[126] This special rule for torts applies both to establishing jurisdictional competence between the regional courts and international jurisdiction.

Under the German rules, it is not entirely clear whether a claimant can sue for the whole loss before the court which has jurisdiction on the basis that this is the place where the tort has been completed, that is, where the direct damage has impacted on the claimant.[127] There is an old decision of the highest civil court of 1909, which found that the tort cannot be split into many separate parts but must be regarded as one single tort, and that therefore the claimant was able to recover the whole loss caused by a print publication in one single action.[128] It would be an extraordinary burden for both the claimant and the defendant to solve their dispute in several separate proceedings before different courts.[129] This is still the prevailing opinion in Germany, although a minority argues that the German rules should follow the *mosaic* rule adopted by the CJEU in *Shevill*.[130]

[116] Case VI ZR 111/10, Judgment 29 March 2011, [2012] ILPr 11, para 6; Banholzer (n 29) para 77.
[117] Zivilprozeßordnung (ZPO).
[118] Ss 12, 13, 17 (domicile), 20 (residence).
[119] See discussion in Chapter 8.
[120] S 21, see BGH NJW 2011, 2056 and Banholzer (n 29) para 86.
[121] S 32.
[122] Specht in Dreier and Schulze (eds), *Urheberrechtsgesetze* (5th edn, 2015 C.H. Beck online) para 31; subject to the specific exception discussed further in this section.
[123] See discussion in section 2.4.
[124] Erfolgsort or Rechtsgutsverletzung, place where the claimant's rights have been injured, the equivalent to the direct damage as interpreted in the jurisprudence of the CJEU, see (n 116); Roth (n 115) 169–72.
[125] BGH, Judgment of June 29, 2010—VI ZR 122/09; BGH, Judgment of September 24, 1986—VIII ZR 320/85, BGHZ 98, 263, 273; BGH, Judgment of November 25, 1993—IX ZR 32/93, BGHZ 124, 237, 240; BGH, Judgment of February 28, 1996—XII ZR 181/93, BGHZ 132, 105, 110; BGH, Judgment of March 2, 2010—VI ZR 23/09, BGHZ 184, 313; Roth (n 115) 168.
[126] Roth (n 115) 174–77.
[127] ibid 298–310.
[128] RGZ 72, 41.
[129] At 45ff.
[130] Roth (n 115) 298–310.

For print publications, the issue of deciding *where the tort has been committed* is tricky and even more so for online publication. However, the CJEU and the German courts have interpreted the place where the tort was committed differently.[131] Like English law the starting point under German law has been the place of publication, but only the starting point. For print publication torts related to personality rights are committed both at *the named place* of the publication[132] and at the place(s) of *purposeful* dissemination.[133] This is called the "flying" jurisdiction as the claimant may sue at each and every place of intended, purposeful publication, of which there may be many,[134] and as discussed earlier in this section, for the whole loss. However, if copies of a publication reach a jurisdiction through coincidence, such as someone taking a few copies of an article into the country, this does not count as publication and hence would be insufficient to establish jurisdiction.[135]

Defamation and insults additionally are criminal offences, which can be prosecuted by private claimants, and the flying jurisdiction originally existed equally in criminal procedural law[136] but was abolished after much criticism in s 7(2) StPO in 1902. This now provides that the courts at the place of (official) publication, and if pursued through private prosecution, additionally, the courts at the place of the private prosecutor's domicile are competent. The rules for civil jurisdiction, however, continue to allow for flying jurisdiction, according to the continuous jurisdictions of the courts and confirmed in the 1977 German Supreme Court Decision.[137] However, the flying jurisdiction has been controversial[138] and in 2013 its abolition was debated in the German Bundestag, however, this debate only led to a (very) partial reform.[139] The jurisdictional rules for copyright infringement were reformed: where the infringer is a private individual acting for non-commercial purposes, jurisdiction is limited to the (registered or unregistered) domicile of the defendant.[140] If the defendant is not domiciled in Germany, the place where the copyright infringement was committed has exclusive jurisdiction.[141]

The flying jurisdiction within the intra-German context of the competence of regional courts had the consequence that claimants pick courts that have specialized in questions of personality rights infringements (and the same applies, for example to intellectual property (IP) infringements). This forum shopping has been criticized as posing the risk of claimants finding the "propitious judge."[142] Furthermore, the flying jurisdiction equally applies to jurisdiction in respect of injunctions, which allows the

131 Banholzer (n 29) para 64.

132 Erscheinungsort (place of publication).

133 BGH, GRUR 1978, 194 = NJW 1977, 1590—profil; Roth (n 115) 173.

134 Consider eg distribution of a national newspaper in Germany.

135 ibid.

136 U Jürgens, "Abgestürzte Gerichtsstände- der fliegende Gerichtsstand im Presserecht" (2014) Neue Juristische Wochenschrift 3061–067, 3061.

137 BGH, GRUR 1978, 194 = NJW 1977, 1590—profil.

138 Danckwerts, GRUR 2007, 104; Solmecke, MMR 2007, 490; Berger, GRURInt 2005, 465; Kaufmann, MMR 2006, 714; Mankowski, MMR 2002, 814.

139 Jürgens (n 136) 3062.

140 S 104a(1) UrhG.

141 ibid.

142 Jürgens (n 136) 3063–64; mentioned as an argument also in J Deister and T Degen, "Darf der Gerichtstand Noch Fliegen?" (2010) NJOZ 1–6, 2 (argument of the lawful judge).

claimant to forum shop to obtain an injunction to prohibit publication,[143] potentially on a worldwide basis. However, the flying jurisdiction also has its proponents who argue that it is in the interests of justice to ensure that claimants have access to a court and that the defendant has chosen the medium of internet communication with full awareness of its global, ubiquitous reach (choice of medium argument, which has also been made in the UK).[144,145]

As far as the flying jurisdiction is concerned, for traditional print publications it has not been sufficient that copies reached a particular destination by coincidence.[146] For cross-border circulation of print publications in a foreign language it is assumed that the publisher did not purposefully intend to disseminate them in Germany.[147] Furthermore, the place of the domicile or presence of the claimant are irrelevant.[148] The equivalent principles apply to broadcasting in respect of spill-over effects, where terrestrial signals coincidentally reach over a land border: such spill-over signals would not mean that a personality infringement contained in the broadcast are committed in the foreign border region.[149]

These principles developed for analogue media can only be applied with difficulty to the publication of personality-infringing content online.[150] For online publications the stakes are raised both for the claimant, because of the increased reach and impact of online publications and the difficulty of obtaining justice at a distance, and for the defendant, since a defendant publishing on the open internet cannot control the reach of the publication.[151] Thus, for online publications the German courts have developed a strand of jurisprudence for deciding the location *where* the tort has been committed, or in other words, *where online publication* takes place.

Applying its jurisprudence developed in the context of trade mark law,[152] in *The New York Times* case, the German Supreme Court[153] balanced these conflicting interests. It held that, for a German court to be competent to hear such a dispute, the conflicts of interests[154] between the claimant and the defendant has to have occurred in Germany.[155] Applying this "conflicts of interests" test means searching for relevant connection factors to Germany.[156] The German Supreme Court held that mere accessibility of the infringing content in Germany is not sufficient for publication,[157]

143 ibid 3.

144 See section 2.4—but the Defamation Act 2013 has not left much space for this argument.

145 Deister and Degen (n 142) 3, 6; Dölling, "Der fliegende Gerichtsstand im Presserecht—Spielball der Interessen?" (2015) Neue Juristische Wochenschrift 124–29, 128.

146 ibid 128.

147 ibid para 32.

148 ibid; BGH, GRUR 1978, 194 = NJW 1977, 1590—profil.

149 ibid.

150 BGH GRUR 2010, 462 Tz 20 f— *The New York Times*; Banholzer (n 29) para 77.

151 Roth (n 115)) 173.

152 BGH, GRUR 2005, 431 = NJW 2005, 1435 [1436]—hotel maritime.

153 BGH.

154 Interessenkonflikt, eg the right to publish versus the claimant's personality or publicity rights.

155 BGH GRUR 2010, 462— *The New York Times*, para 20; Banholzer (n 29) para 77.

156 ibid; see also OLG Karlsruhe GRUR-RS 2016, 115437, para 30.

157 As had been argued in academia in the past: as this would completely imbalance litigation tactics in favour of the claimant.

and additional connecting factors have to be found[158] to ensure that the content complained is in fact likely to reach a German audience and the infringement of the personality rights alleged by the claimant have in fact occurred in Germany.[159] However, the German Supreme Court emphasized that unlike for the law of (unfair) competition, where a court only has jurisdiction if the tort was actively and intentionally targeted at a particular market, for online personality rights infringements jurisdiction is not limited to the place to which dissemination was intentionally targeted, but only requires reach into the territory in the sense that persons in Germany in fact take notice of the illegal content and thereby damage the claimant's reputation.[160] Hence it may be better to refer to impact, rather than targeting in this context, and the test would look at the impact of a statement within a particular jurisdiction.

According to the German Supreme Court, the number of people accessing the infringing content may be one indicative factor of this reach, but was not decisive. It was not decisive for the reason that it was frequently not possible to determine the number of persons having accessed the content on the internet, and, in any case, download figures would not be relevant for an injunction preventatively suppressing the publication.[161] The nature of the online, freely accessible, content is one factor to be taken into account, by looking at who the content is likely to have an effect on or who would be interested in seeking out the content. So there must be factors that suggest persons in Germany will actually access the information and take notice of it.[162] If the content is not addressed to any particular region in Germany, any of the regional courts may assume jurisdiction for intra-German conflicts.[163]

The German Supreme Court applied these criteria in the judgment in *The New York Times* case. This Case concerned an article in the online version and archive of the newspaper claiming that a Russian national domiciled in Germany had engaged in corruption, was part of the Russian mafia and had been barred from entry to the US. The Court reversed the rulings of the two lower instance courts and found that it was highly likely that this article reached a German audience for the reason that *The New York Times* had 14,484 registered subscribers in Germany[164] and that it was an internationally established "big" newspaper read globally, including Germany—the circumstance that the article appeared in the local section was irrelevant, as the subject matter concerned international business affairs.[165] Furthermore, the claimant was

[158] There has to be a special connection between the dispute and Germany, BGH GRUR 2010, 462—*The New York Times*.

[159] BGH GRUR 2010, 462— *The New York Times*, para 20 (Headnote of the Judgment); BGH GRUR 2013, 751- Autocomplete, para 7; BGH MMR 2011, 490; OLG Brandenburg MMR 2017, 261, para 12; OLG Köln BeckRS 2017, 124095 para 20; BGH NJW 2012, 148, para 11.

[160] BGH GRUR 2010, 462— *The New York Times*, para 18.

[161] ibid para 19 and Banholzer (n 29) para 77.

[162] OLG Bremen MMR 2001,53; OLG Brandenburg MMR 2017, 261, para 15; Banholzer (n 29) para 77.

[163] OLG Brandenburg MMR 2017, 261, paras 16–17.

[164] That was 0.5 per cent of its registered subscriber base.

[165] Paras 22, 24.

domiciled and professionally active in Germany—hence this was where the damage occurred. For these reasons the German Supreme Court found that the German courts were competent to issue the injunction.[166] The Court held expressly that there was no *de minimis* threshold regarding the actual or potential access in Germany, as the impact of the article could be felt even if only one person from the claimant's close social circle learned of its contents.[167]

In a later case of 2012, the Bundesgerichtshof (BGH) held that German courts have jurisdiction against the Californian blogger.com host in a defamation claim. The substantial connection to Germany was the fact that the relevant blog post was in German and concerned business activities in Germany, despite the fact that these related to Spanish properties.[168]

These cases can be contrasted with another judgment by the German Supreme Court in *Sieben Tage Moskau* where the Court held that the claimant's domicile in Germany combined with the accessibility of the personality rights infringing report in Germany was not sufficient for jurisdiction.[169] The claimant and the defendant were former classmates and the claimant was a Russian businessman domiciled in Germany. The defendant was domiciled in the US and the personality rights infringement claim arose from a report about a class reunion at the claimant's house in Moscow, written and uploaded by the US domiciled defendant after she had returned there. The allegedly defamatory report was addressed to the classmates who (other than the claimant and the defendant) were still domiciled in Russia, and it was written in Russian, which made it unlikely that anyone other than the claimant had noticed it in Germany. Presumably, although the Court did not say this expressly, this also meant that no damage had occurred in Germany. In these circumstances, the Court held that the connecting factors to Germany were too tenuous and that the claimant's German domicile combined with the accessibility of the report there on their own were too thin as connecting factors to the territory.[170] Interestingly, the Court additionally found it relevant to mention that, if the German court was competent to rule on the claim, it would apply German law, which would be inappropriate given the insufficient links to the territory.[171] In assessing the conflicts of interests test the court took into account the content of the allegedly infringing article to assess whether this provides a sufficient connection to Germany.[172] If defamatory statements about an event in a foreign country are published online in a foreign language without a clear impact on Germany, the German courts are likely to deny jurisdiction.[173] Thus, the approach of the German courts is to assess the impact or effect of a statement in Germany and the likelihood of such a statement coming to the notice to an audience in Germany.

[166] Para 23.
[167] Para 24.
[168] BGH NJW 2012, 148, para 12.
[169] Case VI ZR 111/10 *Sieben Tage Moskau* Judgment 29 March 2011, [2012] ILPr 11.
[170] Paras 15–20.
[171] Para 13; see also OLG Köln OLG BeckRS 2017, 124095 para 22.
[172] OLG Karlsruhe GRUR-RS 2016, 115437 para 30.
[173] OLG Köln BeckRS 2017, 124095 para 23.

2.4 Rules of jurisdiction under English common law

If none of the defendants are domiciled in an EU Member State and none of the other factors[174] for applying the harmonized jurisdiction rules under the Brussels Regulation apply, the English courts apply the common law rules for *in personam* jurisdiction for determining jurisdiction in personality rights disputes. These apply to claims for damages and for claims for an injunction.[175] The English courts have jurisdiction to serve process on a defendant in England, and abroad, only if this is authorized by the court according to the common law rules on civil jurisdiction.[176] Essentially, courts have jurisdiction over persons present in England at the time of service, even if only temporarily, and, where the defendant voluntarily submits to jurisdiction. For corporations the question arises whether a representative within England counts as a presence for the purposes of jurisdiction. In England (by contrast to EU law jurisprudence) a permanent representative with an office does not necessarily amount to corporate presence within the jurisdiction. An office or representative may only count as a presence within the jurisdiction if it has the authority to make binding contracts, acting as an agent binding the corporation.[177]

For service outside the jurisdiction, permission of the court is required.[178] Permission of the court is discretionary and is based on any of the grounds in paragraph 3.1 of Practice Direction 6B (PD6B).[179] An exclusive jurisdiction clause is regarded as binding. With regard to Scotland, for example, in *Clark v Tripadvisor* a hotel operator in Scotland wished to obtain disclosure from Tripadvisor of the identity of two persons who had posted allegedly defamatory comments about the hotel and the question arose whether the Scottish courts could make a third-party disclosure order against the Massachusetts, US-domiciled company. The Scottish Court of Session held that the exclusive jurisdiction clause in favour of Massachusetts in the terms and conditions was binding on the hotel operator.[180]

In personality infringement cases such as defamatory statements pseudonymously posted on a website, the claimant frequently requires a disclosure order against a third-party intermediary, such as the hosting provider to obtain the identity of the putative defendant. In *Clark v Tripadvisor* the Court of Session held that such a disclosure order cannot be made against a foreign hosting provider, as this would be extraterritorial, and the power under section 1(1a)(b) the Administration of Justice (Scotland) Act 1972 is limited to Scotland.[181] A disclosure order should be sought by way of international letters of request to the relevant authorities in Massachusetts under the Hague Convention[182] on the Taking of Evidence Abroad in Civil or Commercial Matters.[183]

[174] Such as the dispute arising out of the operations of a branch, agency or establishment within the EU Art 7(5) or that the dispute is a qualifying consumer dispute Art 17, see further Chapters 8 and 10.

[175] Lord Collins et al (n 26) 371–532, 11-002.

[176] Lord Collins et al (n 26) 11-003.

[177] *Adams v Cape Industries* [1990] Ch 433, 531 (CA); *Harrods Ltd v Dow Jones* [2003] EWHC 1162 (QB), para 22.

[178] Lord Collins et al (n 26) 11-102–11-103, 11-108.

[179] Rule 6.36 of the Civil Procedure Rules; Lord Collins et al (n 26) 11-140.

[180] *Clark v TripAdvisor LLC*, 2014 WL 7255192, Court of Session, para 25.

[181] Para 20.

[182] 18 March 1970, Cmnd 6727 (1977).

[183] *Clark* (n 180) para 19.

If court proceedings are validly served abroad, the English courts have jurisdiction, but maintain discretion to decline jurisdiction if a court in another country is better placed to adjudicate the dispute in the interests of the parties and the interests of justice (*forum non conveniens*).[184] This includes legal and practical considerations as to where the evidence and the witnesses are located, the nature of the dispute, local knowledge required to solve the dispute, and expense of litigation.[185]

For tort claims, the discretionary rule to serve proceedings on a foreign defendant has two prongs, namely that the damage was sustained in England or, alternatively, that the damage sustained resulted from an act committed within England.[186] Thus, similar to the rules in the Brussels Convention/Regulation as interpreted in *Bier*, jurisdiction can be based on the place of the tortious act or the place of where the damage was sustained.[187] However, for injunctions, the jurisdiction of the English courts is limited to order that the defendant do or refrain from doing an act *within England*.[188]

Where the tort is committed by communication (which is particularly relevant to personality rights, including defamation) the courts have held that this is the place where the statements were published and this is the place where they were received (or perceived). For statements made available online, they are published within England, if they are in fact accessed or downloaded within the jurisdiction, with the consequence that the tortious act has been committed in England.[189] Under this interpretation[190] of "publication" the place where the tortious act has been committed frequently merges with the place where the claimant suffered damage to reputation (also place of downloading and access).

For privacy infringement previous actions had been brought under the cause of action of breach of confidence,[191] which is a claim in equity, and thus it was unclear whether for such actions jurisdiction lies at the place of where the damage occurs. In *Vidal-Hall v Google*[192] the Court of Appeal held that misuse of private information and contravention of the statutory data protection requirements is a *tort* and therefore, if damage has been sustained within England, the English courts have jurisdiction and service to the US (California) was proper. This was confirmed in *Ahuja*[193] although in that case the Court concluded that permission to effect service out of the jurisdiction should be set aside, as the tort was centred in Serbia and concerned a Serbian language

[184] Lord Collins et al (n 26) 11-143; based on *Amin Rasheed Shipping Corp v Kuwait Insurance Co* [1984] AC 50; *Spiliada Maritime Corp v Cansulex Ltd* [1987] AC 460 (HL).

[185] Lord Collins et al (n 26) 11-143; *Spiliada* (n 184).

[186] PD6B para 3.1(9) https://www.justice.gov.uk/courts/procedure-rules/civil/rules/part06/pd_part06b accessed on 26/7/2020; Lord Collins et al (n 26) 11R-211.

[187] Lord Collins et al (n 26) 11-214.

[188] PD6B 3.1(2).

[189] *Jameel v Dow Jones* [2005] QB 946, para 48; *Loutchansky v Times Newspapers* [2002] QB 783, paras 58–59; *Harrods* (n 177); *Dow Jones v Gutnick* [2002] HCA 56, (2003) 210 C.L.R 575 paras 44, 46–47 (Gleeson CJ, McHugh, Gummow, and Hayne JJ), 100 (Kirby J); *Lewis v King* [2004] EWCA Civ 1329; *Richardson v Schwarzenegger* [2004] EWHC 2422 (QB), para 19; *Metropolitan International Schools v Designtechnica Corp* [2011] 1 WLR 1743; *Berezovsky v Michaels* [2000] 1 WLR 1004.

[190] Cf the interpretation by the CJEU in *Shevill* (n 24), which held that publication takes place at the publisher's place of establishment.

[191] *Campbell v MGN Ltd* [2004] 2 WLR 1232 (HL).

[192] [2015] 3 WLR 409 (CA).

[193] *Ahuja v Politica Novine* [2016] 1 WLR 1414 (QB) para 75.

publication and this is where the tort had its most real and substantial connection.[194] This is similar to the finding of the BGH in *Sieben Tage Moskau*.

Furthermore, where a computer physically situated in London was hacked by a person from Russia, constituting a breach of confidence, the English courts have jurisdiction as England is the place where the damage was sustained.[195] Hence the starting point is that whenever damage has been sustained in England, jurisdiction may follow.

Given this wide ground for jurisdiction, this raises the question of whether jurisdiction can be limited where a non-domiciled claimant is suing a non-domiciled defendant in respect of an internet defamation on the basis of tenuous business and family links within the jurisdiction, which gives rise to damage in the form of reputational harm within England, and which serves as the relevant jurisdictional gateway.[196] In such cases the claimant must limit its claim to reputational harm within England.[197] But initially, in these cases, the English courts have found jurisdiction despite a small number of publications within the jurisdiction, or despite the fact that the "story" was centred on another jurisdiction.[198] The assertion of jurisdiction by the English courts has been criticized as "libel tourism."

Libel tourism was enabled because of two peculiar features of English defamation law: first, that jurisdiction was in no way confined to the place of *main* publication and, second, that under the *common law* damage to reputation was presumed, in order to establish a cause of action, and was only relevant at the later stage at the assessment of damages to be paid.[199] Section 1 of the Defamation Act 2013 changed defamation law in that damage is no longer presumed—the claimant must show serious harm to reputation to establish a claim *and* for permission to serve outside the jurisdiction. She would have to demonstrate a real prospect of success and good arguable case in this respect.[200]

In early internet cases it was held that even minimal damage to reputation can found jurisdiction.[201] In these cases the courts have also refused to disallow service of claim outside the jurisdiction on the basis of *forum non conveniens*.[202] In *Lennox Lewis v King* the Court of Appeal justified wide claims of jurisdiction on the internet despite the breadth of the reach of this communications medium by saying that the defendant would know that the defamatory statement would be available on a global basis without any restrictions ("choice of a global medium" argument).[203] English courts at that point in time rejected putting the emphasis on the claimant to show that

194 ibid paras 74–75, 78–81, 88–89.

195 *Ashton v OJSC Russian Aluminium* [2006] EWHC 2545 (Comm) para 62.

196 PD6B para 3.1 (9); *Lennox Lewis v Don King* [2005] EMLR 4 (CA): both parties domiciled in the US.

197 *Berezovsky* (n 189); *Richardson* (n 189) para 21.

198 *Harrods* (n 177): offending article omitted from the European edition of the paper (*Wall Street Journal*) and only ten subscribers to this version in the UK; *Richardson* (n 189) publication in the online version of the *Los Angeles Times* in the context of Californian gubernatorial elections.

199 *Berezovsky* (n 189) 1012 per Lord Steyn, 1032 per Lord Hope; *Harrods* (n 177), paras 37–39; *Richardson* (n 189) paras 19-20; *Jameel* (n 189) para 41; *Huda v Wells* [2018] EMLR 7 (QB) para 12.

200 *Euroeco Fuels (Poland) v Szczecin Port Authority* [2018] EWHC 1081 (QB) para 41; *Sobrinho v Impresa* [2016] EMLR 12 (QB) paras 44–51, 95–97; *Altimo Holdings v Kyrgyz Mobil* [2012] 1 WLR 1804 (PC) para 71.

201 *Harrods* (n 177) para 39; *Richardson* (n 189) paras 20–12.

202 *Harrods* (n 177) para 45; *Richardson* (n 189) 22–24.

203 *Lennox Lewis* (n 196) paras 29, 31; *Dow Jones* (n 189) para 39.

the defendant has intentionally targeted the chosen forum as not being compatible with the interests of justice.[204]

However, the Defamation Act 2013 has changed the law for defendants not domiciled in the UK. It now provides in section 9(2), [205] that for defamation jurisdiction to arise "of all the places in which the statement complained of has been published, England and Wales is *clearly the most appropriate place* in which to bring an action in respect of the statement." Thus, the claimant has to show that England is *clearly* the *most* appropriate forum,[206] such that it is no longer sufficient to prove that England is *an* appropriate forum of several.[207] This has displaced the common law *forum non conveniens* test with a statutory test of *the most appropriate forum*. As the first step the courts must take note "of all the places in which the statement complained of has been published," including any statements that convey the same, or virtually the same, meaning.[208] Thus, the preponderance of publication in England is an important factor,[209] and an assessment of whether the statement was *targeted* at England.[210] The court should assess the "global picture" to consider which forum would be the most appropriate for the claim by looking at publication figures.[211] This means that the court should compare respective publication numbers as the Court did, for example, in *Wright v Ver*.[212] However, much also depends on the circumstances of the individual case, and the assessment is not in all cases a pure game of numbers. In some cases, publication to one single person may cause more damage than mass publication, or as has been said by Mr Justice Sharp: "one-well directed arrow [may] hit the bull's eye of reputation."[213] Hence the English courts (like the German courts) undertake an impact analysis. This impact analysis is context-sensitive, and is a multi-factor test, including the place of publication but also including the question of *who* would be the interested audience of the publication, which leads to the impact.[214] This is similar to the German test for assessing whether the publication, which constitutes both the commission of the tort and the ensuing damage to reputation, has taken place in Germany (or a particular region of Germany), albeit that the most appropriate forum test is stricter, due to its superlative nature.

The second step is that the claimant must adduce country-by-country evidence of their reputation and how this reputation is being harmed by the defamatory

[204] *Lennox Lewis* (n 196) para 34.

[205] Neither *forum non conveniens* nor the Defamation Act 2013 apply if the Brussels Regulation applies, see *Euroeco Fuels* (n 200) paras 67, 71–72; subject to the abuse of process doctrine established in *Jameel* (n 189), discussed later. From the 1 January 2021, the EU withdrawal takes effect and the most appropriate place rules also applies in jurisdictional conflicts with the EU, see changed version of the Defamation Act 2013.

[206] *Ahuja* (n 193) paras 25–31 *Huda* (n 199) para 21.

[207] *Wright v Ver* [2019] EWHC 2094 (QB) para 24.

[208] S 9(2) and (3).

[209] *Wright* (n 207) para 26; *Ahuja* (n 193) para 31.

[210] *Wright* (n 207) paras 31–33.

[211] Explanatory Notes to the Defamation Act 2013, para 66; *Wright* (n 207) para 12.

[212] *Wright* (n 207) para 37; but see also caselaw predating the internet such as *Chadha v Dow Jones* [1999] EMLR 724, 732.

[213] Nicklin, J in *Wright* (n 207) para 30 quoting Sharp J in *King v Grundon* [2012] EWHC 2719 (QB) para 40; this is an argument that has also been made by the German courts, see discussion in section 2.3.

[214] *Wright* (n 207) para 32; this is similar to the German jurisprudence and the argument made in relation to the targeting test in the US, see Chapter 9.

publication. In this connection it is not sufficient to merely show that the claimant has substantial connections to England, but the serious harm to reputation in England must be made out.[215] By contrast to the traditional *forum non conveniens* analysis, the general interests of the parties and the interests of justice play only a secondary role under section 9(2) of the Defamation Act 2013. As stated in *Wright v Ver*: "the relative convenience of England and Wales for the parties and witnesses may not, on its own, carry much weight, but could assume importance[216] in a marginal case."[217] However, when assessing the most appropriate forum, the courts should include consideration of whether the claimant would not obtain a fair hearing in the alternative jurisdiction, but that the burden of proof to satisfy this factor is very high.[218] Furthermore, if the limitation period has run out in the most appropriate forum, without the claimant having been tardy in pursuing the litigation, this may be a factor in favour of jurisdiction in England.[219] Thus, in respect of defamation claims, the Defamation Act 2013 has significantly changed the *forum non conveniens* test, particularly for online publications where the claimant has a reputation in multiple states.

But ironically, for those few (?) individuals who have truly international (professional) reputation, this new test of finding the most appropriate forum may not work. There simply may be no "most appropriate forum" if the claim pertains to a global publication by a claimant with a global reputation. This was the problem precisely in *Wright v Ver* where the Bitcoin community is globally spread,[220] without any clear attachment to one jurisdiction. The logic of the Defamation Act 2013 undermines the principle of access to justice in *such* cases.[221] One major criticism of the most appropriate forum test[222] in general, and section 9(2) of the Defamation Act 2013 in particular, is the situation where a person with a genuinely global reputation is suing in respect of a genuinely global publication, as in this specific circumstance no particular jurisdiction may be the most appropriate forum in the sense that it stands out as such.

Even though this new two-step test may impose a heavy burden on a defamation claimant, especially since this burden of proof must be met before permission of service out of the jurisdiction is given, the lower courts have stated, at least at the time of writing, that this would generally not unduly infringe on every claimant's right to access the court, especially where that claimant has the means to sue in other jurisdictions.[223] However, Sir Michael Tugendhat conceded that there may be cases where it is impossible for the claimant to adduce comprehensive evidence about publication numbers:

215 *Wright* (n 207) paras 33–34, 50.

216 The location of witnesses as a relevant, minor factor, especially if located at great distance (eg in Australia): *Huda* (n 199) para 85 (obiter).

217 *Wright* (n 207) paras 34.

218 *Altimo Holdings* (n 200) para 97; *Wright* (n 207) para 34; *Huda* (n 199) para 85 (vi); *Ahuja* (n 193) para 88.

219 *Altimo Holdings* (n 200) para 71; *Huda* (n 199) paras 18(iii), 85.

220 *Wright* (n 207) para 49.

221 Mills (n 55) 5.

222 See the discussion on US jurisdiction in Chapter 9.

223 *Ahuja* (n 193) para 40.

> some ordinary (and otherwise very private) people are the subject of defamations which, for one reason or another, are in fact read or viewed (on media such as You Tube) by thousands or even millions of people abroad. And I would not exclude the possibility that there could be cases where, to require a claimant to put before the court evidence relating to all the jurisdictions where the defamatory statements have been published, might interfere with the claimant's right to access to the court.[224]

An interesting question that has not been addressed yet is this: If section 9 of the Defamation Act 2013 introduces the equivalent to a single publication rule[225] into English law, is the English court the most appropriate forum, can the claimant obtain damages for her total loss worldwide,[226] or is jurisdiction limited to the harm in England?

In summary therefore, the jurisdictional tests are subjected to an analysis of whether England is clearly the most appropriate forum for defamation cases. For claims based on misuse of private information or malicious falsehood, by contrast, the traditional *forum non conveniens* test still applies requiring an assessment of whether England is the appropriate forum in the sense that there has to be a real and substantial connection to the territory.[227]

The Defamation Act 2013 notwithstanding, and, in any case, the Act does not apply to malicious falsehood nor if any of the defendants is domiciled in an EU Member State or the UK, an action with weak links to England may be thrown out at the initial stages of the proceedings. In *Jameel v Dow Jones*[228] the Court of Appeal held that, in order to protect freedom of expression, a defamation action based on a minimal number of publications having occurred in England should be struck out as an abuse of process. The claim concerned an article and hyperlink in the *Wall Street Journal* Online linking the non-UK domiciled claimant to being a financial contributor to Al Qaeda. However, as this content had only been accessed by five subscribers within England[229] the Court held that no real and substantial tort had been committed within England—as publication here is so minimal and any damages would be insignificant in any event—and that the lack of a substantial connection to England and low likelihood of repeated publication also meant that no injunction should be issued.[230] Lord Phillips, MR said that the claimant in this action would achieve minimal vindication and minimal damages: "the game will not merely not have been worth the candle, it will not have been worth the wick."[231] In *Jameel* there was evidence as to how many people had in fact accessed the offending material from England. This raises the question whether for publication on the open internet (without registration or pay wall subscription) it can be assumed that there was substantial online publication in England. This question was answered in the negative in *Al-Amoudi v Brisard*.[232] The

224 ibid para 39.
225 See Chapter 9 for US law.
226 As would be the case under a single publication rule.
227 Paras 50, 78, 80.
228 [2005] QB 946 (CA).
229 Three of whom were agents of the claimant.
230 Per Lord Phillips paras 55, 67, 69, 70, 75–76: arguing from a procedural economy point of view.
231 Para 69.
232 [2007] 1 WLR 113 (QB).

burden of proof rests on the defamation claimant to show that more than a minimal number of persons have accessed and/or downloaded the defamatory material within England.[233] For this purpose the claimant may call a witness, or wider publication can be shown "by establishing a platform of facts from which the tribunal of fact could properly infer that substantial publication within the jurisdiction has taken place."[234] Thus, the court takes into account a number of factors from which inferences can be drawn, including internet traffic data and analytics, and search engines. Likewise in *Davison v Habeeb*[235] the claim was struck out as disproportionate and an abuse of process as the defamation action was based on five individuals unknown to the defendant having accessed the relevant blog that contained the defamation.[236] The Court emphasized that the assessment of publication within the jurisdiction needs to focus on the *actual words complained of*, so that the fact that the overall blogger.com website[237] had an estimated 44 million readers in the UK and was the twelfth most popular internet website was irrelevant for this assessment.[238] In *Sobrinho v Impresa*[239] the reputation of an Angolan banker defamed by allegations of improper loans given by the Angolan subsidiary of a Portuguese bank had been vindicated by a parliamentary inquiry in Portugal whose results were published in England to the same extent as the original Portuguese media coverage complained of, and the Court therefore held that to continue a defamation action in England would be an abuse of process.[240] Therefore the striking out mechanism has been used to terminate proceedings in respect of defamation claims with tenuous links to England.

2.5 Conclusion: jurisdiction

In summary, the starting point under the jurisdiction rules (in England, in Germany, and under the EU harmonized rules) is the place of the commission of the tort and the place of damage. English law (unlike the EU harmonized rules, but like the rules in Germany) locates the commission of personality rights infringements at the place of publication. Since the damage in these types of torts usually occurs at the place of publication, where the information is accessed or downloaded, and therefore impacts on privacy or reputation. Therefore for personality rights infringements the place of the commission of the tort normally coincides with the place of the damage, both being situated at the place of publication, but is limited to the damage suffered in that country. Thus, for online publications, determining the location of publication becomes crucial for determining jurisdiction. Both Germany and England have

[233] Paras 32, 37.

[234] Para 33; however, in *Steinberg v Pritchard Englefield* [2005] EWCA Civ 288 cf para 21 the CA held that a reasonable inference can be drawn that a defamatory letter published on the open internet about the claimant English law firm's charging practices and, which is linked in search results resulting from entering the claimant law firm's name as keyword, is published in England.

[235] [2011] EWHC 3031 (QB); see also *Tamiz v Google* [2013] 1 WLR 2151, para 50.

[236] Paras 24–27.

[237] Hosting many, many blogs of all types.

[238] Para 22.

[239] [2016] EMLR 12 (QB).

[240] Paras 52–94, 98.

developed rules (albeit under very different procedural mechanisms) to find links to the jurisdiction that are closer than mere access or downloading and could be loosely described as impact. In this context impact does not necessarily require that the defendant intentionally directs his or her activities to the place of the forum, so it does not focus on the intention of the communicator, but instead focuses on the recipients, or audience. One aspect of this is the number of times content has been accessed or downloaded (which seems to be the focus of the English line of cases), but also the nature of the content (including the language used and whether the nature of the content would be of interest to the relevant audience in the country concerned). Clearly the most appropriate place test introduced by the Defamation Act 2013 is much stricter in this respect and looks at the "biggest" impact. Furthermore, the Defamation Act 2013 places distinct emphasis on publication numbers.

By contrast, the jurisprudence of the CJEU has located the commission of the tort at the place of establishment of the publisher (which coincides in most cases with the domicile of the publisher) and *not publication*. Thus, it is likely to be in the claimant's interest to sue at the place where the damage occurred, for the harm to reputation or privacy in that country.[241] This limitation that the claimant can only sue for local harm has led the CJEU to develop the centre of interests test whereby the claimant can additionally sue for the whole loss not only at the defendant's domicile (under the general jurisdiction test) but also at the place where the claimant has her centre of interests. This is effectively a targeting test focused on the foreseeability of the claimant's harm.

3. Applicable law

3.1 Applicable law under the Rome II Regulation on the Law Applicable to Non-Contractual Obligations

The Rome II Regulation[242] does not apply to non-contractual obligations arising out of violations of privacy and rights relating to personality, including defamation.[243] Hence the national rules on applicable law continue to be applicable. In the English context, these have been criticized for being old-fashioned and out of date. But harmonization has proved intractable in respect of the law applicable to defamation.[244]

Tort law in general, and defamation law in particular, has two sides. Like contract law, tort law is about private interests and, in particular, compensating a party for harm done by another. This private law aspect allows a legal system to recognize foreign law governing a particular tort case. But tort law is equally connected to the regulation of conduct in society and to public interests, much more so than the law of contract. In the area of defamation, this means balancing freedom of expression with reputational interests in respect of communications. Each society, even within

[241] Banholzer (n 29) para 65.

[242] Rome II Regulation on the Law Applicable to Non-contractual Obligations (EC) 864/2007 of 11 July 2007 OJ L 199/40.

[243] Art 1(2)(g).

[244] Mills (n 55) 15.

the EU, finds this balance at a different point, for cultural and political reasons. It is for this reason that states are reluctant to allow foreign law to govern a defamation action before its courts and this is the reason why the approach in Rome II, which otherwise is open to the application of foreign law, has not been applied to defamation actions—which, like hate speech, involves a delicate and culturally sensitive balance between values such as dignity, privacy, reputation, and free speech. In England the double-actionability rule maintains the influence of the law of the (English) forum (in its role as a filter), thus acknowledging the public law dimension of defamation law.[245]

In some respect this may be more of a problem for online publications *in English* that have a worldwide reach, whereas publications in (some) other European languages may be more confined to the territory of the state concerned, and therefore offer fewer conflicts of law, as the audience may be more clearly identifiable.

3.2 Applicable law under German law

The rules of applicable law are contained in the Introductory Law to the Civil Law Code[246] and in respect of claims based on delict (tort), paragraph 40 provides that the law applicable is the law of the state in which the defendant has acted[247] (*lex loci delicti*). However, the injured party has an option to choose the law of the state, where the damage has occurred at the beginning of the proceedings.[248]

This first rule is, however, displaced in cases where the defendant and the injured party were domiciled in the same state at the time of the tortious event, by the law of that state.[249] In the case of legal persons, their main administration or establishment is to be regarded as the relevant domicile.[250] German law then limits the applicable law if the foreign law provides for damages that go much further than warranted by appropriate compensation of the injured party, or obviously have purposes other than the appropriate compensation of the injured party,[251] or contradict the rules on liability of an international convention that is binding on Germany.[252] If the law applicable to the tort or the law applicable to the insurance contract allow this, the injured party can claim directly from the insurer of the defendant.[253] Article 38 contains the rules on the law applicable to different types of unjust enrichment and provides for three sub-types of claims. First, for claims based on fulfilment of a legal obligation (such as a contractual obligation), these are governed by the law applicable to the legal

[245] ibid 13–14.

[246] Einführungsgesetz Bürgerliches Gesetzbuch (EBGB).

[247] K Thorn, *Beck'sche Kurzkommentare Palandt BGB Kommentar* (76th edn, C.H. Beck 2017) EG 40–42.

[248] S 40(1); Thorn (n 247) EG 40–42.

[249] S 40(2); Thorn (n 247) EG 40–42.

[250] S 40(2).

[251] This would exclude rules on damages that are deterrent, punitive, or excessive, which is contrary to German public policy.

[252] S 40(3).

[253] S 40(4).

relationship under which the obligation arose (such as a contract).[254] Second, claims based on infringement of a legally protected interest (such as privacy or confidence) are subject to the law of the state in which the infringement occurred.[255] Finally, in all other cases of unjust enrichment claims are governed by the law of the state where the unjust enrichment materialized.[256] However, these rules on the law applicable are not binding on the German courts, who may exceptionally apply a different law, if this law has a substantially closer connection (flexible exception).[257] Such a substantially closer connection can result in particular from a special legal or factual relationship between the persons involved in the context of the liability.[258] In the case of unjust enrichment, for types two and three, such a substantially closer connection can also arise from a common domicile of the persons involved, and domicile of legal persons refers here again to main administration or establishment.[259] Finally, the parties may choose the applicable law by mutual agreement, after the tortious event or the unjust enrichment has occurred.[260]

Claims stemming from the infringement of personality rights are subject to these rules. This applies to claims for damages as well as to other claims and injunctions. In the case of torts committed by the media organizations, the place of commission of the tort is the place of establishment of the publisher, this is usually also the place of publication, or the place of broadcast for broadcasters.[261] By contrast, the place of where the tort impacted in the form of damage[262] is every place at which the information was purposefully distributed or disseminated.[263] If the information has been distributed in several states each law applies to the claims in respect of damages that relate to that state (mosaic theory).[264] The mosaic theory also applies to prohibitory injunctions, preventing dissemination.[265] By contrast, the right of contradiction is only subject to the law of the place of the commission of the tort to guarantee a uniform assessment of the balance between freedom of the press and personality rights—this is the place of publication.[266]

For internet torts not committed by media organizations, the commission of the tort may well be the place of uploading the content.[267] For the place where the tort resulted in damage, mere accessibility is insufficient and a further connecting factor to Germany is required. It has been argued, however, that sometimes foreign language publications can cause damage in Germany, depending on the circles in which the claimant moves.[268]

254 S 38(1).
255 S 38(2).
256 S 38(3).
257 S 41(1).
258 S 41(2), No 1.
259 S 41(2), No 2.
260 S 42.
261 Thorn (n 247) EG 40–42.
262 Erfolgsort.
263 "bestimmungsgemäße Verbreitung"—see BGH NJW 96, 1128.
264 Thorn (n 247) EG 40–42.
265 BGH NJW 96, 1128 and 99, 2893.
266 Thorn (n 247) EG 40–42.
267 ibid.
268 ibid.

3.3 Applicable law under English law

The first point to make here is that a distinction must be made between the law applicable to the substantive issues (such as the nature of the claim and liability) and procedural issues. The rules on private international law determine the law applicable to the substantive issues, whereas procedural issues (such as, under English law, the choice of remedies or quantum) are determined by the *lex fori*.[269]

In England, the rules on applicable law to personality rights infringement are governed by the Private International Law (Miscellaneous Provisions) Act 1995, which abolished the traditional common law rules[270] from 1 May 1996.[271] But, since the 1995 Act, in turn, excludes defamation claims from the scope of the 1995 Act, the applicable law to *defamation* under English private international law continues to be governed by common law rules.[272] For this exclusion, defamation includes libel and slander, slander of title, slander of goods or other malicious falsehood ,and any claim under the law of Scotland for verbal injury, or any equivalent claim under foreign law.[273] The reason for this exclusion was a concern for freedom of expression in ensuring that statements potentially defamatory under foreign law that are previously or simultaneously published in the UK could not be suppressed through the application of foreign law.[274] In defamation cases therefore the double-actionability rule prevents that an English court has to apply foreign law that does not recognize defences to defamation law such as fair comment. However, the filtering function of the double-actionability rule only applies to defamation claims, not to other personality rights infringements such as privacy infringements,[275] where English courts may have to apply foreign law to publications regardless of whether the tort would have been actionable if committed in England.

The double actionability works in favour of publishers and media organizations and as *Alex Mills* points out "there is rarely a political will to take on media interests."[276] Essentially, as will be seen, if a publisher is sued before the English courts in respect of a cross-border defamation published abroad, the rule provides defendants with defences applicable under English law *and* defences applicable under the foreign law concerned (eg the "public figure" doctrine in the US). Moreover, since defamation is a criminal offence in some jurisdictions, but not an actionable tort, this means that a case is equally non actionable before the English courts. Thus, the publisher benefits from defences and non-actionability under both legal systems, which makes it harder to bring a successful action.[277]

[269] *Boys v Chaplin* [1971] AC 356 (HL) 379 (Lord Hodson).
[270] Art 10.
[271] SI 1996/995.
[272] Art 13(1).
[273] Art 13(2).
[274] Lord Collins et al (n 26) 35–101.
[275] ibid 35–105.
[276] Mills (n 55), 13.
[277] ibid.

3.3.1 Applicable law to personality rights infringements other than defamation

Claims for privacy infringement such as misuse of personal information or data protection breaches would be governed by sections 11–12 of the 1995 Act. The application of these provisions may lead to the application of foreign law, even for a foreign cause of action, which has no equivalent cause of action under English law or would not be actionable under English law.[278]

The general rule is that the law applicable to a personality rights infringement is the law of the country in which the events constituting the tort or delict occur.[279] The Act contains specific rules on how to apply the general rule if the constituting events occur in several countries. The first specific rule relates to claims in respect of personal injury (or death resulting from personal injury)—in other words, cases where the outcome of the tort (or what would be called "Erfolg" under German law) is personal injury or death. This rule stipulates that the applicable law is the law of the country where the individual was when he or she sustained the injury.[280] The term "personal injury" in this context includes both physical and mental impairments and diseases.[281] While most infringements of personality rights or privacy rights may lead to personal distress and reputational harm, but not to personal injury, in some rare cases claimants are likely to successfully argue mental health impairments as an integral part of a personality rights infringement. Therefore the main specific rule is the third, which states that the law of the country is applicable in which the most significant element(s) of the events constituting the tort occurred.[282] Thus, if a cause of action in respect of a personality rights infringement has elements spread over several countries the English courts have to identify the most significant elements of the events pertaining to the cause of action in order to determine the applicable law.[283] If the privacy infringement is committed by disclosing or publishing of information, presumably this is the act of disclosing or publication. However, in respect of online information flows it may be difficult to pinpoint a particular location, and hence a particular country in which the private information is published. In *KJO v XIM*[284] the claimant had been convicted of forging his grandmother's will and after serving his sentence moved to Hong Kong. His uncle pursued a campaign of informing the professional circles in which the claimant moved and his employers of the conviction in Hong Kong, which by then had been spent under the Rehabilitation of Offenders Act 1974. The claimant sought an injunction to prevent his uncle from continuing his email campaign from the UK by way of summary judgment. Given that this case rose novel issues under the law relating to breach of confidence, misuse of private information, and data protection the Court refused to give summary judgment. However, Mr Justice Eady held *obiter* that breach of confidence and the infringement of privacy rights are committed at

[278] Lord Collins et al (n 26) 35–101.
[279] S 11(1).
[280] S 11(2)(a); *Cox v Ergo Versicherung* [2014] UKSC 22 (SC); *Allen v Deputy International* [2014] EWHC 753 (QB).
[281] S 11(3).
[282] S 11(2)(c).
[283] This is a value judgment see *VTB Capital v Nutritek* [2013] 2 AC 337 (SC) para 199 per Lord Clarke of Stone-cum-Ebony JSC.
[284] [2011] EWHC 1768 (QB).

the *place of publication*, in this case the place where the emails were received and read, namely Hong Kong.[285]

However, the events constituting the tort are not the only connection factors applied to determine applicable law. Once the court has determined the outcome of the test under section 11, it then has to decide whether there are different factors connecting the tort with another country and whether they are substantially more significant than the events constituting the tort. If they are substantially more significant the general rule will be displaced and the law applicable to the dispute is that of the other country.[286] Thus, the court has to compare and weigh different factors and there is flexibility as to which relevant connecting factors dominate in the calculation.[287] The court has to decide whether it is substantially more appropriate, in the light of the significance of the connecting factors, that the law of another country applies and it can decide to apply the law of another country only to some of the issues involved.[288] This displacement rule applies, for example, if the dispute is subject to an express agreement on applicable law.[289] However, this displacement rule only applies by way of exception, and the general rule should not be dislodged easily.[290] For example, the general rule is not automatically displaced where both the claimant and the tortfeasor are English nationals who lived in France at the time of the accident and where the consequences of the accident were mainly felt in England, as the claimant had moved back to England.[291] Displacement may occur where the parties are English and *English domiciled* at the time of the tort.[292]

The Act contains the exceptions common in private international law, namely that the applicable law does not apply to court procedure[293] or where it is against public policy to apply the relevant foreign law.[294] This latter exception protects against the application of foreign law in respect of personality infringements that jeopardize freedom of expression.

Specifically, where a claim is framed on breach of confidence as the underlying cause of action, this is a claim in equity, and therefore the rules on the law applicable to *tort* do not apply directly. It has been argued that a breach of confidence results in a right of restitution, and that this right equally arises at the place of publication.[295] In *Douglas v Hello* the Court of Appeal held that the proper law in respect of the right to restitution for breach of confidence *and* the proper law in respect of tort in relation to privacy

[285] Paras 24–25, 28; however, English law (the Data Protection Act 1998) would however apply to an act of processing of personal data in England, para 33.

[286] S 12; *Roerig v Valiant Trawlers* [2002] EWCA Civ 21 (CA) per Waller LJ.

[287] See the wording of s 12(1)(b): "any factors" and s 12(2) this includes factors relating to the parties, to any of the events constituting the tort, or to any of the circumstances or consequences of those events.

[288] ibid.

[289] *Kent v Paterson-Brown* [2018] EWHC 2008 (Ch) para 186; *Chopra v Bank of Singapore* [2015] EWHC 1549 (Ch) paras 119–24.

[290] *VTB Capital* (n 283) para 205 per Lord Clarke; *Fiona Trust & Holding Corporation v Skarga* [2013] EWCA Civ 275.

[291] *Middleton (A Child) v Allianz Iard SA* [2012] EWHC 2287 (QB), para 19.

[292] *Dawson v Broughton* [2007] 7 WLUK 921.

[293] eg questions of limitation or the assessment of damages (remedy available and quantum): *Harding v Wealands* [2007] 2 AC 1 (HL) para 24, per Lord Hoffmann.

[294] S 14.

[295] *Douglas v Hello (No 2)* [2003] EMLR 28 (CA), para 41.

infringements was the law at the place of publication. The essence of the complaint was held to be the publication in England, with the consequence that English law applied, and not the law of the place (New York), where the photographs were taken.[296] A later court concluded that the proper law of causes of action related to privacy infringements is the place of publication by way of analogy to defamation.[297] However, as already discussed, since *Vidal-Hall v Google* the distinction between privacy-related claims in equity and claims in tort may disappear in many cases, since the Court of Appeal in that case held that misuse of personal information is a tort in any case.[298]

However, not all cases have found the place of publication to be the proper law of an action for breach of confidence. For example, the High Court of Australia in *Attorney-General (UK) v Heinemann Publishers*[299] adopted the approach of examining the law most closely associated with the obligation of confidence and the rights infringed by the unlawful disclosure, which was English law. This approach was approved by Mr Justice Arnold in *Innovia Films Ltd v Frito-Lay North America*.[300] The application of the test is therefore highly fact specific.

3.3.2 Applicable law to defamation

While questions of jurisdiction were discussed during the reform of defamation law in the shape of the Defamation Act 2013, questions of choice of law have received comparatively little attention.[301]

The so-called double-actionability rule continues to apply to the determination of whether a defamation case can be decided in an English court and is more akin to a rule of competence.[302] The rule applies both sets of laws to a case, but it is more than just a rule of applicable law, as it also determines the actionability of the matter in an English court. The rule was established in the case of *Phillips v Eyre* a case following the brutal suppression of a rebellion in Jamaica involving summary execution of protestors, flogging, and false imprisonments,[303] for which Eyre was ultimately responsible as governor.[304] The Court of Exchequer Chamber had to decide whether the governor could be held responsible under English law and liable for compensation. The rule stipulated two conditions for applying English law to a tort that had been committed abroad. First, the tort must be of such a character that it would have been actionable as a tort if it had been committed in England; second, the act must not have been justifiable by the law of the place where it was done (Jamaica).[305] Since the act had been justifiable by the colonial law in Jamaica, the claim was not justiciable before the English courts. The double-actionability rule is therefore a filter in cross-border

[296] ibid: the law of New York may apply to torts constituted by act in New York such as the trespass committed to obtain the photographs by stealth.

[297] *KJO v XIM* (n 284) para 29.

[298] (n 136).

[299] (1988) 165 CLR 30 (High Court of Australia), Brennan J.

[300] *Innovia Films Ltd v Frito-Lay North America* [2012] EWHC 790 (Pat) para 108, Arnolds J.

[301] Mills (n 55) 2.

[302] *Boys* (n 269) 374 (Lord Hodson), 383 (Lord Donovan).

[303] Individuals were removed by force to areas where martial law was in operation—a nineteenth-century extraordinary rendition.

[304] Handford (n 4) 822–60.

[305] (1870) LR 6 QB 1, 28–29 (Willes J).

torts,[306] only if both legal systems recognize the claim can the case successfully proceed.[307] It has to be seen in its historical and socio-political context. Eyre's suppression of the rebellion was a controversy in the public eye with his proponents arguing that he had prevented a massacre, and his opponents pointing to the excessive brutality and human rights violations.[308] At the time, the courts frequently applied the law of the forum, but subject to any legal defences applicable at the place where the tort was committed.[309]

Boys v Chaplin[310] introduced a flexible exception to the double-actionability rule: as long as it was actionable under tort law in the English court, a particular issue—such as heads of damage—could be solely decided by English law if this issue had a closer link to the forum (notwithstanding the second limb of the rule, ie the law at the place where the tort was committed).[311] All Law Lords agreed that this personal injury case arising from a road traffic accident in Malta was actionable in the English courts and English law should apply. But they did so for different reasons:[312] Lord Hodson and Lord Guest held that the *lex loci delicti* (Maltese law) applied to the determination of the substantive issues,[313] whereas Lord Pearson[314] and Lord Wilberforce[315] held that *lex fori* should be applied to the substantive issues. However, the majority held that since both parties were members of the armed forces, ordinarily resident in England and only temporarily stationed on Malta, that English law should apply to the specific issue of whether a particular head of damage should be recoverable. Lord Hudson introduced a flexible extension to the rule in *Phillips v Eyre*.[316] The flexible extension is similar to the "proper law of the tort" developed in US jurisprudence in inter-state torts and has been described by Lord Denning MR in the Court of Appeal in *Boys v Chaplin* as "the law of the place which has the most significant contacts with the matter in dispute."[317] This flexible exception has been applied, for example, in *Kuwait Airways v Iraqi Airways* were Iraqi Airways were not able to rely on the law made by the Iraqi government to justify the confiscation/theft of Kuwaiti aircraft.[318] The exception to double actionability has equally been applied in *Johnson v Coventry Churchill*[319] in a negligence claim made by an injured English joiner who had suffered an accident

306 A Briggs, "What Did Boys v Chaplin Decide?" (1983) 12 Anglo-American Law Review 237–46, 239.

307 Handford (n 4) 823.

308 ibid 834–41—it became the "Jamaica Question."

309 ibid.

310 [1971] AC 356 (HL).

311 See also *Red Sea Insurance Co Ltd v Bouygues SA* [1995] 1 AC 190: exclusive application of *lex loci delicti* to all issues in the case, by way of the flexible exception.

312 It has been argued that there was no *ratio decidendi* in this case at all, Briggs (n 306) 238.

313 Derived from the jurisprudence of the US Supreme Court: *Slater v Mexican National Railroad Co* (1904) 194 US 120, 126 (Holmes, J); *Western Union v Brown* (1914) 234 US 542, 547 (Holmes, J) quoted in *Boys* (n 269) 375–76.

314 At 400 and 406.

315 At 385.

316 Again with reference to US case law on inter-state car accidents where both the injured claimant and defendant originated from the same state (and the car was insured in that state) *Babcock v Jackson* [1963] 2 Lloyd's Rep. 286; *Boys* (n 269) 379–80 (Lord Hudson); Lord Guest did not agree with this test of flexibility, but ruled that heads of damages should be dealt with by the *lex fori*, at 382.

317 [1968] 2 QB 1 (CA) 20 (Lord Denning MR).

318 *Kuwait Airways v Iraqi Airways* [2002] 2 AC 883 (HL).

319 [1992] 3 AllER 14.

during a temporary assignment in Germany against his English employer. German law would not have recognized the claim in Negligence for the reason that German law contained statutory compensation for injuries at work. For this reason the Court solely applied English law disregarding the double-actionability rule.[320]

The case of *Sophocleos*[321] concerned alleged acts of illegal torture by British security forces committed in Cyprus during the Cyprus Emergency 1956–58. The claimants brought a civil action in tort over sixty years later, which was now barred under the rules on limitation in Cyprus. The Court of Appeal applied the double-actionability rule and held that the action was governed by both English and Cypriote law. The Court refused to solely apply English law based on the flexible exception based on a finding that England had the most significant relationship with the tort and the parties. The Court of Appeal held that the exclusive application of the *lex fori* as an exception to the double-actionability rule should be rare and narrow.[322] In particular the Court pointed to the interest of Cyprus to apply its own laws[323] and that there should not be an assumption that English law applied as a matter of public policy in order to extend the limitation period to deal with the alleged atrocious acts of torture.[324]

This discussion now reaches the question of what the double-actionability rule means for defamation cases.

If a libel is actionable as a tort in both the foreign country where it has been published and would be actionable in England but for one of the defences under English defamation law[325] then the rule in *Phillips v Eyre* would mean that the action cannot proceed. In the reverse situation, where the libel is actionable under English law, but not under the tort law of where the libel was published, again the action before the English courts would be unsuccessful. This is precisely why the double-actionability rule was left intact for defamation.

Thus, in a case where an English-domiciled defendant uploads a defamatory statement to an online blog in a foreign language and this blog is not accessed in England but only in this foreign country,[326] the claim is only actionable if the defamatory statement gives rise to a civil action in this foreign country. While there was earlier authority[327] for the proposition that it is sufficient that the statement amounts to a criminally illegal act (criminal defamation) in the foreign country, this is no longer the case.[328] Given that in many civil law jurisdictions defamation is a criminal offence but not a tort, this further limits the availability of the English courts in a defamation action.

320 At paras 24–25.

321 *Sophocleous v Secretary of State for Foreign and Commonwealth Affairs* [2018] EWCA Civ 2167 (CA).

322 Paras 33, 56.

323 Paras 49–51.

324 Paras 62–63.

325 Such as truth, honest opinion, absolute or qualified privilege, responsible publication on a matter of public interest, offer of amends, or innocent dissemination.

326 The English courts could only have *jurisdiction* on the basis that the damage was sustained in England, which will be a rare case.

327 *Machodo v Fontes* [1897] 2 QB 231.

328 *Boys* (n 269) 376 (Lord Hodson *obiter*), 382 (Lord Donovan *obiter*), 384 (Lord Wilberforce *obiter*), and rejected by the High Court of Australia High Court of Australia in *Koop v Bebb* (1951) 84 CLR 629.

Furthermore, internet defamation cases are multi-jurisdictional in many instances. The act of accessing or downloading constitutes publication and, therefore the commission of the tort.[329] Thus, there is potentially a multitude of *loci delicti*—each of which would have to be paired with English law and assessed under the double-actionability rule.

This raises the question of whether the continued insistence on the blunt tool of the nineteenth-century double-actionability rule makes sense in the world of globalized twenty-first-century social media communications.[330] In particular it raises the question of whether the focus on where the defamatory statement was published, that is, accessed and downloaded, makes sense to determine the (second limb of) the rule. A more flexible approach, taking into account multiple factors such as impact (who was the intended and the actual audience of the communication) and identifying the private and public interests involved (place of damage to reputation, state interests), could contribute to finding a balanced approach in the interests of justice.

But the double-actionability rule may not be very relevant for online defamation in practice—in recent defamation cases, where a statement had been published online and downloaded in England and in other jurisdictions, the courts have applied English defamation law in a straightforward manner to deal with that publication in England only, regarding publication in each country as a separate publication and not as a single overall publication giving rise to conflicts of law. Thus, in practice, such cases have been decided without reverting to the double-actionability rule. Perhaps the discussion on the retention of *Phillips v Eyre* in academic and policy debates is therefore no more than a storm in teacup.

3.3.3 Conclusion: applicable law

Under the English rules the applicable law for torts other than defamation is the law of the place where the events constituting the tort occur, or where the most significant factor occurred (a variant of the *lex loci delicti*), subject to another factor being more significant. For personality rights infringements publication is likely to be the most significant factor. For defamation actions the filter of the *double-actionability* rule applies—in other words, the tort must be actionable under both the foreign law and English law. Under the German rules the presumption is that the law of the place where the defendant acted applies to personality rights infringements (also *lex loci delicti*), but the claimant has the option of choosing the law at the place where the damage occurred.

This section has examined how the choice of applicable law frequently has presented itself as, first, the place of the forum, second, the place where the tort was committed, or third, the place where the damage has manifested itself. As we have seen, German rules allow the claimant to choose between the second and the third option. English conflicts rules make a distinction between non-defamation claims, which are governed by a version of the *lex loci delicti* and a flexible rule and defamation claims where the double-actionability rule means that both the first and second options are applicable.

[329] See discussion in section 2.4.
[330] Mills (n 55) 15.

4. Conclusion

In respect of jurisdiction, two basic types[331] of claimants can be distinguished, those whose interests[332] are centred locally in one jurisdiction[333] and those whose interests are spread globally, be it that they are worldwide media and entertainment celebrities or politicians, be it that they have a specific online virtual identity and fame, which is detached from any single jurisdiction but stretches across, multiple jurisdictions. For the first type, a claimant should have a claim, provided their privacy or reputation has been damaged in the jurisdiction concerned, through online publication. Clearly if no-one has accessed or downloaded the damaging publication there or it is clearly not relevant for the audience in the forum state, then no (or only minimal) publication and no (or only minimal) damage has occurred there. This would be the position under the German rules on jurisdiction. And this is what the most appropriate forum rule under the Defamation Act 2013 gets wrong: if the claimant has his or her centre of interests in England (and nowhere else) and publication of a statement damages the claimant's reputation, he or she should be able to sue here, even if the greater part of the *dissemination* of the statement occurred elsewhere, for example, in an online US magazine. Arguably, the US magazine did target this cross-border tort to England as this is where the claimant lives and works and it should have been foreseeable that the defendant may be sued there. However, such a judgment by a German or even English court may not be enforceable in the US because of anti-SLAPP[334] legislation.[335]

Under the EU rules, the claimant could sue for his or her loss in the local jurisdiction both under the *mosaic* doctrine in *Shevill* and the centre of interest doctrine in *eDate Advertising*, both of which would come to the same result, as the totality of the claimant's loss is centred in one jurisdiction anyway. It could be said that for such cases the centre of interest doctrine is not needed in addition to the *mosaic* doctrine, which would consist of only one piece (not much of a mosaic).

For the second type of defendant, an online publication may genuinely infringe his or her privacy or reputation interests in many jurisdictions and this makes the assessment of the "proper" forum so difficult. This assessment should focus on two aspects. The first aspect is the actual or likely[336] number of publications in the relevant country, which I call "impact." The second aspect is localizing the centre of interests of the claimant. Both aspects should be relevant for assessing whether a court is competent and the more the two aspects are concentrated in one country, the stronger the jurisdictional claim should be in that country. While English defamation law after its reform, in my view wrongly, puts too little emphasis on the second aspect and largely limits its analysis to the publication impact, the EU rules on jurisdiction do the opposite, allowing the claimant to sue in a (EU) jurisdiction where only a small part of the

331 In practice this may be more a matter of degrees than two separate types.

332 In this context: private, social, and professional life, relationships, and reputation.

333 And which constitute the greatest part of humanity, though not necessarily the majority of litigants.

334 Strategic Lawsuit Against Public Participation.

335 US SPEECH Act 2010.

336 Assessing the local interest in the publication, language, and other targeting factors concerning the audience or readership.

harm has occurred but the centre of interests of the claimant are concentrated. Both aspects (publication impact and the interests of the claimant) should be balanced in the jurisdictional analysis.

The determination of the applicable law in tort cases presents a number of choices. Historically,[337] the law of the forum presented the main choice, focusing on the public interest and emphasizing state sovereignty, akin to "choice" of law in criminal cases where the court inevitably applies its own law.[338] Moreover, another option is *lex loci delicti*, the law of the place where the tort has been committed—this rule presumes that in most cases this choice is closely connected to the parties and the tort.[339] However, the *lex loci delicti* is very difficult to determine in internet torts.

For internet cases, and in particular in respect of personality rights infringed through remote communication (including on social media), the communication starts in one place (the place of uploading or posting) and is received in another place when it is read (the point of accessing or downloading). Neither place is the obvious and natural place where the tort has been committed, making the search for the *lex loci delicti* elusive. Therefore the law has to make a policy choice between these two places—and this choice involves a policy option: if the focus is on the place of uploading, this usually favours the defendant whose law applies to the tort. By contrast, if the focus is on the place of downloading, this is likely to favour the claimant as this is the place where the harm to reputation, privacy, or dignity may have occurred. Furthermore, a third option is the place of the damage for which compensation is claimed. Again this coalesces in most cases with the place of downloading. If the place of downloading determines the choice of law, the issue of multiple torts arises as the information is likely to have been accessed in many different places with the consequence that many different laws are applicable according to the place of download or access. This inevitably leads to a *mosaic* rule, which makes an assessment of the claim multifarious and complicated, both in terms of evidence and law.

The rules of private international rules are frequently regarded as highly technical rules and therefore the search for such rules in respect of personality rights infringements has been treated purely as a question of finding the correct technical formula. In reality such a formula does not exist—the private international law rules in this area are not a question of technicality but a matter of policy in respect of fundamental values. The question is whether a legal system places more emphasis on freedom of speech, thus favouring the defendant in a personality rights infringement action, or whether the legal system places more emphasis on human dignity and the protection of reputation, in which case it favours the claimant.

However, a further alternative is to apply the law of the place to which the defendant has targeted his or her conduct. A targeting test may not be appropriate for all torts committed on the internet, as frequently conduct online is not targeted to a particular

[337] Handford (n 4) 848, 854.

[338] von Savigny (n 5) 205.

[339] eg in the late twentieth century both Australian and Canadian courts had moved away from the double actionability rule and replaced it with the *lex loci delicti*: *John Pfeiffer Pty Ltd v Rogerson* (2000) 203 CLR 503; *Regie Nationale des Usines Renault SA v Zhang* (2002) 210 CLR 491; *Tolofson v Jensen* [1994] 3 SCR 1022.

destination and may be targeted everywhere and nowhere in particular.[340] However, specifically for personality rights infringement the tortfeasor can normally foresee the identity of the victim and the centre(s) of interests of that person. Thus, it could be argued that personality rights infringements are targeted at a person and thereby at a place associated with that person, regardless of the communications medium used, the place of the commission of the tort, and the subjective intention of the defendant. The centre of interest test should be used to determine applicable law. From a public interest perspective, it is reasonable to argue that the state at whose territory and residents conduct is aimed has a dominant interest in regulating it. In terms of satisfying the private interests of the parties concerned, the claimant's interest in protecting his or her privacy and reputational interests according to the norms prevailing at the place of the centre of the claimant's life is equally satisfied. While the defendant's conduct then may be judged according to foreign norms, arguably, this is a direct consequence of targeting his or her conduct at a foreign jurisdiction (or not caring which jurisdiction they target their conduct to). A targeting test in this area is not straightforward and comes with its own problems, as defendants may be caught out by unexpected stricter legal standards outside their jurisdiction and the centre of interests of the claimant may not be known.

For this reason the question arises whether the targeting test should be coupled to an objective foreseeability criterion, thus protecting the defendant's interests and freedom of expression.[341] Targeting here does not mean that the defendant must have intended to harm the claimant in a particular country (subjective targeting), but that the claimant was aware of where the harm was likely to occur—for example, being aware of where the claimant lived and worked (objective targeting). Naturally, on the internet this will not always be the case, as the defendant may not know or care where the claimant lived and worked, or was domiciled. In such cases the law has to make a policy choice whether foreseeability is required or not and which party should have the burden of suing in a foreign jurisdiction.

Finally, two conclusions stand out. First, that it is necessary to think out of the box and go beyond the traditional connecting factors, in particular the place where the tort was committed (*lex loci delicti*), and develop criteria more relevant to the internet age. I have recommended how the impact analysis and a targeting test based on the centre of interests of the parties should be balanced for personality rights infringements.

Second, private international law rules may have the effect of favouring one party over the other, but it is difficult to formulate abstract rules in such a way that they provide for a fair balance between parties in all cross-border cases. This means that other procedural mechanisms should be used to prevent abusive actions. For example, the claimant should have to show a prima facie case or a good arguable case at the jurisdictional stage to filter out unworthy cases, or public policy of the forum should be used to strike out claims clearly infringing freedom of expression. This would prevent unjustified personality infringement claims being used as a weapon to suppress legitimate speech.

[340] See eg the discussion in Chapter 9 on the US tort cases and jurisdiction or Chapter 10 on consumer disputes.

[341] For the targeting test in US jurisprudence, following *Calder v Jones* see Chapter 9.

12
Intellectual Property—Internet Jurisdiction and Applicable Law

1. Intellectual property and territoriality

This chapter discusses jurisdiction and applicable law in respect of internet cases involving intellectual property (IP). It covers both registered rights (eg trademarks, patents, design rights) and unregistered rights (eg passing off, copyright). Because of their ubiquity and decentralization, internet technologies have enabled a great diversity of cross-border IP infringements, be it infringement by a single defendant, where the damage is spread over several jurisdictions,[1] or be it multiple infringements by multiple defendants in a number of jurisdictions, acting in concert[2] or independently[3] of each other.

The starting point for this examination lies in the nature of IP as a type of intangible *property* and the *territoriality* principle and sovereignty. Since IP is an artificial property, granted by national law, it had traditionally been regarded as being closely aligned to state sovereignty and therefore limited to the territory of the state granting the right.[4] Thus, court actions in IP cases were regarded as local actions and subject-matter jurisdiction only arose for local IP rights. *Bently/Sherman* explain how the notion of IP as property has not been uncontroversial, and different forms of implementation have been developed to mark the boundaries of specific types of IP in different countries.[5] This is one of the reasons why until fairly recently[6] jurisdiction of the courts was limited to decide questions involving validity, scope or infringement

[1] Copyright infringing images or a competitor's trademark protected logo being used on a company's website; a competitor selling a product subject to patent protection via a particular e-commerce channel (trading platform or website); the uploading of a copyright-infringing music video on a YouTube channel.

[2] Peer-to-peer file sharing of copyright infringing films or music; the use of cloud cyberlockers or blockchain technology to share copyright infringing content.

[3] The retweeting or reposting of copyright infringing content on social media platforms; different subsidiaries of the same corporate group using an infringing logo online; counterfeiting of luxury goods on e-commerce platforms.

[4] Mr Justice Vinelott in *Tyburn Productions v Conan Doyle* [1991] Ch 75 (ChD) 83: "that the right of creating a title to such property as land, being vested in the ruler, that is in the sovereign power (. . .) controversies relating to such property can only be decided in the state in which the property is situated. The reason appears equally applicable to patent rights, which (. . .) are created by a similar exercise of the sovereign power" quoting Mr Chief Justice Griffiths in the High Court of Australia, *Potter v Broken Hill* (1906) 3 CLR 479, 496. See also B Ubertazzi, *Exclusive Jurisdiction in Intellectual Property* (Mohr Siebeck 2012) 42ff.

[5] L Bently and B Sherman, *Intellectual Property Law* (4th edn, OUP 2014) 2–4.

[6] See the discussion further in section 3.2.

Internet Jurisdiction. Julia Hörnle, Oxford University Press (2021). © Julia Hörnle.
DOI: 10.1093/oso/9780198806929.001.0001

of IP arising within the court's own jurisdiction.[7] In other words, IP cases before the courts were treated as *in rem* actions, giving the courts at the place where the property is located *exclusive* jurisdiction over the subject matter concerned (exclusive subject-matter jurisdiction), and applying the local law of the forum (*lex fori*).[8] In the English common law this was called the *Moçambique* rule. In a late nineteenth-century case concerning mining rights in Africa the House of Lords held that the English court has no jurisdiction to entertain an action for the recovery of damages for trespass to land situated abroad.[9] While this case concerned physical land (and not IP) it was applied to IP cases, and essentially contained a rule that claims over foreign (intellectual) property are not justiciable before the English courts, drawing a parallel foundation for foreign immovable property (land) and intangible (intellectual) property.[10]

In *Def Lepp Music v Stuart Brown*[11] the Court held that the UK Copyright Act 1956 was confined to the territory of the UK and had no extraterritorial application to infringements outside the UK. The claimant therefore was unable to rely on the statutory rights and hence the Court found that there was no action, and therefore the English court did not have subject-matter jurisdiction in respect of the defendants established in Holland and Luxembourg. The case was decided not on the basis of the rules of private international law but on the basis that no tort had been committed, as the reach of the UK Copyright Act was confined to the UK. It illustrates two levels of jurisdiction that need to be considered in cross-border cases: firstly, territorial or extraterritorial reach of the national law constitutive of the claim, and secondly, competence of the courts (jurisdiction in the narrower sense).[12]

Tyburn Productions v Conan Doyle[13] concerned copyright in a TV programme using the characters of Sherlock Holmes and Dr Watson and Sir Arthur Conan Doyle's daughter and heir threatened to bring copyright proceedings to prevent the distribution of the programme in the US. The production company sought a declaration from the English court that the programme was not a breach of copyright. The Court held that it had no jurisdiction on the question of whether US copyright subsisted in the programme, arguing that copyright was strictly territorial, and therefore not justiciable in the English courts.[14]

As will be discussed, the courts have moved away from the strict territoriality rule in recent years. However, another controversial example of *in rem* jurisdiction is jurisdiction at the place of the registry for domain names.

[7] *Rey v Lecouturier* [1910] AC 262.

[8] In respect of patents, see two Judgments of the Australian High Court in respect of patent, *Potter* (n 4) (validity and infringement of a patent) and *Norbert Steinhardt v Meth* (1961) 105 CLR 440 (threats of proceedings in England in respect of an Australian patent).

[9] *British South Africa Co v Companhia de Moçambique* [1893] AC 602 (HoL) 629 (Lord Herschell), 633 (Lord Halsbury); now limited by s 30 (1) Civil Jurisdiction and Judgment Act 1982.

[10] Ubertazzi (n 4) 207.

[11] [1986] RPC 273 (HC) 274.

[12] See discussion in Chapter 2.

[13] [1991] Ch 75 (ChD).

[14] At 88.

2. Domain names and *in rem* jurisdiction

The legal nature of domain names as either contractual entitlements or property rights has been extensively discussed in the literature, but has not yet been fully settled.[15] If domain names are quasi-property rights, and given the fact that they arise upon formal registration in a domain name registry, this may arguably mean that *in rem* jurisdiction applies, so that the courts at the place of registration have jurisdiction over questions of ownership.

Domain names are *prima facie* web addresses, replacing binary IP addresses with more memorable, alphanumeric combinations, used in order to access resources on the world-wide-web.[16] They are defined by US Federal law as "any alphanumeric designation which is registered with or assigned by any domain name registrar, domain name registry, or other domain name registration authority as part of an electronic address on the Internet."[17]

On the one hand, *prima facie*, registration of a domain occurs through the means of a contract between a registrar and the registrant (the domain name holder), giving rise to contractual not property entitlements. A series of contracts, namely between the domain name registry and the respective registrars, and the registrars and the registrant, control its use. Thus, arguably, domain name registration is a communication service contract, not a proprietary right.[18]

On the other hand, while the registry and the registrars have a real-world presence, the domain name as such is virtual and not territorial, as it has worldwide validity for the reason that domain names are unique in the sense that the same domain name can only be registered once. This uniqueness and the memorability of domain names makes them similar to trademarks to the extent that they function as *source indicators*. Furthermore, domain names are clearly valuable, as they can be auctioned, sold, and transferred for valuable consideration. Moreover, domain names are also exclusive, in the sense that the registrant has exclusive use of the domain name. These features make domain names similar to intangible property.[19]

Several US court decisions have considered whether domain names are a form of intangible property, such as the 9th Circuit US Court of Appelas decision in *Kremen v Cohen*.[20] Under Californian law, at least, internet domain names are considered

[15] A Rački Marinković, "Domain Names: towards a New Form of IP Right" (2011) 6(9) Journal of Intellectual Property Law and Practice 632–37, 633; NM Schottenstein, "Of Process and Product: Kremen v Cohen and the Consequences of Recognizing Property Rights in Domain Names" (Spring 2009) 14(1) Virginia Journal of Law & Technology 1–25; M Bogdan and U Maunsbach, "Domain Names as Property" (2009) 3 Masaryk University Journal of Law and Technology 175–82, 176.

[16] Bogdan and Maunsbach (n 15) 176.

[17] 15 USCA §1127.

[18] Rački Marinković (n 15) 632; Schottenstein (n 15) 6; Bogdan and Maunsbach (n 15) 176.

[19] Rački Marinković (n 15), 633; Bogdan and Maunsbach (n 15) 176.

[20] *Kremen v Cohen* 337 F 3d 1024, 1029–30 (9th Cir 2003): the Court applied a simple three element test to the definition of property: "First, there must be an interest capable of precise definition; second, it must be capable of exclusive possession or control; and third, the putative owner must have established a legitimate claim to exclusivity." See also under District of Columbia law: *Xereas v Heiss* 933 F Supp 2d 1, 6 (2013 US District Court DC), *Domain Protection v Sea Wasp* 12 December 2019, 2019 WL 6782105, 21–23 (US District Court ED Texas 2019).

intangible property,[21] such that they can be the subject of a conversion action.[22] In *Office Depot v Zuccarini* the 9th Circuit US Court of Appeals therefore found that the Californian courts can exercise *quasi in rem* jurisdiction over property situated within their geographical border, and, as the Registry of.com and.net, VeriSign was in the relevant district, allowing the appointment of a receiver to enable the satisfaction of a debt.[23]

By contrast, in *Network Solutions v Umbro International*[24] the Supreme Court of Virginia held that a garnishment order could not be attached to domain names, as they are not a form of liability or chose of action, that is, property.[25] The Court held that the use of a domain name for a certain period is a contractual right, based on the registration agreement.[26] However, it should also be pointed out that the Court did not rule directly on the status of domain names.[27] Likewise the Kentucky Court of Appeals has overturned a ruling by the first instance court, which had ordered the forfeiture of 141 domain names used for gambling websites,[28] on the basis that the wording of the legislation[29] does not include domain names among the items liable to be seized.[30]

The German Supreme Court has held in 2012 that a registered domain name, gewinn.de, does not constitute an absolute property right as defined under German civil law, but only confers relative rights that apply between the parties involved.[31] Thus, while the German courts have recognized economic rights in domain names as protected by the German Constitution, this does not mean that domain names are "property" in a civil law sense.[32] So, while the law may protect certain economic rights in domain names, this does not necessarily equate with domain names being property.[33] The status of domain names as a form of intangible property is ultimately unclear and varies significantly between different jurisdictions.[34]

Under English law no case has been reported on the issue of whether domain names are property or whether an unjustified loss of a domain name could amount to the tort of conversion. In *Patel v Allos Therapeutics*[35] the High Court found no clear basis

[21] *Kremen* (n 20) 1030; *Office Depot Inc v Zuccarini* 596 F 3d 696, 701–02 (9th Cir 2010).

[22] *Kremen* (n 20) 1036 (9th Cir 2003); *CRS Recovery v John Laxton* 600 F 3d 1138, 1142 (9th Cir 2010).

[23] KRS 528.010(4)(b) paras 700, 703.

[24] 259 Va 759, 529 SE 2d 80 (Supreme Court of Virginia 2000).

[25] Paras 769–70.

[26] Para 770: "domain name registration is the product of a contract for services between the registrar and registrant" and that a contract for services is not "a liability" in the meaning of the statute providing for garnishment orders against property.

[27] Bogdan and Maunsbach (n 15) 177.

[28] The trial court had found that the domain names are "gambling devices" subject to forfeiture and seizure.

[29] KRS(n 23) "any other machine or other device, including but not limited to roulette wheels gambling tables and similar devices, designed and manufactured primarily for use in connection with gambling."

[30] *Interactive Media and Entertainment and Gaming Association v Commonwealth of Kentucky*, Kentucky Court of Appeals Decision of 20 January 2009, not reported, 2009 WL 142995 p 3.

[31] [2012] BGHZ 192, 204.

[32] Cf adacta.de [2005] GRUR 2005, 261 German Constitutional Court.

[33] T Mahler, *Generic Top-Level Domains* (Elgar 2019) 112–28.

[34] Rački Marinković (n 15) 637; Mahler (n 33) 112: calling the position "confused" from an international, comparative law point of view and calling for legislation clarifying the status of domain names.

[35] *Patel v Allos Therapeutics* [2008] ETMR 75, para 35.

for a claim by a domain name registrant who had lost a domain name as a result of extra-judicial and extra-legal Uniform Domain Name Dispute Resolution Procedure (UDPR).

The property status of domain names notwithstanding, US Federal law in the shape of the US Anti-cybersquatting Consumer Protection Act (ACPA) provides for *in rem* civil jurisdiction for federal trademark infringement in the courts of the district where the domain name registrar or domain name registry (or other relevant domain name authority) is located.[36] However, this depends on the Court finding that the claimant could not establish the identity of the registrant and/or obtain personal jurisdiction over the registrant.[37]

These provisions have the purpose of enabling a US trademark owner to bring a claim against a *foreign* cybersquatter in the relevant US court where the relevant domain name authority is situated in the US.[38] They were applied in *Porsche Cars North America v Porsche.net*.[39] The US Court of Appeals for the Fourth Circuit held that Virginia's courts have *in rem* jurisdiction under the ACPA[40] over 128 domain names containing the claimants' Federal trademark in "Porsche," despite the fact that they lacked personal jurisdiction over the defendant registrants. The situs of the property itself gave the court jurisdiction, in this case the place where the domain name had been registered. The *in rem* jurisdiction applied despite the fact that the (British) defendants had submitted to personal jurisdiction of the Californian courts three days before the hearing, as the Court essentially argued that this was too late.[41] The domain names as property were the relevant contact with the jurisdiction (of Eastern Virginia) such that the *in rem* jurisdiction did not offend the due process clause of the US Constitution: "In a case that directly concerns possession of the defendant domain names, the registrant's other personal contacts with the forum are constitutionally irrelevant to the assertion of in rem jurisdiction over the domain names he registered."[42]

In *NBC Universal, Inc v NBCUniversal.com*[43] a Korean registrant of the infringing domain name lost the World Intellectual Property Organization (WIPO) dispute resolution under the UDPR. The UDPR is a mandatory, non-binding dispute resolution procedure, to which all registrants of generic-top-level domain names have to submit and that may lead to the cancellation or transfer of the disputed domain name to the complainant trademark holder. The UDPR is implemented through a series of agreements between the relevant domain name registry, domain name registrars, and the

[36] 15 USCA §1125(d)(2)(A).

[37] ibid.

[38] *Standing Stone Media, Inc. v Indiancountrytoday.com*, 193 F Supp 2d 528, 532 (NDNY 2002); *Mattel Inc v Barbie-Club.com* 310 F 3d 293, 298 (2nd Cir 2002).

[39] 302 F 3d 248 (4th Cir 2002); see also *Mattel* (n 38) 24 at 299–304; *Royal Caribbean Cruises v Royalcaribbean.com* 2016 WL 8943172 (MD Fla 2016) 2, *Venetian Casino Resort, LLC v Venetiangold.Com* 380 F Supp 2d 737, 741 (ED Virginia 2005); *Montblanc-Simplo GmbH v Montblancpensale.org* 297 FRD 242, 244 (ED Virginia 2014); *NBC Universal, Inc v NBCUniversal.com* 378 F Supp 2d 715 (ED Virginia 2005); *Harrods v Sixty Internet Domain Names* 302 F 3d 214 (4th Cir 2002); *Globalsantafe Corp. v Globalsantafe.Com* 250 F Supp 2d 610, 615 (ED Virginia 2003).

[40] 15 USCA §1125(d)(1).

[41] At 255–59.

[42] At 260.

[43] (n 39).

domain name holder—thus it is a form of contractually mandated dispute resolution. In order to create a balance of arms between the domain name registrant and the trademark holder, the UDPR provides that, if the domain name registrant loses the domain name, the registrant may bring a case before his or her *local* court,[44] which in this case was a Korean court. However, NBC Universal did not wait for the Korean Court to decide the case, but instead filed a pre-emptive action for federal trademark infringement in the US District Court local to the domain name Registry, arguing for *in rem* jurisdiction under the ACPA. The US District Court for the Eastern District of Virginia held that the trademark owners, NBC Universal, had not waived their right to bring a cybersquatting claim under the ACPA in a Federal US court, when bringing a complaint to a WIPO arbitral panel under the UDPR.[45] The Court held that it had *in rem* jurisdiction.[46]

Moreover, *in rem* jurisdiction in respect of domain names as a form of intangible property has been successfully been argued in respect of claims beyond the cybersquatting context. In *Harrods v Sixty Internet Domain Names* the 4th Circuit US Court of Appeals held that *in rem* jurisdiction also applied to Federal trademark infringement and dilution claims.[47]

Furthermore, in jurisdictions like Sweden providing for jurisdiction in respect of liquidated claims, if the debtor owns assets in Sweden, there may be local jurisdiction if a locally registered domain name is a localized, valuable, and transferable asset. However, the localization raises interesting interpretational issues: should the domain name be located in the place where it is registered and or in the place to which the owner of the domain name targets its business activities?[48]

By contrast, the Austrian Supreme Court has held that cybersquatting ("domain name grabbing"), an act of unfair competition under Austrian law, gave rise to jurisdiction at the place where the damage had occurred under the tort provisions of the Brussels Regulation.[49] The Scottish Court of Session in *Bonnier Media* similarly held that jurisdiction for passing off arising from the registration of a domain name was at the place of the threatened damage.[50] In these cases, European courts have applied tort jurisdiction (instead of *in rem* jurisdiction).

3. Jurisdiction in the EU and UK

In section 1 the strict application of the territoriality principle in IP cases by analogy to immovable property was discussed. In the cases discussed in section 1 the courts have held that the English courts do not have subject-matter jurisdiction in respect of foreign IP infringements. However, in recent years the courts have drilled several holes in the application of this principle. Likewise scholars have also argued that the

[44] D Lindsay, *International Domain Name Law* (Hart 2007) 108.
[45] At 717; see also *Storey v Cello Holdings* 347 F 3d 370, 380 (2d Cir 2003).
[46] At 718.
[47] (n 39) at 227–28.
[48] Bogdan and Maunsbach (n 15) 180–82.
[49] *Re Jurisdiction in Relation to Domain Name Grabbing* 17 OB 2/07D [2007] 3 WLUK 533.
[50] *Bonnier Media Ltd v Smith* [2002] 7 WLUK 3.

sovereignty-based application of the territoriality principle should be abandoned in favour of the proximity principle, ascertaining the closest connection to the dispute instead, in order to guarantee access to justice.[51]

Before the discussion turns to these recent developments, this section explains the jurisdictional rules in the UK, as well as the harmonized EU rules in the Brussels Regulation.

3.1 Harmonized EU jurisdiction rules and IP

The Brussels Recast Regulation[52] guarantees the recognition and enforcement of judgments between EU Member States subject to very narrow grounds of refusal and partly harmonizes the rules on jurisdiction where at least one of the defendants is domiciled in the EU, or one of the exclusive grounds of jurisdiction apply.[53] Furthermore, it recognizes the parties' choice of jurisdiction. Thus, if the parties, regardless of their domicile, have stipulated the court(s) that have jurisdiction in the event of a dispute, for example, in a contract such as a licensing agreement, this choice is respected by a court within the EU.

Essentially, for torts such as IP rights infringement, the Brussels Regulation contains two main rules of *personal jurisdiction*.[54] Firstly, this is the general rule of jurisdiction, namely the courts in the place of the defendant's domicile (regardless of the defendant's nationality).[55] Secondly, the special rule of jurisdiction for torts, including IP infringements, provides that the courts at the place where the harmful event occurred, or for future infringements, may occur, have jurisdiction.[56]

Finally, the Brussels Regulation contains rules regarding connected proceedings involving several defendants. It stipulates that where proceedings are so closely connected that it is expedient to hear them together in order to avoid the risk of irreconcilable judgments, the EU court at the place of domicile of one of the defendants may have jurisdiction over the other defendants.[57] This rule is highly relevant to IP infringements online, as they are frequently spread over a number of states.[58] It is discussed in greater detail in Chapter 11.

In the IP rights context two aspects of the Brussels Regulation deserve further discussion: the question of applying the rules on personal jurisdiction in infringement cases to the internet and the conflict between the exclusive jurisdiction rules for *in rem* property actions and personal jurisdiction.

[51] Ubertazzi (n 4) 180–290.

[52] Regulation (EU) 1215/2012 on Jurisdiction and the Recognition and Enforcement of Judgments in Civil and Commercial Matters (Recast) of 12 December 2012, OJ L351/1, further discussed in Chapter 8.

[53] Art 6(1).

[54] Jurisdiction over the person.

[55] Art 4.

[56] Art 7(2).

[57] Art 8(1).

[58] P Torremans, "Jurisdiction for Cross-border Intellectual Property Infringement Cases in Europe" (2016) 53 Common Market Law Review 1625–46.

3.1.1 Personal jurisdiction—special tort rule in IP infringement cases

The Court of Justice of the EU (CJEU) had to rule on several occasions on the special rule of jurisdiction[59] contained in Article 7(2) that the courts at the *place where the harmful event occurred* or may occur have jurisdiction. Article 7(2) applies to all wrongful actions not amounting to breach of contract, including the non-payment of a copyright levy on recording devices sold by Amazon in Austria, imposed by Austrian Copyright Law.[60]

This rule of jurisdiction[61] was interpreted by the CJEU in *Bier*[62] to mean that this can either be the court where the defendant committed the wrongful act or where the direct damage resulting from the tortious act impacts.[63] The Court pointed out that "it is well to point out that the place of the event giving rise to the damage no less than the place where the damage occurred can, depending on the case, constitute a significant connecting factor from the point of view of jurisdiction"[64] and held that the claimant has the option to sue at either place.[65] Or, as the CJEU has said in a recent case, "Bier thus effectively split the notion of 'harmful event' into two separate notions of cause and consequence: the 'damage' and the 'event giving rise to the damage'."[66]

The reasoning of the CJEU is that the place where the damage resulting from the wrongful act occurs is a connection factor particularly proximate to the dispute and therefore as a connection factor leads to the sound administration of justice and the efficacious conduct of proceedings.[67] Thus, within the EU, for IP infringement the rules have moved away from the territoriality principle to a proximity principle based on the two connecting factors: damage, and the event giving rise to damage.

Article 7(2) therefore includes the place where the damage occurred. The trouble with this interpretation of Article 7(2), generous to the claimant, is that IP infringement in internet cases is frequently spread over a number of states and this wide international distribution of infringement may lead to considerable forum shopping and legal uncertainty as to the forum ("delocalisation of damage"[68]). In some cases access

[59] The general rule of jurisdiction is that the courts at the place of the defendant's domicile have jurisdiction according to Art 4(1) Brussels Bis Regulation.

[60] Case C-572/14 *Austro-Mechana Gesellschaft v Amazon* ECLI:EU:C:2016:286, paras 43–44, 53.

[61] Or its predecessor in Art 5(3) of the Brussels Convention 1968, 1968 Brussels Convention on Jurisdiction and the Enforcement of Judgments in Civil and Commercial Matters, OJ L 299, 31 December 1972, pp 32–42.

[62] Case C-21/76 *Handelskwekerij G J Bier BV v Mines De Potasse d'Alsace SA* [1976] ECR 1735, further discussed in Chapter 8.

[63] Joined Cases C-509/09 *eDate Advertising GmbH v X* and C-161/10 *Oliver Martinez v MGN Ltd* [2011] ECR I-10269, paras 40–41.

[64] Para 15.

[65] Para 19.

[66] Case C-27/17 *flyLAL-Lithuanian Airlines, in liquidation v Starptautiska lidosta Riga VAS* ECLI:EU:C:2018:136, para 29.

[67] *eDate/Oliver Martinez* (n 63) para 40 and C-523/10 *Wintersteiger v Products 4U* ECLI:EU:C:2012:220, paras 18–20, 32: "It is, in particular, established that the place where the event giving rise to an alleged damage occurred may constitute a significant connecting factor from the point of view of jurisdiction, since it could be particularly helpful in relation to the evidence and the conduct of proceedings"; also *Austro-Mechana* (n 60) para 30.

[68] Opinion of Advocate General Cruz Villalón in Case C-441/13 *Pez Hejduk v Energie Agentur* ECLI:EU:C:2014:2212, para 2; K Bercimuelle-Chamot, "Accessibility Is The Relevant Criterion To Determine Jurisdiction In Online Copyright Infringement Cases" (2015) 10(6) Journal of Intellectual Property Law & Practice 406–07.

equates with damage and the concern arises that jurisdiction is almost ubiquitous.[69] In internet cases involving IP the defendant may not be able to control, or foresee, the place of damage.

For unregistered rights such as copyright, the primary infringer may upload and publish copyright infringing materials from one jurisdiction, which is then accessed, downloaded, streamed, or shared in many other jurisdictions, in each of which damage occurs (as well as potentially further acts of copyright infringements). Usually the primary infringer is the target of litigation for a remedy, such as damages or an injunction, as this is a more central point of fighting the infringement. Because of the national treatment principle in Article 5(1)[70] of the Berne Convention[71] and within the EU, the Copyright Directive 2001/29/EC,[72] rights holders have rights under the relevant national copyrights at the place of infringement, hence overcoming the strict territoriality of copyright.[73] Thus, the question arises whether the rights holder can sue the primary infringer in each and every EU Member State in which the infringing material was accessed, downloaded, streamed, or shared and damage has occurred. The jurisprudence of the CJEU in this respect has been inconsistent, as in some, much criticized,[74] cases it has held that accessibility is sufficient[75] for jurisdiction whereas in other cases the Court required a showing of targeting.[76]

In three cases the Court found jurisdiction on the basis that the defendants directed[77] their infringing conduct at the relevant state and thus established a targeting test, which is not contained in Article 7(2) of the Brussels Regulation.

In *L'Oréal v eBay*,[78] in the context of cross-border e-commerce activities carried out on eBay, the CJEU used the concept of "directing" it had developed for consumer jurisdiction in *Pammer/Alpenhof*[79] as the test to be used to decide whether a product is sold outside or within the state of registration of a trademark or the EU, for community trademarks. In other words, the targeting test was used to decide whether a sale

[69] Opinion of Advocate General Cruz Villalón in *Wintersteiger* (n 67) para 22—although he makes a clear distinction between mere "harmful information on the internet" and the disputed information being capable to occasion a trademark infringement—only the latter is sufficient for jurisdiction under Art 7(2), para 25.

[70] "Authors shall enjoy, in respect of works for which they are protected under this Convention, in countries of the Union other than the country of origin, the rights which their respective laws do now or may hereafter grant to their nationals, as well as the rights specially granted by this Convention."

[71] Berne Convention for the Protection of Literary and Artistic Works 1886 (1979), WIPO; 187 members at the time of writing; https://www.wipo.int/treaties/en/ActResults.jsp?act_id=26 accessed on 26/7/2020.

[72] Copyright Directive 2001/29/EC of 22 May 2001, OJ L167/10; see also Case C-170/12 *Peter Pinckney v KDG Mediatech AG* EU:C:2013:635, para 39.

[73] Opinion of Advocate General Cruz Villalón in *Pez Hejduk* (n 68) para 36.

[74] J Smith and Leriche, "CJEU Ruling in Pinckney v Mediatech: Jurisdiction In Online Copyright Infringement Cases Depends On The Accessibility Of Website Content" (2014) European Intellectual Property Review 137–38; Bercimuelle-Chamot (n 68) 407.

[75] *Pez Hejduk* (n 68); Case C-170/12 *Peter Pinckney* (n 72), and for trademarks: *Wintersteiger* (n 67).

[76] Case C-173/11 *Football Data Co v Sportsradar* ECLI:EU:C:2012:642, C-324/09 *L'Oréal v eBay* ECLI:EU:C:2011:474; Case C-5/11 *Donner* ECLI:EU:C:2012:370.

[77] As to the targeting test in respect of act of infringement of the EU Trademark and Community Design, see section 3.4.1.

[78] (n 76).

[79] Joined Cases C-585/08 *Pammer* and C-144/09 *Hotel Alpenhof* ECLI:EU:C:2010:740 para 69, discussed further in Chapter 10.

on an international trading platform was subject to the relevant trademark law and jurisdiction of the court at the place of registration.[80]

Donner[81] concerned an appeal against a criminal conviction for commercial copyright infringement, committed by distribution of Bauhaus furniture from Italy without the respective licences in Germany. The products were manufactured in Italy where they were not protected by copyright, but consumers could order them online via a website in German. Mr Donner was in charge of the delivery company, which was part of the set up. The CJEU confirmed that German copyright law applied, as the distribution scheme was clearly directed at German consumers.[82]

Football Data Co[83] was about an alleged infringement of the *sui generis* database right, giving legal protection from extraction and reutilization of databases.[84] The question[85] before the English Court of Appeal was whether the English courts had jurisdiction under Article 7(2) as the court of the place where the harmful event occurred. A company based in Germany, Sportsradar transmitted database content owned by the Football Data Co to punters using UK and Gibraltar based online betting services and the English Court asked whether this means that any extraction or reutilization occurred at the place of the emission (Germany) or the place where the communication is received (England). The CJEU held that the *sui generis* right is created by national law, approximated by the Directive and therefore territorial, and limited to the territory of each EU Member State.[86] The CJEU pointed out that the transmission of data by Sportsradar is ubiquitous, as website content can be consulted by an unlimited number of internet users worldwide, outside of the control of the website operator.[87] The Court applied *Pammer/Alpenhof*[88] and *L'Oréal v eBay*[89] by analogy, saying that mere accessibility of a website, or the place where the communication was received, was not a sufficient criterion for jurisdiction under Article 7(2): "the mere fact that the website containing the data in question is accessible in a particular national territory is not a sufficient basis for concluding that the operator of the website is performing an act of re-utilisation caught by the national law applicable in that territory."[90] Likewise the CJEU equally held that the place from where the data is emitted or location of the server hosting the data is also not conclusive as to the place where the reutilization takes place.[91] Instead, the CJEU held that the act of reutilization takes place in the state where the defendant intended to direct its conduct to, where "the act discloses an intention on the part of its performer to target persons in that territory."[92] Since the data transmitted by Sportsradar in this dispute contained data about

80 Paras 61–67.
81 (n 76).
82 Paras 27–29.
83 (n 76).
84 Art 7 Directive 96/9/EC on the Legal Protection of Databases of 11 March 1996, L77/20.
85 The case concerned the predecessor to Arts 7(2) and 5(3) Brussels Regulation (EC) 44/2001 of 22 December 2001 (now replaced by the Brussels (Recast) Regulation).
86 Paras 27–28.
87 Para 35.
88 (n 79).
89 (n 76).
90 Para 36.
91 Paras 44, 45.
92 Para 39.

English football league matches, and was in English, the CJEU held that this would be evidence that the conduct was directed at the public in England.[93] Arguably in this case, the CJEU confuses the analysis of the location of the harmful activity (where the reutilization takes place) with the application of the jurisdictional tests in Article 7(2) Brussels Recast Regulation. This is contrary to the jurisprudence starting with *Bier*, which has consistently held that the courts of *both* the place of the event giving rise to the damage (here the reutilization) *and* the place where the damage results (here presumably England) have jurisdiction. The CJEU decided to ignore the second, harm element in order to get to a targeting test for database right cases. A targeting test has also been applied to determine jurisdiction under Article 125(5) of the EU Trademark Regulation.[94]

By contrast, in three cases the CJEU has found explicitly that targeting is not required.

In *Peter Pinckney*[95] an author, composer, and performer domiciled in France found that his songs, originally recorded on vinyl, had been produced on a CD by Mediatech in Austria and the sale of these CDs was promoted online by two companies from Great Britain. The website, which marketed the physical CDs, was accessible in France and Mr Pinckney brought copyright infringement proceedings in France. The French Court[96] referred the following question to the CJEU, namely whether an alleged infringement of copyright committed by means of content placed online on a website gives rise to jurisdiction in each and every Member State where that content is accessible, for damage in that Member State, or whether, for jurisdiction to arise, it is necessary that the allegedly infringing content was directed at the Member State concerned.[97] The CJEU referred to the mosaic rule[98] established in a line of cases starting with *Shevill*[99] and confirmed in relation to internet cases in *eDate Advertising/Martinez*[100] in respect of defamation and privacy-related infringements.[101] The mosaic rule means that the claimant can sue at each and every place where he or she has suffered damage, but can only recover damages for the harm suffered in that particular jurisdiction. *Pinckney* applies the mosaic rule to copyright infringements spread over several EU Member States.[102] Furthermore, the CJEU held that it was *not* necessary that the defendant had directed its conduct to the forum state[103]—mere damage through accessing copyright infringing content online (or in *Pinckney* accessing the website selling the infringing CD to someone in the forum state) was sufficient for a finding of jurisdiction.[104]

[93] Paras 40, 42.
[94] Case C-172/18 *AMS Neve Ltd v Heritage Audio SL* ECLI EU:C:2019:276para 55, see discussion in section 3.4.1.
[95] (n 72)—the case also concerned the predecessor to Arts 7(2) and 5(3) Brussels Regulation (EC) 44/2001 of 22 December 2001.
[96] Cour de Cassation.
[97] Para 15.
[98] Discussed further in Chapter 11.
[99] *Shevill v Press Alliance* [1995] ECR I- 415.
[100] *eDate/Oliver Martinez* (n 63).
[101] However, note that the centre of interests test established in *eDate Advertising* further discussed in Chapter 11 does not apply to intellectual property cases, *Wintersteiger* (n 67) paras 23–24.
[102] Para 45.
[103] *Peter Pinckney* (n 72) para 42.
[104] ibid para 44.

In *Pez Hejduk*[105] a professional photographer authorized an Austrian architect to use her photos of his buildings in a conference organized by Energie Agentur. German-based Energie Agentur used the photos on their website without the photographer's authorization or attribution and she sued them in Austria for copyright infringement. The Austrian Court referred the question of special jurisdiction to the CJEU. As in *Pinckney*, CJEU held that the damage has occurred at each place where the photos were accessed, so that jurisdiction can be based on Article 7(2)[106] but that compensation would be limited to the damage in Austria, applying the mosaic rule.[107] The practical problem with the mosaic rule in cases where there is no sale of a physical item, but viewing and downloading of photos online, is to quantify the damage sustained in a particular jurisdiction.[108] Furthermore, the CJEU stated that there was no requirement that the infringement was directed at an Austrian audience.[109] Thus, again the CJEU held that mere access to a website, which constituted copyright infringement, was sufficient to found jurisdiction in copyright.[110]

By contrast, for registered rights such as patents, trademarks, and design rights, the "internet problem" presents itself differently, as these rights are strictly territorial and thus limited to the state of registration, albeit that the right holder may have registered multiple rights in different jurisdictions. By definition the damage to the right holder's interest can only occur in the state(s) of registration.[111] This means that there is less scattering of damage across a multitude of unforeseeable locations. Nevertheless, for registered rights, there may be a disconnection between the place where the infringer acted and the place where the right is registered, as the internet and its applications have enabled remote infringement. This can be illustrated by a trademark infringement case, *Wintersteiger*.

Wintersteiger is the third case that held that there is no need to show targeting before a court can assume personal jurisdiction under Article 7(2).[112] A competitor of Wintersteiger's had registered the claimant's trademark as a keyword for the purpose of sponsored search results on google.de, effectively advertising the same products (ski and snowboarding servicing tools) under the claimant's trademark on the Germany version of Google. One argument was that the infringement was directed at the German market and that therefore only the German courts had jurisdiction. The CJEU rejected this argument and found that personal jurisdiction merely requires that any damage from the infringement, however small or theoretical, had occurred within Austria.[113] In other words, the CJEU assumed that there could be

[105] ibid.
[106] Art 5 (3) of Regulation (EC) 44/2001.
[107] Paras 36–37.
[108] As pointed out by Opinion of Advocate-General Cruz Villalón in *Pez Hejduk* (n 68) para 39—he recommended that in cases where infringement is delocalized and dematerialized, committed through accessing, streaming, or downloading online, the mosaic rule should be abandoned. In such cases the place where only damage occurred should not have jurisdiction, paras 40–46, however, the Court did not follow this recommendation.
[109] Paras 32–33.
[110] Para 38.
[111] *Peter Pinckney* (n 72) paras 33, 37; *Wintersteiger* (n 67) paras 25, 28, 39.
[112] This case concerned the predecessor to Arts 7(2) and 5(3) of Regulation EC/44/2001.
[113] Para 39.

remote infringement by Austrian internet users searching for Wintersteiger's products on google.de. It, furthermore, held that whether such infringement and the resulting damage had in fact occurred needed not be decided at the preliminary, jurisdictional stage of the case, this could be done at the main stage of the proceedings when the substantive issues were decided.[114]

While trademarks are territorial in the sense that an Austrian trademark cannot be infringed by activities on the German market,[115] according to the CJEU, this territoriality did not mean that for a finding of jurisdiction the infringement had to be directed to Austria, as the Austrian trademark may be infringed by conduct directed to German territory but causing damage in Austria (by Austrian residents using google.de to find the competitor's product, which is likely as both countries share the same language and Germany may have a bigger market for certain products).[116] In fact, Advocate General Cruz Villalón pointed out that, while accessibility on the internet frequently leads to trademark infringement, the two should not be automatically equated. Whether there is in fact a trademark infringement in the state of registration depends on a number of factors such as "language in which the information is expressed, the accessibility of the information, and whether the defendant has a commercial presence on the market on which the national mark is protected."[117] He recommended that these factors needed to be assessed on a case-by-case basis.[118] The CJEU did not take up this recommendation in its judgment, leaving the factual assessment to the national (Austrian) Court. It simply repeated its established jurisprudence as to personal jurisdiction at the place where the damage had occurred. In *Wintersteiger* the place of the alleged damage was the place of registration (Austria). What would have happened if the claimant had decided to sue in the place of the infringement actions (Germany)? In this different scenario the German courts would have equally been competent under Article 7(2) but the question of the relationship between the courts at the place of registration (Austria) and the courts of personal jurisdiction would have arisen.

For registered rights, the infringement action, or in the words of the CJEU "the event giving rise to the damage," may occur outside the state of registration. In these cases the courts at the place of infringement action additionally have personal jurisdiction, despite the territoriality of registered rights such as patents, trademarks, and designs.[119] The relationship between the jurisdiction of the courts at the place of registration (*in rem* or subject-matter jurisdiction) and personal jurisdiction based on the domicile of the defendant or the place of the infringement action is examined in section 3.1.2.

3.1.2 *In rem*, subject-matter jurisdiction and its interplay with personal jurisdiction

Furthermore, the Brussels Regulation contains narrow-tailored rules on *property*, *in rem* jurisdiction based on territory and sovereignty. If these rules apply, the stipulated

[114] Para 26.

[115] *Wintersteiger* (n 67) paras 25, 28; Opinion of Advocate General Cruz Villalón in *Pez Hejduk* (n 68) para 35.

[116] Opinion of Advocate General Cruz Villalón in *Wintersteiger* (n 67) paras 37–38.

[117] (n 68) para 28.

[118] ibid.

[119] The CJEU, *obiter* in *Wintersteiger* (n 67) para 30.

court has *exclusive* jurisdiction trumping the rules of personal jurisdiction, in a similar way to lack of subject-matter jurisdiction depriving the courts, which would have had personal jurisdiction, of being competent. The *in rem* jurisdiction applies even if the court has no personal jurisdiction. The relevant provision for IP rights is currently Article 24(4), which provides that

> in proceedings concerned with the registration or validity of patents, trademarks, designs or other similar rights required to be deposited or registered, irrespective of whether the issue is raised by way of an action or as a defence, the courts of the Member State in which the deposit or registration has been applied for, has taken place or is under the terms of an instrument of the Union or an international convention deemed to have taken place.

This exclusive jurisdiction therefore only applies to cases concerned with registration or validity, and only in respect of registered rights such as patents, trademarks, and design. Thus, it does not apply to proceedings related to infringements, nor does it apply to unregistered rights such as copyright. However, two factors related to registered rights make this provision difficult to apply. First, frequently, it is difficult to clearly delineate infringement actions from validity actions, as questions of subsistence, scope, and the extent of a right might be part of the question of infringement, but equally closely related to validity. Second, when an infringement action is brought, the defence may be precisely that the alleged right is invalid.

There are different ways of overcoming these problems. One is to say that the court that has personal jurisdiction in infringement proceedings is additionally competent to decide the questions related to validity as relevant in the case as an incidental matter, but that this decision is limited in its effect *inter partes*.[120] The upside of this first approach is that it avoids the need for litigation in two different courts in order to solve the dispute. But the downside is that if the validity of the registered patent, trademark, or design right is challenged at the place of its registration, the court at the place of registration may come to a different decision than the court with personal jurisdiction, thus potentially leading to irreconcilable, inconsistent judgments.

The second option is for the court with personal jurisdiction over the infringement action to stay proceedings, refer the questions related to validity to the court of registration, before deciding on infringement.[121] The advantage of this reference procedure is that it avoids irreconcilable judgments, but requires coordination between the two courts (who are operating in different languages and under different procedural rules) and delays judgment considerably.

Finally, the third way of overcoming the jurisdictional conflict between personal jurisdiction and *in rem* jurisdiction is that the court competent to hear the infringement action or the court stipulated in an agreement declines jurisdiction, if the

[120] This is the approach taken by the German courts, discussed in J Fawcett and P Torremans, *Intellectual Property and Private International Law* (2nd edn, Oxford University Press 2011) 7.26.

[121] This separation of issues by way of reference has been rejected by the English courts, *Anan Kasei Co Ltd v Molycorp Chemicals & Oxides (Europe) Ltd* [2017] FSR 13 (Pat) para 27; *Ablynx NV v VHsquared Ltd* [2019] FSR 29 (Pat)) para 43.

action involves questions related to validity. This has been the position of the English courts: if the action is concerned with the validity of a patent, the courts at the place of registration have exclusive competence.[122] For this it must be sufficiently clear that validity is to be put in issue in the future, that is, the court must assess on the balance of probabilities whether validity is one of the issues of the case, even where invalidity has not (yet) been pleaded.[123]

This approach again avoids jurisdictional conflict and irreconcilable decisions, but means that claimants have to bring *two actions in sequence* to obtain a remedy, unless the court at the place of registration is competent to also hear questions of infringement.

The CJEU had to decide between these options in *GAT v LUK*[124] and firmly held that, even where invalidity is raised as a defence within the framework of infringement proceedings, the court at the place of registration has *exclusive* jurisdiction to decide whether or not the patent is valid or invalid. Although the ruling related to the predecessor provision to the current Article 24(4) Brussels (Recast) Regulation, namely Article 16(4) of the Brussels Convention 1968, the ruling is equally applicable. In fact the wording in Article 24(4) Brussels (Recast) Regulation has been updated to include the ruling in *GAT v LUK* by the added phrase "irrespective of whether the issue is raised by way of an action or as a defence." The arguments of the CJEU were that it was necessary to preserve the mandatory and exclusive nature of the *in rem* jurisdiction in respect of registered IP rights,[125] legal certainty,[126] and the need to avoid conflicting, irreconcilable court decisions.[127]

In summary, it is clear that for registered rights such as trademarks or patents *only* the courts in the place of registration are competent to make a decision on the validity of the registered right, even if the issue is raised incidentally, as a defence in the course of an infringement claim.

3.2 English jurisdiction rules

3.3 Recent developments, unregistered rights, and subject-matter jurisdiction

As has been discussed in section 1, the English courts have traditionally held that they are not competent to hear claims in respect of foreign IP rights for lack of subject-matter jurisdiction.

One of the first cases in which the courts have allowed subject-matter jurisdiction in IP cases was *Pearce v Ove Arup*.[128] The claimant brought a claim for copyright

[122] *Coin Controls Ltd v Suzo International (UK) Ltd* [1999] Ch 33 (ChD) 43–44, 51 (Laddie, J); *Fort Dodge Animal Health Ltd v Akzo Nobel NV* [1998] FSR 222 (CA) para 29; *Anan Kasei* (n 121) paras 18, 20, 23–25, 29; *Ablynx NV* (n 121) paras 38–45; 81, 83, 87.

[123] *Knorr-Bremse Systems for Commercial Vehicles v Haldex* [2008] FSR 30 (Pat) para 46; *Ablynx NV* (n 121) paras 45, 81.

[124] Case C-4/03 *Gesellschaft für Antriebstechnik mbH v Lamellen und Kupplungsbau Beteiligungs KG* [2006] ECR I-6509, para 31; also Case C-539/03 *Roche Nederland BV v Primus* [2006] ECR I-6535.

[125] Paras 24, 26.

[126] Para 28.

[127] Paras 29–30.

[128] [2000] Ch 403 (CA) Roch LJ.

infringement in respect of his drawings made as an architectural student. He claimed that a building in Rotterdam constructed by the defendant firm of civil engineers breached his English and Dutch copyrights. The Court of Appeal in this case faced the dilemma that, on the one hand, it was bound to accept personal jurisdiction under Articles 2 and 6(1) of the Brussels Convention 1968,[129] as it was the competent court at the place of one of the defendants' domicile, but that, on the other hand, given *previous* authority[130] infringements of foreign copyright seemed not justiciable in the English courts. The Court of Appeal emphasized that the copyright in the drawings was a local, Dutch copyright, conferred in Holland by Dutch law.[131] The Court of Appeal held that English courts have personal jurisdiction under the Brussels Convention, as the provision on exclusive jurisdiction of the local court for IP rights was limited to "registration or validity of patents, trade marks, designs, or other similar rights required to be deposited or registered"[132] and did not include copyright.[133] The Court of Appeal conceded that the two English conflict of law tests of justiciability (*Moçambique* rule) and, double- actionability (*Phillips v Eyre*[134]) are separate, further tests[135] to be satisfied, in addition to the question of personal jurisdiction. The Court of Appeal stated that the reason for the *Moçambique* rule had been the rule of comity and the principle that "the English courts should not claim jurisdiction to adjudicate upon matters which, under generally accepted principles of private international law, were within the peculiar province and competence of another state."[136] However, it came to the conclusion that comity was ensured by the Brussels Convention as an international treaty, and which led to the reform of English conflict of law rules in the Civil Jurisdiction and Judgments Act 1982, implementing the Brussels and Lugano Conventions.[137] The Court of Appeal held that Article 16(4) of the Brussels Convention guarded against the undue interference with the sovereignty of a foreign state in respect of (registered) IP rights, such as the common law rule in *Potter v Broken Hill Pty*.[138] Furthermore, it held that the Court was not precluded from applying Dutch copyright law and therefore found jurisdiction.[139]

R Griggs Group v Evans was a further case signalling change. In this case, the British footwear company producing Doc Martens boots commissioned a designer to recreate their logo, and this same logo had subsequently been purchased by competitors in Australia. The Court of Appeal held that it was an implied term of the design contract that the person who commissioned the logo owned the *worldwide* copyright in the resulting logo in equity and it upheld the order for assignment of copyrights to the footwear company.[140] Furthermore, the Court of Appeal held in a second judgment

[129] 1968 Brussels Convention on Jurisdiction and the Enforcement of Judgments in Civil and Commercial Matters (n 1).

[130] See discussion in section 1.

[131] At 423.

[132] Art 16(4) now Art 24(4) of the Brussels Recast Regulation.

[133] At 424.

[134] (1870) LR 6 QB 1, discussed in detail in Chapter 11.

[135] ibid.

[136] At 431.

[137] At 432.

[138] At 436, see (n 4).

[139] At 444–45.

[140] *R Griggs Group Ltd v Evans* (No1) [2005] ECDR 30 (CA) paras 19, 25.

that the English courts in this case were exercising personal, not *in rem* jurisdiction, and even though the assignment concerned foreign (Australian) copyright, this was based on contract and that therefore the *Moçambique* rule did not apply in this case.[141] In other words, the English courts had jurisdiction to order the assignment of foreign copyrights and the matter was justiciable and not excluded from subject-matter jurisdiction.[142] The Court of Appeal emphasized that private international law "had moved on"[143] and held *obiter* that the *Moçambique* rule should not apply in IP cases and that deciding a dispute on the subsistence or infringement of foreign copyright was not a question about jurisdiction, but a question of choice of law and if necessary the application of foreign law: "it would merely have been a question of receiving evidence about the will of that sovereign; I doubt that the sovereign could be assumed to be asserting a prerogative to have claims of that sort decided exclusively in its own courts."[144]

In a similar case, which arose from a reference by the Dutch courts, a liquidator of an insolvent company applied for an order that the inventor transfer to the company patents in twenty-two jurisdictions, and the CJEU held that this was a claim *in personam* as it concerned the terms and conditions on the basis of which the inventions were made, and the claim was therefore based on contract, not property.[145]

Further changes were brought by the Brussels and Lugano Conventions, now incorporated also in the Brussels Regulation—these provisions introduced the "novel" concept into the English common law that an English Court *must* accept jurisdiction over foreign IP rights in certain circumstances and cannot disclaim subject-matter jurisdiction.[146]

The Supreme Court in *Lucasfilm v Ainsworth* overruled *Tyburn Productions v Conan Doyle*,[147] discussed earlier.[148] The Supreme Court held that English courts have subject-matter jurisdiction to decide on ownership and infringement of foreign copyright claims, and can hear a case based on the rules of *personal* jurisdiction.[149] The Supreme Court found that the logic of applying the *Moçambique* rule to IP rights was to prevent interference with the *grant of rights* by a foreign sovereign (act of state doctrine[150]), and that therefore it could only ever apply to questions of validity and registration of *registered* rights, not unregistered rights such as copyright.[151] The Supreme Court in *Lucasfilm* referred to[152] Article 24(4) of the Brussels Regulation, discussed earlier.[153]

[141] See also *Crosstown Music Co v Rive Droite Music Ltd* [2012] Ch 68 (CA) paras 56–58.
[142] *R Griggs Group* (n 140) paras 110–16, 121, 140–41.
[143] Para 110 (Peter Prescott QC).
[144] Para 121 (Peter Prescott QC).
[145] Case 288/82 *Duijnstee v Goderbauer* [1983] ECR 3663.
[146] *R Griggs Group* (n 140) paras 123–24.
[147] *Lucasfilm Ltd v Ainsworth* [2012] 1 AC 208 (SC) paras 105–10.
[148] Section 1.
[149] Para 105.
[150] This is a doctrine of US law, see *Voda v Cordis Corp* (2007) 476 F 3d 887 (Fed Cir); *WS Kirkpatrick v Envtl Tectonics Corp* 493 US 400 (1990).
[151] While copyrights must be registered in the US before a claim can be brought, it does not affect subsistence of the right, see *Lucasfilm* (n 147) para 107.
[152] Art 22(4) Jurisdiction Regulation 2001/44 of 22 December 2000, which was the immediate predecessor of the current Recast Jurisdiction Regulation and omitted the words: "irrespective of whether the issue is raised by way of an action or as a defence."
[153] Recast Jurisdiction Regulation (EU) 1215/2012 on Jurisdiction and the Recognition of Judgments in Civil and Commercial Matters of 12 December 2012, OJ L351/1.

The conclusion of this section is that the exclusive *in rem* jurisdiction of the courts at the place of registration, as defined in Article 24(4) is limited to *registered rights and determination of questions of registration and validity*. It does not apply to questions of infringement of registered rights (such as a patent or a trademark), where validity and registration are *not* in issue.[154] The Supreme Court in *Lucasfilm* criticized the application of the *Moçambique* rule to IP rights as a species of intangible personal property bearing no relevant analogy with land. Furthermore, exclusive *in rem* jurisdiction does not apply to copyright that comes into existence automatically when the relevant work is created without a grant, registration, or deposit. The fact that copyright is based on statute does not affect this argument, as under English law, torts that are based on breach of a foreign statutory duty *are* justiciable in the English courts. Finally, the Supreme Court additionally held that there were no issues of policy why foreign copyrights could not be recognized. It pointed to the modern trend in favour of enforcement of foreign IP rights, as exemplified by the Rome Regulation (EC) 864/2007,[155] Recital 26 and Article 8 applying the law of the place for which protection is sought to the infringement of foreign IP rights, thereby clearly assuming that foreign IP rights are justiciable.[156]

3.4 The EU Trademark Regulation, Community Design Regulation and European patent

3.4.1 The EU Trademark Regulation and Community Design Regulation

The community trademark[157] was precisely created in order to overcome the strict territoriality of national trademarks, in addition to the national trademarks of the EU Member States.[158] In a similar fashion, a community design right was created as a unified system, in addition to design rights at national level.[159] The community trademark is now called the EU trademark, and it and the community design right are directly applicable in each EU Member State, involving only one application through the EU IP Office in accordance with a single procedure and thus achieving protection of one design/trademark right for a single territory encompassing all EU Member States.

All EU Member States must designate specialist EU trademark courts,[160] and community design right courts[161] in their jurisdiction, which will be competent to hear

[154] Paras 88–90, 107 quoting *Gesellschaft* (n 124) para 16.

[155] 11 July 2007, OJ 2007 L199 p 40, discussed further in section 4.1.

[156] Albeit that the Rome II Regulation did not apply directly to *Lucasfilm* (n 147), as it only entered into force on 11 January 2009, paras 91–92, 108–09.

[157] Originally created by Council Regulation (EC) 40/94 on Community Trademarks of 20 December 1993, OJ L11/1, then Community Trademark Regulation (EC) 207/2009 of 26 February 2009 OJ L78/1; currently EU Trademark Regulation (EU) 2017/1001 of 14 June 2017, OJ L154/1.

[158] Recitals 5, 7, 8 of the EU Trademark Regulation (EU) 2017/1001.

[159] Community Design Regulation EC/6/2002 of 12 December 2001, OJ L3/1, amended by Regulation EC/1891/2006 of 18 December 2006, OJ L386/14, see Recitals 5, 6, 7, 8, 9.

[160] Arts 123(1) and 124. In addition to infringement actions this includes actions in respected of threatened infringement, declaration of non-infringement (if permitted by national law), compensation for acts after publication (but before registration of the EU trademark) under Art 11(2), or counterclaims for revocation or invalidity.

[161] Arts 80(1) and 81. This stipulates infringement actions, threatened infringement and declarations of non-infringement (if permitted by national law), declaration of invalidity of unregistered Community

validity *and* infringement cases. Jurisdiction for disputes not concerning validity and infringement claims are governed by the Brussels (Recast) Regulation (such as contractual disputes), or if the Brussels (Recast) Regulation does not apply, the courts at the place of the EU IPO Office in Alicante, Spain have jurisdiction.[162]

Special rules of international jurisdiction, contained in the EU Trademark Regulation and the Community Design Regulation apply to these unitary rights. The EU Trademark and Community Design Regulations contain their own rules determining international jurisdiction in respect of validity and infringement cases, which are different from those set out in Articles 4(1) and 7(2) of the Brussels (Recast) Regulation discussed above.

Both the EU Trademark and the Community Design Regulations expressly exclude these and certain other provisions of the Brussels (Recast) Regulation.[163] Other than these specific exclusions, the Brussels (Recast) Regulation is applicable, though. Article 122(1) of the EU Trademark Regulation, provides "unless otherwise specified in this Regulation, the Union rules on jurisdiction and the recognition and enforcement of judgments in civil and commercial matters shall apply to proceedings relating to EU trade marks and applications for EU trade marks, as well as to proceedings relating to simultaneous and successive actions on the basis of EU trade marks and national trade marks." Likewise, Article 79(1) of the Community Design Regulations provides that the Brussels Convention "shall apply to proceedings relating to Community designs and applications for registered Community designs, as well as to proceedings relating to actions on the basis of Community designs and national designs enjoying simultaneous protection." This includes Article 8(1) of the Brussels (Recast) Regulation which states that if one of the defendants is domiciled in an EU Member State, other defendants not so domiciled may also be sued in the same EU Member State court in a joined action, in order to prevent the risk of irreconcilable judgments.[164]

Article 125 of the EU Trademark Regulation and Article 82 of the Community Design Regulation set out the grounds for international jurisdictional competence in validity and infringement proceedings, these are cascading in order or priority so that the one lower in the priority order is only applicable if the previous one is not applicable. The first and main ground is the domicile of the defendant or, if the defendant is not domiciled within the EU, the place where the defendant has an establishment.[165] If the defendant is neither domiciled nor established within the EU, the next rung on the latter down is the place where the claimant has its domicile, or if the claimant is not domiciled in the EU, the place where the claimant has an establishment.[166] Finally, if neither the defendant nor the claimant is domiciled or established

design and for counterclaims for a declaration of invalidity of a Community design, if raised in an infringement action.

[162] Art 134 Regulation (EU) 2017/1001 and Art 93 Community Design Regulation EC/6/2002.

[163] EU Trademark Regulation: Art 122(1), namely Arts 4, 6, and 7(1)-contracts, 7(2)-tort, 7(3)-restitution, 7(5)-branch, agency or other establishment, and Art 35-provisional measures are excluded; Community Design Regulation: Art 79(3) excludes Artes 2, 4, 5(1), (3), (4), (5), 16(4), and 24 of the Brussels Convention 1968.

[164] Joined Cases C-24/16 and C-25/16 *Nintendo v Big Ben Interactive* ECLI:EU:C:2017:724, para 44: "A Community design court (. . .) may therefore, by virtue of that provision (. . .) have jurisdiction to hear an action brought against a defendant not domiciled in the Member State in which that court is situated."

[165] Art 125(1) EU Trademark Regulation; Art 82(1) Community Design Regulation.

[166] Art 125(2); Art 82(2).

in the EU, the courts in the Member State where the EU IP Office (Alicante, Spain) has its seat are competent.[167] The main differences to the jurisdictional rules in the Brussels (Recast) Regulation is that the EU Trademark/community design courts assume jurisdiction even where none of the defendants is domiciled in the EU and that the courts at the place of the claimant's domicile/establishment are competent (*Forum Actoris*).[168] Traditionally there has been a certain degree of reticence against allowing *Forum Actoris* as a ground of jurisdiction.[169] It is assumed that the justification of this ground is the idea that EU trademarks/community design rights are a form of EU property, making this more akin to *in rem* property jurisdiction, justifying that an EU court assumes jurisdiction over a non-EU defendant.

Furthermore, in addition to this cascade of jurisdictional competence, there are three more jurisdictional rules which apply additionally. First, the parties can agree which court has jurisdiction and this choice is accepted under Article 25 of the Brussels (Recast) Regulation.[170] Second, the defendant can submit to the jurisdiction of the court chosen by the claimant, if he or she enters an appearance according to Article 26 of the Brussels (Recast) Regulation.[171] If jurisdiction is based on any of these grounds, the extent of the jurisdiction covers the whole of the EU,[172] even if defendants domiciled in other jurisdictions have been joined.[173]

These grounds of jurisdiction also apply to the competence of the courts for granting provisional measures such as injunctions. No other court is competent to grant provisional measures if these grounds apply.[174]

Finally, and most importantly, the courts of the Member State(s) where an *act of trademark infringement* has been committed or threatened have jurisdiction, but this jurisdiction is then limited to the acts of infringement or threatened infringement on the territory of that particular Member State.[175] This provides an alternative ground of jurisdiction at the claimant's choice (instead of the domicile or establishment of defendant/claimant or the courts at the EU IPO).[176]

Unlike Article 7(2) of the Brussels (Recast) Regulation, which provides for jurisdiction in both the place where the event giving rise to the damage and the place of where the damage occurred, the EU Trademark Regulation Article 125(5) and the Community Design Regulation *only* provide for jurisdiction at the place of *where the act of infringement has been committed*, not in the place where the harm occurred.[177] The CJEU has emphasized that Article 7(2) has been expressly excluded by the

[167] Art 125(3); Art 82(3).

[168] See also Opinion of Advocate General Szpunar in *AMS Neve* (n 94) para 29.

[169] JP Verheul, "Forum Actoris and International Law" in T.M.C. Asser Institute, *Essays in International and Comparative Law* (1983 Springer) 196–209, 197–98.

[170] Art 125(4)(a); Art 82(4)(a).

[171] Art 125(4)(b); Art 82(4)(b).

[172] *AMS Neve* (n 94) para 40.

[173] Art 126 (1); Art 83 (1): "within the territory of any of the Member States"; *Nintendo* (n 164) para 64.

[174] Art 131(2); Art 90(3).

[175] EU Trademark Regulation Art 125(5)—cross-refers to Art 124 with the exception of declarations of non-infringement and Art 126(2); the Community Design Regulation Art 82(5) and Art 83(2); *AMS Neve* (n 94) para 40.

[176] *AMS Neve* (n 94) para 41.

[177] Case C-360/12 *Coty Germany GmbH v First Note Perfumes NV* ECLI:EU:C:2014:1318, para 37.

Community Design Regulation and the EU Trademark Regulation, which provide the *lex specialis* for infringement jurisdiction.[178]

Nevertheless, jurisdiction for claims under national trademark laws[179] is governed entirely by the Brussels (Recast) Regulation, including the tort provisions in Article 7(2).[180] Likewise, claims for unfair competition and passing off (unregistered rights) continue to be governed by Article 7(2) Brussels (Recast) Regulation.[181] Therefore claims under EU Trademarks and Community Design Rights are governed by rules of jurisdiction different than those governing their national counterparts, which may mean that rights holders have to bring separate proceedings.

Furthermore, on the internet, the acts of trademark infringement or Community design right infringement may be difficult to locate. In *Coty*[182] a Belgian entity sold counterfeit goods (perfume) in Belgium to a German reseller who then marketed and sold these products to consumers in Germany. The CJEU held that the German EU Trademark Court did not have jurisdiction in respect of the first seller domiciled in Belgium, as this entity did not act on German territory. Thus, to allow jurisdiction under Article 125(5), the actual acts of infringement have to be committed in the jurisdiction of the court seized and not in the destination country of the goods.[183] The reason for this limitation has been given by the CJEU in *AMS Neve*. Jurisdiction by the courts in the destination country "would be based on an *effect* of the infringement committed by the original seller and not on the alleged unlawful act committed by the original seller, which would be contrary to the sense of the wording 'Member State in which the act of infringement has been committed.'"[184]

The question of where an act of infringement takes place was equally the central issue in *AMS Neve*.[185] A producer of professional audio mixing and recording equipment sued a Spanish competitor for infringement of its EU, and national trademarks. The allegation was that the Spanish company had used the trademark in connection with its own goods and on a website, as well as Facebook and Twitter accounts, targeted to the UK market. The question before the CJEU was whether the English courts had jurisdiction on the basis that this was the place where the act(s) of infringement had been committed. The CJEU described the concept of an "act of infringement" as "active conduct" on the part of the "person causing the alleged infringement."[186] The CJEU then held, with reference to *L'Oréal v eBay*[187] that if the offers for sale and the advertising with the infringing sign were directed to the UK, then these acts of infringement were committed in that territory, notwithstanding the facts that the defendant was established in, and presumably acted from, Spain and that the products

[178] ibid. paras 26–27; Case C-617/15 *Hummel Holding* EU:C:2017:390, para 26; *AMS Neve* (n 94) para 34.

[179] Largely harmonized by the Trademark Directive, currently Directive (EU) 2015/2436 of 16 December 2015, OJ L336/1, in force 15 January 2019.

[180] *AMS Neve* (n 94) paras 35–36.

[181] *Coty* (n 177) paras 42, 59.

[182] (n 177).

[183] Paras 34, 37, 38.

[184] *AMS Neve* (n 94) para 45.

[185] ibid.

[186] At para 44.

[187] (n 76).

themselves were also located in Spain.[188] The mere fact that the advertising and offers for sale were placed remotely online through third-party intermediaries outside the EU (such as web hosts and social media) did not absolve the defendant from committing any acts of infringement in the UK.[189] The Court reasoned that to hold otherwise would render the enforcement of trademark law completely ineffective[190] and that it would be next to impossible for the claimant to identify at which location the defendant has physically acted when placing the offers of sale and advertising online.[191] Therefore the CJEU applied a targeting test in respect of advertising and offering for sale in order to determine whether the infringing acts were committed in the same territory as the court seized.[192] If the advertising and offers were directed to customers in the UK, the acts of infringement were committed there as "apparent from the content of the website and the platforms at issue."[193]

In *Nintendo v Big Ben Interactive*[194] Nintendo, the producer of games, games consoles, and accessories, sued both the French manufacturer of Nintendo-compatible gaming accessories and its German subsidiary in the German courts for infringement of its community design rights under the Community Design Regulation.[195] The German subsidiary marketed the Big Ben products via its website in Germany, which were then directly supplied by the French parent company manufacturer to consumers in Germany and Austria. The question arose as to what are the acts of infringement, but this time in the context of finding the applicable law. The CJEU pointed to several possible acts of alleged infringement: making of the product, offering it, exporting it, importing it, or putting it on the market.[196] The CJEU held that rather than focusing on individual acts of infringement, the court should take an overall view: "the correct approach for identifying the event giving rise to the damage is not to refer to each alleged act of infringement, but to make an overall assessment of that defendant's conduct in order to determine the place where the *initial act of infringement at the origin* of that conduct was committed or threatened."[197] The CJEU held that the act of placing the infringing products on the market by offering them on the website is the event giving rise to the damage and hence the initial infringing act.[198] Since both the provisions on applicable law[199] and the provisions on jurisdiction[200] use the place of where the act of infringement has been committed, one would expect that the determination of the location of the act of infringement is the

188 *AMS Neve* (n 94) para 47.
189 Paras 48–50.
190 ibid.
191 Para 51.
192 Paras 55–56.
193 Para 56.
194 *Nintendo* (n 140).
195 Community Design Regulation (EC) No 6/2002 of 12 December 2001, OJ L3/1; amended by Council Regulation No 1891/2006 of 18 December 2006, OJ L386/14.
196 At para 100.
197 Paras 103, 109.
198 Para 108.
199 Art 88(2) Community Design Regulation EC/6/2002; Art 129(2) EU Trademark Regulation EU/2017/1001 and Art 8(2) Rome II Regulation EC/864/2007 on the Law Applicable to Non-Contractual Obligations of 11 July 2007, OJ L199/40.
200 Art 82(5) Community Design Regulation EC/6/2002; Art 125(5) EU Trademark Regulation EU/2017/1001.

same for both provisions. However, the CJEU in *AMS Neve* held that the purposes of these rules are different. For applicable law it is important that the rules identify only one applicable law and this explains why the CJEU in *Nintendo v Big Ben Interactive* held that only the initial act of infringement was determinative. However, for the question of jurisdiction of the court, there is no particular need to focus on the initial act of infringement[201] and the Court held instead that a targeting test applied.

Furthermore, the EU Trademark/Community Design Regulations also provide for a specific form of *Lis Pendens*: where invalidity or revocation is already pending before the EU IPO or, as a counterclaim in another Member State, proceedings must be stayed, but protective or provisional measures may be ordered for the duration of the stay.[202] The two Regulations also contain *Lis Pendens* rules in respect of parallel actions on national trademarks.[203] Furthermore, the provisions on *Lis Pendens* in Articles 29–34 of the Brussels (Recast) Regulation apply.[204] These essentially provide that where proceedings involve the same parties in the same cause of action, and the courts in two EU Member States are seized of the matter, the court first seized shall hear the case, and the other courts must stay proceedings in favour of the court first seized.[205] Furthermore, courts in the EU must also consider whether to stay proceedings if a court outside the EU is first seized of the action[206] and when the actions are only related (not entirely congruent in the sense that it is not entirely the same parties and the same cause of action) but not staying would lead to the risk of irreconcilable judgments.[207] The CJEU has held that two actions involving the same defendants in respect of the same sign but used in two different trademark territories were not related actions in the *Lis Pendens* sense and that therefore there would be no irreconcilable judgments.[208]

3.4.2 European patents

Three types of patents exist in the EU: national patents under national law (limited to the territory of each Member State), the bundle of national patents in the EU under the European Patent Convention, and the latest addition of the Unitary Patent,[209] which will create a single, unitary patent with its own court, the Unitary Patent Court (UPC), which has exclusive jurisdiction over EU patents and unitary patents.[210] The international jurisdiction of the UPC is determined by the Brussels (Recast) Regulation, as amended by Regulation EU/542/2014.[211] The scope of its decisions is limited to those Member States for which the patent in the dispute has effect. The UPC may assume

[201] *AMS Neve* (n 94) para 64.
[202] Art 132; Art 91.
[203] Art 136; Art 95.
[204] Discussed further in Chapter 8.
[205] Art 29—the only exceptions are exclusive jurisdiction agreements, other courts must stay proceedings in favour of the court stipulated in the agreement, Art 31.
[206] Arts 33, 34.
[207] Art 30.
[208] Case C-231/16 *Merck* EU:C:2017:771, para 42; *AMS Neve* (n 94) para 42.
[209] EU Regulations EU/1257/2012 and EU/1260/2012 entered into force 20 January 2013, but the system will depend on the entry into force of the Unitary Patent Court Agreement, signed on 19 February 2013.
[210] Art 32 Unified Patent Court Agreement.
[211] Art 31.

jurisdiction even where the defendant is not domiciled in the EU under the special grounds of jurisdiction in the Brussels (Recast) Regulation, such as Article 7(2).[212]

The UPC is based on the Unitary Patent Court Agreement, which has been signed by all EU Member States except Poland and Spain. The Agreement will only enter into force after Germany, France, and the UK have ratified it plus at least ten more EU Member States. While the number of ratifications was sixteen at the time of writing,[213] it was not clear when the EU Unitary Patent System would enter into force, as the German ratification had been challenged before its Constitutional Court and the UK's participation[214] may be called into question by its withdrawal from the EU.

4. Applicable law in the EU and UK

In order to determine the rules on applicable law in respect of IP rights, the nature of the underlying claim must be examined and in particular whether the dispute is based on contract, tort, or concerns the creation or subsistence of the intellectual property right.[215] This chapter focuses on the law applicable to tort and, to a lesser extent, to the creation or subsistence of IP rights.

4.1 Rome Regulation

Historically, because of the territoriality of IP rights, and the lack of jurisdiction of the English courts over foreign IP rights under the *Moçambique* rule, the question of the law applicable to adjudicating on foreign IP right infringements did not arise under English law. Traditionally, the double-actionability rule in *Phillips v Eyre*[216] combined with the territoriality of IP rights would have meant that a claim based on foreign IP rights would have been unlikely to be actionable in English courts.[217] The rule in *Phillips v Eyre* has been abolished by section 10 of the Private International Law (Miscellaneous Provisions) Act 1995, which introduced a general *lex loci delicti* for tort actions.[218] This in turn was overridden by the Rome II Regulation[219] providing in Article 8(1) as the law applicable to all "non-contractual obligations arising from an infringement of an IP right (...) the law of the country for which protection is claimed." This has also been termed the *law protectionis*, which applies to national IP rights and has been described as "universally acknowledged."[220] For unitary IP rights harmonized at EU level[221] the relevant Community/EU law instrument applies as the

[212] Art 71b, provided property is located with a Member State with connection to the dispute.
[213] https://www.consilium.europa.eu/en/documents-publications/treaties-agreements/agreement/?id=2013001 accessed on 26/7/2020.
[214] Ratified 26 April 2018.
[215] Fawcett and Torremans (n 120) 12.01.
[216] See (n 134).
[217] As discussed in section 1.
[218] S 11(1) with exceptions further discussed in Chapter 10.
[219] See (n 165).
[220] Recital 26 Rome II Regulation.
[221] Community Design Rights, EU Trademarks and Unitary Patents, see the discussion in section 3.4.

applicable law. For "any question that is not governed by the relevant Community instrument," the law of the country in which the *act of infringement* was committed is the applicable law.[222] The place of infringement of a Community right was interpreted in *Nintendo* as the place where the operator of a website activates the process for offering the products for sale—in other words, the place where the defendant commits the tort and carries out the infringing acts.[223]

The law applicable to IP infringement as stipulated in the Rome II Regulation cannot be contracted out from by way of an agreement.[224] The Rome II Regulation provides expressly in Articles 8 and 13 that these conflict of law provisions apply to IP *infringements*—this can be interpreted as meaning that the provisions do not apply to questions of subsistence and validity of IP rights. For registered rights, the place of registration as the *origin* or *situs* of the right provides the applicable law for questions of subsistence and validity as this is the law of the country where the right was created.[225] Under English case law for patents and trademarks the courts have applied the law of the place where the right could be transferred—the courts in these cases narrowly focused on the transferability question as these cases were about the effects of forced expropriation of trademarks and patents.[226] For copyright the question is answered by the Berne Convention, discussed in section 4.2.

The specific rules on the law applicable to unfair competition in the Rome II Regulation may be relevant for actions concerning unfair competition in respect of branding issues, such as unregistered trademarks and passing off. Article 6 of the Rome II Regulation makes a distinction between acts of unfair competition that affect (1) a specific competitor only, or (2) those which affect the collective interests of consumers or competitive relations in a country more generally. For acts of unfair competition affecting a specific competitor, the applicable law is determined by applying Article 4.[227] This means that the law of the place where this specific competitor suffered the direct damage resulting from the passing off applies,[228] unless the parties are habitually resident in the same country, in which case the law of that country applies.[229] If the act of unfair competition/passing off is manifestly more closely connected with yet another country, then that country's law will apply.[230] However, a contractual relationship and the terms of the contract are not taken into account for this purpose. Therefore when assessing the law applicable the courts must disregard a choice of law contained in a connected contract.[231] For alternative (2), acts of unfair competition affecting the collective interests of consumers/competitive relations in a country, the applicable law is

[222] Art 8(2).
[223] (n 140) para 108.
[224] Art 8(3).
[225] Fawcett and Torremans (n 120) 13.17–13.30, 13.34.
[226] *Wilderman v Berk* [1925] 1 Ch 116; *Rey* (n 7); *Reuter v Mulhens* [1954] 1 Ch 54; *Novello v Hinrichseni* [1951] 1 Ch 595.
[227] Art 6(2).
[228] Art 4(1).
[229] Art 4(2).
[230] Art 4(3).
[231] Case C-191/15 *Verein für Konsumenteninformation v Amazon*, ECLI:EU:C:2016:612 AM paras 46–48.

the law of that country.[232] In practice it will be difficult to find cases where the act of unfair competition merely affects a single competitor, as the collective interests of the customers of that competitor are affected at the same time as the competitor.

4.2 Copyright: Berne Convention

In the field of copyright, the structure of the Berne Convention[233] is that it defines the *country of origin* of a protected work[234] and then deals with conflict of law scenarios arising.

Works by nationals of the country of origin are governed, in the territory of the country of origin, by the copyright laws of that country, and no conflict of law situation arises, as the country of origin is the domestic country in this respect.[235] In any other scenario, a conflict of laws arises, be it by the fact that the author is a foreigner and/or that the work is copied or otherwise exploited in a country other than the country of origin.[236] For these conflict of law scenarios, the Berne Convention establishes two principles, namely the national treatment principle and a principle determining the applicable law.

The national treatment principle in Article 5(1) of the Berne Convention states "authors shall enjoy, in respect of works for which they are protected under this Convention, in countries of the Union other than the country of origin, the rights which their respective laws do now or may hereafter grant to their nationals, as well as the rights specially granted by this Convention." Article 5(3), second Sentence states that "when the author is not a national of the country of origin of the work for which he is protected under this Convention, he shall enjoy in that country the same rights as national authors."

The national treatment principle set out in these provisions essentially embraces the territoriality of IP rights (as property rights) and makes them mutual,[237] by treating foreign authors and foreign works like national authors and domestic works in each territory on the basis of the principle of non-discrimination.[238]

Furthermore, the Berne Convention effectively provides for a rule for the law applicable to copyright infringements in Article 5(2), third Sentence: "the extent of protection, as well as the means of redress afforded to the author to protect his rights, shall be governed exclusively by *the laws of the country where protection is claimed*."[239]

232 Art 6(1).
233 (n 71).
234 Which for lack of space is not further discussed here, but see Arts 3, 4, 5(4) Berne Convention; Fawcett and Torremans (n 120) 12.08–12.14.
235 Art 5(3); Fawcett and Torremans (n 120)12.29–12.30.
236 Fawcett and Torremans (n 120) 12.18ff.
237 Albeit not on a fully reciprocal basis, see later in this section.
238 Fawcett and Torremans (n 120) 12.18.
239 For the equivalent provision in respect of performances etc, see Art 2 of the Rome Convention 1961; a national treatment rule is also contained in Art 2(1) of the Paris Convention for the Protection of Industrial Property 1883 in respect of patents and trademarks, but for registered rights, national registration is constitutive of the national rights, without which no right arises; and in Art 3 of the TRIPS Agreement 1994.

The meaning of this phrase is not entirely unambiguous and a minority opinion has interpreted this as meaning the law of the forum, that is, the law of the place where proceedings have been brought.[240] This interpretation has, however, been strongly opposed and the phrase has instead been taken to mean the law of the country for which protection is sought, as replicated by the Rome II Regulation discussed earlier.[241] It should be pointed out that this interpretation is wider than the place of the commission of the tort (*lex loci delicti*), as the *lex protectionis* may apply even before a tort has been committed, or threatened, or to claims other than tort.[242] In other words, the rule on applicable law for copyright is not just concerned with infringement and its consequences, but relevant to all forms of exploitation and use of copyright. Choice of law questions additionally arise in the non-litigation context, for example, in non-contentious matters such as licensing contracts.[243]

The national treatment principle in the country for which protection is claimed is not merely a rule of applicable law but additionally confers legal *rights* directly under the *lex protectionis*, and it excludes the private international law of that country (no *renvoi*). Thus, the Berne Convention creates a bundle of national copy*rights* for protected works.[244] It is also more generous than a system strictly based on reciprocity, as the author benefits from the law of the country for which protection is claimed regardless of what that law's provisions say compared to the country of origin.[245]

The Berne Convention clearly overcomes some of the limitations of the territoriality of copyright by providing for mutual protection within the states to which the Convention applies. The combination of the principle of national treatment with the *lex protectionis* creates a bundle of national copyrights for authors, which in turn means that authors benefit from a mosaic of differing copyrights with different laws and different terms of protection applying in each country. Having sketched the conflict of law provisions of the Berne Convention the question arises what this means for online copyright infringements. Copyright infringement such as those relating to media content (films, music, games, software) downloaded and shared online will frequently be spread over several national jurisdictions which means that the same act of infringement may be governed by a multitude of national copy*rights*, which means multiple national laws applying, which creates a cost, evidential and enforcement burden in the context of infringement litigation. Thus, while the Berne Convention has overcome the confinement of territoriality of rights, in the sense that copyrights do no longer stop at a national border, it has not created a single unified right and the mutuality of multiple rights creates enforcement difficulties in practice.

[240] Fawcett and Torremans (n 120) 12.25.
[241] ibid 12.25.
[242] ibid 12.26.
[243] ibid 12.26.
[244] ibid 12.31.
[245] Albeit there are some limited exceptions where countries limit the rights granted under their law to the extent of reciprocal rights granted by the country of origin, see ibid 12.35–12.37 (design rights, term of copyright protection, *droite de suite* for artistic copyright).

4.3 Caselaw of the English courts

The Berne Convention raises the difficult question of how to territorialize infringement in order to determine the applicable law. How can we determine the country for which protection is claimed? The English courts have applied a targeting test in respect of the applicability of UK Copyright law.[246] In *Warner Music UK Ltd*, Mr Justice Birss referred to the aforementioned EU "targeting" jurisdiction cases[247] and found that:

> the internet is international. Users accessing the world-wide-web from the UK can gain access to websites all over the world. This is routine. However unlike the internet, intellectual property rights are territorial. In what circumstances therefore does an act undertaken on the internet engage the laws, in particular the intellectual property laws, of a given state? The clear answer to that question is that for the rights in an EU member state to be engaged (at least as far as trade marks and copyright are concerned) the act must be *targeted at the public in that member state*.[248]

He found that UK Copyright Law applied on the basis that the advertising and the business model was objectively targeted at users in the UK.[249] If the service was not targeted at users in the UK, it would be irrelevant that the website could be accessed from the UK (and that there may have been some access in fact).[250]

Similar questions arise in respect of locating the use of a trademark and deciding whether a trademark is used in the UK for the purpose of assessing whether a UK trademark has been infringed under local law. As in copyright cases, the English courts have applied a targeting test. In other words in deciding whether an infringing sign has been used in the UK and thereby infringes on a UK-registered trademark, the English courts have assessed whether the infringing conduct, such as registering a domain name, or using a trademark on a website, has been targeted at the UK.[251] It is clear that the targeting test is a multi-factor test taking into account factors related to the website itself, such as language, currency, context, and customer recommendations or directions, as well as other factors such as the intention of the website operator, advertising revenues, the business model concerned, and the number of unique visitors from the country concerned.[252]

246 *Warner Music UK Ltd v Tunein UK* [2019] EWHC 2923 (ChD) para 12; *EMI Records Ltd v British Sky Broadcasting Ltd* [2013] EWHC 379 (ChD) paras 48–51; *Omnibill (Pty) Ltd v Egpsxxx Ltd (In Liquidation)* [2015] ECDR 1 (ChD) paras 11–13, 15, 33, 37, 40–41.

247 Section 3.1.

248 *Warner Music* (n 246).

249 *Warner Music* (n 246) paras 24–27, 29.

250 *Warner Music* (n 246) paras 13–14.

251 *Argos Ltd v Argos Systems Inc* [2018] EWCA Civ 2211 (CA), paras 51–73; *Merck KG aA v Merck Sharp & Dohme Corp* [2018] ETMR 10 (CA), paras 158, 166–70, 197; *Euromarket Designs v Peters* [2000] ETMR 1025 (ChD) paras 24–25.

252 See cases in (n 246) and discussion in Chapter 13.

5. Conclusion

The rules on jurisdiction and applicable law as applied to the internet are inherently complex and multi-layered. The hitherto distinct fields of private international law and IP have only recently been synthesized for a clearer picture to slowly emerge, but the field continues to be plagued by gaps and opacity.[253] While cross-border trade has always created challenges for IP, traditional marketing and distribution mechanisms were organized along national lines, allowing for territorially based licensing of IP. The internet has fundamentally changed this for good, as e-commerce allows direct marketing and direct cross-border sales to end users and consumers. This trend is likely to increase with ever more sophisticated marketing based on online tracking and profiling. Furthermore, because of the ubiquitous nature of the internet, it has enabled multi-jurisdictional infringements. These multi-jurisdictional infringements occur if the damage is spread over several national territories, for example, through peer-to-peer file sharing or the downloading or streaming of copyright infringing content and/or infringement actions that are carried out in several jurisdictions, such as the use of a trademark on a website.

As we have seen in this chapter, IP rights are territorial and were originally confined to the borders of a country, thus strongly connected to national sovereignty. Traditionally IP rights were seen as a form of property limited to the territory of a country and therefore actions could only be brought in the local courts that had exclusive subject-matter jurisdiction. This binding of IP rights as sovereign rights has recently been softened. This approach has now been limited to the core of claims concerning the *validity* of *registered rights*. It is therefore important to make a distinction between, on the one hand, registered and unregistered rights and, on the other hand, actions concerning validity of a right and infringement actions. For infringement actions (concerning registered or unregistered rights) and for validity claims concerning unregistered rights, courts other than the local courts have subject-matter jurisdiction. Thus, the private international law rules on tort jurisdiction apply to IP infringement actions.

This more modern approach has overcome the territorial limitations of IP rights, but not the problem of connecting claims to territory—thus the territoriality principle continues to apply. For example, because of the *mosaic rule* discussed here, it continues to be necessary to assess *where* the damage arising from infringement has occurred. Furthermore, in order to find the applicable law, it is necessary to identify the place for which protection is sought. Moreover, for registered rights it is necessary to assess whether the infringing conduct occurs within the jurisdiction of registration. For example, for trademarks, the difficult assessment must be made whether the trademark has been used within the jurisdiction. Here, in the *L'Oréal* case, the CJEU has used the concept of targeting originally developed in the context of consumer jurisdiction to connect IP rights to the relevant territory. By contrast, in *Wintersteiger* the CJEU has held that this question does not arise at the point of assessing the jurisdiction of

[253] See eg Fawcett and Torremans (n 120).

a national court, but only at the substantive stage when deciding on the actual infringement after a full assessment of the evidence. Thus, the principles locating IP infringement and connecting it to a particular territory are still not entirely clear and this uncertainty has given rise to inconsistent jurisprudence by the CJEU, which has applied a targeting test in some IP cases, but not others.

13
Conclusion

1. Jurisdiction and disruptive technologies—the jurisdictional challenge

This book explores what I have termed the "jurisdictional challenge" of the internet, that is, the discord between twenty-first-century, disruptive information and communication technologies (ICTs)[1] and laws being made and enforced at the national state level.[2] In what by now amounts to a hackneyed phrase, "the borderless internet" has challenged the ambit of the law, the legal authority of lawmakers, the jurisdiction of the courts, and has built obstacles in the way of law enforcement. The borderless internet has essentially detached the traditional connecting factors linking the human activity and conduct with one sovereign's authority over territory. ICTs allow for the remote processing and storage of data,[3] decentralization of human interaction,[4] and distributed legal harms across state borders.[5] As a consequence, there may be no clear connection to any particular territory or multiple connection points to many territories. The identity or location of online actors are commonly difficult to establish with certainty and tracing defendants (in civil proceedings) or suspects of crime is more difficult and resource intensive. Moreover, if the defendant or suspect, and his or her assets, are not present in the same country as the law enforcement authorities, enforcement across a border may be impossible.

The governance and regulation of modern technology therefore raise issues about the law applicable, jurisdiction, and enforcement. Conventionally the law as a discipline divides these issues related to the interface between national and international law into private international law and (public) international law, two separate legal disciplines.[6] This book cuts across these separate disciplines with a view to gaining insights from comparing the response to the jurisdictional challenge from different areas of law, and across public and private law. This final chapter seeks to tease out these insights in one place.

[1] eg the internet, TCP-IP protocols, client–server architecture, internet applications, cloud computing, blockchain, mobile computing, digital networks, social media, etc.
[2] See Chapter 2.
[3] See the discussion of client–server architecture and cloud computing in Chapter 1.
[4] See the discussion of peer-to-peer file sharing, or blockchain technologies, or user-generated content in Chapter 1.
[5] See the discussion of client–server architecture, cloud computing, the world-wide-web, social media, blockchain, advertising networks, bulletproof hosting in Chapter 1.
[6] Chapter 2.

Internet Jurisdiction. Julia Hörnle, Oxford University Press (2021). © Julia Hörnle.
DOI: 10.1093/oso/9780198806929.001.0001

2. Globalization and identity

Chapter 2 has explained that jurisdiction relates to the authority of making, adjudicating, interpreting, and enforcing the law. It is connected to the rightful lawmaker, law adjudicator, or law enforcer and the rule of law. Jurisdiction is thus connected to the legitimacy of legal institutions and rule-making. Recognition of a government by its people links jurisdiction to identity—to the extent that identity continues to be connected to the nation state, national law determines jurisdiction at its core. The disruptive technologies at the heart of the discussion in this book have speeded up the process of the increased inter-connectedness of the world, in other words, globalization. However, as explained in Chapter 2 people's sense of belonging, their identity has not kept pace with globalization. At a time when greater regional integration and intensified cross-border cooperation is needed between states, and hence less sovereignty, the populist urge is to call for greater national sovereignty. This is the paradox of disruptive technologies: they strike at the heart of national sovereignty, increasing the populist call for more sovereignty at a time when greater international alignment and cooperation is needed *because of these disruptive technologies*, in order to solve the problems arising. The paradigmatic example for this paradox is Brexit. Here the call for "taking back control" has meant that the UK now has less control. The UK has left the close regional cooperation and integration frameworks for data protection, cybersecurity, mutual recognition in criminal matters (including cross-border digital investigations), cooperation in respect of intellectual property laws, as well as coordination in the area of civil jurisdiction through the judgments of the Court of Justice of the EU (CJEU). Albeit that UK law is likely to stay aligned in the sense that large parts of the *EU acquis* already implemented in UK law is likely to stay intact, the benefits of the cooperation mechanisms and clarifying adjudication by the CJEU are liable to be lost, at least partly. The importance of these enforcement cooperation mechanisms have been examined in Chapter 11 (European Data Protection Board), Chapter 6 (Europol, Eurojust, European Arrest Warrant, European Investigation Orders), and Chapter 12 (EU Trademark, Community Design and European Patent).

Arguably, the changes required to improve cross-border enforcement of law means compromise and that states have less sovereignty, individually. However, this is the price to be paid to ensure that states are able to act more effectively across national borders. Arguably, therefore overall, in this interconnected, globalized world, sovereignty is improved through law approximation and cooperation. The current populist backlash endangers this urgently needed international cooperation.

3. Connecting factors and territoriality

Chapter 4 has discussed the principles of jurisdiction recognized under international law. In brief, states connect persons, their actions and criminal results, or unlawful damage *to their territory* in order to assume jurisdiction. It is clear that the territoriality principle plays a pivotal role in the justification of jurisdictional claims based on connecting factors.[7]

Additionally, extraterritorial grounds of jurisdiction exist allowing (some) states to claim jurisdiction over their citizens even when acting abroad or allowing (some) states to claim jurisdiction (more controversially) based on the nationality of the victim harmed.[8] Furthermore, wider grounds of jurisdiction exists enabling assumption of jurisdiction based on the protection of essential interests (protective principle), or universal jurisdiction allowing criminal prosecution in any state where the accused is present (universality principle). As discussed in Chapter 4, the universality principle is recognized in respect of the most heinous crimes such as war crimes and genocide, and crimes that cannot easily be linked to a specific territory such as piracy on the High Seas, but it has not been accepted in respect of cybercrime. One exception to this is Germany applying the universality principle to the dissemination of certain forms of violent, non-consensual pornography.[9]

In the area of *private* international law, one exception to the territoriality principle is that the rules allow the parties to choose the applicable law and the competent court. Choice of the parties is well established in respect of contract law (subject to protection of the "weaker" party in EU law as discussed in Chapter 10), but likewise exists in tort law, for example, Recital 31 and Article 14 Rome II Regulation.[10] Furthermore, in the area of private international law, the territoriality principle allows connecting to the domicile of the defendant, which is where the courts are competent to adjudicate on a civil dispute, as a general principle of jurisdiction.[11]

For crime and torts, the territoriality principle requires the identification of certain connecting factors. Such connecting factors identify the place (situs) of the crime or tort, by examining where the defendant acted (conduct) or where the results manifested, if the results are part of the definition of the crime, or, for tort cases, localizing where the damage caused by the tort take place.[12] For investigatory jurisdiction, the application of the territoriality principle requires location of the data. Determining the location of (1) conduct, (2) results/damage, and (3) location of data leads to interpretational and factual uncertainties.

Determining the location of conduct in the online environment is difficult, as the place where the accused acted may be different from the place where the action impacts. Furthermore, in early academic debate, the location of the server processing and storing data has been considered as the place of the *virtual* conduct, but given the complexities of layers of network architecture and cloud computing, this approach is no longer tenable.[13] But the basic constellation that a defendant acts remotely through a chain of computers continues to be relevant. The defendant may carry out

[7] See further Chapter 2.

[8] Discussed in Chapter 4.

[9] See Chapter 5.

[10] Rome II Regulation (EC) 864/2007 on the Law Applicable to Non-contractual Obligations of 11 July 2007, OJ L199/40.

[11] See Chapters 8 and 9 (for the EU and US respectively).

[12] Art 7(2) Recast Brussels I Regulation (EU) 2015/12 on Jurisdiction in Civil and Commercial Matters of 12 December 2012, OJ L351/1 and the *Bier* case, discussed in Chapter 8, see also Chapter 5.

[13] See discussion in Chapters 1 and 5.

commands on a laptop while physically being in State V, which launches an attack on computers in States X and Y leading to a criminal result in State Z (such as a denial of service attack or intrusion).[14] Furthermore, the mobility of computers makes it factually and evidentially difficult to ascertain the location of a person while acting online. If a person uploads illegal user-generated content (such as hate speech) to a social media platform, it is difficult to pin this conduct to a particular territory, especially if the defendant uses a mobile device, for example while travelling. Determining the territory of where this device connected to the internet requires disclosure of traffic and location data from the relevant (foreign) service providers. Thus, while persons of course continue to have a physical presence, this physical presence can give raise to forensic and evidential challenges. Moreover, interpretational difficulties arise in respect of corporate acts: in *Shevil* the CJEU held in the context of defamation that a publisher acts at the place of its establishment and that this is the place where the wrongful act takes place, ignoring the *actual* place where an employee of the publisher has in fact acted, thus avoiding these evidential problems.[15]

Determining the location of the results of a crime or damage in tort cases for the purposes of applying the territoriality principle is equally challenging. The first interpretational challenge is the distinction between the criminal conduct and the result as discussed in Chapter 5. For example, is publication an activity or is publication a result of conduct? Thus, the categorization of offences into "result crimes" and "conduct crimes" is riddled with inconsistencies and uncertainty.[16] In tort cases the difficulty has been to distinguish between the direct damage caused by the unlawful act, which can give raise to territorial jurisdiction, and the indirect damage (such as financial implications), which does not.[17] Furthermore, in tort and criminal cases where the damage is spread across very many countries, this potentially leads to multiple courts being competent to adjudicate. In intellectual property (IP) infringement and personality rights cases the CJEU solved this dilemma through the *mosaic doctrine*, which allows a claimant to sue the defendant in each and every jurisdiction where the claimant has suffered harm, but only to the extent of harm suffered in that jurisdiction.[18] Thus, the territoriality principle allocates jurisdiction to different states according to the proportions of the damage. But, in practice, this means the risks of multiple suits and evidential burdens when assessing the amount of damage in each jurisdiction. In the criminal law sphere multiple suits in different jurisdictions in respect of criminal results spread across several countries raises the concern of double (or even multiple) jeopardy.[19] Albeit that from the perspective of due process for defendants and procedural efficiency, multiple suits across different jurisdictions in respect of the same criminal act or the same tort are undesirable, they are the direct result of territorial sovereignty and the state's function to provide redress or retribution for harms suffered *locally*.[20]

[14] See eg the *Levin* case discussed in Chapter 5 or the arguments of *virtual* presence in the Belgian *Yahoo!* case discussed in Chapter 6.

[15] See Chapter 11.

[16] See Chapter 5.

[17] See Chapters 8 and 11.

[18] See Chapters 11 and 12.

[19] See Chapter 4.

[20] See further in section 5 on changing the territoriality principle.

Finally, determining the location of data in the cloud for investigative purposes may be impossible and, arguably remote, cross-border investigations are extraterritorial, even if they do not involve physical access of law enforcement officers on foreign territory. The territoriality principle restricts the actions of states to carry out cross-border investigations thereby limiting the conflicts between different legal procedures and standards for human rights safeguards.[21]

Thus, the territoriality principle connects actions, events, and results with territory thereby determining competence of a sovereign, and the applicable law. Its functions are to provide for redress and retribution according to local laws, and to ensure that local procedures and safeguards apply. While these functions continue to be important in the twenty-first century, it is equally clear that the connection between conduct or results/damage and territory does not work well in the interconnected online environment. Finding solutions to overcome these problems caused by the "unterritoriality of data" and loss of location is more difficult. The way forward consists of rule changes and systemic changes, as will be discussed here. Before discussing these changes, it is necessary to consider the jurisdictional scope of any remedies ordered by the courts, as well as the role of intermediaries in overcoming the jurisdictional challenge.

4. Worldwide remedies or localized remedies?

Jurisdiction is about the competence of the courts, but in this connection also about the scope of the remedy ordered by the competent court. Under the EU rules, a claimant may sue in the defendant's domicile, or at the place where the defendant acted, in order to recover the whole loss in damages.[22] However, under the *mosaic theory*, the claimant has the additional option to sue at the place(s) where the localized damage occurred, to the extent of the loss in that jurisdiction.[23]

The territorial scope of the remedy is particularly interesting in respect of injunctions. In *Eva Glawischnig-Piesczek v Facebook* the CJEU examined a reference on the scope of the obligation to remove insulting content illegal in Austria, imposed by an injunction. The Court held that EU law does not prevent worldwide injunctions permissible under national law, but that such injunctions have to comply with principles of international law.[24] The Advocate General had counselled self-restraint of national courts under the international doctrine of *comity*.[25]

Court have considered the scope of delisting injunctions in orders requiring Google to delist search results on both sides of the Atlantic. In *Google v Equustek* the Canadian Supreme Court upheld an interlocutory worldwide injunction to delist search results linking to a competitor's offering allegedly infringing Equustek's IP rights.[26] In *Google LLC v CNIL* the CJEU had to decide on the scope of a delisting order in the context of

[21] See Chapter 6.
[22] See Chapter 8.
[23] See Chapters 8, 11, and 12.
[24] See Chapter 3.
[25] See Chapter 3.
[26] Discussed in Chapter 3.

compliance with the EU data protection legislation. The Court acknowledged that the right to dereferencing is not recognized by all countries and therefore the scope of the injunction had to be limited to the territory of the EU.[27]

The Canadian Supreme Court and the CJEU in these three examples of juris prudence on worldwide injunctions have acknowledged the problematic nature of global orders, as they effectively impose the applicable law on the rest of the world. These three courts have also considered that in some instances an injunction needs to have global effect in order to provide effective protection to the claimant in IP, defamation, and data protection infringement cases, because of the global nature of social media and search services. The courts have held that the competent court should exercise restraint and balance the interests of all affected parties under an interest of justice and comity analysis before imposing injunctions with global effect.

5. Enforcement: the role of private gatekeepers

Judgments that are not voluntarily complied with and cannot be enforced are of limited practical value. Thus, a state's assumption of jurisdiction without having concomitant enforcement powers is a pointless exercise of sovereignty. Multilateral conventions harmonizing the rules on jurisdiction in civil and commercial cases have the ultimate purpose of ensuring recognition and enforcement of judgments in another contracting state.[28] Furthermore, civil judgments are sometimes enforced under the notion of comity, according to a state's domestic law, subject to reciprocity and the public policy exception. Such enforcement takes place only if the foreign court had jurisdiction and the defendant was properly served with proceedings.[29] However, State A does not customarily enforce the *public* law of State B in its territory.[30] This non-enforcement of public law applies to criminal jurisdiction and investigatory measures.[31] The limited enforcement of foreign laws leads to states searching for internet intermediaries for enforcement purposes who are local in the sense that they are established on the territory of the enforcing state.[32] This book has examined two aspects of this gatekeeper enforcement. First, the liability of gatekeepers and the move towards a positive duty of care to regulate certain types of content online in Chapter 3. Second, Chapter 6 has examined the role of online communication service providers in processing and storing communications data and their role in disclosing data to law enforcement authorities in the context of criminal investigations. Thus, private gatekeepers play a pivotal role in law enforcement.

[27] Discussed in Chapter 7.

[28] See eg the Hague Convention of 2 July 2019 on the Recognition and Enforcement of Foreign Judgments in Civil or Commercial Matters; or the EU process starting with the Brussels Convention of 1968 to the current Recast Brussels Regulation of 2012, discussed in Chapter 8.

[29] eg para 328(1) of the German Civil Procedure Code.

[30] Discussed in Chapter 2.

[31] See Chapter 6.

[32] Gatekeeper enforcement is discussed in detail in Chapter 3.

6. Changing the territoriality principle: closed systems and their interfaces

Just as the proverbial man with a hammer in his hand sees nails that need hammering into a wall everywhere,[33] lawyers tend to believe in the fallacy that (all) problems can be solved through legal rules and regulation. One example of this is the argument that we should somehow change the territoriality principle,[34] linking jurisdiction to the territory where a legal element (such as an element of the criminal offence or a tort) occurs. According to this view, since the existing rules are no longer adequate, the solution lies in changing the legal principles and rules, adapting them to modern technology. In my opinion, this view is a misconception, as law is one system, the geo-political interplay of states is a second, and technology is a third, and while they interface this interface is not without friction. The discussion on changing the territoriality principle, or not applying it to internet cases, takes me back to Baron von Münchausen and his story of lifting himself and his horse out of a swamp by pulling on his hair, mentioned in the Introduction.

Most lawmaking and law enforcement continues to occur at the level of nation states intimately linked to the current geo-political system frequently describes as the "Westphalian" system of nation states[35] and the concept of sovereignty.[36] Changes of law (whether through nations' lawmaking processes or treaties etc) do not directly effect changes to the geo-political system or to the disruptive technologies. The social systems theorist Niklas Luhmann has created the foundations for the legal concept of law as an autopoietic system interacting with other social sub-systems.[37] Gunther Teubner analyses in his work how the law continually redefines the perception of legal problems and how it responds to changes in other sub-systems, but that these systems are autonomous and closed. Therefore each system's own construction of the reality of the surrounding systems clashes with the operative reality of each system.[38] The challenge for law is that it must be interoperable with its surrounding systems (such as the law of other states[39] or disruptive technologies), yet remain compatible with its own values and internal structure.[40] This tightrope walk is exemplified by the doctrine of comity, discussed in Chapters 4 and 9.

There is a parallel in the interface between autonomous social systems such as law, communication, and technology and between the different territorial legal systems. All are separate, autonomous systems closed off to each other, but mutually influencing and conflicting with each other. Norms of international law and private international law have traditionally smoothed the conflicts between different national legal

[33] Attributed to Mark Twain.

[34] D Svantesson, *Solving the Internet Puzzle* (Oxford University Press 2017) 225.

[35] Named after the Peace Treaty signed in the Westphalian town of Münster, which ended the terrors of the Thirty War in 1648, see further Chapter 2.

[36] See Chapter 2.

[37] N Luhmann, *Systemtheorie der Gesellschaft* (2nd edn, Suhrkamp 2018).

[38] G Teubner, *Law as an Autopoietic System* (Blackwell 1993) 100–02.

[39] This is what the doctrine of comity attempts to achieve.

[40] Teubner (n 38) 104.

systems, creating an interface between different systems of national law.[41] However, disruptive technologies have massively scaled up these conflicts with the consequence that the international legal system does not function well currently, which is the core of the jurisdictional challenge. Therefore it is more helpful to regard jurisdictional conflicts as a "*systems interface*" problem, rather than a "*rule problem*."

The international legal system is tied to the geo-political system, which does not react easily or quickly to changes in technology. The territoriality principle is fixed, as it is too firmly attached to the Westphalian system of states, their power, and their sovereignty. Because of the limited influence one social system has over another, and the inability of international law to change the geo-political situation, criticisms of the territoriality principle contribute little towards solving the jurisdictional challenge of the internet. At best, tweaks in how states assume jurisdiction under the territoriality principle are one small factor in improving the conflict, but do not solve the problem holistically. In my view, an argument in this direction is as an unconvincing as the gravity-defying tales of Baron von Münchausen.

Viewing the legal systems as independent, closed systems allows one to identify two types of responses to the jurisdictional challenge: first, rule-level responses that make changes inside the legal system (changes in the law) and, second, more importantly, systemic responses, which make changes to the interface between law and other sub-systems or changes to systems outside the law completely. Having explained the limited effectiveness of rule-level responses, this book has largely focused on the problems associated with applying the traditional rules on jurisdiction and applicable law in different sectors.[42] It is for this reason that I examine insights in respect of the rules themselves first.

7. Rule-level changes

The goal of rule-level changes is to improve the various rules on jurisdiction contained in national legal systems and to reduce jurisdictional overreach. One concept, which seems to be an overarching theme in all the different sectors, is the concept of targeting or directing. Its main purpose is to limit the assumption of jurisdiction in cases where the link to the territory is marginal.

7.1 Targeting and directing

The rationale for targeting as a rule of jurisdiction is that if a defendant targets the effects of his or her conduct to a particular country remotely, that defendant should be answerable to stand (civil, criminal) trial in that country. Targeting has been discussed

[41] ibid 110.

[42] Chapters 5 (Criminal Jurisdiction), 6 (Criminal Enforcement Jurisdiction), 7 (Data Protection Jurisdiction), 8 (Private International Law in the EU), 9 (US Conflicts of Law), 10 (Consumer Jurisdiction), 11 (Jurisdiction in Privacy and Personality Rights Cases), and 12 (Intellectual Property Rights and Jurisdiction).

as a rule in order to limit the application of the territoriality principle and thereby reduce the amount of jurisdictional overreach and duplication and in order to identify the most appropriate jurisdiction. However, it is not one simple unifying concept and is used in multiple ways in different sectors and legal systems.

Chapter 9 has discussed US Conflicts of Law, where targeting has evolved from the *minimum contacts test*, which has been part of the jurisdictional analysis under the due process clause of the US Constitution. US courts use the *Calder v Jones* effects test to find jurisdiction in tort cases where the defendant has *purposefully directed* their tortious conduct to the forum state. However, as discussed in Chapter 9, conduct online is not always directed at specific countries and it is the deliberate and purposeful, but non-specific targeting of a larger geographical areas which makes it difficult to apply the targeting test. By contrast, in the EU the targeting test has not achieved the same amount of prominence, as jurisdiction is based on connecting factors allocating the proper *seat* of a dispute. Chapter 8 has discussed the harmonized special rules for jurisdiction in tort cases in Article 7(2) of the Recast Brussels Regulation (EU) 1215/2012. This connects jurisdiction to the place where the defendant acted or to the place(s) where the damage occurred, irrespective of the defendant's purpose or intention, and irrespective of whether the defendant targeted the claimant's domicile. The place where the damage occurs can of course be entirely fortuitous. Even if the place of the damage was entirely fortuitous and unforeseeable, the courts at that place may still assume jurisdiction. Notwithstanding this general position under EU law, the targeting test has gained some traction on EU territory.

First, under national law, the test has been used in legislation in order to delineate regulatory competence, by focusing on the reach of regulated activities. For example, in the UK under section 21 FiSMA 2000 a person must not communicate an invitation or inducement to engage in financial investment or claims management without authorization in the course of business, as this is a regulated activity. For communications originating outside the UK, this prohibition only applies if the financial communication is capable of having an effect in the UK.[43] A further example is the territorial scope of the British Gambling Act 2005. The regulation (including the licensing requirements) applies to remote gambling, if the punters use the gambling facilities in Great Britain and the operator knows or should know that the facilities are being used, or are likely to be used, in Great Britain.[44] Thus, a business who makes available remote gambling facilities to persons in Great Britain is subject to the licensing requirements and regulation by the Gambling Commission, as the operator's intention is irrelevant.

Moreover, the targeting test has influenced the harmonized civil jurisdiction rules under the EU Brussels Regulation for determining the jurisdiction of the courts in *consumer disputes*.[45] The Explanatory Memorandum to the original Brussels Regulation[46] makes a distinction between interactive and passive websites and has clearly been

[43] See also *Financial Services Authority v Bayshore Nominees Ltd & Others* [2009] EWHC 285 (Ch)—the prohibition was applied to marketing calls to UK investors from abroad inducing investment in shares as being under FSA jurisdiction.

[44] S 36(3)(b) and (3A).

[45] Discussed in Chapter 10.

[46] COM(1999) 348 Jurisdiction and the Recognition and Enforcement of Judgments in Civil and Commercial Matters, Explanatory Memorandum of 14 July 1999.

influenced by US conflicts of law doctrine and in particular *Zippo*.[47] The consumer protection provisions in EU private international law apply if the business "directs" its activities to the consumer's country, which is clearly a targeting test. The consequence of such targeting is that the courts at the consumer's domicile are competent and the consumer can rely on the mandatory provisions of consumer protection law at the place of his or her domicile.[48] In *Pammer/Alpenhof* the CJEU held that this targeting test is an objective test in the sense that the courts must take into account all circumstances of the business activity to assess whether it is directed to the consumer's domicile and the subjective intention of the business is irrelevant.[49]

Pammer/Alpenhof in turn has influenced the jurisprudence of the CJEU in privacy and personality rights cases, and in IP cases. In *eDate Advertising* the CJEU introduced the centre of interests test, which additionally gives the courts at the place where the claimant has his or her centre of their life jurisdiction in respect of privacy and defamation claims.[50] This centre of interests is the place where the defendant lives, works or has other professional interests, and is similar to the *Calder v Jones* targeting test, equally based on foreseeability.[51]

In IP cases the CJEU has referred to the targeting test in *Pammer/Alpenhof*, by way of analogy, even though these cases did not concern consumer disputes.[52] In *L'Oréal v eBay*, *Donner*, and *Football Data Co* the CJEU held that the defendant directed its IP infringing conduct to the claimant's domicile and that therefore the courts had jurisdiction there.[53] The targeting test is used here to restrict jurisdiction by distinguishing between jurisdiction based on mere access and jurisdiction based on targeting. However, as discussed in Chapter 12, the jurisprudence of the CJEU has not been consistent: in other cases mere access to websites and resulting damage was sufficient.

Finally, the analysis in Chapter 5 in respect of the jurisdiction of the criminal courts in Germany and England has similarly shown that courts have tried to restrict jurisdiction by a type of targeting test, in order to prevent mere accessibility being the basis for jurisdiction. The German approach to criminal jurisdiction in publication cases is to connect the elements of the criminal offence to German territory. As we have seen, the courts do not require targeting as such, but reached a "compromise" in *Töben*, which classified the Holocaust Denial offence as an offence endangering of an identifiable *protected interest in Germany* (namely the memory of victims and the public peace). The Court's reasoning, which focuses on the defendant's intended results in Germany, *de facto* amounts to a targeting test.[54] In England, the courts have developed the substantial measure test, which weighs up all factors and circumstances of a criminal case

[47] Discussed in Chapter 9.

[48] Discussed in Chapter 10.

[49] ibid.

[50] Discussed in Chapter 11.

[51] Although the difference between the US and EU jurisprudence is that some courts in the US (*Burdick*) have focused more on the targeted "audience" and held that mere knowledge on the defendant's part that the claimant lives in a particular jurisdiction is insufficient for targeting, whereas in the EU the fact that the claimant lives and works in a particular place is sufficient, see Chapters 9 and 11.

[52] Discussed in Chapter 12.

[53] ibid.

[54] Discussed in Chapter 5.

when assessing jurisdictional competence and, as applied in *R v Sheppard v Whittle*, is similar to a targeting test.[55]

Thus, the concept of the defendant targeting the claimant's or victim's jurisdiction has been an overarching theme in the jurisdictional analysis, limiting the assumption of jurisdiction based on the territoriality principle, in order to prevent overreach. As already mentioned, though, jurisdictional restraint on its own does not prevent concurrence in, and conflict of jurisdiction. Therefore more important is coordination of jurisdiction and international cooperation of states, discussed further in section 8.

7.2 Jurisdictional restraint: comity, extraterritoriality, and reasonableness

A second type of change at the level of rules is the exercise of restraint in applying domestic law and in assuming jurisdiction. This principle of restraint has reappeared in different guises and variations in a number of doctrines at the interface between a state's domestic law with the domestic law of another state. The doctrines discussed in this book are the following: comity,[56] public policy,[57] the presumption against extraterritoriality,[58] non-justiciability,[59] forum non conveniens,[60] and the reasonableness tests.[61] These doctrines balance the assumption of jurisdiction to adjudicate in a conflict of law situation or the assumption of jurisdiction to enforce a foreign judgment on domestic territory with negative effects on the foreign state, on the domestic legal order, or on the parties themselves. In applying these tests, the courts balance the interests of justice, state interests, and the interests of the parties in a conflicts of law scenario, recognizing that legal systems are closed and independent, but that they are equally systemically interdependent.

8. Systemic changes

Although rule-level changes are an important part of the jurisdictional puzzle they are not sufficient. Out-of-the-box thinking is required, which involves systemic changes going beyond changes in the nitty-gritty of jurisdictional rules and principles. Three themes stand out from the discussion of the jurisdictional challenge in the book. The most important of these three themes is the need for international coordination of jurisdiction and transnational enforcement cooperation. The second systemic change is technology, namely the use of geo-location and geo-blocking to counter some of

[55] See further Chapter 5.
[56] Discussed in Chapters 2 and 9.
[57] Discussed in Chapter 8.
[58] Discussed in Chapter 2.
[59] Discussed in Chapter 12.
[60] Discussed in Chapter 8, 9, and 11.
[61] Discussed in Chapter 9.

the negative effects of the jurisdictional challenge and reconnecting internet activities to territorial states. The final systemic change is the development of complementary self-regulation as a form of private regulation, which is enforceable across national borders.

8.1 Coordination, coordination, coordination

Coordination is concerned with states agreeing which states take regulatory enforcement action, precisely to prevent lack of enforcement or multiple enforcement actions. International cooperation, more generally, can take many different forms, exchanging information, exchanging intelligence, exchanging best practices, or pooling resources for enforcement of law.

Chapters 4 and 6 have emphasized the importance of coordination of jurisdiction. This has been discussed in the context of transnational digital investigations pointing out the role of Eurojust and joint investigation teams.[62] The importance of coordinating criminal jurisdiction has been explored with the example of the Eurojust Guidelines and EC Framework Decision.[63] Chapter 7 has explained the significance of the coordination mechanism within the European Data Protection Board, in order to ensure consistency of enforcement of EU data protection law. The argument here is that effective coordination mechanisms can reduce overlapping, multiple claims of jurisdiction and reduce the risk of multiple jeopardy or, conversely, the lack of enforcement because of lack of jurisdiction. Both multiple claims of jurisdiction and lack of enforcement of the law are problems in practice. Chapter 4 has discussed the risk of overlapping jurisdiction in the context of multiple prosecutions for the same criminal offence (*Ne Bis in Idem*). Chapters 11 and 12 have examined the issue of overlapping jurisdiction in the context of civil jurisdiction of the courts, in defamation, privacy, and IP cases. Chapter 3 has discussed the lack of enforcement of public, regulatory laws in the context of gatekeeper regulation. One of the main conclusions here and in our EU Study on the cross-border enforcement of online gambling regulation, is the need for more efficient international cooperation mechanisms, both between regulators of different countries *and* between regulators and social media companies.[64] Finally, for civil and commercial disputes, bilateral and multilateral conventions on jurisdiction and recognition ultimately have the function of ensuring the enforcement of civil judgments, which indirectly leads to coordination of overlapping jurisdiction through the *lis pendens* principle.[65]

[62] Chapter 6.

[63] Chapter 4.

[64] J Hörnle et al, EU Study "Evaluating Regulatory Tools for Enforcing Online Gambling Rules and Channelling Demand towards Controlled Offers" (29 January 2019) DOI 10.2873/253036, https://publications.europa.eu/en/publication-detail/-/publication/6bac835f-2442-11e9-8d04-01aa75ed71a1/language-en/format-PDF/source-98923888 accessed on 26/7/2020.

[65] In the EU context, see Chapter 8; in the international context, the Hague Convention of 2 July 2019 on the Recognition and Enforcement of Foreign Judgments in Civil or Commercial Matters (not yet in force and not further discussed in this book).

8.2 Geo-location and geo-blocking

Geo-location and geo-blocking technologies are controversial, as they limit the availability of products and services along national lines, thereby destroying the key benefit of the "borderless" internet. For those commentators regarding the internet as a great tool to disseminate and share information *globally*, these technologies are anathema. Authoritarian regimes use these technologies in order to prevent access to information, in particular information critical of the government. Geo-location and geo-blocking technologies reterritorialize the internet, carving up national or regional territories out of global internet applications such as websites, social media platforms, search engines. and other applications. Thus, the use of such technologies leads to a fragmented internet, defeating the network effects of global interconnectedness:

> a global, singular and universal system with maximum end-to-end connections produces a greater positive impact and potential than would a set-up that was composed of largely discrete intranets, national or otherwise.[66]

By the same token, these technologies allow localizing conduct online, thus reducing conflicts of national laws.[67] They allow states to apply national law on their territory thereby solving the everywhere and nowhere in particular problem of the internet. Geo-location technologies determine the location from where a person accesses the internet. By contrast, geo-blocking disallows access to certain internet applications (most commonly websites or part of websites) from certain countries—for example, if an online product (such as gambling or pornography) is illegal in that country. In this way, geo-blocking enables website operators to manage the risk of liability exposure in certain countries. Website operators can determine the likely physical location of a user accessing their services and block users from certain countries. The absence of geo-blocking may also indicate to a regulator of tightly regulated services that the operator targeted their operations to a particular state and this equally applies to advertising. For example, a Maltese online betting operator was admonished by the UK Advertising Standards Authority for allowing a Croatian gambling affiliate to target non-compliant advertising to UK punters. One of the factors for assessing whether the affiliate targeted the advertising to the UK was that he had not employed geo-blocking.[68]

Website operators additionally use geo-blocking in an anti-competitive way in order to segment markets along geographical lines coupled with differential pricing, or staggered release dates for products.[69] This is particularly relevant for multimedia

[66] G Berger, "The Universal Norm of Freedom of Expression- Towards an Unfragmented Internet" in U Kohl (ed), *The Net and the Nation State* (Cambridge University Press 2017) 27–38, 28.

[67] D Svantesson, "Time for the Law to Take Internet Geolocation Technologies Seriously" (2012) 8(3) Journal of Private International Law 473–87, 475.

[68] See https://www.asa.org.uk/rulings/bet-at-homecom-internet-ltd-a15-321776.html accessed on 26/7/2020.

[69] Unjustified geo-blocking by business has been made illegal within the EU by Regulation (EU) 2018/302 on Addressing Unjustified Geo-blocking of 28 February 2018 OJ L601/1.

products, such as films, games, and music, where territorial licensing prevails.[70] Geo-location tools additionally play an important role in the targeting of advertising.[71]

Geo-location and geo-blocking reduce the problem that national law has become unenforceable as far as internet activities are concerned. Arguably, a (democratic) country, which does not enforce its (criminal) laws, equally does not protect free speech within its borders, as online bullying, hate, and abuse stifle free and equal debate. Even citizens in a democratic state, which is not able to protect its citizens, are likely to lose their freedom over time. This is precisely the dilemma of online harms and balanced internet regulation.

A whole range of technologies are used for geo-location: IP address mapping, GPS, cellular data and Wi-Fi-access information for mobile devices, billing and delivery addresses used in e-commerce, language choices, and tracking and profiling technologies used in determining users' preferences.[72] Geo-blocking is implemented at different levels, for example, at the level of website operators as mentioned earlier, individuals' broadband accounts to opt out from certain types of content, for example, for parental filters or gambling filters, or within an employer's network, or at the level of internet access providers. Furthermore, as explained in Chapter 3, the courts may order all internet access providers in a country to implement geo-blocking technologies to prevent users in that country from accessing certain specific websites with illegal content. Regulators can order internet access providers in their country to block certain domain names, IP addresses, or URLs, in order to make it more difficult to access certain websites from a particular country. Used in this way, website blocking becomes a strategy for law enforcement, using local internet access providers as gatekeepers.[73] It is equally clear, however, that users can and do circumvent geo-blocking, so that geo-blocking has little effectiveness towards users *who are determined* to access a website[74] but may be helpful to inform users who are not aware that the website they are trying to reach contains illegal content.[75] Furthermore, geo-blocking can lead to the collection of privacy sensitive information if governments collect data on users attempting to access certain blocked websites or URLs. Thus, it is a slippery slope from the implementation of mandatory geo-blocking at internet access level to surveillance of citizens' internet access.

In summary, therefore, the benefits of geo-location and geo-blocking technologies are that they enable website operators to manage their regulatory compliance and liability risks. They may provide for greater legal certainty as to the law applicable to a particular internet activity. Furthermore, they reduce international conflicts of law while allowing local laws (and indirectly local values) to govern online conduct. By

[70] D Hilliard, "Evaluating the Legitimacy of Geo-location Circumvention in the Context of Technical Protection Measures" (2015) 5(2) Queen Mary Journal of Intellectual Property 157–82, 159ff.

[71] As recognized in the famous *Yahoo!* case, see Chapter 4.

[72] It should also be pointed out that geo-location technologies are not 100 per cent accurate; their accuracy depends on the population density in a country (especially near a border), the size of countries in a region and the level of investment in such technologies.

[73] See Chapter 3.

[74] The metaphor of "cybertravel" has been used for circumvention and a strong argument is made for its legality in M Trimble, "The Future of Cybertravel: Legal Implications of the Evasions of Geolocation" (2012) 22 Fordham Intellectual Property Media & Entertainment Law Journal 567–657, 572.

[75] See further Chapter 3.

reterritorializing the internet they guard against the extraterritorial application of the law, and thus jurisdictional overreach. They enhance law enforcement and the effectiveness of regulation. In respect of civil jurisdiction these technologies help to achieve a fair allocating of the burden of jurisdiction, by determining whether conduct was targeted at a country.[76] The serious disadvantages of geo-location and geo-blocking technologies[77] are that they fragment the internet and reduce the benefits of global connectivity. They raise serious issues of freedom of speech and access to information, as well as increasing the risk of state surveillance of netizens' conduct online. Therefore, the benefits and negative impacts need careful balancing for each particular instance of geo-blocking. Such technologies should be used in a transparent and accountable way.[78]

8.3 Private law systems: depleting sovereignty and states within states

A further element in overcoming the jurisdictional challenge on a systemic level is the increased use of private law systems in regulating online conduct and resolving disputes between internet actors.[79] These private law systems take on public functions, which traditionally the state has carried out, such as content regulation or dispute resolution. Chapters 3 and 5 have discussed the difficulties of regulating online content across borders. Chapter 3 has shown how social media companies employ policies in respect of acceptable content and their mechanisms for policing such content. This form of self-regulation has *de facto* become a separate, quasi-legal system, which has now been recognized as a form of "voluntary" co-regulation in states' legislative initiatives, complementing the criminal law for content regulation.[80] Chapter 6 has demonstrated how voluntary, extra-legal cooperation between foreign law enforcement and communication services providers has been used in digital investigations in order to overcome the territorial limitations of investigative powers.

Furthermore, the use of alternative dispute resolution and online dispute resolution is another example of private law systems replacing public legal mechanisms (in this case formal adjudication) in order to overcome the jurisdictional challenge of the internet.[81] As has been pointed out in Chapter 2, contracts and private law play an ever-increasing role in regulating transborder transactions and relationships. Some of these forms of governance are laws in a traditional, doctrinal sense—for example, contract law—but used in a field where one would expect state-made, public law to govern. Private law is more easily enforced across a border, since comity mechanism in private international law are more developed to ensure the recognition and enforcement of judgments, for example.[82] The power of (some) social media companies also means

[76] Svantesson (n 34) 486.
[77] See further ibid 213.
[78] See further Chapter 3.
[79] Teubner (n 38) 112.
[80] Chapter 3.
[81] Discussed elsewhere, see J Hörnle, *Cross-border Internet Dispute Resolution* (Cambridge University Press 2009).
[82] Contrast the discussion in Chapters 8, 9, 11, and 12 with the discussion in Chapters 6 and 7.

that their content governance systems have created a state within all states and the increased use of private law systems has depleted the monopoly of power of sovereign states to a degree. In sum, one could argue that we are moving towards more pluralistic legal systems where several legal systems exist within the same nation state. Legal pluralism and systemic inconsistency raises the question of how to protect fundamental human rights within this complex interaction between different legal systems.

9. The relationship between jurisdiction, the rule of law, and fundamental rights

One of the most fascinating aspects of writing this book was the changing relationship between jurisdiction, the rule of law, and fundamental rights in view of the jurisdictional challenge caused by the internet. As we have seen, the jurisdictional challenge and cross-border enforcement problems have caused systemic changes in the law (international coordination, private law systems), which have moved regulation outside the national legal system. However, the rule of law and fundamental rights are anchored in the national legal system albeit that the extent of the protection of the rule of law and fundamental rights vary significantly between countries. Jennifer Daskal has pointed to new ways of international lawmaking whereby countries with higher fundamental rights standards enter into bilateral agreements with other countries negotiating a mechanisms for them to comply with the higher standards, citing the General Data Protection Regulation (GDPR) and the Cloud Act as chief examples for this.[83] She argues that this has the potential to lead to the adoption of augmented fundamental rights standards.[84] While this argument has *some* force to it, it overlooks that political considerations frequently govern international law making through treaties where standards are agreed at the international level, but are not implemented into the national legal system.[85] This is again due to national and international law being separate, independent legal systems with a political interface when governments negotiate international treaties. Furthermore, this argument additionally overlooks that the rule of law and human rights protection do not merely depend on substantive law standards but more importantly on the implementation of effective accountability mechanisms and judicial redress to ensure effective implementation.

For countries with a high level of protection therefore, this move away from the national legal system presents a problem as it raises the question of how to guard the rule of law and preserve fundamental rights protection in private law systems and the international law interface.[86] Chapters 2 and 9 have analysed how the doctrines of the presumption against extraterritoriality and comity have been used by US courts, in order to prevent holding US based multinational companies accountable for their unlawful actions on foreign territory. Chapter 6 has examined how the lack

[83] J Daskal, "Microsoft Ireland, the Cloud Act, and International Lawmaking 2.0" (2018) 71 Stanford Law Review Online 9–16, 15; see Chapter 6.
[84] Daskal (n 83).
[85] See eg the discussion of data sovereignty or the US Judicial Redress Act in Chapter 6.
[86] See Chapters 2, 3, 6, and 12.

of judicial redress and accountability mechanisms in international digital investigations and direct cross-border access to cloud data has created a serious loophole in the implementation of protection. Chapter 10 has explained the difficulty of cross-border consumer redress in civil cases and the unaccountability of private law systems, as consumers do not read lengthy terms and conditions and therefore cannot be said to have consented to them in any meaningful sense of the word. Chapter 3 analysed the lack of safeguards in self- and co-regulation of social media content.

These examples demonstrate that the real challenge behind the jurisdictional challenge is the implementation of cross-border accountability and legal redress mechanisms in order to guard fundamental rights and the rule of law.

Index

For the benefit of digital users, indexed terms that span two pages (e.g., 52–53) may, on occasion, appear on only one of those pages.

Note: Cases and legislation only appear in the index where mentioned at length. These appear in separate tables.

Tables and figures are indicated by *t* and *f* following the page number